Sociolinguistics
Theoretical Debates

Sociolinguistics is a dynamic field of research that explains the role and function of language in social life. This book offers the most substantial account available of the core contemporary ideas and arguments in sociolinguistics, with an emphasis on innovation and change. Bringing together original writing by more than twenty of the field's most influential international thinkers and researchers, this is an indispensable guide to the newest and most searching ideas about language in society. For researchers and advanced students it gives access to the field's most pressing issues and debates and provides a platform for new initiatives in sociolinguistic research.

NIKOLAS COUPLAND is an elected Fellow of both the UK Academy of Social Sciences and the Australian Academy of the Humanities. He has published more than 20 books and more than 150 articles and chapters on wide-ranging aspects of sociolinguistics and discourse analysis. His volume *The Handbook of Language and Globalization* (2010) was the winner of the British Association for Applied Linguistics annual book prize.

Sociolinguistics

Theoretical Debates

Nikolas Coupland

Cardiff University and Copenhagen University

CAMBRIDGE
UNIVERSITY PRESS

CAMBRIDGE
UNIVERSITY PRESS

University Printing House, Cambridge CB2 8BS, United Kingdom

Cambridge University Press is part of the University of Cambridge.

It furthers the University's mission by disseminating knowledge in the pursuit of education, learning, and research at the highest international levels of excellence.

www.cambridge.org
Information on this title: www.cambridge.org/9781107635753

© Cambridge University Press 2016

First published 2016

Printed in the United Kingdom by Clays, St Ives plc.

A catalogue record for this publication is available from the British Library.

Library of Congress Cataloging-in-Publication Data
Names: Coupland, Nikolas, 1950– editor.
Title: Sociolinguistics: Theoretical Debates / edited by Nikolas Coupland.
Description: Cambridge; New York: Cambridge University Press, [2016] | Includes bibliographical references and index.
Identifiers: LCCN 2016000249| ISBN 9781107062283 (Hardback) | ISBN 9781107635753 (paperback)
Subjects: LCSH: Sociolinguistics.
Classification: LCC P40 .S564 2016 | DDC 306.44–dc23 LC record available at https://lccn.loc.gov/2016000249

ISBN 978-1-107-06228-3 Hardback
ISBN 978-1-107-63575-3 Paperback

Contents

Contributors

JANNIS ANDROUTSOPOULOS is Professor of German and Media Linguistics at the Institute for German Studies and the Institute for Media and Communication at Universität Hamburg, Germany.

ROBERT BAYLEY is a Professor in the Department of Linguistics at the University of California, Davis, CA, USA.

ALLAN BELL is Professor of Language and Communication, and Director of the Institute of Culture, Discourse and Communication, at Auckland University of Technology, and Visiting Research Professor, School of English, University of Hong Kong.

JAN BLOMMAERT is Professor of Language, Culture and Globalization and Director of the Babylon Center at Tilburg University, The Netherlands. He is also Professor of African Linguistics and Sociolinguistics at Ghent University, Belgium. He holds honorary appointments at University of the Western Cape (South Africa) and Beijing Language and Culture University (China) and is group leader of the Max Planck Sociolinguistic Diversity Working Group.

DAVID BRITAIN is Professor of Modern English Linguistics in the Department of English at the University of Bern in Switzerland.

MARY BUCHOLTZ is Professor in the Department of Linguistics at the University of California, Santa Barbara, CA, USA. She is also affiliated with UCSB's Department of Education, the Department of Feminist Studies, the Department of Spanish and Portuguese, and the Latin American and Iberian Studies Program and is the director of the Center for California Languages and Cultures.

NIKOLAS COUPLAND is Honorary Professor at the Department of Nordic Studies and Linguistics, Copenhagen University, Denmark, and Emeritus Professor at the Centre for Language and Communication Research at Cardiff University, Wales, UK.

ALEXANDRE DUCHÊNE is Professor of Sociology of Language, Head of Department of Multilingualism Studies at the University of Fribourg (Switzerland), and Co-Director of the Swiss National Research Center on Multilingualism.

DIANA EADES is Adjunct Professor in Linguistics at the University of New England, Australia.

PENELOPE ECKERT is Albert Ray Lang Professor of Linguistics and (by courtesy) of Anthropology at Stanford University, Stanford, CA, USA.

SUSAN GAL is Mae and Sidney G. Metzl Distinguished Service Professor in the Departments of Anthropology and Linguistics at the University of Chicago, Chicago, IL, USA.

KIRA HALL is Associate Professor in the Department of Linguistics and the Department of Anthropology at the University of Colorado, Boulder, CO, USA.

MONICA HELLER is Professor at the Ontario Institute for Studies in Education and the Department of Anthropology, University of Toronto, Canada.

ALEXANDRA JAFFE is Professor of Linguistics and Anthropology at California State University, Long Beach, CA, USA.

BARBARA JOHNSTONE is Professor of Rhetoric and Linguistics at Carnegie Mellon University, Pittsburgh, PA, USA.

HELEN KELLY-HOLMES is Professor of Sociolinguistics and New Media at the School of Modern Languages and Applied Linguistics, University of Limerick, Ireland.

CEIL LUCAS is Professor of Linguistics, Emerita, at Gallaudet University, Washington, DC, USA.

ALASTAIR PENNYCOOK is Professor of Language in Education at the University of Technology Sydney, Australia.

SARI PIETIKÄINEN is a Professor of Discourse Studies in the Department of Languages, University of Jyväskylä, Finland.

BEN RAMPTON is Professor of Applied and Sociolinguistics at King's College London, UK, where he also directs the Centre for Language, Discourse and Communication.

MICHAEL SILVERSTEIN is the Charles F. Grey Distinguished Service Professor of Anthropology, Linguistics, and Psychology at the University of Chicago, Chicago, IL, USA, where he is also Director of the Center for the Study of Communication and Society.

LIONEL WEE is a Professor in the Department of English Language and Literature at the National University of Singapore.

Preface and acknowledgements

I would like to express my thanks to the many people who have shown confidence in this book project and patience in the face of delays in its completion. I had originally envisaged this book as a short review of 'sociolinguistic theory', written in my own name. As time went on, and as the field expanded and theory proliferated, I came to realise the impossibility of shouldering even the core of this task myself. It was once possible to argue that there was rather little theoretical ambition in sociolinguistics. Even if originally true – not true any longer!

The project then evolved into one based on 'theoretical debates', necessarily so because many of the emerging theory-rich perspectives came from different parts of what I take to be sociolinguistics – the fertile and shifting multi- and interdisciplinary fields of enquiry where language and society come into contact with each other in so many ways. This made any single theoretical vision contentious in its wider context. What was needed, I latterly realised, was to bring as many as possible of the leading researchers into this debate, and I am again grateful that so many of them have been willing to play along.

In the pages of this book many different voices interact with each other, sometimes harmoniously, sometimes less so, but in all cases with importantly distinctive ways of representing what we know in the field of sociolinguists, what we need to know, what we can generalise about, what generalising means, where we are heading, and what next, with a modicum of 'so what' thrown in too. In some cases the debates in question have been actual collaborative discussions based around first drafts of the chapters that appear here. Regrettably, I was not able to realise my ambition of circulating all or even most of such drafts around the full set of contributors, theme by theme. Coordinating the timing of different contributors' writing, and my own, and getting to a finishing line, proved to be enough of a challenge. But a *spirit* of debate certainly comes through the chapters: All contributors are striving for consolidation and clarification, and often genuine innovation and agenda-setting, and to this extent the book serves as an opportunity to take stock across many of the central fields of sociolinguistic research and to conceive of future developments.

The six sections are not exactly the same as the ones I had planned when designing the book, nor are the authors allocated to them exactly as planned. I felt it was essential to encourage contributors to set their own theoretical and metatheoretical targets for their chapters, and I am sure that what may have been lost (relative to planned structure), as the book's chapters evolved, is more than compensated for by the sharpness and originality of what the contributors provide. Any significant omissions are of course my own responsibility.

I am grateful to Cambridge University Press, and to Andrew Winnard in particular, for allowing me the flexibility to shape-shift the book over time; also to Stephanie Sakson for her expert and very supportive input into preparing the manuscript for publication. One or two planned chapter contributions did not make it into the final collection, because of the sorts of human and professional exigencies that we all know about. I have been sorry to miss out on those contributions.

Different universities have supported me in the preparation of the book. It began its life when I was chair of the Centre for Language and Communication Research at Cardiff University, and continued through my time as Visiting Professor at the University of Technology Sydney and Research Professor at the University of Copenhagen. Without that support, plus the continuing support of esteemed colleagues at these three locations, the project would certainly have foundered.

The Press has agreed to set the chapters of the book in a mix of USA-based and UK-based house styles for academic English, to reflect, at least to some degree, individual authors' preferences. These styles include not only the familiar distinctions in spelling but also some distinctions in punctuation. The setting of Chapter titles, Part titles and running heads has, on the other hand, been regularised.

NIKOLAS COUPLAND

1 Introduction: Sociolinguistic theory and the practice of sociolinguistics

Nikolas Coupland

Theory and practice

Theory and practice are terms that are often set in opposition to each other, but not for very good reasons. This is a book about theory, but it is not a book that is, one might say, 'couched in abstractions with little relevance to the real world of language use'. Who needs theory, if that's what theory is? On the contrary, theory is about what we see and experience in the social world of language, and about how we impute meaning to actions. As language users, we are all theorists, although the discipline of sociolinguistics has particular responsibilities in fostering, through its theory, awareness of what happens at the interface between language and society, and in reviewing what we know and what we have not yet adequately explained. So this is actually a book about practice too – practices of using language and practices of interpreting language in society.

My main task in the chapter is to set the scene for the nineteen chapters that follow; I introduce the chapters and the structure of the volume in the second half of this chapter. Before that it may be useful to comment in quite general terms on 'theory', and then on 'sociolinguistic theory', the object of debate in this volume, and its historical status in the field. That will lead to an overview of the types of theory that sociolinguistics has aligned with to date, and might profitably align with in the future. This is a necessary debate in itself, especially if it is right to observe that sociolinguistics has entered a phase where 'theory is everywhere' and that this is radically influencing what sociolinguistics is and what it does. But we are also arguably in a phase where discussion of what counts as theory, and why it matters in so many practical regards, is still generally lacking. In other words, we need to keep revisiting some basic *meta*theoretical questions about sociolinguistics, following a line of reflexive commentary started by Figueroa over twenty years ago. Figueroa (1994) set out the different principles and assumptions that supported the research of three of the 'founding fathers' of sociolinguistics, Labov, Gumperz, and Hymes. She wanted to explain (or theorise, if you like) the theoretical stances that underpinned early sociolinguistics. That reassessment was particularly

1

useful in helping us to appreciate points of similarity and difference across these sociolinguistic 'traditions', and greater awareness is a prerequisite for innovation. That idea is a key motivation for the present book.

As sociolinguistics has expanded and indeed innovated, the need for this sort of reflexive reassessment has become more urgent. This book has been designed to bring many influential researchers and perspectives more closely into focus with one another. The book is framed as a series of 'debates' about sociolinguistics and theory – debates in the sense that contributors reflect on their own and others' research, asking fundamental questions about the concepts and assumptions that underlie sociolinguistic analysis and interpretation. The overall picture that emerges is one of rapid change and increasing theoretical ambition in sociolinguistics – quite contrary, then, to the older suggestion that sociolinguistics was deficient in the area of theory. But we also get a picture of sociolinguistics as a contested field, being pulled in different directions and subscribing not only to different theories (which is a fairly normal condition for any academic discipline) but also to different types of theory. So these are dynamic and exciting times. New theoretical stances (even if they are sometimes reassertions of older ideas, though more commonly reinterpretations of them) have the potential to radically strengthen the field, but they also come with some risks attached, which I touch on below.

Contemplating sociolinguistic theory

In its sporadic existence so far, 'sociolinguistic theory' has referred to several different kinds of endeavour. Not surprisingly, then, people have made very different judgements of how sociolinguistics has stood at different times in its history, and how it stands now, in relation to theory. There was an early period when sociolinguistics was linked to descriptivism, and when descriptivism was apparently a 'good thing' (at least in its oppositional relationship to prescriptivism). This, however, left the possibility hanging in the air that 'descriptive' might imply 'atheoretical', which was presumably *not* such a good thing. Rampton notes that novice linguists were regularly indoctrinated into the view that 'linguistics [as a whole] is descriptive not prescriptive' and that this view fed into a dominant ideological commitment in sociolinguistics to study 'tacit, unself-conscious language use' in the ambition to find 'the regularity, system and consistency that defines their professional interest' (Rampton 2006: 16).

This stance prioritised descriptive adequacy over theoretical adequacy. Burke (2005: 101) traces the slogan 'who says what to whom, and with what effects' to political scientist Lasswell (1935). He also notes Fishman's (1965) influential re-rendering of it – 'the study of who speaks what language to whom, when' – as an agenda-setting dictum for the sociology of language, which was another descriptively oriented 'wing' of early sociolinguistics (cf. García et al. 2012). This emphasis on the distributional patterning of languages (also on attitudes to languages) mirrored Labov's structuralist emphasis on the distribution of (dialectal) sociolinguistic variables. While important principles could be induced from both initiatives, the descriptive endeavour (in Labov's case inherited in part from the systematicity of early dialectological fieldwork) was viewed as a credentialising characteristic in its own right.

At one point I dared to ask the question 'What is sociolinguistic theory?' (Coupland 1998) in a context where sociolinguistics had been criticised for having a theoretical deficit, and for perhaps not knowing what sort of theory it could aspire to. Williams (1992), Romaine (1994), and Coulmas (1997) had all commented on the status of sociolinguistic theory, mainly in support of the view that, up to those dates of publication, sociolinguistics needed *much more theoretical impetus* than it had achieved. In an introduction (Coupland 2001b) to a book on sociolinguistics and social theory (Coupland et al. 2001),[1] I had tried to take the edge off this criticism. Several fields of sociolinguistic research were mentioned that were theoretically rich in their ambitions and achievements. They included some obvious examples, such as Hymes's (1972) theorising of the social and cultural contexts of language use, elaborated, for example, in Duranti and Goodwin's (1992) constructionist approach to social context. Gumperz's (1982) inferential perspective on intercultural encounters was another clear instance, as were Bauman's (1977) theorising of performance and Milroy and Milroy's (1992) reinterpretation of social class–based linguistic variation in terms of social networks. Many other contributions deserved to be mentioned. But it is worth noting that sociolinguistic theory, as illustrated by these instances, was eclectic and that particular theoretical contributions made very little effort to speak to each other. It certainly was not the data-based inductive theorising that 'scientific theory' classically demanded either. Labov's theoretical contribution, from its earliest phases (1963, 1966), was indeed based in induction, inducing general principles from extensive empirical research. But in this case the challenge related to how variationism constructed its *social* theory, and therefore its theorising of language–society relations. In an early and unfair critique, Halliday (1978) had suggested that variation research was providing sets of answers to questions that hadn't been adequately formulated.

In any event, the accusation of theoretical deficit was not so easily countered. Hudson (1980/1996) had lamented the absence of a *unifying* sociolinguistic theory; he seemed to be looking for sociolinguistic theory that

---

[1] The book considered relationships between sociolinguistics and the ideas of several social theorists, mainly Bourdieu, Foucault, Habermas, and Bakhtin.

was more inclusive and entertained on a larger scale. He wrote that 'we badly need a general framework of ideas to integrate the facts into a whole that makes some sort of intellectual sense' (1996: 228). Romaine's (1994) point had been similar, arguing that we needed theory that oriented more to social conflict and discrimination than implying social consensus (which was also one of Williams's points). What was sociolinguistics contributing to the pressing sociological problems and debates of the day? Similarly, Coulmas (1997) saw an un-self-critical sociolinguistics that was lost between linguistic theory and social theory, managing only to formulate its own local 'mini-theories', with little impact on either mainstream linguistics or the social sciences. Did sociolinguistics lack theoretical ambition of this grander sort? Did sociolinguists lack appreciation of where their own distinctive contributions to the human and social sciences could be made, and were they/we generally ignoring social theory as it was being articulated in the social sciences, and critical theory in the humanities? Maybe yes, quite possibly.

Yet 'theory' is a troublesome concept for all disciplines. Aristotle's *theoria* refers to 'contemplation', 'looking at' or 'becoming aware of' – minimally, then, the idea of being a spectator at the events of one's own research and having a commitment to scrutinising what research is achieving, relative to other instances and types of research. Are we doing something useful? What are the principles that we agree should be defended? Are we headed in the best direction? Theory is (still in that minimal interpretation of it) reflexive engagement with research, something beyond the techniques and apparatuses that enact particular research projects and deliver research findings. Of course, no research project will be totally devoid of theory in this sense, and the criterion of theoretical adequacy therefore needs to be entertained both qualitatively and quantitatively: Are we reflexively 'contemplating' our field of research and its social contribution in the right way, and to an adequate extent? Greek *theoria* had assumed a moral character, and later became a religious imperative (MacIntyre 2007), and this is partly reflected in the above questions.

If we look at some of the particular sociolinguistic initiatives that have branded themselves as contributions to sociolinguistic theory, we immediately see a wide range of interpretations of what theory might mean. Chambers has used the title *Sociolinguistic Theory* for his comprehensive overview of variationist sociolinguistic research (Chambers 1995/2009). He has interpreted his title to mean something like 'foundational concepts in the quantitative study of language variation and change' plus 'generalisations supported by this sort of research'. Chambers's book is contemplative and reflexive about research, but specifically about research conducted in the Labovian paradigm of variationism, in its quest to generalise about language (dialect) variation and change. Chambers does not substantially engage with the much wider project of sociolinguistics, which, for the purposes of the present volume, refers to the broad inter- and multidisciplinary terrain where 'language', or 'the linguistic', meaningfully interacts with 'society', or 'the social'. Nor does Chambers comment on what sort of social theory underlies the variationist paradigm. Yet Labov's orientation to social class came to be considered 'Parsonian' (Parsons 1952), and, as above, it has been critiqued for being overly structuralist and consensus oriented (Kerswill 2007; Block 2014).

Other sociolinguistic paradigms have been referred to as 'theories' too. Politeness theory (Brown and Levinson 1987) identified the relational principles according to which speakers orient to considerations of 'face': positive face, a speaker's desire for his or her public image to be well regarded by others, and negative face, a speaker's desire to avoid intrusions on her or his personal autonomy. The fact that Brown and Levinson saw face-work as a universal pragmatic dimension of social interaction, whose general principles could (they argued) be induced from comparative observations across different language communities, was probably important in politeness research being able to claim its status as 'a theory'. This was in some ways paralleled by accommodation theory (Giles and Powesland 1975; Giles et al. 1991), even though in this case principles were induced (and stated as axioms) from extensive experimental studies of how speakers showed different degrees of convergence or divergence in interaction, or how observers associated convergence and divergence with particular sociopsychological motivations.

So these are two examples of theories, developed in specific corners of sociolinguistics, that submit (at least to some extent) to classical conceptions of theorising in the scientific tradition – theory that initially finds its principles and axioms inductively, from regular patterns observed in extensive data. In this classical mode, theoretical generalisations could then stand as hypotheses, generalising statements which might provide a basis for predicting as-yet unobserved outcomes. Another trait that united politeness theory and accommodation theory is that they can be considered 'rational choice' (or 'rational action') theories, presuming that speakers make ongoing assessments of their speaking environments (and specifically their speaking partners) and are then able to make strategic choices from known sets of discursive options in the service of particular motivations and goals. Rational choice theories have, however, come under criticism in several disciplines (e.g. Schram and Caterino 2006) for overinvesting in people's capacity to navigate their social worlds on the basis of knowable choices.

The immediately relevant point here is that the examples of 'sociolinguistic theorising' we have considered so far do not have application across the whole of sociolinguistics. Nothing that we can call 'a unified sociolinguistic theory' has emerged from any of them. We need not go into further detail about classical 'scientific method and theory' as a basis for sociolinguistics, from Popper to Hawking or beyond, because it is already obvious that, overall, it bears limited relevance to sociolinguistics in most of its current manifest-ations. Sociolinguistic research has always incorporated a wide range of different methods, from quantitative surveys, through ethnographic observa-tional studies and interviews, to in-depth single-case analyses (Milroy and Gordon 2003; Holmes and Hazen 2014). Sociolinguists continue to pride themselves on the level of detail with which language data are scrutinised in empirical studies. But (for better or worse) there has been a general (by no means exception-less) retreat from large-scale survey-type designs, as socio-linguistic investigations have increasingly favoured theory-heavy, empirically smaller-scale, qualitative investigations that mainly claim the status of ethnog-raphies. Under these circumstances we need to ask what types of theory can be in question.

Theory for the humanities and social sciences

If sociolinguistics wants to maintain its 'reflexive contemplation', as it must, how should this sort (or these sorts) of theory be formulated? Taking a lead from social scientific perspectives on theory (Schutt 2014), we would expect sociolinguistic theory to be formulated as sets of statements, generalising where possible, about social reality, couched in concepts whose definitions and interrelationships would be made explicit. Preferred theoretical contribu-tions – 'good theories' – would, as in classical scientific theory, have wide reach and applicability, but not necessarily 'wide reach' in relation to empirical data. (A key justification for establishing a narrower empirical focus is that social situations and the discursive events transacted within them are unique.) We might maintain the hope that theories should be expressed simply and parsimoniously, but once again, the social world is generally too complex to hold simplicity as a high priority. Like all theory, theory in the social sciences and sociolinguistic theory should still involve abstracting away from particular data contexts and instances. But distinctively from classical scientific theory, it might also be conceived as providing a guide to social action (the moral agenda of 'theory' returning to prominence), so that explanation may be insufficient in itself as a priority.

There would be a recognition that social phenomena (including linguistic/discursive phenomena) are not amenable to very reliable categorisation, and to this extent generalisations will be unlikely to be reliably predictive, which presents a challenge over what 'generalisation' can actually mean. Because meaning is always at issue in language-related research, generalisation might, for example, mean generalising about how meanings *can* be made under particular conditions, rather than about *how* they *are* (always or typically) made. There have been metatheoretical initiatives to explain and justify the value of small-scale social investigations, including case studies. One of these is MacIntyre's (e.g. 2007) lobbying for a phronetic social science (see also Flyvbjerg 2002; Flyvbjerg et al. 2012).

Phronesis is another Aristotelian term, referring to intellectual thought that attends to values and 'value-rationality', in ways that go beyond analytic ('scientific') knowledge (*episteme*) and technical knowledge (*techne*). In Flyvbjerg et al.'s conception, 'From a phronetic perspective, social science works best not when it tries to give us the unrealizable perfection of expert knowledge, such as that which comes from abstract models, but instead when it strives for the 'adequation' of what works for any collective as it struggles to decide things for itself' (Flyvbjerg et al. 2012: 2). The quotation makes it clear that there are political and demotic nuances to this view of social research that are strongly echoed in 'critical' conceptions of theory (see below). There is also explicit recognition that value-linked meanings are only ever detectable in close and context-rich forms of analysis, which echoes ethnographic priorities (Hammersley 1992) and what is sometimes called 'ethnographic theory' (cf. Wilson and Chadda 2009). Without being so-named, a lot of sociolinguistics is showing signs of being reoriented around phronetic-type approaches to theory. This raises further interesting questions about the scale and weight of sociolinguistic theorising. Phronetic social science accepts a relatively humble role for itself – any one of its theoretical interpretations is 'just one voice among many'. It eschews theory as authoritative generalisation.

What then of 'social theory'? This is an ambiguous term that sometimes refers to the full range of social scientific efforts at reflexive 'contemplation' and generalisation, including 'scientifically oriented' theories (cf. Harrington 2005), while at other times referring to efforts to generalise in profound ways about 'how society is now' – that is, in its historical context, prioritising aspects of social change. Turner says that '[s]ocial theory broadly encompasses the general concern with the nature of the social in modern society' (1996: 2). A prominent example is Giddens's treatise on 'living in a post-traditional society' where, for example, he theorises processes of de-traditionalisation, and then how globalisation entails the 'evacuation of tradition' (Giddens 1996: chapter 2). Social theory of this sort addresses the 'big questions' of social change, and these have steadily moved to the forefront of sociolinguistic research.

Many chapters in the present volume illustrate this movement, in reference to change-related concepts such as globalisation, mediatisation, individualisation, reflexivisation, conversationalisation, and so on (cf. Coupland 2010b). There is a striking disjunction between the theoretical 'scaling up' of social theory in this sense and the empirical 'scaling down' of phronesis, and this is paralleled in contemporary sociolinguistics. The fate of sociolinguistic theory is increasingly tightly entwined with the (sociologically) theorised transition from modernity into late modernity. It would be wrong to claim that what sociolinguistic theory is and what it does have changed *exclusively* as effects of social change or in the desire to model language-related social change, and there is the familiar query (which surfaces in several later chapters) about the extent to which theory reflects real social change versus changes in intellectual fashion, and then how those two sorts of shift relate to each other. Also, social changes labelled by '-isation' nominals are far from clear-cut and conclusive. As we also see in several later chapters, theorists commonly refer to late modernity as an epoch of nonlinear transition out of modernist priorities into other priorities, with considerable contestation over priorities and normativities (including many that centre on language). But social change cannot be avoided in sociolinguistic theory, if only because we need to review earlier theoretical stances (and possibly theoretical deficits) as possibly being 'products of their epoch'. (I will come back to these issues in Chapter 20.)

Social theory in its sociological life also tends to disconnect theorising from the large-scale, wide-reach empirical approaches that might be expected to be its basis. At least, theory often tends to have a viable existence prior to large-scale empirical investigation. Do big questions require big data? On the other hand, are the big questions of social theory simply impossible to address according to the classical principle that generalisations should emerge from extensive data? Whatever line we take on this, we end up with difficulties in defining theoretical adequacy. 'Good theory' whose reach is broad enough to capture the radical social changes we are currently experiencing may necessarily have to 'go beyond the data'; theory that tentatively and self-critically explains accumulated observations of human and social experience may not be 'grand' enough. In the context of critical theory in the humanities, other important priorities come into play too. Critical theory, or theory through critique, is supported by a metatheory in which 'elaborate existential judge-ment' by individuals or groups (Therborn 1996: 57) has come to be accepted as an alternative to theory based in direct processes of induction and deduction. The 'judgement' in question is of course the judgement of critical theorists themselves. But theory that is *not* tied closely to inductive generalisation, speculative though it might be, is able to open up new research perspectives which can then become foci for empirical projects. Recent sociolinguistic work on heteroglossia (e.g. Blackledge and Creese 2014), stylisation and authenticity (e.g. Eckert 2003; Rampton 2006; Coupland 2010a, 2014) are examples of theoretical projects that have arisen in large part from literary traditions of critical research.

Critical theory has found it legitimate, and necessary (because of the political urgency of many of its themes), to provide something close to free-floating critique, particularly when it moves away from its literary origins in the critical examination of texts. Its emphasis is not simply on understanding social and cultural processes, but also on interrogating those processes in order to point up and *challenge* the systems of dominance and hegemony that they can be shown to espouse. 'Critical' in this context therefore implies a critique of 'interested-ness', and 'theory' implies a cogency and social progressiveness on the part of theorists, viewed from their own perspectives. Those perspectives may be neo-Marxist, and critical theory is quite widely based in opposition to late-capitalist processes and systems, which it often opposes under the banner of postmodernism. Although critical theory was associated with the Frankfurt School from as early as the 1920s, it has strongly influenced the nature of disciplinary theory across the humanities and social sciences for many decades. The recent upsurge in sociolinguistic theory is to a large extent a reorientation towards sociocultural critique via the analysis of language and discourse. This has made it possible to construe (and to critique) a *critical sociolinguistics* (e.g. Singh 1996; Gregersen 1998; Muysken 1998; Blommaert 2005, 2010; Mesthrie and Deumert 2009).

In this short overview of theory in the social sciences and the humanities I have been struggling to *exclude* theoretical perspectives that have had language, discourse, meaning, symbolic action, or semiotics close to their centres. To exclude them is ultimately impossible, of course, because 'language' has been a key consideration in many of them and certainly in any approach to theory that can be called 'critical'. Some of these are briefly mentioned below. My main intention, so far, has been to ask an open-ended question. If it is true that sociolinguistics is moving away from classically 'scientific' conceptions of theory, then which of the conceptions adopted in neighbouring fields are sociolinguists aligning themselves with, and why? Many clues (and some direct metatheoretical assessments) emerge in the main chapters of the book. When we look at the character and foci of theories that have emerged from within the field of sociolinguistics (again broadly conceived) relatively recently, we can reflect on whether and to what extent sociolinguistics in fact *needs* to align itself with one or several 'outside' approaches to theory (cf. Wodak's [2000] question: 'does sociolinguistics need social theory?'), as opposed to generating its own distinctive body (or bodies) of theory.

Sociolinguistic theory 'from within' rather than 'from without'

There is no doubt that many of the most influential theoretical innovations in the area of language and society have come from linguistic anthropology. In his review of the scope of linguistic anthropology, Duranti identifies 'three major theoretical areas that ... [had] been developed within linguistic anthropology in the ... [previous] few decades'; they are performance, indexicality, and participation (in the sense of what it means, culturally speaking, to participate as a speaker in communicative interaction) (Duranti 1997:

14–21). As we shall see in later chapters, each of these themes has maintained its status as an important and evolving focus of sociolinguistic theory. This is particularly true in the case of indexicality, which is shared as the main topic of the four chapters in Part I. But performance too has also expanded its theoretical range in sociolinguistics in connection with the concepts of style and stylisation, voicing and quotativity, ritual, language display, and so on, not least in relation to mediatised language and interaction. Participation is a less eye-catching construct, but it has been receiving attention in a wide array of sociolinguistic contexts, for example in relation to linguistic landscape research, minority languages, and media discourse analysis.

Sociolinguistics (in the name of linguistic anthropology) is undoubtedly the 'home territory' for the three theoretical 'nuggets' that Duranti discusses, even though many other disciplines will lay legitimate claim to them – for example, performance will certainly be claimed by literary, media, and theatre studies, but also by sociology (see Alexander et al. 2006 on 'social performance'). The question then arises of whether sociolinguistic theory might be further enhanced by developing its 'nuggets' in ways that map more closely onto neighbouring theoretical tendencies elsewhere in the humanities and social sciences. Would it be productive, for example, to incorporate more critical perspectives into the theorising of indexical relations, or more social-theoretic (e.g. globalisation-linked) perspectives into performance theory (which might indeed be productive for the sociolinguistic account of mediation and mediatisation – see Chapter 20)?

There is no shortage of home-sourced sociolinguistic theory and theories, and only a few obvious others can be mentioned here. Critical discourse analysis (CDA) developed out of critical linguistics to be the major interdisciplinary orientation to linguistically and textually mediated power relations (see, e.g., Fairclough 1992, 1995; Blommaert 2005; Wodak 2012). Its prevalence has been one of the main stimuli for sociolinguistics as a whole to 'go critical'. Similarly, and although sociologists will assert that he 'belongs to them' rather than to something called sociolinguistics, Bourdieu has been remarkably influential within recent decades of sociolinguistic research. In fact Bourdieu is the prime example of how permeable the boundary between sociolinguistics and the social sciences can be. Blommaert (2015) provides a critical review of the impact of Bourdieu's research (and one which goes well beyond Bourdieu's now-familiar concept of symbolic capital; Bourdieu 1991) on different thematic areas of sociolinguistics, including linguistic ethnography and language-ideological theory.

Language ideology research itself (e.g. Silverstein 1979; Irvine and Gal 2000) shares CDA's critical perspective, but it originated at the intersection of linguistic anthropology and semiotics. Language ideology, a concept that is so heavily represented in later chapters, has become a major paradigm (while lacking a conventional acronym). Once again it can be thought of as a 'home-grown' paradigm, but one that has impacted on all strands of sociolinguistics, including dialectology and the study of language variation and change. One of the most successful sociolinguistic achievements in recent years has been to develop perspectives that infuse critical/ideological sensibilities regarding gender, race, and class into interactional sociolinguistics and studies of dialect variation/performance, which of course are sociolinguistic concerns of old, with a strong spine of social theorising also in evidence (as exemplified in Rampton 2006; Mendoza-Denton 2008; Madsen 2015; and Madsen et al. 2015). Critical and ethnographic work with a historical focus has also emerged to transform the sociology of language, for example, in its coverage of minority language politics, policy, and revitalisation (e.g. Duchêne and Heller 2011; Pietikäinen et al. 2016). New sociolinguistic approaches to mediation and mediatisation are challenging our conceptions of 'everyday language' and creating distinctive ways of approaching media data (e.g. Johnson and Ensslin 2007, Androutsopoulos 2014). All of these developments and several overlapping others are reviewed, debated, and extended in the following chapters.

So, if sociolinguistics is displaying its internal theory-generating mechanisms so vividly and so successfully, should sociolinguists seek to contain their theory within the bounds of sociolinguistics itself? This is a metatheoretical question that needs to be considered in light of the full contents of this book. My own initial response is, however, no. While sociolinguistics needs to resist plucking its theory off the shelves of other disciplines, it is certainly the poorer when it fails to engage with substantial theoretical debates in neighbouring disciplines. As CDA, language ideology research, and semiotically informed approaches to variation have all demonstrated, sociolinguistics is able to advance core ideas in the humanities and social sciences based on its own distinctive modes of research and offer them back to those wider constituencies in stronger, more explicit, and often more rigorously evidenced forms.

Another reason for answering 'no' is that a boundaried sociolinguistics can easily become internally unstable. I have knowingly overstated the degree of unity represented by the word 'sociolinguistics' in this chapter (and, with colleagues, elsewhere, e.g. Coupland and Jaworski 2009a,b). We know that sociolinguistics was born as a multidisciplinary field, and in some ways it continues to function that way. Vested interests (understandably enough) continue to make it desirable to represent segments of the field under different names, for example, as variationist sociolinguistics (usually 'language variation and change'), the social psychology of language, linguistic ethnography, sociocultural linguistics, discourse analysis, linguistic anthropology, media studies, even communication studies. There is a risk, then, of sociolinguistics losing its coherence and, in consequence, losing such influence as it now has (with far greater potential influence in the future) as a distinctive voice in dialogue with many other voices in the humanities and social sciences. The most striking theoretical innovations in sociolinguistics have come at the intersections between different (or what historically were differently named) subfields, both 'within' and 'without'. Again, examples of this abound: reengagement with Peircean semiotic theory, finding important new resonances with Bakhtin's heteroglossia, exploring links between linguistics and economics or linguistics and human geography, and so on. It is to be hoped that this book will facilitate more coherence (which is not at all the same as uniformity), more border-crossing, and in consequence more loci and impetus for innovation.

There is another risk, which we might refer to as premature internal revolution. Nowadays we read about the need for radically new perspectives in sociolinguistics and explicit calls for paradigm shift. (There is no need to cite sources because these issues are explicitly debated in the following chapters, to be introduced shortly.) Sociolinguists' recent enthusiasm for theoretical innovation and change is admirable, engaging, and often inspiring. As suggested earlier, the best theorists and the best theories locate problems and perspectives which, possibly because of theoretical entrenchment and an academic 'metaculture of tradition' (Urban 2001), others have failed to identify. The contrary case is that progressive evolution can be more productive than abrupt revolution. In many cases what we arguably need is to reinflect and retheorise older concepts (community, variety, diversity, identity, standard and vernacular, mediation, etc.) rather than dispense with them altogether. In fact, it is not obviously the case that concepts of this sort and the theory that binds them *can* be summarily disinvented. Theory is never ideology free, but one element of the 'contemplation' that theory represents must be reflexivity, including making sure that theory does not overreach. Conventionally, theorising has been said to be better when it is cumulative, new contributions 'standing on the shoulders' of others. This convention can also lead to complacency, especially under changing social and sociolinguistic conditions which then do need to be freshly theorised.

Sociolinguists of all stripes will agree with Labov's early dictum that we should design our research (and our theory) in such a way that 'we encounter the possibility of being right' (Labov 1972: 259). 'Being right' is a pretty good criterion for theoretical adequacy, although of course it begs important questions about the *respects* in which theoretical generalisations are and are not true. We surely maximise the possibility of 'being right' if we keep in view as broad a range of contemplatory insights as possible. The above sections convey some aspects of the rich, complex, and shifting context into which the chapters of the book make their very wide-ranging pitches, for and against particular theoretical stances, across many of the most prominent themes in contemporary sociolinguistic research. I now introduce the individual chapters, section by section, pointing to some of the continuities and discontinuities across them.

Part I: Theorising social meaning

One of the strongest currents of sociolinguistic theorising in recent decades has been the systematic reconsideration of 'social meaning' in relation to language. The idea of social meaning is by no means unique to sociolinguistics – it is a phrase that many of the social sciences use to summarise their theoretical quests: 'the social meaning of money', 'the social meaning of civic space', and so on. In sociolinguistics, social meaning has been approached in several different ways, such as in language attitudes research (and the social psychology of language, generally) and in folk linguistics. But the most intensely productive reconsideration of social meaning in sociolinguistics has been undertaken in relation to semiotic theory and from a broadly anthropological standpoint. It is appropriate, then, that the first section of the book is devoted to new issues and debates about how social meaning should be theorised and analysed.

The authors represented in Part I have all previously made key contributions to our understanding of social meaning – Silverstein through his theorising of indexicality, metapragmatics, and enregisterment; Eckert through her radical rethinking of sociolinguistic variation as a resource for situated meaning-making, particularly among 'style groups' in educational settings; Gal through her pioneering work on language ideology in relation to sociolinguistic diversity; and Jaffe through her research into language in education, media, and diverse contexts of cultural performance.

In Chapter 2 Silverstein offers a critical retrospective on how the sociolinguistic concepts of indexicality, register, and enregisterment emerged to challenge classical 'law-based' perspectives on language change (particularly sound change) in historical linguistics. Silverstein's review points to, for example, historical continuities between system-focused theoretical concepts (such as co-occurrence) and socially focused concepts (such as register). It explains how theoretical ideas that we now consider to lie at the heart of sociolinguistics, including the distinction between context-generated and context-generating modes of meaning, were developed in early anthropological reinterpretations of classical theories of language change. We also get insights into the origins of Silverstein's substantial personal contributions to these issues, such as how he came to see semiotics as a unifying perspective able to reconfigure the variationist project of researching language change.

Silverstein's chapter then provides a sharp critique of variationism, when viewed through the lenses of indexicality and metapragmatics. He discusses problems associated with variationism's near-exclusive engagement with standard-language communities, its problems of ecological validity (since it relies on sets of demographic categories that are likely to be locally unwarranted), its weak theorising in the area of social identity, and so on. Many of these observations have been made elsewhere, but Silverstein then inverts his critique, summarising how a sociolinguistics of change needs to be framed, once we set aside the mechanistic perspective that, he suggests, variationism inherited from the Neogrammarians.

Change is a theme entertained in many chapters in this volume, and it is a primary interest in Eckert's chapter (Chapter 3). Eckert starts by putting the case that change is central to the semiotic function of language, in the sense that the structure of language is either reproduced or potentially changed in the practice of using indexically salient linguistic forms. The meaning potential of forms and styles (or registers; see Agha 2007), she argues, is continually changing, and Eckert's examples of change are markedly *social* and *cultural* as well as linguistic. Variation is interpreted as part of a semiotic system that is flexible enough to bring social change (new identity formations, new ways of being in the world) into lived practice through new ways of speaking.

Eckert makes it clear that she writes from the disciplinary position of being a variationist, and to that extent her account of contemporary ('third wave') variationism is a view of a classical sociolinguistic paradigm having expanded to incorporate many new assumptions and priorities. Far from the state of affairs where, she says, 'social meaning has been an untheorized subtext of all work on variation', she characterises a perspective on variation that is remarkably open and closely consonant with Silverstein's priorities. New points of consensus that Eckert discusses include the view that variationists need to study (and indeed are studying) practice and pragmatic processes, not just statistics abstracted from practice; they can profitably attend to styles and stylistic creativity, and not be bound to conceptions of 'speech' and 'variables' (although Eckert persists with the term 'variable', but in a widened sense); variation research is enriched when it *integrates* the social and the linguistic/ semiotic; it needs to take a dynamic approach to social meaning, as emergent and potentially focused around new and local social formations; it must embed change in a thoroughgoing manner.

The breadth and inclusiveness of these ideas implies that variationism no longer needs to be viewed as a clearly distinct subfield of sociolinguistics. In tracing its diverse origins, and particularly in locating variationism within the broader study of linguistic signs (and hence with reference to Peirce and Saussure, also Halliday and Bakhtin), contributors to Part I of the book review and reformulate the very foundations of social meaning, which itself is a concept at the heart of any version of sociolinguistics. In that same spirit, Jaffe (in Chapter 4) opens a perspective on 'indexicalization' – the process by which indexical relations come to exist. While we know that indexical relations (contingent associations between signs and referents/objects) can easily become naturalised or iconicised (as Gal elaborates in her later chapter), Jaffe is particularly interested in circumstances where the contingency and context-restrictedness of meaning (i.e. indexicality minus iconicity) is key to how specific interactional effects are achieved. She is therefore interested in a range of meaning effects where indeterminacy is a key quality of semiosis (cf. Eckert, this volume, on 'underspecification' of social meaning).

Elaborating Eckert's (2008) concept of the indexical field, Jaffe coins the idea of 'fields of indexicalities', applying this to how prior clusters of indexical meaning are referenced and reworked in the blog *Stuff White People Like*. In the data, for example, 'funny or ironic tattoos' and 'Moleskine notebooks' are juxtaposed as elements in a putative list of desiderata for 'White people', so that the new juxtaposition is itself an indexical overlay on preexisting possible indexical relations. Jaffe argues that creative, mediatised play of this sort can function to build new stances towards class and race, for example, by inviting readers of the blog to find indexical parallelism across the itemised instances of 'stuff white people like'. By allowing readers to see its own indexicalising procedures (similarly, then, to the process of stylisation; Coupland 2001a), Jaffe explains that the blog allows readers to also see the indexicalities of whiteness and of upper-class existence as something other than natural: They are merely constructed indexes, even if they might otherwise be held to be 'natural' and iconic relations.

In Chapter 5 Gal rethinks the focal sociolinguistic idea of difference, or differentiation. She looks beyond the concept of indexicality that is Jaffe's focus to consider other Peircean concepts that help to theorise differentiation: iconicity, rhematisation, and qualisign. Like the previous three contributors, she provides an integrative account that builds new theory on older sociolinguistic foundations. Gal emphasises language ideology and metapragmatics – and indeed, ideology *as* metapragmatics – and she shows how the concepts of style, persona, register, and enregisterment all depend on a 'meta' conception of language in use.

Overviewing her own recent theoretical work and her collaborative work with Irvine, Gal then lays the ground for closer sociolinguistic engagement with the concepts of iconicity (resemblance between a sign and its referent), rhematisation (slippage between indexical and iconic types of relationship), and qualisigns (signs organised around holistic qualitative experiences or qualia). This is a decisive broadening and enriching of the traditional remit of 'social meaning' in sociolinguistics. It also demonstrates the importance of drawing on an interdisciplinary theoretical base (anthropology, linguistic semantics, semiotics, politics, and philosophy, allied to existing subfields of sociolinguistics itself) in order to advance sociolinguistic theory. The examples that Gal uses to demonstrate the importance and utility of less well-exploited Peircean concepts are themselves strikingly diverse: studies of rape jokes, glossolalia, and (returning us to traditional concerns) language change. In all cases she points to meaningful change that is intelligible only once complex and shifting axes of differentiation are brought to light.

Part II: Language, markets and materiality

The theme of change assumes a larger-scale character in Part II, which deals with the commodification of language in a range of different senses, including the marketisation and embodiment of language. Heller's research has been of central importance in refocusing the sociology of language, where strong paradigms have been developed as a basis for researching diverse aspects of 'languages in communities' (e.g. Heller 2011). Themes include the distribution of languages within and across communities, accounts of minority/majority relations in bilingual and multilingual settings, practical as well as theoretical approaches to language policy and planning, and models of ethnolinguistic vitality which could be applied in initiatives to 'revitalise' minority languages. All of these themes remain important for sociolinguists, just as sociolinguistic input remains important in negotiating these 'real-world' processes. Even so, the theoretical bases of earlier sociolinguistic work in these areas have also been challenged. Heller's contributions have been influential in this regard, perhaps mainly for her critical stances on (what have been understood as) minority languages, on how social change impacts on languages and language in general, and on languages as shifting economic resources.

It was formerly possible to refer to the sociology of language and variationism as the twin pillars of sociolinguistics: the macro versus the micro, and the 'more sociological' versus 'the more linguistic' perspectives, respectively. The sociology of language has come to be associated with 'Fishmanian sociolinguistics' (García et al. 2012). Distinctions of this sort have become less appropriate, however, as 'practice' (e.g. in the senses of Bourdieu 1977; Eckert 2000; Pennycook 2012) has come to the fore. The apparently macro category of 'minority languages', similarly, can usefully be viewed as an object of discursive stance, locally interpreted (cf. Pietikäinen et al. 2016). The status and meaning of 'language', 'languages', and all other generalising concepts of this sort need to be *not* taken for granted in *any* sociolinguistic project (as the Part I chapters have already argued). Heller and her colleagues' contribution to these important realignments has partly been to track the shifts in capital value (in Bourdieu's sense of 'capital'; cf. Kelly-Holmes, this volume, Chapter 7) that are associated with the globalised, neoliberal economies of the present era.

In Chapter 6 Heller and Duchêne first provide a short overview of their earlier research on multilingualism in late-capitalist circumstances, taking francophone/bilingual Canada and multilingual Switzerland as particular cases. They then introduce three angles from which their research has been criticised by others, before giving their reactions to these critiques. In other words they stage their own self-reflexive 'sociolinguistic debate' about the commodification of language – a process which they have argued is accelerating, as language and languages are repositioned under new market conditions. The debate brings to the surface many of the tensions between older (nation-state-linked, identity-based, category-driven) and newer (globalisation-linked, 'profit'-based, discursively framed) conceptions of language, but also conceptions of how sociolinguists should engage with these issues. This sets the scene for Kelly-Holmes's critical review (Chapter 7) of how sociolinguistics has more generally dealt with issues of economic value and 'the market'.

Kelly-Holmes reviews two main theoretical traditions that have brought language and the market into systematic relationship with each other, one inspired by Bourdieu's ideas on language as symbolic capital, the other associated with Fairclough's development of CDA. She then addresses Heller's arguments about the commodification of language and argues that sociolinguistics currently sustains two related but distinguishable senses of this phrase. Kelly-Holmes makes the interesting observation that growing concern with the market has influenced the data sites that sociolinguists tend to examine, so that media texts, for example, are deemed increasingly important because of the close association between mediatisation and marketisation as social and sociolinguistic changes (see Chapter 20). She also links linguistic commodification to new semiotically informed perspectives on language variation and change (cf. Part I), when she explains the increasing role of visual symbolism ('visual multilingualism') and creative styling of other sorts in marketised discourses.

Bucholtz and Hall (Chapter 8) explore diverse points of contact between bodily semiosis, seen as a dimension of language's materiality, and existing sociolinguistic (sociocultural-linguistic) themes. They ask how sociolinguistic theory changes when embodiment is placed at the centre of sociolinguistic concerns, while acknowledging that there is already a substantial history of engagement with the communicating body, for example, in linguistic anthropology, conversation analysis, social psychology, critical theory, and elsewhere. Several of Bucholtz and Hall's examples relate to sexualised indexicalities of body and voice (the voice, as the authors say, being grounded in the body), and the long-running sociolinguistic concern with the social meaning of gender and sexuality will surely be invigorated by bringing visual and linguistic/metapragmatic indexicality into a much more integrated perspective. Bucholtz and Hall cite a wealth of recent research where this is beginning to be accomplished.

In discussing 'embodied experience', Bucholtz and Hall review important new approaches that can re-theorise bodily normativity and non-normativity, which will be a high-priority topic of future research. A serious, critical approach to bodily meaning-in-interaction, as they imply, should no more assume what is 'normal' and what is 'competent' than any sociolinguistic approach to linguistic 'normality' and 'competence' does. Bucholtz and Hall are therefore testing the boundaries of how 'the linguistic' should be construed in sociolinguistics. Many other chapters in this collection do the same, and this reflects not only a broadening of the field but a greater confidence to rethink these boundaries. A question like 'Can we transcend the boundaries of the linguistic?' is, however, being rapidly overtaken by a different question: 'How can we *not* situate our view of language within the wider frameworks of semiosis, agency, and value?'

Part III: Language, place and mobility

Sociolinguistic theorising of space and place has been reconsidered in several important recent treatments (e.g. Jaworski and Machin 2010, 2013; Auer 2012; Joseph 2012; Pennycook 2012). This sort of reappraisal is extended in Part III. In Chapter 9 Pennycook takes on the tasks of explaining and evaluating the welter of new terminology that has been spawned in the wake of globalisation, which has sensitised – and arguably hypersensitised – sociolinguists to mobility and to the limitations of social and linguistic categories of different sorts. 'Translanguaging', for example, is a concept that, as Pennycook explains, emerged in order to highlight the fluidity of actual linguistic practice (e.g. Jørgensen and Møller 2014), particularly in the context of quite large-scale demographic and ethnic mobility, and consciously to oppose the potentially damaging implications of a term like 'bilingualism', which might imply that two languages in contact actually do, or normatively should, retain their character as 'whole languages', discretely associated with different groups. To what extent is this a response to real social change or, on the other hand, a change in perspective that could have been applied to mobility in an earlier epoch? Pennycook rejects the idea that this is merely 'old wine in new bottles'.

The perception that long-established sociolinguistic terms like bi- and multilingualism serve to discriminate against those who use 'mixed' languages (although, as Pennycook notes, 'mixing' as a concept itself conceptually implies prior separation), particularly in educational settings, might be enough to motivate researchers to 'cleanse' their terms. On the other hand, Pennycook makes the important observation that overstating fluidity risks seeming to deny the fact that newly created ways of speaking can indeed *become* enregistered as baseline practices (whether we mean this in a descriptive sense – accepting that baseline styles, or vernaculars [in one sense of this further troublesome term, see Coupland forthcoming], really do exist – or in an ideological sense – that we want to imply that baseline styles should be recognised as legitimate).

Terminological innovation is often a marker of more substantial theoretical realignment, although Pennycook also notes the risks inherent in having too many competing terms with overlapping meanings, particularly where prefixes to new terms (as in the cases of 'super-' and 'trans-') carry different specific meanings. One relevant metatheoretical question is whether key concepts in any discipline can *ever* transparently capture the ideological priorities that theorists want them to bear. If they *could* so align, then there would be no need to progressively critique disciplinary 'keywords' (cf. Williams [1976] in relation to keywords in critical and cultural studies). Pervasive refining and reinterpreting of theoretical terms has always featured in reflexive academic work. It is also clearly not the case that mobility was ignored in sociolinguistics before the concepts of superdiversity and globalisation came into wide circulation, nor the case that perspectives on multilingualism ignored the issues of repertoires and so-called mixing before 'trans-' and 'metro-' prefixed terms were posited. It may well be the case that these considerations were not *adequately* foregrounded, but the 'evolution versus revolution' issue is certainly relevant in this case (cf. Blommaert, this volume, Chapter 11).

One interesting aspect of Britain's argument in Chapter 10 is that, in his considered view and contrary to prevailing assumptions (and contrary to Blommaert's belief that we are experiencing 'a new level of globalized mobility'), the world has *not* 'become more mobile' in any simple sense. Britain's claim is, at first blush, remarkable, particularly in view of the massive 'European migration crisis' being experienced at the time of my writing this chapter (which postdates the writing of the main chapters). A 'sociolinguistics of mobility' and of superdiversity (as reviewed by Pennycook) therefore, in Britain's view, needs to be circumspect about the social tendencies on which it is apparently premised. In the section of his chapter titled 'Mobility unleashed?', Britain gives a nuanced reinterpretation of available statistics, concluding that what is new may be our (the West's) *sensitivity* to mobility, rather than levels of mobility themselves.

Britain's chapter is organised around the concepts of 'sedentarism' and 'nomadism' – two antagonistic ideologies, the first of which privileges stasis and 'fixed abodes', the second of which privileges mobility. Britain explains how *each* of these ideological stances (with sedentarism having come under severe critical assessment across the social sciences recently) can easily be overplayed, to the detriment of the other. Theoretical pendulum swings of this sort are disconcerting. They raise the spectre of theory being formulated as ideology, and they bring Wee's point (see below) about the risk of 'theoretical vanguardism' into view. Britain reviews different sociolinguistic approaches to spatial/areal variation, drawing particular attention to how they have generally sustained an ideology of sedentarism. But he makes a convincing case for the sociolinguistics of dialect needing to adopt a self-critical approach, as espoused in 'the new mobilities paradigm', which does not fixate on either (myopic) sedentarism or (romanticising) nomadism.

Rampton (see below) and Blommaert, in their separate contributions as well as sometimes in collaboration (e.g. Blommaert and Rampton 2011), have shouldered a large part of the responsibility for reassessing sociolinguistic theory over the two last decades. Their work has been remarkable, in terms of productivity, range, and sharpness of critique. It has been at the centre of a substantial European wave of theoretical and metatheoretical reworking of sociolinguistics, addressing the relationship between sociolinguistics and neighbouring disciplines, in particular. Alongside the profoundly influential work of linguistic anthropologists based mainly in North America (discussed at many points in this volume and elsewhere in this Introduction), this European input has reconfigured the field.

Blommaert's metatheoretical incursions into sociolinguistics and discourse studies might be called unremitting. In a flood of major publications (amply referenced across the chapters of this book), he has goaded sociolinguists of all persuasions into radical reflexive reconsiderations of their work and its disciplinary history. Blommaert, along with Rampton and others, must also be credited with setting up and overseeing new international research networks and online resources[2] that have been remarkably productive for the dissemination of new, critical sociolinguistic ideas and analyses, and for building capacity in European and global sociolinguistics. Blommaert has been vociferous in calling for paradigm shift in sociolinguistics; he does so again in Chapter 11. Many other chapters in this book find their orientation by either supporting or challenging Blommaert's positions on the adequacy of 'traditional' theoretical stances or presumptions. We have just seen, in Britain's chapter, how (following Eckert's [2003] initiative towards critiquing 'the authentic speaker') Britain recognises the value of root-and-branch reassessment of the sociolinguistics of place – in general and as regards the

---

[2] The series of online publications referred to as *Working Papers in Urban Language and Literacies* hosted at King's College London has been a particularly strong resource for critical, theoretical, and interdisciplinary innovation in language and society. Tilburg University's Babylon Centre and International Consortium for Language and Superdiversity network have made a similar contribution. Macquarie University hosts the *Language on the Move* Web resource and publishing site, coordinated by Ingrid Piller. All three of the above focus on language and mobility as a key theme.

particular issue of dialectological research. In so doing, we saw how, agreeing with Blommaert, he argues that sedentarism has been too influential as a motivating sociolinguistic ideology. But Britain also vigorously challenges the idea of superdiversity, a perspective that Blommaert has explicitly championed.

In his chapter Blommaert repeats his view that serious engagement with mobility and superdiversity have found sociolinguistics wanting. Earlier theoretical models and analytical frameworks are, he says, 'deficient', although (to my mind, contentiously) Blommaert also sees the reorientation as having been 'largely accomplished'. The new challenge, he asserts, is to move beyond mobility to complexity – constructing a version of sociolinguistics centred on images and metaphors inspired by complexity theory. In his chapter Blommaert then goes on to introduce many such concepts, in a tantalising way. The challenge Blommaert offers us here is indeed inspiring, rich, suggestive, and provocative, but many of the specific claims he makes will necessarily remain partial and controversial until they can be clarified and pursued in detail, both theoretically and empirically. For the moment it is difficult to gauge the precise respects in which '[c]ontemporary repertoires are tremendously complex' and 'messy' in superdiverse circumstances (the definition of which, as Britain suggests, is not yet sufficiently watertight). New images and metaphors may well inspire new theories, but, as Blommaert notes, they do not constitute theories in themselves.

Blommaert sees implications for method as well as for theory itself, and he links his ideas about increasingly complex sociolinguistic environments to the need to frame research ethnographically. Ethnography does indeed seem best suited to exploring infinitely complex environments, although there is nowadays rather little sociolinguistic research, outside of traditional variationism and corpus approaches, that is *not* framed as ethnography. But also, where does complexity end? Even the most detailed and sensitive ethnographic investigation cannot aspire to capturing the full complexity (whatever that might mean) of a single interactional moment – in its historical and local contextualisation, from all relevant points of view. This raises several further questions. Which dimensions of complexity should we target, against which criteria, and what is the optimal balance between opening up complexity and defending workable generalisations on the basis of data analyses? How can we reconcile Blommaert's focal idea of a sociolinguistic 'system' (or 'a universe of complex systems') with the hostility to structural formalism that is his point of departure? To anticipate issues of sociolinguistic intervention that arise in Part V, how can solutions to sociolinguistic problems based in a theoretical appeal to complexity be communicated to people and institutions that might be willing to engage with our research? We will hear more from Blommaert about complexity in other publications.

For the moment, the sheer scale of the theoretical revolution for sociolinguistics that Blommaert is countenancing makes it difficult to evaluate.

Part IV: Power, mediation and critical sociolinguistics

Relationships of power, authority, hegemony, and status have been structured into sociolinguistics since the field originally coalesced. Sociolinguists have been drawn to their work partly out of personal commitments to researching and redressing power imbalances and relationships of subordination of one sort or another – the critical agenda. Most of the grand themes of sociolinguistics, organised around dimensions of class, gender, race, nation, and so on came to prominence in the discipline because of the social and (as could be demonstrated) the sociolinguistic inequalities that were in evidence. Domains such as education, minority group politics, and the law were some of the fields of engagement in which linguistic aspects of inequality were researched, and these infrastructural characteristics may still exist (cf. Blommaert 2012). On the other hand, a good deal of early sociolinguistics was relatively inexplicit about power. It was possible to develop theoretical principles about dialect variation and about multilingualism, for example, with very little reflexive theorising of power.

As noted earlier, however, critical perspectives now predominate in sociolinguistics, in the wake of CDA and the theorising of language ideology. Globalisation has been treated as generating new contexts and modes of linguistic and cultural subordination, ripe for critical engagement. Important countercurrents have been the ideas that sociolinguistics may have tended to romanticise minoritised groups (the working classes, minority language groups, mobile minorities) and that the discipline's political stances were themselves 'uncritical' in another sense – insufficiently worked through at the interface between theory and actual data. In this climate it is particularly helpful to reinstate basic questions, such as, What do we really mean by 'critical'?, which is Pietikäinen's central question in Chapter 12, and What are the roots of particular critical orientations in sociolinguistics?, which is Rampton's question in Chapter 14. Pietikäinen identifies three broad interpretations of critique – emancipatory, ethnographic, and carnivalesque – supporting three modes of critical engagement. She discusses how they are sustained at the level of discursive practice in relation to Sámi communities, the indigenous northern peoples of Finland and neighbouring states. Pietikäinen shows how emancipatory critique relies on there being fixed categories and fixed centre–periphery relations, not least the category of 'Sámi speaker' identifying a peripheral sociocultural group, around which policies seeking to protect Sámi minority rights are organised. Yet applying these categories can also lead to the active marginalisation of particular individuals and subgroups, a process which sometimes defeats emancipatory intentions.

Ethnographic critique, on the other hand, is relativist, establishing specific entitlements in local instances and seeking to recognise historically specific considerations (e.g. in relation to who might be considered 'a Sámi speaker'), in the manner of a situated ethnographic inquiry. Pietikäinen recognises that it risks being perceived as *too* relativist to succeed as the basis of political intervention. Carnivalesque critique (following Bakhtin and Foucault) is transgressive, subverting dominant ideologies via playful or parodic performances. It is based in transcending boundaries (see Pennycook's discussion of 'trans' perspectives, this volume, Chapter 9) rather than resisting them. Mediated parodic interventions are new in relation to Sámi language and culture, and Pietikäinen explains how particular instances, while they are undoubtedly 'risky', can challenge existing orthodoxies.

Androutsopoulos's chapter is included in this section of the book partly because of the obvious role of mass media in both reflecting and promoting language-ideological values. The history of language standardisation is a case in point (cf. Agha 2007; Kristiansen and Coupland 2011). Androutsopoulos cites Agha's distinctive definition of mediatisation, which draws in the idea of 'commoditization' and emphasises how the scale of mass-mediated involvement creates conditions for coordinated understandings of media discourses in terms of their metapragmatic meanings and values. Androutsopoulos critically reviews how sociolinguistics has put up with particularly loose conceptualisations of media, mediation, and mediatisation, and his chapter does important theoretical ground-clearing work for future studies.

Several significant conclusions emerge from this review. One is that sociolinguistics has allowed itself to erase most considerations of 'the media' simply because it has theorised this apparently basic term so loosely. In fact Androutsopoulos lobbies us to set aside the concept of 'the media' in favour of far more nuanced definitions of mediation and mediatisation. When we clarify these concepts, it becomes necessary to also set aside the phonocentric perspectives that have prioritised spoken/audible language use as the main (and sometimes the only legitimate) target of sociolinguistic analysis. Technologically mediated, keyboard-based (and hence 'written') communication is subject to its own logics, norms, and patterns of variability and should not be seen as a recoding of 'real' spoken language. As other chapters have also argued, sociolinguistics needs to engage more wholeheartedly with visual semiosis and the interplay between visual and textual/linguistic dimensions of meaning. The trajectories of mediated exchanges also need to come into view, extending earlier approaches to 'media texts'. It becomes clear that there will be rather few sociolinguistic projects to which mediatisation will not be relevant.

In addition to his own extensive empirical research, Rampton's work has been distinctive for its interdisciplinary range and its commitment to metatheoretical review and reinterpretation. Rampton has kept questioning what the sociolinguistic project amounts to, how it is subdivided, how it has changed, and how it might cohere around specific principles. His chapter here typifies this contribution. Rampton goes back to Foucault for a theoretical account of power and governmentality, then comments on how North American versus European sociolinguistic traditions (referring more specifically to North American linguistic anthropology and European CDA) have elaborated Foucault's ideas in empirical terms. Rampton's main focus of attention is Gumperz and the field of interactional sociolinguistics that Gumperz nurtured.

Rampton is able to draw out several 'points of quite profound connection' between Foucault's and Gumperz's theoretical framing of power, but also between their priorities for how power needs to be researched (the main point being that it was Gumperz who pioneered the necessary empirical approaches through interactional sociolinguistics). The chapter then develops as a review of social-theoretic ideas about social change and new forms of governmentality, to which Rampton adds ideas about how key parts of Gumperz's interactional perspective can be applied in modelling these new circumstances, including new technologically mediated modes of social and commercial interaction. The chapter therefore gives us a way to understand power-coded interactions in contemporary life through the lens of Gumperz's theory – 'neo-Gumperzian theory' – although this mix is also distinctively Ramptonian in its breadth and willingness to embed several disciplines' best theoretical sensibilities into a single account.

Part V: Sociolinguistics, contexts and impact

As mentioned at the outset, in the designing of the book it seemed important not to accept a clear and simple distinction between theory and practice, or for that matter between theory and application. After all (and as Bell notes in Chapter 18), so many of the concerns that have driven sociolinguistics, particularly issues of social inequality with language either at their centre or involved in some less central way, are ones where ideological structures are already in place and impacting on lived experience. A good deal of sociolinguistic research output has taken the form of 'writing against' dominant ideologies, of race, class, gender, and age, spurred on by explicit theorising of the role of the researcher (Cameron et al. 1992), also by the explicitly political agenda of CDA and the subfields it has influenced (reviewed in Part IV).

Under these circumstances, sociolinguistic theory needs to include theorising of the positionality of sociolinguistic professionals in relation to the issues and contexts that they address. This is therefore another mode of metatheory, because we have to theorise how the first-level theoretical frameworks that we build and defend have their impacts on language users, other language-interested people, and institutions. In Chapter 15 Wee draws on Lo Bianco to explain how, with late modernity's quite pervasive scepticism about how academic research can function in fields (like language policy) where vested interested are acknowledged to exist, it becomes impossible to take 'language problems' at face value. In arguing this case, Wee echoes Heller and Duchêne's (Chapter 6) account of how they have not acquiesced to their critics' views that they, as sociolinguists, should wade in on behalf of threatened minority languages. The question is how we should – in theoretical but also in practical terms – define the role of sociolinguists confronting 'sociolinguistic problems in the real world'. Can we avoid aligning with (as Wee puts it) 'class interests or political factionalism'?

There has of course been fairly widespread sociolinguistic discussion of 'intervention' and issues of 'debt' or 'responsibility to the community' or so-called gratuity (cf. *Journal of Sociolinguistics* 1999, vol. 3, outlined in Chapter 18 by Bell; also Wolfram 2013). But the rights and wrongs of linguistic subordination (Lippi-Green 2011) are rarely clear-cut, and ideological self-critique is a prerequisite. In this connection Wee urges caution about theoretical revolution in sociolinguistics, making the point that it is relatively easy to argue for radical realignments in theory and perspective when working in the genre of 'theoretical debate', but that it is much less easy, and perhaps often not desirable or possible, to defend those realignments when modes of intervention will be influenced by them. Wee mentions the problem of 'scholarly vanguardism' – a potential academic error in metatheoretical stance-taking, when academics anticipate social and ideological changes that have not yet infused the whole (or even most) of the populations to whom they apply. It relates to theory as ideology, where progressively minded theorists theorise language–society relations as they want them to be, rather than as they are.

In Chapter 16 Lucas and Bayley orient to the powerful impact of variationist sociolinguistics on our understanding of signed languages. One basic achievement has been in establishing that signed languages are 'normal languages' – a conclusion that lies at the heart of all manner of consequential, practical implications for Deaf communities. (With close relevance to this issue, in Chapter 8, Bucholtz and Hall considered a wide range of political issues associated with different communicative modalities and abilities.) It has been of crucial importance to be able to demonstrate that, for example, the variation that is attested within and across particular signed codes parallels the variation that we know exists within and across spoken codes. But there is also the theoretical affordance that, in comparing signed and spoken languages, we begin to recognise significant truths about *each* of these language types. Lucas and Bayley show, for example, that morphology in sign languages is 'by and large not a boundary phenomenon', as it is in many spoken languages, grammatical person being indicated by the degree of proximity a hand movement has to the signer; a particular gestural path can indicate aspectual meaning. Quantitative comparisons are also able to shed light on language change, for example, the emergence and development of the variety that Lucas and Bayley refer to as Black American Sign Language. This dialectal perspective maps onto the history of racial segregation and progressive integration in the United States.

A cautionary note about sociolinguistic theorising also exists as a subtext in Lucas and Bayley's chapter. They are sensitive to the fact the sociolinguistics of signing still takes its inspiration from classical variationist approaches, which may be partly explained by the relative lack of basic descriptive research into sign language use until recent times. But Lucas and Bayley also argue that smaller-scale, ethnographic perspectives need to be set against large-scale survey research that can determine broad trends in language variation and change. This point is also made by some researchers who prioritise ethnographic methods. They include Eckert (Chapter 3), if we assume that her three waves of variation (Eckert 2012) are not simply scaled as successive 'improvements' to the variationist model, but represent variationism asking successively more subtle questions, which need to be set against wider-reach accounts of sociolinguistic distribution. Similarly, Rampton is explicit about the need to locate his local ethnographic episodes in the wider content of general trends in his data (2006: 253ff.). Mooney (2010: 339) is among those who ask whether sociolinguistics may be in danger of setting aside what it has shown itself to be good at.

Eades (Chapter 17) takes a more direct line on intervention. She demonstrates that legal processes (in Australia but far more generally too) are premised on, and sustain, an ideology of 'referentialism', presuming language to be a transparent medium for the passing on of propositional meaning. How can sociolinguists intervene to challenge this institutional norm that involves the bracketing off of social context? The scale of the challenge involved in intervention varies enormously, context by context, relating to the extent of the gap between 'real-world' ideologies and the value systems that sociolinguistic research and theory seek to inculcate. For educational or government institutions to adopt an ideology of flexible as opposed to fixed bilingualism (in Wee's example, building on Blackledge and Creese's [2014] theoretical perspective) amounts to a very substantial realignment, particularly when linguistics and even traditional sociolinguistic conceptions of bilingualism have endorsed fixed bilingualism. In Eades's context too, referentialist ideology is deeply entrenched. Not only has it been naturalised through years of legal practice; it is (as Eades explains) formally enshrined in the law itself. It allows legal systems to ignore all manner of contextual considerations in how meanings are made in court and in the giving of evidence to the police.

There is also the central problem of 'complexity' (which both Wee and Eades touch on). That is, theory considered to be adequate, particularly in increasingly complex social environments (cf. Blommaert, Chapter 11), will inevitably be 'more complex' in its latest articulations than in earlier versions. Institutional systems very commonly have to rely on category systems – typologies of people (e.g. 'minority language users', 'Aboriginal children'. . .), of language (e.g. 'Welsh' versus 'English' languages, taken to define school types and norms), or of pragmatics (e.g. a 'yes' versus a 'no' response to a question in court) – that are far less sensitive and nuanced than sociolinguists know to be theoretically justifiable. To challenge them is to challenge basic institutional presumptions.

Even so, Eades is optimistic that sociolinguistics *can* change legal systems for the better, so long as we develop strategies for explaining the tenets of sociolinguistic theory in the most effective ways. Eades notes, for example, that the term 'ideology' has unfortunate resonances which are likely to impair intervention initiatives with lawyers; is ideology still interpreted as 'false consciousness'? The idea of 'researching with' as opposed to 'researching on' or 'for' social actors (Cameron et al. 1992) is what Eades recommends, so that sociolinguists do not see themselves as authoritative experts relative to 'lay' ('nonlinguist') others, many of whom have their own professional principles to uphold. The scope of sociolinguistic theory needs to be broad enough and 'meta' enough to encompass the consequences of proposing theoretical positions in relation to the social ecology in which those positions will need to be entertained, and on which they will impact.

Part VI: The evolution of sociolinguistic theory

The final section of the book includes three personal perspectives on how sociolinguistic theory has evolved in recent decades and continues to evolve. Bell (Chapter 18) and Johnstone (Chapter 19) are ideally placed to comment on such changes from their standpoints; both have been principal editors of two leading journals in the field, *Language in Society* and *Journal of Sociolinguistics* for substantial periods of time. In my own concluding chapter (Chapter 20) I have the benefit of being able to react not only to disciplinary changes that have been evident in my own editorial and collaborative research over the years, but also to changes reflected both in the chapters of the present book, and in Bell's and Johnstone's synthetic summaries.

It is interesting to see how both Bell and Johnstone take Hymes as their primary discipline-internal reference point for sociolinguistic theory. This is not because other discipline-internal contributors were less original or less weighty – several of them are still writing influentially, not least in the pages of this book. It might have been because Hymes's ideas were particularly programmatic, setting out principles that could be progressively filled in and adapted over following decades. Bell focuses, for example, on Hymes's idea of socially constituted linguistics (which, for some good reasons, Bell ends up repositioning as socially constituted *socio*linguistics), and a concept of this sort stands as an apt cover term for the theoretically explicit social and cultural treatments of language and semiosis that we see in so many of the present book's chapters (certainly for Rampton's reinterpretation of the Gumperz-Foucault relationship, for example).

Hymes's ideas on genre and communicative key opened up a theoretical space where perspectives on 'style' could thrive and where contexualisation (and its prefixed elaborations; see Bauman and Briggs 1990) would continue to be central to interaction-focused sociolinguistics. This continually refreshed theorising of context in turn (along with Hymes's idea of communicative 'instrumentalities') offered opportunities to develop new accounts of mediation and mediatisation, including technological mass-mediation and 'new' social media which Hymes could not have anticipated. In retrospect, multimodality seems like another Hymesean concept, or at least one that his visionary programme for sociolinguistics could easily absorb.

Johnstone points to other foundational ideas that we have inherited from Hymes and kept at the centre of sociolinguistics, including his ambition to move beyond conceptions of 'dialect' and 'languages' towards the more inclusive and malleable idea of 'linguistic resources' articulated in modes of social practice. Johnstone reviews research papers published under her editorship that have been important in establishing current sociolinguistic theories of style and stylisation, the enregisterment of styles and voices, growing momentum around the semiotic concepts of indexicality and iconicity (very largely under the influence of Silverstein's elaborations of Peirce; cf. Silverstein, this volume, Chapter 2), the view of languages and speakers as ideological rather than descriptive constructs, and new critical orientations to place and identity.

The two reviews (Chapters 18 and 19) suggest far more similarity than difference in theoretical trajectory across the two journals. Together they establish that, despite the two journals' different geographical home bases and their different circumstances and times of origin, sociolinguistics has been evolving rapidly in complex, interrelated ways: There has progressively been more consistent attention to interactional contexts of language, more refined and more multimodally framed semiotic theory, more reflexive use of key terms and categories, more confidence in the critical range and power of sociolinguistics, more integrative approaches to variation and diversity, and more attention to social change, mobility, cultural hybridity, and mediatisation. Chapters 18 and 19 of course reflect only two of the many journals that support and advance international sociolinguistics, and the fact that it is increasingly difficult to come up with a comprehensive list of 'sociolinguistics journals' is telling in its own right. There is considerable overlap between outlets that could be included in such a category and many other socially oriented journals in discourse analysis, as well as linguistically interested journals in sociology, media studies, social psychology, and indeed social theory.

For the moment, however, one point emerges in relation to Bell's and Johnstone's reviews, relating to Labov's place in sociolinguistics and to the importance of what has been known as variationism (and 'Labovianism') for many years. The variationist model was the first truly cohesive perspective on linguistic diversity to gel in sociolinguistics, and under Labov's inspiring leadership, it has evolved to be the most clearly principled perspective at the interface between language and society. This explains why it has become a pervasive point of reference, but also a target of critique. To have had anything to say – in sociolinguistics since 1966 – that might meaningfully add to or qualify Labov's work has had unique symbolic capital for sociolinguists. Most of the theoretical tendencies that Bell and Johnstone identify of course move the central impetus of sociolinguistics away from classical Labovianism. But it is also necessary to ask whether these movements would have been possible without having had Labov's work to articulate with. In very many regards they could not, and this applies equally to the semiotic re-theorising of social meaning and style (cf. Part I of this volume); issues of social inequality around class, race, and gender (e.g. Lucas and Bayley, this volume, Chapter 16; Eades, this volume, Chapter 17); the interactional analysis of group relations (e.g. Rampton, this volume, Chapter 14); and the critical/political framing of sociolinguistics in general and sociolinguists' potential to intervene in social problems (e.g. chapters in Part V). This is also the case for the sociolinguistic theorising of language change and social change (cf. Eckert, this volume, Chapter 3), which I pick up as the main theme of Chapter 20.

REFERENCES

Agha, Asif. 2007. *Language and Social Relations*. Cambridge: Cambridge University Press.

Alexander, Jeffrey C., B. Giesen, and J. L. Mast. 2006. *Social Performance: Symbolic Action, Cultural Pragmatics and Ritual*. Cambridge: Cambridge University Press.

Androutsopoulos, Jannis (ed.). 2014. *Mediatization and Sociolinguistic Change*. Berlin: de Gruyter.

Auer, Peter (ed.). 2012. *Space in Language and Linguistics*. Berlin: de Gruyter.

Bauman, Richard. 1977. Verbal art as performance. *American Anthropologist* 77, 2: 290–311.

Bauman, Richard, and Charles Briggs. 1990. Poetics and performance as critical perspectives on language and social life. *Annual Review of Anthropology* 19: 59–88.

Blackledge, Adrian, and Angela Creese (eds.). 2014. *Heteroglossia as Practice and Pedagogy*. Dordrecht: Springer.

Block, David. 2014. *Social Class in Applied Linguistics*. Abingdon and New York: Routledge.

Blommaert, Jan. 2005. *Discourse: A Critical Introduction*. Cambridge: Cambridge University Press.

2010. *The Sociolinguistics of Globalization*. Cambridge: Cambridge University Press.

2012. Investigating narrative inequality: African asylum seekers' stories in Belgium. In R. Wodak (ed.), *Critical Discourse Analysis*. London: Sage, 55–96.

2015. Pierre Bourdieu and language in society. *Working Papers in Urban Language and Literacies* 153, King's College London. Available at www.kcl.ac.uk/innovation/groups/ldc/publications/workingpapers/.

Blommaert, Jan, and Ben Rampton. 2011. Language and superdiversity: A position paper. *Working Papers in Urban Language and Literacies* 70, King's College. Available at www.kcl.ac.uk/innovation/groups/ldc/publications/workingpapers/.

Bourdieu, Pierre. 1977. *Outline of a Theory of Practice*. Cambridge: Cambridge University Press.

1991. *Language and Symbolic Power*. Cambridge: Polity.

Brown, Penelope, and Stephen C. Levinson. 1987. *Politeness: Some Universals in Language Usage*. Cambridge: Cambridge University Press. First published 1978 as part of Esther N. Goody (ed.), *Questions and Politeness: Strategies in Social Interaction*. Cambridge: Cambridge University Press.

Burke, Peter. 2005. *History and Social Theory*. Ithaca, NY: Cornell University Press.

Cameron, Deborah, Elizabeth Frazer, Penelope Harvey, Ben Rampton, and Kay Richardson. 1992. *Researching Language: Issues of Power and Method*. London: Longman.

Chambers, J. K. 1995/2009. *Sociolinguistic Theory*. Oxford: Wiley-Blackwell.

Coulmas, Florian. 1997. Introduction. In F. Coulmas (ed.), *The Handbook of Sociolinguistics*. Oxford and Cambridge, MA: Blackwell Publishers, 1–12.

Coupland, Nikolas. 1998. What is sociolinguistic theory? *Journal of Sociolinguistics* 2, 1: 110–117.

2001a. Dialect stylisation in radio talk. *Language in Society* 30, 3: 345–375.

2001b. Introduction: Sociolinguistic theory and social theory. In Nikolas Coupland, Srikant Sarangi, and Christopher N. Candlin (eds.), *Sociolinguistics and Social Theory*. London: Longman, 1–26.

2010a. The authentic speaker and the speech community. In Carmen Llamas and Dominic Watts (eds.), *Language and Identities*. Edinburgh: Edinburgh University Press, 99–112.

(ed.). 2010b. *Handbook of Language and Globalization*. Malden, MA, and Oxford: Wiley-Blackwell.

2014. Language, society and authenticity: Themes and perspectives. In Véronique Lacoste, Jakob Leimgruber, and Thiemo Breyer (eds.), *Indexing Authenticity: Sociolinguistic Perspectives*. Berlin: Mouton de Gruyter, 14–39.

Forthcoming. Labov, vernacularity and sociolinguistic change. *Journal of Sociolinguistics*.

Coupland, Nikolas, and Adam Jaworksi (eds.) 2009a. *The New Sociolinguistics Reader*. Basingstoke and New York: Palgrave Macmillan.

2009b. *Sociolinguistics: Critical Concepts in Linguistics* . 6 vols. London: Routledge.

Coupland, Nikolas, Srikant Sarangi, and Christopher N. Candlin (eds.). 2001. *Sociolinguistics and Social Theory*. London: Longman.

Chambers, J. K. 1995/2003. *Sociolinguistic Theory: Linguistic Variation and Its Social Significance*. Oxford: Blackwell.

Duchêne, Alexandre, and Monica Heller (eds.). 2011. *Language in Late Capitalism: Pride and Profit*. London: Routledge.

Duranti, Alessandro. 1997. *Linguistic Anthropology*. Cambridge: Cambridge University Press.

Duranti, Alessandro, and Charles Goodwin (eds.). 1992. *Rethinking Context: Language as an Interactive Phenomenon*. Cambridge and New York: Cambridge University Press.

Eckert, Penelope. 2000. *Linguistic Variation as Social Practice*. Oxford: Blackwell.

2003. Elephants in the room. *Journal of Sociolinguistics* 7, 3: 392–397.

2008. Variation and the indexical field. *Journal of Sociolinguistics* 12, 4: 453–476.

2012. Three waves of variation study: The emergence of meaning in the study of sociolinguistic variation. *Annual Review of Anthropology* 41: 87–100.

Fairclough, Norman. 1992. *Discourse and Social Change*. Cambridge: Polity.

1995. *Critical Discourse Analysis*. Boston: Addison Wesley.

Figueroa, Esther. 1994. *Sociolinguistic Metatheory*. Oxford: Pergamon.

Fishman, Joshua. 1965. *Yiddish in America: Socio-linguistic Description and Analysis*. Bloomington: Indiana University Press.

Flyvbjerg, Bent. 2002. *Making Social Science Matter*. Cambridge: Cambridge University Press.

Flyvbjerg, Bent, Todd Landman, and Sanford Schram. 2012. Important next steps in phronetic social science. In Bent Flyvbjerg, Todd Landman, and Sanford Schram (eds.), *Real Social Science: Applied Phronesis*. Cambridge: Cambridge University Press, 285–297.

García, Ofelia, Gella S. Fishman, and Joshua Fishman (eds.). 2012. *International Journal of the Sociology of Language: Cultural Autonomy and Fishmanian Sociolinguistics*. Berlin: de Gruyter, Number 213.

Giddens, Anthony. 1996. *In Defence of Sociology: Essays, Interpretations and Rejoinders*. Cambridge: Polity Press.

Giles, Howard, and Peter F. Powesland. 1975. *Speech Style and Social Evaluation*. London and New York: Academic Press.

Giles, Howard, Justine Coupland, and Nikolas Coupland (eds.). 1991. *Contexts of Accommodation: Developments in Applied Sociolinguistics*. Cambridge: Cambridge University Press.

Gregersen, Frans. 1998. Review of R. Singh (ed.), 1996. *Towards a Critical Sociolinguistics*. John Benjamins. *Acta Linguistica Hafniensia* 30: 241–253.

Gumperz, John J. 1982. *Discourse Strategies*. Cambridge: Cambridge University Press.

Halliday, M. A. K. 1978. *Language as Social Semiotic: The Social Interpretation of Language and Meaning.* London: Edward Arnold.

Hammersley, Martyn 1992. *What's Wrong with Ethnography? Methodological Explorations.* London: Routledge.

Harrington, Austin (ed.). 2005. *Modern Social Theory: An Introduction.* Oxford: Oxford University Press.

Heller, Monica. 2011. *Paths to Postnationalism: A Critical Ethnography of Language and Identity.* Oxford: Oxford University Press.

Holmes, Janet, and Kirk Hazen (eds.). 2014. *Research Methods in Sociolinguistics: A Practical Guide.* Oxford: Wiley-Blackwell.

Hudson, Richard A. 1980/1996. *Sociolinguistics.* Cambridge: Cambridge University Press.

Hymes, Dell. 1972. On communicative competence. In J. B. Pride and J. Holmes (eds.), *Sociolinguistics.* London: Penguin, 269–293.

Irvine, Judith T., and Susan Gal. 2000. Language ideology and linguistic differentiation. In P. Kroskrity (ed.), *Regimes of Language.* Santa Fe, NM: SAR Press, 35–84.

Jaworski, Adam, and David Machin. 2010. *Semiotic Landscapes: Language, Image, Space.* London: Continuum.

  2013. *The Sociolinguistics of Space and Semiotic Landscapes. Semiotix* (online edition, available at Semioticon.com).

Johnson, Sally, and Astrid Ensslin (eds.). 2007. *Language in the Media: Representations, Identities, Ideologies.* London: Continuum.

Jørgensen, J. Normann, and Janus Møller. 2014. Polylingualism and languaging. In Constant Leung and Brian V. Street (eds.), *The Routledge Companion to English Studies.* Abingdon: Routledge, 67–83.

Joseph, John E. 2012. Role of language and place in language policy. In Carol A. Chapelle (ed.), *The Encyclopedia of Applied Linguistics.* Oxford and New York: Wiley-Blackwell.

Kerswill, Paul. 2007. Socio-economic class. In Carmen Llamas and Peter Stockwell (eds.), *The Routledge Companion to Sociolinguistics.* Abingdon and New York: Routledge, 51–61.

Kristiansen, Tore, and Nikolas Coupland (eds.). 2011. *Standard Languages and Language Standards in a Changing Europe.* Oslo: Novus.

Labov, William. 1963. The social motivation of a sound change. *Word* 19: 273–309.

  1966. *The Social Stratification of English in New York City.* Washington, DC: Center for Applied Linguistics.

  1972. *Sociolinguistic Patterns.* Philadelphia: Pennsylvania University Press.

Lasswell, Harold. 1935. *World Politics and Personal Insecurity.* New York: Free Press.

Lippi-Green, Rosina W. 2011. *English with an Accent: Language, Ideology, and Discrimination in the United States.* London: Routledge.

MacIntyre, Alasdair. 2007. *After Virtue: A Study in Moral Theory,* 3rd ed. Notre Dame, IN: University of Notre Dame Press.

Madsen, Lian Malai. 2015. *Fighters, Girls and Other Identities: Sociolinguistics in a Martial Arts Club.* Clevedon: Multilingual Matters.

Madsen, Lian Malai, Marha Sif Karrebæk, and Janus Spindler Møller (eds.). 2015. *Everyday Languaging: Collaborative Research on the Language Use of Children and Youth.*

Mendoza-Denton, Norma. 2008. *Homegirls: Language and Cultural Practice among Latina Youth Gangs.* New York: Blackwell.

Mesthrie, Rajend and Ana Deumert. 2009. Critical sociolinguistics: Approaches to language and power. In Rajend Mesthrie, Joan Swann, Ana Deumert, and William L. Leap, *Introducing Sociolinguistics,* 2nd ed. Edinburgh: Edinburgh University Press, 309–342.

Milroy, Lesley, and Matthew Gordon. 2002. *Sociolinguistics: Method and Interpretation,* 2nd ed. London: Wiley-Blackwell.

Milroy, Lesley, and James Milroy. 1992. Social network and social class: Toward an integrated sociolinguistic model. *Language in Society* 21: 1–26.

Mooney, Annabelle. 2010. Has God gone global? Religion, language and globalization. In Nikolas Coupland (ed.), *Handbook of Language and Globalization.* Malden, MA, and Oxford: Wiley-Blackwell, 323–345.

Muysken, Pieter. 1998. Review of Singh 1996. *Journal of Pragmatics* 30, 6: 771–773.

Parsons, Talcott. 1952. *The Social System.* London: Tavistock.

Pennycook, Alastair. 2010. *Language as a Local Practice.* London: Routledge.

2012. *Language and Mobility: Unexpected Places.* Clevedon: Multilingual Matters.

Pietikäinen, Sari, Helen Kelly-Holmes, Alexandra Jaffe, and Nikolas Coupland. 2016. *Sociolinguistics from the Periphery: Small Languages in New Circumstances.*

Rampton, Ben. 2006. *Language in Late Modernity: Interaction in an Urban School.* Cambridge: Cambridge University Press.

Romaine, Suzanne. 1994. *Language in Society: An Introduction to Sociolinguistics.* Oxford: Oxford University Press.

Schram, Sanford F., and Brian Caterino (eds.). 2006. *Making Political Science Matter: Debating Knowledge, Research and Method.* New York and London: New York University Press.

Schutt, Russell K. 2014. *Investigating the Social World: The Process and Practice of Research,* 8th ed. Thousand Oaks, CA: Sage.

Silverstein, Michael. 1979. Language structure and linguistic ideology. In P. R. Clyne, W. F. Hanks, and C. L. Hofbauer (eds.), *The Elements: A Parasession on Linguistic Units and Levels.* Chicago, IL: Chicago Linguistics Society, 193–247.

Singh, Rajendra (ed.). 1996. *Towards a Critical Sociolinguistics.* Amsterdam: John Benjamins.

Therborn, Göran. 1996. Critical theory and the legacy of twentieth-century Marxism. In Bryan S. Turner (ed.), *The Blackwell Companion to Social Theory.* Cambridge, MA: Blackwell, 53–82.

Turner, Bryan S. 1996. Introduction. In B. S. Turner (ed.), *The Blackwell Companion to Social Theory.* Oxford: Blackwell, 1–19.

Urban, Greg. 2001. *Metaculture: How Culture Moves through the World.* Minneapolis: University of Minnesota Press.

Williams, Glyn. 1992. *Sociolinguistics: A Sociological Critique.* London: Routledge.

Williams, Raymond. 1976. *Keywords: A Vocabulary of Culture and Society.* London: Croom Helm.

Wilson, William J., and Anmol Chadda. 2009. The role of theory in ethnographic research. *Ethnography* 10, 4: 549–564.

Wodak, Ruth. 2000. Does sociolinguistics need social theory? Paper presented at Sociolinguistics Symposium, Bristol, 27 April.

   (ed.). 2012. *Critical Discourse Analysis*. London: Sage.

Wolfram, Walt. 2013. Community commitment and social responsibility. In J. K. Chambers and Natalie Schilling (eds.), *Handbook of Language Variation and Change,* 2nd ed. Malden, MA, and Cambridge: Wiley-Blackwell, 557–575.

Part I

Theorising social meaning

2 The "push" of *Lautgesetze*, the "pull" of enregisterment

Michael Silverstein

Without question the enterprise of linguistics was decisively transformed, in Leipzig, Halle, and elsewhere, by what flowed from the comparative-historical study of Indo-European and other recognized language families. By the last quarter of the nineteenth century, serious scholars in the discipline sought to base generalizing theories about the nature of language on these results, intending to make the speculative philosophizing of Enlightenment savants disappear in the brighter and better light of empirical generalizations about language change that evidence, in turn, how language must function. By the post–Great War twentieth century, language change itself, once the central focus of linguistics – "diachrony" of linguistic systems, in Ferdinand de Saussure's terminology – came to be viewed counterdirectionally through the lens of "synchronic" structural states immanent in the actualized forms and functions of language.[1] And indeed, for the rest of the century until the current day, the presumption of such immanent structural systematicity in relation to the actualized and experienced forms and functions of language has played the central role in investigating language change. Understood as change of the way forms code denotational meanings of language, it is seen as an inevitable outcome of the universal fact of variation in discursive performance within a language community. The synchronically based reimagination of Neogrammarian *Lautgesetze* has been in this respect variationist sociolinguistics' key affordance, both in phonology and, more problematically, beyond.

In light of a Foucauldian genealogy of ideas, I will counterpose a more semiotically and social anthropologically informed view of what is termed "variation" in terms of indexicality – the quality of signs such as phonetic parameters to point to aspects of their context of production and

---

[1] Thus note that by the mid-1920s, Leonard Bloomfield could summarize Neogrammarian doctrine in his parsimonious postulate H3, "Phonemes ... gradually change" (1926: 162); see also 1933: 354), relying on the consolidation of (synchronic) phonological theory as a model for linguistic structure. See also Sapir (1925: 49–50; 1949: 180–186). Parallel structuralist developments in Europe beginning with Baudouin de Courtenay were consolidated in Praguean structural-functionalism by the end of the 1920s, as will be pointed out below.

reception – and of variation's enregisterment[2] – the frequently only intuitively felt property of textual ("stylistic") coherence of indexical and other compatible signs one with another in the flow of discourse that defines an abstractable schema, a subgrammar, for context-appropriate and context-effective modes of communicating. Observe that enregisterment partially structures the norms immanent in any measurable indexical effects in the real-time use of language by filtering such indexicality through the lens of form in denotational code. Such enregisterment frequently cuts across analytic planes and levels of linguistic structure, so that, for example, certain morpholexical expressions tend to have certain phonetic realizations all the while as well occurring in grammatically conforming phrasal collocations with particular other morpholexical expressions. But enregisterment operates as well on each distinguishable plane of language, so that phonological registers, morphological registers, lexical registers, syntactic registers, and so on are all recognizable for any language. But more later on indexicality and enregisterment as the best theoretical practices for the study of variation in the light of the signal contributions of several generations of students of language change.

I wish here critically to trace some of the perhaps unrecognized currents of best theoretical practice in this flow of ideas that has lead from Neo-grammarian insights to contemporary sociolinguistic views of variation. I want to point out the extraordinary – indeed, almost puzzlingly ironic – continuities involved as diachronically focused comparative philology gave way to synchronically focused linguistics, and to revisit and recuperate some of the key ideas along the way that, though puzzlingly lost from the intellectual patrimony of sociolinguistic variationism, are compatible with and indeed necessary to a more sophisticated, semiotically and ethnographically informed sociolinguistics – whether of the "Third Wave" (Eckert 2012; this volume, Chapter 3) or beyond – in which key concepts of indexicality, of linguistic 'register' and the dialectical sociolinguistic processes of 'enregisterment'

---

[2] I introduced this clumsy but necessary term in the mid-1980s (Silverstein 1992: 320) within the constraints of available English derivational morphology in order to emphasize the dynamic and dialectical aspect of how native speaker intuitions of variation – always, of course, ideologically informed – operate as an ever-present biasing vector in the operation of indexical semiosis. Enregistered indexicality is always what I have termed second- or higher-order indexicality. A denotational register is, in effect, a model of the grammar underlying and specific to how one can "say 'the same thing'" as one otherwise could, appropriate to and effective in a particular social context, for example, characterized by what kind of individuals (in one or more schemata of social differentiation and characterological types) currently inhabit the roles of Sender, Receiver, Audience, etc., and in what kind of communicative event. Observe that in language communities like current American English, "dialect" has become to a significant degree functionally enregistered so as to index affiliation-to-place, a kind of human *appellation d'origine contrôlée*" (see Johnstone et al. 2006; Johnstone 2013; Silverstein 2014a).

refocus this enterprise. On this basis, I would argue, we can found a more realistic view of linguistic variation than the dominant one in much variationist work; this view, in turn, dissolves the rigid synchrony/diachrony distinction in the sphere of *langue* in favor of a rather more dialectical and perhaps explanatory view of language form and function centered on indexicality and enregisterment, *language thus to be seen as a structured, semiotically functional envelope of enregisterment moving along in socio-space-time.*

Sound law, speech, and structure

To be sure, "the Neogrammarian – or *Lautgesetz* – controversy," as it has come to be called,[3] arraying Leskien et al. against Schuchardt et al., centered on the ontological and epistemological aspects of the exceptionlessness of sound laws (for how could there be a "law," even one paradoxically specific to time and place, if there were unpredictable exceptions to it? And how could one inductively infer the prior operation of such a "law" in the messy and disparate textual data from which one worked?). But the longer term significance of Neogrammarianism is its clear concept of the relative autonomy of phonology as a plane of language, that is, the "duality of patterning" (Hockett 1958: 574–575; 1977: 152–155) or "double articulation" (Martinet 1949; 1955: 157–158) of language structure. If the sounds of a language's lexical stock, whatever their nature, could systematically transform over time in some community of users independent of any other properties of their words and expressions – morphological complexity, syntactic distribution in phrases, frequency of occurrence, textual (and contextual) affinities – there must be something integral and distinctive to them as a type of linguistic phenomenon. Two great classes of ideas emerged about such "sounds": one essentially reductive, the other essentially structural.

The reductive idea rested on the fact that sound laws invoked to derive 'regular' descendent forms from earlier ones seemed, on the whole, to involve the change of sound segments as a function of the sequential context in which such segments occurred in the (sometimes only reconstructed) ancestral form and that such change, as an adjustment of the overall sequence of sounds, seemed to have a kind of general phonetic rationale. Sound laws were in fact classifiable into phonetic types, such as assimilation, dissimilation, metathesis,

---

[3] See the useful compilation by Terence H. Wilbur (1977) that reproduces several important publications of the mid- to late 1880s, including Georg Curtius's, Hugo Schuchardt's, and Otto Jespersen's critical doubts about Neogrammarian doctrines, as well as explanatory expositions thereof by Karl Brugmann, Hermann Osthoff, and Hermann Collitz. Wilbur adds an extensive biographical and bibliographic contextualization of Neogrammarianism in nineteenth-century linguistics. See also the excellent survey of Morpurgo Davies (1998).

and syncope, and, moreover, seemed to recur in distinct language families and even in distinct and independent language branches within a family. If such sound changes manifest results of a gradual accumulation of minute, physiologically driven changes, it sent researchers to the phonetics laboratory to demonstrate in living articulatory performance the minute tendencies of this sort congruent or consistent with sound laws as discovered in the archive of completed history, the philologically grounded comparative etymological dictionary. Needless to say, such psychophysiological and psychophysical explanations run into extraordinary problems (though there are still determined advocates of reduction!) both of an empirical sort – the eminent phonetician Paul Passy (1890: 152, 224, 226) no less than the eminent comparatist Antoine Meillet pointed, for example, to the change (with no intermediates) from tongue-trilled r to uvular r in one generation in Paris[4] – and, of course, of a more profound conceptual sort: The "sounds" at issue in "sound laws" are not, in fact, mere token event occurrences, a sample or swatch of which can be collected purely as articulatory data-points in the laboratory and then studied for same-subject and cross-subject characteristics (variationists, take note!); the "sounds" of "sound laws" are not even segments as such, but what we now term "features."

The irony in all this is that the young Leipzig student Ferdinand de Saussure had already, in his brilliant if opaque *Mémoire* of 1878 (1879), intuited the essentially syntagmatic character of an abstract structure of syllables realizing serially concatenated allomorphic forms of roots and suffixes underlying anything one might wish to call "sounds" in the articulated language forms of Indo-European languages.[5] It was on the basis of a theory of the reconstructed morphology of lexical classes inferred for the Indo-European parent language that Saussure could see the distributional necessity for certain non-obstruent "*coéfficients sonantiques*" – 'laryngeals' we call them today – to fill out the syllabic and morpholexical pattern of the reconstructed parent language – and in this way to *save* the concept of the regularity of "sound

---

[4] Though it would appear that Meillet considered the change not quite exemplary of "sound law" so much as of another kind of process, suggesting, in fact, its status as a register shibboleth: "*Dans une grande partie des langues de l'Europe, et à ce qu'il semble, sous l'action de la civilization, la vibrante r [de la pointe de la langue qui va toucher le palais] trop éclatante, tend à s'éliminer, soit que l'articulation tend vers zero, comme en anglais, soit qu'elle soit remplacée par une articulation de l'arrière-gorge, comme en français et en allemand*" (1995 [ca. 1910]: 55; cf. also 1995: 189, §146).

[5] An added irony is that by the time of his early twentieth-century Geneva lectures underlying the *Cours de linguistique générale* of 1916, he seemed not to make much of the relevance of the existence of this structure of 'syntagmatic' and 'paradigmatic' relations among sound segments in phonology itself, in addition to these relations among the simplex and complex linguistic signs he attended to at the level of morphology and syntax.

law" in respect of the vocalic correspondences across Latin, Greek, Sanskrit, Gothic, and so on that otherwise were then in puzzling disarray.[6]

In short, the doctrine of the abstract sequential combinatorics of phonological or phonemic segments in syllable-measured forms (later doubled by recognition of the Boolean combinatorics of phonological features manifested by each such segment) turns out to be necessary to making sense of the very possibility of the "exceptionlessness" of "sound law." But, beyond the naïve identification of graphemes in a written source with phonological segments, how do we find or discover what are the actual phonological units of a language in the history of which we may be interested? Empirical phonology, a way of establishing, for a newly encountered language, the "grammar" of sound immanent in the articulatory events of its users, is the essential breakthrough, undertaken in part by field dialectologists of nonstandard variants in Europe and more essentially by anthropological linguists mapping the "exotic" languages of the world. For all this, of course, we thank Saussure's coeval who had come to America, Franz Boas, and his successors in the study of the "American Native languages," as he always termed them, the founders of descriptivism Edward Sapir and Leonard Bloomfield and their many followers. And we thank equally the European pioneers of feature phonology, Jan Baudouin de Courtenay, Nikolaj Trubetskoj, and Roman Jakobson, who, along with Daniel Jones and his school, reintegrated a concern for phonetic reality into a model of phonological structure: linguistically implemented not merely as an algebraic inventory of occurring phonological segments but a dimensionalized organization of them in respect of a phonologico-phonetic space that corresponds to and projects from their distributional properties in syllables and word forms.

"Phonemes ... change"

So Bloomfield, with his reverence for Pāṇinian conciseness, sums up the Neogrammarian theory in his "Postulates" of 1926 ("Assumption H3"). If phonological units (segmental and other "phonemes") are the targets and loci of *Lautgesetze*, this at once explains the autonomy and ubiquity of any particular "sound" change: It is a diachronic process operating sui generis and affecting every occurrence in the language of particular targeted units of a structural plane, that of phonological representation, as part of the grammatical

---

[6] See Saussure 1922: 1–268. Kuryłowicz (1927) demonstrated that the then recently deciphered Hittite showed correspondences of the segments the youthful Saussure had postulated. At the same time, Bloomfield and Sapir showed similar predictive power for comparative reconstructions in the indigenous languages – Algonquian and Athapascan, respectively – of North America. See Silverstein 2014b and references therein.

norms of a community. Yet at the same time this renders even more mysterious how so-called idiolectal quirks of speakers at the level of measurable variant token phonetic realizations of type phonemic sequences might ever cumulate in a structural (paradigmatic) change – a merger or split of phonemes, for example – in the language community's systemic norm. And in such a model, to be sure, the focus is on individual changes, to be described using formulae of the usual sort, p > q /r__s '[phoneme] p (at an earlier stage) becomes [phoneme] q (at a later stage) in the (earlier-stage syntagmatic) context of following r and preceding s.' With some concern for rule inputs and rule outputs from mergers and splits, such changes could be ordered step-by-step into a model of overall phonological change that, when assembled, seems to recapitulate the relative chronology of the totality of changes differentiating temporally earlier and later inventories of expressions. Beyond renaming "sounds" as phonological segments, however, such a model is, in fact, no different from the prephonemic models of the Neogrammarians – only now complicated by the essential stadialism of the presumption of a single structural norm: If "subphonemic" phonetic variance in token realizations of phonological structures is a universal condition within a language community, when and how can it cumulate so as to lead to what must be, by stadial logic, sudden change in that structure?

If phonemes are the loci and fulcra of *Lautgesetze* as earlier formulated, they are also the loci and fulcra of what Baudouin (1972 [1895]) – and after him, Saussure (1916: 215–220) – termed 'alternations,' to be captured by statements of synchronic variation in the shape of morphemes in their various combinations, that is, (morpho-)phonological rules, that look precisely like those of historical change applied in a more-or-less recapitulative order.[7] There was a seamless – almost puzzling – continuity in the discipline moving from diachronic to synchronic phonology in this respect, seemingly reflecting the common logic of both kinds of empirical investigation. The investigation of contextually conditioned subphonemic variance in synchronic terms, by which one was able to eliminate complementary distribution so as to group distinct, phonetically similar sound-types into a single phonemic category, or the criteria for grouping distinct phonemes under partial neutralization into a more abstract "morphophonemic" one, followed an operational logic that was precisely the same as the earlier logic of induction, the "method of residues," by which *Lautgesetze* had been recognized (see Silverstein 2013). This inevitably encouraged thinking about the kinds of synchronic phonological rules in precisely the same phonetic terms as had earlier students of diachrony

---

[7] Bloomfield's classic observation of this in his "Menomini morphophonemics" (1939: 105–106) has resonated through the years of first "item and process" phonemic structuralism – see Hockett 1954: 211 – and then generative phonology – see Chomsky and Halle 1968: 249–251.

(palatalizations, velarizations, labializations, and other assimilations, positionally driven strengthenings vs. weakenings, etc.) and, in fact, thinking respectively about morphophonological and subphonological synchronic variance as
the recapitulative trace of history, in the first instance, and the prospective
promise of change, in the second. And scholars from Baudouin to Bloomfield
to Chomsky and Halle and beyond continue to "discover" the first, where
"underlying" forms are equatable to "earlier" (surface) forms, and scholars
from Leskien to Hockett to Labov and beyond continue to "discover" the
second, where today's "allophones" and "phonological variables" are harbin-
gers of tomorrow's phonemes.

But such models, however focused on a "law"-by-"law" or rule-by-rule basis
on the phonetic underpinnings, do not essentially move beyond the consideration of one phonological phenomenon at a time, surface form yielding surface
form, more or less as it had always been thought. In an insightful final
paragraph in his paper on sound law, Sapir (1949: 82 [1931]) suggested that
perhaps phonological systems – such as he had theorized in detail in his
1925 "Sound Patterns" paper – themselves were structures in time the properties of which *as systems* motivate and explain phonological persistence as well
as change. It was Jakobson's *Prinzipien* of 1931 (reprinted in its French version
in 1962: 202–220), of course, following on the 1929 *Thèses* at the Slavists'
Congress (Vachek 1964: 33–58), that first seriously developed this structural-
functional idea that it was not the – as he later liked to say in lectures –
"atomistic and blind" phonetic laws affecting individual-segments-in-context
that were the locus of change, so much as the relational structures, the oppositions, of phonetically projectable but nonetheless still phonological categories.

Hence, processes of phonologization, dephonologization, and rephonologi-
zation as structural characteristics of particular subparts of systems over time
become the analytic and descriptive tools for this kind of historical phonology.
And what might be the factors that drive and shape these processes at the level
of systems then becomes the key question. Can we discern which oppositions
in a system are more "central" and hence fundamental, and which more
peripheral? On what grounds can we discern centrality and peripherality?
If we think of the phonological structure, the principles organizing the inventory and relative distributions of phonemic units as such, we might interrogate
historical transformations of the system with considerations such as the
following: Is it the case, for example, that more central oppositions – for
example, Trubetskojan 'correlations' of multiply applicable, parallel, binary
(and generally privative) contrasts – of a system tend to be constantly repho-
nologized over time (think Grimm's Law), while marginal oppositions, unique
contrasts isolated by their pertinence only in a small region of the system,
come and go without consequence? Given that phonological units are the
syntagmatic building-blocks of syllabic structures, of an integral number of

which every linguistic form consists, what distributional constraints – a kind of 'functional load' – may as well contribute to the maintenance or elimination or even compensatory resituating of phonologic contrasts subject to the statistical fluctuations of variability in performance?

Note, all these questions about systemic structures as such had long been central to dealing with historical change at the nonphonological planes of language, where changes of "analogies" and structural and semantic "contamination" of one expression-type by another necessarily invoked properties of morphosyntactic systematicity among the elements of language directly bearing denotational meanings.[8] Thus, for example, the shifts from case-marked nominal phrases in older Indo-European languages as the expression of grammatical relations to fixed constituent orders and adpositional phrases have long been interpreted in terms of functionally compensatory regrammaticalization of universally obligatory semantic content, like 'Agent' and 'Patient' indications within a clause-level morphosyntactic form.[9] Ideas about predictable (or at least retrodicted) directions of analogical influences in "regularizing" one kind of form on the basis of another prominently include relative distributional ubiquity and parsable categorial transparency of the forms in question (as well, sometimes, as raw token frequency, for example, invoked to rationalize the persistence of irregular forms of common words).[10] In other words, ideas of universal and system-specific structural-functional markedness, relatively homeostatic or eufunctional structural states at the sense-coding morphosyntactic plane,[11] were not only in the explanatory conceptual vocabulary even of Neogrammarians as they contemplated all of historical change outside

---

[8] Thus the rigid "great divide" of explanatory theory and method embraced down to the present day by those, like Bloomfield and his followers, e.g., Hockett and Hoenigswald, whom we may term 'structuralist Neogrammarians' in matters of language variation, change, and history. Classic sociolinguistic variationism belongs here as well, notwithstanding ungrounded attempts to document morphological and syntactic "change in progress" with the data-collecting methods of phonology, not understanding "where the sociolinguistic variable [must] stop" (Lavandera 1978).

[9] Students of the relatively modern Indo-European branch languages, such as Otto Jespersen (see 1909: 138–278) for English, or Ferdinand Brunot (see 1966: 498 [1906]) for French, observed such cumulative "analytic" tendencies for fixed-order syntactic constituent organization of the proposition-coding clause as over against the "free word-order" earlier stages. Jespersen, in particular, understood this as an example of unidirectional evolutionary tendencies to "progress" and simplification in language away from the morphological hypercomplexity – "(poly) synthesis" – seen in the classical Indo-European languages, Anglo-Saxon, Latin, etc.

[10] Kuryłowicz's (1945/1949) foundational work constitutes a watershed here, grounding "so-called 'analogic' laws" of morphosyntactic change in asymmetries of systemic status of forms as to internal constituency, distribution (and hence frequency), and paradigmatic complexity.

[11] Joseph Greenberg (1957: 86–94; 1966; 1969: 147–159) is the modern exemplar of such "typological" universals and near-universals, oriented in particular to determining historical transitions across such systemic "states."

"sound laws"; such properties of language were consciously invoked on the side of the great divide between the merely mechanical in language – phonological history as a kind of natural science to be studied in the unconscious psycho-physiology revealed by the phonating individual – and the admittedly mental plane of grammatical (morphosyntactic and lexical) structure coding cognitive and affective values in forms – the historical processes of which are bound up in collective normativities of "meaning-making" of a thus very different sort.[12]

When "sound change," too, is properly viewed as part of language in the same way, the Neogrammarian ways become laughably inadequate, though asymptotically special cases, as do also approaches that do the modern synchronically based but reductive equivalent in considering variation.

From potential to neutralization: structural enregisterment

Wilém Mathesius it was, the older cofounder, with Jakobson, of the Prague Linguistic Circle, who already in 1911 (translated in Vachek 1964: 1–32) proposed a rather more interesting view of language as a system of structures of covariation of units, what he termed the multiplex structural "potential" within the norms of a language community, the covariant "static [= synchronic] oscillation" of what we would now term cross-subject dialectal and sociolectal characteristics and, much more important for him, intrasubject stylistic or context-indicating characteristics. The idea is that under the empirical gaze at samples of actual *parole*, the norm of Saussurean *langue* does not look like a single invariant form actualizable anywhere as such, so much as an envelope of variance with two properties: covariation of sets of describable, even measurable parametric characteristics one with another, and contextual distribution of such covariation for "stylistic" ends.

Mathesius has, in an early conceptualization, thus hit upon the manifesting phenomena of 'register' that underlie the observable statistics one can gather from samples of actual linguistic usage. He notes, for example, that (British) English stressed vowels in monosyllabic words covary in duration with tongue height, the high vowels systematically shorter than the low, all other conditions being equal. Furthermore, high vowel tokens and those of lax

---

[12] Sociolinguistic variationism illustrates the great divide in the way of asserting a distinction between apparent change in phonological forms via mechanisms of "lexical diffusion" vs. those of real – as it were – "sound change." Arising as a controversial concept in the 1970s (see Wang 1969, 1977 for example, and Labov 1981; Labov 1994: 421–471, 502–543), the former unfortunately merges what in Neogrammarian terms were distinguished as "sporadic phonetic change" vs. "contamination," the first being incompletely pervasive due to unknown causes of blockage, the second being the influence of semantically, morphologically, or collocationally "close" forms.

vowels show a greater overall range of variation in length than lower and tense syllable nuclei. So within the dichotomous phonological opposition of tense and lax, a particular systematic "oscillation" can be observed, one that will give a particular phonetic silhouette to connected speech as native and natural or calling attention to itself as marked within this envelope of parametric regularity. Again, looking at the statistics of how words retain or lose their lexical stress in German prose text in relation to lexical category, one finds that substantives and adjectives are overwhelmingly more likely to be stressed than personal pronouns, and lexical verbs overwhelmingly more likely to be stressed than modals and auxiliaries. To be sure, in running text, where major and minor stresses ultimately fall is largely a function of syntactic organization of constituents, but nevertheless such a pattern as Mathesius describes sets an expectation of a sequential unfolding of, in effect, beats, from which stylistic deviation, when it does occur, has functional value.

Such covariations may be more or less characteristic and sharp in distinct dialects and sociolects and come to be implemented in different styles as functional (contextual) alternatives. I think it is important to see that, in Mathesius's first example, the opposition tense versus lax, strongly associated with the redundant feature of duration of nucleus, tends in this sense toward phonetic suppression in the high vowel nuclei. Tense and lax tend toward phonetic overlap, as it came to be called, and thus toward the phenomenon of structural neutralization. Imagining a dialect or a style where this oscillatory phenomenon is extremely pronounced (!), it would be like a distinct subsystem of vowels where low vowels fully implement the tense/lax opposition, and high vowels do not. (There are numerous phonological systems, e.g., Yokuts [California Penutian], where what structurally should be /i:/ and /u:/ are phonetically [e:] and [o:], in fact.) If the envelope of -lectal and stylistic oscillations sorts itself out in this way, one would then expect that within the "potential" of a language community, many such typologically possible registers, of distinct oscillatory configurations with stylistic, that is, contextualizing potential do, in fact, make up the totality of what speakers consider to be their "language."[13]

----

[13] In this respect, one should take note as well of an early formulation of Meillet (1893: 320–321): "*[L']unité linguistique ... existe partout où se trouvent les mêmes tendances phonétiques, visibles ou latentes. Deux paysans de la France du nord, séparés par de grandes distances et dont chacun parle un patois peu intelligible pour l'autre ont pourtant la même langue, non seulement parce que ces patois ont la même origine, mais aussi parce que certaines tendances phonétiques sont communes à tous les deux. ... C'est sur cette communauté, d'autant plus que personne n'en a conscience, que repose l'unité linguistique.*" (I thank Pierre Swiggers for a reference to this paper.)

This understanding of not merely textually but syntagmatically determinate distinct inventories – and of *phonological* units – was very much on the mind of the American linguist W. Freeman Twaddell, whose dissertation, "On Defining the Phoneme," was published by the Linguistic Society of America as a 1935 supplement to *Language*. Indeed, very much aware of the work of the Prague Circle (to the *Travaux* of which he subscribed), Twaddell observes that to implement the Saussurean understanding of the phonemic segment as a minimal element of syntagmatic form in a paradigmatic structure of oppositions, two kinds of facts complicate matters. One is the simple fact of syllabic syntagmatic distributions; the other is what was termed "neutralization." For example, before tautosyllabic [r] in American English, there occur only a very reduced number of stressed vocalic nuclei, as compared with those before syllable-final obstruents of other sorts. It is as though the set of contrasting vocalic "microphonemes" in this syntagmatic environment comprises a reduced, though coherent *sui generis* paradigmatic structure, but one the elements of which can be identified only problematically – except by brute phonetic considerations – with any of the larger preobstruent paradigmatic set of vocalic "microphonemes." And yet, of course, phonemicists do identify the elements across these different contexts as belonging to the same overall systemic set of "macrophonemes."

One can see the problem. Such considerations should lead us back to the notion of distinct paradigmatic subsystems each syntagmatically distributed according to its own privileges of occurrence – a *structural*, rather than merely phonetic, "oscillation" of parametric covariation rather than a merely infrastructural one. The Pragueans, the Bloomfieldians, and their successors in generative phonology started from a single inclusive macro-system of units and invoked neutralization between members of a single abstract 'archiphoneme' (or 'morphophoneme') to account for the syntagmatic peculiarities of positionally reduced inventories of opposed elements (think of the classic case of word-final devoicing of expected voiced obstruents). From the perspective of what can be observed along the temporally unfolding linear surface of language, what this results in is a set of structures of opposed formal units of different 'degrees of delicacy' – paradigmatic division – in particular co-occurrent positions within a larger syntagmatic construction type, some positions admitting of a greater number of contrasting forms than others, but (for phonology, at least) the experienced tokens being clustered in one particular region of phonologico-phonetic space. Thus, consider cases of final syllables in which occur only three possible vowels rather than the five of non–final syllable nuclei, or final (or closed) syllables with only short, not long vowels. Note, by contrast, that in areas of phonologico-phonetic space where no positional neutralizations obtain in a language, there is unrestricted distribution of the units subject only to general syllable canons of a language.[14]

Here, of course, is the basic formal machinery necessary to characterize linguistic registers, each such register a paradigmatic set of elements occurring in a context within a total grammar defined by position-specific formal elements that co-occur syntagmatically in actual text in characteristic and recurrent patterns with other, perhaps distributionally unrestricted paradigmatic material. We will return to this in respect of the concept of *sociolinguistic register*, where the paradigms are pragmatic (indexical) in semiotic loading rather than a function of denotational constituent structure alone.

Economie – Symmétrie – Inégalité

We have already noted that in reaction to Neogrammarianism – even Saussure's own hybrid pedagogical stance in his last lectures – structural approaches to language change refocused not on physiological forces bearing on individual phonetic segments but rather on structures or constellations of relationships among phonological segments. Structural analysis ultimately developed the insight that phonological units can be defined in terms of "bundles" – Boolean combinations – of simultaneous values along scales of differentiation that map into and are realized in articulatory–acoustic–auditory space. With this understanding of a correspondence between distributional classes and their manifestation, one can begin to look for properties of such phonologico-phonetic structures relevant to understanding patterns of historical persistence and change in them. To be sure, in "process"-oriented, derivational, or "generative" phonological models, investigators have concentrated on properties of the relationships of such derivational processes – the ones that to a great extent recapitulate as derivational "rules" the kinds of historical "sound changes" Neogrammarian approaches postulated – but most of such properties involve domains of applicability and ubiquity of neutralization effects at – derivationally

---

[14] In morpho-syntax, as well, such positional neutralizations of (elsewhere) maximal paradigmatic distinctions have long been well known and have long been treated via "transformations" and their equivalent, parallel to – and arising from – the morphophonological model. Note, for example, that however many case-marking distinctions accrue to the nominal arguments of the predicate of an independent clause – 'John is hunting the deer' – its corresponding maximally telescoped "deverbative nominalization" admits of only one, whatever case-marking is used for 'Possessor' – 'John's hunting [of the deer],' 'The deer's hunting [by John].' The adnominal genitive (or equivalent) thus neutralizes the grammatical (and sometimes additional nongrammatical) case-markings that are paradigmatically distinct for the corresponding nominal phrases occurring as verbal arguments in full finite clause structures. (See Benveniste 1962.)

speaking – intermediate stages between "underlying" and "surface" form, in addition to concern with final, "target" states of derivation.[15]

In historical phonology, one such structural approach involves, as in studies of "analogic" or morphosyntactic change, trying to understand structural-functional load and configuration as factors in furthering or impeding phonologization (split); and re- (shift) or de-phonologization (merger) of oppositions in the system used for denotational communication. Jules Gilliéron's (1921) famous dialectological studies based on the linguistic atlas of France had already convinced historical linguists that homeostatic preservation and renewal of denotational distinctions at the level of lexical form played a role in renewal of forms in the face of lexeme homophony threatened by phonological mergers. Applied more generally to emerging ideas about structures of phonologico-phonetic systems, a cluster of ideas emerged about diachronic effects of tendencies to *systemic homeostasis* as a structural-functional reinterpretation – a structural rarefication – of earlier mechanical ideas – ones that had invoked physical "least effort" in pronunciation and raw token frequency – interpreting functional tendencies underlying changes to linguistic forms in the way of sound laws.

André Martinet summed up a good deal of this literature – invoking Passy, Jespersen, Frei, Zipf, Trubetskoj, and others – in his 1955 *Traîté* on diachronic phonology, *Economie des Changements Phonétiques*. Here are reviewed the tendencies manifested in the history of phonological systems to 'series' [= place of articulation] x 'order' [= manner of articulation] paradigmatic symmetries (Trubetskoj's 'correlations,' as noted above); to minimally overlapping, even equidistant spacings of actualized phonetic distinctiveness;

---

[15] Indeed, as linguists – and especially phonologists – came during the 1960s to see historical change, for example, dialect differentiation, as change of *grammars*, i.e., derivational systems, rather than change merely of forms (the focus of earlier etymology, to be sure), important questions arose as to such conditions on the interaction of derivational rules within grammars, their fixity of ordering, their stability, their mutability. Thus, how the derivational inputs to and outputs of certain rules are related to corresponding characteristics of other rules moved to the center of theorizing, as historical change in derivational grammars was reconceptualized as intergenerational rule addition, rule insertion, rule reordering, rule deletion, etc. One can trace such concerns in Robert D. King's 1969 textbook, *Historical Linguistics and Generative Grammar* as well as in Chomsky and Halle's earlier – but long in circulation – *The Sound Pattern of English* of 1968, through a long line of attempts, e.g., Kiparsky 1971; 1973; 2003; Andersen 1973, to characterize permissible kinds of rule interactions ("bleeding," "feeding," etc.) and therefore expected and unexpected changes in such rule interactions in history. (Such concerns were also coevally evident among students of generative syntax, as evidenced in John Robert Ross's 1967 dissertation, "Constraints on Variables in Syntax," which constituted a field-transforming watershed of thinking about derivational grammars in terms of abstract 'constraints' on possible input and output constituent structures as related by derivational rules.) Weinreich, Labov, and Herzog's 1968 paper, "Empirical Foundations for a Theory of Language Change," manifests cognizance of the generative phonological framework and speaks of "constraints" on change.

and to token statistical profiles as a function of type-level syntagmatic distributional regularities ("functional load" in various possible contexts of syllabic and word distribution and thence, overall within a system). Against this are the inherent asymmetries of parametric realization (cf. Mathesius) in particular areas of phonetic space, for example, the "stoppier" stop-ness of [k, kh, g] when compared with [p, ph, b] (the latter everywhere tending more to weakening or disappearance), or the tighter space for structural degrees of height differentiation of back vowels as opposed to front vowels (so /u/ and /o/, or /o/ and /a/ recurrently tend to merge even where their anterior counterparts do not). Martinet shows the diachronic effects of such tendencies, where, for example, "holes" in phonological patterns have a tendency to be filled, classes of sounds in a series tend to change order together, correlational structures renew themselves as mutations of order, and so on. In particular, Martinet introduces the concepts of 'push chains' and 'drag chains' where structurally central phonological oppositions are phonetically preserved when one phonological unit shifts its actualization and others linked to it follow suit, whether by moving to a new "available" space or by drawing another unit into its "former" space. Note that such "chains" in diachrony may take some time to form, though the driving force must involve threats to or opportunities of synchronic actualization of structural distinctiveness within a phonological system.

We should be particularly interested in such "pushes" and "pulls," it seems to me, because these depend essentially on 'functional load' properties of phonological structures; they are not mere phonetic facts but seem, rather, to reveal distributionally relative paradigmatic structures – cf. registers – that preserve distinctiveness across a "chain" notwithstanding positionally relative shifts in phonetic realization of some particular precipitating phonological unit. It should thus become clear that *the enregistered paradigm of differentiae is the actual functional and diachronic locus of such "chain" effects* and that such effects are not pre- or retro-dictable merely on the basis of the overall phonological inventory of a linguistic system.

A structural-functional historical phonology, then, is very much of a piece with the historical study of grammar. Recall, for example, in my teacher Jerzy Kuryłowicz's rules of thumb for the directionality of morphosyntactic reshapings – "so-called 'analogical' changes," he terms them in sanitary quotes – that the influencing ("founding") and influenced ("founded") forms emerge in competition from their distributional properties in syntagmatic environments, from their compositional transparency (or its lack), and from their ubiquity or denotational centrality modulo syntagmatic environment. Older and newer systems coexist as registers until the tension is resolved in favor of the one over the other, with various emergent effects that themselves tend to create tensions elsewhere – in short, a "chain" of morphosyntactic transformations.

All this has long been recognized when focused on *denotational* systems from a structural-functional point of view. But what if we wish to bring in broader functional characteristics of language? What if we wish to think seriously about how sociolinguistic variation functions as the "empirical foundation" for language change?

Indexicality and the "First Wave"

It was, of course, the tragically short-lived Uriel Weinreich, the student at Columbia of Martinet, of Jakobson, and of other emigré European linguists, who thought deeply about reconciling structural-functional approaches to language in the first instance to matters of 'dialect' (Weinreich 1954) and thence to other kinds of variability within what is considered to be a single-language community (or in a plurilingual speech community, for that matter, such as is treated in his dissertation based on work in Switzerland). To be sure, these were matters that worried many American structuralists of the postwar period as well, especially those, like my teacher Einar Haugen (see Haugen 1953; 1956), who worked in bilingual situations of "languages in contact" with an unstable trajectory of ultimate replacement of one "system" by another. But, as Weinreich and his students William Labov and Marvin Herzog came to see (1968), one must embrace variability – recall Mathesius and Meillet supra – as inherent in every language community, and see its implications for those norms called *langue* in the Saussurean idiom. Weinreich himself had the benefit of direct connection to Prague School structural-functionalism in the person of Roman Jakobson, whose ideas about the language norm of a community as a functionally (= contextually) differentiated and stylistically deployable structure of registers developed in the milieu of Mathesius and others; the 1929 *Thèses*, as I noted, already develop these concepts. In the translation into compatibility with the American generativist idiom, however, around the time of Weinreich's death, much of this became confused and conceptually incoherent.

It should be pointed out that a rather more anthropological concern with "sociolinguistics" as socially and culturally contextualized use of language emerged coevally in the "ethnography of speaking/communication" (see Gumperz and Hymes 1964, 1972), where concern for norms of conducting interpersonal social life via the medium of verbal and other semiotic systems leads one to construe what the structural-functionalist would see as infra-structural "variation" as the very essence of language – doing interpersonally effective things, as it were, with words in subjectively strategic, nondisinterested ways. Himself trained originally as a dialectologist and student of bilingualism, John Gumperz was a key figure here (along with Dell Hymes, Susan Ervin-Tripp, Erving Goffman, John Searle, et al., all then at Berkeley).

Writing of the aggregate of language forms in a population, he formulated (Gumperz 1968: 383–384) a dichotomy about the nature of such variability, as being either "dialectal" – where contrasting forms differentiate the envelope of usage of socially, geographically, and so on different groups of people within a community (and from which we can generalize to '-lectal' variation) – or "superposed" – where members of a group tend to control such contrasting forms for contextually strategic communicative deployment. In the light of speech act theory, one can now see that at any given period, there must be a cline along the polarities of which any "variant" form is positioned, from the -lectal, that is, differential identity-indexing features of one's utterance (pointing reliably to one's social identity in one or more respects), to the superposed, that is, context-creating or -effectuating, whether as to achieved identity or other alignment to interaction. It is fairly obvious that Labov's (1972: 237) "sociolinguistic indicators," statistically significant differences of rates of forms-as-produced across describable social categories of speakers, are scales of -lectal indexicality and that his "sociolinguistic markers," a second-order structure crossing the first according to contextual task demands, reveal superposed indexicality, though *such effects themselves tend to show -lect-like distributions into socially definable repertoires*, as I will elaborate below. Labov's "stereotypes" are ideologically (ethnometapragmatically) infused, seemingly full-tilt versions of sharply -lectally distinguished "markers."

It was clear to me even on initial encounter with both these approaches that they cried out for immersion in a semiotic perspective that joined two concerns separately elaborated but unfortunately not joined by my teacher Jakobson: the functional and componential analysis of events of communication in the Karl Bühler–to–Shannon and Weaver mode, as in his "Linguistics and Poetics" (1960: 353), and the semiotics of indexicality in language, generalizing via C. S. Peirce's reconstruction of meaning and logic from "Shifters, Verbal Categories, and the Russian Verb" (1957; reprinted 1971: 130–147). It has long been clear that shifters – indexical denotationals – contribute to reference or predication by characterizing something in computable relation to the presumed-upon characteristics of one or more components of the communicative event qua situated event. What is needed, however, is a concept of a nondenotational or merely indicative relation of linguistic token form to some component(s) of the context in which it occurs: the nondenotational index, whether strongly 'presupposing' of some dimensions of the context – looks to Gumperz's -lectal pole, where what is indexed is a language-independent and situationally relevant social characteristic of one or more of the participants – or strongly 'entailing' of them – for which Gumperz's envelope of superposed variation is an affordance. *Variationism's sociolinguistic variables are particular groupings of token forms such that something about the profile of such tokens' frequency or density of occurrence-in-context itself constitutes a nondenotational index.*[16]

I need not review the wild institutional success of correlationist variationism, but wish to point out what are, to my mind, some fatal conceptual inadequacies and incoherences, before going on to compare this family of approaches to investigating "change in progress" with what I have traced above. These involve the problems of "variable" scale construction, cultural ecological validity, communicative task demands and "consciousness," and so on.

At the plane of phonology, variably realized tokens of pronunciation in performance imply an immanent target in competence, a phonological form of some identifiable morphosyntactic unit, the phonological shape or form of which is in some sense known. The heuristic in variationist work in phonology is based on identifying lexical items and their denotations, and scoring pronunciations of token occurrences of those lexical expressions, whether monomorphemic or more complex (e.g., in English suffixed or ablauted 'past tense' tokens of lexical verbs; in French auxiliated tense–mood–aspect forms of lexical verbs). The idea is that one can create a phonetic scale or measure for such tokens in a sample of speech, either a linear scale between two polarities or a landmark-based central moment around which variance in the use of tokens clusters. (The first approach characterizes earlier work; the second, implementing spectrographic laboratory technique, characterizes more recent work.) In either case, an assumption about an identifiable target realization, where the phonological structure of *langue* is transparently "executed" in *parole*, is necessary.

Unfortunately, a massive confusion emerges almost immediately because most variationist work has been done in standardized language communities: Instead of a model of the phonological structure of word forms, the forms of *standard register*, itself an emergent product of a complex institutionalization of sociolinguistic authority, substitute for a model of the community norm in the Saussure-to-Chomsky sense of the term. (Worse, a reconstructed standard register of some presumed ancestor state preceding variation and change seems

---

[16] Given that such measures are empirically derived from aggregating tokens of performance in a within- or across-subject sample of, presumably, a statistically significant sort, for such an indexical signal to be informative to an interlocutory other in some single communicative event, there must be a kind of frequency or density or similarly behaviorist model of signal detection surely implying reenforcement or extinction of indexical effects classifying or categorizing a speaker over the course of a relevant interval of a listener's short-term memory. The field of sociophonetics attempts to grapple with at least laboratory stimuli as indexes of identity, recuperating classic themes of the early to mid-1960s work of social psychologist Wallace Lambert and his group that used -lectally and linguistically differentiated stimuli to probe social stereotypes associated with those whom research subjects heard but did not see. More recent experiments reveal a complex interaction of indexical effects across perceptual modes.

to haunt the definition of variables.[17]) To be sure, it is the very essence of standardization that what we as linguists seek in the way of evidence for a community norm is informed and biased by a reflexive unconscious, an ethnometapragmatic anxiety, in respect of the standard register. Such orientation or allegiance to the standard is itself a differentiated characteristic among community members as a function of their position in social structure and its functional organization. Allegiance to standard is an ideological fact, central to the sociolinguistics of language communities such as ours. This is precisely what Labov discovered, differentially distributed as predicted, in measuring what he termed "stylistic" variation (1966: 90–135; 1972: 70–109, 237) as the anxiety-inducing demands on speakers in respect of standard register production shift in the course of an encounter (see below).

But absent a fixed or publicly institutionalized register model of this sort, establishing baseline norms for phonology depends on having worked out a phonologico-phonetic model relative to which Mathesian "oscillation" can be measured. Every anthropological linguistic field worker has had this experience, of encountering variance even in elicitation (let alone connected spoken performance) of lexical forms, of sometimes subtle – and sometimes not so subtle (e.g., [véys] : [vɑ̇·z] for English orthographic <vase>; cf. Labov 1972: 251n.42) – segmental substitutions, characteristic phonetic overlaps, and so on. No less a figure than Bloomfield, with his obsessive concern for inductive operationalism, was much disturbed by this in working on Menomini, but finally realized that postulating the structure of the phonology as the necessary model for asserting the community norm was a prerequisite to understanding variance, overlap, and so on. (See Bloomfield 1939: 115; Hockett 1970: 367–368; Goddard 1987: esp. 181–196.) It is perhaps no wonder that one can count on the fingers of one hand the attempts to do serious variationist phonetic analysis in the absence of a standardized register or its equivalent, as for example indicated by orthography or other socially licensed authority. Or complementarily, one can note the lack of a serious, locally relevant autonomous phonological – or grammatical – analysis serving as a prerequisite to doing variationist correlations. (See now Dorian 2010 on the character of sociolinguistic variation in local, nonstandardized languages.)

But the confusion of a sociolinguistic structure of enregisterment with the normative order of *langue* at the heart of earlier historical linguistics is not

---

[17] Thus, a baseline presumed phonetic point of departure never synchronically established for the vowel system (but perhaps based on historical graphic practice) allows the rather ambiguous use of process concepts such as "fronting," "raising," and "tensing" as at once descriptors of speaking subjects' measurable articulatory behaviors *divergent from* the baseline and their interpretation in "apparent time" as evidence for "sound change in progress" in a community of speakers. While moving beyond the synchrony/diachrony dichotomy is salutary, the methodology here is, if anything, reductively circular.

the only problem. When we think of how phonetic performance characteristics covary with something that defines the context of communication, most variationist work seizes on what one recognizes as the ready-to-hand official macrosocial characteristics of identity by which governments and similar institutional forms of the public sphere describe people and which are, like standard registers for languages, inculcated as norms of self- and other-definition in people's reflexive consciousness as a function of their very social condition. We have here the problem of what psychologists have long termed the "ecological validity" of these social categorizations of people, such that various attempts at correctives have been made within the limits of small, ethnographically tractable social groups (note: not mere categories!), such as network structures (according to the salience of mutual knowledge individuals have of each other and rates of their various communicative transactions) or so-called communities of practice (scored by intensity and kind of coparticipation of individuals at sites of mutually reinforcing social action defining a social group and its interests).[18]

The problem is one that many anthropologists and sociologists have theorized and investigated through fieldwork for a century and more but that somehow seems not to have risen to consciousness of variationists: Through investigations of actual social relations on the ground, one must map the variety and local identifiability of types of groups to which humans belong and the statuses that define them, to only some of which are attached labels, and with respect to which locally significant communicative variation is organized – frequently locally recognized by an ethnometapragmatics of enregisterment, and so on. One can consider any area of social life and note that the scales, categorizations, and even descriptive terms of official censuses or of marketing surveys cut everything the wrong way insofar as they attempt to describe people's actual arrangements into communicationally significant social groups. How does the structure of a "household" vary as a function of a complex social organization involving kinship, residence and labor patterns, gender and sexuality, and so on? Why does chronological age sampled at any given calendric moment reveal nothing without considering the nature of generation ($\neq$ demographic cohort!), age-grade (or even age-set), and so on as the socioculturally significant divisions of a community's social structure?

---

[18] To be sure, Leslie and James Milroy's early Belfast work (see Milroy 1980) centrally uses the concept of speakers' positions in local social networks as an independent variable indexed by dependent phonetic characteristics. Note Labov's (2001: 229–232) attempt at refutation. Eckert and McConnell-Ginet (1992; 2003: 57–58, 98–99) invoke communities of practice in discussing issues of language and 'gender,' in particular, but it is not clear how such coparticipation in and of itself differs from measures of networked connectivity among individuals, save when – as the very notion of 'community' indicates – they are talking about a Weberian social group (see also Sapir 1932) with reflexive consciousness of membership and institutionalized corporateness.

The list goes on and on of what one might term, on analogy with physics, massive error factors (like friction) which are involved in mere demographics-driven variationist models of what phonetic and other kinds of "oscillation" might, in fact, be indexing at particular social sites at which individuals interact one with another.[19]

Finally, from the perspective of correlation-as-indexing, we must consider one of the more puzzling aspects of this work, the notion that at one extreme of a gradual cline of consciousness we are unaware of our speech and how it operates indexically to situate us as social beings, and at the other extreme we are extremely aware of it, at least as targeted behavioral form. Within the sociolinguistic structure of standardization, to be sure, we might say that there are situations in which, plausibly and a priori, there is less or more pressure to produce public-sphere standard forms, such pressure differentiating how one speaks with an intimate in-group friend from childhood (where indexing the continuing relevance of the long-term relationship is generally to the fore) versus how one gives a public lecture in one's own language as a professional expert on it (see Goffman 1981: 160–161). But note: In every possible communicative situation, one is at all times speaking *as someone*, that is, indexing all manner of sociological category-types made relevant – made, as it were, flesh – in the here-and-now of the communicative event as not just speakers but interlocutory social beings inhabiting particular relational roles one with another.[20] And there is thus no possible communicative situation in which, reflexively, one does not orient by stance-taking, to the verbal and other semiotic inhabitance of these context-appropriate and – if they "secure uptake," as Austin (1975: 116–120) would say – these context-effectuating aspects of identity, one's own and as well one's interlocutor's/-rs' and one's audience's/-s'. Such aspects of identity – and of alterity (cf. Hastings and

---

[19] Eckert's (2000) investigations among Detroit-area public high school students constitute a notable example of trying to establish locally ecologically relevant – even named – social groupings and their behavioral norms and imaginaries in relation to which measures of sociolinguistic variability can be interpreted. At least some of that variability involves phonetic clines in what has been termed the "Northern Cities Vowel Shift" (see Wolfram and Schilling-Estes 2006: 147–149), an apparently long-term east-to-west trend involving linked shifts in vowel norms of nonelite urban and periurban registers. The local salience of such shifts, among the high school student subjects serving as shibboleths of (dis)affiliation and (non-) identification with school social groups, perhaps exemplifies one mechanism for their cumulative persistence.

[20] It is nothing short of astounding that correlational variationism remains for the most part uninformed by multiple disciplinary lines of work on the structural analysis of discursive interaction, much in fact relevant to understanding the parameters and dynamics of face-to-face situations such as "sociolinguistic interviews" from which raw numerical performance data are abstracted and extracted. Goffman (1974; 1979) is, of course, central here, especially as it has been of use to linguistic anthropological understanding of how variation is 'entextualized' and 'contextualized' in relation to enregisterment. See Agha 2007.

Manning 2004) – are made relevant to the course of discursive interaction; at particular phases they become "in play" as armatures of mutual social coordination and calibration and then, at a later phase, may take on a fixed or settled "background" character. We come to interaction as partially legible social types, recruited, as one says, to role relationality, and we generally enrich legibility over interaction's time course, reinforcing or, as the case may be, transforming identities in and by how we say what we say. Demographic measures of individuals are hardly to the point.

It is interesting that in early interview-based sociolinguistic research a protocol of so-called stylistic variation involved ordering frequency samples of phonetic production along a postulated monotone increase of interviewee's "attention to language." When one considers the task-demands of the production formats, ranging from out-of-interview surreptitious recordings of people with intimates – no longer allowable in the United States under ethical guidelines for research – all the way to being presented with a minimal graphic pair to read aloud, it is clear, however, that such a cline, were it even linear, is really one that ratchets up the possibilities of a speaker's anxieties in respect of standard register, the latter taught as a grapheme-to-phoneme transduction in the first instance, and thus maintained in ethnometapragmatic consciousness. "Reading aloud" produces register anxiety not uniformly in society, but, as Labov's New York City work definitively demonstrated (1966: 455–481; 1972: 122–142), minimally at the bottom and top of a scale of social stratification – he used government figures for household socioeconomic stratification – where rates of production change moderately across all task-demands and maximally in a region of social stratification near but consciously striving to be at the top. (Labov identified such people as members of the "lower middle class" in the New York City context.) But this is just as we would expect for any ideologically driven stratification where some behavioral characteristic is considered the neutral, top-and-center standard, considered to be the universal social solvent in institutions of the public sphere, and anchored by massive inculcation that itself is differentially successful among distinct segments and sectors of the population. Indeed, the so-called upper-middle-class professionals who earn their living and the esteem of their consociates through verbal skills centered on standard, are privileged to speak this register endowed with ideological neutrality, while those speaking otherwise can be negatively located in social space along one or another axis of differentiation, as "speaking like a ..." indexed by these very forms.[21] The matter here, in other words, has nothing to do with attention to or

---

[21] There is, of course, a vast literature touching one or another aspect of the phenomenon of standardization, that is, enregistering a standard register. (Bloomfield (1927; 1933: 48–52, 482–487) was concerned with these matters, as also Otto Jespersen (1946 [1925]), and the

consciousness of how we self-present in the verbal channel; the sharpness and degree of shift from nonstandard toward standard is the index of one's position within this sociolinguistics of orientation to and anxiety before standard register. No wonder "covert [or negative] prestige" (Trudgill 1972), a ridiculous coinage expressing the surprise that sometimes people spoke – and wanted to speak – in highly nonstandard ways, was encountered in those for whom affiliations with local social structures permeated people's primary reference groups (a finding, one might add, not only in Norwich, but earlier – though unnamed – in Martha's Vineyard [Labov 1963]).

The notion of an individual's "natural" and "unmonitored" phonetic modality is, of course, useful in the instance of misguided attempts to resuscitate the Neogrammarian concept of mechanical sound change, change that goes on essentially unrecognised by surreptitiously spreading across a community from individual innovators through a kind of Tardean "social contagion" in vernacular contexts of usage, standardization and its institutions notwithstanding. Hence, at any given moment, the profile of variation within a language community, sampled with everything controlled but stratified by "unaware" usage of calendric age cohorts (so-called apparent time) should give a synchronic picture of diachronic ("real time") Neogrammarian change-in-progress. To my knowledge, nothing of the sort has ever been demonstrated with methodological or statistical reliability. Nor, moreover, does this model ever move beyond Neogrammarian models of what we now term "additive change," where phonetic laws applying to earlier phonetic outputs result in newer phonetic forms. And what are the "phonetic" forms to which such putative additive changes have applied to yield current vernacular innovations? They are forms of standard register transparently realized as such, or a historical linguistic reconstruction of a putatively earlier norm value. Thus, the only kind of change countenanced here is change by those sociologically far from the standard-producing top-and-center of the stratificational cone, the kind of change postulated for an urban lumpenproletariat that looks very much like the anonymous "*Volk*" out there in the nineteenth century countryside that dialectologists studied in Neogrammarian times – and imagined for proto-Indo-European times – to see the leading edges of phonetic law, unspoiled by urban – and urbane – standardization. Or, perhaps, do even standard registers change, among elites? This sad model, alas, takes us back to a prestructural understanding of phonetics (and the rest of language), to a

---

Prague School linguists of the 1920s trying to locate standard Czech in a functional order (see Garvin 1964). Agha (2007: 190–232) traces the complex route by which Received Pronunciation became established as a phonologico-phonetic standard in Great Britain, and Silverstein (2014a) discusses contemporary New York City and other "regional" nonstandard American English in relation to "General American."

preempirical sociology or social anthropology, and to a social psychology of "contagion" among "the people" that might have been propounded 150 years ago.

Register and the dialectics of chronotopy

So let us, at length, put up or shut up, as I like to say. I want to draw together what I see as the central points about phonological structures being the loci of change, not individual phonemic segments as "variables"; about the relationship of indexicality to enregisterment and thence to functional load in the historical dynamics of languages; and about the implications for overcoming the synchrony/diachrony divide in modeling the relationship of sociolinguistic variation to the dynamics of language communities.

Let us start with the semiotic and functional understanding of registers. The modern concept was first applied to phonology, I believe, by Eugénie Henderson in 1952, in describing two systematic indexical realizations of vocalic nuclei of Cambodian (Khmer);[22] consistent with this, but more central to sociolinguistic usage is the line of terminologization from T. M. R. Reid (1956) through the MacIntosh–Halliday (1964) understanding of essentially contextual variation observable in a single speaker adapting his or her usage to the demands of communicative context. The term alludes to the pipe organ, where different registers provide distinct timbral envelopes for what is otherwise precisely the same melodic sequence of pitch-over-time. For language, the idea is that there is a mode of folk consciousness (an ethnometapragmatics) of "superposed" (Gumperz) indexical variability that posits the existence of distinct, indexically contrastive ways of saying what counts as "the same thing," that is, communicating the same denotational content over intervals of text-precipitating discourse that differ as to their appropriateness to and effectiveness in conceptualized contexts of use. These contexts may be defined along any of the usual sociolinguistic dimensions describing who communicates with what forms to whom about whom/what where and under what institutional conditions.

Language users evaluate discourse with intuitive metrics of coherence of enregistered features of form co-occurring in text-in-context across segmentable stretches of discourse such as an individual's contribution to a discursive interaction, generally focusing on highly salient 'register shibboleths'[23]

---

[22] I am indebted to Anthony Woodbury for calling my attention to this usage that pre-dates the 1956 Reid usage I had located and to which I had attributed primacy.

[23] In work on "Pittsburghese," Johnstone (2013; cf. Johnstone et al. 2006) has emphasized the linked lexical-phonological shibboleths of local affiliation, such as the absence of diphthongs in both syllables of 'downtown', the 'second plural' pronoun 'yinz', etc. New Yorkers identify "fuhgeddabadit," the illocutionary form 'Forget about it'! as such a constructional shibboleth

that reveal a basic register setting around which cluster the untroubled compatibility or indexically marked lack of compatibility of other aspects of usage. Kiksht (the easternmost Chinookan language; see Silverstein 1994) has a phonological gradation from so-called augmentative usage to so-called diminutive usage via a neutral register, indexing a speaker's affective stance with respect to the matters being denotationally communicated; as one would expect, in general the implementation is highly "variable," though some of these affective stance-indexations have been lexicalized for particular areas of denotation. "Standard" registers, too, are gradient in nature, denoting, within sloppy margins of performance, the coherent co-occurrence in someone's usage of a sufficient number of prescriptive 'standard'-shibboleths and the nonoccurrence of the preponderance of proscribed 'nonstandard' ones within the cultural order of institutionalized standardization. (On this fact the entire covariationist enterprise has rested, as noted above.) Registers, it should be noted, have all the properties of languages as structures immanent in denotational discourse; since registers are, however, indexically particular to context, whether in positive or negative stipulation, the set-theoretic union of the elements of all registers in a community, sociolinguistically viewed, thus constitutes the inclusive envelope of the community's 'language' and its "oscillations" (cf. Meillet quoted in n. 13 supra).

To be sure, indexically loaded variance goes on constantly and at all degrees of inclusiveness of speakers; there is, indeed, always a cloud of variance one samples around any targeted prototype realizations of grammatical and phonological categories in construction, nondirectional and noncumulative. Speakers have intuitions – sometimes even explicit normative stipulations – of how one or more elements of such paradigmatically differentiated indexes can appropriately – congruently – co-occur across textual stretches. Such principles define a *denotational textual register* for the users of language, an intuition (or stipulation) of which textual elements go together with which others, and which ought to be excluded from textual co-occurrence – save for producing (entailing) special effects by violation. Where sociolinguistic variability turns into movement of a language's norms, in every case we find register shibboleths – in essence, Labovian "markers" becoming "stereotypes" – that anchor an ethnometapragmatically identifiable aspect of social identity (see Jaffe, this volume, Chapter 4, and Gal, this volume, Chapter 5), the co-occurrence of which with particular forms linked in enregisterment is the way that "drags" and "pulls" manifest in the economy of change as languages – unstable and always changing structures of interlocked registers – move along in time within the population of their users.

of locale, and others as well, illustrating some of the phonological shibboleths like variable absence of standard syllable-coda segmental /-r/.

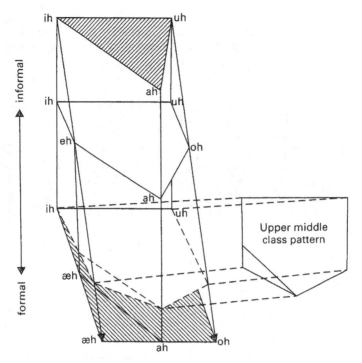

Figure 2.1: Structure of New York City vowel system: Stylistic variation (after Labov 2006: 368, Figure 14.9).

Indeed, one of the most striking demonstrations of enregisterment is in what became a still-born part of Labov's dissertation (1966: 507–575), based on his Lower East Side survey in New York's borough of Manhattan in the early 1960s. After reviewing the various correlations in overall performance profiles on a more-or-less variable-by-variable basis, Labov synthesizes his results in the final chapter – making reference to Martinet, by the way – with a striking set of reconstructions of what we can understand are covariations within vocalic registers strongly associated with the twentieth century's dynamics of class stratification, with ethnic differentiation, and so on. He is able to diagram an interpretation of the crystal structure–like envelope of register variation in performance as a set of planar targets of phonological differentiation that speakers seem to be attempting to hit, as it were, in their identity-indexing usage. (See Figures 2.1 and 2.2, reproduced from Labov 2006.[24]) Working-class white ethnics – principally Jews and Italians at the time – seem

---

[24] I am grateful to William Labov for authorizing these reproductions.

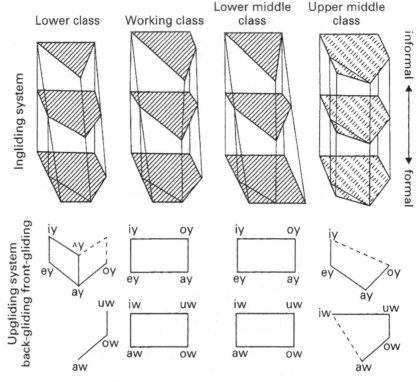

Figure 2.2: Three-dimensional structure of New York City vowel system: Stylistic variation for four class groups (after Labov 2006: 371, Figure 14.11).

to have a three-vowel "ingliding" enregistered system, /ah/ : /ih/ : /uh/;[25] upper-middle-class professionals index their identity by a corresponding five- or six-vowel vocalic register. The details can be studied in the original work, but what is important to note is that the statistical measures needed are not per-subject overall scores of one phonological variable at a time, but scores of production over stretches of coherent speech of *co-occurring values of the paradigmatic members constituting such identity-indexing registers* so as to reveal the stylistic silhouette, as it were, which a speaker is attempting, oriented to self-expression through such indexically significant projection – what Labov himself, prefiguring Pierre Bourdieu (1991: 81–89), terms "articulatory gesture ... phonological posture" (1966: 567).

---

[25] Thus, differentiating three vocalic nuclei in opposition, as for the words orthographically park : clear, Clare : poor, pour (recall as well the absence of a syllable-coda rhotic in all of these).

In short, when a proper sociolinguistics of indexicality and its enregisterment is undertaken, the claim that variation is both structured and always in dynamic movement over time can be properly demonstrated in a framework for what Coupland terms 'sociolinguistic change' (2014). It is a movement of a sociological structure of repertoires of enregisterment – with or without explicitly standardized ones – distributed over a language community, always changing but always immanent in the variance of *parole* in which people perform their context-relevant identities via indexical semiosis. This will finally realize a dialectical and simultaneously socio- and historical linguistics conceptually adequate to succeed the would-be mechanism of "mindless" – really, unminded – Neogrammarian additive phonological change. At the same time it would avoid the structuralist's *langue*-focused stadialism and its trap of sundering a synchronic grammatical abstraction from its diachronic fate only to fail in the task of putting them back together again – the very path sought by Weinreich, Labov, and Herzog (1968).

REFERENCES

Agha, Asif. 2007. *Language and Social Relations*. Cambridge: Cambridge University Press.

Andersen, Henning. 1973. "Abductive and deductive change." *Language* 49, 4: 765–793.

Austin, John L. 1975. *How to Do Things with Words*, 2nd ed. J. O. Urmson and Marina Sbisà, eds. Cambridge, MA: Harvard University Press.

Baudouin de Courtenay, Jan. 1972. An attempt at a theory of phonetic alternations. In Edward Stankiewicz (trans. and ed.), *A Baudouin de Courtenay Anthology: The Beginnings of Structural Linguistics*. Bloomington and London: Indiana University Press, 144–212. (Originally published in 1895.)

Benveniste, Emile. 1962. Pour l'analyse des fonctions casuelles: le génitif Latin. *Lingua* 11, 1: 10–18.

Bloomfield, Leonard. 1926. A set of postulates for the science of language. *Language* 2, 3: 153–164.

1927. Literate and illiterate speech. *American Speech* 2, 10: 432–439.

1933. *Language*. New York: Holt, Reinhart & Winston.

1939. Menomini morphophonemics. *Travaux du Cercle linguistique de Prague* (Special issue: *Etudes Phonologiques Dédiées à la Mémoire de M. le Prince N. S. Trubetzkoy*) 8: 105–115.

Bourdieu, Pierre. 1991. *Language and Symbolic Power*. John B. Thompson (ed.), Gino Raymond and Matthew Adamson (trans.). Cambridge, MA: Harvard University Press.

Brunot, Ferdinand. 1966. *Histoire de la Langue Française des Origins à Nos Jours*. Tome 1. *De l'Epoque Latine à la Renaissance* (nouvelle edition). Paris: Armand Colin. (Originally published in 1906.)

Chomsky, Noam, and Morris Halle. 1968. *The Sound Pattern of English*. New York: Harper & Row.

Coupland, Nikolas. 2014. Language change, social change, sociolinguistic change: A meta-commentary. *Journal of Sociolinguistics* 18, 2: 277–286.

Dorian, Nancy C. 2010. *Investigating Variation: The Effects of Social Organization and Social Setting*. New York: Oxford University Press.

Eckert, Penelope. 2000. *Linguistic Variation as Social Practice: The Linguistic Construction of Identity in Belten High*. Malden, MA: Blackwell.

2012. Three waves of variation study: The emergence of meaning in the study of sociolinguistic variation. *Annual Review of Anthropology* 41: 87–100.

Eckert, Penelope, and Sally McConnell-Ginet. 1992. Think practically and look locally: Language and gender as community-based practice. *Annual Review of Anthropology* 21: 461–490.

2003. *Language and Gender*. Cambridge: Cambridge University Press.

Garvin, Paul, L. (trans. and ed.) 1964. *A Prague School Reader on Esthetics, Literary Structure, and Style: Selected and Translated from the Original Czech*. Washington, DC: Georgetown University Press.

Gilliéron, Jules. 1921. *Pathologie et Thérapeutique Verbales*. Paris: Champion.

Goddard, Ives. 1987. Leonard Bloomfield's descriptive and comparative studies of Algonquian. *Historiographia Linguistica* 14, 1/2:179–217.

Goffman, Erving. 1974. *Frame Analysis: An Essay on the Organization of Experience*. New York: Harper & Row.

1979. Footing. *Semiotica* 25, 1: 1–29.

1981. *Forms of Talk*. Philadelphia: University of Pennsylvania Press.

Greenberg, Joseph. 1957. *Essays in Linguistics. Viking Fund Publications in Anthropology*, no. 24. New York: Wenner-Gren Foundation for Anthropological Research.

1966. Some universals of language with particular reference to the order of meaningful elements. In Joseph Greenberg (ed.), *Universals of Language*, 2nd ed. Cambridge, MA: MIT Press, 73–113.

1969. Some methods of dynamic comparison in linguistics. In Jaan Puhvel (ed.), *Substance and Structure of Language*. Berkeley and Los Angeles: University of California Press, 147–203.

Gumperz, John. 1968. Linguistics, III: The speech community. In David L. Sills (ed.), *International Encyclopedia of the Social Sciences*. New York: Macmillan and Free Press, vol. 9: 381–386.

Gumperz, John, and Dell Hymes (eds.). 1964. *The Ethnography of Communication. American Anthropologist* 66, 6, part 2.

(eds.). 1972. *Directions in Sociolinguistics: The Ethnography of Communication*. New York: Holt, Rinehart & Winston.

Halliday, M. A. K., Angus McIntosh, and Peter Strevens. 1964. *The Linguistic Sciences and Language Teaching*. London: Longman.

Hastings, Adi, and Paul Manning. 2004. Introduction: Acts of alterity. *Language and Communication* 24, 3: 291–311.

Haugen, Einar. 1953. *The Norwegian Language in America: A Study in Bilingual Behavior*, 2 vols. Philadelphia: University of Pennsylvania Press.

1956. *Bilingualism in the Americas: A Bibliography and Research Guide. Publications of the American Dialect Society*, no. 26. University: University of Alabama Press.

Henderson, Eugénie. 1952. The main features of Cambodian pronunciation. *Bulletin of the School of Oriental and African Studies, University of London* 14, 1: 149–174.
Hockett, Charles F. 1954. Two models of grammatical description. *Word* 10, 3: 210–231.
1958. *A Course in Modern Linguistics*. New York: Macmillan.
(ed.). 1970. *A Leonard Bloomfield Anthology*. Bloomington: Indiana University Press.
1977. Logical considerations in the study of animal communication. *The View from Language: Selected Essays, 1948–1974*. Athens: University of Georgia Press, 124–162. (Originally published in 1960.)
Jakobson, Roman. 1931. Prinzipien der historischen Phonologie. *Travaux du Cercle Linguistique de Prague* 4: 247–267. (Reprinted in French translation, "Principes de phonologie historique," in *Selected Writings of Roman Jakobson*, vol. 1. *Phonological studies*, 202–220. The Hague: Mouton & Co., 1962.)
1957 [1971]. *Shifters, verbal categories, and the Russian verb*. Mimeograph. Cambridge, MA: Department of Slavic Languages and Literatures, Harvard University. (Published in *Selected Writings of Roman Jakobson*, vol. 2, *Word and Language*, 130–147. The Hague: Mouton & Co., 1971.)
1960. Closing statement: Linguistics and poetics. In Thomas A. Sebeok (ed.), *Style in Language*. Cambridge, MA: MIT Press, 350–377.
1964. Thèses présentées au Premier Congrès des philologues slaves. In Josef Vachek (ed.), *A Prague School Reader in Linguistics*. Bloomington: Indiana University Press, 33–58. (Originally published in 1929.)
Jespersen, Otto. 1909. *Progress in Language, with special Reference to English*, 2nd ed. London: Swan Sonnenschein & Co.; New York: Macmillan.
1946. *Mankind, Nation and Individual from a Linguistic Point of View*. London: Allen & Unwin. (Originally published in 1925.)
Johnstone, Barbara. 2013. *Speaking Pittsburghese: The Story of a Dialect*. Oxford and New York: Oxford University Press.
Johnstone, Barbara, Jennifer Andrus, and Andrew E. Danielson. 2006. Mobility, indexicality, and the enregisterment of "Pittsburghese." *Journal of English Linguistics* 34, 2: 77–104.
King, Robert D. 1969. *Historical Linguistics and Generative Grammar*. Englewood Cliffs, NJ: Prentice-Hall.
Kiparsky, Paul. 1971. Historical linguistics. In William O. Dingwall (ed.), *A Survey of Linguistic Science*. College Park: University of Maryland Linguistics Program, 576–642.
1973. Abstractness, opacity, and global rules. In Osamu Fujimura (ed.), *Three Dimensions of Linguistic Theory*. Tokyo: TEC, 57–86.
2003. The phonological basis of sound change. In Brian D. Joseph and Richard D. Janda (eds.), *Handbook of Historical Linguistics*. Malden, MA: Blackwell, 313–342. (Originally published in 1995.)
Kuryłowicz, Jerzy. 1927. ə indoeuropéen et ḫ hittite. In Witold Taszycki et al., *Symbolae grammaticae in honorem Ioannis Rozwadowski*. Cracow: Drukarnia Uniwersytetu Jagiellońskiego, vol. 1, 95–104.
1945/1949. La nature des procès dits "analogiques." *Acta Linguistica [Hafniensia]* 5, 1: 15–37.

Labov, William. 1963. The social motivation of a sound change. *Word* 19, 3: 273–309.
    1966. *The Social Stratification of English in New York City.* Washington, DC:
    Center for Applied Linguistics.
    1972. *Sociolinguistic Patterns.* Philadelphia: University of Pennsylvania Press.
    1981. Resolving the Neogrammarian controversy. *Language* 57, 2: 267–308.
    1994. *Principles of Linguistic Change,* vol. 1, *Internal Factors.* Oxford: Blackwell.
    2001. *Principles of Linguistic Change,* vol. 2, *Social Factors.* Oxford: Blackwell.
    2006. *The Social Stratification of English in New York City,* 2nd ed. Cambridge
    and New York: Cambridge University Press.
Lavandera, Beatrice. 1978. Where does the sociolinguistic variable stop? *Language in
    Society* 7, 2: 171–182.
Martinet, André. 1949. La double articulation linguistique. Recherches structurales:
    interventions dans le débat glossématique. *Travaux du Cercle Linguistique de
    Copenhague* 5: 30–37.
    1955. *Economie des changements phonétiques: Traîté de phonologie diachronique.*
    Bern: A Francke.
Mathesius, Wilém. 1964. On the potentiality of the phenomena of language. In Josef
    Vachek (ed.), *A Prague School Reader in Linguistics.* Bloomington: Indiana
    University Press, 1–32. (Originally published in 1911.)
Meillet, Antoine. 1893. Les lois du langage: I, Les lois phonétiques. *Revue
    Internationale de Sociologie* 1, 4 : 311–321.
    1995. *Pour un manuel de linguistique générale.* A cura de Fiorenza Granucci.
    Atti della Accademia Nazionale dei Lincei, Memorie, ser. 9, vol. 6, no. 1. Rome:
    Accademia Nazionale dei Lincei.
Milroy, Lesley. 1980. *Language and Social Networks.* Oxford: Blackwell.
Morpurgo Davies, Anna. 1998. *Nineteenth-Century Linguistics.* Giulio Lepschy (ed.),
    History of Linguistics, vol. 4. London: Longman.
Passy, Paul. 1890. *Étude sur les changements phonétiques et leurs caractères généraux.*
    Paris: Firmin-Didot.
Reid, T. B. W. 1956. Linguistics, structuralism, and philology. *Archivum Linguisticum*
    8, 1: 28–37.
Ross, John Robert. 1967. Constraints on variables in syntax. PhD dissertation, MIT.
Sapir, Edward. 1925. Sound patterns in language. *Language* 1, 2: 37–51.
    1932. Group. In Edwin R. A. Seligman (ed.), *Encyclopaedia of the Social Sciences.*
    New York: Macmillan, vol. 7, 178–182.
    1949a. The concept of phonetic law as tested in primitive languages by Leonard
    Bloomfield. In David G. Mandelbaum (ed.), *Selected Writings of Edward Sapir in
    Language, Culture, and Personality.* Berkeley and Los Angeles: University of
    California Press, 73–82. (Originally published in 1931.)
    1949b. *Language: An Introduction to the Study of Speech.* New York: Harcourt,
    Brace & World. (Originally published in 1921.)
Saussure, Ferdinand de. 1879. *Mémoire sur le système primitif des voyelles dans les
    langues Indo-Européennes.* Leipzi[g]: B. G. Teubner.
    1916. *Cours de linguistique générale.* C. Bally and A. Sechehaye (eds.). Paris &
    Lausanne: Payot.
    1922. *Recueil des publications scientifiques de Ferdinand de Saussure.* C. Bally and
    L. Gautier (eds.). Lausanne: Payot.

Silverstein, Michael. 1992. The uses and utility of ideology: Some reflections. *Pragmatics* 2, 3: 311–323.

1994. "Relative motivation" in denotational and indexical sound symbolism of Wasco-Wishram Chinookan. In Leanne Hinton, Johanna Nichols, and John J. Ohala (eds.), *Sound Symbolism*. Cambridge: Cambridge University Press, 40–60.

2013. From inductivism to structuralism: The "method of residues" goes to the field. *History and Philosophy of the Language Sciences*. http://hiphilangsci.net/2013/09/11/from-inductivism-to-structuralism-the-method-of-residues-goes-to-the-field.

2014a. In praise of "exceptionlessness": Linguistics among the human sciences at Bloomfield and Sapir's Chicago. *History and Philosophy of the Language Sciences*. http://hiphilangsci.net/2014/11/26/in-praise-of-exceptionless-linguistics-among-the-human-sciences-at-bloomfield-and-sapirs-chicago.

2014b. The race from place: Dialect eradication vs. the linguistic "authenticity" of terroir. In Véronique Lacoste, Jakob Leimgruber, and Thiemo Breyer (eds.), *Indexing Authenticity: Sociolinguistic Perspectives*. Berlin: Walter de Gruyter, 159–187.

Trudgill, Peter. 1972. Sex, covert prestige and linguistic change in the urban British English of Norwich. *Language in Society* 1, 2: 179–195.

Twaddell, W. Freeman. 1935. *On Defining the Phoneme*. Language Monographs no. 16. Baltimore, MD: Linguistic Society of America/Waverly Press.

Vachek, Josef (ed.). 1964. *A Prague School Reader in Linguistics*. Bloomington: Indiana University Press.

Wang, William S. Y. 1969. Competing changes as cause of residue. *Language* 45, 1: 9–25.

(ed.). 1977. *The Lexicon in Phonological Change*. The Hague: Mouton.

Weinreich, Uriel. 1954. Is a structural dialectology possible? *Word* 10: 388–400.

Weinreich, Uriel, William Labov, and Marvin I. Herzog. 1968. Empirical foundations for a theory of language change. In W. P. Lehmann and Yakov Malkiel (eds.), *Directions for Historical Linguistics: A Symposium*. Austin: University of Texas Press, 95–195.

Wilbur, Terence H. (ed.). 1977. *The Lautgesetz-Controversy: A Documentation*. Amsterdam: John Benjamins.

Wolfram, Walt, and Natalie Schilling-Estes. 2006. *American English: Dialects and Variation*, 2nd ed. Oxford: Blackwell.

3   Variation, meaning and social change

Penelope Eckert

Introduction

The perspective that I will develop in these pages,[1] what has come to be referred to as the "Third Wave" approach to variation,[2] takes as basic that the meaningfulness of sociolinguistic variation is not incidental, not a by-product of social stratification, but a design feature of language. Sociolinguistic variation constitutes a system of signs that enables the nonpropositional expression of social concerns as they unfold in interaction. It allows people to say things without putting them into words, making it essential to social life and part of the pragmatics that link speech to the wider social system. I will argue further that language is not just a system that *happens* to change, but a system whose change is central to its semiotic function. Variation is a system of signs that enact a continually changing social world, and it is the potential for change in the meanings of these signs that makes language viable for human life.

This perspective appears to conflict with some of the basic tenets of the view of variation that emerged from work in the First Wave and that endure in much current work in variation. To some extent, this is because the First Wave grew out of the structuralist study of sound change and is primarily concerned with presocial cognitive forces giving rise to change and with macrosocial patterns of variation as structuring the regular social contact that accounts for the spread of change. This limits the view of social meaning to forces deriving from the macrostructure of society, hence external to language. My argument will be that social meaning in variation is an integral part of language and that macrosocial patterns of variation are at once the product of, and a constraint on, a complex system of meaning.

---

[1] I am immensely grateful to Nik Coupland, Chris Potts, and Michael Silverstein for their detailed and penetrating comments on this chapter. I have done my best to incorporate their suggestions, but there remain some that I will continue to muddle over in the months and years to come. And as always, I owe a great debt of gratitude to Miyako Inoue and Rob Podesva, for their continuing starring roles in my intellectual life.

[2] See Eckert (2012) for a fuller account of the three waves of variation study.

Three waves real quick

The First Wave of survey studies found a robust and repeated pattern of variation correlating with macrosociological categories, showing that change enters communities at the lower end of the socioeconomic hierarchy, and spreads upward. According to the model that emerged in the First Wave, sound change is presocial, originating in the most unconscious and systematic reaches of the speaker's linguistic system and emerging in the speaker's most unmonitored speech, the vernacular. But the global prestige and stigma of class lend social evaluation to patterns across this hierarchy, which intrudes in production, interrupting the natural flow of the vernacular when speakers' attention is drawn to their speech. In this way, the class stratification of variation is embedded in each speaker's range of variation, which constitutes a small slice of the community pattern. The finding that several apparently stable variables show a similar social distribution solidified the idea that variables all range along a single vector of formality or attention to speech. Intensity of contact was the underlying cause of the spread of change, but the class origins of change were explained by orientation to the standard language market (e.g., Kroch 1978; Sankoff and Laberge 1978).

The Second Wave delved under the large social aggregates of the First Wave, uncovering the local categories and configurations in which change takes place at the local level and drawing attention to the day-to-day social practice in which macrosocial patterns emerge. Work in the Second Wave adopted a more constructivist view of the relation between variation and social categories and called into question the relation between style and attention to speech, emphasizing the positive value of the vernacular in local practice. In its later stages, it drew attention to the importance of style in the construction of social categories, and this ultimately led to the beginnings of the Third Wave.

The Third Wave departs from the first two by viewing variation as a system of signs, whose meanings emerge in their role in styles that enact social personae or types. These types, in turn, are both constrained by, and contribute to, macro-social patterns. Thus variables connect only indirectly to the macrosocial. The first two waves viewed social locations and their social evaluations as broadly consensual and stable, while the Third Wave views them as emergent.

In other words, the study of variation and change until now has been exclusively a study of change in form, with the social structuring the broad path through which change in form travels, and the boundaries around aggregates of people who use variable forms in similar ways. The promise of Weinreich, Labov, and Herzog (1968), by locating change in the orderly heterogeneity of the speech community, was to break down the distinction between synchrony and diachrony, moving us away from the stadial (see

Silverstein, this volume, Chapter 2) treatment of change. If work in variation has not achieved this transcendence, it is because it has been hamstrung by its treatment of the social as static. I will argue in what follows that change involves the entire sign – content as well as form.

Variation as a semiotic system

To examine the nature of social meaning in variation, I begin with three properties of variables that are particularly important to their functioning:

Implicitness. Unlike much of the propositional meaning that preoccupies semantics, the meaning of variables[3] is implicit, only rarely overtly constructed, and eminently deniable. In this way, variation enables speakers to signal things about themselves and the social world without saying them "in so many words," and allowing things to be left "unsaid." This also allows a speaker to make small indexical moves, for example to try out the identity waters with less risk to face.

Underspecification. A design feature of language more generally, underspecification allows a small number of forms to serve a large number of purposes. Individual variables never have a single meaning, but a broader meaning potential. In this sense, they are like other linguistic signs, as more specific meanings emerge only in context. This need for interpretation binds language to social action, and it lies at the core of language's capacity for flexibility, nuance, creativity and change.

Combinativeness. Finally, these underspecified variables do not take on meaning in isolation, but as stylistic components. They connect to the social through their role in enacting and re-enacting personae, which are visible marks of the distinctions that make up the social fabric. As these personae and the world they construct are not static, a kind of infinite semiosis continually affects a variable's meaning potential or indexical field. (Eckert 2008)

These three properties make the meaning of variation eminently mutable, as the means of expression moves with the social world it engages. In this way, variation is not just a reflection of the social, but essential to its construction. Central to the Third Wave is the emphasis on practice. The First Wave is based in a theory of linguistic structure, rendering change problematic and maintaining separation between language and the social. But it is in practice that we reproduce, and in the process change, the structure of language. And this is inseparable from our more general practice that reproduces the social. Giddens (1979: 2) sums up social reproduction simply: "In and through their activities agents reproduce the conditions that make these activities possible." The macrosocial categories of variation studies – class, gender, ethnicity, age, and so on – structure the conditions under which each of us

---

[3] For the sake of brevity, I use *variable* to mean *sociolinguistic variable,* but do not claim that all linguistic variables have a social function.

lives and to which our actions respond. In the process, we reproduce, potentially changing, that structure.

Variation and change

The macrosocial categories of class, gender, ethnicity, and age are abstractions over an infinite range of activities and conditions that constitute the lives in and for which people use variation. In their day-to-day lives, people do not experience class as a stratification of economic and status indicators, gender as a simple binary, or age as a biological or calendric continuum – even if they can learn to think of them in these ways. Correlations of formal linguistic variation with these categories can point to, but cannot explain, the discursive use of variation. The important issue is not whether we recognize the importance of abstract social patterns, but what we take their significance to be for a theory of variation. Gender, class, age, and ethnicity will always emerge as supremely important in the study of variation because they are central aspects of our social order. But what is their relation to the use of variation? Are they cause or result? Is it more important to us that they structure interaction or that they are the outcome of interaction? From her perspective, does a person mop floors every day for a living because she is working class or is she working class because she mops floors every day? And does her way of speaking have more to do with the fact that she is working class or with the fact that it unfolds in the course of mopping floors? Is she more likely to be marking her class status as she speaks, showing annoyance about her boss, showing worry about her car breaking down, or being polite or confrontational with her children's teachers? And does sound change just roll through her social networks or is it part of what happens as she engages in these conversations? In other words, is she an intermediary or a mediator – does she just pass changes along or does she do something with them, hence to them, in the process?[4] The crux of the matter lies in agency which, as I will discuss below, does not require conscious intention. And if we view variables as signs, we need to consider that the meaning can change as well as the form.

Having no denotational meaning of their own, phonological units are not signs in the received Saussurean sense. But once a piece of phonetic form comes to be associated with some social indexical meaning, it becomes a sign. The emergence of a sign, whether a new sign or a change in an existing sign, opens an order of indexicality (Silverstein 2003). Orders of indexicality are most commonly described as steps in a linear progression – a first order indexing a category of speakers, the next order indexing some association or

---

[4] See Latour (2005) for a discussion of the distinction between mediator and intermediary.

stereotypic quality of that category, and so on. Thus in Labov's (1963) Martha's Vineyard study, (ay) with a centralized nucleus, originating as a regional ("first" order) index 'Vineyarder,' was appropriated to index a particular stance in the struggle with mainland incursion, yielding a "second" order index – a particular claim about what constitutes an 'Authentic Vineyarder.' In fact, it's almost impossible for an index to be first order (see Silverstein 2003), since the moment a form becomes indexical, it is flush with meaning. The Vineyard (ay) no doubt had long had other associations on the mainland (such as some quaint associations with island people) that would not have been affected by what went on on the Island. In other words, orders of indexicality involve interpretive orders – the socially located meaning systems within which construal takes place. This is particularly important because it keeps our focus on the multiplicity of interpretations. Once the centralized nucleus indexed an anti-incursion stance on the Vineyard, it was available for reuse, for example, indexing a strong stance on some other issue – possibly local or otherwise. This continuous reinterpretation of variables results in indexical fields (Eckert 2008), or ranges of potential meanings that can be called up depending on the context. While an indexical field encompasses variability of meaning, it does not imply boundedness – one person's indexical field for a variable will change continually and will presumably be continuous with those of people with long-shared experiences (Jaffe's chapter in this volume, Chapter 4, offers an expansion of the indexical field construct). In other words, just as the forms themselves are continuously variable across time and space, the meanings may be as well.

At the very microlevel, meaning is constructed where production and interpretation come together. Peirce's (1931) triadic theory of the sign involves three components: the sign-vehicle (roughly form), the object (roughly meaning), and the interpretant[5] – the in-the-moment construal of the sign. The interpretant, in turn, launches a new sign. Signs, in other words, are in a continual process of enregisterment. This is crucial to any theory of language, underlying change at all levels. We simply do not have a viable theory of linguistic change if we separate the sign vehicle from the object and if we view some signs as changing, others as stable. By their very nature, signs are unstable. While some may be continually maintained, that maintenance is best seen as a kind of change. Needless to say, some parts of language, and some meanings, are more volatile than others. We expect the meaning of *table* to be more stable than that of *hipster*. We also can observe that words denoting women (e.g., *hussy*) change faster than equivalent terms denoting men, given the enduring tendency to render terms for women pejorative. Here, once again, change of

---

[5] Strictly speaking, as I understand Peirce's distinctions, a *dynamic interpretant*.

meaning takes place within an interpretive (in this case gender) order. And the effect of the gender order is not abstract but is played out in the continual situated use of the word. The shift of the etymon from 'housewife' (thirteenth-century *huswif*) to 'slattern' (McConnell-Ginet 1984) took place in repeated social moves in particular kinds of situations on the part of particular kinds of people. And the gender order within which this took place accounts similarly for shifts of meaning such as *mistress* and *bitch*.

Like the rest of language, variation does not simply reflect the social but enacts it, and in the course of this enactment, it participates in social change[6]. Social distinctions such as gender, class, age, and ethnicity are instantiated through day-to-day activity that includes linguistic variation. But while they are being instantiated, they are also changing. Gender is not the same as it was in my mother's generation, and in recent years, we have seen the technology industry rearrange class in significant ways. It certainly does not mean the same thing to be African American today as it did when I was a kid, and of course sixty is the new forty. The character of cities and geographic regions is unstable as well – urban gentrification and the industrialization of agriculture bring consequences for the use and perception of dialect features. And the movement of people to and away from areas brings about new perceptions as well (e.g., Johnstone et al. 2006). The distinctions remain, even sometimes labeled the same, but they are not static. Society and the people who make it up are always works in progress, so if variation is to do semiotic work, it has to be a dynamic resource.

Who we are and what we do changes over time because who we can be and what we can do changes over time. The persona that I present every day as an academic woman was impossible when I was a thirty-year-old Assistant Professor,[7] both because I had the mind and body of a thirty-year-old and because the world around me was the world of the 1970s. Like the sprinkling of female Assistant Professors around me, I consciously lowered my vocal pitch (F0) in order to be taken more seriously – a move that some young female academics nowadays feel they can afford to resist. Granted that changes in academic gender balances were brought about to some extent through legislation, and institutional change made room for new kinds of female Assistant Professors, those high-level changes were the result of action on the ground, and the way of "doing being" female Assistant Professor emerged on the ground as well. In other words, much social change is brought about through changes in personae – modifications of existing personae, and the emergence of new ones. Skaters, Valley Girls, Bros, and Hipsters are all young

---

[6] This is one aspect of Coupland's (2014) *sociolinguistic change*.

[7] And this female academic persona barely existed in my mother's generation, which is why in my entire undergraduate and graduate career I had only three tenure-track female professors.

white personae that have emerged in the current generations and that personify issues in millennial social life. The Kogals (Miller 2004) and Gothic Lolitas (Gagné 2008) of Japan were not even imaginable fifty years ago. Their stylistic innovations, including their linguistic innovations, are integral to social change in Japan.

To the people on the ground, stylistic change does not place us in a ready-made spot but carves out a new spot in a structure that is itself in flux – or that we would like to put into flux.[8] I probably raised my F0 when I went home at the end of my Assistant Professor day – but over time, aspects of my Assistant Professor self spread to the rest of my life. The Gothic Lolitas leave home in their school uniforms and a matching demeanor, changing into Lolitas in their free public space. And no doubt becoming – and ceasing to be – Gothic Lolitas is part of their movement through life. Heath, the gay doctor of Podesva's (2007) study, switches styles radically as he moves from the clinic to the barbecue with his friends. Most likely Heath did not have a "gay diva" style as a young boy, nor could he have envisioned the possibility of the personae he would develop. Rickford and McNair-Knox (1994) warned against taking one recording as evidence of a person's "habitual" speech – or differences between recordings at two points in time as evidence of change in that person's "habitual" speech. Indeed one's change over time is an unfolding of identity work that is always in motion moment-by-moment, situation-by-situation. And Heath's particular ensemble of personae is not only part of his moving into adulthood, but also, importantly, part of social change. Not only has change in sexual and gender ideologies brought about increasing performances of sexual and gender diversity, but each such performance brings about change in these ideologies.

Personae and the semiotic landscape

The development of new personae is social change at a basic level, and variation does its semiotic work in the stylistic practice that puts these personae flexibly into the landscape. Coupland introduced the notion of *persona* into the study of style and variation, pointing out the relation between personae and macrosociological categories. This perspective lies at the origins of the Third Wave:

Dialect style as persona management captures how individuals, within and across speaking situations, manipulate the conventionalized social meanings of dialect varieties – the individual through the social. But it is the same process of dialectal self-projection that explains the effect of dialect stratification when the speech of social groups is aggregated in sociolinguistic surveys. Individuals within what we

---

[8] This is what Silverstein (1976) terms *creative* indexicality.

conventionally recognize to be meaningful social categories enact dialect personas with sufficient uniformity for survey researchers to detect numerical patterns of stratification. (Coupland 2001: 198)

The attention to personae shifts the focus away from the social aggregate to individuals as they move through identities and situations. However, it amounts to a study not of the individual but of the structure within which individuals find and make meaning. This structure can be viewed as a semiotic landscape, in which styles and the linguistic features that constitute them connect to the social. This is a slippery spatial metaphor, with many of the problems of the metaphorical socioeconomic hierarchy, but it focuses us on styles rather than individual variables, thus foregrounding the social basis of meaning. Rather than seeking out variables that correlate with class, we will seek out variables that play a role in this landscape, but needless to say, abstractions like class will emerge as areas in this landscape. This will greatly expand the number and kind of variables we examine, and in the process we may find other abstractions, intersecting or not, with class. This multiplicity of variables does not mean that the study of style moves us into disorderly heterogeneity, but it puts new demands on us to find order. It is crucial that we recognize that there is nothing random about variation – that when we move on from our focus on the macrosocial, we continue to find patterns that explicate, rather than conflict with, the macrosocial.

Order in the First Wave comes in treating all variables as moving continuously along a single vector of formality, which conditions the speaker's attention to speech. Thus the raising of (eh) in New York City can be expected to co-occur with the raising of (oh), apical pronunciations of (-ING), and even (th/dh) stopping. Although this covariation is not strict,[9] a general class and formality stratification applies to all. This treatment of relative formality as the social impetus for changing states of attention is in support of the theory of the vernacular, but to the extent that covariation is not strict, this cannot be a theory of style. The essence of style is difference, and the study of style needs to focus on the novel patterns of co-occurrence that bring about difference. Such patterns have been treated extensively over the years in discussions of alternation and co-occurrence (Ervin-Tripp 1972), register (e.g., Halliday 1978; Agha 2003), and heteroglossia (Bakhtin 1981), all of which are defined by distinctive combinations of alternative forms, whose use corresponds to some combination

---

[9] These variables show different class patterns; there are differences between and among changes in progress and stable variables. While movement of (eh) and (oh) is constrained by their structural relations, differences correspond to ethnic differences, with Italians raising (eh) more than Jews, with consequences for the pronunciation of (ah) (Labov 1966: 511ff.). Labov speculated that the Jewish lower (eh) might be due to Yiddish substrate. But is this purely a cognitive phenomenon or did Jews hold back on (eh) because the lower version sounded "Jewish"?

of social type and situation. In most of these cases, quite explicitly in Halliday's case, registers are treated as emergent in the situations that structure the social world and are tied to situations through the meanings in play in those situations. Registers are styles with broad recognition, and whatever the breadth of that recognition, they give shape to the semiotic landscape.

Agha's register (2003) is a sign at a particularly high level of consensuality and metadiscursivity – a style that is enduringly associated with some widely recognized character type such as Posh Brit or Surfer Dude. Silverstein's and Agha's notion of enregisterment emphasizes the processual, the creation of a sign through the linguistic bringing-into-being of a characterological figure. And this bringing-into-being is where variation comes in. From the perspective of variation, registers are an outcome of stylistic practice, in which speakers make small or large interactive moves. A girl on the Fields Elementary School playground (Eckert 2011a) who wants to talk about "who's going with who [hɪːw]," and her classmate who, upon the approach of someone she's shunning, says, "I better move [mɪwv]," are advancing an element of the California vowel shift as they fashion themselves as players with attitude in the emerging popular crowd. These girls, in these stylistic moves, can be said to be modifying their personae, modeling themselves as someone quite distinct from their less popular peers and from their own childhood personae. But there is nothing random or particularistic about what they are doing, as it all takes place within and with respect to a cultural paradigm yielding a particular configuration of youth, gender, ethnicity, class, attitude, and region. And while they are using a resource that is even still commonly associated with Valley Girls, they are not using a Valley Girl register, but drawing on, and referring to, that register and its persona.

Based on the patterns we encounter, we construct our own patterns, engaging in stylistic activity as we move through and make places for ourselves in the social landscape. Styles are put together in a continual process of bricolage (Hebdige 1984 adapting Lévi-Strauss 1967), which may take place in minute and quite unconscious moves (e.g., a slightly longer voiced onset time or slightly shifted vowel) or in more intentional moves (e.g., a more drastic vowel shift or an intense use of creak). A skinny white boy may start saying "yo!" Indeed, at some point in recent years, some white frat boy ventured to call one of his brothers "bro." Depending on how these moves come off, one might use them again, refine them, back off from them. A stylistic move is always creative – people do not make stylistic moves to replicate what is already there but to move on.[10] And these moves are the microorganisms of linguistic and social change and stability.

---

[10] Hodder (1982) emphasizes that stylistic innovations are linked to ideologies and "strategies of legitimation."

The perception of social meaning involves a reverse process. When we see a new person, we perceive a style – a combination of clothing, facial expression, posture, movement, speech, and so on – that helps us place this person in the social landscape and predict how he or she might think and act, both in the present situation and in others. Campbell-Kibler (e.g., 2008) has shown that hearers interpret variables on the basis of their understanding of what kind of person is speaking and what a particular variant can mean coming from that person to that hearer in that situation. In other words, the hearer's model of the speaker in the situation is the basis from which he or she interprets the use of a particular linguistic variant. While perceptions vary from person to person, patterns emerge, as people with similar experiences tend to have similar interpretations.[11] The more similar the participants' semiotic systems, the better the match is likely to be. People who are socially closer will have more similar experiences, more mutual concerns, and more similar interpretations of the semiotic landscape. As a result, they are more likely to give and take small stylistic innovations. And to the extent that individuals participate in the same communities of practice, they are likely to reach out jointly into the wider stylistic landscape to appropriate resources from more distant styles. These similarities accumulate into larger social patterns, which ramp up into macrosocial differences. In this way, our social landscape comprises a stylistic continuum.

Agency does not equal awareness

Some view the focus on style and persona as separate from the "mainstream" quantitative tradition in variation both because it examines variables that are not primarily associated with the macrosocial and because it brings in intentional uses of variables. But the status of these "other" variables cannot be established a priori. First, these "other" variables are not random but engage social issues that are part of the same structured social world as the macropatterned variables. Given that frontliers in changes in progress that are not markers or stereotypes can clearly be produced for stylistic emphasis, the line between the intentional and the unintentional, the conscious and the unconscious, is a problematic one.

The theory of the vernacular protects the autonomy of sound change by presupposing a clear line between the conscious and the unconscious. While the regularity of sound change and the automaticity of speech are central to any theory of variation, this line between the conscious and the unconscious, and the strict separation of the social from the linguistic, are not. Social motivations

---

[11] This is the habitus (Bourdieu 1997) writ small.

have been snuck into discourses about variation from the start. For example, Trudgill (1972) developed Labov's notion of "covert prestige" to account for the spread of change upward from the working class. As a leading denier of the role of the social in sound change, Trudgill presumably found this bit of social meaning acceptable because it is "unconscious."

But consciousness and awareness are not simple matters, and agency does not equal or require awareness. A central source of this problem is the common belief that the social is somehow external to cognition, or at a "higher" level. People talk about social constraints as "top-down" constraints. Such spatial metaphors can facilitate scientific discourse, but in doing so they often render problematic generalizations as given. Anyone who has thought carefully about the social will know that the social is every bit as interior and basic as the linguistic. The social is embedded in the unconscious to the same extent, in the same way, and along the same timeline, as the linguistic. Bourdieu's (1977) notion of the *habitus* is a cognitive embedding of the social, developed from the earliest years as a function of one's location in society. The habitus has even been described (Wacquant 2005) as the social equivalent of linguistic competence. This is a problematic analogy, since the vernacular does not encompass the full range of variation, and one would be better off speaking of a linguistic habitus. Experimental work is showing that a speaker's percep-tion of the social meaning of variables can operate at a very unconscious level, whether the variables are stereotypes (e.g., Hay and Drager 2010) or recent sound changes in progress (D'Onofrio 2014). Most importantly, D'Onofrio (2015) has shown that social information enters the process of perception from the very start and is inseparable from phonological processing. This perspective on stylistic practice does not erase the importance of the systematicity and automaticity of sound change but raises the question of when and how that automatic sound change becomes a sign.

Labov proposes a continuum of awareness, among indicators, markers, and stereotypes, on the basis of (1) the presence or absence of stylistic use and (2) the presence or absence of metapragmatic awareness. These are, presumably, stages in the process of enregisterment and can be part of the development and progress of sound change, as the progress from indicator to marker is a gradually emerging pattern sensitivity, eventually leading to recognition. At the same time, very intentional stylistic moves may eventually become auto-matic. White boys with little contact with African American peers who adopt features of African American Vernacular English (Bucholtz 1999) know what they're doing. The skinny white kid saying "yo!" knows what he's doing. The result may be a little jerky, but if the innovation works – that is, if it goes over in the right circles – it may over time become integrated into his style, eventually becoming smoother and more automatic. It will not be the same sign that his African American peers use (and may hence cease to use), but it will be a new one whose meaning includes the conditions of borrowing. In other words, change can progress from unconscious to conscious, and vice-versa. Certainly we do things unconsciously all the time, and our lack of consciousness does not mitigate its effect or our role in its effect. Personae are not necessarily entirely intentional. Even involuntary tics become part of a person's style, whether that person likes it or not, since the style is not in the intent but in the intersubjective space between production and perception.

Kinds of meaning

The objects of study of variation and pragmatics together make up a social-indexical system, but having emerged from different directions, they remain disciplinarily separate. Pragmatics compensates for a decontextualized semantics, which concerns stable but underdetermined meanings. But nothing in language is stable, and semantic change is a product of regular patterns of the contextualized use that is the subject matter of pragmatics. The division of labor between semantics and pragmatics is an analytic convenience – one might say, an analytic requirement – but stability is a matter of degree. Similarly, the line between pragmatics and variation is fluid. Acton (2014) and Gardner and Tagliamonte (2015) have shown, for example, how the presence or absence of the definite article patterns socially but along pragmatic lines. This is as it should be, and the question is to what extent the meanings associated with more traditional variables are significantly different.

Over the years, the move from phonological to syntactic and discourse variables has broadened meaning preservation to include functional equivalence (e.g., Coupland 1983; Cheshire 2005; Buchstaller 2006), which leads into classic pragmatic territory. The emphasis, though, has been on abstracting away from pragmatic force. Social stratification, in these cases, seems to be what qualifies something as a sociolinguistic variable. The fact that Labov and Weiner (1983) didn't find social constraints in the use of the agentless passive may mean not that it is not a sociolinguistic variable but that they have not found the right social constraints (Romaine 1985). Whatever social differentiation there is to be found will be a function of social differences in pragmatic strategies. Perhaps there is a category of people, for instance, the compulsively transgressive and cowardly (see, e.g., Ehrlich 1998), who are more likely than others to background their own agency. But as long as this tendency does not align with macrosocial categories, they will not be considered sociolinguistic variables. Acton has shown that when referring to a group of people, the use of *the* rather than a bare plural (*the Americans* vs. *Americans*) "tends to depict the group as a monolith of which the speaker is not a part" (2014: iv). People inclined to engage in othering, or individuals when they are in "othering mode," then, may be more likely to use this variant (Melnick and Acton 2015).

But one does not have to go to syntax to see the pragmatic potential of variation. To take the simplest interpretation of its meaning, people will agree that apical pronunciations of (-ING) are more casual than velar ones. So, is the social stratification of this variable an otherwise meaningless difference in how people pronounce this morpheme? Or does stratification reflect class differences in participation in situations that call for casualness and/or correspond to differences in ideologies about casualness and formality? Campbell-Kibler (2008) has shown that listeners hear the apical variant as condescending if they believe the speaker is educated, and the velar variant as pretentious if they believe the speaker is not educated. If a college student tells his friends he can't go out for a beer with them because "I'm studyin'," are his friends more likely to urge him to go, inferring that he's less serious about not going out than if he had said "I'm studying"?

Crossing another disciplinary boundary, variation plays an important role in the expression of emotion, which, although commonly relegated to psychology, is eminently social. Although emotion is thought of in terms of states, it is also a practice. People "do" affect just as they "do" gender or other category memberships (see, e.g., Eckert 1996). Affect interacts with, is part of the construction of, macrosocial categories, as certain populations find themselves in particular affective states more often, are expected to display or to not display particular affective states, or have come to distinguish themselves on the basis of those states. The mutually opposed high school communities of Belten High in the Detroit suburbs (Eckert 1989), the Jocks and the Burnouts, distinguished themselves among other things on the basis of affect. The Burnouts considered themselves a problem culture, the have-nots, and resented what they saw as the Jocks' fake smiles. Many Jocks, meanwhile, prided themselves on presenting a happy face at all times (regardless of how they felt). One might ask to what extent this is responsible for the fact that the Jocks favored the fronting (hence lip-spreading) components of the Northern Cities Shift while the Burnouts favored the backing (hence lip-rounding) components. This raises the question of what exactly constitutes a variable.

The traditional focus in variation has been on individual units, primarily segments, and when we turn to prosody we generally focus on specific intonational contours (e.g., Guy et al. 1986) or rhythmic patterns (e.g., Carter 2005). But one might consider that the Jocks' and Burnouts' preference for fronting versus backing changes involves a difference in articulatory setting, extending the variable to multiple related segments. Similarly, fortition can index anger and may affect a variety of segments. In this case it may be the process that is the variable. And some instances of fortition might also be hyperarticulations, and index clarity or carefulness along with other forms of hyperarticulation (as discussed at greater length in Eckert 2008). This also introduces embodiment and iconicity. Certainly prosody is closely tied to affect, and the relation is in large part iconic, but iconicity creeps into segmental phonology as well. The frequency code (Ohala 1994) has been shown to relate front vowels with positive affect and back vowels with negative (Geenberg 2010; Eckert 2011b). Prosodic expressions of affect can generally be said to not change propositional value, but they can disambiguate. Nygaard and Lunders (2002), for example, found that emotional tone of voice affects the processing of tokens of homophonous lexical items, so experimental subjects are more likely to process [flæwə] as *flower* when hearing it in a happy voice, and *flour* when hearing it in a neutral voice, and to process [daɪ] as *die* when hearing it in a sad voice and *dye* when hearing it in a neutral voice. Indeed, it would be strange if iconicity were not frequently at work in the indexical realm. Although sound symbolism is conventional, once conventionalized it brings ready-made meaning potential to the enregisterment process.

Conclusion

Perhaps because my intellectual roots are in the Labovian tradition, I think of the Third Wave study of meaning as part and parcel of a larger variationist endeavor. If there are two robust facts about variation, they are that (1) variation is socially meaningful, and (2) variation patterns socially on both the macro- and the microsocial scale. A robust theory of variation will integrate these facts, tracing the links between local stylistic practice and macrosocial patterns, examining meaning-making on the ground in view of the conditions of life represented by macrosocial categories. A theory of variation will also have to deal with the contributions to meaning of different kinds of variables, from sound changes in progress to segmental and prosodic indexes of affect.

And we will have to recognize questions that are still open. Social meaning has been an untheorized subtext of all work on variation, tempered by a commitment to protecting the autonomy of sound change. The focus on macrosociological categories has played an important role in this protection, as it foregrounds mechanical contact and distance. And arguments against the role of the social in sound change have fixated on macrosociological notions of identity. Trudgill (2008) argues that identity played no role in dialect mixture in a variety of historical situations of contact, based on the lack of evidence that the mixture was ever associated with a new colonial identity. Identity, he claims, does not have the power to drive change but is parasitic upon automatic, unconscious, interactional synchrony. Labov (2001: 191) questions the importance of identity, setting forth density of contact as the most powerful force in the spread of change:

The Martha's Vineyard study is frequently cited as a demonstration of the importance of the concept of local identity in the motivation of linguistic change. However, we do not often find correlations between degrees of local identification and the progress of sound change. (Labov 2001: 191, cited in Trudgill 2008: 244)

However, this was meant to raise the issue rather than reject the social motivation. But as in Trudgill's case, the social force that Labov is questioning is a kind of identity based on macrosociological constructs – nation, region, island. But it is not at all clear that local identity is what was at issue in the Martha's Vineyard case. Rather, a variable that had been a local marker was used in taking an ideological stance within – and dividing – the local community. The fisherfolk may have been laying claim to greater local authenticity as a way of bolstering their stance, but not to local identity. Accommodation in colonial situations may have more to do with emerging local social types or stances in the colonial situation than with some abstract colonial identification. It seems that there is an 'it-must-be-like-that' school (Trudgill 2014: 220) on both sides of the issue, when in fact we are faced with open questions.

Certainly we cannot ignore the automaticity of sound change and the possibility that where change is involved, social meaning may well be only parasitic on internally constrained processes, at least in the early stages. But sound changes also make up a minority of the sociolinguistic variables at any given time, possibly even of the phonological variables, so a theory of variation cannot be just a theory of sound change. It isn't always clear which variables are actually changes in progress, but there is no question that while some variables are very obviously changing over time, others show greater durability as variables. The meaning potential of variables as a function of their durability is an open and interesting question. No doubt an apparently long-term stable variable such as (-ING) or negative concord has had a greater possibility of setting down more widely consensual and possibly well-defined indexical meanings (Haeri 1994: 103). But I also believe that a central question is where changes in progress fall in the ecology of meaning. What kinds of social meanings can sound changes take on as they progress?[12] The serious study of variation calls for the unification of the macro- and micro-perspectives, which will no doubt require reconsideration of assumptions that lead to, and theoretical constructs that emerge in, the study of variation at any single social-structural level.

---

[12] These are questions that have been considered at the macrosociological level (e.g., Labov's "Eckert progression" [2010: 192ff.]) and are being considered at the stylistic level (Podesva and Van Hofwegen [forthcoming]).

REFERENCES

Acton, E. 2014. Pragmatics and the social meaning of determiners. PhD dissertation, Stanford University.

Agha, A. 2003. The social life of a cultural value. *Language and Communication* 23: 231–273.

Bakhtin, M. M. 1981. *The Dialogic Imagination*. Michael Holquist (ed.), Caryl Emerson and Michael Holquist (trans.) Austin and London: University of Texas Press.

Bourdieu, P. 1977. *Outline of a Theory of Practice*. Cambridge: Cambridge University Press.

Bucholtz, M. 1999. You da man: Narrating the racial other in the production of white masculinity. *Journal of Sociolinguistics* 3 (4): 443–460.

Buchstaller, I. 2006. Diagnostics of age-graded linguistic behavior: The case of the quotative system. *Journal of Sociolinguistics* 10: 3–30.

Campbell-Kibler, K. 2008. I'll be the judge of that: Diversity in social perceptions of (ING). *Language in Society* 37: 637–659.

Carter, Phillip M. 2005. Prosodic variation in SLA: Rhythm in an urban North Carolina Hispanic community. *Penn Working Papers in Linguistics* 11, 2: 59–71.

Cheshire, Jenny. 2005. Syntactic variation and beyond: Gender and social class variation in the use of discourse-new markers. *Journal of Sociolinguistics* 9, 4: 479–508.

Coupland, Nikolas. 1983. Patterns of encounter management: Further arguments for discourse variables. *Language in Society* 12: 459–476.

2001. Language, situation and the relational self: Theorizing dialect-style in sociolinguistics. In P. Eckert and J. Rickford (eds.), *Stylistic Variation in Language*. Cambridge: Cambridge University Press, 185–210.

2014. Language change, social change, sociolinguistic change: A meta-commentary. *Journal of Sociolinguistics* 18, 2: 277–286.

D'Onofrio, A. 2014. Sociolinguistic knowledge of a sound change in progress: Perceptions of California TRAP backing. Paper presented at 88th Annual Meeting of the Linguistics Society of America, Minneapolis, MN.

2015. Persona-based information shapes linguistic perception: Valley Girls and California vowels. *Journal of Sociolinguistics* 19 (2): 241–256.

Eckert, P. 1989. *Jocks and Burnouts: Social Categories and Identity in the High School*. New York: Teachers College Press.

1996. Vowels and nailpolish: The emergence of linguistic style in the preadolescent heterosexual marketplace. In J. Ahlers, L. Bilmes, M. Chen, M. Oliver, N. Warner, and S. Werhteim (eds.), *Gender and Belief Systems*. Berkeley, CA: Berkeley Women and Language Group.

2008. Variation and the indexical field. *Journal of Sociolinguistics* 12, 3: 453–476.

2011a. Language and power in the preadolescent heterosexual market. *American Speech* 86, 1: 85–97.

2011b. Where does the social stop? In J. Parrott (ed.), *Language Variation: European Perspectives III*. Amsterdam and Philadelphia: John Benjamins, 13–30.

2012. Three waves of variation study: The emergence of meaning in the study of variation. *Annual Review of Anthropology* 41: 87–100.

Ehrlich, S. 1998. The discursive reconstruction of sexual consent. *Discourse and Society* 9: 149–171.

Ervin-Tripp, S. 1972. On sociolinguistic rules: Alternation and co-occurrence. In J. Gumperz and D. Hymes (eds.), *Directions in Sociolinguistics: The Ethnography of Communication*. New York: Holt, Rinehart and Winston, 213–250.

Gagné, I. 2008. Urban princesses: Performance and "women's language" in Japan's Gothic/Lolita subculture. *Journal of Linguistic Anthropology* 18, 1: 130–150.

Gardner, Matt Hunt, and Sali Tagliamonte. 2015. The bike, the back, and the boyfriend: Confronting the "definite article conspiracy" in Canadian and British English. Paper presented at Linguistic Society of America Annual Meeting, Portland, OR.

Geenberg, K. 2010. "Poor baby, you got a boo-boo!": Sound symbolism in adult baby talk. Talk delivered at NWAV 39, San Antonio, TX.

Giddens, A. (1979). *Central Problems in Social Theory: Action, Structure and Contradition in Social Analysis*. Berkeley and Los Angeles: University of California Press.

Guy, G., B. Horvath, J. Vonwiller, E. Daisley, and I. Rogers. 1986. An intonational change in progress in Australian English. *Language in Society* 15: 23–52.

Haeri, Niloofar. 1994. A linguistic innovation of women in Cairo. *Language Variation and Change*. 6: 87–112.

Halliday, M. A. K. 1978. *Language as Social Semiotic*. London: Edward Arnold.

Hay, J., and K. Drager. 2010. Stuffed toys and speech perception. *Linguistics* 48, 4: 269–285.

Hebdige, D. 1984. *Subculture: The Meaning of Style*. New York: Methuen.

Hodder, I. 1982. *The Present Past*. London: Batsford.

Johnstone, B., J. Andrus, and A. E. Danielson. 2006. Mobility, indexicality, and the enregisterment of "Pittsburghese." *Journal of English Linguistics* 34: 77–104.

Kroch, A. S. 1978. Toward a theory of social dialect variation. *Language in Society* 7: 17–36.

Labov, W. 1963. The social motivation of a sound change. *Word* 18: 1–42.

    1966. *The Social Stratification of English in New York City*. Washington, DC: Center for Applied Linguistics.

    1972. Some principles of linguistic methodology. *Language in Society* 1, 1: 97–120.

    2001. *Principles of Linguistic Change: Social Factors*. Malden MA. and Oxford: Blackwell Publishers.

    2010. *Principles of Linguistic Change: Cognitive and Cultural Factors*. New York: Wiley-Blackwell.

Labov, W., and E. J. Weiner. 1983. Constraints on the agentless passive. *Journal of Linguistics* 19: 29–58.

Latour, B. 2005. *Reassembling the Social*. New York: Oxford University Press.

Lévi-Strauss, Claude. 1967. *The Savage Mind*. Chicago, IL: University of Chicago Press.

McConnell-Ginet, S. 1984. The origins of sexist language in discourse. In S. J. White and V. Teller (eds.), *Discourses in Reading and Linguistics. Annals of the New York Academy of Sciences*. New York: New York Academy of Sciences, vol. 433, 123–135.

Melnick, R., and E. Acton. 2015. Function words, power, and opposition: A socio-pragmatic "deep" corpus study. Poster presented at the 89th Annual Meeting of the Linguistic Society of America, Portland, OR.

Miller, L. 2004. Those naughty teenage girls: Japanese Kogals, slang, and media assessments. *Journal of Linguistic Anthropology* 14, 2: 225–247.

Nygaard, L. C., and E. R. Lunders. 2002. Resolution of lexical ambiguity by emotional tone of voice. *Memory and Cognition* 30, 4: 583–593.

Ohala, J. 1994. The frequency code underlies the sound-symbolic use of voice pitch. In L. Hinton, J. Nichola, and J. J. Ohala (eds.), *Sound Symbolism*. Cambridge, NY: Cambridge University Press, 325–347.

Peirce, Charles Sanders. 1931. The Collected Papers of Charles S. Peirce, vols. 1-6. Eds. C. Hartshorne, P. Weiss, and A.W. Burks. Cambridge: Harvard University Press.

Podesva, R. 2007. Phonation type as a stylistic variable: The use of falsetto in constructing a persona. *Journal of Sociolinguistics* 11, 4: 478–504.

Podesva, Robert J., and Janneke Van Hofwegen. Forthcoming. On the complementarity of the three waves: The acoustic realization of /s/ in inland California.

Rickford, J., and F. McNair-Knox. 1994. Addressee- and topic-influenced style shift: A quantitative sociolinguistic study. In D. Biber and E. Finegan (eds.), *Sociolinguistic Perspectives on Register*. New York: Oxford University Press, 235–276.

Romaine, S. 1984. On the problem of syntactic varation and pragmatic meaning in sociolinguistic theory. *Folia Linguistica* 18: 409–437.

Sankoff, D., and S. Laberge. 1978. The linguistic market and the statistical explanation of variability. In D. Sankoff (ed.), *Linguistic Variation: Models and Methods*. New York: Academic Press, 239–250.

Silverstein, M. 1976. Shifters, linguistic categories, and cultural description. In K. H. Basso and H. A. Selby (eds.), *Meaning in Anthropology*. Albuquerque: University of New Mexico Press, 11–55.

2003. Indexical order and the dialectics of sociolinguistic life. *Language and Communication* 23, 3–4: 193–229.

Trudgill, P. 1972. Sex, covert prestige and linguistic change in the urban British English of Norwich. *Language in Society* 1: 179–195.

2008. Colonial dialect contact in the history of European languages: On the irrelevance of identity to new-dialect formation. *Language in Society* 37: 241–280.

2014. Diffusion, drift, and the irrelevance of media influence. *Journal of Sociolinguistics* 18: 214–222.

Wacquant, Loïc. 2005.

Weinreich, U., W. Labov, and M. Herzog. 1968. Empirical foundations for a theory of language change. In W. Lehmann and Y. Malkiel (eds.), *Directions for Historical Linguistics*. Austin: University of Texas Press, 95–188.

4 Indexicality, stance and fields in sociolinguistics

Alexandra Jaffe

Introduction

In the recent history of the field of sociolinguistics, the concept of indexicality has been a productive lens for a central disciplinary focus on conventional/ stereotypical relationships between linguistic forms and social meanings. These conventionalized associations have been the basis for studies of a wide range of communicative practices, where they are building blocks or resources in performance and stance-taking and components of styles or registers. They also underpin many critical sociolinguistic projects focused on the social evaluation of communicative practice and its social, political, and ideological implications.

Indexicality has also been central to the understanding of linguistic practice as *context-sensitive* and *context-creating* (see Kiesling 2009: 177) and the companion perspective on meaning as both *conventional* and *emergent*. In this chapter, I review these principles with an emphasis on *processes of indexicalization*: how indexical meanings accrue to particular forms, how indexicals at one level (or "order") are projected onto subsequent orders (Silverstein 2003), and how indexicals are organized into fields (Eckert 2008). I argue that taken together, these approaches constitute a motivated, empirically grounded framework for documenting and understanding sociolinguistic continuity and change.

In this examination of processes of indexicalization, I join many other scholars in focusing on ideology. I make a modest effort to expand this conversation by drawing attention to the sometimes implicit ways in which analyses of indexicality and indexicalization in sociolinguistic analyses have been framed in relation to iconicity and iconization. In doing so, I treat Peirce's famous trichotomy of sign modalities into symbol, index, and icon according to the relationship between the sign and what it stands for (its "object") not just as a typology but as itself a set of dynamic relationships that frame the production and interpretation of meaning.

The distinction that Peirce formalized between indexes and icons revolves around the degree to which particular signs are treated as "fused" with their objects. Indexes have a relationship of contiguity (pointing/association) with what they stand for; icons have relationship of formal ("natural") similarity or resemblance; icons are thus more "fused" with their objects than indexes. Much sociolinguistic work on processes of indexicalization has focused on the way in which indexical associations come to be conventional, potentially so conventional as to undergo iconization as "styles" (Coupland 2007), "persona styles" (Coupland 2002; Eckert 2008: 456), or "registers" (Agha 2007). Iconization (or rhematization), as Gal and Irvine (2000) have emphasized, functions ideologically to naturalize connections between language and the social world that are in fact social and political creations. Viewed in this light, the process of indexicalization itself can be the target of processes of "erasure," to use another of Gal and Irvine's terms. That is, iconization can be understood as erasing the situated, contingent, and political nature of indexical links between language/semiotic practice and aspects of the social world. In this respect, the process of indexicalization (whereby signs acquire social indexicalities) can be viewed as a potential way-station on a path to iconization (in which signs are perceived as coterminous with their social objects). The implication of this line of reasoning is that, in addition to viewing indexical signs as emergent and socially contingent, we also have to understand the *status of a sign as indexical* as emergent and socially contingent. Put another way, a given sign (a sociolinguistic variable) may be interpreted by some social actors as having an essential, natural, "given" relationship with, for example, a social type, and by others as indexing social identities in a less deterministic way.[1]

This attention to meta-indexicality follows from the focus on process and can be traced, as Ball (2014) has recently pointed out, to Pierce's second (and less well-known) trichotomy, which is concerned with the way the relationship between a sign-vehicle and its object is reflexively mediated by an interpretant (see also Eckert, this volume, Chapter 3). "Dicentization" frames an interpretant as an index, as having a connection with its object that is motivated by some empirical relationship (contiguity/causality) in the world. "Rhematization," by contrast, frames the interpretant as an icon, as being a "pure" representation/description of its object. Dicentization, as we will see in several examples below, draws attention to the social and situated way in which signs acquire meanings; rhematization presupposes those meanings as given, natural, or transparent.

The premise of this chapter is that iconization/dicentization and indexicalization/rhematization exist in a dynamic tension in social life, a tension that revolves around the extent to which *semiotic practices* draw attention to *semiotic processes*. One of its goals, then, is to look at communicative

---

[1] As Johnstone has also recently emphasized, the same sign may have no social associations for still other social actors (2013).

practices in which sign–object–interpretant relations *are* the focus of the linguistic and semiotic acts under analysis. Complementing longstanding attention to the social outcomes of iconization/rhematization in the fixing and naturalization of social categories and ideologies, I ask, *What social and ideological projects are advanced when indexicalization is foregrounded rather than erased, and when the contingent and contextual relationships between linguistic forms and social meanings are emphasized?* For this part of the discussion, I draw on data from the blog and book *Stuff White People Like* (hereafter, SWPL) that I have previously analyzed with Shana Walton (2011) and that I reinterpret here as a deliberate, reflexive (or "meta") indexical project.[2]

Second, I consider the dynamics of relationships between indexicals as they are packaged together in *indexical fields* (Eckert 2008): the indexes associated with a particular linguistic form or variable (what kinds of people and stances are associated, for example, with the use of "dude"). Drawing on Silverstein's notion of *orders of indexicality* (2003), I consider how these fields are internally ordered, what conditions favor or disfavor their expansion or contraction, and how relationships of contiguity within these fields may affect individual elements' meaning potentials. I go on to introduce the term *fields of indexicalities* to look at these same processes as they obtain within packages of indexicals associated with the same social object, again drawing on data from SWPL, which constitutes a field of indexes of Whiteness.

Social indexicalities: given and created

The indexical relations that have been of the most interest to sociolinguists and linguistic anthropologists have been social and sociolinguistic ones related to how both speakers and persons figured in a discourse are positioned and position themselves *socially* and *situationally*. The metaphor of "pointing" captures the way that the relationship of the indexical sign to its object is contingent on the positionality of the speaker or writer: An indexical sign is a sign that is anchored in the temporal, spatial, and social context of the linguistic act. Indexes point *to* aspects of the social world and point *from* socially situated vantage points. Some referential indexicals have built-in social salience, establishing the standpoint or stance of speakers/signers/ writers as well as their relationships to other social actors. Pronouns and honorifics are prototypical indexes of this kind and have multiple social

---

[2] This parallels Silverstein's use of "metapragmatic" to refer to "linguistic signs that are about the pragmatic code, about how to interpret the extrasemantic meanings encoded in speech" (Urban 2006: 90); here, the "meta" refers to linguistic and semiotic practices that are about the processes of indexicalization.

and interpersonal functions related to the quality and nature of relationships/ social hierarchies and degrees of social inclusiveness and specificity. In Silverstein's terms, we can think of them as having *first-order* social indexicality. They have been especially productive, for this reason, in the analysis of identity claims and forms of inclusion/exclusion in a wide range of discourse and interactional data. Other referential indexes (spatial and temporal ones) have potential *second (and nth)-order* social indexicalities, a point to which we will return below.

This potential is shared with all other linguistic or semiotic forms. The social indexicals that have been of the most interest to sociolinguists are in fact ones that are *not* given in language but are either purposefully attributed to or accrue in less intentional ways to linguistic forms in temporal and social context. As Ochs writes in her seminal piece, "Socialization is in part a process of assigning situational, i.e., indexical meanings (e.g. temporal, spatial, social identity, social act, social activity, affective or epistemic meanings) to particular forms (e.g. interrogative forms, diminutive affixes, raised pitch and the like)" (1996: 410). Social indexicalities are often, as Ochs demonstrated, mediated by *stance* in combination with statistical/behavioral frequencies. That is, patterns of use make it possible for speakers both to notice (Johnstone 2013) a feature as significant and to establish an indexical association (first-order) between such a feature – for example, high rising terminal intonation (HRT) with a stance (uncertainty or other-orientation). An empirically higher frequency of HRT use by women then creates conditions for potential "noticing" and the establishment of a second-order gender indexicality, such that HRT comes to index gender.

Indeterminacy, multiplicity, and situated/emergent meanings

As Ochs's focus on socialization underscores, indexicality plays a role in the establishment of conventional associations that become part of the backdrop of the shared sociolinguistic knowledge that competent (socialized) social actors use to produce and interpret meaning. At the same time, the dynamics of that socialization process illustrate a wider principle: the *indeterminacy* of the relationship between signs and social meanings. It is due to this indeterminacy that the meaning of social indexicals has to be understood as contextual and emergent. One of the reasons for this fundamental indeterminacy is that regimes of conventional meaning always underdetermine practice. Second, indeterminacy is the outcome of processes *over time*, in which norms and meanings accumulate in a piecemeal fashion, are inherently multiple (and not necessarily coherent), and are anchored in different (and only partially articulated) domains of practice with different historical depth (Jaffe 2009; Johnstone 2013).

To illustrate, let us take one of the linguistic forms mentioned in the Ochs citation above: diminutive affixes. In Spanish, one of these diminutives is the -ito(a)/-cito(a) suffix, which can function as a term of endearment. For example, "pobrecito" – poor little guy – can be used for sympathy, as in this exchange used in the Urban Dictionary as an illustration of usage:

Extract 1:[3] Urban Dictionary Illustration[4]
BOY: "I've got a papercut"
FRIEND: "Aw, pobrecito!"

The stance of sympathy is related to typical speakers (adults) and recipients (children) of a diminutive and the associated benevolent affect of this relationship. This is the (first-order) and conventional indexicality of the ending. However, in a particular interaction, "pobrecito" can also be used sarcastically. This is in fact a possible interpretation of the exchange above even in the absence of any information about the relative ages of the boy and his friend, given the minimal (though very annoying) nature of the injury. If we changed the participants and made them both adult men, this interpretation would become not just possible but likely. Following the logic established by Ochs, a first-order social indexicality in Extract 1 links a linguistic form (-cito) with a stance and, through it, to a type of speaker associated with that stance. In "pobrecito," a stance of sympathy for someone small indexes adulthood (or relative seniority). That stance also presupposes and thus indexes the stance (pitiableness) and identity (child or junior status) of the recipient/target of the utterance. As Silverstein points out, these multiple indexicalities of different orders or levels coexist and interact, sometimes in competition (2003).

An empirical example of such competing indexicalities is shown in Extract 2, where further social meanings potentially accrue to "pobrecito" when uttered by a Spanish-speaking grandmother to her grandchild in front of the child's non-Latina mother. The example is the text of a post to a discussion board on the website CafeMom, where participants exchange opinions and advice on variety of topics related to children. The mother of the baby in question (OP) seeks out feedback on the possible indexicalities of this situated use of "pobrecito":

Extract 2: CafeMom post
For those of you who don't know Spanish this means "poor baby." Every single time my mother-in-law comes around she constantly calls my son "Pobrecito"
Wtf!!?
Can someone please help me understand why she keeps saying this?

---

[3] Here and below, all texts cited from the Internet retain original spellings and punctuation.
[4] www.urbandictionary.com/define.php?term=pobrecito.

There is absolutely no reason for her to refer to my son that way. He's well behaved, healthy, and well taken care of.

Is this just something that Hispanic moms/grandmas just say..? I'm really confused.

If I hear her say it one more time, I'm going to ask her why she does that. Unless, someone on here helps me out with this.

I'm white so I definitely have no idea what this could mean. If she's saying it because of the fact that she doesn't like me then we'll problems. Lol

–OP

The 86 replies to this posting gave mixed answers, a small sample of which are reproduced in Extract 3, below. Many commenters, like #1, asserted that saying "pobrecito" was just a form of endearment, directed entirely at the baby.

Extract 3: CafeMom Responses

#1 My MIL and SIL and BIL always say that too. It's not a big deal. They say it to every baby I've noticed.

#2 (IamMex11) naw, naw….tell her the truth…. Hey OP…they just trying to make you feel better. Anytime an older woman in my family says pobrecito, it is to show disapproval of something. I dont know what that something is in your case, but……she is incinuating something. Just ask her.

#3 I'm Spanish and usually people don't say it unless they feel sorry for someone, im mx & pr.

#4 Ummm no….. I'm Mexican and if my ex mil would have said that it would mean she thought something was wrong…or that she felt sorry for one of my kids…. I wouldn't like.

#5 It could also be a left over thing based on the superstition that if you praise a child too much the evil spirits will be attracted to it and will harm the child. So saying "Poor Baby" would not attract the attention of the evil spirits, some families will find something "wrong" with the baby, like "It's a shame that her feet are so long." or "Poor thing has his Dad's ears."

But another forum participant whose screen name was IamMex11 posted response #2, which offers an alternative and negative reading of the stances indexed by the use of "pobrecito" in this particular context. IamMex11 is then asked her or his nationality, and replies "Puerto Rican." This leads to posts #3 and #4, which also include forms of national/ethnic identification ("Spanish," "mexican" and "puerto rican"). Post #3 contradicts IamMexx11 by interpreting the mother-in-law's use of "pobrecito" as "being sorry"; #4 sides with IamMex11 by telling OP she has a right to feel criticized or insulted. Post #5 suggests yet another cultural frame that treats the utterance as formulaic and culturally conventional and, therefore, not an index of interpersonal stance at all.

In this very brief glance at the comments and interactions in the responses, we can see that there are multiple possible indexicalities of the mother-in-law's utterance: term of endearment, formulaic/superstitious verbal routine, *or* critique of the daughter-in-law. It is interesting to consider these data in light of

Eckert's notion of the "indexical field," which she defines as a "constellation of ideologically related meanings, any one of which can be activated in the situated use of the variable" (2008: 454; see also Coupland 2007). The challenge is to reconcile the contradictory nature of these multiple indexicalities and the notion of the field as hanging together ideologically. What we see is that all of the possible indexical meanings in the field are *indirectly* related to the indexical term "pobrecito" and have to be traced through other known situations, social uses, and stances. In other words, the ideological coherence or relatedness of the field is not a formal property of the field itself but, rather, a property of socially situated uses and interpretations of that field. The latter is a "meta" property that involves attention to processes of indexicalization.

In the discussion on the CafeMom board that ensues, we find participants engaged in exactly this process: trying to tease out indexical potentials by doing such things as evoking different Spanish-speaking communities of practice and querying the writer of the original post for additional details of her relationship with her mother-in-law. In other words, we see these participants orienting to a foundational principle of indexicality by treating it as *necessarily* interpreted against a variety of temporal/historical, relational, and sociolinguistic contexts. In doing so, they echo Ochs's statement that "the indexical valence of a form derives from a history of usage and cultural expectations surrounding that form" (Ochs 1996: 418) and Wortham, who writes that, "depending on which features of the context are in fact salient at the moment of utterance, participants will interpret the sign differently. This is what Silverstein calls 'contextualization,' the fact that signs come to have meaning only as they and co-occurring signs index aspects of the context" (Wortham 2008: 86, citing Silverstein 1992).

The description of the interaction between the woman and her mother-in-law on the blog also points to the way in which indexical use is not just context-sensitive but context-creating. That is, while there is a history of relationship between the two women that precedes this interaction, what it is to be in that moment and going forward is shaped in no small part by the terms that they use to refer to one another and to the baby. The tenor of that relationship, strained in OP's account on the forum, would have been different had she reported her mother-in-law had called the baby "cariño" instead of "pobrecito" or if the mother had directed the baby to "say hi to Abuelita" (all presuming "sincere" tone of voice). This constitutive role is related to the role of indexicality in accounting for both reproduction and change in sociolinguistic meanings. That is, since indexical relations are constantly being produced and reproduced in particular contexts, these moments of reproduction are sites of possible shifts in those relations that can be picked up and redeployed in subsequent interactions and, over time, regularized or conventionalized.

Orders of indexicality and sociolinguistic change

The potential for indexical change has been illustrated in several recent analyses. Through an analysis of a corpus of social media discourse using the term "lady pond" (referencing lesbian sexual activity), Squires documented a phenomenon she calls "indexical bleaching" (Squires 2014). The phrase and its stance potentials were initially tightly associated with the Bravo TV personality who launched the term in the mediascape. That is, both Bravo and this personality were co-located in, and played a dominant role in, the phrase's indexical field in its first phase of distribution. Over time, however, the use of the phrase spread to a wider range of users who were not necessarily oriented to the TV program in question. As the indexical field of "lady pond" contracted over time, Bravo TV and the TV personality were "bleached" from that field; that is, they receded or disappeared. A similar process can be seen in another Spanish-language example studied by Bucholtz (2009): the use of "guey" as a rough equivalent to "dude." Following the success of Bud Light commercials that portrayed twenty-something guys using "dude" in a variety of male, heterosocial ways, Coors brewing company produced a Coors Light commercial in Mexico depicting the same young male demographic engaged in very similar uses of "guey." This sparked a controversy among some middle-aged Spanish-speaking viewers, for whom "guey" had primarily pejorative meanings. This controversy is reflected in Extract 4, which shows two online comments regarding the ad campaign that illustrate the indexical change-in-progress. That is, we see that at a particular point in time – 2004, when the ad first aired – the indexical field of "guey" had at least two, competing meanings. In an example of what Johnstone (2013) has labeled "indexical layering," some older speakers insisted that the pejorative meaning was dominant; others conceded that new meanings had already accrued to it – its indexical value had shifted and expanded to include "dude-like" meanings, at least for younger speakers.

Extract 4: Guey comments
#1 For as long as I've been on the border the word "guey" is slang for "idiot." It is usually used in conjunction with the word pinche which roughly translates to "[Fornicating] Idiot." I wonder which pinche guey at Coors came up with the idea for this ad? #2 [My younger co-workers] said guey is used pretty much as a friendly salutation now instead of an insult.

What we see, then, is Silverstein's principle that all first-order indexes are subject to second (and "nth")-order indexicalization, which links them to widespread social evaluations/stereotypes about the categories of people they index. This means that those linguistic forms can be redeployed by members both inside and outside the group to take up, or project, a stance relative to those social, evaluative meanings. In the case of the use of "pobrecito," we have seen that it can embody more or less "sincere" positions toward the stance of sympathy that is a first-order index of "pobrecito": It can be used to project a stance of childlikeness on an interlocutor (with positive or negative overtones), assume a patronizing role, and so on. Because of the interaction of different orders of indexicalization, as the social evaluations of categories of speakers shift, so too can the indexical values of the linguistic forms. Alternatively, as linguistic forms come to be used by and thus associated with wider or different categories of speakers and socially evaluated in different ways, those linguistic forms' indexicalities can widen, contract, or shift with respect to stance. We have seen the widening, for example, in the case of "guey"; another example is HRT, whose increasing use by younger men makes it subject to indexical change. In this respect, the concept of indexicality provides a socially motivated account of intertwined processes of social and linguistic change and continuity that may result in new linguistic practices/normativities as well as new meanings attached to stable practices (see Androutsopoulos 2014: 6–7, Coupland 2014, and this volume, Chapter 20, on the concept of sociolinguistic change).

It also points to the ideological siting of these processes. First, indexical associations are constructed within language-ideological fields, which motivate social/evaluative meanings. Second, as mentioned above, indexical associations are subject to ideological processes such as iconization. Returning for a moment to HRT, its indexical association with women is not just a statistical account of behavior but is also constructed within gender hierarchies that devalue women's ways of speaking and within (also gendered) language ideologies that negatively evaluate HRT as "uncertain" against a (gendered) standard of assertiveness rather than positively evaluating it as "other-oriented" against a standard of inclusion or modesty. We could say, then, that HRT became an index of gender and subsequently moved toward iconic status as "intrinsically" or "naturally" female. Its increasing use by young men is suggestive relative to the interaction between social and linguistic ideologies. That is, reduction of (gendered) stigma may have played a role in making it attractive or possible as a discursive tool for young men. Their use of this form, in turn, may contribute to indexical shift: the decoupling of HRT and gender.

The outcomes of this process – to return to the indeterminacy principle – could include the reindexicalization of HRT at the level of stance and/or social category. We might speculate, for example, that uncertainty could drop out or recede in importance in the indexical field associated with HRT while other-orientation, and its positive values for self-presentation and narrative may become more dominant. In a period of change-in-progress, it might lose gender but gain age indexicalities; over time generational change might reduce its indexical field to stance alone. This suggests the utility of looking at the (changing) content of indexical fields as themselves indexes of continuity and change in the social sphere.

Stuff White People Like

Stuff White People Like is a blog started in January 2008 by Christian Lander, a self-described White person and aspiring comedy writer from Toronto, and his friend Myles Valentin, a half-Filipino and fellow Canadian. The blog was a viral success, with more than 23 million hits by April of that year. The following year, Lander published *Stuff White People Like* with Random House; the book was on the *New York Times* bestseller list for more than seven weeks. A second book, *Whiter Shades of Pale*, was published in 2010, the year in Lander stopped adding to the online blog, which is now fixed at 136 entries. In the following analysis of the blog as a whole (Lander's authored pieces and reader comments on them), I look at the way that meaning within fields of indexicalities is both internally structured by stance and structured by the relationships between fields that are presupposed or proposed by the multiple authors on the blog.

The framing texts on the website make tongue-in-cheek reference to the "unique" taste of millions and represent the blog as "insider" data to be used by non-Whites who wish to "infiltrate" White social groups. Explicit references on the blog to its agenda state that it is "partially about race, but it's funda-mentally about class. It's about a generation and class that values authenticity and credibility more than monetary wealth." A brief sampling of the titles of the entries on the blog illustrates its flavor. White people like: Funny or Ironic Tattoos, Moleskine Notebooks, Ray Ban Wayfarers, Taking a Year Off, Hummus (or Houmous), Black Music That Black People Don't Listen to Anymore, Grammar, Free Health Care, Multilingual Children, Coffee, Not Having a TV, Apple Products, *The Colbert Show*, Diversity, and Kitchen Gadgets (a full list can be consulted at http://stuffwhitepeoplelike.com/full-list-of-stuff-white-people-like/).

We can consider Lander's blog as a whole as a *field of indexicalities*. In other words, if *indexical fields* map the varied social indexicalities associ-ated with a particular linguistic (or other semiotic) variable, *fields of indexi-calities* map the linguistic and semiotic variables associated with a particular social object. Put in another way, the blog makes a claim that White people (as "objects") are indexed by an array of signs that include consumables of various kinds, practices, places, political causes, values, attitudes, and a variety of social and epistemic stances. The humor of the blog depends simultaneously on prior histories of indexicalization and the productive, cre-ative meaning potential of the packaging of indexicalities into a field, clustered around what Eckert (2008) would call persona styles and social categories and what Agha would call a register (2007). We will take these up in turn.

Indexical histories

First, prior histories of indexicalization are presupposed by and constitute shared ground for the interpretation of the blog itself. This point has been underscored by Hill's work on mock Spanish (or other languages/varieties), whose humor or stance potential depends on a set of shared, taken-for-granted second-order indexicals connected to the language being mocked (Hill 2011). In this respect, the fact that people "get" the blog reflects preexisting indexicalities associated with personal styles or registers that it then creatively leverages for comedic effect. That is, the rapid success of the blog depended on Whiteness already having been thematized in social discourse and indexically linked to ways of speaking, thinking, and acting.

Against this backdrop of prior indexicalization of Whiteness, SWPL engaged in a new operation: the systematic, mediatized juxtaposition in the same field of first-order indexes that are potentially empirically confirmable (White people like coffee) and second-order indexes (White people like diversity). Here, we have to take an indexical perspective on the internal ordering of the blog. My argument is that the meaning of each specific index in the field of indexicalities is also an indexical one, in that it is crucially contextualized by its shared location in that field with other indexes. If we consider the entry on coffee, for example, its inclusion in the blog serves first to identify it as an item of consumption that is a social index. Since coffee is a generic product that is "liked" by many people, both White and non-White, its identification as a social index of a specific category of people presupposes greater specificity as a product type (it cannot be just any coffee), which in turn presupposes that it is doing some work of distinction. The content of the blog entry for coffee confirms this: White people like special/elite coffees prepared in special/elite ways. Over time, as Lander added new entries to the blog, the field of indexicalities was populated with other things White people like, and the theme of elite food and drink consumption became solidified with other entries, like organic foods, farmers' markets and microbreweries.

Stance as governing index

Even more crucially, "Coffee" got brought into contact with entries that are much more overt, second-order indexes of a variety of White stances and ideological agendas, for example, "Having Two Last Names," "Hating Their Parents," and "Multilingual Children." Within this assortment of ideological stances, we find several that are explicitly about race: "Having Black Friends,"

"Black Music That Black People Don't Listen to Anymore," "Diversity," "Barack Obama," "Being an Expert on Your Culture." One alludes to class through (avoidance of) a product: "Hating People Who Wear Ed Hardy T-Shirts."

By proposing coherence among all of the indexes in the field of the blog and by including overt/recognizable stances along with other entries, SWPL invites its audience to read *all* the items in the field as being fundamentally about stance. That is, all the items in SWPL that are not in and of themselves overt stances must, within the overall logic of the blog, be read as stance objects through which White people take up public stances and position themselves with and in opposition to other social types. This is in fact the thematic thread of the blog entries. So, for example, Moleskine notebooks are described as vehicles for the display of an important, creative life of the mind and literacy practices that implicitly distinguish White people from others. All the generic foods listed (coffee, tea, wine) are represented opportunities for the display of elite or expert stances, like connoisseurship and its links to scarce or under-appreciated commodities.

This suggests that within indexical fields and fields of indexicalities, there is a hierarchical sensitivity. Once a given example of linguistic or metalinguistic behavior is identified as being part of a *field*, the highest-order indexicals in that field prevail as an overarching theme or focus. Second, because the indexical field is proposed as coherent, readers are invited to track that coherence at the level of stance – to view the subject positions that are created through stance-taking vis-à-vis all of these stance objects as being similar.

Thus the SWPL audience, in addition to being invited to read first-order indexes as indirect (second-order) indexes of stance, is also invited to read the second-order stance indexicalities in light of the first-order ones. Here, the co-location of trivial instances of stance-taking through consumption of elite products with nontrivial stances like appreciation of diversity has the potential to trivialize those social attitudes or orientations as superficial. That is, placing coffee snobbery in the same field as "Religions Your Parents Don't Belong To," "Diversity," and "Having Black Friends" implicitly casts these latter positions as primarily *public displays* or *performances* oriented at securing or consolidating social position. One effect of this is to disrupt dominant, individualist notions of the unified speaker whose words and other semiotic practices represent a true "inner" self. In doing so, it both names and destabil-izes a "sincere" White subject positionality.

Indexicality, iconization, and risk

White subject positions are further unsettled in the blog by the tension between indexicality and iconization. Here it is instructive to briefly consider the sociolinguistics of performance, media, and comedy as related to minority or ethnicized groups. One of the focuses in this literature is on acts of stance-taking (Jaffe 2011) – in particular, those involving role alignment (Agha 2007: 177) – in which writers/performers do not just evoke but take up a reflexive position vis-à-vis the conventional indexicalities deployed as comic material (see, e.g., Barrett 1999; Jaffe 2000; 2015; Coupland 2001; Chun 2004). In other words, this kind of humor is often about the reentextualization of semiotic relations that circulate as *icons* (ethnic or racial stereotypes), as objects of reflexive evaluation and resources for creative performance. To the extent that this process reveals those semiotic relations as situated, emergent, and political, we can say that it *indexicalizes* them. Herein lies much of the potential of this kind of humor to be transgressive or to resist dominant ideologies: by revealing processes of iconization as *social* and *political* rather than *natural* truths.

If this kind of metasemiotic awareness is a form of empowerment for minority groups, it is just the opposite for dominant ones. Herein lies the ideological dynamic of SWPL. We can see that it exposes White readers/audiences to the risk of iconization: It reveals Whiteness as a non-innocent, collective project rather than as a natural, individual subject position.

These risks are exemplified in comments on the blog both by readers who identify themselves as White and by readers who identify themselves as non-White, three of which are extracted below:

Extract 5: Moleskine notebooks
I have a Moleskine notebook and planner ... and unfortunately I cannot argue with a single point made in the post. I carry my notebook with my MacBook in a computer bag that's covered in patches of countries I've been to, and yes, I use the journal to jot down ideas for an amateur novel. I never knew how white I was until I saw this website...
(Response to blog entry on Moleskine notebooks, posted by Renard, July 13, 2009)

Extract 6: I feel so White
I've never felt so White as when I am reading your blog. I, like many other White people, tend to think that I am somehow different–you know, not as White as my bretheren. Thanks for reminding me of where I come from and for making me ROTFL-MAO. The truth is that so many people still exist in a world of White privilege where they view their perspective as the norm, not a culturally constructed reality that not everyone shares. The ability to ignore one's privilege, and hence its impact on others, may be the most insidious aspect of privilege. Thank you for illustrating what is so often overlooked. (Response to blog as a whole, posted by Aerynn on November 20, 2008)

Extract 7: You White people are all alike
i am black, i am at work and was looking for coffee to order for my boss who is white and lo and behold, here i am here at this website. very interesting and funny. your site describes ALL the white people i've EVER worked with. i've worked in many different areas from accounting (very white) to colleges and universities (white on white)!!! this

is funny. you hit it right on the nose. i never realized that whites and their tastes, attitudes, etc. are the same wherever you go...exactly the same!! with blacks, we have diversity–in color, how we speak and attitude. but with you whites, you are all in one category. sorry, but that's just the way i've seen it for many years!! take it how you want! :-) (Response to blog on Music Black People Don't Listen to Any more, posted by on October 14, 2008)

The first extract is a personal confirmation of the "ethnographic truth" of the first-order indexicalities. In it, Renard adds his own example as evidence that White people like Moleskine notebooks. By writing that he "never knew how white he was" until he read the blog, he indicates that accepts a collective subject position as White and reveals that doing so involves a shift from a preferred, more individualist stance. However, he remains silent on the second-order, collective indexical implications of Whiteness as a stance. In the second extract, we find a White reader who names and accepts the *second-order* stance indexicalities of the blog. Like Renard, Aerynn evokes the experience of having her individuality reframed as collective Whiteness; unlike Renard, Aerynn explicitly characterizes this experience as related to a collective stance of White Privilege, taken at the expense of others. In the third extract, a reader who identifies as Black responds to the post on coffee by saying that it confirms the truth of his/her understanding of White people as completely homogenous in both their tastes (first-order indexes) and attitudes (second-order indexes).

Risk to White readers is evidenced first by the fact that Extract 5 is by far the most common kind of White response to the blog and that comments like those in Extract 6 are relatively rare. In other words, the risk of being aggregated and deindividualized on the basis of "innocent" practices is smaller than the risk of having one's behaviors understood as indexing stances and attitudes that reflect and reproduce a privileged social position. Second, risk is exemplified in the person of the non-White commenter in Extract 7. The comment in this extract dramatizes the process of iconization at work: First-order indexes (practices) are fused with second-order indexes (attitudes/stances), and the whole semiotic assemblage is naturalized. This extract dramatizes the risks that accrue to public dissemination of "insider" appropriations of negative stereotypes. This public circulation allows for less-than-benevolent framings by outsiders, who can read the content as straightforward confirmations of simple "truths." This is the difference between Lander's tongue-in-cheek claim that the blog represents the "unique taste of millions" and the Black comment- er's assertion that White people really *are* all the same, in contrast to the diversity of Black people. These outsider readings can also forego the original humorous or parodic framing. This is made visible in the SWPL comments, where we find many self-identified White commenters taking up Lander's parodic voice to propose new entries, or to riff on the existing entries, thus aligning with Lander and the blog's overall key. Commenters who identify as non-White, however, never enact or align with the non-White figure he sets up as the fictive audience for the blog (the novice outsider learning about White culture for purposes of ingratiation). On the contrary, like the commenter in Extract 7, when they identify as outsiders, they display that they already have (stereotypical) knowledge about White people.

Reflexivity and strategic stance indeterminacy as social capital

We have seen how the prioritization of second-order/stance indexicalities in the field of indexicalities set up by SWPL around Whiteness destabilizes an innocent and sincere White subject position and exposes White readers to the risks associated with iconization. This raises the question of whether there are any "safe" or legitimated White positionalities offered by the blog.

As I have argued with Shana Walton (2011), a candidate for such a position is the reflexive stance embodied by Lander, as the author of a blog that lays open the processes by which White Privilege is established. This reflexive stance involves the display of both metalinguistic/metasemiotic awareness and a political/ideological awareness of the self as positioned in relation to wider social categories, discourses and hierarchies.

This is the position with which Aerynn, the commenter in Extract 6, explicitly aligns. It allows for the exercise of *stance indeterminacy*, which I define here as the ability to align to various degrees with fields of indexicalities associated with an insider group while maintaining the flexibility of distancing oneself from their status as iconic.

To explore the potential and the limits of reflexivity as social capital in the blog, we need to examine in more detail the social categories and figures/personas that are indexed by the blog. This will allow us to focus on how the *fields of indexicalities* that are set up by Lander's blog entries *evoke or constitute other such fields,* some of which are nested, some of which are distinct.

First, let us consider the quasi-ethnographic frame of the blog – an insider documenting and explaining the practices of White "others" to an imagined/fictive non-White audience. In addition to "othering" the objects of observation, this frame implicitly constitutes them as immersed unself-consciously in their cultures – as having a nonreflexive experience or perspective. These objects are racialized as White, but they are also, as we have seen above, characterized explicitly as being about class. This framing introduces several other categories of White and non-White people, who, I will argue, are defined and ranked with respect to reflexivity and are attributed different degrees of stance indeterminacy (see Figure 4.1). First, there is Lander's position as reflexive middle class (MC)/upper middle class (UMC) White. As a White

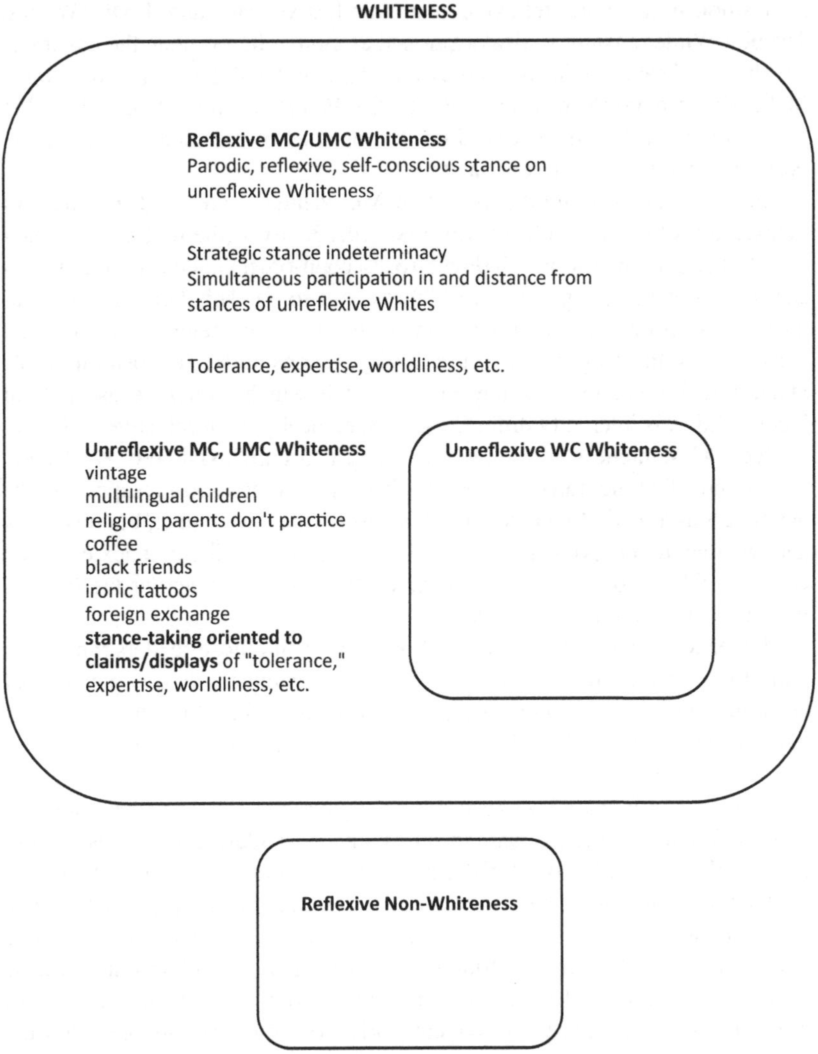

WHITENESS

Figure 4.1. Strategic stance indeterminacy.

insider, he is authorized to speak about unreflexive MC and UMC Whites but is differentiated from them by his displayed reflexivity (and thus partial distance) from their practices and stances. Then there is the putative audience for the ethnography: the non-White outsider who reads SWPL for information about White people in order to exploit that information for social benefit. This deliberately implausible figure, while less knowledgeable than Lander, is positioned as more reflexive than unreflexive MC and UMC Whites. The non-White outsider is also positioned as more reflexive than the unnamed, or "shadow," category introduced by the frame of the blog in opposition to the MC/UMC: the White working class (WC). Figure 4.1 thus depicts the blog not as a unified field of indexicalities but as a set of indexical fields that are positioned with respect to one another.

The blog targets – unreflexive MC/UMC Whites – are sited in a field of indexicalities that is populated with first-order indexes (the topics of the blog posts) that are themselves indirect (or second-order) indexes of a set of stances – tolerance, expertise, worldliness, and so on. This field of indexicalities in its entirety is in turn a stance *object* for the reflexive author and consumers of the blog. In this sense, it plays a constitutive (oppositional) role in defining those people. So stance is one way in which Whiteness, as a field of indexicalities, is internally differentiated. Specifically, both reflexive and unreflexive MC Whiteness are defined in contrast to unreflexive WC Whiteness. We can note that the framework established by the blog itself presupposes WC Whiteness as a field of indexicalities that has no specific content, but it is ready and waiting to be populated with both direct and indirect indexicals that contrast with the ones in the unreflexive MC White field, and/or the (also as yet unpopulated) non-White field.

The stance indeterminacy enjoyed by Lander and those readers who align with him thus allows them to enjoy and participate in the patterns of consumption, practice, and discourse described in the blog while resisting being fully categorized by them, to enjoy privilege but be (at least partially) redeemed by being able to laugh at themselves. This strategic indeterminacy is one of the tools that allow readers to mitigate the risks identified above, to claim tolerance, expertise, and so on as sincere, enduring positions *in contrast to* those (unreflexive MC/UMC Whites) who only perform them. Put another way, strategic stance indeterminacy is a kind of prophylactic against being identified as being engaged in the process of stance-taking, here defined in opposition to enacting a "true" self. It is also clear that strategic stance indeterminacy for one set of social actors is built on the back of oppositions with other personas or categories whose stances are presupposed, essentialized, and fixed.

Returning to the reader comments, we find additional evidence for the prioritization of stance in the field of indexicalities: A reflexive voice is often presented as a trump card in interaction with commenters who engage in literal ways with the content of the site and, in particular, those who bypass the humor and take up serious discourses related to race, class, and privilege. This is illustrated in two exchanges illustrated below taken from comments to the "About" section, where people debate the purpose and point of the site.

Extract 8: Feeling bad
I picked this up and at first i was amused.
"oh haha i get it, i'm white."
but then the comments were hitting a little close to home.
i don't really feel all that original anymore.
it kinda hurts to be generalized and put down the way this book has put me down. (from the "About" section, posted by Kelly on November 30, 2008)

Extract 9 (response to Extract 8): Calling out White sensibilities
White person reaction = getting offended, and thinking that your feelings should somehow matter.
Oh. And outsmarting someone purporting to be smarter. . . ("Cart" December 8, 2008)

Extract 10: Accusations of reverse racism
My point is that it's suddenly pc to stereotype white people, but god forbid anyone mentions watermelon and blacks, or mexicans and beans in the same sentence. Give it a couple more decades, when whites are actually the minority in the US, then we'll talk – you intellectually stunted idiot. ("White girl" on December 14, 2008)

Extract 11 (response to Extract 10): Girl, we need to talk
I'm embarassed reading this post from my white, misguided sister. Girl, we need to talk. First latte's on me. ("Whitish guy" December 16, 2008)

In Extract 8, Kelly claims that she is hurt and takes up a discourse of reverse discrimination. Cart, in Extract 9, responds using reflexive stance to dismiss "getting offended" and "thinking your feelings should matter" as "just" more examples of White stance-taking as opposed to legitimate sentiments. About a week later (Extract 10), "White girl" pursues even more overtly the theme that the site is racist. She is quickly countered by a post from "Whitish guy" (Extract 11), written from a stance of humorous reflexivity, who uses a classic hip/cool "other" voicing ("sister," "girl") to simultaneously invoke an ethnicized intimacy and to invoke (and critique) her equation of White and non-White victimhood.

Finally we can look at an exchange that took place in comments about a brief blog post about "Assists" in basketball.

Extract 12: Ethnographic falsehood
Personally, as a white person I do not get offended by almost any stereotype mainly because that is just my personality. What people say has never really bothered me. However, this stereotype sounds completely bizarre. Saying that great white athletes only care about assists in sports because they feel guilty over slavery is one of the most unpractical arguments I have ever heard. There is absolutely no validity to this claim. (Michael on April 18, 2011, at 4:01 p.m.)

Extract 13 (response to Extract 12): Dude, it's comedy
dude the purpose of this website is comedy ("chill" on May 4, 2011, at 1:11 a.m.)

In Extract 12, Michael personally disaligns with an "offended white person stance" but questions the truth value of the overt reference to White domination and guilt. In Extract 13, "chill" writes back to tell him he is humorless (lacks a reflexive understanding of the blog as comedy). These three pairs of comments and responses represent bids to consolidate reflexivity as core/ dominant cultural capital. They presuppose that this stance blocks, subordinates, or backgrounds other kinds of indexicalities in the field.

I have deliberately used the word "bids," because the success of such bids can be assessed only contextually, as they emerge across the corpus of comments where readers and Lander engage with indexicality, iconizaton, and the interaction of fields of indexicalities associated with different social types. In the next section, we look more closely at these conversations.

Stance indeterminacy in question

One of the things that reader responses to the blog do is make explicit many of the blog's implicit presuppositions. The following three extracts illustrate that one of these presuppositions is the strategic stance indeterminacy of a reflexive White stance.

Extract 14: Chains of callings out
But I do like the white people that comment about how white other white commenters are. What I love is that white people love to call out other white people as white and thus prove that they aren't so white themselves. White people also like to call out other white people that call out white people for being white. And on and on. . ... (Response to blog entry Black Music That Black People Don't Listen to Anymore, posted by beb, November 19, 2008)

Extract 15: Doubtful sincerity
The only thing better than the people offended by this site are the people that defend themselves by expounding on how "its so true how some people pretend to like jazz but others, like myself, truly appreciate it." It makes the blog even more relevant. (Response to blog entry Black Music That Black People Don't Listen to Anymore, posted by matt, November 22, 2008)

Extract 16: SWPL as a potential entry in SWPL
i'm sure someone has said this already, but its ironic that stuffwhitepeoplelike.com is now on the list of stuff white people like. (Response to blog overview, posted by cody on August 30, 2009)

These three extracts make explicit reference to the stance potentials of being reflexive and being metareflexive by calling out other Whites for their Whiteness and calling out those who call out. By naming reflexivity (and SWPL

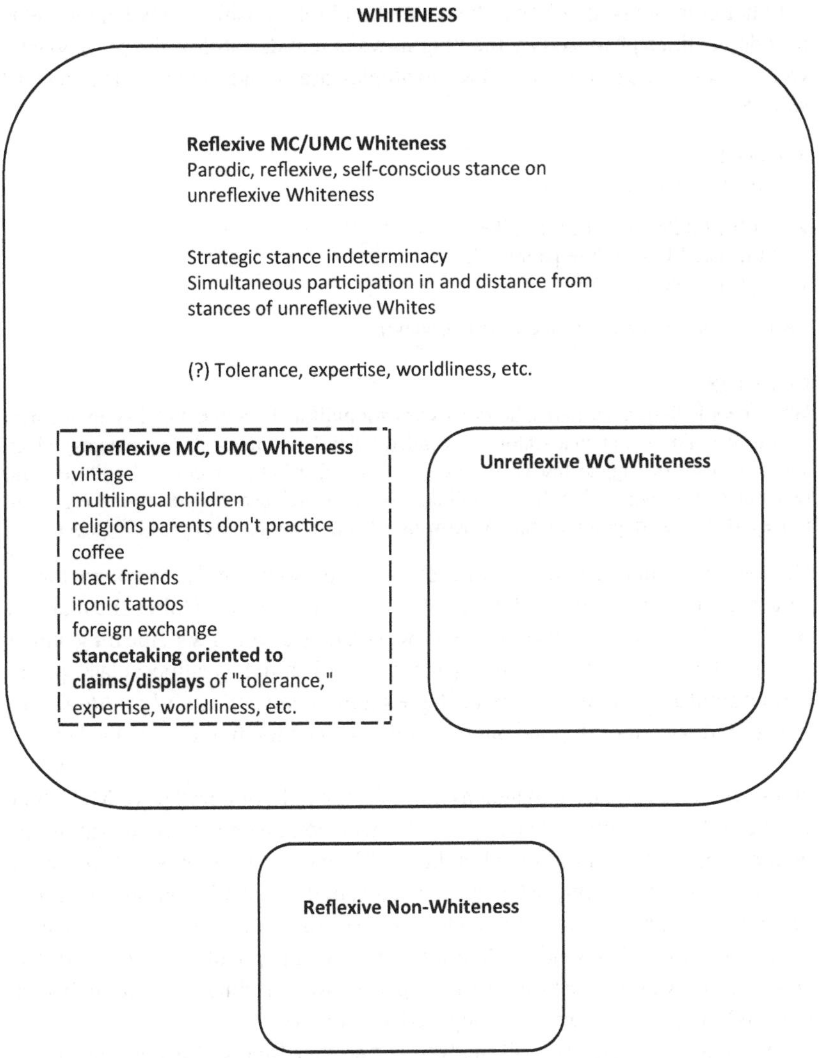

WHITENESS

Reflexive MC/UMC Whiteness
Parodic, reflexive, self-conscious stance on
unreflexive Whiteness

Strategic stance indeterminacy
Simultaneous participation in and distance from
stances of unreflexive Whites

(?) Tolerance, expertise, worldliness, etc.

Unreflexive MC, UMC Whiteness
vintage
multilingual children
religions parents don't practice
coffee
black friends
ironic tattoos
foreign exchange
**stancetaking oriented to
claims/displays** of "tolerance,"
expertise, worldliness, etc.

Unreflexive WC Whiteness

Reflexive Non-Whiteness

Figure 4.2. Porous boundaries.

itself) as one of the things that White people like, its potential to mitigate both
iconization/stereotypes and attributions of hegemonic privilege is undermined.
The reflexive stance, in these comments, is opened up to the same critical eye
as the stance bids of nonreflexive White people. Put another way, this discourse represents the boundaries between the reflexive and nonreflexive White
people as porous, as reflected in Figure 4.2.

Other comments also frame the content and relationships between the fields of indexicalities proposed by the blog in ways that destabilize the prophylactic value of the reflexive stance. Two examples are found below in Extracts 17 and 18.

Extract 17
This blog should be renamed:

- "Stuff Middle Class People Like"
- "Stuff LIBERAL white people like"
- "Stuff rich people like"

(Anonymous comment to the blog overview)

Extract 18
White people like trailer parks, ho-downs, tractor pulls and Nascar. Yet they're nowhere in your list. You've taken a sector of so-called 'white' culture (or its implements) which are, like sushi or raggae music, the best pickings from other races and cultures, and reinvented it as white. You're not talking about 'white' people; you're talking about moneyed, educated, young, white Americans. (Zack, in comments to the blog overview)

On the one hand, comments like these adopt some of Lander's rhetorical strategies (titling the site, making a list of proposed entries). Unlike the majority of those who engage in this practice, however, they disalign with the blog and its parodic stance. They also explicitly name unspoken indexicalities: class, privilege, cultural appropriation. Extract 18 goes further, *activating and populating* the field of indexicalities implied but left empty by the blog framework: the "other," working-class White people. Once that field has a few items – NASCAR, trailers, and so on – it becomes activated as a foil for the field of unreflexive MC White people and is then subject to being filled in with contrasting elements – monolingual as opposed to multilingual children, RV vacations as opposed to foreign travel, non-ironic as opposed to ironic tattoos, traditional religions as opposed to religions their parents don't belong to, and so forth. Following the logic we have explored above, that field is then *subject to* being populated by contrastive *stances*, for example, parochialism as opposed to worldliness, traditionalism as opposed to openness, racism as opposed to diversity.

The final comment we will analyze is one that followed a long discussion about Lander's blog entry on multilingual children. It is of interest because it proposes a new indexicality that undercuts the strategic indeterminacy of the reflexive position and the structure of relations between the indexical fields we have examined so far. Extract 19 excerpts Lander's post; Extract 20 is a reader comment.

Extract 19 (Lander, in SWPL #73, "Multilingual Children")
All white people want their children to speak another language. There are no exceptions. They dream about the children drifting in between French and English sentences

as they bustle about the kitchen while they read the New York Times and listen to Jazz... Generally, white people prefer their children to speak French... Languages such as German, Spanish, Swedish, or Italian are also acceptable, but are considered to be poor substitutes (especially Spanish). At the time of writing, it is still considered expert-level white person behavior to have white children speaking Asian and African languages.

Extract 20 (response to Extract 15)
White people, while adoring photo ops with brown folks and trumpeting "diversity", nevertheless secretly think European cultures and languages to be vastly superior to all others. Yes, Spanish is a European language, but it makes white people uncomfortable because so many brown people speak it. The language is associated not with Spain, but rather with Latin America, where so many newly arrived Americans come from, people whose brown skin makes white people uncomfortable. (N, February 28, 2008)

Early comments to Lander's post on multilingual children included ethno-graphic alignments by self-identified White people who reported on the languages they or their children spoke. There was also debate related to the status and use of Spanish – some agreeing with the blog that it was devalued, others reporting on its popularity and value as cultural capital for White people. Like several comments we have seen, N's post in Extract 20 names indirect stance indexicalities of the blog. However, this comment is different – and relatively rare in the corpus – in that it explicitly identifies *racialization* as a second-order index of a White stance. In doing so, it exposes all forms of White privilege as requiring (and implying) opposition not just to "other White people," but also to other *non-White* people. This blurs the line between MC White people and the other White people (see Figure 4.3). Put another way, it places these two kinds of White people within a shared, expanded indexical field where racism (previously located only in the "Other White people" field) and racialization are not cleanly demarcated. Choosing French is not just a humorous choice of a prestige language, but avoidance of a language uncomfortably associated with brown skin. In this framework, wanting multilingual children gets poten-tially co-located in an indexical field along with advocating for monolingual-ism, resisting bilingual education, or complaining when you hear Spanish spoken on the street. This is represented by the shared highlighting in these two fields in Figure 4.3.

Even further, Figure 4.3 suggests that the blurring of implicit class and stance boundaries between unreflexive MC and WC Whites also has the potential to trouble the boundary between reflexive MC Whites and those two groups, because it opens up all stances of Whiteness (including reflexiv-ity) for scrutiny as implicated in racializing processes. We see that stance flexibility is a tenuous resource, subject to being reduced or regimented by voices and forces outside the individual's control. In short, stance

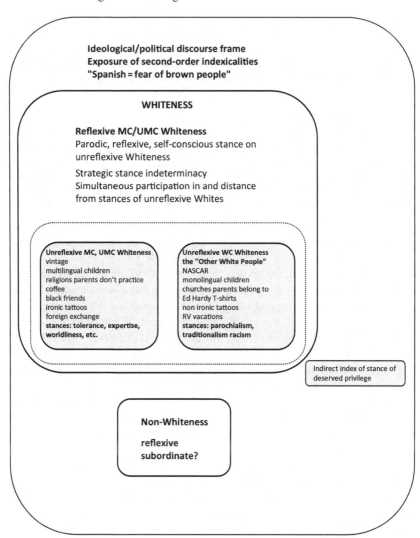

Figure 4.3. Stance instability.

indeterminacy and flexibility is one side of a coin that, when flipped, reveals *stance instability*.

What we see, then, is that the blog sets up but also *underspecifies* a range of stance potentials, possible indexical fields, and their contents. That is, the blog creates spaces for both Lander and those who comment on the blog to exploit strategic indeterminacy or, alternatively, to propose new stances and figures/personas. In doing so, they do not just respond to existing fields of indexicalities, but play an active role in populating them (with both direct and indirect indices) and proposing relations between them. This perspective is consistent with Eckert's view of indexical fields as emergent in interaction and as objects of stance or style. At the same time, we can see the ways in which, over time, the corpus of comments that collect in response to the blog *name what Lander leaves implicit*. The diverse set of reader comments thus draws attention to semiotic processes of indexicalization and iconization and, in doing so, restricts the "looseness" or openness of the field of indexicalities and the subject positions available to its readers as scripted by its author.

Conclusions

We owe to Ochs (1996) the crucial insight about the mediating role of stance in the creation of sociolinguistic indexes. In the analyses above, I have further suggested that stance plays a similar role in the internal ordering of both indexical fields and fields of indexicalities. When people reflect on what it means to say "pobrecito," they review the social types in its indexical field. But more critically, they evaluate the stance potentials of the utterance given those social types, the identity of the speaker, and the history and context of the focal utterance. Power and ideology are never far away; it is no accident that most of the examples used in this chapter involve majority/minority or dominant/nondominant relationships that shape both how sociolinguistic indexes are interpreted and their implications for specific categories of people (Latino/a, White/non-White, male/female, etc.). In SWPL, stance acts as a hub for interpretation of fields of indexicalities associated with Whiteness, coloring other (potentially more "innocent") elements in the field.

This analysis of stance in SWPL hinges on the blog being set up by its author as a *coherent* field of indexicalities. Not all fields, of course, are set up with this kind of presupposed coherence. The SWPL site thus raises, questions about the implications of greater or lesser overt coherence among the elements in a given field for its meaning potential in use. From a different and more significant perspective, it points to coherence in these fields as a focus for sociolinguistic agency. That is, instead of positing coherence (and consensus) as a *feature of* fields (or registers or styles), we can view it as an *emergent property of social action* with respect to those fields. Representations of fields as being more or less coherent can then be seen as forms of political action and/or as foci for ideological debate. Thus, where I have nominalized "indexical fields" and "fields of indexicalities," we might want instead to talk about the process of "fielding" of indexes into supposed coherent complexes. This raises implications for sociolinguistic and, more broadly, semiotic change. It may be that one motor of change is the gradual destabilization of representations of coherence associated with particular fields.

In this chapter, I have also put forward the notion that a process-based approach to indexicalization as it is engaged in particular social contexts benefits from a broader semiotic framework that accounts for the dynamic tension between indexicalization and iconization on the ground. That is, if we look at the discursive complex formed by the SWPL blog as a whole, one of the key things at stake for the author and his readers/commenters is whether particular signs and collections of signs will be characterized as indexes versus as icons. This fielding of SWPL as a coherent complex of indexicalities poses risk because it is a potential step along a path to iconization. That iconization has the potential to limit the agency of White subjects, in particular with respect to the strategic stance indeterminacy offered to them through engagement with the reflexivity of the parodic agenda. Agency for White subjects is also attenuated by the "meta" semioticity of the blog: By drawing attention to processes of indexicalization, the blog destabilizes unreflexive claims to essential, sincere, unreflexive stances by revealing them as situated and political.

Finally, I have drawn attention to the way that indexical fields and fields of indexicalities themselves exist in situated (indexical) relations of comparison and contrast with one another. These relationships, as we have seen, are mutually constitutive. Their relationships, as we have seen in SWPL (Figure 4.3), are an integral part of the dynamics of meaning for any given element in any given context of use and warrant our continued attention as *meta-orders of indexicality* that are created in situated use.

REFERENCES

Agha, Asif. 2007. *Language and Social Relations*. Cambridge: Cambridge University Press.
Androutsopoulos, Jannis. 2014. Mediatization and sociolinguistic change. Key concepts, research traditions, open issues. In Jannis Androutsopoulos (ed.), *Mediatization and Sociolinguistic Change*. (FRIAS Linguae and Litterae series.) Berlin: Mouton de Gruyter, 3–48.
Ball, Christopher. 2014. On dicentization. *Journal of Linguistic Anthropology* 24, 2: 151–174.
Barrett, Rusty. 1999. Indexing polyphonous identity in the speech of African American drag queens. In Mary Bucholtz, A. C. Liang, and Laurel Sutton (eds.), *Reinventing Identities*. Oxford: Oxford University Press, 313–331.
Bucholtz, Mary. 2009. From stance to style: Gender, interaction, and indexicality in Mexican immigrant youth slang. In Alexandra Jaffe (ed.), *Stance: Sociolinguistic Perspectives*. New York: Oxford University Press, 146–170.

Chun, Elaine. 2004. Ideologies of legitimate mockery: Margaret Cho's revoicings of
    mock Asian. *Pragmatics* 14: 263–289.
Coupland, Nikolas. 2001. Dialect stylisation in radio talk. *Language in Society* 30, 3:
    345–375.
    2002. Language, situation and the relational self. In Penelope Eckert (ed.),
    Style and Sociolinguistic Variation. New York: Cambridge University Press,
    185–210.
    2007. *Style: Language Variation and Identity*. Cambridge: Cambridge University
    Press.
    2014. Sociolinguistic change, vernacularization and broadcast British media.
    In Jannis Androutsopoulos (ed.), *Mediatization and Sociolinguistic Change*.
    Berlin: Mouton de Gruyter, 67–98.
Eckert, Penelope. 2008. Variation and the indexical field. *Journal of Sociolinguistics*
    12, 4: 453–476.
Gal, Susan. 2005. Language ideologies compared: Metaphors of public/private. *Journal*
    of Linguistic Anthropology 15, 1: 23–37.
Gal, Susan, and Judith Irvine. 2000. Language ideology and linguistic differentiation.
    In Paul V. Kroskrity (ed.), *Regimes of Language*. Santa Fe, NM: School of
    American Research, 35–84.
Hill, Jane. 2011. *The Everyday Language of Racism*. Malden, MA: Wiley-Blackwell.
Jaffe, Alexandra. 2000. Comic performance and the articulation of hybrid identity.
    Pragmatics 10, 1: 39–60.
    2009. Indeterminacy and regularization: Sociolinguistic variation and language
    ideologies. *Sociolinguistic Studies* 3, 2: 229–251.
    2011. Sociolinguistic diversity in mainstream media: Authenticity, authority
    and processes of mediation and mediatization. *Language and Politics* 10, 4:
    562–586.
    2015. Staging language on Corsica: Stance, improvisation, play and heteroglossia.
    Language in Society 44: 1–26.
Johnstone, Barbara. 2013. *Speaking Pittsburghese: The Story of a Dialect*. Oxford:
    Oxford University Press.
Kiesling, Scott. 2009. Style as stance: Stance as the explanation for patterns of
    sociolinguistic variation. In Alexandra Jaffe (ed.), *Stance: Sociolinguistic*
    Perspectives. New York: Oxford University Press, 171–194.
Ochs, Elinor. 1996. Linguistic resources for socializing humanity. In John Gumperz
    and Stephen Levinson (eds.), *Rethinking Linguistic Relativity*. New York:
    Cambridge University Press, 407–437.
Silverstein, Michael. 1992. The indeterminacy of contextualization: When is enough
    enough? In P. Auer and A. di Luzio (eds.), *The Contextualization of Language*.
    Amsterdam: John Benjamins, 55–76.
    2003. Indexical order and the dialectics of sociolinguistic life. *Language &*
    Communication 23: 193–229.
Squires, Lauren. 2014. From TV personality to fans and beyond: Indexical bleaching
    and the diffusion of a media innovation. *Journal of Linguistic Anthropology* 24, 1:
    42–62.
Urban, Greg. 2006. Metasemiosis and metapragmatics. In Keith Brown (ed.),
    Encyclopedia of Language and Linguistics. Oxford: Pergamon Press, 88–91.

Walton, Shana, and Alexandra Jaffe. 2011. *Stuff White People Like*: Stance, class, race and internet commentary. In Crispin Thurlow and Kristine Mroszek (eds.), *Language in the New Media: Sociolinguistic Perspectives*. New York: Oxford University Press, 199–216.

Wortham, Stanton. 2008. Linguistic anthropology. In Bernard Spolsky and Francis Hult (eds.), *The Handbook of Educational Linguistics*. Oxford: Blackwell, 83–97.

5   Sociolinguistic differentiation

Susan Gal

Introduction

Early work in sociolinguistics offered key insights for studying the social meanings of linguistic differentiation. Three of these remain strong inspirations for current research programs. First, there was a deep understanding that many apparently different disciplinary approaches were closely related and together would shed light on linguistic variation and change. Dialectology, ethnographies of communication, conversation analysis, and studies of standardization and of language politics sat comfortably side-by-side in the early edited collections (Hymes 1964; Bright 1966).[1] In a second insight, researchers proposed that all social signaling occurs in interaction of some kind: Linguistic changes correspond to shifts in the social situation (Fischer 1958; Hymes 1962; Labov 1963; Gumperz and Hymes 1964). In studies of communication, a concern with reflexivity was present from the start. Anthropologist Bateson (1955) highlighted the necessity of metasignals that give cues to listeners about how they should understand or respond to utterances. Jakobson (1960) discussed the metalinguistic (i.e., reflexive) function of language. Both theorists recognized that many levels of linguistic structure can carry metamessages, and such signaling occurs in every kind of interaction and social group. A third insight followed: If the selective display of linguistic variants can signal the definition of situation, it can also reconstruct it. Linguistic variation does not simply reflect but also performatively creates social meaning that is a spur and enactment of social differentiation (Labov 1963; Blom and Gumperz 1972). In this way, linguistic variation participates in sociocultural as well as linguistic change.

---

[1] This insight is being revived, for instance, by Bucholtz and Hall (2008) in announcing "new coalitions in sociocultural linguistics" and welcoming closer connections between sociolinguistics as practiced in linguistics departments and in linguistic anthropology. See also Eckert's (2012) hailing of a "Third Wave" of more integrative sociolinguistic study that relies on ethnography as one of its methodologies. For an example of such studies, see Johnstone's (2013) book about Pittsburghese, which includes, along with sociolinguistic analysis of variables, a consideration of the city's social history and the formation of cultural emblems and media representations.

In the sociolinguistics research that developed from these early insights, metasignaling has been understood as a semiotic process: A metasign is one that regiments how it itself and other signs are to be interpreted; it is a framing.[2] Language ideologies in all their more-and-less explicit forms do just this work. Among all the many possible effects of metasignaling, this chapter focuses on the achievement of similarity and difference – between linguistic forms, speaker personae, social roles, situations, objects of talk. Similarity and difference are like two sides of a coin; they result from mutually implicated sociolinguistic processes. My question is: How are the resemblances and contrasts of sociocultural and linguistic practices actively constructed by framings and uptakes of signs? The sign relation of indexicality has been most thoroughly examined in sociolinguistics so far. Fundamental work has explored its role in presupposing and performatively recreating situations, role relations, identities, and stance. My goal here is to build on that literature to explore *other* concepts, also inspired by Peircean semiotics, that help us understand the making of similarity/difference. This chapter discusses the analytic usefulness of three linked concepts: iconicity, rhematization, and qualisign, also showing their relation to a fourth: axes of differentiation. I seek to show that these are productive tools for analyzing how social and political projects of diverse kinds are created and pursued through linguistic differentiation, how the values of social life are configured and reconfigured via language practices. Linguistic forms themselves are changed in the process. Recent empirical studies have been analyzing an increasingly diverse range of linguistic and expressive materials. I draw on a selection of such studies to illustrate the work of sign relations as ingredients in ideologies and thus in the semiotic organization of difference and similarity.

From speech variety to enregisterment via metasemiosis

A brief glance backward will help to locate my themes. Despite the early recognition of reflexivity by Jakobson and others, later work took a less interpretive and more positivist turn. Although Labov's study of Martha's Vineyard explored the frames with which speakers interpreted utterances, his New York City research adopted an objectivist approach in which speakers' perspectives were sidelined. The handling of sociolinguistic variables shows this. In the NYC study, linguistic variation was defined by the linguist, not through speakers' perceptions. Speaker identities were also

---

[2] See Lucy (1993) for a clear overview of metacommunication and the history of its development as a concept. The notion of "frame" is an old one; Bateson used it for discussing metacommunication; Goffman (1974) developed it considerably further.

investigator-defined, often with ready-to-hand survey categories of age, education, gender, and income, not speakers' culturally defined distinctions among person-types. The variation observed was treated as behaviors "given off" by speakers, not expressions performed, taken up, and interpreted by them. Situational variation was seen as relatively mechanical, a result of the different amounts of attention that speakers paid to their speech. Ironically, even the values speakers attributed to variables were measured with preset categories. In interviews, the goal was not to figure out how speakers' self-awareness and interpretations might affect linguistic practices but to eliminate self-awareness, since it was seen as a pernicious investigator effect.[3]

Other approaches, however, soon focused on speakers' understandings. Interactional sociolinguistics, conversation analysis, and ethnomethodology all relied on ethnographic methods to explore speakers' linguistic repertoires, as these were used to achieve interactional "moves" (Goffman 1967). Some early studies had assumed that physical settings or tasks would define situations and therefore elicit one type of speech rather than another. By contrast, interpretive scholars took a more dynamic approach. They used ethnographic observation to reveal that participants were co-constructing what they took to be the situation at hand (Schegloff 1972; Bauman and Sherzer 1974; Goffman 1974). Even in contexts like schools, which have fairly rigid linguistic norms, speakers creatively changed their speech and other expressive forms, thereby signaling their belonging to social groups and enacting momentary interactional intentions or effects (Gumperz 1982; Eckert 1989; Duranti and Goodwin 1992). The effects were achieved through metasignaling, which received attention in concepts such as Goffman's (1974) "framing," Gumperz's (1982) "contextualization cues," and conversation analysts' "pair parts" (Schegloff et al. 1974). These terms were ways of highlighting how participants relied on (often minor) differences in speech to change roles and situations in interaction. As Goffman said, these devices transform "what is going on." Analysts observed that a switch in nondenotational features of speech – often involving the sociolinguistic variables investigated by quantitative sociolinguistics – could signal a change in frame and in effect, implicitly claiming that, for instance, "this event is not a discussion but a debate"; "not a conversation but a fight." Researchers were faced with conceptualizing this remarkable and ubiquitous achievement. How is it possible?

---

[3] These epistemological assumptions were typical of the social science of that era. Tellingly, even John Gumperz, the most interactionally and culturally sensitive of early sociolinguists, wrote in the early 1970s that speakers' "attitudes will interfere with their response" to questions about variation (1972: 21). By contrast, in his later work on contextualization cues, he turned to analyzing those "attitudes," i.e., participants' own interpretations of styles, varieties, and interaction (1982).

The concept of "linguistic ideology" (or language ideology or, more broadly, "semiotic ideology") has been one way of approaching this question.[4] Though language ideology has become a familiar term, it is still worth emphasizing that it labels a form of reflexivity: It is metacommunication, participants' talk about talk, or their reflections, signals, and presuppositions about linguistic forms and their use. Sometimes this reflection is explicitly formulated, as in corrections ("don't say ain't"), generalizations ("dropping your r's makes you sound like a New Yorker"), or nomic statements ("proper people do not curse"). More often it is simply an unspoken inference that participants make on the basis of prosody, intonation, the frequency of socio-linguistic variables, or shibboleths. Such inferences are evident to observers through participants' reactions in situ. The often hard-to-express interpretation of subtle cues is a crucial part of language ideologies. These are ideologies of language-in-use, metapragmatic discourses and functions.

Nevertheless, explicit statements about some aspect of language structure have been more readily seen as examples of language ideology. For instance, the widespread Euro-American assumption that denotation is the most import-ant aspect of speaking is one such ideological tenet that is evident among ordinary speakers' commonsense discussion and is also a topic in philosoph-ical discourse. It has shaped linguistic theory.[5] Another commonly observed notion is that speakers' national or ethnic belonging is signaled by "*their* language" or "dialect." Indeed, forms of speaking are often characterized as property, linked to cultural categories (stereotypes) of person, place/time, and activity ("those kinds of people speak in X way"). Yet "explicitness" is a complex dimension. Stereotypes often remain unspoken or constitute a taboo subject. They can be presupposed categories that become evident in speakers' uptakes and role alignments in particular settings.

---

[4] In this lineage of research, ideology has been understood as a mediator and a matter of perspective, not deception nor false consciousness. The key review (Woolard and Schieffelin 1994) and the earlier impetus (Silverstein 1979) make this point, although "rationalization" and systematization are still important, as in erasures (Irvine and Gal 2000) that deny what does not "fit" the expectations evoked by ideology. For discussion of metapragmatic discourse and function as further mediating terms, connecting ideology and interaction, see Silverstein (2003), which is also the source for second-order indexicality, mentioned later in this chapter. Keane (2003) extended these to "semiotic ideology" to embrace material signs that are not specifically linguistic.

[5] The recognition of speakers' language ideologies has led to studies of researchers' own ideolo-gies of language. Although I do not discuss it here, research that explores the sources and effects of the professional ideologies of linguists, sociolinguists, and linguistic anthropologists is an indispensable field for questioning presumptions and thereby sharpening analysis. It reveals the way we as linguists understand the ideologies of others (Lucy 1993). Philosophical, linguistic, and other professional discourses about language are themselves usefully thought of as language ideologies; they often authorize and justify projects in politics, aesthetics, economics, and other spheres of activity (see Gal and Irvine 1995; Irvine and Gal 2000; Bauman and Briggs 2003).

So far I have said little about the linguistic forms that are the signs evoking (pointing to) presuppositions about speakers and speaking or inspiring corrections and normative statements about speaker-types and speaking. Long ago, Gumperz (1972) proposed that instead of starting with linguistic forms and then asking how these are distributed across speakers, sociolinguists should start with a group of speakers and their cultural notions to discern what sets of linguistic features alternate meaningfully in their speech events. In this way, he argued, researchers would find clusters of co-occurring features that had social significance for those speakers. This methodological innovation was necessary because, as became clear in empirical work, linguists' categories and those of speakers were rarely parallel. The clusters of forms that speakers treated as unified, and that alternated in complementary distribution with meaningfully different clusters, often did not constitute any single category from the perspective of traditional linguistic analysis (Ervin-Tripp 1972). In sociolinguistics, however, the categories of traditional linguistic analysis were less important than the function of forms in signaling social contrasts for some population of speakers. Sociolinguists proposed that sets of alternating clusters be analyzed as "varieties" or "codes." This nomenclature, focused on social meanings and effects, integrated under a single rubric the many different forms of variation that linguists had long noticed and classified by provenance or structural level (Gumperz and Hymes 1972: 21, 63).[6]

Despite this attempt to rethink and unify all kinds of variation, many scholars maintained a distinction between varieties that were linked to situation of use (then called "registers") and those linked to speaker identities or geography (e.g., "social dialects," "regional dialects"). Yet the differences were hard to disentangle empirically. Indeed, Irvine (1990) argued that in particular cases, the same variants that distinguished speakers also distinguished situations of use – as Labov too had found in the NYC studies. With an African example, Irvine showed that a cultural model distinguished named categories of speaker-types and the speech forms that were associated with each. Among the Wolof, the stereotyped speech of "nobles" was regularly contrasted with that of "griots" (praise singers). The labels identified speaker-types, yet typified personal features of speakers; their typical values, activities, and interactional roles were also implied and evoked. The cultural model organized and ordered the normative relationship between speaking, social identity, situation, and social function, as perceived by speakers. Taking up U.S. and British data in the same spirit, Agha (2007) showed that *all* meta-pragmatic labels about speech operate in this way. Labels like 'literary usage,' 'upper-class speech,' 'legalese,' and 'radio-announcer talk,' all name speech

---

[6] See Haugen (1966) for a history of the usage of labels such as "language" and "dialect," by linguists and in national politics.

varieties that speakers recognize and distinguish. Although some labels link speech to event-types (e.g., literary), others to typical speakers (e.g., announcer, upper-class), and still others to function (e.g., legal), they each evoke/ imply all these dimensions of variation. In all cases, a cultural model associates speaker types, their typified features, activities, practices, and values with a way of speaking: a register. Such models are metasemiotic or language ideological phenomena.

With this innovation, what early sociolinguistics rightly saw as co-occurrences and correlations could be reconceptualized as the *result* of speakers operating with cultural models that organize conceptions about variation, making variation meaningfully interpretable with reference to a model. Accordingly, the term "register" has been retheorized, extending its earlier use by Reid, Halliday, and others. Scholarly attention has focused on *enregisterment* (Silverstein 2003), the metasemiotic process by which such a cultural model is assembled, so that indexical associations of typified speaker, occasion, speech variety, and values are recognized by some population of language users. Novel registers are constructed all the time, while others disappear. Recent examples include "nerdy speech" or "a vent." The first one names a person-type, but also evokes stereotyped expectations about speech, demeanor, and character, as well as typical activities. The second names a speech form and function, but people-types and situations are also evoked (Manning 2012). Speakers themselves are not embodiments of such stereotypes. Rather, speakers construct identities – with varying degrees of awareness and success – by drawing on their own knowledge of such models and relying on that of their interlocutors.

Of course, what sociolinguists examine in empirical research is not models but their instantiations in the interactions of speakers. As researchers watch and record scenes, they notice – as do other speakers – that some linguistic forms are enregistered, that is, they conventionally *index* cultural models. The models are inferred from the way linguistic variants are taken up, reacted to, discussed, and interpreted by speakers. Since all such uptake necessarily occurs in interactions, it is organized according to participation frameworks (Goffman 1981). A useful way to think about the invocation of models in interaction is through Bakhtin's (1981) notions of "persona" and "voice." For Bakhtin, a label such as "nerd" names a "persona" (a person-type) imagined, from some perspective, to speak and act in particular ways in a heteroglossic world of contrasting personae that are all conventionally indexed by speech forms (registers). When a speaker uses some fragment or aspect of speech associated with a persona in a real-time interaction, he or she "voices" (enacts or invokes) some aspect of that persona, as known by some population of speakers. Voicing is an action that others interpret through their own perspective, in keeping with their knowledge of the model invoked, the situation of use, and the history of relationships among speakers.

Here then is a further reconceptualization that departs from the theories of early sociolinguistics. Rather than seeing speakers as simply revealing their identities when they talk, analysts now view speakers as aligning with (or against) stereotypes, simultaneously aligning with and against interlocutors – as they pursue interactional goals. Speaking involves adoption of a perspective vis-à-vis models as well as interlocutors. Although I am using the term 'register' here, the recasting of 'style' in sociolinguistics has taken a parallel route (Irvine 2001; Eckert 2012). Most generally: Linguistic variation indexes the speaker-as-role-inhabitant as well as the model (persona), bringing them into alignment, when viewed from the perspective of some population of interlocutors, while also accomplishing alignments or disalignments with other speakers in the scene, as they too orient to models, although they may not actually know or invoke the same ones.

Many phenomena are illuminated by the conceptual move to enregister-ment, in which cultural models (typifications) and their real-time voicings (tokens) are analyzed as separate yet related. The separation leaves a space of indeterminacy; role distance, creativity, differential perspectives, and diver-gent knowledge operate in that space. This gives proper weight to studies of crossing and stylization (e.g., Rampton 1999; Coupland 2001). Speakers typify the speech of others, in contrast to their own, thereby creating and drawing on models. They adopt fragments of the stereotype in specific inter-actions; they may be "voicing" personae they do not necessarily inhabit in the long run. Analysis of interactions unfolding in time is necessary to determine whether a voicing is imitative, parodic, ironic, or an official performance, and/ or to what degree it is a knowing or a sincere enactment. Moreover, utterances can be double-voiced, simultaneously enacting more than one persona, designed for more than one audience. To choose among these possibilities of analysis, researchers focus on the way an utterance is taken up by others, noting its interactional effect as teasing, solidarity, competition, aggression (or something else), and to what degree. By separating persona/model from voicing and insisting that participation frameworks mediate interaction, we gain subtler analyses of how relationships develop over time. By specifying that knowledge of person-types is specific to populations of speakers – and that knowledge/ideology changes over time – we have a way of grasping the indeterminacies, clashing perspectives, and open-endedness that are always part of interactional uptake and exchange.

This brief historical sketch suggests that analysis of variation has increasingly relied on a metasemiotic – language ideological – approach in which knowledge of cultural stereotypes mediates between biographical individuals and the "voices" they enact. We assume that speakers are as adept as researchers at typifying speech and in making new models that can, in turn, be indexed and invoked in interaction as part of motivated social projects and political activity.

Aspects of enregistered signs: icons, rhemes, qualia

Indexicality – pointing, contiguity, co-occurrence – is clearly a key sign relation in enregisterment. Yet there are many questions opened up by this approach that indexicality alone does not handle. For example, it has long been a salient finding in studies of variation that linguistic features (or, more broadly, expressive features) do not simply co-occur as register phenomena. Rather, speakers regularly perceive the co-occurring features as naturally "belonging together," as in some sense resembling each other, even when they are different in modality (sound vs. sight vs. touch), in linguistic level (phonology vs. syntax vs. lexicon), or even in ontology (speech vs. food vs. bodily demeanor). Perhaps the earliest example of this observation was Hebdige's classic study of the way "punk" and "teddy boy" youth styles in Britain were matters not only of music, but also of dress, speech, objects, rituals, and demeanor. In all these realms, the styles of "teds" shared qualities of "plain [ness] and ... puritanism" and thereby contrasted with those of "punks" (1979: 123), as seen by the youth themselves. Scholars also noted that such linguistic or expressive registers/styles are perceived to display the attributes of their stereotyped speakers or situations of use. Importantly, these are matters of resemblance and contrast; they go beyond indexicality.

To see how this is so, let us recall that indexicality is one of the ways that signs may be related to the "objects" they represent, within the system of Peircean sign-relations. The term "object" deserves scare quotes because it is not some predetermined category of things in the world, nor is "sign". Rather, a sign is anything taken to be one; anything that provokes a hypothesis about what it might stand for. That hypothesis is an uptake (interpretant) that links the presumed sign to the proposed object for speakers who adopt that interpretant. Such hypotheses always derive from and are fully embedded in cultural knowledge. That means knowledge of stereotypes/models, or at least guesses about them, must preexist interpretation of signs. As a next step, whatever act or response signals a speaker's uptake or interpretation of a sign can itself become a sign, for some further interpretant. (My uptake of your r-dropping as a sign of your origin in NYC is itself a sign that can be interpreted as indexical – a second-order index – that might point to me as a speaker who knows a thing or two about "regionalisms" or as a co-New Yorker; perhaps it is also an interactional attempt at solidarity or insult). Such active picking out of something-as-sign and something-as-object implies, indeed requires, comparison and contrast. No r-dropping without some notion of r-fulness; no punk styles without teds. Indeed, a complex of signs (register) that is linked to a persona in a model *never* stands alone. It is defined by its contrast to other registers, as taken up in speakers' perspectives. That is why it is important to emphasize that registers do not simply coexist; they stand in co-constitutive, mutually defining relation.

This is where it is helpful to draw on other aspects of Peirce's (1955) three semiotic trichotomies. Any sign can be characterized in accord with each of these; each does different work yet intersects analytically with the others. Index is part of the trichotomy that distinguishes signs in accordance with how they are related to the objects they represent, always within some framework. We have already seen that indexes are those signs apprehended as contiguous with their objects, representing them by pointing or evocation. Icons, on the other hand, are signs that represent by being taken as in some way similar to their objects. Yet as philosophers have long argued, there are potentially unlimited ways in which two phenomena may be similar. Similarities (iconicity) never simply inhere in objects, whether the objects are linguistic, material, or more broadly cultural practices (Goodman 1971). Instead, particular similarities must be defined and picked out as relevant by virtue of some framing, some ideology.

Moreover, as Judith T. Irvine and I (2000) have emphasized, similarities are construed in the context of differentiation (and vice versa). Similarity and difference are mutually defining. Registers are products of contrast; contrasting registers each index some category of personae (and associated times, places, events). In such a configuration, the relation of contrast between the signs/ registers provides a template that invites the perception of contrast between the images/personae that they index. Alternatively, some culturally salient contrast among personae invites the perception that there are distinct registers, each associated with a persona. This configuration constitutes what Peirce called a diagrammatic icon. It is the semiotic scaffolding for *axes of differentiation*, organized according to *qualities* picked out as shared by the expressive features that make up the register and also by the persona it indexes, in contrast with another such pairing. That is, sign-clusters constituting registers are distinguished from other such clusters by qualitative contrasts; these qualities are perceived as resembling the qualities that characterize the persona and other "objects" that the register represents. The qualities picked out are ones that are culturally and often politically significant in the world that participants inhabit. Thus, a register comes to seem particularly apt for representing the category of person (and/or time, place, and situation) that it indexes because it seems to resemble the category, to share its qualities. Indeed, participants observing co-occurrences in interaction *search* for ways in which the signs might "cohere" and "belong together," so that they make ideological sense. They ignore (erase) signs that do not "fit" preexisting cultural images/ models of personae.

It is clarifying to characterize this process in semiotic terms. Peirce proposed that a sign relation may be represented as iconic rather than indexical (or both), depending on the ideological framework (interpretant) with which it is interpreted. Drawing on this notion, Irvine and I have argued that axes of differentiation are reinterpreted, making "linguistic features that index social groups or activities appear to be iconic representations of them ... picking out qualities supposedly shared by the social image and the linguistic image" (2000: 37). That is, once links between sign and object are socially established in a diagrammatic iconic configuration, the same sign may be represented as iconic or as indexical (or both) of the persona it represents, depending on the framework (interpretant) through which it is interpreted. Peirce used the term "rheme" for signs represented by their uptake as icons. In recognition of this source, we have dubbed as *rhematization* the process of creating iconic signs out of indexical ones.[7] The concept captures the way registers that seem like indexes from one ideological perspective can (also) be construed as icons in another ideological frame (Gal 2005). The transformation can work in the opposed direction as well. Perceived similarities between, say, images of person-types and registers can be reinterpreted as mere co-occurrences, rather than resemblances (Ball 2014). Cultural knowledge (as linguistic ideology), social positioning, and political project define which kind of sign relation is made salient.[8]

The transformation from co-occurrence to similarity is particularly striking when the signs come from realms recognized by participants as ontologically distinct (as in Hebdige's examples of matching person-type, clothing style, and music-type). How can speech be similar to food or clothing? It is significant that across the globe, participants often name the opposing poles in axes of differentiation with the lexicon of sensual qualities. Common examples include "plain" versus "florid," "hard" versus "unhard," "narrow" versus "embroidered," or "cool" versus "uncool" expressions.[9] Such contrasts occur repeatedly in ethnographic accounts of how participants characterize their own linguistic differentiation. There may be just one or sometimes several such axes in a social group, accompanied by debates about their relative importance or the relative value of the qualities. Disputes occur because registers are swept up in contrasts of qualities that are part of wide-ranging systems of cultural value and political conflict. The qualities and values projected onto social categories, expressive forms, and speech emerge from and are harnessed to

---

[7] In an earlier version of these semiotic processes, Irvine and I called this step "iconization." That was a more transparent term, since it named the process of turning an index into an icon. Rhematization names the same process. We changed the term in order to better reflect the precise Peircean inspiration.

[8] The difference is one of cultural knowledge that is deemed relevant. A yardstick is evidently in iconic relation to a yard of cloth; they are similar. Yet as Peirce notes, for those who know the yard as a standard of measure, any yard-long object must be indexical – in a real chain of contiguity – with the prototype held in the Royal Observatory in Greenwich, England.

[9] This last comes from Bucholtz's (2011) analysis of a California high school. For the others, see full citations in Gal (2013): plain/florid is a nineteenth-century distinction in American public speaking described by Cmiel; hard/unhard is a Kaluli contrast described by Schieffelin.

sociopolitical projects. Justifications and explanations for such projects – their ability to be persuasive, to motivate action – hinge in part on the taken-for-granted, seemingly self-evident experience of the qualities associated with the projects (Munn 1986). One can cite, for instance, the significance of a "tough/ soft" axis of differentiation in Cold War–era U.S. diplomacy and the accompanying persuasiveness of arguments for the diplomatic use of a register colloquially labeled "tough talk."

Another of Peirce's trichotomies is useful in further understanding such qualitative metaphors and in unpacking how speech can be experienced as similar to ontologically various phenomena as food or clothing. Peirce considered signs to differ in their "degree of reality," distinguishing between abstract qualities, real-time occurrences, and conventions. The three come together in actual experience. As he noted, abstract qualities (e.g., softness) can be experienced only when embodied in real-time objects and occurrences (e.g., a pillow). Moreover, real-time embodiments of abstract qualities are necessarily shaped by conventions: They are cultural categories. By convention, some examples of pillows are recognized as soft. The embodied, conventional, and hence experienceable forms of abstract qualities he termed 'qualia.' Qualia can become signs (qualisigns) and can be instantiated across modalities. The notion of qualisigns is useful in reminding us that it is not the linguistic forms nor objects that are inherently of some quality, but rather that *attributed qualities* can act as signs if they are so interpreted (Chumley and Harkness 2013). So the relative softness of a consonant or vowel can seem experientially similar to the softness of a pillow or a tone. Crucially, speakers must learn such sensual metaphors and through instruction come to understand what "counts" in their social world as a conventional instantiation of an abstract quality like softness or lightness, as it is manifest in various modalities. Pedagogical demonstrations and instructional discourses are needed to socialize speakers into perceiving qualisigns across modalities (hearing, sight, smell, taste) and across different media (Gal 2013).

Once learned as part of sociocultural knowledge, the qualia and sensual metaphors that make up an axis of differentiation can be put to further interactional use. The axis can be invoked repeatedly to differentiate among the phenomena earlier characterized as belonging to one or the other "side" of an axis. For instance, all those registers, objects, practices, personae seen as "plain" (in co-constitutive contrast, perhaps, to "florid") may themselves be divided in accordance with (roughly) the same criteria, thereby making more distinctions of plain versus florid, but now sorting only among the plain. In this new comparison, some of those earlier deemed plain will seem relatively florid. The process is multiply iterable. Participants can make ever more distinctions applying the same axis of differentiation within itself, as in my example, or they can propose to unify phenomena otherwise seen as distinct, via more encompassing categories compared along the same axis. This analogical process of fractal recursivity (Gal and Irvine 1995; Irvine and Gal 2000) allows an axis and its qualia to organize a wide range of activities and relations in diverse scales of social life.

It is worth noting that the perception of similarity (iconism) that unifies the features of a register and that often connects a register with the person-type it indexes does not itself necessarily imply an "essentialization" of the person-type or the linguistic form. Iconicity may be an armature for creating ideologies of essence, but it is not sufficient. As McIntosh (2005) has noted, essentialisms are not merely perceived similarities but elaborate discourses that purport to explain why or how the resemblance exists and what processes or substances are presumed to create or underlie the similarity. Explications of the similarity may involve attributions of inner traits on the basis of outer behavior. Or similarity can be narrativized as a result of lifestyle and learning, rather than shared essence. "Naturalization" too is an elaboration of perceived iconicity that deserves detailed examination in ethnographic studies. Both of these are further semiotic steps in explicating differentiation and its attendant ways of establishing similarity.

In recent sociolinguistic research, a great range of linguistic and behavioral signs is being investigated in semiotic terms, in addition to the traditional subject matter of phonological variables, lexical sets, and morphosyntactic alternations. Studies in sociophonetics show that variables such as voice quality, timing of stop-release, and the relative steepness of falling pitch in intonation all contribute to indexing typified personae in specific social contexts of contrast, even though speakers are hardly conscious of these variations (Mendoza-Denton 2011). As I noted earlier, an uptake, a noticing, makes any behavior into a sign in a Peircean sense. The noticing constitutes a hypothesis that there is meaning, a move that seeks to guess how it might fit into a cultural model of differentiation. Thus, any *reaction* to, say, voice quality or vowel height is already ideological, whether or not speakers can provide exegesis. As another kind of example, scholars have analyzed denotational codes (named languages) as registers, and code-switching itself as an enregistered phenomenon, indexing specific person-types (Eisenlohr 2006) and often rhematized. Orthographic differences can be understood in the same way, with diacritics and shapes interpreted as indexical and rhematized signs arranged in axes of differentiation, linking sets of graphic choices to contrasting values and political commitments (Schieffelin and Doucet 1998; Jaffe 2012).

Thus, by shifting attention to participants' categories and language ideologies, and to semiotic principles, sociolinguistics has discovered social meaning in types of variation that were not noticed before or were not thought to be socially significant signs. In what follows, I draw on recent literature in linguistic anthropology and sociolinguistics, deliberately choosing studies that examine expressive forms falling outside the familiar sociolinguistic variables, in order to demonstrate the wide array of phenomena that can be analyzed in terms of these semiotic processes. In some of these cases, the original investigators did not propose the kind of analysis I suggest. Nevertheless, they have provided empirically rich and culturally insightful accounts that make reanalysis possible. The next section focuses on what icons, indexes, and rhematizations reveal about the construction and reproduction of cultural values and political conflicts. The final section proposes some ways in which these same sign relations, combined in axes of differentiation, are involved in linguistic change.

Linguistic differentiation as sociopolitical process

My first example is an exploration of political discussions in the contemporary United States and shows how sign relations organize and reproduce conflicts, sometimes through the intentional activities of participants, but also in ways that participants deny. Discourse analyses of political speech too often take disputes at face value – as disagreements about issues/content or as matters of deception. As a result, the semiotic process that drives and reproduces them remains unanalyzed. Yet it is a dynamic that occurs in many places and times of political discussion and therefore deserves the close attention of sociolinguists.

Kramer's (2011) study analyzes reactions to rape jokes on U.S. Internet sites and tells a complex story about ideologies of language and of humor. I wish to focus on the aspect of her argument that bears on icons and rhematization. Kramer considers threads of Internet commentary that emerge when a rape joke is posted. Because individuals cannot be traced on these sites, nor can comments be tied to particular demographics, Kramer looks at *types* of comments and finds that they sort into two sides, like a virtual debate. There are pro comments ("rape jokes can be funny") and con positions ("rape jokes are never funny"). Surprisingly, both sides invoke the same ideological principles about humor and language. Among the most important of these is the judgment that laughter is automatic, so that those who do not laugh are either unable to "get" the joke or suppressing a natural urge. Once the joke type has been made a conventional sign – as it was by Second Wave feminism's campaign against rape jokes – any reaction provides the opportunity for a second-order index, sorting responses into those that approve of laughing at rape jokes and those that do not.

Instead of the more usual phonology or grammar, Kramer shows us the enregisterment of lexical and denotational materials. The registers (comments that justify laughing vs. comments that justify not laughing) can be analyzed as constituting an axis of differentiation; they are given co-constitutive *qualities*, as seen from opposed perspectives. Commenters who say they refuse to laugh were characterized by the laughing commenters as showing a lack of humor; those who said they laugh were characterized by the refusing commenters as showing a lack of concern for rape victims. The qualities of the two reaction-types (registers) were projected onto the persona that each supposedly indexes, so that lack of sensitivity to others and humorlessness became qualities of speaker types, not simply of posted reactions. The perceived personal qualities of the two stereotypes are modeled on the perceived qualities of the posted reactions. Refusing to laugh was rhematized as a general bodily hexis of "holding in." Those who refuse to laugh are "uptight," "priggish," "anal-retentive," and "sexual[ly] and emotional[ly] withholding." Those who justify laughing are rhematized in the opposite way: "they do not hold in enough; they . . . lack self-restraint, lack maturity" (2011: 161).

Furthermore, rhematization allows the invention of a causal story by participants in these disputes: "[O]ne's response to rape jokes becomes inextricably tied to [imagined] political views and social grace[s] because they are all seen as resulting from the same intrinsic personal qualities" (2011: 160). This identity work and personalization, Kramer argues, is the real social task at hand, reproducing each side's claim to moral superiority. I add that rhematization systematically allows registers to be taken as *evidence* for the very contrast in identities and morality that supposedly produced them. This circular logic adds an aspect of "proof" to the claims and enhances the power of this process to reproduce social conflict and polarization, erasing details of perspective and the possibility of more nuanced political positions.

My second example is not political in the conventional sense but involves cultural values that are – if anything – more deeply held and socially central. Language ideology is crucial here as well. The study is not about disputes but about making palpable the qualia of something that is considered beyond experience. Tomlinson (2012) describes a U.S. Pentecostal preacher's teachings about glossolalia in a Fijian public park. This preacher emphasized a full-body style of worship with dancing and shouting that ended in his speaking in tongues. A key part of the event was the translation of the preacher's words into Fijian by a Fijian-speaker who shared the platform with him, even though the audience largely understood the Texan's English. The event enacted a relationship between English and Fijian as demonstrably intertranslatable. However, both were set in contrast to glossolalia, which was not translated when it occurred. Indeed it was presented as untranslatable, when placed within the significant contrast set of other languages. English and Fijian indexed human speakers, in contrast to glossolalia, which indexed the decidedly superhuman. As Tomlinson explains, "glossolalia . . . [was] semantically unintelligible, pointing to the otherworldly, even [the] miraculous . . . In Pentecostal understandings, [glossolalia's] linguistic otherness points to the presence of something exceeding the human, namely the Holy Ghost" (2012: 274, 284).

Tomlinson notes that the contrast between glossolalia and ordinary languages such as English or Fijian provides a model (a diagrammatic icon) of the relationship between divinity and humans, a model of radical difference. But I suggest we should also consider how rhematization projects the qualities of the registers (English/Fijian vs. glossolalia) onto the personae indexed in this axis of differentiation. Because such resemblances and qualia are never self-evident, metadiscourse provides exegesis. As Tomlinson emphasizes, the preacher's acts are pedagogical, instructing the audience in how they should experience the glossolalic register: They should hear it as an instance of unknowable, mysterious words arriving in the speaker's consciousness from elsewhere. It is to be understood as having a higher meaning. These are the experienceable qualia of the glossolalic register and (by rhematization) of the divine. While the translator provided semantic meaningfulness from English to Fijian, glossolalia (god-to-human) required no such mediation by a translator. Each participant would directly receive the voice of the Holy Ghost, who would be "speaking through you," as the preacher said.

If Kramer's study showed central political values at issue – indeed reproduced, psychologized, and polarized – through Internet interaction, Tomlinson gives us a communicative scene in which central cultural values, hardly in dispute, are reproduced by enactment. Both involve turning indexes into icons (contiguity into resemblance) and attributing qualities to speakers on the basis of such sign relations, as interpreted by participants' ideological presuppositions. In addition, in Tomlinson's study, people are taught, through the event itself, how to experience the signs that will then count as evidence of otherwise ineffable phenomena.

Linguistic change and transformation of axes

With three more examples I wish to show how axes of differentiation and speakers' handling of them illuminate linguistic variation and change. Woolard (2008) has noted that many mechanisms of change involving language ideology have already been identified in the scholarly literature. I offer the following readings of others' research in the hope of adding yet another process to our tool kit. The metasemiotic approach suggests that the linkages – indexical and iconic – between cultural categories, on the one hand, and linguistic forms, on the other, are shaped by political economic and cultural changes that affect speakers' images of social groups and the linguistic clusters that represent them (Irvine and Gal 2000). It is significant that, contrary to traditional linguistic presumptions, contact between groups is a powerful source of *differentiation*, not similarity. I suggest that this is often the result because contact – as in migration or colonialism – produces a reorganization of the contrast among registers via a change in the operative axes of differentiation.

It has become a truism in studies of variation and change that variants conventionally indexing contrasts of place or region are often reindexicalized and come to represent contrasting class positions (or vice versa). These are clearly cases in which axes of differentiation have shifted. For instance, Agha (2007) has shown how regional markers in UK English were refunctioned as class markers. Johnstone et al. (2006) have argued that some of what had been class markers in Pittsburghers' speech have been reconceptualized by local speakers as distinctive signs of speakers' connection to the city. But "class" and "place" are themselves sociological categories with cultural significance, implying qualities that deserve attention but are more often taken for granted. Therefore it is instructive to turn to a case of change in axes of differentiation that is far removed from Western sociological categories. Kuipers's (1998) discussion of sociolinguistic distinctions in Weyewa (Sumba, Indonesia) presents the difference between everyday talk and ritual speech as the most salient cultural contrast about speaking. Ritual speech, especially in major ceremonies, was filled with syntactic and phonological features that were specific to it. Ritual speech was understood in terms of a set of qualia: "Whole," "full," dense with meaning; everyday speech was a mere derivative, just the "tip" of what was considered the ritual "trunk." Ritual speech was also heard as "angry" and powerful, in contrast to the emotional flatness and calmness of everyday speech.

Yet ritual speech – especially its major genres – gained quite a different interpretation when, during the colonial period, it was no longer contrasted to ordinary Weyewa speech in an axis of differentiation but instead paired to contrast with Dutch public discourse. The Dutch (and later Weyewa too) understood the "anger" of the central genre of ritual speech as a (rhematized) feature of Weyewa discourse. When compared with Dutch rituals, Weyewa ritual speech was interpreted as an icon of the supposedly overaggressive, out-of-control, "savage" condition of Weyewa leadership, in contrast to that of the Dutch (Kuipers 1998: 11). The Dutch used this interpretation to buttress their demand that Weyewa men act more "civilized" by giving up their major, "angry" ritual. The "fullness," "wholeness," and completeness of the "trunk" receded as qualia of importance. When the rituals were abandoned, many syntactic and phonological patterns that were key features of ritual speech went out of use. Later attempts to create grammars and dictionaries for Weyewa had relied on the "tips" – everyday speech and still-existing minor rituals. The grammars lacked the phonological and syntactic forms of the major rituals. When used to teach Weyewa children in Western-style schools, they produced far-reaching and unanticipated linguistic reductions in what was understood to "be" the Weyewa language. The effects of colonialism were mediated by language ideologies in contact, by a reanalysis of the indexical and rhematized values of ritual speech in a newly constructed axis of differentiation: not ritual versus everyday speech, but ritual speech versus Dutch public speaking.

Another example similarly highlights the changes in the social meaning of a single linguistic variable as it was shaped by the axis of differentiation through which the feature was understood. Single features are never meaningful on their own, but one can be singled out as the focus of attention, identified as shibboleth within some array of signs constituting a register. Mendoza-Denton's (2011) discussion of creaky voice starts by carefully defining this nonmodal speech quality in phonetic and distributional terms and tracking its co-occurrence with other features, before exploring changes in its social meaning. On the one hand, creaky voice – linked to other stylistic features – indexed a "hard" persona in the narrative told to Mendoza-Denton by a young girl, a Chicana gang member in a northern California high school in the 1990s. On the other hand, and surprisingly, creak indexed *"male* Chicano gangster personae" in the media genre of Chicano gangster rap that was separately emerging at just about the same time. As Mendoza-Denton notes, it may seem odd that creak contributed to indexing a "hardcore" stance for the gang *girls*, while in contemporaneous, mediatized performance it enacted a stereotype of "brown *masculinity*" (2011: 270, emphasis in original), yet, as she shows, cross-gender contrasts were not relevant for either speaker.

For the narrating girl, creaky voice had a place in what Mendoza-Denton tellingly identifies as a *"locally-defined* economy of affect." In this economy, among gang girls, "[C]lose metalinguistic attention is paid to the management of emotional responses displayed in a given situation," and it is "centered around being silent, being hard of heart (hardcore), and being toughened by experience" (2011: 266, 269). This vividly reveals the qualia understood to be shared by the feature and the ideal persona it indexes. But "hard" compared with what? Creaky voice may well be metaphorical of "tension under control" (269), as Mendoza-Denton suggests. But I propose that the effect of "hardness" and "toughness" is also achieved through an axis of differentiation that relies on an evoked contrast with the qualia of some other persona and other register in the same *locally defined* economy, that of the high school the girl attended. Perhaps, as Mendoza-Denton implies in her ethnography of that school, there was a contrast with the more mainstream, conventionally gendered style of the "trendy Euro-American" girls, who criticized "those Mexicans" for their dress and makeup, with the very term "hard" (2008: 152).

The rapper, by contrast, was not operating in this local economy but evidently had his own. It is one in which creaky voice participated in what seems like the same axis of differentiation, but that gained contrastive value via a different local comparison. Writing about the early recordings of the rapper-artist who is credited with inventing Chicano rap, Mendoza-Denton observes that, "at the time, he was the only rapper who was using this sustained voice quality [creak] in his raps, and created a distinctive sound which set him apart from others ... like his African American contemporar [ies]" (2011: 271). For the rapper, the salient contrast was not with a typified Euro-American girl, and neither hardness nor masculinity would have distinguished him from his African American counterparts. It was creaky voice, interpreted as Chicano-ness, that did. Further circulations and uptakes of creaky voice by other populations were doubtless constrained and shaped by such reevaluations in these and other "local economies."

A final example shows how multiple axes of differentiation can be projected simultaneously onto a single contrast, with palpable effects on its social meanings. Harkness (2012) describes South Korean vowel harmony, noting that traditional analyses of it in Korean relied on ancient philosophies of yin/yang (in the Korean scheme this corresponds to dark/light) as a basic ontological contrast, projecting culturally significant qualities onto sound contrasts (and vice versa). Korean vowel harmony allows limited denotational iconism (i.e., onomatopeia). In words that differ only in having vowels categorized as yang [a] (light) in contrast to yin [ɔ] (dark, heavy), the difference can denote miniaturization or augmentation of the denoted object or action: light = smaller, dark = bigger. For this and a number of other reasons, the distinction between "light" and "dark" vowels remains a strongly felt one for Korean speakers. Harkness argues that these contrasts continue to have a lively effect on understandings of speech sound, even though more recent ideologies emphasize "modern/traditional" as a dimension of contrast for speech, as people highlight the vast political and economic changes of recent decades.

A delicate locus of linguistic change is the borrowing of English loan words. During the Japanese colonization of Korea in the twentieth century, English loans came into the Korean language via the Japanese language. In the representation of English mid-vowels, [a] (yang, light) was used, and this unintentionally intersected with the quality distinctions of Korean vowel harmony. Since the end of colonialism, although the old system of yin/yang persists, a campaign of eliminating Japanese linguistic influence has tried to represent English words in what seem like more "accurate" ways, using [ɔ] for the same English sound. The Japanese era's loans with [a] are heard no longer as indexing colonial influence, but rather as indexing the speakers who use those forms. They are speakers who tend to be survivors of the colonial period; therefore, they are now old people.

The contrast between loan words with [a] (old form) and the same loans pronounced with [ɔ] (new form) is now interpretable as exemplary of two different axes of differentiation. For many speakers, both old people and the vowels they emit in the relevant context ([a]) sound "old," in contrast to new vowels ([ɔ]), indexing young people. But the contrast of loans pronounced with [a] versus [ɔ] is also interpreted as light/dark. Thus, to many people, [a] (yang, light) sounds diminutive; its use is not only indexical but rhematically evokes a "smaller," more "trivial" speaker as well as an old one. The combined effect is transformative: old, quaint, provincial, even infantile is contrasted with young, heavy, big, and important. Harkness notes the multiply ironic result: the old ideology of yin/yang – now distinguishing speakers as well as sounds – contributes to a way of hearing contrasts that accords with – even strengthens – a new, global theory of modernization in which, moreover, "the speech of seniors becomes infantile, and the speech of young people becomes mature" (2012: 376).

It has long been a truism in sociolinguistics that the uptake of linguistic forms and their consequent spread are dependent on the social meanings speakers convey with them. Registers gain meaning when they are understood to stand in co-constitutive opposition to each other, along specific axes of differentiation. When registers/styles are placed in typified comparative sets with newly available images or simply different ones, the register is resignified; linguistic features gain new social meanings. They evoke different personae and in that way contribute to the meaning and spread of linguistic changes. Identifying the axes of differentiation (and constitutive qualia) that are relevant for a population of speakers – and for the interactional practices being studied – is therefore crucial in understanding processes of linguistic change.

Conclusion

Evidence from diverse sociohistorical and cultural contexts demonstrates how the ideological/semiotic processes I have highlighted contribute to differentiation and the creation of similarity in the social worlds analyzed. Linguistic differentiation is a crucial part of sociocultural differentiation; these same processes create the social meaning of variants that contributes to linguistic change.

The principles and processes I have discussed require no review here. I would like to close instead by highlighting a number of implications of this approach when compared with the early sociolinguistic works with which this chapter began. Language ideological approaches resist the temptation to assume that the "linguist knows best" or that there is a "view from nowhere" that would allow investigators to determine what are the important variables extant in a population. It forces analysts to listen to the valuations of speakers. By the same token, it presumes that all speakers, including linguists, orient to others with the help of ideological presuppositions, metacommunication. We all take positions, with the help of presumed models, in interactional scenes. Therefore, ethnographic investigations must include the ethnographer and his or her role. As Bucholtz (2011: 210–235) has pointed out, even the "background questions" she at first presumed to be innocent and easy tasks for the California high school students she was studying turned out to reveal the kinds of differentiations that she wished to analyze. Requesting "your age, sex, ethnicity and year in school" in a scene of racial tensions invited hostile reactions equivalent to "Who wants to know?" In this sense, language ideological approaches recognize the deeply political nature of all sociolinguistic and ethnographic investigation.

In addition, some of my examples analyze the processes of political discourse itself. Kramer, for instance, has a different relation to her materials than Bucholtz, since Kramer did not encounter her evidence in face-to-face interaction. Yet she too must take a position with reference to the virtual "sides" she analyzes. She resists being drawn into the debate, which would simply reproduce the arguments, nor does she presume to condemn or laud the participants. Rather, she takes a metaperspective. Her goal is to show the way statements of opinion are systematically turned into attributed identities and qualities, thereby revealing the unspoken stakes of the Internet encounters and showing how the conflict is exacerbated. This semiotic process is typical of much political discourse, especially in a period of identity politics. Kramer's analytical strategy is effective in specifying the poetics by which discursive conflicts operate. It is itself political by providing tools for those inspired to engage in further struggles.

Finally, I have suggested that the fundamental indexicality of linguistic variation that the early studies of language-in-social-context discerned and analyzed should be enhanced by paying attention to qualities and resemblances, seen as ideological and interactional achievements. These processes organize a great deal of sociolinguistic variation. Contrasts of attributed qualities – hard/soft, full/incomplete, tight/loose, dark/light, and innumerable others that are constantly invented – are conceptualized through culturally specific narratives. These are the sorts of qualitative differences that create contrasting and value-laden images of people-types. At the same time, they also unify diverse modalities of experience by linking the images of speech registers to typified practices and, most importantly, to the values and thus to the moral principles and often contentious politics of participants.

REFERENCES

Agha, A. 2007. *Language and Social Relations*. New York: Cambridge University Press.
Bakhtin, M. M. 1981. *The Dialogic Imagination*. Austin: University of Texas Press.
Ball, C. 2014. On dicentization. *Journal of Linguistic Anthropology*. 24, 2: 151–173.
Bateson, G. 1972 [1955]. *Steps to an Ecology of Mind*.: San Francisco: Chandler.

Bauman, R., and C. Briggs. 2003. *Voices of Modernity*. New York: Cambridge University Press.

Bauman, R., and J. Sherzer (eds.) 1974. *Explorations in the Ethnography of Communication*. Cambridge: Cambridge University Press.

Blom, J.-P., and J. J. Gumperz. 1972. Social meaning in linguistic structures: Codeswitching in Norway. In J. J. Gumperz and D. Hymes (eds.) *Directions in Sociolinguistics: The Ethnography of Communication*. New York: Holt, 407–434.

Bright, W. (ed.) 1966. *Sociolinguistics: Proceedings of the 1964 UCLA Sociolinguistics Conference*. The Hague: Mouton.

Bucholtz. M. 2011. *White Kids*. New York: Cambridge University Press.

Bucholtz, M., and K. Hall. 2008. All of the above: New coalitions in sociocultural linguistics. *Journal of Sociolinguistics* 12, 4: 401–431.

Chumley, L., and N. Harkness. 2013. Introduction: QUALIA. *Anthropological Theory*. 13: 1–2.

Coupland, N. 2001. Dialect stylisation in radio talk. *Language in Society* 30, 3: 345–375.

Duranti, A., and C. Goodwin (eds.). 1992. *Rethinking Context*. New York: Cambridge University Press.

Eckert, P. 1989. *Jocks and Burnouts*. New York: Columbia University Press.

2012. Three waves of variation study. *Annual Review of Anthropology* 41: 87–100.

Eisenlohr, P. 2006. *Little India*. Berkeley: University of California Press.

Ervin-Tripp, S. 1972. Alternation and co-occurrence. In J. J. Gumperz and D. Hymes (eds.), *Directions in Sociolinguistics: The Ethnography of Communication*. New York: Holt, 218–250.

Fischer, J. L. 1958. Social influences on the choice of a linguistic variant. *Word* 14: 47–56.

Gal, S. 2005. Language ideologies compared. *Journal of Linguistic Anthropology* 15: 23–37.

2013. The taste of talk. *Anthropological Theory* 13, 1–2: 31–48.

Gal, S., and J. T. Irvine. 1995. The boundaries of languages and disciplines. *Social Research* 62, 4: 967–1001.

Goffman, E. 1967. Face-work. In E. Goffman, *Interaction Ritual*. Chicago, IL: Aldine.

1974. *Frame Analysis*. Philadelphia: University of Pennsylvania Press.

1981. *Forms of Talk*. Philadelphia: University of Pennsylvania Press.

Goodman, N. 1971. Seven strictures on similarity. In N. Goodman, *Problems and Prospects*. Indianapolis, IN: Bobbs-Merrill, 437–447.

Gumperz, J. J. 1972. Introduction. In J. J. Gumperz and D. Hymes (eds.), *Directions in Sociolinguistics: The Ethnography of Communication*. New York: Holt, 1–25.

1982. *Discourse Strategies*. New York: Cambridge University Press.

Gumperz, J. J., and D. Hymes (eds.). 1964. Special issue of *American Anthropologist*.

(eds.). 1972. *Directions in Sociolinguistics*. New York: Holt.

Harkness, N. 2012. Vowel harmony redux. *Journal of Sociolinguistics*. 16, 3: 358–381.

Haugen, E. 1966. Language, dialect, nation. *American Anthropologist* 68, 4: 922–935.

Hebdige, D. 1979. *Subculture: The Meaning of Style*. London: Methuen.

Hymes, D. 1962. The ethnography of speaking. In T. Gladwin and W. C. Sturtevant (eds.), *Anthropology and Human Behavior*. Washington, DC: Anthropological Society of Washington.

(ed.). 1964. *Language in Culture and Society*. New York: Holt.

Irvine, J. T. 1990. Registering affect. In L. Abu-Lughod and C. Lutz (eds.), *Language and the Politics of Emotion*. New York: Cambridge University Press.

2001. "Style" as distinctiveness: The culture and ideology of linguistic differentiation. In P. Eckert and J. Rickford (eds.), *Style and Sociolinguistic Variation*. New York: Cambridge University Press, 21–43.

Irvine, J. T., and S. Gal. 2000. Language ideology and linguistic differentiation. In P. Kroskrity (ed.), *Regimes of Language*. Santa Fe, NM: SAR Press, 35–84.

Jaffe, A. (ed.) 2012. *Orthography as Social Action*. Boston and Berlin: Mouton.

Jakobson, R. 1960. Closing remarks. In T. Sebeok (ed.), *Style in Language*. Cambridge, MA: MIT Press.

Johnstone, B. 2013. *Pittsburghese: The Story of a Dialect*.New York: Oxford University Press.

Johnstone, B., J. Andrus, and A. E. Danielson. 2006. Mobility, indexicality and the enregisterment of "Pittsburghese." *Journal of English Linguistics* 34: 77–104.

Keane, W. 2003. Semiotics and the social analysis of material things. *Language and Communication* 23: 409–425.

Kramer, E. 2011. The playful is political: The metapragmatics of internet rape joke arguments. *Language in Society* 40: 137–168.

Kuipers, J. 1998. *Language, Identity and Marginality in Indonesia*. New York: Cambridge University Press.

Labov, W. 1963. The social motivation of a sound change. *Word* 19: 273–309.

Lucy, J. 1993. Reflexive language and the human disciplines. In J. Lucy (ed.), *Reflexive Language: Reported Speech and Metapragmatics*. New York: Cambridge University Press, 9–32.

Manning, P. 2012. *Semiotics of Drinks and Drinking*. New York: Continuum.

McIntosh, J. 2005. Language essentialism and social hierarchies among Giriama and Swahili. *Journal of Pragmatics* 37: 1919–1944.

Mendoza-Denton, N. 2008. *Homegirls*. New York: Blackwell.

2011. The semiotic hitchhiker's guide to creaky voice. *Journal of Linguistic Anthropology* 21, 2: 261–280.

Munn, N. 1986. *The Fame of Gawa*. Durham, NC: Duke University Press.

Peirce, C. S. 1955. Logic as semiotic: The theory of signs. In J. Buchler (ed.), *The Philosophical Writings of Peirce*. New York: Dover, 98–115.

Rampton, B. (ed.). 1999. Special issue on *Styling the Other*. *Journal of Sociolinguistics* 3.

Schegloff, E. 1972. Notes on a conversational practice: Formulating place. In D. Sudnow (ed.), *Studies in Social Interaction*. New York: Free Press.

Schegloff, E., G. Jefferson, and H. Sacks. 1974. A simplest systematics for the organization of turn-taking in conversation. *Language* 50: 696–735.

Schieffelin, B. B., and R. C. Doucet. 1998. The "real" Haitian creole: Ideology, metalinguistics and orthographic choice. In B. B. Schieffelin, K. Woolard, and P. Kroskrity (eds.), *Language Ideologies*. New York: Oxford University Press, 285–316.

Silverstein, M. 1979. Language structure and linguistic ideology. In R. Clyne, W. F. Hanks, and C. L. Hofbauer (eds.), *The Elements: A Parasession on Linguistic Units and Levels*. Chicago, IL: Chicago Linguistics Society, 193–247.

2003. Indexical order and the dialectics of sociolinguistic life. *Language and Communication* 23: 193–229.

Tomlinson, M. 2012. God speaking to God: Translation and unintelligibility in a Fijian Pentecostal crusade. *The Australian Journal of Anthropology* 23: 274–289.

Woolard, K. 2008. Why dat now. *Journal of Sociolinguistics*. 12, 4: 432–452.

Woolard, K., and B. Schieffelin. 1994. Language ideology. *Annual Review of Anthropology* 23: 55–82.

Part II

Language, markets and materiality

6   Treating language as an economic resource: Discourse, data and debate

Monica Heller and Alexandre Duchêne

1.   Can language be a commodity?

In recent years, along with other colleagues, we have developed arguments that language is increasingly treated as a commodity in late capitalism (Tan and Rubdy 2008; Heller 2010; Duchêne and Heller 2012; Park and Wee 2012).[1] This argument has been the subject of three major types of critique: The first comes from linguistic minority theorists, the second from the field of "language economics," and the third from Marxist approaches to language and commodification. We begin by briefly summarizing our argument and by making explicit the assumptions behind it, specifically those that orient us to the material we discuss in ways which differ from those of our critics (rendering straightforward 'debate' actually quite difficult). We conclude with a discussion of how the consideration of whether language (or, as we prefer to say, communicative resources) can be commodified opens questions for further research.

We should begin by saying that one thing that frequently arises as an issue in these debates is what idea of language underlies them. We draw on Bourdieu (1982) to argue that language can be understood as a social practice that consists of circulating communicative resources. Those resources are modes of meaning-making that include social organization and therefore lie at the heart of the ways in which the social, cultural, political, and economic are inherently intertwined. Having said that, we need to recognize that the processes of commodification we claim to observe usually are based on a quite different idea of what language is; namely, they draw on the idea of language as an autonomous system that can be constructed both as an emblem of authentic identity and as a technical skill – an idea that crystallized around industrial capitalism and its connection to the nation-state (Heller 2007). Our critics, as we shall see, themselves grapple with the question of the ontological

---

[1] Research on which this chapter was based was supported by the Social Sciences and Humanities Research Council of Canada and the Swiss National Science Foundation. We would like to thank Nik Coupland, Bonnie McElhinny, and Jackie Urla for their insightful comments on an earlier version of this chapter. Errors remain our own.

status of language, albeit not necessarily from the same position as each other or from the position that we authors adopt.

The next section details how our ideas about linguistic commodification emerged in an attempt to account for phenomena we saw emerging as we were looking at something else. Our longstanding interest in different forms of nationalism has meant tracking ways in which discourses on language and linguistic practices are tied to the production of ideas of the nation and of the nation-state, and so to examination of the discursive spaces in which such discourses and practices are produced (and contested) and of the social actors who produce (or contest) them. As we watched, dominant discourses of political rights, citizenship, and governance became increasingly challenged by discourses of economic development, in which linguistic material of a variety of forms was increasingly presented as an element of economic exchange. It was this process that, as we will summarize, led us to look for a way to understand what was happening.

Our conclusion, as we will explain, was that this was no metaphor. Rather, as Bourdieu pointed out long ago (Bourdieu 1982), while language has always been part of complex systems of exchange among symbolic and material resources, with differing values depending on the sociohistorical conditions of the market, the conditions of late capitalism extend the commodification of language in ways that make it available for work it has not had to do before. Moreover, for our purposes, this extension shifts the bases for how we think of the relationship between language and nations, for how they both are valued, and for how their intertwined existence is justified or challenged. In particular it introduces economic value as a newly important basis for legitimizing claims that undermines previous bases linked to discourses of political rights.

The third section of the chapter details the three main critiques that this argument has triggered. They are interestingly disparate, in that they emerge from very different ideas about the relationship between language, nation, and economy. What they have in common is a set of beliefs regarding that relationship which differs from ours, and a concomitantly different set of positions regarding what our role in exploring it as sociolinguists should be. The final section of the chapter discusses the implications of these differences for orienting research priorities at this particular historical moment, notably for situating commodification in a broader economic and social context.

2.   Following the data

Working in francophone Canada and in Switzerland, both of us began noticing the emergence of economistic arguments about language in the 1990s concerning language proficiency, marketing, and branding. Not that language has never been understood as linked to the economy; it has often been argued that economic progress and development are tied to the reproduction of the linguistically homogeneous community. That ideology, however, understands the two as distinct realms of activity; the new practices, both discursive and material, construct language directly as an economic resource.

We have discussed elsewhere (Heller and Duchêne 2012) the historical shifts in political economic conditions that help explain why the realignment between nation-state and capital (or what we think of as the shift to neoliberalism and globalization) led to a shift in discourses and practices of language; we can summarize here by saying that the extension and intensification of capitalism led to the incorporation of the semiotic products of nationalism (among them "language") into processes of commodification, in particular in the rapidly growing tertiary sector, with its emphasis on the value of the intangible (knowledge, culture, and services).

As Appadurai (1986) pointed out in an edited volume on the commodification of material culture, capitalism can potentially commodify pretty much anything. He also recognized that, while his own work and that of the contributors to the volume focused on material objects (Oriental carpets, medieval relics, prehistoric kingly wealth in gold objects), the same reasoning could be applied to services or, to put it in our current terms, to what is exchanged in the tertiary sector (such as information, experiences, expertise).

At the same time, he argued, commodification is a process. Things can become commodified, that is, newly used in a transaction where value is accorded and made commensurate across a set of exchangeable things, but they can also become decommodified; that is, their status as commodities can shift. And so language is at least available for attempts to construct it as a commodity, although those attempts may be contested, may fail, or may enter a more complicated process of commodification, decommodification, and recommodification, as conditions and interests shift.

The economistic arguments and concomitant practices we witnessed in the 1990s (shortly after Appadurai's observations) emerged strongly in the arena of education, where decisions over language teaching (which languages to teach, to whom to teach them, and how) began to move quickly, albeit not without controversy, from questions of cultural distinction, cohesive citizenship, and intercultural understanding to questions of access to resources of value in the globalized new economy. We can see this as part of a general neoliberal trend in education, as it has moved from its nation-state origins as a site for the production of the national citizen and the industrial worker (Weber 1976; Bowles and Gintis 1977) to a site for the production of the neoliberal entrepreneurial, flexible self (Urciuoli 2008; Allan 2013).

But this neoliberal trend has also increasingly characterized the discursive construction of the nation-state itself, whether of established states like Canada or Switzerland or among minority movements claiming their own state-like rights to autonomous governance (as in francophone Canada, or Catalunya), from major state-level campaigns to the smallest localities. Stakeholders, like language planners, minority language advocates, or language educators, stop treating ethnolinguistic diversity as a problem to be solved or, at best, as a symbol of national "tolerance" and "democracy," and begin to provide arguments for how it generates national wealth (including how that wealth may be redistributed to its citizens). Ethnolinguistic diversity hence figures more and more prominently in the ways in which political entities increasingly construct themselves.

State and civil society stakeholders thus encourage linguistic minorities to stop fighting for their rights, and instead to point out how their linguistic and cultural resources represent "added value" to their regional or national economies. States also argue that the linguistic resources of their citizens allow for distinctive forms of access to markets (including small niche markets) – that is, both to consumers and to the people who control valued resources (those who produce them, who distribute them, and who sell them), as well as to the circulation of knowledge about them. For example, as the authenticity produced by older forms of romantic nationalism becomes marketable in the growing and lucrative tourism industry (Heller et al. 2014), language becomes one key way to add value to a tourism product as a marker of that authenticity, while multilingualism allows that product to be widely consumed. States such as Canada and Switzerland even market their metaknowledge about language: beyond having access to multiple linguistic resources, they argue that they have experience in managing linguistic diversity, through, for example, expertise in translation and interpretation. Finally, linguistic diversity gets incorporated in the branding in which states increasingly engage, as they become more closely aligned to the private sector.

These practices and discourses focusing on the economic value of languages also circulate more and more widely at the supranational level, notably in the European Union. For example, the Division of Language Policy of the Council of Europe currently argues that linguistic diversity is an economic asset for Europe as a whole (in terms of market access and expansion) and for individual Europeans (in terms of job access and mobility) (Zappettini 2014). In related developments in the private sector, advertisements for language courses have promised significant increases in personal income; the market for machine translation has increased; and multinational firms have emphasized the multilingualism of their workers as a key asset.

Figure 6.1 shows one example from Switzerland (see also Flubacher and Duchêne 2012; Duchêne and Flubacher 2015). The table is part of a promotional brochure entitled "Savoir-faire Biel/Bienne," published in 2008 by the city council of the German-French-Italian multilingual city of Biel/Bienne

Marché du travail attrayant et polyvalent

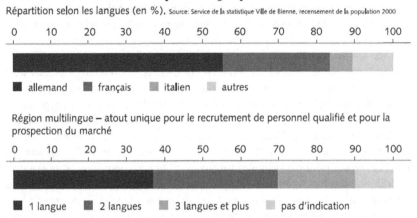

Figure 6.1: Promotional brochure, City of Biel/Bienne.

and aimed at attracting economic investors to the city, especially companies from the tertiary sector.

Several things are notable about this figure. The heading advertises an "attractive and polyvalent labour market," while the body is about multilingualism: The brochure fuses the linguistic and the economic. The reference to "polyvalence" takes up neoliberal notions of the importance of flexibility, that is, a labor pool, and indeed individual workers, skilled at many things, not just the one specialized task typical of Taylorized industrial production chains. The city shows us, first, that it is economically attractive and polyvalent, simply by virtue of the co-presence of multiple languages. Further, its labor pool comprises a majority of bilingual or multilingual individual workers; individual multilingualism is announced as an "advantage for the recruitment of qualified personnel and for exploration of the market." The city thus markets itself as economically attractive on the basis of the multilingualism of its labor pool.

To sum up, the increased presence of the economic – the economic turn – takes three forms. First, we see discourses of rights increasingly confronted with, or alternatively melding with, discourses of added value (or, as we said in an earlier publication, discourses of pride are confronted with discourses of profit; Duchêne and Heller 2012). Second, the semiotic resources produced by the nationalism characteristic of industrial capitalism (such as flags, the distinction between standard and vernacular linguistic varieties, traditional costume, heroic or iconic personages, and high and popular culture forms) are mobilized in economic activities to create niche markets or add value to products or are mobilized as products in and of themselves. Finally, the phenomena constructed as problems by nationalisms and industrial markets focusing on boundaries and uniformity, such as multilingualism and variability, are recast as economic assets and as brands, although their earlier existence as problems may persist alongside the increasingly prominent neoliberal discourses.

Thus we find tensions over authority, authenticity, and legitimacy. To give one example, in November 2014 the city of Québec, a political capital as well as a major tourist destination, unveiled a new tagline. In addition to its traditional symbol (a boat whose outline recalls the arrival of Europeans in the seventeenth century), it now labels itself *l'accent d'Amérique* ("the accent of America"), using its Frenchness to make distinction within North America and its Americanness to sell itself as familiar but exotic to Europeans. In Québec, where political struggles for sovereignty still loom large, this exercise in branding has had to be cast as "positioning," in order to avoid too obvious a reference to economic frames, that is, to selling Québec (as opposed to constructing its authority and authenticity as the political capital of a nation). In Switzerland, on the other hand, we do not find similar hesitation.

Linguistic commodification, then, is something we became interested in by "following the data," that is, by observing processes in our fieldwork that turned out to be unevenly distributed, contested, and nonlinear but nonetheless neither purely local nor ephemeral. Our job, as we see it, has been to try to account for both the emergence of the phenomena we observe and their complex contours, in order better both to explain them and to understand their consequences for how we imagine such traditional objects of sociolinguistic scrutiny as linguistic variability, community, and identity, as well as the relationship between these concepts and the idea of the nation. Certainly, the idea of variability as abnormal corresponds less and less to how we experience the world, as we can see in the turn in the social sciences to the study of *relations* between process and fixity, flow and stasis, mobility and immobility, variability and uniformity (Giddens 1990; Appadurai 1996; Castells 2000; Sheller and Urry 2006). The question is how the tension between language as commodity and as relation plays out.

The idea of language as commodity helps us understand part of what people are trying to do with language (whether successfully or not is another matter), not just in how they think of it but in how they concretely try to turn it into an exchangeable resource with measurable value in economic terms (from choosing one place to invest in, or one person to hire over another, to calculating hourly or monthly wages, training fees, or gross national product). In and of itself, that challenges the modernist nation-state idea of language as a whole, bounded, and principally cognitive system, and orients to an understanding of language as part of a complex set of communicative resources that circulate in flows – although the resources in question remain recognizable largely in the form in which the nation-state produced them, that is, as elements of whole, bounded autonomist systems or as those systems themselves. The commodification of communicative resources under contemporary conditions raises a tension between understanding those resources as unified objects, somehow outside human agency, obedient only to the laws of the market, or as inalienable aspects of social action.

As we will see in the next section, these tensions surface in several different ways in the critiques formulated to date of the argument we make that language is observably commodifiable and commodified (albeit perhaps sometimes not that well), with equally observable challenges to currently dominant ways of understanding language, identity, and nation. They surface with respect to analytic stance and to the ontological status accorded to language, market, and nation.

The next section takes up three major lines of critique, the three of which we are aware. What they have in common, we believe, is a discomfort with the ontological status we accord language and its commodification. We see commodification of language as a (not necessarily linear or universal) process in which elements of the ideological construction of the nation-state are inscribed more directly into the workings of capitalism than they were before. Those elements relate to both Romantic and Enlightenment dimensions of nationalism – the first capitalizing on the idea of language as symbol of national authenticity, and iconic of national values, the second regarding language as an autonomous system and technical skill to be brought to bear on the makings of democratic citizenship. We are trying to account for how and why that is happening, and with what consequences for both dominant ideas of language, and therefore also to the idea of the nation. The different perspectives brought to bear in the debate as to whether language can be thought of as a commodity and, if so, of what kind, result also in disagreement about our relationship as analysts to language and economic activity.

Our claims to see attempts at commodification are not the same as claims to witnessing a fully realized commodification process. Indeed, it is the tension between the conditions that produced the semiotic resources of "identity," "language," and "culture" and those that make them available to be put into play as commodities that is most characteristic of our times. While we have no particular investment in the vocabulary of "late" versus "high," we do argue that intensification of capitalism has consequences for the possibility of reproduction of political economic conditions. At the same time, critiques of our work do lead us to open up further avenues of inquiry, notably to ask in what different ways the semiotic resources of nationalism are in fact treated, in areas and for people differentially positioned with respect to the globalized new economy, and with respect to the process of production, circulation, and consumption of products. We will end the next section with a discussion of what further investigations of these processes might look for, with an emphasis on moments of conversion or, put differently, on those sites where the ability to deploy linguistic and cultural resources makes a real difference to people's lives.

3.   Engaging with the critiques

The first critique concerns language as commodity, national emblem, or mode of governance. It is less a direct critique of our work than an expression of concern over the ways in which states have changed their rationale for providing funding for linguistic minority communities or multilingualism, away from the demonstration of the political rights of collectivities toward the demonstration of the economic value of linguistic resources. Our work figures in the discussion insofar as it is understood to implicitly support this shift by virtue of its attention to it, rather than to what is expected of us as intellectuals, that is, to struggle against it in the service of minority nation-building.

The concern is clearly evident in Canada, from within the movement for francophone national political rights. We use as an exemplar a text by Forgues and Doucet (2014), produced by a linguistic minority think-tank that has a role of commenting on government policy. We consider this text useful partly because it is the most clearly written example of this concern we have come across, and partly because, not coincidentally, it was produced within the context of a research institution founded within the frame of francophone linguistic minority rights, which drives the discourse that, as we said above, is most directly challenged by the state's turn toward economic, rather than political, modes of discursive legitimation of the state and its institutions. The discourse takes language to be inalienable from national bodies, and national development as the reason to be interested in the relationship between language and the economy.

Forgues and Doucet take issue with efforts on the part of the state to change the basis for providing funding to "linguistic minority communities" (see Silva and Heller 2009 for a detailed discussion of this change), for these reasons. They say:

En effet, si on suit cette nouvelle logique de financement, ce n'est plus tant le droit qui fonde l'intervention de l'État, mais la valeur ajoutée produite par les organismes et leur rendement mesurée à la lumière de leur capacité d'atteindre leurs objectifs. Il s'agit moins pour l'État d'assurer une forme de réparation et de rattrapage, que de financer les organismes les plus performants qui contribuent à la prospérité du pays, quitte à aller du côté des organismes de la majorité pour ce faire. On crée un marché qui dissocie les services de l'organisme qui les offre. Ce que l'État finance n'est pas tant des organismes que des services. (p. 18)

Les droits linguistiques garantissent une aide de l'État peu importe le rendement des organismes et leur valeur ajoutée. Il ne faut pas perdre de vue que le modèle de la concurrence est incompatible avec celui qui vise la réparation des torts du passé. Ce dernier modèle demande de développer les capacités des organismes qui ont peut-être un moins bon rendement. (p. 21)

Our translation:

Indeed, if we follow this new logic of financing, it is not so much the law that underlies State intervention, but the added value produced by organizations and their performance measured in the light of their ability to reach their objectives. It is not so much an issue of the State ensuring a form of reparation and "catch-up," as of financing the organizations that perform the most strongly in their contributions to the prosperity of the country, even if that means going over to majority organizations in order to do so. This creates a market that dissociates services from the organization that offers them. What the State finances is not so much the organizations as services. (p. 18)

Language rights guarantee support from the State whatever the performance of organizations and their added value. We must not lose sight of the fact that the competition model is incompatible with the model that is oriented to repairing the wrongs of the past. This means developing the capacities of organizations that might perform less well.

The movement for francophone national political rights is mostly concerned with understanding why linguistic minorities are marginalized, and with searching for the best conditions for the rectification of that situation. The link between language and economy is thus best understood in that frame as a question of what resources are possessed by people who identify (e.g., in the census) as speakers of a specific language. The movement is deeply critical of neoliberalism, which it sees as an assault on collective rights (Silva and Heller 2009), and therefore on francophone Canada's possibilities for self-governance and self-determination.

While Forgues and Doucet's critique is squarely aimed at the neoliberal state, it intersects with our work in terms of how our role as analysts of francophone Canada is seen. Within their framework, we should orient to the protection of a liberal welfare state discursive regime, and its support for a specific understanding of language as needing to be "preserved" and "transmitted" within a community defined in national terms. From that perspective, it is only possible to decry the shift to neoliberalism. It makes no sense to undertake a description and analysis of the ideological, discursive, and material shifts that comprise neoliberalism. Indeed, it becomes difficult to see the analytic apparatus of "commodification" and "resource" as anything other than mimetic (and therefore supportive) of the neoliberal state.

Alexandre has encountered similar critiques in Switzerland. The dominant Swiss discourse of multilingualism (including academic discourse) constructs it as both more democratic and more just toward minorities than traditional

European monolingual regimes. His work has explored what we might call the "darker side" of multilingualism, notably the link between the exploitation of workers' linguistic resources and the increasing precariousness of immigrant and working-class labor. He has shown how Swiss multilingualism can indeed be seen to be linked to profits and productivity, but not necessarily to the benefit of the direct producers of the resource themselves. We would argue that most of Alexandre's work has shown that, while public and political discourse constructs multilingualism as an economic asset, the convertibility of linguistic, financial, and material capital is more complex than generally recognized. As a result, his work is frequently taken up as a threat to the mainstream discourse focusing on the positive valorization of linguistic diversity. One reason offered for this concern is that critiques of the discourse and practice of Swiss multilingualism are potentially recuperable by traditional, conservative, nationalist movements, with their preference for the domination of ideologies of monolingualism and standardization and their resistance to immigration or other forms of linguistic and cultural diversification. From that perspective, any critique of Swiss multilingualism risks undermining minority efforts to be recognized and to exercise their collective rights.

But these critics speak from a position different from the one we take. For us, our job as intellectuals is not straightforwardly to work toward the self-determination of nations. Rather, we understand our job to be to examine under what circumstances varied ideas of the nation (and the nation-state) emerge, do or do not become hegemonic, are modified, or disappear. In that sense, our interest in the economic mobilization of linguistic nationalism is intended to ask what is actually happening, and what its consequences might be for the idea of the nation and for the social actors invested in or marginalized by it.

The second critique emerges from the field of economics, in particular from the work of Swiss economist and language policy analyst François Grin. Grin was trained by François Vaillancourt, a Montréal-based economist who developed some of the most widely used measures for analyzing whether specific linguistic groups have better or worse chances than average to earn income, and that are part of the analytical apparatus used by the francophone political movement to which Forgues and Doucet contribute (e.g., Vaillancourt 1985). Grin therefore shares with them the idea that language can be understood as a variable, the relationship of which to the economy relies on understanding it as a property of producers and consumers. As with Forgues and Doucet, his goal is concomitantly different from ours; it focuses on the development of a model of economic activity, which he calls "language economics." His concern with our work is primarily that it does not provide the resources for language economic modeling, and therefore is unable to generate estimates of just how much being able to use a language is worth, whether to individuals or to the agglomerated economy in which they participate.

The field of "language economics" is defined by Grin and Vaillancourt (2012: 1) as situated within "the paradigm of mainstream theoretical economics"; it "uses the concepts and tools of economics in the study of relationships featuring linguistic variables." Its main areas of inquiry have included the link between language proficiency and income, economic development, and minority languages or national languages and gross domestic product (see Grin 2014 for an overview). Grin's perspective on language economics has been very influential in public policy discussions in Switzerland and the European Union.

Grin argues that our analysis has nothing to do with what economists feel is central to what they do. He argues that our use of terms like "market," "resource," and "commodity," inspired by the work of Bourdieu (1982), can be understood only as metaphorical, and hence we really should not be using them or claiming to have anything to say about the workings of capitalist economies. At best, we can be cited as having tracked the emergence of economistic discourses, but this should not be confused with any shift in the actual economy:

It [our work] offers an (otherwise very stimulating) analysis of some aspects of language from a sociolinguistic angle, but it offers no economic angle – it simply happens to formulate propositions with reference to a macro-level context that presents some economic features. This is not to say that there are no genuine language economics questions in the background of such contributions, but a fair amount of work remains necessary to bring them to light, and language economics may prove useful to this end. (Grin 2014:19)

We disagree both on what counts as data and on what the purpose of analysis should be. The goal of Grin's language economic approach is to provide predictive models of the interaction among variables understood as distinct entities. Where language is concerned, such an economic approach does not in fact seek to measure anything connected to an object called "language," but rather seeks to examine what difference it might make to individual income and to regional or national productivity in the context of (individually or collectively) possessing language skills. This requires abstracting out the problem of what it means to claim to possess language skills, and how they actually relate to income and economic productivity. More importantly, for Grin (2014), this requires grappling with how to turn language into a quantifiable variable, a problem, he agrees, that is not easily solved.

Although Grin does agree that a fine-grained understanding of communication processes, for which very micro-, and even "'nano-level' applied linguistics is useful," he is not convinced that such data can be of value except "heuristically" (2014: 19). Put differently, the language economics approach requires the assumption that we know what the market is and what knowing a language is, as well as reducing both to quantifiable variables. It does so in order to discover how resources are allocated and what difference that makes to individual or collective wealth. The approach we take, inspired by Bourdieu and anthropological conceptions of language, requires us to ask how people organize their economic exchanges, and how those exchanges are intertwined with (and precisely *not* separable from) the accumulation of social, cultural, and political capital. Our approach does share Grin's interest in understanding what difference access to linguistic resources makes to people, individually and collectively. However, we work with a broader idea of what kinds of resource distribution might be involved and what kinds of differences could be made (e.g., effects on status, prestige, and meaning).

Put differently, we do share an interest in some central questions, involving what difference something called "language" or "linguistic proficiency" makes to the ability of a person to earn a living or own property of some kind, the ability of a group of people to produce commodities and profit, how value is assigned to linguistic commodities, and the role of language in the functioning of the market. Where we differ is in how we think those things can be observed and accounted for, namely, as processes rather than as unified variables.

Where we differ further is in what we want to do with this information. We do not seek to develop a static, universal, predictive model. Rather we seek to discover what conditions make some ideas of language (as emblematic of cultural authenticity or a technical skill) interesting as potential zones of commodification. We further seek to discover what consequences commodification of language in those ways has for the ability of certain kinds of people to attribute value to it or to exchange it profitably; for the principles of political, social, and cultural organization with which it is intertwined; and even for our very ideas about what language is.

The third critique comes from a Marxist perspective on political economy and has been summarized by Kenneth McGill (2013). The concern within this frame has been to compare our use of the notion of commodity with that in general circulation in Marxist theory. Put differently, this critique suggests that if we have not shown that language acts purely as a commodity on clearly bounded and identifiable markets, it is misleading to use the term. Further, this critique argues that our work assumes, rather than demonstrates, that conditions are in some ways different from those we have known from the emergence of capitalism.

In a recent review of our book *Language in Late Capitalism*, McGill (2013) suggests, following Polanyi (2001/1944), that "commodities only exist within functioning markets, and Heller's approach does not clearly specify that heritage tourism itself constitutes a functioning market in Ontario, much less that assembled instances of heritage tourism can be legitimately labeled as constituting a market in French language production" (2013: 85). In other words, it would be legitimate to refer to "commodities" only if we could show how they are produced and are consumed within a market whose conditions explain their value or, more importantly, their impact on "rents" (or, broadly, profits relative to those of competitors).

For McGill, it is necessary for the analyst to quantitatively measure the exchange value of linguistic resources in order to show that they are commodities. The argument is that, in our perspective, we need to show how social actors attempt to quantitatively measure linguistic resources in order to demonstrate an attempt at commodification. However, as we argue in Section 4, McGill's critique does point us to the importance of examining exactly in what ways linguistic resources are treated as commodities, and whether or not they are actually successfully convertible as such.

Nonetheless, it is important to reiterate that we do not consider that language is now completely understandable, and only understandable, as a commodity, but rather that it seems, under specific historical conditions, to be increasingly inscribed (albeit not always successfully and not always in exactly the same ways) in processes of commodification (and decommodification). We do agree that there remains much work to be done on both how those processes work and what their implications for social change (or reproduction) might be. In particular, it is clear that we can learn a great deal from a closer ethnographic examination of the processes of commodification, circulation, contestation, and decommodification as they unfold over time and across space, with particular attention to processes of conversion. McGill does point us to an important concern: We need to distinguish between linguistic commodification and some of the other ways in which language is part of economic activity, just as it forms part of the unfolding of any other social activities. Just because we see attempts at linguistic commodification, that does not mean that acting as a commodity is the only way in which language is economically relevant.

The three sets of concerns we have outlined in this section leave us with two kinds of conclusions. In the next section, we draw out what we think needs to be done from within the perspective that underlies our work on this subject so far, responding as best we can, without radically shifting our epistemologies, to the need articulated by both Grin and McGill to explore further to what extent attempts at linguistic commodification are in fact successful, under what market conditions, and with what impact on the market. This does require, we agree, closer attention to the workings of markets across sectors of activities, especially in those areas where we believe language plays the greatest role: in the development of niche products and niche markets, in the construction of the flexible worker, and in the management of globalized networks of production, exchange, and consumption. It additionally requires attention to the processes of commodification, decommodification, and recommodification (following Appadurai) and in particular to the attribution of value to them. More broadly, it requires attention to the role of language in the distribution of resources more generally.

In developing this line of thought, we respond indirectly to the first set of critiques, taking the position that we are better off understanding how shifting conditions challenge legitimating discourses and practices (like distribution of state funds) of linguistic nationhood than fighting against them. For it is by understanding what is happening, and why, that we can make out what the consequences might be and for whom. It is also in this way that we can better understand what a political economic approach to language does and does not permit.

4.   Beyond commodification

We have identified several sets of questions that we believe deserve more empirical attention. A first set relates to the fluctuating nature of commodification attempts. Indeed, not every speaker and not every language skill has the same value everywhere and at all times. Having Japanese in her language repertoire may help a manager get a better job in a multinational company, and being a multilingual in French, German, English, and Italian may ease a tourism worker's entry into the job market. At the same time, being fluent in Portuguese and Spanish in Switzerland does not necessarily constitute capital useful for gaining access to interesting positions; on the contrary, this particular multilingual repertoire can be easily constructed as problematic – even as a deficit – since it does not encompass the country's official languages.

In addition, specific language skills may be needed only in relation to particular markets. For instance, a call center that wants to expand its clientele to include the Turkish market may be looking for employees with Turkish in their repertoire. Yet there is no guarantee that the new market will succeed, and the Turkish-speaking employee will likely be fired quickly if the targeted benefits are not attained. As another example, certain competences are capitalized on in daily practice but are not officially acknowledged. For instance, a hotel maid could be asked to translate an email from a Polish client into French. Her language skills are capital for the hotel, but they do not provide her personally with any form of added value. In such cases, multilingual expertise entails variable forms of (mis)recognition; that is, in this case her skills are recognized as important but are misrepresented as a central asset for her as an employee. Indeed, it is only under certain conditions that language emerges as economic capital; under other conditions, a multilingual repertoire can instead become the object of exploitation. We need to better examine the specific processes that allow for the conversion of linguistic capital into other forms, particularly financial ones. In that sense, we need to go beyond economists' correlations of claimed proficiency and income to see what is actually worth what, how, and why.

A second set of questions has to do with a better understanding of what counts as a resource in linguistic terms, and how these resources are managed and regulated by the economic sectors, given the messiness of the market, ever-changing consumer expectations, and the shifting nature of work. By documenting and analyzing the various economic appropriations of linguistic resources, we might be able to better explain how language is inscribed in the mechanisms of exchange and production in late capitalism, and how it becomes the object of control in relation to attempts to locate measurable criteria of productivity (such as the number of phone calls answered in X languages, the number of successful transactions fulfilled, the number of words translated, or the number of seconds needed to understand instructions). However, we will argue, possibly contra McGill, that such measures have to be understood in relation to ideologies of language and work in contexts that pertain to them.

A second dimension of looking at what it means to treat language as a resource requires examining the ways in which language skills operate as selection criteria, and how they get alternately emphasized and marginalized in relation to the fluctuation of the market (i.e., what this particular form of its trajectory in commodification-decommodification-recommodification looks like). This includes discovering how the idea of language "skill" is concretely operationalized.

The third dimension involves using the lens of linguistic resources to shed light on the ways in which the other symbolic and material resources with which they are convertible are valued or not, how they circulate, where, and for what purposes. The linguistic resource lens also opens up investigation of the dynamic process linking the exploitation of resources and the producers of these resources, thereby shedding light on possible asymmetrical interests and outcomes. As we have already mentioned, linguistic resources might become a source of profit for the economy, but they are not necessarily a profit for those who produce them. They also lead us to reexamine the precarious and unpredictable nature of the linguistic market (cf. Kelly-Holmes, this volume, Chapter 7).

A third set of questions has to do with resistance to profit and to attempts to commodify language. If we have been interested so far at looking at the ways in which language has been gradually treated as an economic resource, we believe that there is a need to examine the processes by which people, communities, and organizations of various kinds might resist these new trends, why they do so, and what alternatives they propose.

Fourth, we can ask whether there is anything empirically new in what we are seeing, or whether we are simply asking questions we could have asked long ago. We think both are true. The ways we have been formulating questions need to be extended, understood as a process in which (among other things, of course) conversion happens (or fails to), under certain conditions. We can do a better job of connecting the dots, following the process, seeing where it comes from and where it leads, and under what conditions, that is, when specific kinds of resources are available. At the same time, the economy-expanding conditions of late capitalism also intensify competition and heighten the economic role of language in a number of ways. What is new, then, is perhaps extension and intensification rather than an entirely new phenomenon, but with increasing tensions between nation-state and postnational ideologies of language. Closer attention to processes, and to the interrelationship between discourses and practices, as well as specifically the discourses and practices of pride and profit, would allow us to better understand the consequences of change and continuity in the ways language operates in social life and the ways in which language inequalities and differences might be both challenged and/or reproduced under current social and economic conditions.

More broadly this requires linking the study of linguistic commodification to the study of governmentality (Urla 2014; see also Rampton, this volume, Chapter 14), that is, to the conditions under which it makes sense or not to try to treat language as commodity. Framing linguistic commodification in this way allows for the exploration of the cultural organization of symbolic and material markets. By looking at the ways in which forms of knowledge production and the regulation of social actors shift or remain the same, we can pinpoint to what extent the conditions of late capitalism change the grounds for social and economic mobility.

REFERENCES

Allan, Kori. 2013. Skilling the self: The communicability of immigrants as flexible labour. In Alexandre Duchêne, Melissa Moyer, and Celia Roberts (eds.), *Language, Migration and Social Inequalities: A Critical Sociolinguistic Perspective on Institutions and Work*. Bristol, UK: Multilingual Matters, 56–78.

Appadurai, Arjun. 1986. Introduction: Commodities and the politics of value. In Arjun Appadurai (ed.), *The Social Life of Things: Commodities in Cultural Perspective*. Cambridge: Cambridge University Press, 3–63.

1996. *Modernity at Large: Cultural Dimensions of Globalization*. Minneapolis: University of Minnesota Press.

Bourdieu, Pierre. 1982. *Ce que parler veut dire*. Paris: Seuil.

Bowles, Samuel, and Herbert Gintis. 1977. *Schooling in Capitalist America*. New York: Basic Books.

Castells, Manuel. 2000. *The Information Age: Economy, Society and Culture.* 3 vols. Oxford: Blackwell.

Duchêne, Alexandre, and Mi-Cha Flubacher. 2015. Quand légitimité rime avec productivité: La parole d'œuvre plurilingue dans l'industrie de la communication. *Anthropologie & Société* 39, 3: 173–196.

Duchêne, Alexandre, and Monica Heller (eds.). 2012. *Language in Late Capitalism: Pride and Profit.* London: Routledge.

Flubacher, Mi-Cha, and Alexandre Duchêne. 2012. Eine Stadt der Kommunikation?: Mehrsprachigkeit als wirtschaftliches Argument. *Bulletin Suisse de Linguistique Appliquée*, 95: 123–145.

Forgues, Éric, and Michel Doucet. 2014. *Financer la francophonie canadienne: faire société ou créer un marché de services?* Moncton: Institut de recherche sur les minorités linguistiques.

Giddens, Anthony. 1990. *The Consequences of Modernity.* Berkeley: University of California Press.

Grin, François. 2014. 50 years of economics in language policy. Critical assessment and priorities. ELF (English as a Lingua Franca) *Working Papers* 13, Université de Genève.

Grin, François, and François Vaillancourt. 2012. Multilingualism in economic activity. In Carol Chapelle (ed.), *Encyclopedia of Applied Linguistics.* Wiley-Blackwell (on line) DOI: 10.1002/9781405198431.wbeal0808.

Heller, Monica. 2007. Bilingualism as ideology and practice. In Monica Heller (ed.), *Bilingualism: A Social Approach.* London: Palgrave, 1–22.

   2010. The commodification of language. *Annual Review of Anthropology* 39: 101–114.

Heller, Monica, Lindsay Bell, Michelle Daveluy, Hubert Noël, and Mireille McLaughlin. 2014. La mobilité au coeur de la francophonie canadienne. *Recherches Sociographiques* 55, 1: 79–104.

McGill, Kenneth. 2013. Political economy and language: A review of some recent literature. *Journal of Linguistic Anthropology*, 23, 2: 84–101.

Park, Joseph, and Lionel Wee (eds.). 2012. *Markets of English: Linguistic Capital and Language Policy in a Globalizing World.* London: Routledge.

Polanyi, Karl. 2001/1944. *The Great Transformations: The Political and Economic Origins of Our Time.* Boston: Beacon Press.

Silva, Emanuel da, and Monica Heller. 2009. From protector to producer: The role of the state in the discursive shift from minority rights to economic development. *Language Policy* 8, 2: 95–116.

Sheller, Mimi, and John Urry. 2006. The new mobilities paradigm. *Environment and Planning* 38, 2: 207–226.

Tan, Peter, and Rani Rubdy (eds.). 2008. *Language as Commodity: Global Structures and Local Marketplaces.* London: Continuum.

Urciuoli, Bonnie. 2008. Skills and selves in the new workplace. *American Ethnologist* 35, 2: 211–228.

Urla, Jackie. 2014. Landscapes of language ideology: Pride, profit and governmentality. Plenary address given at 2nd International Symposium, New Speakers in a Multilingual Europe, Barcelona, November 20–22, 2014.

Vaillancourt, François. 1985. *Économie et langue*. Québec: Conseil supérieur de la langue française.
Weber, Eugene. 1976. *Peasants into Frenchmen*. Stanford, CA: Stanford University Press.
Zappettini, Franco. 2014. "A badge of Europeanness": Shaping identity through the European Union's institutional discourse on multilingualism. *Journal of Language and Politics* 13, 3: 375–402.

7   Theorising the market in sociolinguistics

Helen Kelly-Holmes

More than forty years since it first appeared, it is interesting to speculate about how Labov's (1972) department store study would be reviewed, received, and perhaps framed in a sociolinguistics journal today. Reading his paper from a contemporary perspective, the three department stores used in the study come across as sites primarily selected for finding and observing socially distinguishable groups interacting in three differently stratified shops. This is, I would argue, in contrast to the current approach which might place the commodification of accent at the heart of the analysis. In this chapter, I would like to explore what has happened in the intervening forty-plus year period, both in sociolinguistics and in society, to transform the market from one of a number of domains of everyday interaction to an overriding concern in contemporary sociolinguistic studies.

The chapter starts with a brief overview of the treatment of the market in early sociolinguistic research, using Labov's study as an illustration to show how markets were treated in much the same way as other domains where sociolinguistic data could be gathered. I then go on to argue that two main developments challenged this treatment of market domains. The first was Bourdieu's (1991) conceptualisation of the linguistic market, in which he advocated on the one hand a recognition of the economic foundations of all linguistic exchanges, whilst on the other arguing for the treatment of economic exchanges as just another type of exchange. The second was the development of Critical Discourse Analysis (CDA), particularly the British School, led by Norman Fairclough (e.g.1995; 2001), a key objective of which was the unmasking of the pervasiveness of market discourses across society. This period in sociolinguistics can be seen as one in which the domain of the market was put under a critical spotlight, largely in response to increasing marketisation of society and neoliberalism in the global political economy.

Having reviewed these two developments, the chapter moves on to the current period, in which the market is no longer restricted to a particular domain, but potentially impacts on all aspects of language in society. This corresponds with a societal transition from marketplaces as bounded physical spaces to a concept of the marketised society (Slater and Tonkiss 2000), and an acceptance among social theorists and sociolinguists of the increasing commodification of all aspects of life, including linguistic aspects (see Heller and Duchêne, this volume, Chapter 6).

Markets as sites

What is striking about early sociolinguistic research is that markets come across as simply another site for sociolinguistic fieldwork. If we look at Labov's (1972) study, for example, he describes how he chose the relevant department stores:

> to observe the public use of language in everyday life apart from any interview situation – to see how people use language in context when there is no explicit observation ... [to provide] an account of the systematic use of rapid and anonymous observations in a study of the sociolinguistic structure of the speech community. (p. 49)

So, for his study, a shop is chosen as an unremarkable domain of 'public use of language in everyday life' and an integral part of the speech community. In his contextualisation of the department stores, Labov acknowledges their functions, describes their respective niche markets and key distinctiveness in relation to each other (in terms of the class of customer they attract and their location in stratified areas of New York City), using market texts, for example advertising, as one of the sources for this. He comments on the prices and types of product on sale, and he also gives us information about wage structures and unionisation in the stores. What he does not do, and what I think would be very hard for a study of this type in the contemporary era not to do, is theorise this market domain and link the buying and selling that happens in the store – the market processes – to the production of the particular speech varieties. For the original study, the data could conceivably have been collected in a school or on public transport in the vicinity of the respective department store. The use of department stores, in the case of all three of Labov's locations and in order to access the speech of three distinct social categories of speaker, narrows the uncontrollable variables, and the choice is based on convenience and representativeness rather than on the economic activities taking place there.

The approach in Labov's study is illustrative not just of the approach in sociolinguistics, but also of consumer culture and social conditions of the time. In terms of the former, Eckert (2012) points out that the focus in early sociolinguistics was on 'filling cells defined by macro-sociological categories' (p. 88). In her words, such studies:

> interpreted the social significance of a general understanding of the categories that served to select and classify speakers rather than through direct knowledge of the speakers themselves and their communities. (Eckert 2012: 90)

So, we can see in Labov's study how upper-middle-class speech production is expected in the store that is deemed to target and attract upper-middle-class shoppers. Shoppers are assumed to stick to their designated social stratification, and this dictates their shopping and habits and linguistic behaviours. There is no evidence here of the boundary-transgressing, late modern consumer who may frequent all three stores and who is unpredictable and unclassifiable in his or her habits.

The department stores could reasonably be considered as unremarkable field sites for the observation of stratified speech because of the consumer culture of the time. It can be argued that the department store of the 1970s could still be seen as a 'marketplace' – a physical and public place, spatially and temporally located and bounded. The physical marketplace has, however, given way over time to the 'abstract notion of the market' (Slater and Tonkiss 2000: 9). The growing marketisation of society involves this transition from physical marketplaces to the abstract, ubiquitous market:

Rather than a specific place, time or institution ... the modern, abstract market is not visible as an event, but constituted through an instrumental gaze concerned with opportunities to buy and sell. (Slater and Tonkiss 2000: 19)

While the society of the 1970s was certainly not a premodern era or a premarket society in the United States, Slater and Tonkiss (2000) argue that it is 'the neoliberal restructuring of advanced capitalist and transnational economics since the 1980s' that has made the market idea central to Western societies. So, it could be argued that, at the time of the early variationist studies, marketplaces were still bounded field sites, 'local and public', which constituted unremarkable sites for sociolinguists. Shoppers went to marketplaces to shop, and the activity was demarcated and delimited to that place.

It is important to point out that this approach to marketplaces as normal, bounded sites for the collection of data has continued, for example, in sociolinguistic studies of workplaces (e.g. Coupland 1980; Clyne 1994), in interactional sociolinguistics (e.g. Holmes and Marra 2002; Holmes 2006), and in language policy research (cf. Spolsky [2009], who has consistently argued for a broadening of domains in which sociolinguists work), particularly in the language management strand of language policy theory (Neustupný and Nekvapil 2003; Nekvapil 2006).

This chapter, as outlined above, argues that two developments in particular have changed the way in which markets are treated compared with this early period: The first is Bourdieu's linguistic market, and the second is the evolution of CDA. Both took place at the start of the 1990s, a time of language-rich social sciences, with the so-called linguistic turn, both in academe and elsewhere.

Bourdieu and the linguistic market

Bourdieu sees linguistics as at the root of the problem in social sciences. In his words:

The linguistic model was transposed with such ease into the domain of anthropology and sociology because one accepted the core intention of linguistics, namely the intellectualist philosophy which treats language as an object of contemplation rather than as an instrument of action and power. (Bourdieu 1991: 37)

This resulted in a predictable and unproductive 'opposition between economism and culturalism' (Bourdieu 1991: 37), and, as a consequence, the market was largely ignored by linguists, who were exclusively concerned with the latter. He critiques the earlier approaches outlined above and accuses linguists of being focused solely 'on one of the factors involved – a strictly linguistic competence, abstractly defined, ignoring everything that it owes to the social conditions of its production – it tries to give an adequate account of discourse' (Bourdieu 1991: 38). His argument was that linguists were content with 'bracketing off' economic conditions (Bourdieu 1998: 94–95).

Bourdieu advocated, on the one hand, that 'mercantile exchange' be treated simply 'as a particular case of exchange in all its forms' (Bourdieu 1986: 84). On the other, he stressed that economic capital was 'at the root of all the other types of capital and that these transformed, disguised forms of economic capital [e.g. cultural and social capital] . . . produce their most specific effects only to the extent that they conceal the fact that economic capital is at their root' (Bourdieu 1986: 91). So, economics is at the root of everything, but economic exchange is just one part of our economy of practices, which is, however, underpinned by economics.

He argued for the conceptualisation of an economy of symbolic exchanges and a reintroduction of the concept of capital,

in all its forms and not solely in the one form, recognised by economic theory. Economic theory has allowed the economy of practices which is the historical invention of capitalism; and by reducing the universe of exchanges to mercantile exchanges, which is objectively and subjectively oriented towards the maximization of profit, i.e. [economically] self-interested, it has implicitly defined the other forms of exchange as non-economic and therefore disinterested. (p. 83)

By allowing special status for economic exchanges, bracketing off market conditions, and pursuing 'culturalism', linguists had allowed elites to get off too lightly. This also resulted in a romanticizing of the pursuit of sociolinguistics. As Bourdieu puts it, 'the world of bourgeois man with his double-entry account cannot be invented without producing the pure perfect universe of the artist and the intellectual and the gratuitous activities of art-for-art's sake' (Bourdieu 1986: 84). His argument echoes and has been echoed by other linguists, who have critiqued the romanticisation of the objects of sociolinguistic inquiry and their positioning as 'apart' from markets. Indeed, Rampton (2013) has warned of a similar danger in the new concern with superdiversity in sociolinguistics. In contrast, what Bourdieu was arguing for was:

a general science of the economy of practices, capable of re-appropriating the totality of the practices, which, although objectively economic, are not and cannot be socially recognised as economic, and which can be performed only at the cost of a whole labour of dissimulation or more precisely euphemization, [that] must endeavour to grasp capital and profit whereby the different types of capital change into one another. (1986: 84)

His thesis of the linguistic market was deliberately intended to counteract 'partial views' such as 'economism, which, on the grounds that every type of capital is reducible in the first analysis to economic capital, ignores what makes the specific efficacy of the other types of capital, and, on the other hand, semiologism, which reduces social exchanges to phenomena of communication and ignores the brutal fact of universal reducibility to economics' (Bourdieu 1986: 91). This is despite the realisation that 'in reproducing linguistic expressions speakers take into account – in varying ways and to differing extents – the market conditions within which their products will be received and valued by others' (Thompson 1991: 19). Building on this, Heller (2010) points out that while Bourdieu's market is metaphorical, it does have an economic start and an economic finish, since 'how one speaks, and writes is one basis for deciding one's worth as a scholar, an employee, or a potential marriage partner' (p. 102).

We can also see that this applies to language choice in more concrete market domains. For example, linguistic (code, accent) choices, metalinguistic comments and framing, and discourse choices are decided on the basis of there being more or less chance of profit from these choices (e.g. accent catalogues which are used by radio stations to match particular voices to particular products in advertising). Thompson (1991) reminds us that 'the distribution of linguistic capital is related in specific ways to the distribution of other forms of capital (economic capital, cultural capital, etc.) which define the location of an individual within the social space' (p. 18). The profit of distinction (Thompson 1991: 18), which previously applied only to speakers, perhaps, now applies more generally to languages in a broad sense (see Heller 2010; Heller and Duchêne, this volume, Chapter 6).

Fairclough and Critical Discourse Analysis

CDA, understood by Fairclough (2001) to be 'part of a broadly conceived sociolinguistics' (p. 6), railed against the very invisibility and taken-for-grantedness of the marketplace that was a feature of the invisibility era outlined above. The mission of CDA, which itself was the product of a growing concern with discourse rather than language alone in the 1980s, has been to examine the 'connections between language use and unequal relations of power' (Fairclough 1992: 1). CDA therefore set about uncovering and abnormalising commonsense and everyday practices, and its focus has been on taken-for-granted practices that in their very ordinariness 'do ideological work' every day on the ground in unremarkable ways. The advertisements seen and heard, the commercial landscape encountered, interactions in shops, and the familiar aisles of supermarkets add up to a type of 'banal capitalism' (borrowing from Billig's 1995 concept of banal nationalism).

Fairclough (2001) describes how he came to develop CDA as a response to sociolinguistic approaches to date, which had, in his view, echoing Bourdieu's concern, been content with attempting to 'describe prevailing sociolinguistic conventions in terms of how they distribute power unequally'. In contrast, he wanted to 'explain these conventions as the product of relations of power and struggles for power' (2001: 1). So, in his view, sociolinguistics was strong on 'what' with a 'positivist orientation to facts' (p. 6–7) but weak on 'why'.

Fairclough (2001) identified a 'turn to language' in academe and in society in general which has forced a more in-depth engagement in linguistic issues for other social sciences, and with economic and societal issues for linguists: 'The "turn to language" means that the struggle to impose or resist the new order is in large part a struggle for or against a new language' (p. 203). He defined this new order as 'a shift in the relationship between the market and the state which has characterised capitalism for most of the twentieth century, freeing the market from state controls and undermining the role of the state in providing social welfare and converting the state into a local advocate and agent for the free market' (p. 204). He saw two main roles for language in this new order: first, as part of the knowledge economy, so part of the product (p. 205); second, as part of the means of maintaining some sort of order within the complexity of this new order (pp. 204–205). He saw language as 'doubly involved in the struggle to impose the new neo-liberal order': on the one hand because language is a main way of participating in this new order; secondly because language is a main way of representing and winning acceptance for this new order (2001: 205).

A key driver for the development of CDA was a recognition of the growing marketisation of society, and the gradual replacement of marketplaces with the market:

one major tendency in current sociocultural change ... is marketization – the reconstruction on a market basis of domains which were once relatively insulated from markets, economically, in terms of social relations, and in terms of cultural values and identities. I argue that marketization is to a significant degree a discoursal process – it is partly constituted through colonization by the discursive practices of market domains, such as advertising. (Fairclough 1995: 19)

Fairclough's work, in particular, has been responsible for defamiliarising everyday market practices, setting them into relief for critical examination and deconstruction. The class relations taken for granted in Labov's study are thus subject to exposure through linguistic analysis in CDA, since domination by one class – in collusion with ruling private and public institutions – over another 'is exercised through discourse' (Fairclough 1992: 27). Language is considered 'both a site of and stake in class struggle, and those who exercise power must constantly be involved in struggle with others to defend (or lose) their position' (p. 29).

In such an understanding, a department store could never just be another field site or place to observe everyday language. In line with Bourdieu, Fairclough sees the approach in variationist sociolinguistics as 'descriptive' rather than 'explanatory', which CDA sets out to be, particularly in relation to the capitalist economic system that underlies all aspects of social interaction.

A key objective in CDA has been to show the ubiquity of marketisation and associated discourses, which involves the invasion of a whole range of non-market domains (family and personal life, childhood, education, charity and welfare, health) by the ideological discourses of the market domain:

the capitalist economic domain has been progressively enlarged to take in aspects of life which were previously seen as quite separate from production. The commodity has expanded from being a tangible 'good' to include all sorts of intangibles: educational courses, holidays, health insurance and funerals are now bought and sold on the open market in 'packages' rather like soap powders. And an ever greater focus has been placed upon consumption of commodities, a tendency summed up in the term consumerism. As a result, the economy and commodity market massively impinge upon people's lives, including especially through the medium of television, their private lives in the home and the family. (Fairclough 1992: 29)

CDA thus developed in response to growing marketisation, and the transition, as mentioned above, from the concrete marketplace to the ubiquitous yet nebulous market, a society in which 'one mode of exchange – based on market transactions – has come to dominate, restructure or marginalize all others' (Slater and Tonkiss 2000: 8). Thus, one of the concerns of CDA has been to examine – partly with a view to offering emancipatory alternatives and/or at least empowering people through awareness (see e.g. Clark et al. 1990) – the discursive colonisation by the market domain of other domains such as education and public institutions (e.g. Fairclough 1993 regarding higher education institutions).

This unmasking of the banality of the market and its discourses meant that market processes could no longer be seen as just another 'normal' domain of language use, as in the early period outlined above. CDA and the discourse analysis shift from which it grew introduced a much greater level of engagement with written texts and mediated texts than had previously been the case in sociolinguistics, which had a fairly exclusive focus on oral, ideally naturally occurring or elicited data. Media texts are seen in CDA as tied up in the same relations of domination and as vehicles for reproducing the taken-for-grantedness of market conditions. Thus, their treatment tended to be in terms of critiques of representations and the uncovering of commonsense ideologies in texts, rather than in terms of sites of sociolinguistic practice. However, this mainstreaming of media texts in sociolinguistics can be seen as, at least in a limited way, contributing to the subsequent mainstreaming of the domain of the market, since mediation and the market are inextricably linked in contemporary society, and so many media texts are also at the same time market-driven texts. The growing engagement with media texts as a result of the expansion of (written) discourse analysis, and CDA in particular, necessarily led to a greater engagement with and mainstreaming of the market domain.

Political economy of language versus variation in the marketised society

Reflecting on these two key theoretical developments in relation to markets and commodification, we can see that both had seemingly contradictory effects on the treatment of the market. Bourdieu's impact is felt in the ubiquity of the market and its mainstreaming as a topic; Fairclough's and CDA's in general can be seen to have resulted in an othering of the market as negative agent. With both of these in mind, we move on to look at current studies involving markets and commodification.

Heller (2010) highlights the dual nature of the current preoccupation with markets in sociolinguistics:

The recent interest in language as commodity points to a specific and emergent form of the exchange value and requires explanation on two levels. One level relates to the extent to which forms of exchanges (standardized language for jobs, for example) that used to be treated discursively as matters of breeding, taste, etc. are now treated as directly exchangeable for material goods, and, especially, for money. The other concerns the extent to which the circulation of goods ... now depends on the deployment of linguistic resources. (p. 102)

Heller sees two ways in which languages are commodified, and these are reflected in current concerns of sociolinguistics: The first is as a technical skill that can be measured, while the second is as a sign of authenticity and a way of adding distinction to niche markets (2010: 102). She identifies tourism, marketing and advertising, language teaching, translations, call centres, and performance art as 'areas of particular salience for illustrating the ways in which the commodification of languages is tied to late capitalism, as well as [illustrating] some of tensions and contradictions of commodifying language' (p. 107).

Building on Bourdieu and Fairclough, Heller (2010) hints at the need to acknowledge the ubiquity of the market for sociolinguists in the following:

> This material also suggests that the attention linguistic anthropology has traditionally paid to the fine-grained working of semiosis in specific sites needs to be tied to analyses of political economic condition, and more particularly to the circulation of symbolic and material resources, to their active (albeit constrained) deployment, and to the complex interpenetrations of the construction of subjectivities of categorization (that is, of social difference), and of relations of power (that is, of social inequality). (p. 110)

Likewise, Chouliaraki and Fairclough (1999) remind us of 'the potency of economic discourses in shaping economic realities' (p. 4) in the current era. This is primarily the result of a growth in cultural commodities, which constitute 'an important and growing category of commodities in contemporary capitalism' (p. 10). Cultural commodities 'consist of signs – they are semiotic. What is produced, circulated and consumed in the case of cultural commodities is words and images ... What is different about cultural commodities ... is the increased salience of discourse within them' (p. 10). They argue that 'within this shift, language becomes increasingly commodified – it comes to be treated, worked, according to the logic of commodities' (p. 10). Furthermore, they identify, in common with Heller, 'a process of extending the market economy and the language of the market economy, of social and linguistic normalization' (p. 12). They conclude that 'in late modernity, boundaries between social fields and therefore between language practices have been pervasively weakened and redrawn, so that the potential seems to be immense' (p. 12).

These developments are reflected in two main strands of work in contemporary sociolinguistics: political economy/commodification of language studies and sociolinguistic studies which take place in a marketised society. This focus on commodification of language is not surprising in the current era. The transformation from marketplace to 'the abstract concept of the market' outlined above, the transitional crisis of which was perhaps witnessed during the era of the emergence of the linguistic market and CDA, now seems complete. The contemporary era is deemed to encompass two kinds of dependency on markets: 'the production of things and services is profoundly governed by the need to sell things on the market; and the reproduction of everyday life and culture is governed by the need to buy things in markets' (Slater and Tonkiss 2000: 24). Consequently, we are witnessing the commodification of 'things that were normally viewed as inalienable' and the 'transforming into saleable objects, of social phenomena which were previously not framed in that manner' (p. 24). It seems clear then that language, like other inalienable objects, can be commodified (but see Heller and Duchêne's careful reconsideration of this issue in this volume, Chapter 6). The market domain is therefore not just another area of sociolinguistic practice, or another domain for the reproduction of unequal economic, social, and power relations exercised through language (as in CDA), but instead a necessary prerequisite for contextualising how 'the globalized new economy is bound up with transformations of language and identity' (Heller 2003: 473).

Heller (2003) is particularly concerned with the commodification of language through its functioning as both product and process in the 'new economy' of late capitalism. The new economy can be understood in terms of the abstract notion of 'the market' – the opposite of the marketplace: It involves private, shifting spaces, which are temporally and territorially unbound, and it is characterised by language-rich service industries. Heller (2003) sees this market as actually changing the fundamental nature of the relationship between language and identity. In her work on francophone Canada, she argues that there has been 'a shift in understanding language as being primarily a marker of ethnonational identity, to understanding language as being a marketable commodity on its own, distinct from identity' (p. 474). Tourism, as pointed out above, is the exemplar domain for demonstrating this, and many of the current studies of language and the market domain focus on global tourism (e.g. Pujolar 2006; Heller and Pujolar 2009; Jaworski 2009; Jaworski and Thurlow 2010; Duchêne and Heller 2012). In addition, a focus on the role of English in the global political economy of language has also enhanced our understanding of language and market relations (see, e.g. Rubdy and Tan 2008).

Variationist sociolinguistic studies now take place within a marketised society. Eckert (2012) characterises the current era in terms of a move 'from a view of variation as a reflection of social identities and categories to the linguistic practice in which speakers place themselves through stylistic practice' (p. 94). Thus, speakers are agentive, creative, transgressive, and unpredictable, and cannot be relied upon to produce speech appropriate to their social categorisation upon elicitation or observation – upper-middle-class shoppers do not always shop in upper-middle-class department stores. Replicability, representativeness, and predictability, which can be considered important criteria in early studies, are also no longer considered seminal. Rather than looking for typical patterns and typical speakers, instead, one-off, 'spectacular' (Sweetland 2002) uses of language are no longer simply dismissed as 'an accidental event, but [treated as] a continuous process in which linguistic features of all sorts are continually imbued with a variety of meanings'. 'Spectacular' uses of language, what Sweetland (2002) also terms 'inauthentic language', have thus recently become 'prized for understanding the social meanings that adhere to language varieties and the many ways in which speakers can put such ideologies to work' (Sweetland 2002: 138). This shift from an interest in patterned, authentic, group language behaviour to random, 'inauthentic' (in terms of an essentialised understanding of language and identity), individual, and one-off performances also favours the market domain and commodified displays, as it is here that we find some of the most creative and ideologically astute examples of language play, primarily in advertising, which has been a major focus (e.g. Haarmann 1989; Gerritsen et al. 2000; Piller 2001; 2003; Martin 2002; 2007; Dimova 2012). For example, the concept of linguistic fetish (Kelly-Holmes 2000; 2005; 2014) builds on the Marxian concept of commodity fetish to explain variation in economically driven displays, such as marketing and advertising texts. In linguistic fetish, the symbolic or visual value of a language takes precedence over its communicative value, and this symbolic value is the product of existing linguistic hierarchies and semiotic regimes, including ways of seeing. Linguistic fetish, then, results in a highly refined version of multilingualism, informed by a culturally determined gaze. It is a type of decoration or linguistic 'colour by numbers', which has everything to do with the producer's perception of the consumers' own linguistic culture or habitus. Linguistic colour by numbers describes, for example, the very contained, prescribed parameters by which words from other languages are used in advertisements. The choice is driven primarily not by what the word means, but by how it looks, what associations the language may have among target addressees, and how these can be triggered by the appearance of the foreign word.

Consequently, the contemporary market society throws up much that is of interest to the sociolinguist: 'commercialization has produced – for whatever nefarious reasons of its own – an unprecedented range of symbolic resources for common (everyday) culture through which people necessarily construct their own symbolic universe' (Slater and Tonkiss 2000: 185). Not surprisingly, all of this has resulted in what Stamou (2014) has described as 'a shift of contemporary sociolinguistic research towards media and pop cultural discourse' (p. 119). Thus, unlike the early era, when marketplaces were simply taken-for-granted domains of language practice, and the critical era, when the transition from marketplace to market society and the emergence of CDA rendered the market an invalid domain of sociolinguistic activity, the current era has to engage with the market domain and consider it pertinent in almost every area of sociolinguistic practice.

Discussion

Like Bourdieu, Slater and Tonkiss (2000: 33) trace an 'intellectual division of labour' between economics and business, on the one hand, and the other social sciences and humanities, on the other, which had a common origin, but which diverged into opposing intellectual forces. 'Culture', a preoccupation for sociolinguists, has 'played a strategic role in defining the 'other' of rational economic action in a market society' (p. 149; see also Bourdieu 1986). This concern with rationality in economics has made it the 'other' for sociology and, by extension, sociolinguistics: 'While economists occupied themselves with rational, maximising behaviours in markets, the study of "irrational" (affective, rule-governed, ritual, deviant, customary) behaviour was left to sociologists and anthropologists' (Slater and Tonkiss 2000: 92). Gal (2012; cf. Chapter 5) argues similarly in relation to linguistic forms that an 'axis of differentiation' between 'pride' and 'profit' developed over time, and it could be argued that sociolinguists were traditionally interested in the former, namely 'pride', which was 'aligned with particularities of emotion/passion, creativity and specificity in time and place', with the latter, 'profit', being the domain of market rationality and economics 'aligned with supposedly universal time, place and interest' (Gal 2012: 27).

Early sociolinguistic studies could be seen either to have developed in isolation, along an already diverged path in the humanities, in which the market domain was not of concern, or, quite the opposite, in fact, to have developed with a more holistic view of all aspects of society, including the market domain. The CDA era certainly can be seen to have developed much more in line with thinking in the other social sciences, where rationality consciously (as opposed to subconsciously) represented the other, and on the basic principle of a 'belief that pre- or post-market societies allow a wholeness of both individual and society' and 'the desire for a return to a mythic, premodern past' (Slater and Tonkiss 2000: 34).

Current variationist studies acknowledge the centrality of the market society in sociolinguistic practice, with 'a view of modern consumer capitalism . . . in which marketed goods [are] at the centre of a new cultural populism, and markets appear . . . as places of diversity, play and anti-elitism' (Slater and Tonkiss 2000: 168). Thus, in this approach, variation is still the primary focus, but the society which is being studied has changed, and the approach and focus acknowledge that 'consumer culture provides a very particular set of material circumstances in which individuals come to acquire a reflexive relation to identity' (Lury 2010: 29; see also Coupland 2007; Blommaert 2010; Pennycook 2010; Rampton 2010; Bell and Gibson 2011).

The other contemporary strand, which could broadly be termed political economy and commodification studies in the contemporary era, although it developed very differently, can nevertheless be seen to be much more closely aligned with the view of society espoused in the CDA era, and with other social sciences, particularly sociology, in terms of its view of 'the market'. Here, the problematic of the marketisation of society is the primary focus, and the commodification of language is one example of this. In a review of recent work on political economy of language, McGill (2013; see also discussion in Chapter 6) concludes that while 'in recent years sociolinguists have made the claim that language has achieved the status of commodity on a broad scale' (p. 85), 'problems regarding the clear designation of language as a commodity continue to exist' (p. 87). He argues that what sociolinguists are terming 'commodification of language' or 'linguistic commodification' may in fact be better understood as the 'framing' of language as a commodity or an economic resource in the language policies of governments, companies, tourist agencies, schools, and so on. He takes the literalist position that there has to be an actual exchange of money for 'language', and sociolinguistic studies have to show how the use of a particular language, variety, and so on actually attracts money and/or an enhanced price (cf. Johnstone 2009).

McGill's literalist stand, however, is in contrast to Bourdieu's metaphorical use of 'the market' for language, which has been so influential in contemporary sociolinguistics, and we can see a particular line of influence from Bourdieu to the current work on political economy and commodification studies. Therefore, the use of the term 'commodification' in contemporary sociolinguistics can be seen in the tradition of sociology, the 'other' of economic science, which treats the term as a macro-process.

So, the first approach in contemporary sociolinguistics could be said to be about *language in/and the market*. The market as a domain is of central and increasing importance in contemporary society and a site where many of the phenomena of interest to contemporary sociolinguists can be found; to study variation (multilingualism, accents, dialects, sociolects, heteroglossia) in contemporary society is necessarily to engage with its marketisation, and this can lead to enhanced understandings of these phenomena (linguistic fetish, impersonal bilingualism, bilingual display, etc.). The second, the linguistic commodification/political economy approach, could be seen to be about the *market in/of/for language*. Linguistic practice is just one area in the social sciences where we can see the contemporary and ubiquitous processes of marketisation and commodification at work (see, e.g. Erreygers 2005; Duchêne 2009).

From an original treatment as just another field site for sociolinguists, therefore, the market domain has evolved to one that is ubiquitous in sociolinguistics. As a result, we can see a healthy level of engagement with the market, albeit in two parallel, complementary strands: One has its origins in early variationist studies and works with and within relevant domains of contemporary society, this being the marketised society of the current era; the other continues a critical and problematizing treatment of market relations and language as a special case, effecting sociolinguistic change and dominating all other domains. Although there is a tendency and temptation to treat both as sharing an interest in processes of commodification, each offers different insights into sociolinguistic theory. The former, I would argue, continues to inform our understanding of the micro-level functioning of linguistic variation in contemporary society, whereas the latter offers macro, sociology-of-language perspectives on how the dominant paradigm of contemporary society – the market – impacts on language.

REFERENCES

Bell, Allan, and Andy Gibson. 2011. An introduction to the sociolinguistics of performance. *Journal of Sociolinguistics* 15: 555–572.
Billig, Michael. 1995. *Banal Nationalism*. London: Sage.
Blommaert, Jan. 2010. *The Sociolinguistics of Globalization*. Cambridge: Cambridge University Press.
Bourdieu, Pierre. 1986. The forms of capital. In J. Richardson (ed.), *Handbook of Theory and Research for the Sociology of Education*. New York: Greenwood, 241–258.
    1991. *Language and Symbolic Power*. Oxford: Polity Press.
    1998. *Acts of Resistance against the Tyranny of the Market*. New York: The New Press.
Chouliaraki, Lilie, and Norman Fairclough. 1999. *Discourse in Late Modernity: Rethinking Critical Discourse Analysis*. Edinburgh: Edinburgh University Press.
Clark, Romy, Norman Fairclough, Roz Ivanič, and Marilyn Martin-Jones. 1990. Critical language awareness. Part I: A critical review of three current approaches to language awareness. *Language and Education* 4, 4: 249–260.
Clyne, Michael. 1994. *Intercultural Communication at Work: Cultural Values in Discourse*. Cambridge: Cambridge University Press.
Coupland, Nikolas. 1980. Style-shifting in a Cardiff work-setting. *Language in Society* 9: 1–12.
    2007. *Style: Language, Variation and Identity*. Cambridge: Cambridge University Press.
    2012. Bilingualism on display: The framing of Welsh and English in Welsh public spaces. *Language in Society* 41: 1–27.
Dimova, S. 2012. English in Macedonian television commercials. *World Englishes* 31, 1: 15–29.
Duchêne A. 2009. Marketing, management and performance: Multilingualism as a commodity in a tourism call center. *Language Policy* 8, 1: 27–50
Duchêne, Alexandre, and Monica Heller (eds.). 2012. *Language in Late Capitalism: Pride and Profit*. London: Routledge.
Eckert, Penelope. 2012. Three waves of variation study: The emergence of meaning in the study of sociolinguistic variation. *Annual Review of Anthropology* 47: 81–100.
Erreygers, G. 2005. *Language, Communication and the Economy*. Amsterdam: John Benjamins.

Fairclough, Norman. 1992. *Discourse and Social Change*. Cambridge: Polity Press.

1993. Critical Discourse Analysis and the marketization of public discourse: The universities. *Discourse and Society* 4: 133–168.

1995. *Critical Discourse Analysis*. Boston: Addison Wesley.

2000. Discourse, social theory, and social research: The discourse of welfare reform. *Journal of Sociolinguistics* 4: 163–195.

2001. *Language and Power*, 2nd ed. London: Longman.

Gal, Susan. 2012. Sociolinguistic regimes and the management of 'diversity'. In Alexandre Duchêne and Monica Heller (eds.), *Language in Late Capitalism: Pride and Profit*. London: Routledge, 22–42.

Gerritsen, M., H. P. L. M. Korzilius, W. F. J. van Meurs, and I. Gijsbers. 2000. English in Dutch commercials: Not understood and not appreciated. *Journal of Advertising Research* 40, 4: 17–31.

Haarmann, H. 1989. *Symbolic Values of Foreign Language Use: From the Japanese Case to a General Sociolinguistic Perspective*. Berlin: Mouton de Gruyter.

Heller, Monica. 2003. Globalization, the new economy, and the commodification of language and identity. *Journal of Sociolinguistics* 7, 4: 473–492.

2010. The commodification of language. *Annual Review of Anthropology* 39: 101–114.

Heller, Monica, and Joan Pujolar. 2009. The political economy of texts: A case study in the structuration of tourism. *Sociolinguistic Studies* 3, 2: 177–209.

Holmes, Janet. 2006. *Gendered Talk at Work: Constructing Gender Identity through Workplace Discourse*. Malden, MA, and Oxford: Blackwell.

Holmes, Janet, and Meredith Marra. 2002. Having a laugh at work: How humour contributes to workplace culture. *Journal of Pragmatics* 34, 12: 1683–1710.

Jaworski, Adam. 2009. Greetings in tourist-host encounters. In Nikolas Coupland and Adam Jaworski (eds.), *The New Sociolinguistics Reader*. Basingstoke and New York: Palgrave, 662–679.

Jaworski, Adam, and Crispin Thurlow. 2010. Language and the globalizing habitus of tourism: Towards a sociolinguistics of fleeting relationships. In Nikolas Coupland (ed.), *Handbook of Language and Globalisation*. Oxford: Wiley-Blackwell, 255–286.

Johnstone, Barbara. 2009. Pittsburghese shirts: Commodification and the enregisterment of an urban dialect. *American Speech* 84: 157–175.

Kelly-Holmes, Helen. 2000. Bier, parfum, kaas: Language fetish in European advertising. *European Journal of Cultural Studies* 3: 67–82.

2005. *Advertising as Multilingual Communication*. Basingstoke and New York: Palgrave-MacMillan.

2014. Linguistic fetish: The sociolinguistics of visual multilingualism. In David Machin (ed.), *Visual Communication* (Handbooks of Communication Science). Berlin: de Gruyter, 135–150.

Labov, William. 1972. *Sociolinguistic Patterns*. Philadelphia: University of Pennsylvania Press.

Lury, Celia. 2010. *Consumer Culture*. Cambridge: Polity Press.

Martin E. 2002. Cultural images and different varieties of English in French television commercials. *English Today* 18, 4: 8–20.

2007. 'Frenglish' for sale: Multilingual discourses for addressing today's global consumer. *World Englishes* 26, 2: 170–188.

McGill, Kenneth. 2013. Political economy and language: A review of some recent literature. *Journal of Linguistic Anthropology* 23, 2: E84–E101.

Nekvapil, J. 2006. From language planning to language management. *Sociolinguistica* 20: 92–104.

Neustupný, J. V., and Jiří Nekvapil. 2003. Language management in the Czech Republic. *Current Issues in Language Planning*, 4, 3–4: 181–366.

Pennycook, Alastair. 2010. *Language as a Local Practice*. London: Routledge.

Piller, Ingrid. 2001. Identity constructions in multilingual advertising. *Language in Society* 30, 2: 153–186.

2003. Advertising as a site of language contact. *Annual Review of Applied Linguistics* 23: 170–183.

Pujolar, Joan. 2006. *Language, Culture and Tourism: Perspectives in Barcelona and Catalonia*. Barcelona: Turisme de Barcelona.

Rampton, Ben. 1995. *Crossing: Language and Ethnicity among Adolescents*. London and New York: Longman.

2010. Speech community. In Jürgen Jaspers, Jan-Ola Östman, and Jef Verschueren (eds.), *Society and Language Use* (Handbook of Pragmatics Highlights 7). Amsterdam: John Benjamins.

2013. Drilling down to the grain in superdiversity. *Working Papers in Urban Language & Literacies* 98, www.kcl.ac.uk/ldc.

Rubdy, R., and P. Tan (eds.). 2008. *Language as Commodity: Global Structure, Local Marketplaces*. London: Continuum.

Slater, Don, and Fran Tonkiss. 2000. *Market Society: Markets and Modern Social Theory*. Oxford: Polity Press.

Spolsky, Bernard. 2009. *Language Management*. Cambridge: Cambridge University Press.

Stamou, Anastassia. 2014. A literature review on the mediation of sociolinguistic style in television and cinematic fiction: Sustaining the ideology of authenticity. *Language and Literature* 23: 118–140.

Sweetland, Julie. 2002. Unexpected but authentic use of an ethnically-marked dialect. *Journal of Sociolinguistics* 6: 514–538.

Thompson, J. B. 1991. Editor's introduction. In Pierre Bourdieu, *Language and Symbolic Power*. Oxford: Polity Press.

8   Embodied sociolinguistics

Mary Bucholtz and Kira Hall

Introduction: *Habes corpus!*

Bodies and embodiment are central to the production, perception, and social interpretation of language.[1] In spoken languages, the body is the locus of the speaking voice and the listening ear, while in the case of sign languages the body supplies the grammar for the entire linguistic system (cf. Lucas and Bayley, this volume, Chapter 16), a fact that has important consequences for theorizing language in general as an embodied phenomenon. Embodiment is also enlisted in a variety of semiotic practices that endow linguistic communication with meaning, from the indexicalities of bodily adornment to gesture, gaze, and other forms of movement. And just as bodies produce language, so the converse also holds: Language produces bodies. That is, language is a primary means by which the body enters the sociocultural realm as a site of semiosis, through cultural discourses about bodies as well as linguistic practices of bodily regulation and management. Moreover, even as technologically mediated forms of communication may seem to displace physical bodies as sources of linguistic production, the body insistently reasserts itself in communicative practices in the spheres of technology and the media.

Despite the crucial role of embodiment in producing social meaning through language and vice versa, a broad-based discussion within sociocultural linguistics concerning the theoretical relationship between language and embodiment is largely lacking. Hence what we engage here is not a current debate but a needed interdisciplinary conversation that includes sociocultural linguists of all stripes (see Coupland and Gwyn 2003, inter alia, for one valuable starting point for this dialogue).

In part this lack of dialogue among research traditions can be attributed to methodological and analytic differences, which often prevent scholars

---

[1] Our thanks to Nik Coupland for providing us the opportunity to explore these ideas in this volume and for his valuable comments on earlier drafts of this chapter. Thanks are also due to Brenda Farnell and Joshua Raclaw for offering useful feedback and reference suggestions. Our failure to heed these readers' sound advice on a few key points should not be construed as their fault in any way.

investigating embodiment in one domain from drawing on work in other areas. But it is also due to a tendency in much sociolinguistic research to conceptualize the body as secondary to language rather than as the sine qua non of language. Perhaps this is unsurprising given that the discipline of linguistics as conventionally practiced is logocentric almost by definition. Within generative linguistics in particular, most embodied phenomena have been ignored or viewed as background noise or "performance" rather than as part of the abstract grammatical system of "competence" imagined to be the proper subject of linguistic scholarship. Empirical work in embodied cognitive science departs from this view by arguing that linguistic knowledge is grounded in the body's perceptual and motor systems (e.g., McNeill 1985; 1992; Bergen et al. 2003; Bergen 2007), yet dominant theoretical perspectives continue to characterize language production and comprehension as based in mental representations involving the manipulation of abstract symbols. Professional language ideologies notwithstanding, embodiment is quite literally how language works. Hence the subtitle of this section revises the familiar legal phrase to remind readers of a fundamental truth: 'You have a body!'

In this chapter, we call for an embodied sociolinguistics – or, more precisely, an embodied sociocultural linguistics (Bucholtz and Hall 2008).[2] Drawing on scholarship from a variety of approaches that contribute to this interdisciplinary field, we discuss work on embodiment that centers on several important analytic areas: the voice; the bodily semiotics of style and self-presentation; discourses and counterdiscourses of the body; embodied motion, action, and experience; and the mediation of embodiment by material objects and technologies. Although we focus primarily on embodiment, the body participates in a wide array of material contexts and processes, and so we do not sharply distinguish embodiment from other aspects of materiality (Shankar and Cavanaugh 2012; Cavanaugh and Shankar forthcoming). The primary goal of our discussion is to bring different perspectives into dialogue with one another. A second goal is to suggest the sorts of analytic issues that an embodied sociocultural linguistics can address – topics that may be viewed as marginal to or entirely outside some branches of sociocultural linguistics yet are crucial to the advancement of the field as a whole. A final goal is to explore the theoretical consequences of placing embodiment at the center of sociolinguistic inquiry. In the five realms we examine, we consider in particular how a

---

[2] In this chapter, as in our other work, *sociocultural linguistics* is a cover term for the broad interdisciplinary study of language, culture, and society, similar to the inclusive spirit in which the term *sociolinguistics* is intended in this volume. Although most of the scholars we discuss in this chapter do not use the label *sociocultural linguistics* for what they study, we find the term useful for highlighting the social and cultural dimensions of such scholarship. The adjective *sociolinguistic* is used without disciplinary or subdisciplinary implications to describe any phenomenon or activity involving language, culture, and society.

focus on bodies broadens sociocultural linguists' understanding of the key concepts of indexicality, discourse, and agency. Recognizing that these and other core concepts are both material and linguistic is crucial to the ongoing development of sociocultural linguistics as a fully embodied field of inquiry.

Indeed, in some ways sociocultural linguistics is ideally positioned to quite literally incorporate the body into the study of language, given many researchers' theoretical predisposition to see these two domains as integrated rather than antithetical. By contrast, the scholarly perception of a fundamental division between discourse and materiality has long driven debate in other fields. However, a number of theorists have challenged this dichotomy, most influentially – and controversially – Judith Butler (1990; 1993), via her insight that the gendered body is the product of discourse rather than biology.[3] This and related ideas have helped spark sociolinguistic research on the politics of embodiment and especially of bodily difference on the basis of gender assignment or identity, sexual identities and practices, racial categorization, and ideologies of health, ability, and physical normativity or acceptability. Through such work, sociocultural linguists from various traditions have already advanced the linguistic understanding of embodied processes and phenomena. Before we turn to research that illustrates the simultaneously embodied and linguistic processes of indexicality, discourse, and agency, however, we first consider early work in the field that introduced an integrated perspective on language and the body.

Finding the body in sociocultural linguistics

The body has been of enduring interest to researchers of language, culture, and society, as attested by a range of early agenda-setting interdisciplinary volumes that included at least some attention to embodiment (e.g., Hymes 1962; Gumperz and Hymes 1964; Giglioli 1972; Pride and Holmes 1972; Bauman and Sherzer 1974). The 1950s saw the emergence of areas of inquiry sometimes known as *kinesics*, *proxemics*, and *paralanguage*, which drew on ideas from structural linguistics, anthropology, and other fields to investigate the cultural workings of gesture, gaze, and the arrangement of bodies in space, usually based on the meticulous analysis of film recordings of face-to-face interaction (e.g., Hall 1959; Birdwhistell 1970; Key 1975; Kendon 1990). Alongside such research, the work of Erving Goffman offered wide-ranging analyses of embodied phenomena derived primarily from sociological field observations,

---

[3] As noted below, a number of material feminists have critiqued Butler for what they view as her privileging of discourse and erasure of the material realities of embodiment; in our reading, however, Butler's theories recognize the importance of the body without reducing it to a precultural prime.

including such issues as the role of embodiment in the social management of the self (1967; 1971), bodily and behavioral stigma (1963), and the visual representation of the gendered body (1979).

Ethnomethodology, as a related line of research within sociology, has also addressed embodiment as part of its focus on social norms as interactional accomplishments. This issue was explored most famously through the case study of a young trans woman, Agnes, who presented herself to clinicians as intersex in order to receive gender-corrective surgery (Garfinkel 1967); this study inspired later feminist-informed ethnomethodological work on the accomplishment of gender that arguably anticipated and provided an empirical grounding for Butler's perspective (West and Zimmerman 1987).

Developing from ethnomethodology, conversation analysis focuses on interactional norms at an even finer level of detail, but aside from a few pioneering scholars who habitually used film and/or video data and incorporated embodiment into their earliest analyses and continue to do so (e.g., Goodwin 1981; Heath 1986), most early work stemming from conversation analysis drew on audio recordings or analyzed film recordings without close attention to embodied action. A great deal of data was taken from telephone conversations, which were seen as obviating the need to consider bodily phenomena in any detail. However, in more recent years, conversation analysts have been at the forefront in investigating the use of the body in interaction. In addition, a second strand of early embodied research in conversation analysis focused on prosody (French and Local 1986; Local and Kelly 1986), a line of investigation that has continued in later scholarship (e.g., Couper-Kuhlen and Selting 2006).

Meanwhile, within anthropology the ethnography of communication and interactional sociolinguistics also attend to the relationship between language and embodiment, informing contemporary research on the body in linguistic anthropology. The ethnography of communication takes as its starting point the question of what counts as communicative in particular cultural contexts (Gumperz and Hymes 1964; Bauman and Sherzer 1974; Hymes 1974), including not only speech but also embodied and material phenomena ranging from drumming to movements of the body to claps of thunder. Interactional sociolinguistics, which in some ways built on the 1950s work on face-to-face interaction but typically offers greater ethnographic and linguistic nuance, examines how fine-grained aspects of talk, including intonation as an embodied aspect of linguistic structure, may be used to perform culturally specific interactional functions (Gumperz 1982).

Another strand of scholarship, rooted in M. A. K. Halliday's theory of social semiotics (e.g., Halliday 1978; Hodge and Kress 1988), has long given sustained attention to material and embodied phenomena through the lenses of critical linguistics and critical discourse analysis (Kress and Hodge 1979;

Fairclough 1989), multimodality and visual communication (Kress and van Leeuwen 1996; 2001), and mediated discourse analysis (Scollon 2001). This broad research tradition focuses more closely on textual and mediatized materialities than the frameworks discussed above; consequently, embodiment itself has been less central to these perspectives than the semiotic representation of materiality generally (but see Norris 2004; Norris and Jones 2005).

By contrast with these early sociolinguistic engagements with bodily and material phenomena, for many years the study of language within variationist sociolinguistics was for the most part a disembodied undertaking. This situation can be understood as the result of both methodological constraints and theoretical orientation. By the 1960s variationist sociolinguistics was becoming an increasingly technology-dependent field, using relatively inexpensive and portable audio recording equipment (at the time, reel-to-reel recorders; later, analog cassette recorders and eventually digital formats) to elicit vernacular language in situ in speakers' neighborhoods and homes. Examination of embodied linguistic practices would have been impeded by the greater bulkiness and cost of film recording technology, particularly given the quantity of data typically required for variationist analysis compared with early interactional microanalyses. In addition, the prospect of filming may have raised concerns about participant self-consciousness and the resulting effect on the data in an era when even audio recording was still a novelty (cf. Labov 1972).

The central obstacle to examining language as an embodied phenomenon within early variationist sociolinguistics, however, was theoretical, not methodological. To begin with, a focus on language as traditionally conceived was necessary to gain legitimacy as a still young and marginalized field within the discipline. Moreover, early analyses gave priority to phonological variation at the segmental level, with secondary attention to morphological and syntactic variation; hence less well-understood embodied linguistic phenomena, such as intonation, were largely set aside (for an important exception see Guy and Vonwiller 1984; Guy et al. 1986). But most significantly, early variationist sociolinguistics viewed its primary task as the investigation of variation as language change in progress; hence, many of the most influential researchers in the field concerned themselves with ongoing changes in linguistic patterning rather than with the place of language in a broad communicative field encompassing the full range of embodied practices. However, more recent developments in what are sometimes termed *second-wave* and *third-wave sociolinguistics* (cf. Eckert, this volume, Chapter 3; Bell, this volume, Chapter 18) have introduced the body into variationist sociolinguistics as part of a larger reframing of the field around social semiosis (Eckert 2012). We next examine how this new line of work, along with contemporary research in linguistic anthropology and other areas, offers theoretical purchase for an embodied sociocultural linguistics via its focus on the semiotic process of indexicality.

Embodied indexicality

The notion of indexicality, or the production of contextualized meaning, arises from bodily engagement with the world. In his various formulations of the three basic sign relations, Charles Sanders Peirce consistently characterizes indexicality as a fundamentally material relation that includes "all natural signs and physical symptoms"; he offers "a pointing finger" as the exemplar of the index (1885: 181). Sociocultural linguists have extended Peirce's original idea of indexicality to encompass the ideologically saturated semiotic processes that produce social meaning, giving rise to a long tradition of research on language ideologies (Silverstein 1979; Woolard and Schieffelin 1994; see also Part I of this book, Chapters 2–5).

However, as scholars recognize, language ideologies go beyond indexicality, readily enlisting an iconic dimension that links social categories to a bodily hexis that is imagined to be the source of socially marked linguistic forms or practices; iconicity thus positions language as a symptom of bodily disposition (Irvine and Gal 2000; Silverstein 2003; 2005; Eckert 2008; Woolard 2008). In other words, sociocultural beliefs about language rely on indexical iconization (Carr 2011; cf. Silverstein 2003; 2005), an ideological process that rationalizes and naturalizes semiotic practice as inherent essence, often by anchoring it within the body. Indeed, the body may be physically deployed in the service of furthering language ideology, such as when speakers perform stereotyped "gay speech" through the flap of a limp wrist or parody "teenage girl talk" with the accompanying embodied posture of taking a selfie with a cellphone. The iconic dimension of indexicality is therefore a central issue for an embodied sociocultural linguistics, as shown especially in studies of the voice as well as research on style.

The voice

The voice is the embodied heart of spoken language: It emerges from the body, and through indexicality it auditorily locates the body in social space as being of a particular kind.[4] Recent sociophonetically informed scholarship on the

---

[4] By *voice* we refer to the production of speech via phonation and related physical processes. We do not intend the problematic liberationist metaphor of voice as empowerment (cf. Bucholtz, Casillas, and Lee forthcoming) nor the Bakhtinian metaphor of voice as a socially distinctive style that can be interwoven with other styles (e.g., Bakhtin 1981), although voice and style are often connected, as discussed below.

voice examines how such phenomena as phonation type, pitch, and the articulatory production of phonemes are employed by speakers as well as interpreted by listeners, especially in relation to categories of gender, sexuality, and race. While most research on the gendered and sexualized indexicalities of the voice in particular has been experimental in nature (Munson and Babel 2007), the social meaning of the voice cannot be ascertained without consideration of the local cultural context within which it is used and heard (Weidman 2014). Ethnographically based studies of the semiotics of the voice (Podesva 2007; Mendoza-Denton 2011; Zimman 2013; Harkness 2014) demonstrate that it does not directly index race, gender, or sexuality; rather, voice phenomena, like all linguistic acts, in the first instance perform specific cultural and interactional functions (Nielsen 2010; Sicoli 2010; Podesva 2013), yet in so doing they also come to be ideologically associated with specific social categories (cf. Ochs 1992).

Such research clearly illustrates the role of indexical iconization in the relationship between language and embodiment. For example, Robert Podesva's (2013) study of gender, race, and phonation type argues against the sociobiological claim put forth by John Ohala (1994) that high pitch is iconic of smallness, femaleness, and nondominance, an association that Ohala asserts is innate across species. Podesva's finding that African American women, more than African American men or European American women, use falsetto to take negative evaluative stances reveals instead a far more complex indexical field (Eckert 2008), in which falsetto, as an extreme form of phonation, becomes iconically linked to particular kinds of powerful stances. More generally, because the voice is grounded in the body, it can be ideologically linked to particular ways of using the body (e.g., to display power) or to particular types of people who are believed to use their bodies and voices in those ways (e.g., African American women). But because the association of the voice with social qualities is fundamentally indexical and gains an iconic overlay only through ideological processes, any such association is a historically contingent sociopolitical construct, not an innate biological fact.

Style and embodied self-presentation

Much of the recent sociophonetic work on the indexical iconization of the voice emerges from the retheorizing of sociolinguistic style as a set of practices for displaying social stances and personae in local sociocultural contexts (e.g., Rampton 1995; Eckert 2003; Coupland 2007).[5] This shift placed embodiment squarely on the research agenda of sociocultural linguists concerned with

---

[5] The notion of stance is of course itself also a partly embodied concept, as explored in some recent sociolinguistic research on this topic (e.g., Jaffe 2009).

language variation. From this perspective, the stylistic meaning of a linguistic variant cannot be determined in isolation; instead, stylistic analysis requires examination of the place of specific semiotic forms within a wider system of social meaning. This may involve attention to sociolinguistic variation at multiple levels: segmental phonology, grammar, prosody, and the lexicon (e.g., Mendoza-Denton 2008).

More radically, from the standpoint of semiosis there is no conceptual difference between stylistic variables based in language and those based in (other forms of) embodiment. As Eckert (1989; 2000) demonstrates in her study of U.S. high school students, which is deeply influenced by Dick Hebdige's (1979) visual study of youth styles, style is produced not only through speakers' use of a locally innovative versus conservative vowel or a standard versus nonstandard grammatical form but also through the color and cut of their clothing, their usual lunch hangout – even their preferred controlled substance. Likewise, Latino teenage boys in Chicago index their ethnonational identities as either Mexican or Puerto Rican through finely observed differentiation of their hairstyles (Rosa forthcoming), while young Tamil men in urban South India adorn themselves with counterfeit brands and cheap brand-inspired clothing to establish a peer-oriented aesthetics that downplays class and caste hierarchy (Nakassis forthcoming). In styles, linguistic and embodied practices align to produce a culturally meaningful whole (even if the assemblage of features exploits semiotic dissonances between established stylistic meanings). Thus the semiotics of style includes all dimensions of language as well as material and embodied resources of self-presentation, which together yield ideologically cohesive semiotic packages available for interpretation by others (see also Bucholtz 2015).

Here again, indexical iconization is at work, for it is embodied variables that give semiotic meaning to linguistic variables rather than the reverse. That is, to make semiotic sense of themselves and others, social actors link specific embodied ways of being in the world to ideological expectations regarding specific ways of speaking. To use the categories at the heart of Eckert's high school study, a bubbly, clean-cut jock girl who favors pastels should not talk like a tough, black-clad, chain-smoking burnout. By the same token, a nonstandard form like multiple negation, which linguistically iconizes the nonconformity of the burnout style, cannot be indexical of jock identity without a reconfiguration of the entire semiotic system. Although such iconicity is always ideological, it may have a physical basis: In later work, Eckert (2010) argues that early adolescent girls may exploit sound symbolism within the vowel system to make themselves variously sound small and childlike or more grownup and knowledgeable about teen activities. Given the acoustic properties of these vowels, it is unlikely (but not impossible) that they could be assigned the contrasting indexicality.

This and other research on style and the bodily presentation of self is often ethnographic in its approach, for it is only through a deep understanding of local semiotics that the sociocultural meaning of embodiment can be recognized. Such scholarship demonstrates that although the social meaning of bodily practices is contingent on situated cultural and historical factors, via ideology this contingency is erased and meaning is instead viewed as inherent and fixed in the body. This process of ideologization depends on the establishment and circulation of hegemonic discourses of embodiment. We turn now to a consideration of how discourses of the body categorize and evaluate bodily difference, as well as how these discourses may be countered through the agentive discursive work of embodied social actors.

Embodied discourse

The idea that the body is discursive as well as material is pivotal to much of the recent sociolinguistic scholarship on embodiment, especially within the field of language, gender, and sexuality. The poststructural theorizing of the body as a discursive construction is most closely associated with Butler's (1990; 1993) critique of feminism's traditional distinction between biological sex and social gender (see also Zimman and Hall 2009). For Butler, the sexed body, though imagined to be a biological truth, is meaningful only because discourse makes it so. Her work draws heavily from Michel Foucault's (1970; 1978) genealogical critique of the classification schemes of science not as objective fact, but rather as constituted through disciplinary histories of discourse (cf. Rampton, this volume, Chapter 14). As Foucault shows, whether a homosexual act is construed as sin or sickness – or, more recently, as part of the normal range of human sexuality – depends on the prevailing discourses in a given era. Similarly, Butler argues, bodies become intelligible as female or male by entering discursive systems that recognize them as such.

Although some critics charge that Butler and similar theorists reduce intractable material realities to "mere words," the recognition of the intimate connection between discourse and materiality in fact advances scholarly understanding of both concepts by foregrounding the very real material consequences of discursive regimes. This general perspective informs a wide range of sociolinguistic scholarship focused not only on gender and sexuality but also on such embodied categories as race, health, and disability. Bringing together linguistic analysis of the details of discursive structure and Foucauldian notions of discourses as systems of productive power and knowledge, a wealth of linguistic scholarship on the categorization, evaluation, and regulation of varied body morphologies demonstrates the central role of discourse in maintaining and challenging the borders of ideologically recognized and valued kinds of bodies.

Discourses of the body

One of the clearest examples of the discursive dimension of embodiment is the lexicon of gendered body parts investigated by researchers of language, gender, and sexuality. Work in this vein focuses on how speakers bring meaning to the body by conspiring with dominant discourses on gender – for example, men who access metaphors of violence and conquest when coining terms for the penis (Cameron 1992) or students who use patterns of slang that perpetuate homophobia and misogyny (Sutton 1995; Armstrong 1997; Thurlow 2001). Such research establishes how normative discourses of gender inform dichotomous understandings of female and male embodiment as well as the sexual acts that gendered bodies are expected or permitted to perform. In an echo of Foucault, Virginia Braun and Celia Kitzinger's (2001) study of dictionary definitions of women's and men's genitals reveals that even scientific genres such as medical dictionaries rely on such ideological dichotomies. Whereas female genitals are described by these texts in terms of their location in the body, male genitals are described in terms of function, reinforcing popular understandings of men's sexuality as more active than women's. Such binary representations are slow to change, sedimented through discursive iteration and perpetuated across discourse genres. For this reason, the quantitative methods of corpus linguistics are particularly suited to investigating the repetitive reach of these constructions (Baker 2008; Motschenbacher 2009).

Sociolinguistic research on the medicalized body likewise offers empirical evidence in support of Foucault's claim that biomedical categorizations are created in discourse. Charles Briggs (2011) has coined the term *biocommunicability* to highlight the ways that illness is transformed when medical discourses leave the laboratory and travel into the media domains of public health and journalism. His work illustrates that even "virtual epidemics" such as the West Nile virus in San Diego or, more recently, the Ebola virus in Houston can be made "real" through the discourses of mediatization. The embodied effects of mediatization can also be seen in multimodal analyses that show how photographs of the human body become semiotic resources in mediatized discourses that range from tourism advertising (Caldas-Coulthard 2008) and war journalism (Chouliaraki 2007) to representations of sexual citizenship (Milani 2015). Other potential discursive transformations of the body arise when medical information moves – or fails to move – across cultural and linguistic borders. Scientific discourses on HIV/AIDS, for example, do not enter easily into cultural contexts in which talk about sex is taboo (Pigg 2001; Brookes 2011; Black 2013). In such cases, the body is shaped and reshaped by the linguistic systems available and the language ideologies that inform them.

From discourse to counterdiscourse in body talk

Although a focus on hegemonic discourse reveals how the body is regimented, language users do much more than unthinkingly repeat discursive hand-me-downs. The body is far from stable, shifting across time and space as speakers collaboratively construct new investments in the semiotics of physicality. For example, discourses of aging as loss of beauty may be both circulated and challenged in talk among older professional dancers (Coupland 2013). Further, researchers have documented how discourses of the body change across generations, as seen in studies of talk about body size (Wetherell 1996; Guendouzi 2004) and of new bodily discourses emergent within the context-ualized identity concerns of social groups. The trans men discussed by Lal Zimman (2014), for example, disrupt normative ideologies of the body when they describe their surgically unaltered genitals as "transcocks," "boycunts," and "bonus holes." By remapping the expected links between sex and gender, these men authenticate themselves as masculine even if their embodiment is not normatively male. In contrast, India's hijras, a group historically recog-nized as a "third" biological sex, publicly reproduce the popular myth that they are asexuals "born without genitals" in order to prevent further marginaliza-tion, even as they engage privately in sexual acts with men (Hall 2005). As in queer theory, much of this research involves persons whose bodies do not easily materialize within female/male binaries of social gender (see also Hall 2009; King 2015).

The above examples indicate that any analysis of the categorizing power of bodily discourses must consider the audience's role in shaping discursive production. As shown in the many embodied categories commonly discussed in sociocultural linguistics – race, ethnicity, gender, sexuality, class, age – as well as categories that are now gaining attention, such as ability, the body is a dialogic product, co-constructed in the back and forth of speakers and hearers. Susan Speer and Richard Green's (2007) conversation analysis of an inter-action between a trans woman seeking sexual reassignment surgery and her evaluating psychologist – a study that explicitly recalls Garfinkel's classic work with Agnes – brings this issue into sharp focus. In this pressure-laden institutional setting, the patient's multimodal presentation of her appearance – or more poignantly, her attempt to display a "passing" femininity – is contin-gent on the type of participation enacted by the psychologist. Likewise, H. Samy Alim's (forthcoming) discussion of his own experiences of transra-cialization demonstrates how racial classification is read through situational logics of language, culture, and sociopolitical relations. The regulatory power of bodily discourses can also be seen in teenagers' collaborative and audience-oriented evaluative talk about the body size of others, as well as the responses by the targets of such teasing (Taylor 2011). Such studies of the jointly constructed and emergent nature of bodily categorizations indicate that an exclusive focus on culturally dominant discourses of the body misses the crucial role of agency in producing and circulating counterdiscourses of embodiment.

Embodied agency

As the preceding discussion suggests, discursive agency is not merely a matter of language. The relationship between the body and discourse is more productively viewed as bidirectional or even recursive (Edelman and Zimman 2014). That is, as a material entity that is both enabled and constrained by physical possibility, the body offers certain affordances that shape the trajectory of semiosis, even if a particular outcome cannot be predicted in advance. Thus, agency is produced through a network of entities – or interactants (Latour 2005) – that are both semiotic and material. A new line of scholarship from interactional analysis and embodied cognitive science even argues that the body has its own agency separate from the speaker, based on accumulated tactile and haptic experiences and skills (Streeck 2013). This focus on embodied motion and experience expands sociolinguistic theory to recognize and accommodate the distribution of agency beyond language to include human bodies as well as nonhuman entities, such as animals, other living beings, material objects, and the physical world.

Embodied motion

Perhaps the most basic mechanism of embodied agency is the process through which fleeting embodied phenomena such as eye gaze and gesture as well as more sustained movements of the body work with and without talk to perform particular social actions (e.g., Streeck et al. 2011; Haddington et al. 2013). By examining the moment-to-moment sequential progression and social coordination of embodied motion, interactional researchers are able to show in fine detail how minute movements such as the flash of an eyebrow, the twist of a torso, or the lifting of a finger are consequential for ongoing talk and other activities. A different perspective on embodied motion is offered by the anthropology of human movement (e.g., Farnell 1999; 2012), which combines detailed analysis with theoretical insights from cultural and linguistic anthropology. Both traditions of research convincingly demonstrate that the body is not simply a supplement to language but a basic element of communication.

Embodied motion has been theorized as the primordial source of indexicality, given Peirce's assertion that the most basic indexical form is the pointing gesture. Linguistic-anthropological research on culture- and setting-specific deictic processes conceptualizes spatial deixis as a situated interactional practice rather than as a linguistic system of context-dependent reference (Hanks 1990; Haviland 1993; Enfield 2002; 2009). This line of scholarship positions the body as the origo of indexicality, the deictic center, around which social relationships and cultural space are brought into interactional play through the coordination of speech and gesture. Iconicity is also an important semiotic phenomenon in interactional research on embodiment, due to the prevalence of gestures that physically resemble their referents in some way (e.g., Kendon 2004).

The habituality and apparent lack of deliberation involved in such mundane embodied actions as pointing may seem to preclude viewing them as evidence of agency. However, ethnographic researchers argue against this perspective. Frequently targeted in such critiques is Pierre Bourdieu's (1978) concept of habitus, or the set of socialized and socially distinguishing dispositions that shape the use of the body. Although this concept has been productively applied in sociocultural linguistics, Bourdieu's work is viewed by many scholars as too deterministic in its representation of bodily practice as largely beyond the reach of human awareness – indeed, it has been argued that habitus is best analyzed as an agentive process of habituation (Mahmood 2005). Habitus is far more than an unconscious logic, for physical acts as mundane as crossing the street or jumping on a moving bus can be brought into systems of signification (Farnell 2000; Elyachar 2011). The process whereby embodied habit becomes socially meaningful is illuminated by a variety of contextualized studies showing that even routinized bodily actions may operate in highly agentive ways to inscribe the ideological boundaries of social difference (e.g., Goodwin and Alim 2010; Hoenes del Pinal 2011; Arnold 2013).

Embodied experience

Building on research on discourses of embodiment as well as studies of embodied movement, one of the most important developments in sociolinguistic scholarship on the body is the growing attention to bodily experience. This work has been especially driven by researchers of illness, disability, and impairment who argue for experiential agency as a crucial counterpoint to the prevailing discourses of disability. Under these discourses, persons with ailments or nonnormative bodies or bodily experiences are constructed as outliers to physical normalcy, and this construction in turn affects the perceived and sometimes even actual physical capacity of such persons to act (McPherron and Ramanathan 2010; Ramanathan 2010). In Elinor Ochs and Olga Solomon's (2005) view, practice-based paradigms enable an alternative discourse of ability by recognizing the place of both structure (dispositions) and agency (practices) in the production of subjectivity. If sense is "culturally organized competence in meaning making" (Solomon 2010: 243), then persons with alternative configurations of sense have different, not deficient, competences (see also Keating and Hadder 2010). This perspective motivates a new strand of research that explores how persons with nonnormative bodily experiences of the world, as active participants in communities and social groups, navigate normative expectations of competence in everyday practice. For example, how does a Seattle Deaf woman in the process of losing her sight transition from a primarily visual to a primarily tactile mode of communication (Edwards 2012)? How does a quadriplegic man in Islamic Oman make use of digital media to manage interpersonal and social isolation (Al Zidjaly 2015)? How do child cancer patients negotiate adult communication – and lack of communication – about their illness (Clemente 2015)? Or, to pose a broader line of inquiry, how do persons with marginalized bodily experiences instantiate themselves as agents within discursive systems that deny them agency?

Such research also offers an important reminder that even unmarked embodied acts are imbued with social meaning, since physicality can never escape the semiotics of normativity. Hence the scholarship on disability and agency has also opened the gateway to a general sociolinguistic examination of how embodied experiences and sensations – the perception of color, smell, touch, sound, and feeling – gain their meaning both from cultural discourses of the sensing body and from physical encounter with the world (Harkness and Chumley 2013). These experiences include scientists' perception of color (Goodwin 1997), listeners' experiences of speech registers as tactile (Gal 2013), the affective touching of families in interaction (Goodwin forthcoming), and the enjoyment of food and flavor as a social activity (Ochs et al. 1996; Wiggins 2002). In short, even the experiences that seem most fundamentally physical and biological are thoroughly social, cultural, and ideological at their core.

Objects, technologies, and language

The research cited above is indicative of a larger shift across the humanities and social sciences to rethink agency as emergent from the interactions of entities that are both abstract and concrete. In this perspective, the body is imbricated in complex arrangements that include nonhuman as well as human participants, whether animals, epidemics, objects, or technologies. This pan-entity approach has been labeled *posthumanist* by a number of scholars (e.g., Hayles 1999; Barad 2003), but the decentering of human signification as the site of agency does not make posthumanism any less a theory about humanity. As Bruno Latour (2005) has argued in his development of actor–network theory within anthropology, an important touchstone for posthumanist approaches, the recognition that agency is distributed across mutually evolving arrays of material and discursive interactants can lead to highly dynamic accounts of social life.

Linguists have understandably been hesitant to engage overtly with these paradigmatic shifts. Just as critical theory's discursive turn once validated our object of study, the posthumanist turn may seem to threaten to undermine it. And there are certainly concerns to be raised about Latour's rather schematic understanding of agency. Yet scholars working across varied fields in sociocultural linguistics have contributed to a general posthumanist perspective for some time now, even if they rarely identify them as such and may not entirely align with these theoretical frameworks. At the leading edge of this development are studies of embodied human engagements with built objects and technologies of various kinds – whether involving archaeological tools (Goodwin 2000), digital video communication (Jones 2008; Licoppe and Morel 2012), photo and video sharing websites (Jones 2009; Thurlow and Jaworski 2011; 2014), mobile phones (Arminen and Weilenmann 2009), online gaming worlds (Keating and Sunakawa 2010), or surveillance monitors (Goodwin 1996). This area of scholarship dissolves the discourse–materiality dichotomy by analyzing semiosis as a process that emerges in the mutually constitutive actions that take place between human bodies and the other entities with which they interact. In these studies, objects and technologies may be seen not as static "things" that remain distinct from the bodies that deploy them but as participants that are complexly intertwined in the production of action, social meaning, and subjectivity (Nevile et al. 2014; Goodwin forthcoming). If agency is "the socioculturally mediated capacity to act," as Ahearn (2001: 112) states, then certainly built objects and technologies – as material entities that have profoundly altered communicative and social arrangements throughout human history – are integral partners in this mediation.

Research on computer-mediated communication has offered some of the richest analyses of the relationship between the body, technology, and language. Media theorists have long idealized cyberspace as holding the potential to liberate users from the constraints of physicality. But this perspective relies on a dichotomous understanding of the "virtual" and the "real" as separate interactional domains, with bodies seen as fluid in one but concrete in the other (Campbell 2004). Several innovative lines of research within sociocultural linguistics challenge this view by exploring how bodily practices are transformed in the interplay between these two domains. For instance, Rodney Jones (2009) examines the recursive feedback that takes place between the bodily practices of skateboarders and the digital images of their performances that they edit and upload to video-sharing sites. Such research considers not just how the body materializes in virtual environments, but also how virtual environments affect embodiment offline, a point that is especially dramatically illustrated by interactional research on the activity of cybersex (Jones 2008;

Adams-Thies 2012). From a different perspective, Elizabeth Keating (2005) illustrates how Deaf signers innovate new forms of communication and participation, and hence subjectivity, as they adapt their bodies to the constraints and affordances of online webcams. Following Donna Haraway (1989) and other theorists, Keating demonstrates in fine detail how technologies are not objects that remain distinct from the users that deploy them, but rather prostheses that extend and augment human capabilities. This scholarship convincingly shows that relationships between virtual and nonvirtual bodies, as well as the discourses in which they are embedded, are both contingent and dynamic.

The increasingly prominent role of multimodal communicative technologies in twenty-first-century sociality compels sociocultural linguists to develop new theoretical perspectives on identity, including a deeper consideration of the body's role in subjectivity. The sociohistorical emergence of communicative technologies such as stenography (Inoue 2011), the phonograph (Weidman 2007), the telephone (Bauman 2008), and the sound film (Taylor 2009) has the potential to produce dramatic shifts in language and subjectivity by facilitating the separation of voice from body (Bucholtz 2011). Indeed, the technologically augmented conversations that characterize sociality for much of today's middle-class youth are also having their effects on language and subjectivity, as localized engagement in social media circulates into discursive systems of identification, participation, and spectatorship that did not exist in previous generations (Gershon 2011; Mortensen 2015). In short, as technology extends our senses into the social world in new and unpredictable ways, it changes not just the way we interact but also our sense of self – a situation that demands the attention of an embodied sociocultural linguistics.

Conclusion

The wide range of research topics examined here – the voice, style and self-presentation, discourses and counterdiscourses of the body, embodied motion and experience, and language, objects, and technology – demonstrates that an embodied sociocultural linguistics is already under way from a variety of analytic and theoretical standpoints. While such work has been fruitful in advancing specific subfields of sociocultural linguistics, we have argued that bringing these different areas of scholarship into dialogue with one another can further sociolinguistic theorizing of such fundamental concepts as indexicality, discourse, and agency.

In addition to the topics and concepts we have highlighted here, some of the issues that we see as especially important for an embodied sociocultural linguistics to take up are the following: What counts as a body, and as embodiment, for sociolinguistic theory? What would a comprehensive sociolinguistic theory of embodiment look like? How does a recognition of the role of the body in communication force a reconceptualization of language and linguistics? How does the emergence of new technologies, such as the central role of digital media in late modernity, shape cultural understandings of the relationship between language and the body, and vice versa? How are embodied actions and practices ideologically linked to types of bodies, on the basis of race, gender, sexuality, age, (dis)ability, and other social categories, as well as culturally and interactionally specific roles? How does a focus on embodiment expand sociolinguistic theories of agency to recognize and accommodate the distribution of agency across human and nonhuman entities, such as animals, objects, and the environment? How does sociolinguistic research on the body help shift the field away from a mentalist theory of cognition by enabling a retheorizing of affect, perception, and knowledge as social stances performed through bodily action and interaction?

Although we do not have space here to discuss how a sociolinguistic theory of embodiment might begin to address these and other questions, investigations of all of these matters have already been taken up in different areas of sociocultural linguistics. As the field continues to reveal the close connections between language and the body, we urge researchers to enter into conversation with scholars examining this relationship from other analytic, theoretical, and disciplinary perspectives. Only through such dialogues can sociocultural linguistics develop a comprehensive understanding of language as a fully embodied, fully material phenomenon.

REFERENCES

Adams-Thies, Brian. 2012. Fluid bodies or bodily fluids: Bodily reconfigurations in cybersex. *Journal of Language and Sexuality* 1, 2: 179–204.
Ahearn, Laura. 2001. Language and agency. *Annual Review of Anthropology* 30: 109–137.
Al Zidjaly, Najma. 2015. *Disability, Discourse and Technology: Agency and Inclusion in (Inter)action*. Basingstoke: Palgrave Macmillan.
Alim, H. Samy. Forthcoming. Who's afraid of the transracial subject?: Transracialization as a dynamic process of translation and transgression. In H. Samy Alim, John R. Rickford, and Arnetha F. Ball (eds.), *Raciolinguistics: How Language Shapes Our Ideas about Race*. New York: Oxford University Press.
Arminin, Ilkka, and Alexandra Weilenmann. 2009. Mobile presence and intimacy: Reshaping social actions in mobile contextual configuration. *Journal of Pragmatics* 41: 1905–1923.
Armstrong, James D. 1997. Homophobic slang as coercive discourse among college students. In Anna Livia and Kira Hall (eds.), *Queerly Phrased: Language, Gender, and Sexuality*. New York: Oxford University Press, 326–334.
Arnold, Lynnette. 2013. Reproducing actions, reproducing power: Local ideologies and everyday practices of participation at a California community bike shop. *Journal of Linguistic Anthropology* 22, 3: 137–158.
Baker, Paul. 2008. *Public Discourses of Gay Men*. New York: Routledge.

Bakhtin, M. M. 1981. *The Dialogic Imagination*. Austin: University of Texas Press.

Barad, Karen. 2003. Posthumanist performativity: Toward an understanding of how matter comes to matter. *Signs* 28, 3: 801–831.

Bauman, Richard. 2008. "It's not a telescope, it's a telephone": Encounters with the telephone on early commercial sound recordings. In Sally Johnson and Tommaso M. Milani (eds.), *Language Ideologies and Media Discourse: Texts, Practices, Politics*. New York: Continuum, 252–273.

Bauman, Richard, and Joel Sherzer (eds.). 1974. *Explorations in the Ethnography of Speaking*. Cambridge: Cambridge University Press.

Bergen, Benjamin, Schweta Narayan, and Jerome Feldman. 2003. Embodied verbal semantics: Evidence from an image-verb matching task. In Richard Alterman and David Kirsh (eds.), *Proceedings of the Twenty-fifth Annual Conference of the Cognitive Science Society*. Mahwah, NJ: Lawrence Erlbaum Associates. 139–144.

Bergen, Benjamin. 2007. Experimental methods for simulation semantics. In Monica Gonzalez-Marquez, Irene Mittleberg, Seana Coulson, and Michael J. Spivey (eds.), *Methods in Cognitive Linguistics*. Amsterdam: John Benjamins. 277–301.

Birdwhistell, Ray L. 1970. *Kinesics and Context: Essays on Body Motion Communication*. Philadelphia: University of Pennsylvania Press.

Black, Steven P. 2013. Stigma and ideological constructions of the foreign: Facing HIV-AIDS in South Africa. *Language in Society* 42, 5: 481–502.

Bourdieu, Pierre. 1978. *Outline of a Theory of Practice*. Trans. Richard Nice. Cambridge: Cambridge University Press.

Braun, Virginia, and Celia Kitzinger. 2001. Telling it straight? Dictionary definitions of women's genitals. *Journal of Sociolinguistics* 5, 2: 214–232.

Briggs, Charles L. 2011. On virtual epidemics and the mediatization of public health. *Language and Communication* 31, 3: 217–228.

Brookes, Heather. 2011. *Amangama amathathu* 'The three letters': The emergence of a quotable gesture. *Gesture* 11, 2: 194–217.

Bucholtz, Mary. 2011. Race and the re-embodied voice in Hollywood film. *Language and Communication* 31: 255–265.

   2015. The elements of style. In Ahmar Mahboob, Dwi Noverini Djenar, and Ken Cruickshank (eds.), *Language and Identity across Modes of Communication*. Berlin: De Gruyter Mouton, 27–60.

Bucholtz, Mary, Dolores Inés Casillas, and Jin Sook Lee. Forthcoming. Beyond empowerment: Accompaniment and social justice in a youth research program. In Robert Lawson and Dave Sayers (eds.), *Sociolinguistic Research: Application and Impact*. London: Routledge.

Bucholtz, Mary, and Kira Hall. 2008. All of the above: New coalitions in sociocultural linguistics. *Journal of Sociolinguistics* 12, 4: 401–431.

Butler, Judith. 1990. *Gender Trouble: Feminism and the Subversion of Identity*. New York: Routledge.

   1993. *Bodies That Matter: On the Discursive Limits of "Sex."* New York: Routledge.

Caldas-Coulthard, Carmen Rosa. 2008. Body branded: Multimodal identities in tourism advertising. *Journal of Language and Politics* 7, 3: 451–470.

Campbell, John Edward. 2004. *Getting It On Online: Cyberspace, Gay Male Sexuality, and Embodied Identity*. New York: Haworth Press.

Carr, E. Summerson. 2011. *Scripting Addiction: The Politics of Therapeutic Talk and American Sobriety*. Princeton, NJ: Princeton University Press.

Cavanaugh, Jillian R., and Shalini Shankar (eds.). Forthcoming. *Language and Materiality*. New York: Oxford University Press.

Chouliaraki, Lili. 2007. *The Spectatorship of Suffering*. London: Sage.

Clemente, Ignasi. 2015. *Uncertain Futures: Communication and Culture in Childhood Cancer Treatment*. Malden, MA: Wiley-Blackwell.

Couper-Kuhlen, Elizabeth, and Margret Selting (eds.). 2006. *Prosody in Conversation: Interactional Studies*. Cambridge: Cambridge University Press.

Coupland, Justine. 2013. Dance, ageing and the mirror: Negotiating watchability. *Discourse and Communication* 7, 1: 3–24.

Coupland, Justine, and Richard Gwyn (eds.). 2003. *Discourse, the Body, and Identity*. Basingstoke: Palgrave Macmillan.

Coupland, Nikolas. 2007. *Style: Language Variation and Identity*. Cambridge: Cambridge University Press.

Duranti, Alessandro. 2003. Language as culture in U.S. anthropology: Three paradigms. *Current Anthropology* 44, 3: 323–47.

Eckert, Penelope. 1989. *Jocks and Burnouts: Social Categories and Identity in the High School*. New York: Teachers College Press.

2000. *Linguistic Variation as Social Practice*. Oxford: Blackwell.

2003. The meaning of style. In Wai Fong Chiang, Elaine Chun, Laura Mahalingappa, and Siri Mehus (eds.), *SALSA XI: Proceedings of the Eleventh Annual Symposium about Language and Society – Austin (Texas Linguistic Forum 47)*. Austin: University of Texas Department of Linguistics, 41–53.

2008. Variation and the indexical field. *Journal of Sociolinguistics* 12, 4: 453–476.

2010. Affect, sound symbolism, and variation. *University of Pennsylvania Working Papers in Linguistics* 15, 2. Available at http://repository.upenn.edu/pwpl/vol15/iss2/9.

2012. Three waves of variation study: The emergence of meaning in the study of sociolinguistic variation. *Annual Review of Anthropology* 41: 87–100.

Edelman, Elijah Adiv, and Lal Zimman. 2014. Boycunts and bonus holes: Trans men's bodies, neoliberalism, and the sexual productivity of genitals. *Journal of Homosexuality* 61: 673–690.

Edwards, Terra. 2012. Sensing the rhythms of everyday life: Temporal integration and tactile translation in the Seattle Deaf-Blind community. *Language in Society* 41, 1: 29–71.

Elyachar, Julia. 2011. The political economy of movement and gesture in Cairo. *Journal of the Royal Anthropological Institute* 17, 1: 82–99.

Enfield, N. J. 2002. "Lip-pointing": A discussion of form and function with reference to data from Laos. *Gesture* 1, 2: 185–211.

2009. *The Anatomy of Meaning: Speech, Gesture, and Composite Utterances*. Cambridge: Cambridge University Press.

Fairclough, Norman. 1989. *Language and Power*. London: Longman.

Farnell, Brenda. 1999. Moving bodies, acting selves. *Annual Review of Anthropology* 28: 341–373.

2000. Getting out of the habitus: An alternative model of dynamically embodied social action. *Journal of the Royal Anthropological Institute* 6, 3: 397–418.

2012. *Dynamic Embodiment for Social Theory: "I move therefore I am."* Abingdon: Routledge.

Foucault, Michel. 1970. *The Order of Things: An Archeology of the Human Sciences.* New York: Pantheon Books.

  1978. *The History of Sexuality,* vol. 1: *An Introduction.* Trans. Robert Hurley. New York: Random House.

French, Peter, and John Local. 1986. Prosodic features and the management of interruptions. In Catherine Johns-Lewis (ed.), *Intonation and Discourse.* London: Croom Helm, 157–180.

Gal, Susan. 2013. Tastes of talk: Qualia and the moral flavor of signs. *Anthropological Theory* 13, 1–2: 31–48.

Garfinkel, Harold. 1967. *Studies in Ethnomethodology.* Cambridge: Polity.

Gershon, Ilana. 2011. Breaking up is hard to do: Media switching and media ideologies. *Journal of Linguistic Anthropology* 20, 2: 389–405.

Giglioli, Pier Paolo (ed.). 1972. *Language and Social Context: Selected Readings.* Harmondsworth: Penguin.

Goffman, Erving. 1963. *Stigma: Notes on the Management of Spoiled Identity.* New York: Simon & Schuster.

  1967. *Interaction Ritual: Essays on Face-to-Face Behavior.* New York: Pantheon.

  1971. *Relations in Public.* New York: Harper & Row.

  1979. *Gender Advertisements.* New York: Harper & Row.

Goodwin, Charles. 1981. *Conversational Organization: Interaction between Speakers and Hearers.* New York: Academic Press.

  1997. The blackness of black: Color categories as situated practice. In Lauren B. Resnick, Roger Säljö, Clotilde Pontecorvo, and Barbara Burge (eds.), *Discourse, Tools, and Reasoning: Essays on Situated Cognition.* Berlin: Springer, 111–140.

  1996. Transparent vision. In Elinor Ochs, Emanuel A. Schegloff, and Sandra A. Thompson (eds.), *Interaction and Grammar.* Cambridge: Cambridge University Press, 370–404.

  2000. Action and embodiment within situated human interaction. *Journal of Pragmatics* 32: 1489–1522.

  Forthcoming. *Co-operative Action.* Cambridge: Cambridge University Press.

Goodwin, Marjorie Harness. Forthcoming. Haptic sociality: The embodied interactive constitution of intimacy through touch and voice. In Christian Meyer, Jürgen Streeck, and J. Scott Jordan (eds.), *Intercorporeality.* New York: Oxford University Press.

Goodwin, Marjorie Harness, and H. Samy Alim. 2010. "Whatever (neck roll, eye roll, teeth suck)": The situated coproduction of social categories and identities through stancetaking and transmodal stylization. *Journal of Linguistic Anthropology* 20, 1: 179–194.

Guendouzi, Jackie. 2004. "She's very slim": Talking about body-size in all-female interactions. *Journal of Pragmatics* 36: 1635–1653.

Gumperz, John J. 1982. *Discourse Strategies.* Cambridge: Cambridge University Press.

Gumperz, John J., and Dell Hymes (eds.). 1964. The Ethnography of Communication Special issue of *American Anthropologist* 66, 6, part 2.

Guy, Gregory, Barbara Horvath, Julia Vonwiller, Elaine Daisley, and Inge Rogers. 1986. An intonational change in progress in Australian English. *Language in Society* 15, 1: 23–52.

Guy, Gregory R., and Julia Vonwiller. 1984. The meaning of an intonation in Australian English. *Australian Journal of Linguistics* 4, 1: 1–17.

Haddington, Pentti, Lorenza Mondada, and Maurice Nevile (eds.). 2013. *Interaction and Mobility: Language and the Body in Motion*. Berlin: De Gruyter.

Hall, Edward T. 1959. *The Silent Language*. Garden City, NY: Doubleday.

Hall, Kira. 2005. Intertextual sexuality: Parodies of class, identity, and desire in Delhi. *Journal of Linguistic Anthropology* 15, 1: 125–144.

2009. Boys' talk: Hindi, moustaches, and masculinity in New Delhi. In Pia Pichler and Eva Eppler (eds.), *Gender and Spoken Interaction*. Basingstoke: Palgrave Macmillan, 139–162.

Halliday, M. A. K. 1978. *Language as Social Semiotic: The Social Interpretation of Language and Meaning*. London: Edward Arnold.

Hanks, William F. 1990. *Referential Practice: Language and Lived Space among the Maya*. Chicago, IL: University of Chicago Press.

Haraway, Donna J. 1989. *Primate Visions: Gender, Race, and Nature in the World of Modern Science*. New York: Routledge.

Harkness, Nicholas. 2014. *Songs of Seoul: An Ethnography of Voice and Voicing in Christian South Korea*. Berkeley: University of California Press.

Harkness, Nicholas, and Lily Hope Chumley (eds.). 2013. Qualia. Special issue of *Anthropological Theory* 13, 3.

Haviland, John B. 1993. Anchoring, iconicity, and orientation in Guugu Yimithirr pointing gestures. *Journal of Linguistic Anthropology* 3, 1: 3–45.

Hayles, N. Katherine. 1999. *How We Became Posthuman: Virtual Bodies in Cybernetics, Literature, and Informatics*. Chicago, IL: University of Chicago Press.

Heath, Christian. 1986. *Body Movement and Speech in Medical Interaction*. Cambridge: Cambridge University Press.

Hebdige, Dick. 1979. *Subculture: The Meaning of Style*. London: Methuen.

Hodge, Robert, and Gunther Kress. 1988. *Social Semiotics*. Ithaca, NY: Cornell University Press.

Hoenes del Pinal, Eric. 2011. Towards an ideology of gesture: Gesture, body movement, and language ideology among Q'eqchi'-Maya Catholics. *Anthropological Quarterly* 84, 3: 595–630.

Hymes, Dell (ed.). 1964. *Language in Culture and Society: A Reader in Linguistics and Anthropology*. New York: Harper & Row.

1974. *Foundations in Sociolinguistics: An Ethnographic Approach*. Philadelphia: University of Pennsylvania Press.

Inoue, Miyako. 2011. Stenography and ventriloquism in late nineteenth century Japan. *Language and Communication* 31, 3: 181–190.

Irvine, Judith T., and Susan Gal. 2000. Language ideology and linguistic differentiation. In Paul V. Kroskrity (ed.), *Regimes of Language: Ideologies, Polities, and Identities*. Santa Fe, NM: School of American Research Press, 35–84.

Jaffe, Alexandra (ed.). 2009. *Stance: Sociolinguistic Perspectives*. New York: Oxford University Press.

Jones, Rodney H. 2008. The role of text in televideo cybersex. *Text and Talk* 28, 4: 453–473.

2009. Dancing, skating, and sex: Action and text in the digital age. *Journal of Applied Linguistics* 6, 3: 283–302.

Keating, Elizabeth. 2005. Homo prostheticus: Problematizing the notions of activity and computer-mediated interaction. *Discourse Studies* 7, 4–5: 527–545.

Keating, Elizabeth, and Chiho Sunakawa. 2010. Participation cues: Coordinating activity and collaboration in complex online gaming worlds. *Language in Society* 39, 3: 331–356.

Keating, Elizabeth, and R. Neill Hadder. 2010. Sensory impairment. *Annual Review of Anthropology* 39: 115–129.

Kendon, Adam. 1990. *Conducting Interaction: Patterns of Behavior in Focused Encounters*. Cambridge: Cambridge University Press.

2004. *Gesture: Visible Action as Utterance*. Cambridge: Cambridge University Press.

Key, Mary Ritchie. 1975. *Paralanguage and Kinesics*. Metuchen, NJ: Scarecrow Press.

King, Brian W. 2015. Reclaiming masculinity in an account of lived intersex experience: Language, desire, and embodied knowledge. In Tommaso Milani (ed.), *Language and Masculinities: Performances, Intersections, Dislocations*. London: Routledge. 220–242.

Kress, Gunther, and Robert Hodge. 1979. *Language as Ideology*. London: Routledge & Kegan Paul.

Kress, Gunther, and Theo van Leeuwen. 1996. *Reading Images: The Grammar of Visual Design*. New York: Routledge.

2001. *Multimodal Discourse: The Modes and Media of Contemporary Communication*. New York: Oxford University Press.

Labov, William. 1972. Some principles of linguistic methodology. *Language in Society* 1, 1: 97–120.

Latour, Bruno. 2005. *Reassembling the Social: An Introduction to Actor–Network Theory*. New York: Oxford University Press.

Licoppe, Christian, and Julien Morel. 2012. Video-in-interaction: "Talking heads" and the multimodal organization of mobile and Skype video calls. *Research on Language and Social Interaction* 45, 4: 399–429.

Local, John, and John Kelly. 1986. Projection and "silences": Notes on phonetic and conversational structure. *Human Studies* 9, 2–3: 185–204.

Mahmood, Saba. 2005. *Politics of Piety: The Islamic Revival and the Feminist Subject*. Princeton, NJ: Princeton University Press.

McNeill, David. 1985. So you think gestures are nonverbal? *Psychological Review* 92, 3: 350–371.

1992. *Hand and Mind: What Gestures Reveal about Thought*. Chicago, IL: University of Chicago Press.

McPherron, Paul, and Vaidehi Ramanathan (eds.). 2010. *Language, Body, and Health*. Berlin: Walter de Gruyter.

Mendoza-Denton, Norma. 2008. *Homegirls: Language and Cultural Practice among Latina Youth Gangs*. Malden, MA: Blackwell.

2011. The semiotic hitchhiker's guide to creaky voice: Circulation and gendered hardcore in a Chicana/o gang persona. *Journal of Linguistic Anthropology* 21, 2: 261–280.

Milani, Tommaso. 2015. Sexual cityzenship: Discourses, spaces, and bodies at Joburg Pride 2012. *Journal of Language and Politics* 14, 3: 431–454.

Mortensen, Kristine. 2015. A bit too skinny for me: Women's homosocial constructions of heterosexual desire in online dating. *Gender and Language* 9, 3: 461–488.

Motschenbacher, Heiko. 2009. Speaking the gendered body: The performative construction of commercial femininities and masculinities via body-part vocabulary. *Language in Society* 38, 1: 1–22.

Munson, Benjamin, and Molly Babel. 2007. Loose lips and silver tongues, or projecting sexual orientation through speech. *Language and Linguistics Compass* 1, 5: 416–449.

Nakassis, Constantine V. Forthcoming. *Doing Style: Youth and Mass Mediation in South India.* Chicago, IL: University of Chicago Press.

Nevile, Maurice, Pentti Haddington, Trine Heinemann, and Mirka Rauniomaa (eds.). 2014. *Interacting with Objects: Language, Materiality, and Social Activity.* Amsterdam: John Benjamins.

Nielsen, Rasmus. 2010. "I ain't never been charged with nothing!": The use of falsetto speech as a linguistic strategy of indignation. *University of Pennsylvania Working Papers in Linguistics* 15, 2: 111–121. Available at http://repository.upenn.edu/pwpl/vol15/iss2/13.

Norris, Sigrid. 2004. *Analyzing Multimodal Interaction: A Methodological Framework.* New York: Routledge.

Ochs, Elinor. 1992. Indexing gender. In Alessandro Duranti and Charles Goodwin (eds.), *Rethinking Context: Language as an Interactive Phenomenon.* Cambridge: Cambridge University Press, 335–358.

Ochs, Elinor, Clotilde Pontecorvo, and Alessandra Fasulo. 1996. Socializing taste. *Ethnos* 61, 1–2: 7–46.

Ochs, Elinor, and Olga Solomon. 2005. Practical logic and autism. In Conerly Casey and Robert B. Edgerton (eds.), *A Companion to Psychological Anthropology: Modernity and Psychocultural Change*, Malden, MA: Blackwell, 140–167.

Ochs, Elinor, Tamar Kremer-Sadlik, Olga Solomon, and Karen Gainer Sirota. 2001. Inclusion as social practice: Views of children with autism. *Social Development* 10, 3: 399–419.

Ohala, John J. 1994. The frequency code underlies the sound-symbolic use of voice pitch. In Leanne Hinton, Johanna Nichols, and John J. Ohala (eds.), *Sound Symbolism.* Cambridge: Cambridge University Press, 325–347.

Peirce, C. S. 1885. On the algebra of logic: A contribution to the philosophy of notation. *American Journal of Mathematics* 7, 2: 180–196.

Pigg, Stacy Leigh. 2001. Languages of sex and AIDS in Nepal: Notes on the social production of commensurability. *Cultural Anthropology* 16, 4: 481–541.

Podesva, Robert J. 2007. Phonation type as a stylistic variable: The use of falsetto in constructing a persona. *Journal of Sociolinguistics* 11, 4: 478–504.

2013. Gender and the social meaning of non-modal phonation types. In Chundra Cathcart, I-Hsuan Chen, Greg Finley, Shinae Kang, Clare S. Sandy, and Elise Stickles (eds.), *Proceedings of the 37th Annual Meeting of the Berkeley Linguistics Society*, 427–448. Available at http://elanguage.net/journals/bls/issue/view/377.

Pride, J. B., and Janet Holmes (eds.). 1972. *Sociolinguistics: Selected Readings.* Harmondsworth: Penguin.

Ramanathan, Vaidehi. 2010. *Bodies and Language: Health, Ailments, Disabilities.* Tonawanda, NY: Multilingual Matters.

Rampton, Ben. 1995. *Crossing: Language and Ethnicity among Adolescents.* London: Longman.

Rosa, Jonathan. Forthcoming. *Looking like a Language, Sounding like a Race: Exclusion and Ingenuity in the Making of Latin@ Identities.* New York: Oxford University Press.

Scollon, Ron. 2001. *Mediated Discourse: The Nexus of Practice.* New York: Routledge.

Shankar, Shalini, and Jillian R. Cavanaugh. 2012. Language and materiality in global capitalism. *Annual Review of Anthropology* 41: 355–369.

Sicoli, Mark A. 2010. Shifting voices with participant roles: Voice qualities and speech registers in Mesoamerica. *Language in Society* 39: 521–553.

Silverstein, Michael. 1979. Language structure and linguistic ideology. In Paul R. Clyne, William F. Hanks, and Carol L. Hofbauer (eds.), *The Elements: A Parasession on Linguistic Units and Levels*. Chicago, IL: Chicago Linguistic Society, 193–247.

  2003. Indexical order and the dialectics of sociolinguistic life. *Language and Communication* 23, 3–4: 193–229.

  2005. Axes of evals: Token versus type interdiscursivity. *Journal of Linguistic Anthropology* 15, 1: 6–22.

Solomon, Olga. 2010. Sense and the senses: Anthropology and the study of autism. *Annual Review of Anthropology* 39: 241–259.

Speer, Susan A., and Richard Green. 2007. On passing: The interactional organization of appearance attributions in the psychiatric assessment of transsexual patients. In Victoria Clark and Elizabeth Peel (eds.), *Out in Psychology: Lesbian, Gay, Bisexual, Trans and Queer Perspectives*. Chichester: Wiley, 335–368.

Streeck, Jürgen, Charles Goodwin, and Curtis LeBaron (eds.). 2011. *Embodied Interaction: Language and Body in the Material World*. Cambridge: Cambridge University Press.

Streeck, Jürgen. 2013. Interaction and the living body. *Journal of Pragmatics* 46: 69–90.

Sutton, Laurel. 1995. Bitches and skankly hobags: The place of women in contemporary slang. In Kira Hall and Mary Bucholtz (eds.), *Gender Articulated: Language and the Socially Constructed Self*. New York: Routledge. 279–296.

Taylor, Jessica. 2009. "Speaking shadows": A history of the voice in the transition from silent to sound film in the United States. *Journal of Linguistic Anthropology* 19, 1: 1–20.

Taylor, Nicole. 2011. "Guys, she's humongous!": Gender and weight-based teasing in adolescence. *Journal of Adolescent Research* 26, 2: 178–199.

Thurlow, Crispin. 2001. Naming the "outsider within": Homophobic pejoratives and the verbal abuse of lesbian, gay, and bisexual high-school pupils. *Journal of Adolescence* 24: 25–38.

Thurlow, Crispin, and Adam Jaworski. 2011. Banal globalization? Embodied actions and mediated practices in tourists' online photo-sharing. In Crispin Thurlow and Kristine Mroczek (eds.), *Digital Discourse: Language in the New Media*. New York: Oxford University Press, 220–250.

  2014. "Two hundred ninety-four": Remediation and multimodal performance in tourist placemaking. *Journal of Sociolinguistics* 18, 4: 450–494.

Weidman, Amanda. 2007. Stage goddesses and studio divas in South India: On agency and the politics of voice. In Bonnie McElhinny (ed.), *Words, Worlds, and Material Girls: Language, Gender, Globalization*. Berlin: Walter de Gruyter, 131–155.

  2014. Anthropology and voice. *Annual Review of Anthropology* 43: 37–51.

West, Candace, and Don H. Zimmerman. 1987. Doing gender. *Gender and Society* 1, 2: 125–151.

Wetherell, Margaret. 1996. Fear of fat: Interpretive repertoires and ideological dilemmas. In Janet Maybin and Neil Mercer (eds.), *Using English: From Conversation to Canon*. London: Routledge, 36–42.

Wiggins, Sally (2002). Talking with your mouth full: Gustatory *mmms* and the embodiment of pleasure. *Research on Language and Social Interaction* 35, 3: 311–336.

Woolard, Kathryn A., and Bambi B. Schieffelin. 1994. Language ideology. *Annual Review of Anthropology* 23: 55–82.

2008. Why *dat* now?: Linguistic-anthropological contributions to the explanation of sociolinguistic icons and change. *Journal of Sociolinguistics* 12, 4: 432–452.

Zimman, Lal. 2013. Hegemonic masculinity and the variability of gay-sounding speech: The perceived sexuality of transgender men. *Journal of Language and Sexuality* 2, 1: 1–39.

2014. The discursive construction of sex: Remaking and reclaiming the gendered body in talk about genitals among trans men. In Lal Zimman, Jenny Davis, and Joshua Raclaw (eds.), *Queer Excursions: Retheorizing Binaries in Language, Gender, and Sexuality*. New York: Oxford University Press. 13–34.

Zimman, Lal, and Kira Hall. 2009. Language, embodiment, and the "third sex." In Dominic Watt and Carmen Llamas (eds.), *Language and Identities*. Edinburgh: Edinburgh University Press, 166–178.

Part III

Sociolinguistics, place and mobility

9   Mobile times, mobile terms: The trans-super-poly-metro movement

Alastair Pennycook

It is evident that something has been going on recently in sociolinguistics with a sudden upsurge – to the pleasure of some and the chagrin of others – of new terminology. Alongside *superdiversity* (Vertovec 2007; Blommaert 2010) as a new term to address the intensification of diversity, we now have *translanguaging* (Garcia 2009a; Blackledge and Creese 2010; Li Wei 2011) and *translingual practice* (Canagarajah 2013), *transglossia* (García 2013, 2014; Sultana et al. 2015), *polylingual languaging* (Jørgensen 2008a,b; Møller 2008), and *metrolingualism* (Otsuji and Pennycook 2010; 2014), amongst others. According to Blommaert (2013; see also this volume, Chapter 11) the old "Fishmanian" framing of sociolinguistics has been profoundly questioned with this proliferation of new terms signalling "an epistemological rupture with past approaches" (p. 621). All share a desire to move away from the language of bi- or multilingualism, castigating earlier work for operating with the idea that multilingualism is the sum of several, separate languages.

The first aim of this chapter is to provide an overview of these different frameworks, weighing up the different approaches and discussing their similarities and differences. All focus on contexts of multiple, mixed language use (while also trying to escape these notions of multiplicity and mixing) with an interest in talking in terms of repertoires of linguistic resources rather than bilingualism, code-mixing, or code-switching. While there are some differences between these different approaches, they have much in common. Their irruption into the world of sociolinguistics raises at least two questions: To what extent do these new terminologies reflect a changing sociolinguistic world marked by greater diversity, mobility, and language contact (as the notion of superdiversity suggests), or to what extent is this rather a shift in theory that could apply to all eras of sociolinguistic interaction? Does this signal a major paradigm shift in the way we think about languages, or is this rather a case of old wine in new bottles or, worse still, merely a case of "uncouth neologisms and dysfluent phrasings" that "don't represent an advance" (Edwards 2012: 37)? The chapter concludes by evaluating these arguments about whether there is anything new or worthwhile going on here.

Translanguaging

Among this proliferation of new terms, translanguaging has emerged as the term of choice, so much so that it has already become a common and unmarked term referring to instances of language mixing. Canagarajah (2013) suggests that *translingual practice* in fact serves as an umbrella term for the many currently emerging orientations, including, in addition to trans-, poly-, and metrolingualism, translingual writing (Horner et al. 2010), code-meshing (Canagarajah 2011), transcultural literacy (Lu 2009), hetero-graphy (Blommaert 2008), dynamic bilingualism, and pluriliteracy (García 2009a). To this list (see Blackledge and Creese 2014, for another catalogue), we might add 'flexible bilingualism' (Creese and Blackledge 2011) and 'contemporary urban vernaculars' (Rampton 2011) as well as multilingua or metrolingua francas (Makoni and Pennycook 2012; Pennycook and Otsuji 2014a).

García and Li Wei (2014) suggest that we are witnessing a 'translanguaging turn' (p. 19) with the term now referring to "both the complex language practices of plurilingual individuals and communities, as well as the peda-gogical approaches that use those complex practices" (p. 19). The impetus behind the development of translingualism, then, has been as much peda-gogical as sociolinguistic. It has emerged from sociolinguistic studies of classrooms and has been applied to classrooms based on an understanding of the sociolinguistic context of education. García points to the need for peda-gogical practices "firmly rooted in the multilingual and multimodal language and literacy practices of children in schools in the 21st century" (2009: 8). This translanguaging approach to education makes central "the act performed by bilinguals of accessing different linguistic features or various modes of what are described as autonomous languages" (García 2009a: 141).

Translanguaging thus "requires an epistemological change in which stu-dents' everyday languaging and school languaging is expanded and integrated, and in so doing blends ways of knowing which are traditionally found in different spaces" (García and Li Wei 2014: 69). In Canagarajah's (2013) view, pedagogy needs to "be refashioned to accommodate the modes of performative competence and cooperative disposition we see outside the classroom. Rather than focusing on a single language or dialect as the target of learning, teachers have to develop a readiness in students to engage with the repertoires required for transnational contact zones" (p. 191). Likewise, based on their studies of the mixed language practices of heritage language classes, Blackledge and Creese (2010) advocate "teaching bilingual children by means of a bilingual pedagogy" and argue for a "a release from monolingual instructional approaches" (p. 201) through translanguaging.

Central to these proposals is an acknowledgement of the complex and mixed language practices of bilingual worlds and the need for language classes to start to resemble these worlds more. In relation to literacy, Hornberger and Link (2012) call for the need to focus on "practices that recognize, value, and build on the multiple, mobile communicative repertoires, translanguaging and transnational literacy practices of students and their families" (p. 274). For Li Wei (2011) it is important to think in terms of *translanguaging spaces* that allow for and are produced by translanguaging practices (p. 1234). While a more general take-up of the idea of translanguaging has now come to refer to mixed language practices outside educational contexts, the central focus has remained a pedagogical drive to make language classes more accountable to the sociolinguistic worlds that are both part of the wider context in which such classes occur and part of their internal dynamics. Thus the focus of much of the work on translanguaging is oriented towards a critique of the narrow focus on separable languages in educational contexts and the need instead to understand that "[e]ngaging in translanguaging may hold transformative power to shift students' and teachers' dominant monolingual ideologies toward more plural-ist understandings of the wider linguistic repertoire students bring to literacy practices and beyond" (Martin-Beltrán 2014: 226)

Jacquemet's (2005) work on *transidiomatic practices* – "the communicative practices of transnational groups that interact using different languages and communicative codes simultaneously present in a range of communicative channels, both local and distant" (p. 265) – or his more general concept of *transidioma* (Jacquemet forthcoming) have also been influential in the devel-opment of these ideas. Transidiomatic practices, Jacquemet explains, "are the results of the co-presence of multilingual talk (exercised by de/reterritorialized speakers) and electronic media, in contexts heavily structured by social indexi-calities and semiotic codes." For Jacquemet, such practices are dependent on "transnational environments," the mediation of "deterritorialized technolo-gies", and interaction "with both present and distant people" (p. 265). García (2009a: 304) meanwhile suggests a move from diglossic (via 'transdiglossic') to *transglossic*, to capture the way languages are blended and mixed rather than used in isolation. She goes on to argue that transglossia "could offer flexible spaces for language practices that are associated with making meaning and improving communication among participants who are different, and yet participate more equally" (2009b: 148).

The term 'translanguage' García and Li Wei (2014) trace back to the Welsh *trawsieithu*, coined by Cen Williams (1996). In its original use, it referred to a pedagogical practice where students are asked to alternate languages for the purposes of receptive or productive use. While tracing the term back to an original use serves a certain purpose, a more useful approach may be to think in terms of multiple origins, especially since all these terms have emerged around the same time from various directions. Li Wei and Zhua Hua (2013) suggest at least three meanings of the 'trans' here – going between and beyond (linguistic) systems and structures, transforming current structures and practices, and employing transdisciplinary perspectives on society and cognition. As García and Li Wei observe, we also need to understand the evolution of the *trans* prefix, which they trace back to the idea of *transculturación* developed in the 1940s by Fernando Ortiz and subsequently taken up by Mignolo (2000) and others. This work leads to a more dynamic, transgressive understanding of transglossia in García's subsequent formulation where "transglossia releases ways of speaking of subaltern groups that had been previously fixed within static language identities and are constrained by the modern/colonial world system" (2013: 161).

A slightly different approach to transglossia developed by Sultana et al. (2015) derives from heteroglossia rather than diglossia, combining a broader transgressive theory (an alternative to other critical approaches to applied linguistics) and a transanalytic framework (including transculturation, transmodality, and transtextualization) (Pennycook 2007). This transglossic approach, then, draws together Bakhtinian heteroglossia (Blackledge and Creese 2014; and see further discussion below) and some of the current 'trans' approaches to language, culture, and modality, with a view to both "unveiling the voices" young adults draw on and "unzipping the translinguistic complexities of meanings" in their language use (Sultana et al 2015: 95). Like related ideas such as 'translingual activism' (Pennycook 2008) drawing on Venuti's (1998) critical approach to translation, the emergence of translanguaging, translingualism, and transglossia can be seen not only as deriving from Williams's (1996) *trawsieithu*, but also as part of the general interest in 'trans' concepts over the last twenty years, a reaction possibly to the temporally oriented and backward-looking 'post' orientations (poststructuralism, postmodernism, postcolonialism).

Poly-, metro-, and other terms

In their studies of mixed language use in Copenhagen schools (Jørgensen 2008a,b), similar questions arose for the researchers concerning the use of descriptions such as bi- or multilingual. "What if the participants do not orient to the juxtaposition of languages in terms of switching?" Møller (2008) asks. "What if they instead orient to a linguistic norm where all available linguistic resources can be used to reach the goals of the speaker?" If this is the case, Møller argues, "it is not adequate to categorise this conversation as bilingual or multilingual, or even as language mixing, because all these terms depend on the separatability of linguistic categories. I therefore suggest the term polylingual instead" (p. 218). Ritzau (2014) uses this polylingual framework to suggest that learners of Danish at the tertiary level use features associated with languages other than Danish because "their linguistic repertoires do not match the ideologies of the institution" (p. 13). One aspect of this framework to interpret data from the remarkable longitudinal Amager project in Copenhagen is an emphasis on *features*, which avoids talking in terms of languages. Like Blommaert's unfortunately negative-sounding term *truncated multilingualism* – intended to describe the ways we only ever have a "partial competence" (2010: 103) of a broader linguistic repertoire – the focus here is on the use of linguistic resources rather than of languages.

A second significant aspect of this framework is the idea of enregisterment (drawing on Agha 2007; and see Part I of this book, Chapters 2–5), which enables the researchers to focus on how certain forms of youth street language can be both fluid yet also sedimented as a locally used and recognized register (Møller and Jørgensen 2011). This point that an overemphasis on flexibility and fluidity may miss the ways in which young urban language use can also become recognized as a particular way of speaking – both fixed and fluid ascriptions of language and identity are constantly in play – was also part of the argument behind the idea of *metrolingualism* (Otsuji and Pennycook 2010; Pennycook and Otsuji 2015). Metrolingualism is an attempt to understand linguistic resources in relation to the city, to show how everyday language practices are related to urban space and how the spaces and rhythms of the city operate in relation to language. Metrolingualism drew inspiration originally from Maher's (2005) *metroethnicity*: "a hybridised 'street' ethnicity deployed by a cross-section of people with ethnic or mainstream backgrounds who are oriented towards cultural hybridity, cultural/ethnic tolerance and a multicultural lifestyle in friendships, music, the arts, eating and dress" (Maher 2005: 83). Eschewing the possibly voluntaristic and playful overtones of this notion (Coupland 2007), however, metrolingualism makes central the relations between language and place (*spatial repertoires*), language and activity (*metrolingual multitasking*) (Pennycook and Otsuji 2014b), and the broader context of the city.

Like trans- and poly-languaging the focus is on the mixed resources people deploy in daily interaction, while the contexts of study are places of work across the city rather than educational contexts. Central to many of these new terms has also been the idea of mobility, nowhere more obviously than in the work of Blommaert (2010): "Mobility is the great challenge," according to Blommaert, since it draws attention to "the dislocation of language and language events from the fixed position in time and space attributed to them by a more traditional linguistics and sociolinguistics" (2010: 21). As can be seen in a number of the quotations above (e.g. Hornberger and Link 2012; Canagarajah 2013), mobile resources and repertoires are very much part of the background to the idea of translanguaging. Blommaert has also developed much of his work around the much more commonly used *superdiversity* (see also Møller and Jørgensen 2011) as well as *supervernacular*, referring to the ways in which vernacular language practices such as texting have become global practices. As Makoni (2012) notes, however, not only is the use of these terms alongside each other confusing (one 'super' is an intensifier of diversity, the other points to ways in which new vernaculars can operate above and across other language domains), but they also convey a "powerful sense of social romanticism, creating an illusion of equality in a highly asymmetrical world" as well as disconcertingly promoting an "open celebration of diversity in societies marked by violent xenophobia, such as South Africa" (p. 193).

These approaches generally share a number of features: They move away from talking about languages, bilingualism, multilingualism, code-switching, and so forth, and instead talk in terms of language practices and repertoires of linguistic (and nonlinguistic) resources (or *features*, in Jørgensen's and Møller's terms). García and Li Wei (2014) explain translanguaging as "an approach to the use of language, bilingualism and the education of bilinguals that considers the language practices of bilinguals not as two autonomous language systems as has been traditionally the case, but as one linguistic repertoire with features that have been societally constructed as belonging to two separate languages" (p. 2). There is also a largely shared view that we need to think in terms of *languaging* to capture the fact that "human beings use language to change the world" (Jørgensen, 2008a: 180). Li Wei (2011) likewise aligns his use of the term translanguaging with this understanding of an active process of achieving things through language. While the broader notion of translingualism therefore refers to the general idea of translingual language use, the idea of translanguaging suggests an active, transformative process.

The notion of repertoires, as an enabling term to avoid talking about languages or codes, has received rather less attention than expected, given the work it is now being called on to do. Unlike Gumperz's (1964: 137) original formulation of repertoire as "the totality of linguistic forms regularly employed in the course of socially significant interaction", this more recent adoption of the term tends to view the repertoire in terms of individual accumulation rather than community resources. As Benor (2010: 161) notes, "recent work on sociolinguistic style sees individuals as making use of a repertoire of sociolinguistic resources." Repertoires are thus commonly conceived in terms of how "different resources enter into our subject's repertoire" (Blommaert and Backus 2013: 26), or the "resources individuals use to create their own space" (Li Wei 2011: 1223). Even though these accounts of the development of linguistic repertoires may involve bodily (*leiblich*), emotional, and historico-political dimensions of life trajectories in Busch's (2012; 2013) poststructuralist understanding of the subject, the social nature of the idea of repertoire as the resources available to groups of people has shifted towards the accumulation of resources in the individual, what Orman (2013) calls a 'mental warehouse' view of language resources stored in the mind ready for deployment. The possibility of talking of speech or language communities that also allowed for a more stable concept of bi- or multilingualism has thus given way to a more individualised relation between speakers and resources.

Paradigm shift or barren verbiage?

Canagarajah (2013) argues that the term *translingual* "highlights two key concepts of significance for a paradigm shift" (p. 6): On the one hand, "communication transcends individual languages," that is to say, we use repertoires of linguistic resources without necessary recourse to the notions of languages, and on the other hand, "communication transcends words and involves diverse semiotic resources and ecological affordances" (p. 6), that is to say, we draw on a wide set of possible resources to achieve communication. Blommaert and Rampton (2011) also argue that we are in the midst of a paradigm shift in terms of how we think about languages, language groups, and communication: "Rather than working with homogeneity, stability and boundedness as the starting assumptions, mobility, mixing, political dynamics and historical embedding are now central concerns in the study of languages, language groups and communication" (p. 3). For Blommaert (2013: 621) the recent shifts in sociolinguistic thinking – amounting to a ' post-Fishmanian' turn that is reorienting thinking about language, culture, and identity and bringing in new understandings of social-semiotic practices in contemporary contexts – suggest a "paradigm shift in sociolinguistics" comprising a socio-linguistics aimed at understanding society as well as language (an echo in some ways of Williams's [1992] trenchant critique of the inadequate sociology of sociolinguistics), viewing language as one among "a richer and more faceted configuration of semiotic resources deployed in events" and a richer understanding of contexts in temporal, spatial, and mobile terms.

Others, however, are less convinced, suggesting that this mushrooming of terms is little more than "Jargon and neologism to no useful purpose. Preten-tiousness and barren verbiage. Lack of novelty coupled with inelegant expres-sion" (Edwards 2012: 37–38). One direction from which the 'nothing very new' argument may be made is the long-standing focus on heteroglossia. As Blackledge and Creese (2014) suggest, the recent observations about mobility, resources, repertoires, and unbounded languages might just as readily be approached through "Mikhail Bakhtin's theoretical and practical notion of 'heteroglossia' as a lens through which to view the social, political and historical implications of language in practice" (p. 1). Thus, given that the *glossia* of heteroglossia was never a concern with languages but rather with voices and variability in speech, and as Bailey (2007) explains has to do with understanding the social meaning of talk "rather than in terms of formal systems, such as codes, that can veil actual speakers, uses and contexts"

(p. 272), it is equally possible either to look at translanguaging from within a framework of heteroglossia (García and Leiva 2014; Lin 2014) or to follow a framework of heteroglossia without reference to translanguaging or the other current terminologies (Pietikäinen 2013; Pietikäinen and Dufva 2014). While some may critique this as "ham-handed reminders of Bakhtin's well-known arguments about 'heteroglossia'" (Edwards 2012: 37), a case can be made that the notion of heteroglossia has been available to do this work all along.

The argument that we communicate across languages and with semiotic means beyond languages is also, from an *integrationalist* point of view (Harris 1990; 1998), nothing new. According to Harris, integrationalism "rejects any a priori attempt to circumscribe the phenomena of language or to draw a distinction between language and non-language which will be valid in each and every case. Instead, it delimits its own sphere of investigation by reference to dimensions of communicational relevance which apply to all forms of sign behaviour in human communication" (1990: 50). From this point of view, there is no good reason for linguistics to postulate the existence of languages, and there is "no longer any need to postulate, as in the Classical Model, that A and B must both know the same language in order to engage in verbal communication" (2009: 74). All two people need to know, Harris goes on, "is how to integrate their own semiological activities with those of their interlocutor" (p. 75).

From this standpoint, which "resists and rejects attempts to reduce human linguistic and communicative endeavours to an analysis based on the postulation of rules, objects and systems" (2013: 91), Orman critiques the "increasingly emergent emphasis in current sociolinguistic theorising" to "develop a new metaterminology" on the basis of a "perceived inadequacy of more traditional concepts and categorisations to satisfactorily capture the 'mixed' or 'hybrid' nature of much modern discourse, be it verbal or the product of digital literacy practices" (p. 90). Focusing particularly on polylanguaging, he argues that this is largely old wine in new bottles, suggesting that "when it comes to linguistic analysis," these new approaches fall back on fairly traditional approaches to linguistics, "hence the continued reference to codes, systems, etc." (p. 97). While aspects of this critique are not entirely convincing – Orman picks on particular aspects of the polylingual argument to show it adheres to traditional linguistic formulations – this nevertheless points to an important concern: To the extent that these frameworks employ traditional terminology or talk of 'mixing' languages (as do many of the quotes in the previous sections), they struggle to escape the linguistics that still defines the objects of critique.

It could be argued, therefore, that to claim that translanguaging rests on processes of language mixing is only to rename the process while maintaining the idea of mixed languages. Indeed, to talk of translanguaging is arguably to maintain a notion of distinct languages that are then mixed. This is a dilemma of any transgressive philosophy: Transgression simultaneously reinforces the very boundaries it aims to cross (Foucault 1977; Pennycook 2007). A similar point has been made about the notion of hybridity: While the idea points to the mixing of language, identity, or culture, it simultaneously implies the existence of entities that become hybridised (Otsuji and Pennycook 2014). Translanguaging, it might be argued, has started to become for sociolinguistics what hybridity became for cultural studies: Once hybridity or translanguaging have been observed, the analysis is over. More broadly, in its continued use of notions such as language mixing as well as its rejection of terms such as code-switching, it potentially maintains a notion of separable languages while also overlooking the implications of the shifts in meaning that the older terminology has undergone.

The notion of code-switching, which is often held up as one of the sociolinguistic concepts the new approaches aim to supersede, was originally intended as more diverse than current debates suggest. An open-ended term for the alternation of registers, genres, styles, dialects, and other varieties – see, for example, Blom and Gumperz (1972) on situational and metaphorical code-switching in Norway – the idea was reinscribed into normative sociolinguistics (or perhaps even more so in applied linguistics) and came to refer to the mixing of languages. Thus Davies's (2005: 22) definition of code-mixing becomes "switching between two or more languages within sentences and phrases," and elsewhere code-mixing and code-switching could be defined as "changing from one language to another within sentences, and across sentences, and larger language domains" (Kachru and Nelson 2006: 85). The more flexible notion of a code that does not predefine what kind of variety is under investigation became redefined in terms of language under the normative weight of socio- and applied linguistic orthodoxies. Indeed it might be argued that the greater flexibility in the idea of codes allows for a broader understanding than the 'language' element of translanguaging, polylanguaging, or metrolingualism.

In some ways, the intention of the idea behind code-switching was not dissimilar to the intention behind translanguaging, and it is arguable that we are already seeing the same processes of normalization with translanguaging. When Vaish and Subhan (2014), for example, equate a "translanguaging pedagogy" with a "bilingual approach to teaching reading" (p. 2) in their study of the use of Malay as a scaffold to teach English in Singapore, it would seem that translanguaging may have already become synonymous with official (rather than informal) notions of Singaporean bilingualism. While one aspect of translanguaging has been its attempt to describe everyday, subaltern, informal, vernacular use of multiple codes – 'contemporary urban vernaculars' in Rampton's (2011) terms – descriptions of translanguaging as bilingual pedagogies in official languages (even if such pedagogies transgress educational dogmas of the state) have surely been reincorporated into standard language ideologies. Although translanguaging has been used in contradistinction to a notion of standard language, here its nonstandardness has become only a rejection of the monolingual norms of certain pedagogical doctrines.

Makoni (2012; 2014) suggests that languaging and translanguaging cannot escape the idea of a language itself, since this approach to language is "founded on a deterministic framework of language and communication and a non-dynamic way of understanding interaction that runs contrary to the idea" (2012: 191). On the other hand, Sayer argues that a translanguaging approach to language mixing "provides a way to conceptualize dynamic bilingual practices beyond the scope of the linguistic or even sociolinguistic analysis of code-switching" (2013: 68–69). The difficulty here, then, is that these terms have been developed to escape what has happened to terms that were themselves developed to do not dissimilar things. These terms have been put to use within the contexts of a sociolinguistics that has been unable, particularly in European and North American scholarship, to escape its statist language ideologies, limiting the scope of multilingualism or code-switching in ways that were often not intended. Yet the new terminologies may already be in the process of inscription into the same language ideologies, rendering them equally susceptible to normative conceptualizations.

As Makoni (2012) suggests, the new "mantra of sociolinguistics" (p. 189) that languages are not clearly defined entities echoes many earlier observations, including Chomsky's (2000) view of the fuzziness of the idea of languages. Canagarajah, on the other hand, suggests that a translingual approach may turn Chomsky on his head since "we are all translinguals" (2013: 8). When contemporary calls are made to recognize that "No one knows *all* of a language . . . no one needs all the resources that a language potentially provides" (Blommaert 2010: 103), such a view echoes sociolinguistic truisms of forty years ago: No-one "commands a knowledge of any language 'as a whole'" but rather "possesses a repertoire, or set of overlapping codes" (Corder 1973: 66). Yet ultimately the 'old wine in new bottles' metaphor suggests that the new wine that was once poured into the bottles has itself changed. There is nothing intrinsic to the ideas of language, code-switching, or bilingualism that render them static and fixed, nor is there anything about translanguaging that will guarantee its more transgressive meanings.

Conclusion

Sociolinguists have long fought to argue in the public domain that bi- and multilingualism are natural, normal, and beneficial. A reconfiguration of terminology potentially threatens these arguments as well as possibly having little traction for a broader audience. Yet to the extent that sociolinguistics has all too often operated on the same terminological terrain as statist language ideologies while promoting a vision of tolerant diversity, it has perhaps been equally part of the problem. For many (socio)linguists the 'bilingual myth' remains the perception in some quarters that bilingualism is abnormal, dangerous, or damaging. Yet in fighting this myth so assiduously, there has been a reification of bilingualism into something positive yet static. To be sure, there have been a few 'language myth' objections – from Harris's (1981) critique of the 'fixed code' and 'telementational' fallacies of the Saussurean legacy of linguistics (the capacity to convey ideas from one mind to another through a fixed system of linguistic signs) to the more recent book of the same title (Evans 2014) critiquing the idea of a language instinct or universal grammar in favour of an understanding of language as an integrated communicative capacity – but studies of multilingualism have rarely gone far enough in seeing bilingualism as a set of social practices.

Canagarajah (2013) argues for the idea of translingual over multilingual because of the associations of separate languages, separate cognitive compartments, and separate language groups that have become aligned with the term *multilingual* which "doesn't accommodate the dynamic interactions between languages and communities envisioned by translingual" (p. 7). The term translingual, Canagarajah argues, not only gets us away from the mono/multi dichotomy, but also questions the very possibility of this approach to the countability of languages. "If languages are always in contact and communication always involves a negotiation of mobile codes, we have to ask if the term monolingual has anything more than an academic and ideological significance" (Canagarajah 2013: 8). From this perspective the construction of the idea of monolingualism is a central part of the problem (Yildiz 2012; Busch 2013; Pennycook and Otsuji 2015). The way forward from a translingual point of view is not to decry monolingualism in favour of multilingualism but to critically analyse the discursive history of enumerative approaches to language (Makoni and Pennycook 2007), from pernicious zerolingualism (a term used to denigrate minority languages as well as their speakers' supposedly inadequate grasp of Dutch in Belgium) (Jaspers 2011) and the well-meaning but unfortunate semi-lingualism (Skutnabb-Kangas 1981) to the unlikely idea of monolingualism and the beloved bilingualism, trilingualism, and multilingualism of sociolinguistics.

We should of course be sceptical about proclamations of turns and paradigm shifts, and we might also wonder whether a new paradigm is likely to be ushered in by such a plethora of new terms. At the same time, however, there is certainly something afoot here. Bell (2014) identifies a shift from Fishmanian 'sociology of language' studies – a 'macro-sociolinguistic' orientation to "whole languages and their distribution and usage within society" (p. 8) – to 'critical-constructivist sociolinguistics' wherein language is understood as a "social practice, with speakers drawing on all kinds of linguistic resources for their own purposes" (p. 9). This "post-Fishmanian" (Blommaert et al. 2012: 18) position can be seen as a reconciliation of some of the dichotomies of modernist linguistics (language and society, language and mind, society and culture), the coming together of sociolinguistics and linguistic anthropology (Bucholz and Hall 2008), and a turn away from the abstractions of languages and their isolation from other semiotic modes towards an understanding of language as a local practice (Pennycook, 2010).

We are indubitably witnessing rather more than "important lapses of under-standing", "infelicitous phrasing", and an "ignorance of the very well-known and long-established findings, from sociology and social psychology, bearing upon multiple social identities, roles and allegiances" (Edwards 2012: 37). It may well be the case that the claims to newness have been overstated and that issues raised by Gumperz, Hymes, and others in the 1960s and 1970s may not be so different. It is also clear that integrational linguistics – despite its lack of empirical work – has been saying something similar for a long time. Rather than translanguaging and polylingual approaches operating with a fixed code version of language (Orman 2013), it can be argued they share a number of characteristics with integrational linguistics. While we might object to the proliferation and the aesthetics of these new terminologies, we need at the same time to understand that terms such as 'diversity', 'bilingualism', and 'multilingualism' have become burdened by their history of use both within academic texts and across social life more broadly.

When a bilingual language policy can mean little other than support for English language teaching (de Mejía 2012), we can either struggle to reclaim the idea of bilingualism as dynamic and flexible (Creese and Blackledge 2011) or we can try to open up new territory by talking in new terms. A wide number of authors, sometimes through mutual influence, sometimes independently, have been seeking to throw off the shackles of sociolinguistic and pedagogical frameworks that do not seem to deal adequately with contemporary language practices. That our perception of such realities is linguistically mediated – an understanding gained perhaps from the 'linguistic turn' that possibly preceded the 'translinguistic turn' – may necessitate the search for new terms. Whether these are new terms for new times – brought about, that is, by changing social realities, as the superdiversity argument would have it – or whether these are new terms for new ways of thinking – epistemological changes that may not be causally linked to empirical changes – remains an open question. But we do seem to be witnessing a moment of disciplinary upheaval. Whether the terms themselves last or become reinscribed into sociolinguistic orthodoxies may not be the point; rather, we may learn from the broader insistences that language mixing is the norm and does not need explanation, that communication occurs across what have been thought of as languages, that speakers draw on reper-toires of semiotic resources, and that language is best understood in terms of social practices.

REFERENCES

Agha, A. 2007. *Language and Social Relations.* Cambridge: Cambridge University Press.

Bailey, B. 2007. Heteroglossia and boundaries. In M. Heller (ed.), *Bilingualism: A Social Approach.* New York: Palgrave Macmillan, 257–274.

Bell, A. 2014. *The Guidebook to Sociolinguistics.* Chichester: Wiley Blackwell.

Benor, S. B. 2010. Ethnolinguistic repertoire: Shifting the analytic focus in language and ethnicity. *Journal of Sociolinguistics* 14: 159–183.

Blackledge, A., and A. Creese. 2010. *Multilingualism: A Critical Perspective.* London: Continuum.

2014. Heteroglossia as practice and pedagogy. In A. Blackledge and A. Creese (eds.), *Heteroglossia as Practice and Pedagogy.* Dordrecht: Springer, 1–20.

Blom, J-P, and J. J. Gumperz. 1972. Social meaning in linguistic structure: Code-switching in Norway. In J. J. Gumperz and D. Hymes (eds.), *Directions in Sociolinguistics: The Ethnography of Communication.* New York: Holt, Rinehart and Winston, 407–434.

Blommaert, J. 2008. *Grassroots Literacy: Writing, Identity and Voice in Central Africa.* London: Routledge.

2010. *The Sociolinguistics of Globalization.* Cambridge: Cambridge University Press.

2013. Complexity, accent, and conviviality: Concluding comments. *Applied Linguistics* 34, 5: 613–622.

Blommaert, J, and A. Backus. 2013. Super diverse repertoires and the individual. In I. de Saint-Georges and J-J. Weber (eds.), *Multilingualism and Multimodality: Current Challenges for Educational Studies.* Rotterdam: Sense Publishers, 11–32.

Blommaert, J., and B. Rampton. 2011. Language and superdiversity. *Diversities* 13: 1–21.

Blommaert, J., S. Leppänen, and M. Spotti. 2012. Endangering multilingualism. In J. Blommaert, S. Leppänen, P. Pahti, and T. Räisänen (eds.), *Dangerous Multilingualism: Northern Perspectives on Order, Purity and Normality.* London: Palgrave Macmillan, 1–21.

Bucholz, M., and K. Hall. 2008. All of the above: New coalitions in sociocultural linguistics. *Journal of Sociolinguistics* 12, 4: 401–431.

Busch, B. 2012. The linguistic repertoire revisited. *Applied Linguistics* 33: 503–523.

2013. *Mehrsprachigkeit.* Wien: Facultas Verlags.

Canagarajah, S. 2011 Codemeshing in academic writing: Identifying teachable strategies of translanguaging. *Modern Language Journal* 95: 401–417.

2013. *Translingual Practice: Global Englishes and Cosmopolitan Relations.* New York: Routledge.

Chomsky, N. 2000. *Knowledge of Language: Its Nature, Origins and Use.* New York: Praeger.

Corder, S. P. 1973. *Introducing Applied Linguistics.* Harmondsworth: Penguin.

Coupland, N. 2007. *Style: Language Variation and Identity.* Cambridge: Cambridge University Press.

Creese, A., and A. Blackledge. 2011. Separate and flexible bilingualism in complementary schools: Multiple language practices in interrelationship. *Journal of Pragmatics* 43: 1196–1208.

Davies, Alan. 2005. *A Glossary of Applied Linguistics*. Edinburgh: Edinburgh University Press.

de Mejía, A-M. 2012. English language as intruder: The effects of English language education in Colombia and South America – a critical perspective. In V. Rapatahana and P. Bunce (eds.), *English Language as Hydra: Its Impacts on Non-English Language Cultures*, 244–254.

Edwards, J. 2012. *Multilingualism: Understanding Linguistic Diversity*. London: Continuum.

Evans, V. 2014. *The Language Myth: Why Language Is Not an Instinct*. Cambridge: Cambridge University Press.

Foucault, M. 1977. A preface to transgression. In Donald F. Bouchard (ed.), *Language, Counter-memory, Practice*. Ithaca, NY: Cornell University Press, 15–52.

García, O. 2009a. *Bilingual Education in the 21st Century: A Global Perspective*. Oxford: Wiley.

2009b. Education, multilingualism and translanguaging in the 21st century. In T. Skutnabb-Kangas, R. Phillipson, A. Mohanty, and M. Panda (eds.), *Social Justice through Multilingual Education*. Bristol: Multilingual Matters, 140–158.

2013. From diglossia to transglossia: Bilingual and multilingual classrooms in the 21st century. In C. Abello-Contesse, P. Chandler, M. López-Jiménez, and R. Chacón-Beltrán (eds.), *Bilingual and Multilingual Education in the 21st Century: Building on Experience*. Bristol: Multilingual Matters, 155–175.

2014. Countering the dual: Transglossia, dynamic bilingualism and translanguaging in education. In Rani S. Rubdy and Lubna Alsagoff (eds.), *The Global-Local Interface and Hybridity: Exploring Language and Identity*. Bristol: Multilingual Matters, 100–118.

García, O., and C. Leiva. 2014. Theorizing and enacting translanguaging for social justice. In A. Blackledge and A. Creese (eds.), *Heteroglossia as Practice and Pedagogy*. Dordrecht: Springer, 199–216.

García, O, and Li Wei. 2014. *Translanguaging: Language, Bilingualism and Education*. Basingstoke: Palgrave Macmillan.

Gumperz, J. J. 1964. Linguistic and social interaction in two communities. In J. J. Gumperz and D. Hymes (eds.), The ethnography of communication. *American Anthropologist* 66, 2: 137–153.

Harris, R. 1981. *The Language Myth*. London: Duckworth.

1990. On redefining linguistics. In H. Davis and T. Taylor (eds.), *Redefining Linguistics*. London: Routledge, 18–52.

1998. *Introduction to Integrational Linguistics*. Oxford: Pergamon.

2009. *After Epistemology*. Gamlingay: Authors Online.

Hornberger, N., and H. Link. 2012. Translanguaging and transnational literacies in multilingual classrooms: A biliteracy lens, *International Journal of Bilingual Education and Bilingualism*. 15, 3: 261–278,

Horner, B., M. Lu, J. Royster, and J. Trimbur. 2010. Language difference in writing: Towards a translingual approach. *College English* 73, 3: 303–321.

Jacquemet, M. 2005. Transidiomatic practices: Language and power in the age of globalization. *Language and Communication* 25: 257–277.

Forthcoming. *Transidioma: Language and Power in the Age of Globalization*. John Wiley.

Jaspers, J. 2011. Talking like a 'zerolingual': Ambiguous linguistic caricatures at an urban secondary school. *Journal of Pragmatics* 43: 1264–1278.

Jørgensen, J. N. 2008a. *Languaging: Nine Years of Poly-lingual Development of Young Turkish-Danish Grade School Students*. 2 vols. Copenhagen: University of Copenhagen.

2008b. Polylingal languaging around and among children and adolescents. *International Journal of Multilingualism* 5, 3: 161–176.

Kachru, Y., and C. Nelson. 2006. *World Englishes in Asian Contexts*. Hong Kong: Hong Kong University Press.

Li Wei. 2011. Moment Analysis and translanguaging space: Discursive construction of identities by multilingual Chinese youth in Britain. *Journal of Pragmatics* 43: 1222–1235.

Li Wei and Zhu Hua. 2013. Translanguaging identities and ideologies: Creating transnational space through flexible multilingual practices amongst Chinese university students in the UK. *Applied Linguistics* 34, 5: 516–535.

Lin, A. 2014. Hip-hop heteroglossia as practice, pleasure and public pedagogy: Translanguaging in the lyrical poetics of "24 Herbs" in Hong Kong. In A. Blackledge and A. Creese (eds.), *Heteroglossia as Practice and Pedagogy*. Dordrecht: Springer, 119–136.

Lu, M. 2009. Metaphors matter: Transcultural literacy. *Journal of Advanced Composition* 29: 285–94.

Maher, J. 2005. Metroethnicity, language, and the principle of Cool. *International Journal of the Sociology of Language* 11: 83–102.

Makoni, S., and A. Pennycook. 2007. Disinventing and reconstituting languages. In S. Makoni and A. Pennycook (eds.), *Disinventing and Reconstituting Languages*. Clevedon: Multilingual Matters, 1–41.

Makoni, S. 2012. A critique of language, languaging and supervernacular. *Muitas Vozes, Ponta Grossa* 1, 2: 189–199.

2013. An integrationist perspective on colonial linguistics. *Language Sciences* 35: 87–96.

2014. 'The Lord is my Shock Absorber': A sociohistorical integrationist approach to mid-twentieth-century literacy practices in Ghana. In A. Blackledge and A. Creese (eds.), *Heteroglossia as Practice and Pedagogy*. Dordrecht: Springer, 75–98.

Makoni, S., and A. Pennycook. 2012. Disinventing multilingualism: From monological multilingualism to multilingua francas. In Marilyn Martin-Jones, Adrian Blackledge, and Angela Creese (eds.), *The Routlledge Handbook of Multilingualism*. New York: Routledge, 439–453.

Martin-Beltrán, M. 2014. "What do you want to say?" How adolescents use translanguaging to expand learning opportunities. *International Multilingual Research Journal* 8, 3: 208–230.

Mignolo, W. D. 2000. *Local Histories/Global Designs: Coloniality, Subaltern Knowledges and Border Thinking*. Princeton, NJ: Princeton University Press.

Møller, J. S. 2008. Polylingual performance among Turkish-Danes in late-modern Copenhagen. *International Journal of Multilingualism* 5: 217–236.

Møller, J. S., and J. N. Jørgensen. 2011. Enregisterment among adolescents in superdiverse Copenhagen. In J. S. Møller and J. N. Jørgensen (eds.), *Language*

Enregisterment and Attitudes. University of Copenhagen: Copenhagen Studies in Bilingualism 63, pp. 99–121.

Orman, J. 2013. New lingualisms, same old codes. *Language Sciences* 37: 90–98.

Otsuji, E., and A. Pennycook. 2010. Metrolingualism: Fixity, fluidity and language in flux. *International Journal of Multilingualism* 7: 240–254.

2014. Unremarkable hybridities and metrolingual practices. In Rani S. Rubdy and Lubna Alsagoff (eds.), *The Global-Local Interface and Hybridity: Exploring Language and Identity*. Bristol: Multilingual Matters, 83–99.

Pennycook, A. 2007. *Global Englishes and Transcultural Flows*. London: Routledge.

2008. English as a language always in translation. *European Journal of English Studies* 12, 1: 33–47.

2010. *Language as a Local Practice*. London: Routledge.

Pennycook A., and E. Otsuji. 2014a. Market lingos and metrolingua francas. *International Multilingual Research Journal*. 8, 4: 255–270.

2014b. Metrolingual multitasking and spatial repertoires: 'Pizza mo two minutes coming'. *Journal of Sociolinguistics*, 18, 2: 161–184.

2015. *Metrolingualism: Language in the City*. London: Routledge.

Pietikäinen, S. 2013. Heteroglossic authenticity in Sámi heritage tourism. In S Pietikäinen and H. Kelly-Holmes (eds.), *Multilingualism and the Periphery*. Oxford: Oxford University Press, 77–94.

Pietikäinen, S., and H. Dufva. 2014. Heteroglossia in action: Sámi chidren, textbooks and rap. In A. Blackledge and A. Creese (eds.), *Heteroglossia as Practice and Pedagogy*. Dordrecht: Springer, 59–74.

Rampton, B. 2011. From 'multi-ethnic adolescent heteroglossia' to 'contemporary urban vernaculars'. *Language and Communication* 31: 276–294.

Ritzau, U. 2014. Learner language and polylanguaging: How language students' ideologies relate to their written language use. *International Journal of Bilingual Education and Bilingualism*. DOI: 10.1080/13670050.2014.936822.

Sayer, P. 2013. Translanguaging, TexMex, and bilingual pedagogy: Emergent bilinguals learning through the vernacular. *TESOL Quarterly* 47, 1: 63–88.

Skutnabb-Kangas, T. 1981. *Bilingual or Not: The Education of Minorities*. Avon: Multilingual Matters.

Sultana, S., S. Dovchin, and A. Pennycook. 2015. Transglossic language practices of young adults in Bangladesh and Mongolia. *International Journal of Multilingualism* 12, 1: 93–108.

Vaish, V., and A. Subhan. 2014. Translanguaging in a reading class. *International Journal of Multilingualism*. DOI: 10.1080/14790718.2014.948447.

Venuti, L. 1998. *The Scandals of Translation: Towards an Ethics of Difference*. London: Routledge.

Vertovec, S. 2007. Super-diversity and its implications. *Ethnic and Racial Studies* 30, 6: 1024–1054.

Williams, C. 1996. Secondary education: Teaching in the bilingual situation. In C. Williams, G. Lewis, and C. Baker (eds.), *The Language Policy: Taking Stock*. Llangefni, UK: CAI, 39–78.

Williams, G. 1992. *Sociolinguistics: A Sociological Critique*. London: Routledge.

Yildiz, Y. 2012. *Beyond the Mother Tongue: The Postmonolingual Condition*. New York: Fordham University Press.

10   Sedentarism and nomadism in the sociolinguistics of dialect

David Britain

Introduction

Perhaps one sign of a maturing discipline is a willingness on the part of its practitioners to introspect, self-critique and reflect upon what the field has taken for granted in its quest for progress.[1] As Eckert (2003: 392) has argued, 'we have to take a look at the givens and consider their implications for what we've done, and for what we will do in the future'. There comes a point, she says, when theoretical and methodological assumptions that have previously been swept under the carpet 'have done their work and it is now time to pull them out and examine what they have helped us take for granted' (2003: 396). One particular 'elephant in the room' that has come in for considerable unpacking in recent years is the concept of the 'authentic speaker' (in addition to Eckert 2003, see Bucholtz 2003; Coupland 2010), the 'ideal' informant with all of the 'right' social characteristics that suit the analysis to be conducted. In dialectological theory and practice, the 'authentic speaker' has been a particularly large elephant.

In this spirit, I turn the attention to another elephant and present an account of the ways in which differing stances towards *mobility* have permeated theory and practice in dialectology, from the early nineteenth-century studies through to the present. In assessing how ideologies of mobility have shaped dialectological practice, I draw heavily from contemporary debates in cultural geography that have explored 'the way the geographical imagination ... provides an underlying metaphysics that influences and informs thought and action' (Cresswell 2006: 25). I begin, therefore, by outlining recent discussions about one particularly powerful underlying metaphysics that concerns 'imaginations of mobility', discussions which examine 'the mobilization of mobility as a root metaphor for contemporary understandings of the world of culture and society'

---

[1] The work presented in this chapter has been conducted with the help of funding from the Swiss National Science Foundation ("Contact, mobility and authenticity: language ideologies in koineisation and creolisation": 100015_146240). I am extremely grateful to Nik Coupland for his sensitive and detailed close reading and commentary of an earlier draft of this chapter. The final product has improved immeasurably thanks to his critique.

(Cresswell 2006: 25–26). I highlight, first, the ongoing geographical critique of how mobility is imagined, conceptualised and 'managed' at two opposing poles – at one end 'the propensity to see the world in fixed and bounded ways', at the other 'a way of seeing that takes movement as its starting point' (Adey 2010: 40) – pointing to contemporary mobility theorists' attempts to carve out a more nuanced middle path between the two, sensitive to the concerns of each. Second, I will suggest that some of the methodological and theoretical assumptions that underlie sociolinguistic approaches to the study of dialect can productively be explored through the ways in which they align with these powerful ideological ways of 'seeing' mobility. In earlier research (Britain 2010), I compared the perhaps unsurprisingly parallel, but somewhat later development of theoretical conceptualisations of *space* in social dialectology with those in its 'home' discipline of human geography. The ways that dialectologists were imagining space were following the same epistemological trajectory as that of the human geographers and were, with a slight delay, entirely typical of their time. In many ways I am performing the same task here, attempting to demonstrate that the ways in which social dialectologists have engaged with mobility suggest a parallel alignment to that in the other social sciences. Like Eckert (2003: 396) in relation to the authentic speaker, however, I agree that we must accept when long-held ideological assumptions 'have done their work and it is now time to pull them out and examine what they have helped us take for granted'.

Imaginations of mobility

Cresswell's (2006) book *On the Move: Mobility in the Modern Western World* has become an extremely influential text in the articulation of what has come to be known as the 'new mobilities' paradigm in the social sciences, an attempt both to challenge what it sees as the a-mobile focus of much social science research and to present a new sociology that engages with and attempts to understand, *whilst not fetishizing*, mobility (also Urry 2000; 2007; Adey 2010). In this book he presents two ways of seeing the world, in relation to mobility, that have been especially dominant – what he and others (e.g. Malkki 1992: 26) have labelled a *sedentarist* in contrast to a *nomadic* metaphysics.

Sedentarism has been especially influential. It 'sees mobility through the lens of place, rootedness, spatial order and belonging ... conceptualized through the lens of fixity as an ideal' (Cresswell 2006: 26, 28; also Sheller and Urry 2006: 208, Hall 2009: 575). It is one of the fundamental claims of the new mobilities paradigm that mainstream sociology has largely theorised society from a sedentarist perspective. Sedentarist approaches see place as the 'phenomenological starting point for geography', as a 'moral world, as an insurer of authentic existence and center of meaning for people ... mobility is often the assumed threat to the rooted, moral, authentic existence of place' ... playing 'second fiddle to the overriding concern with place' (Cresswell 2006: 30–31), 'the often implicit underbelly of the place' (Cresswell 1997: 361).

As a result, mobility more generally from this perspective 'is seen as morally and ideologically suspect, a by-product of a world arranged through place and spatial order ... a threat, a disorder in the system, a thing to control ... as suspicious, as threatening and as a problem ... as anachoristic'[2] (Cresswell 2006: 26, 55). Cresswell and others (e.g. Adey 2010) have demonstrated that this mobility-as-threat pervades public discourses and points to the way that 'modern states have preoccupied themselves with the ordering and disciplining of mobile peoples. Think of the role of the outsider in modern life ... the drifter, the shiftless, the refugee and the asylum seeker have been inscribed with immoral intent ... These have all been portrayed as figures of mobile threat in need of straightening out and discipline' (2006: 26). Kabachnik (2010: 95, 102–103) talks of an 'unquestioned privileging of fixed abodes' and a 'hegemonic sedentary norm', according to which 'nomads and others without a fixed place are particularly terrifying and disruptive ... nomads – be they capitalists, refugees or migrant workers – threaten the stability of places by crossing borders and disrupt the normative order'.

Ignoring the mobile is another manifestation of sedentarism. Mobility theorists have highlighted how societies depend on an ever more complex and interconnected series of 'mobility systems' that enable, regulate and bring together flows of people, goods, capital, ideas, communications and waste. Sedentarist approaches have downplayed the critical role of these systems, yet Cresswell and Martin highlight how 'the often invisible networks of mobility' are made visible when the 'smooth laminar flow' (2012: 516) of societal systems of mobility falters. Cresswell (2014: 712) labels such events '"critical mobilities" – (im)mobilities which interrupt the taken-for-granted world of flows and force us to question how things move and the meanings given to those movements'.

One such event was the disruption caused by the ash cloud from Iceland's Eyjafjallajökull volcano in 2010. The eruption of the volcano triggered an eruption of academic papers pointing to how it revealed not only the taken-for-granted nature of international movement – of people, goods, and services – but also the knock-on effects of when the smooth laminar flow is suddenly disrupted. With fewer than 20 percent of normal flights operating in European airspace in mid-April 2010 (Budd et al. 2011: 32), business people were stranded, tourists forced to spend another week in

---

[2] Anachorism is the spatial equivalent of anachronism – a term for denoting something that is in the wrong place (rather than at the wrong time).

Majorca, and perishable goods rotted in warehouses, with Tanzanian green beans and Peruvian blackberries unable to reach Western dinner tables. Kenyan factory workers lost their jobs as tonnes of flowers they were preparing for European vases had to be dumped.[3] The panic that followed the eruption, according to Budd et al. (2011: 35), 'owed much to the strategic contribution of air transportation to capital accumulation in the contemporary post-Fordist economy'. Furthermore, the media presentation of the volcano's effects as unprecedented also foregrounded the eurocentricity of reaction to the event. Jensen notes that 'hitting the trans-Atlantic nerve system made these nature-aeromobility systems' vulnerabilities specific to Europe and America as if this was the first time that flights were ever grounded due to volcanic activities' (2011: 71). The volcano also, at least temporarily, changed mobilities within Iceland's own tourism industry, not only limiting arrivals in the immediate aftermath of the eruption, but also triggering changes in tourist activity on the island – with many wanting to watch the volcano in action and drive through the ash – with risk-seeking acting 'as inspiration for travel and a deepening of the travel experience' and enabling Iceland's tourism industry to recruit the eruption as a branding opportunity (Benediktsson et al. 2011: 78). It also caused 'stranded' travellers to suddenly feel *emotionally* vulnerable, even in perfectly hospitable surroundings. Drawing upon Heidegger's idea (1962: 102) that only when a tool is damaged does its functioning become conspicuous, Jensen argued that 'the "breakdown" triggered by the volcanic activity illustrates vulnerabilities at a very practical level, but equally that emotions are tied to our relationship to global mobility and finally that such abnormalities are windows into technology and the ontology of mobilities' (Jensen 2011: 68). These authors (and many others) all agree that it is often only when the system breaks down that the network is suddenly revealed (Adey and Anderson 2011: 11).

The primary goal of the new mobilities paradigm has been to overturn this sedentarist perspective, to question the 'perceived prioritization of more rooted and bounded notions of place as the locus of identity', and to persuade us 'not to start from a point of view that takes certain kinds of fixity and boundedness for granted' (Cresswell 2011: 551). Place should not be seen as an 'arena of static rootedness but as an achievement of dwelling, constructed through the intricate, repeated and habitual movements of people . . . the collective effect of

---

[3] Even those not directly affected by this temporary immobility noticed its consequences. Jeffries (2010: 9, cited by Budd et al. 2011: 37) talks about being able, in central London, to be able to "savour the birdsong [and other] . . . restful sounds, so long obliterated by Virgin Atlantics laden with victims of global Disneyfication and Lufthansas packed with businessmen who could just as well conduct their fatuous meetings via Skype from Munich".

individual bodies moving through space' (Cresswell 2006: 45–46). Later, I argue that sedentarist approaches have been overwhelmingly predominant in dialectological theory and practice, from the early traditional dialectological accounts of the nineteenth century, right through to the present.

Mobility has not always, however, been seen in such a negative and threatening light – it has long also been presented as a sign of emancipation, freedom, and progress, and place and fixity seen as stifling, restrictive, far from ideal. Frequent (decontextualized) reports that the world is 'becoming more mobile' are usually presented in positive terms, as signs of advancement and civilisation, as liberating for the citizen (though not necessarily good for the planet). Cresswell has argued that 'ways of thinking that emphasise mobility and flow over stasis and attachment have come to the fore. As the world has appeared to become more mobile, so thinking about the world has become *nomad thought*' (2006: 43, emphasis in original), and he and others have pointed to the way in which 'scholars have increasingly turned to anti-essentialist and post-structuralist thinking, and there has been an emerging interdisciplinary interest in themes such as migration, diasporic cultures, cosmopolitanism[,] … performance, globalisation and post-colonialism' (Merriman 2012: 4–5). Some mobility theorists, however, working within the new paradigm, warn against a descent into an opposing 'nomadic meta-physics'; a stance which sees mobility as 'unremittingly positive' and 'puts mobility first, has little time for various notions of attachment to place and revels in notions of flow, flux and dynamism. Place is portrayed as stuck in the past, overly confining and possibly reactionary' (Cresswell 2006: 25–26).

A number of criticisms have been levelled at such nomadism. One is that 'by critiquing one perspective of place and then ignoring place altogether, a nomadic metaphysics is throwing the baby out with the bathwater' (Kabachnik 2010: 95). A number of 'new mobilities' scholars have argued for a recognition of the interconnectedness of 'moorings' and 'mobilities', appreciating the centrality of mobility in social life but recognising that 'all mobilities entail specific often highly embedded and immobile infrastructures' (Sheller and Urry 2006: 210). For mobility in the car, for example, think of the petrol station; for air travel, think of the airport. Concepts of place survive in the mobilities paradigm but are theorised in a progressive sense (Massey 1993), which 'conceptualizes places as constructed, dynamic, relational, and intercon-nected with other places' (Kabachnik 2010: 91). Secondly, it has been argued that nomadic approaches have presented a *decontextualised* mobility, abstract, dehistoricised, generalised, homogenised, ungrounded, and unbounded (Cress-well 2006: 53; 1997), an approach that does not sufficiently recognise who is mobile (and who is not), who has the resources to be mobile (and who does not), who is moving out of free will (and who is not). Cresswell has charged that 'the postmodern nomad is a remarkably unsocial being – unmarked by the traces of class, gender, ethnicity, sexuality, and geography ... little attention has been paid to the historical conditions that have produced specific forms of movement' (2006: 53–54). Nomadism, it has also been suggested, runs the risk of 'romanticis[ing] the lives and transgressive movements of subjects such as the nomad or migrant ... diverting our attention away from the task of identifying the complex politics underpinning the production and regulation of mobilities' (Merriman 2012: 5).

The new mobilities paradigm has positioned itself, therefore, by problematising 'both "sedentarist" approaches in the social science that treat place, stability and dwelling as a natural steady state, and deterritorialised approaches that posit a new grand narrative of mobility, with fluidity and liquidity as a pervasive condition of postmodernity or globalisation' (Hannam et al. 2006: 5). My aim in what follows is to subject dialectology to such a critique, unpacking the largely sedentarist approaches of much work in the field and highlighting the potential for nomadism in an emergent dialectology of superdiversity. In considering how sedentarism and nomadism have shaped dialectological practice, I examine its underlying stance towards mobility.

It is at this point important to delimit what kinds of mobilities I will be addressing here. Recent sociological and geographical work on mobilities has recognised that a full appreciation of mobility necessitates an examination of the movement not just of people, but also of 'objects, images, information and wastes' (Urry 2000: 1). Given that research in dialectology, historically, has overwhelmingly relied on face-to-face interaction as the conduit of linguistic change, diffusion and transmission, I restrict my discussion here to physical human mobility. Very recently, relative to the historical depth of dialectology, some have argued for a greater sensitivity towards the potential for change to be transmitted via the media, though this potential remains controversial in the discipline (see Sayers 2014 and commentaries on this article published in the same journal issue). A dialectology of mobile communication, by which I mean non-co-present *voice* interaction (i.e. *not* entextualised computer- or phone-mediated communication), appears to be almost entirely absent. To make an initial evaluation of social dialectology's stances towards mobility, therefore, I restrict myself here to examining the kinds of mobilities with which it has theoretically engaged.

In doing so, I focus on a number of prominent themes and approaches within dialectology: the 'traditional' approach, Labovian variationism, the diffusion and transmission of linguistic features, contact dialectology and, finally, the dialectology of superdiversity. As we will see, until very recently, a strong sedentarism prevails: Mobility is either ignored, seen as peripheral to models of linguistic change, or positively shunned and treated as suspect.

Sedentarism in dialect data collection: the study of *Homo dormiens*?

Before examining the more theoretical sedentarism of dialectology, it is worth making the very practical, methodological point that almost the entire dialectological enterprise, in collecting data for analysis, has involved the recording of people who are kept as *still* as possible. Dialectological recordings are routinely conducted in informants' homes (TV turned off, parrot moved to another room) or in quiet classrooms, seated, literally face-to-face, rather than in the busy workplace, walking down the street, sitting on the train, or driving the car to the mall. We know little about the patterning of language variation when we are *literally* on the move, yet potentially, for example, the lack of (literal) face-to-face interaction that talk en route often entails could well have, for example, phonological implications for the marking of turn management (Britain 2013b). Occasionally, in some more ethnographically oriented work, researchers have recorded on the move (e.g. Mendoza-Denton's 2008: 66–73 car journey with some of her Latina informants) or recorded within relatively restricted spatial domains that enable some movement, for example within school playgrounds, but the overwhelming norm is for recording to take place seated in a quiet room (see, e.g. Schilling 2013: 239–243). The approach clearly represents a prioritisation of optimal recording conditions over capturing human interaction in all its different mobile forms. But if dialect variant choice itself is constitutive of and not simply reflective of identities and is used constructively in the ongoing management of talk, the sedentarism of recording norms in dialectology could be deemed problematic, preventing us from gaining insight into an informant's fuller repertoire of variant adoption.

Traditional dialectology

It is important to state here, at the start of an examination of dialectological imaginations of mobility (and since it remains true for most of the approaches to the study of dialect that are broached in this chapter), that sedentarism is not *unaware* of mobility – quite the contrary, it has a particularly heightened sense of consciousness about its impact on dialect. Its impulse, however, is to shun it, ignore it, or treat it as secondary, as we will see. The methodological approach of the first dialectologists has routinely come in for sharp critique, and it is clear that many scholars in this tradition took a strictly sedentarist approach to, for example, informant choice. For Ellis (1889), a pioneer of English dialectology, the very word 'dialect'[4] implied a particular sort of speaker – uneducated, native

---

[4] 'This is a treatise on the existing phonology of the English dialects, meaning simply peasant speech' (Ellis 1889: 7).

(1889: 1), 'old and if possible illiterate' (1889: 4). His analysis of the resulting data, especially in the areas surrounding London, showed that he felt mobility was antithetical to the very existence of 'dialect':[5]

> the composite nature of a very shifting population in this district renders the growth of any dialect proper impossible (Ellis 1889: 129) ... the enormous congeries of persons from different parts of the kingdom and from different countries, and the generality of school education, render dialect nearly impossible. (1889: 225)

Later, the sedentarist trope of 'mobility as suspicious' was explicitly raised in motivations of the sample for the Survey of English Dialects:

> The kind of dialect chosen for study was that normally spoken by elderly speakers of sixty years of age or over belonging to the same social class in rural communities, and in particular by those who were, or had formerly been, employed in farming, for it is amongst the rural populations that the traditional types of vernacular English are best preserved to-day ... *dialect speakers whose residence in the locality had been interrupted by significant absences were constantly regarded with suspicion.* (Orton and Dieth 1962: 14–16, emphasis added)

The tendency for the traditional dialectologists to focus on *rural* areas has also not infrequently been seen as a symptom of an avoidance of mobility. Cresswell has pointed out that, more generally, 'the rural was theorised as a place of rest and rootedness – of community – the urban was a site of movement and alienation – a space of "society"' (2006: 36; see also Woods 2011: chapter 2).

The idea that place is an *authenticating* aspect of language is also particularly salient in this early dialectological work. Both the rural geographical and linguistic authenticity literatures have noted how the rural is seen as untainted and traditional. Woods (2011: 27) argues that 'the rural was portrayed as fragile, vulnerable to urban incursions, either physical ... or socio-cultural', whilst Bucholtz, for example, has argued 'the authentic speaker as remote from urban modernity has remained a core element of much research on regional and social dialects' (2003: 399).[6] Concerns about mobility, furthermore, have contributed centrally to the framing of a critique of the authentic speaker. Eckert (2003: 392) points, for example, to the ideal 'poster-child' informants of dialectology being 'locally located and oriented', 'untainted by the interference of ... social agency', and Bucholtz (2003: 404) posits 'linguistic isolationism' as another ideal in the hunt for 'authentic' data: 'the most authentic language is removed from and unaffected by other influences, and thus the most authentic speaker belongs to a well-defined, static, and relatively

---

[5] See Britain (2009) for further examples of Ellis's sensitivity to mobility-triggered dialect levelling.

[6] For a consideration of how 'rural' and 'urban' have been handled in dialectology, see Britain (2012a, forthcoming).

homogeneous social grouping that is closed to the outside. In the logic of this ideology, the effects of social and linguistic contact are problematic – hence, the normal state of linguistic affairs is often understood as a difficulty for sociolinguistic analysis'. While these authenticities are characteristic of most forms of dialectology, they are sharpest in focus amongst the earliest dialectologists. Traditional dialectology was unashamedly and overtly sedentarist; mobility was suspicious and made 'dialect' impossible.

Variationist sociolinguistics

Dialectology's shift to the city in the 1960s went hand in hand with a number of methodological and theoretical developments in the discipline (Labov 1966/ 2006; Weinreich et al. 1968). A broader sweep of speech community members was sampled, and the capturing of continuous speech enabled analysis that entailed a closer inspection of the constraints on variability. Despite this expansion of who was an 'acceptable' informant, however, community nativeness remained a central and core criterion for selection. The young, the female and the urban were now acceptable, but mobile people were (still) not. Labov's pioneering study of New York (1966/2006: 110–111) excluded those who had arrived after the age of eight, and most surveys of a similar kind since continue to incorporate such eligibility benchmarks. But calculations by Kerswill (1993: 35) have suggested that Labov's exclusion of mobile individuals meant that 'well over 50 percent of the original sample are excluded by various nativeness related criteria'.

That this is problematic for our understanding of linguistic change has become especially evident, however, since the publication of work demonstrating that nonlocal mobile members of the community can be at the vanguard of language changes that affect longer-term members of the same communities. Horvath's (1985) work in Sydney that took into account the immigrant Italian and Greek populations found that 'the inclusion of migrants in the study proved to be rewarding in a number of ways ... the study ... can be seen as a description of how migrants enter into a speech community; the formation of a peripheral community by the first generation and then the movement into the core speech community by the second generation. *The attendant effects on the speech community in general cannot be fully comprehended unless the peripheral community is included in the study*' (1985: 174–175, emphasis added). Fox's (2007; 2015; Britain and Fox 2009) ethnographic work in an East London youth club, too, has demonstrated how linguistic innovations generated within the migrant Bangladeshi community spread through network connections to local 'Anglos'. Observing social network ties contracted within the club, she was able to analyse the transmission of linguistic changes via network ties within the club. One such development is the variable loss of allomorphy in the definite article *the*, shifting from a system sensitive to whether the sound following the article was a vowel or a consonant (i.e. *the melon* [ðə mɛlən] versus *the apple* [ði æpɫ]) to one which lacked such sensitivity (*the melon* [ðə mɛlən] versus *the apple* [ðəˀæpɫ], with a glottal stop functioning to break the hiatus between the two vowels). In analysing (see Fox 2015) the network transmission of this lack of allomorphy across different friendship groups within the club, she finds its use highest amongst the older Bangladeshi males, and ever lower use with greater social distance from this network group in the club. Such work is the exception, rather than the rule, however.[7] The continued exclusion of the mobile from much place-based variationist work has had, as we will see, ongoing sedentarist consequences for theory development.

Geographical diffusion

One area of the variationist enterprise where one might expect to find a more robust and central role for mobility is the examination of the intergenerational transmission and spatial spread of linguistic innovations. I examine two aspects of diffusion here – firstly, approaches to the spread of innovations and, secondly, Labov's (2007) differentiation between community-internal 'transmission' and community-external 'diffusion'. The most influential model in accounting for geolinguistic innovation diffusion has been the urban hierarchy model, which suggests that innovations spread down an urban hierarchy from metropolis to city to town to village to countryside. The rationale for this model is that transportation networks tend to link urban with urban, and the socioeconomic and consumer infrastructure tends to be based in and oriented towards urban centres, so that while distance plays some role, interaction between urban centres is likely to be greater, and therefore a more frequent and effective channel for innovation transmission, than between urban and rural (see Britain 2012b,c for a critique of work on innovation diffusion in dialectology). Quantitative gravity models were piggybacked onto the urban hierarchy model, leading some dialectologists to attempt to mathematically calculate the likely linguistic influence of Place A on Place B by examining solely the populations of the two and the distance between the two (see, e.g. Trudgill 1974; 1983; Larmouth 1981; Hernández Campoy 2003; Inoue 2010). Note here, however, how 'the line that connects A to B is explained *by* A and B' (Cresswell 2006: 29, emphasis in original), and the mobilities between the two are, actually, factored out of the explanations of diffusion. Two places

---

[7] For example, in the extensive recent surveys of 'Multicultural London English' (e.g. Cheshire et al. 2011) all the children who formed the core informant sample in the two surveys either were born in London or arrived as preschoolers.

exist, they are connected (or not) by potential channels of communication, and population and distance are deemed to account for interaction between the two. Gravity model approaches assume that everyone in A has an equal chance of transmitting an innovation and that everyone in B has an equal chance of adopting it. Gravity models, then, 'continued to relegate movement to something curiously inhuman, empty of social and cultural content and logically secondary to the arrangements of space and place' (Cresswell 2012: 573–574; Gregory 1985; Britain 2012b,c). Gravity models have generally been accused of more generally being insensitive to social structure, leading Gregory (1985: 304) to argue that there had been 'no serious discussion of the structures of social relations and systems of social practices through which innovations filter'. This critique applies equally to linguistic work on innovation diffusion, which has tended to foreground the geographical and the places that donate and receive and often ignore the social and the mobilities that enable the transmission.

As outlined in Britain (2012b,c), when one zooms in to the neighbourhood level, the picture of transmission becomes somewhat more socially rich, with social network–based (e.g. Milroy 1980; Milroy and Milroy 1985; Milroy 1992; Labov 2001) and community of practice–based techniques (Eckert 2000; Fox 2007; Mendoza-Denton 2008) demonstrating routes of intralocality or intracommunity transmission. The work of Lesley and James Milroy (especially 1985) has highlighted which sorts of social networks are especially vulnerable (weak networks) or resistant (strong networks) to outside linguistic influence. Furthermore, they have 'projected up' this finding to propose, for example, that the more mobile central social classes are likely to be both the most vulnerable to outside influence and the most likely to diffuse change and that communities with historically relative social equality and close social network ties – such as Iceland – are less likely to develop dialectal fragmentation and diversity than socially unequal countries with variable degrees of social and geographical mobility, such as Britain. The model is sensitive to the impact of mobility on local social network structure but has less to say about how linguistic features embedded in networks of different strength nevertheless are projected geographically across space. As a result of their work, we can better gauge what sorts of people in A are likely to be diffusers, and what sorts of people in B are likely to be willing recipients, but how the distance between them is overcome is less well developed.

Labov very explicitly sees variation in space as distinct from variation in society (Labov 1982: 20) and, robustly defending his conceptualisation of the speech community, argues that 'the primary source of diversity is the transmission (and incrementation) of change within the speech community, and that *diffusion is a secondary process of a very different character*. Such a clear dichotomy between transmission and diffusion is dependent upon the concept of a speech community with well-defined limits, a common structural base and a unified set of sociolinguistic norms' (Labov 2010: 309, emphasis added). He (2007, 2010) presents evidence from fine-grained differences in the pronunciation of /a/ in five U.S. cities – New York, North Plainfield, Albany, Cincinnati, and New Orleans – to demonstrate that whilst the system in the four latter locations has undergone various types of simplification and regularisation, changes of a different kind have taken place in New York as the system is, with some 'incrementation', transmitted 'faithfully' from one generation to the next through an 'unbroken sequence of native-language acquisition by children' (2010: 307). One might ask at this point who is and is not part of the New York speech community, and therefore who is indeed incrementing and transmitting. Labov states (2007: 369) that 'the speech communities described so far – New York, Albany, Cincinnati, New Orleans – are formed by the population defined in American society as the white mainstream ... differentiated internally by social class, but separated sharply from the African American and Latino populations in the same cities.'

An exploration of the demographics of New York is rather informative. In 2010, the 'White-alone not Hispanic or Latino' category in the U.S. Census accounted for 33 percent of the population of New York City.[8] Given that not all of this 33 percent are likely to be native to New York (indeed, 11.2 percent of the population were not even living in the same place a year before the census[9]), then the 'New York speech community' represents a clear minority of the population of New York. Clearly, sedentarism is a significant determiner of membership here, where authenticity is strongly related to white, multigenerational, stable residence. But this point has been made before (Kerswill 1993). What clearly nails home the sedentarist metaphysics underlying this approach, however, is the idea that somehow the changes that have affected the other cities are secondary, of lesser theoretical importance to an account of change than the processes affecting a (shrinking) minority that has, apparently, not been subject to contact and diffusion. This approach, firstly, ignores the undoubtedly disruptive role of what Hall (2009: 574) calls 'the small and (seemingly) trivial practices and movements that constitute the urban everyday' (see also Britain 2013a). Subverting the concept of the city as a bounded site, a view that is nevertheless fairly overt in Labov's account (2001: 226–227), Hall (2009: 573–574) goes on to argue that

place as a primary container for social life and a basic unit of social research and analysis ... is the domain and object of a sedentary social science ... No longer a spatial clot – of place, power, people, dwelling and situated economy – the city is

---

[8] http://quickfacts.census.gov/qfd/states/36/3651000.html (accessed December 1, 2014).
[9] Ibid.

opened up to fluidity and transitivity; thus cities may be reconsidered 'as much spaces of flows as they are spaces of place' (Yeoh, 2006: 150) ... Routine urban undulations – mundane recurrences, people and objects making the rounds and doing the usual, practices started over and over again – are as much a part of the flow of the city as are translocal circuits of movement, and, as such, equally disruptive of a sedentarist social science.

Secondly, in presenting these types of linguistic development as 'normative' for 'internal' change in a community, this approach prevents the changes that are taking place from being interpreted in the full light of the sociodemographic developments of the city, where researchers would be cognisant of the ongoing flows that together create New York. How can we interpret these 'community-internal' changes socially, when the majority of New Yorkers are not implicated in them? Thirdly, when the linguistic consequences of mobility are relegated to a secondary position, mobility is treated again as disruptive of some static social realm in which 'normal transmission' can take place, and is therefore deemed to be of peripheral importance to our understanding of change.

Contact dialectology

Contact – 'the effect of one system on another' (Labov 2001: 20) – has been largely peripheral to Labov's own work until very recently (see Labov 2001: 20), although it has been central to another strand of dialectology that gained momentum following the publication of Trudgill's (1986) *Dialects in Contact*. Building upon the subtle linguistic changes that take place when speakers interact, and recognising the implicit mobility involved in interactional co-presence, this approach has placed the linguistic consequences of especially *geographical* mobility at its core, with some even suggesting it as a potential alternative to Labovian explanations of change (e.g. Milroy 2002). It has largely been the dialect outcomes of large-scale, long-distance and mixed-origin acts of migration, for example colonial settlement migrations (e.g. Trudgill 2004 for [mainly Southern Hemisphere] English, Mougeon and Beniak 1994 for Canadian French, Penny 2000 for Latin American Spanish, Matsumoto and Britain 2003 for Micronesian Japanese, etc.), indentured labour movements (Barz and Siegel 1988), urbanisation (Bortoni-Ricardo 1985; Kerswill and Williams 2000; etc.), and individual migration (e.g. Chambers 1992), that have provided the evidence for theory building in this approach. The model has also been applied to the outcomes of more mundane forms of mobility (e.g. Britain 2013a), such as commuting, local house moves, moves for education and training, consumption choices – short in distance, but massive in scale – which trigger a dialect-contact-inducing demographic churn that is leading to (socially differentiated) dialect supralocalisation and the levelling of more conservative local nonstandard features. The dialect contact approach is, in some respects, impossible without mobility. It is not difficult to see, however, how, in a number of ways, this approach too has succumbed to sedentarism:[10]

- The model attempts to explain how acts of mass migration disrupt the continuity of a community's dialect, but how over time a new variety crystallises from the mixture of dialects that were brought with immigration. A focused new dialect eventually emerges. Stability and continuity are implicitly assumed to be the normative state that a community 'returns to' once the impact of the mobility event has been absorbed. Just as in the case of Labov's approach to transmission, mobility is seen as something external to the normal conditions under which dialects are transmitted through time.
- Similarly, the approach examines the acquisition of a 'second dialect' by individual migrants, measuring, for example, their success at adopting the traditional local patterns of variation as used by speakers born and bred (and often whose parents are born and bred) in the community. Note here how it is those with historical roots in the community whose varieties are deemed to be the target, and the success of the mobile is measured in terms of how well these people meet the linguistic norms of the static. The varieties of the long-term rooted are seen as the baseline against which others are measured – a textbook case of sedentarism.
- As in the case of innovation diffusion, contact dialectology has largely been asocial. There have been relatively few attempts to examine it through a social filter, in other words to address the social embedding problem (Weinreich et al. 1968) – how are linguistic changes embedded in and spread through social structure? This is partly, and understandably, because in many cases the outcomes of dialect contact have been observed post hoc. But even in those studies attempting to examine new dialect formation in progress, the research design has not been framed to address these questions.[11] This gap in the literature is all the more surprising given Trudgill's controversial deterministic approach to new dialect formation that shuns the role of 'identity' in explaining the genesis of new varieties (Trudgill 2004). Similarly, contact-induced changes at a more local level, such as supralocalisation, are not infrequently accounted for as a result of 'an increase in geographical mobility' without pointing to whose mobilities they are or where these mobilities are most evident (see Britain 2013a for a critical discussion).

---

[10] I willingly accept, of course, that I have been guilty of this myself (e.g. Britain 1997).

[11] One exception is Woods's (1997) research on early New Zealand English, which suggested women led the process of koineisation.

Sedentarism, then, has reigned pretty much continually through the last century and a half of dialectology, even when, seemingly, mobility has played an important role in the genesis of the changes under investigation. Mobility has been seen as 'external', peripheral, even suspicious, and, often as a result, shunned, ignored, or factored out. Place, rootedness, stability, meanwhile, have played a central role as the internal, the core, the starting point, the norm, the determining factor in the direction of dialect change.

Mobility unleashed?

In work on the sociolinguistics of globalisation, Vertovec's (2007) concept of 'superdiversity' has become especially influential, and although there has been relatively little dialectological analysis drawing explicitly upon this concept (though see Rampton 2013), there is nevertheless an emergent body of literature examining the apparent dialectological outcomes of such diversity in the shape of so-called multiethnolects that have apparently fused as a result of large-scale migration to the West. Superdiversity and multiethnolects share a good deal of theoretical baggage. Firstly, both are presented as new, as artefacts of both globalisation and a rapid increase in mobility, and emerging at some point in the late twentieth century. Second, both are presented as *urban*, as if there is some critical and specific characteristic of the urban condition that engenders them. Third, there is common cause against traditional (presumably Labovian) notions of the speech community – superdiversity undermines such approaches, and the sociolinguistic repertoires that underlie multiethnolects are claimed to better capture how linguistic variation works than traditional notions of a community, place-based dialect (e.g. Sharma 2011).

Superdiversity, however, has not been uncontroversial, and much of the critique raises the spectre of a nomadic approach that revels in flow at the expense of place, that romanticises the mobile in ways that smack of orientalism, that presents mobility rather than the academic recognition of that mobility as new, and that fails to recognise the diversity of the mobile.

For Vertovec, superdiversity emerged after the Second World War; for Blommaert (2014), much later, at the point in the late twentieth century when the Cold War ended, the Soviet Communist Bloc collapsed and fragmented, and the geopolitical order of the previous forty years was reframed. One index of superdiversity is that 'over the past twenty years globally more people have moved from more places to more places'[12] (see also Vertovec 2007: 1025). The phenomenon is, then, apparently, new and on a scale like

---

[12] www.mmg.mpg.de/research/all-projects/super-diversity/.

never before. Piller (2014) takes issue with these claims. She points to work on the diversity of nineteenth-century Uruguay as evidence that the phenomenon reaches further back in time than suggested. Even further back, Hellenistic Alexandria comes to mind as a city that qualifies for the label, two thousand years ago.

Although Vertovec recognises that the mobile peoples that have created superdiversity are not all alike, it is the ways in which host countries differentially *regulate, police* and *react to* migrants from different countries that represent his principal parameter to distinguish the mobile. He argues that

the proliferation and mutually conditioning effects of additional variables shows that it is not enough to see diversity only in terms of ethnicity ... Such additional variables include differential immigration statuses and their concomitant entitlements and restrictions of rights, divergent labour market experiences, discrete gender and age profiles, patterns of spatial distribution, and mixed local area responses by service providers and residents ... The interplay of these factors is what is meant here ... by the notion of 'super-diversity'. (2007: 1025)

Vertovec's dating of superdiversity as a post-1945 phenomenon is motivated by the idea that this year was a turning point in terms of migration policy. This too is arguable. Certainly in Britain, the control of the migrant had been on the political agenda for many centuries before the twentieth and is evidenced by a raft of legislation to that effect: For example, the 1290 expulsion of Jews, the Egyptians Act of 1530, the Jewish Naturalization Act of 1753, and the British Nationality Act of 1772 are all early examples of the regulation and policing of immigrants of various kinds.

As Urry states (2007: 3), at the very start of his book-length articulation of the new mobilities paradigm, it sometimes seems as if all the world is on the move. He notes that, for example, by 2010 one billion legal international arrivals were expected (cf. 25 million in 1950), that 4 million passengers fly every day and at any one time 360,000 are in flight above the United States, that 31 million refugees roam the globe, and that in 1800 people in the United States travelled on average 50 metres per day and at the time of his writing they travelled 50 kilometres per day. Whilst recognising these quite amazing statistics, mobilities scholars have argued forcefully that we need to carefully deconstruct these figures and nuance our view of whether the *whole* world really is on the move. Urry points to evidence, for example, that people are not spending more time travelling than before or making more journeys (2007: 4), but are travelling further and faster. Mobilities scholars' caution about hyping mass global mobilisation appears to hinge around three main factors, and these all impact on how we can interpret the superdiversity literature's imaginations of mobility.

Firstly, and perhaps most importantly, they point to the fact that there is extreme social differentiation in terms of who is mobile. Urry (2007: 4) partly cites Schivelbusch (1986: 197) in arguing that for 'the twentieth century tourist, the world has become one large department store of countrysides and cities, although of course most people in the world can only dream of voluntarily sampling that department store on a regular basis'. Not everyone is equally mobile.

Secondly, there is a question about perception. Is it true that more people have moved from more places to more places in recent years, or does it seem to be that way because 'we' have been disproportionately benefitting from it and affected by it? Zlotnik, back in 1999, showed that the percentage of people living outside their country of origin is 'remarkably small and has been relatively stable for a long period' (1999: 42). More recent evidence, cited in Piller (2014), comes from Czaika and De Haas (2014), who demonstrate that Vertovec's claims about the scale of human movement need to be nuanced. They show that the percentage of the world's population that is internationally on the move *fell* between 1960 and 2000 from 3.06 percent to 2.73 percent, and that, while international migrants do come from an increased array of countries,[13] they are moving to ever *fewer* places: predominantly Western Europe, North America, Australia and the Gulf, with Europe receiving more of what Czaika and De Haas call 'phenotypically and culturally distinct' (2014: 32) migrants. Their work appears to show that we may be *perceiving* an increase in mobility because Western countries have been disproportionately affected by it.

Thirdly, we are reminded that most people, most of the time, are engaged in relatively short-distance mundane mobilities, 'the taken-for-granted mobility of everyday life – a mobility seldom reflected upon, which plays a large role in the possibilities and potentials that individuals experience in creating the good life' (Freudendal-Pedersen 2009: 9), and that we need to put long-distance international mobility into context and resist fetishising it. The sheer scale of mundane mobility and local migration in the West is startling. In the United Kingdom, for example, between April 2000 and April 2001, 11 percent of the population moved home (ONS 2005: 3) – more than 2,500,000 moves. ONS (2012: 2) shows that this annual rate has not changed much since that date and has remained above 2,500,000 every year since 2001 – just under half of that number moving to a different local authority area. There were more than 25 million house moves in the first decade of this millennium, therefore (see Britain 2013a for the scale of other such mobilities). Pooley, Turnbull and

---

[13] Though note that there are more countries today than there have ever been – almost twice as many in 2014 (201) as in 1950 (105).

Adams, examining changes in mobility across the twentieth century, argued that, for most people, 'everyday mobility consists mainly of local travel connected to essential everyday tasks ... *this aspect of mobility* has changed little over time ... [there has been] too little emphasis on important elements of stability in everyday mobility' (2005: 1, 224, emphasis added). Levels of mobility, they claim, have been relatively stable in the United Kingdom over the past century. What has changed is *how* people are mobile – automobility, for example, is certainly up, but predominantly in rural areas where cars are needed, and not so much in the 'superdiverse' city.[14]

The argument overall, here, is not to deny that long-distance mobility is significant but to recognise the diversity within the mobility figures, to suggest that we are, in the West, at the present time, especially sensitised to it and that we should not overestimate the extent to which people's mobilities are long-distance.

Despite these cautions, what Arnaud and Spotti (2014) call 'superdiversity discourse' is most definitely on the increase in sociolinguistics. The lack of clear definitional parameters for what is and is not superdiverse, however, has led to a considerable broadening, bleaching and slippage of the term. Cynics might argue that pretty much any place with some migrants is being labelled as superdiverse in the literature right now. One could ask, Where *isn't* it superdiverse? For the past decade I've been carrying out dialectological research with Andrea Sudbury on a community that meets all the criteria for superdiversity – 49% of the population not locally born (in Europe, only Andorra and Monaco have a higher proportion of immigrants), with more than sixty countries represented in the population (with different legal statuses, restrictions on rights, etc.), thirty different home languages, and so on. In fact, the community in question is the Falkland Islands. As Adey has argued, 'if mobility is everything, then the concept has little purchase' (2006: 76), and one wonders what the concept of superdiversity buys us in this context. It appears not to be so new or so remarkable (or even so necessarily urban – rural superdiversity is there but largely ignored[15]). It has certainly reoriented

---

[14] Internal migration in the United Kingdom, for example, has also been disproportionately affecting rural areas, which have experienced significant net increases in in-migration since at least the 1950s (see Britain 2013b).

[15] In Britain (forthcoming), I provide evidence of: the demographic impact of post-2004 migration from the EU accession states of Eastern Europe and the Baltic on rural areas in southern England, a number of rural southern English towns whose "non-White British" populations have risen from less than 4 percent of the total in 2001 to well over 20 percent in 2011, and significant international migration to rural areas of England during the medieval period. I argue that as we expect multiethnolects in the city, but not in the countryside, there are no studies of

the sociolinguistic spotlight, such that other, more mundane, perhaps less visible, less ideologically contentious, but certainly no less intense mobilities have gone out of view.

One could also argue that superdiversity research smacks therefore of nomadism. Despite Makoni's (2012: 193) warning that it 'contains a powerful sense of social romanticism, creating an illusion of equality in a highly asymmetrical world' (see also Rampton 2013: 3), the international migrant, it could be argued, has indeed rather become fetishised yet undifferentiated in contemporary sociolinguistics. Cresswell argues that this fetishisation is not infrequently 'raced', repeating 'centuries of Western romanticization of the non-Western other ... it is a thoroughly Orientalist discourse investing the ... non-sedentary population with desire and romance ... its advocates often overlook the colonial power relations that produced such images' (2006: 54). It is certainly the non-Western, noncosmopolitan migrant who is subjected to the greatest degree of linguistic gaze, within both superdiversity and multiethnolect research. It also not infrequently presents an asocial perspective on the migrant (something else Rampton 2013 warns against) – in work on multiethnolects, it is not uncommon to find migrants lumped together as one group,[16] in an assumption of similarity, when in fact different ethnic groups in the community and different members of the group may well have distinct migration histories and different degrees of exposure to the host language, and when they pull differently from the ambient dialect repertoire. To what extent there exist fused multiethnolects is an empirical question and should not be an a priori assumption. If, as is claimed, urban speakers in superdiverse neighbourhoods are fusing a new distinctive and multiethnic code, researchers should be able to demonstrate that a speaker's ethnic background is *not* a significant predictor of the patterning of language variation – if it is, the fusion has not been successful. This is what, for example, Papazachariou (1998) demonstrated in his examination of what, had his work appeared ten years later, could have been called the rural multiethnolect of Goumenissa in northern Greece. This small town had witnessed the arrival of a number of different ethnic groups at different times, speaking different varieties of Greek, but he demonstrated that, today, variant choice in the new fused dialect does *not* correlate with ethnic origins. When scholars have teased apart different ethnic groups in work on

---

Multicultural Rural Englishes in the literature, not because they don't or can't exist, but because we haven't looked.

[16] It is not always possible to record a large enough sample from a large enough range of different ethnic groups in studies of multiethnolects, so there are practical limitations on the extent to which this empirical question can be fully addressed.

multiethnolects, considerable interethnic diversity has been found. Cheshire and Fox (2009: 18), for example, in work on the past tense of the verb *be* in Multicultural London English found large differences between different ethnic groups in their data, suggesting both a lack of a fused system (for this variable at least) and the preservation of distinctive ethnic variation. So while the black Caribbean speakers in their sample produced nonstandard first-person plural forms ('we was') in 80 percent of all potential tokens, the Bangladeshi speakers only did so 14 percent of the time. To go one step further, we could ask why we need labels like 'multiethnolect', when we already have well-established terms that capture the relevant linguistic process and outcome, such as koine and koineisation. To label them as distinct fetishises the ethnic other in ways reminiscent of claims of creole exceptionalism.

Conclusion

Dialectology has long been, and largely remains, locality based, and it is therefore not at all surprising that the discipline looks at the world through place-coloured spectacles. Sedentarism is one of the most important authenticators of dialect, and shapes both how practitioners collect their data and how they theorise resulting analyses of them. And there is little evidence yet of an engagement, for example, with what have come to be known as 'mobile methods' (e.g. Büscher et al. 2011), ways of observing the mobile. Perhaps more surprising are the underlying sedentarist ideologies at work in sociolinguistic accounts of dialect that is apparently on the move – the ways in which innovations diffuse across communities, the ways in which new dialects form as a result of migration, the ways in which individual migrants linguistically adapt to new dialect landscapes. But as we have seen, these too are sedentarist – in the case of new dialect formation, for example, mobility is seen as an external event that causes momentary social and linguistic disruption that is eventually rationalised to a state where 'normal service resumes'. This externalisation of mobility, particularly evident in Labovian distinctions between transmission and diffusion, problematically presents it as something which might under certain circumstances not prevail.

Merriman argues that 'uncritical celebrations of the incessant movements constituting the world are said to be in danger of diverting our attention away from the task of identifying the complex politics underpinning the production and regulation of mobilities' (2012: 5). There is certainly a need in contemporary dialectology to heed Merriman's warning, both, as I have shown elsewhere, in examining the consequences of mundane mobilities (Britain

2013a) and in work on multiethnolects, lest we indeed be guilty of an overfascination with flow, at the expense of a more socially sensitive account of the mobilities that underpin the apparently (super)diverse. Multiethnolect scholarship, for example, slips into nomadism in not itself sufficiently celebrating and taking account of the diverse ethnic backgrounds of its speakers, and it is ironic, in this age of heightened sociolinguistic sensitivity to 'identity', that the identities of individual speakers are lost as they are amalgamated into the multiethnic whole. Multiethnolect speakers appear to be stereotypical examples of Cresswell's 'postmodern nomad ... a remarkably unsocial being – unmarked by the traces of class, gender, ethnicity, sexuality, and geography' (2006: 53). It is the task of emergent work both on superdiversity and on contemporary linguistic change to ensure that, in moving the field forward, we do not lurch it from a long-standing sedentarism to an equally problematic nomadic stance towards mobility. What for me further nails down the problematic nomadism of superdiversity, however, is the overcelebration of the long-distance traveller. While refugees and the cosmopolitan jet-set are especially visible, the mobilities with which they engage are exceptional relative to the vast majority of the population's everyday toing and froing.[17] It fetishises the (especially "non-White") international migrant, while failing to take into consideration the general local population churn that proceeds, quietly, but at a far, far greater magnitude. It is this local mundane mobility which more intensively orients people to places, neighbourhoods, homes. Scale is important.

While critiquing uncritical celebrations of incessant movement, Merriman argues that such a lack of discrimination is not a necessary result of placing mobility centre stage (2012: 5). A dialectology that welcomed mobility but avoided the extreme poles of sedentarism and nomadism would need to embrace – methodologically when collecting data as well as theoretically in model building – the fact that humans are all mobile, that mobility is not external, or secondary, but also appreciate that mobilities are overwhelmingly mundane, 'socially differentiated and unevenly experienced' (Adey 2010: 92).

---

[17] Today, I moved around my flat a lot, took the tram to the office, walked around various rooms at work a lot, walked home via the supermarket to buy tomatoes and bread, then moved around the flat a lot. Tomorrow will be very similar, as will the next day and the next. Hardly exotic, but these are extremely well-worn, routine paths. Peters, Kloppenburg, and Wyatt nicely capture the rather mundane nature of much movement in suggesting that "[m]obility can be understood as the ordinary and everyday achievement of planning and organising co-presence with other people and with material objects such as tables, chairs and occasionally also cake" (2010: 349).

238   Sociolinguistics, place and mobility

REFERENCES

Adey, P. 2006. If mobility is everything, then it is nothing. *Mobilities* 1: 75–94.
   2010. *Mobility*. London: Routledge.
Adey, P., and B. Anderson. 2011. Anticipation, materiality, event: The Icelandic ash
   cloud disruption and the security of mobility. *Mobilities* 6: 11–20.
Arnaut, K., and M. Spotti. 2014. Superdiversity discourse. *Working Papers in Urban
   Language and Literacies* 122: 1–11.
Barz, R., and J. Siegel (eds.). 1988. *Language Transplanted: Development of Overseas
   Hindi*. Wiesbaden: Harrassowitz.
Benediktsson, K., A. Lund, and E. Huijbens. 2011. Inspired by eruptions?
   Eyjafjallajökull and Icelandic tourism. *Mobilities* 6: 77–84.
Blommaert, J. 2014. From mobility to complexity in sociolinguistic theory and method.
   Tilburg Papers in Culture Studies 103: 1–24.
Bortoni-Ricardo, S. 1985. *The Urbanization of Rural Dialect Speakers*. Cambridge:
   Cambridge University Press.
Britain, D. 1997. Dialect contact and phonological reallocation: 'Canadian Raising' in
   the English Fens. *Language in Society* 26: 15–46.
   2009. One foot in the grave? Dialect death, dialect contact and dialect birth in
   England. *International Journal of the Sociology of Language* 196/197: 121–155.
   2010. Conceptualisations of geographic space in linguistics. In A. Lameli, R.
   Kehrein, and S. Rabanus (eds.), *Language and Space: An International Handbook
   of Linguistic Variation*, vol. 2: *Language Mapping*. Berlin: De Gruyter Mouton.
   69–97.
   2012a. Countering the urbanist agenda in variationist sociolinguistics: Dialect
   contact, demographic change and the rural-urban dichotomy. In S. Hansen,
   C. Schwarz, P. Stoeckle, and T. Streck (eds.), *Dialectological and Folk
   Dialectological Concepts of Space*. Berlin: De Gruyter, 12–30.
   2012b. Diffusion. In A. Bergs and L. Brinton (eds.), *English Historical Linguistics:
   An International Handbook*. Berlin: Mouton de Gruyter, 2031–2043.
   2012c. Innovation diffusion in sociohistorical linguistics. In J. M. Hernandez
   Campoy and J. C. Conde Silvestre (eds.), *Handbook of Historical Sociolinguistics*.
   Oxford: Blackwell, 451–464.
   2013a. The role of mundane mobility and contact in dialect death and dialect birth. In
   D. Schreier and M. Hundt (eds.), *English as a Contact Language*. Cambridge:
   Cambridge University Press, 165–181.
   2013b. Space, diffusion and mobility. In J. Chambers and N. Schilling (eds.),
   Handbook of Language Variation and Change, 2nd ed. Oxford: Wiley, 471–500.
   Forthcoming. Which way to look?: Perspectives on 'Urban' and 'Rural' in
   dialectology. In E. Moore and C. Montgomery (eds.), *A Sense of Place: Studies in
   Language and Region*. Cambridge: Cambridge University Press.
Britain, D., and S. Fox. 2009. The regularisation of the hiatus resolution system in
   British English: A contact-induced 'vernacular universal'? In M. Filppula,
   J. Klemola, and H. Paulasto (eds.), *Vernacular Universals and Language Contacts:
   Evidence from Varieties of English and Beyond*. London: Routledge, 177–205.
Bucholtz, M. 2003. Sociolinguistic nostalgia and the authentication of identity. *Journal
   of Sociolinguistics* 7: 398–416.
Büscher, M., J. Urry, and K. Witchger. 2011. *Mobile Methods*. London: Routledge.

Budd, L., S. Griggs, D. Howarth, and S. Ison. 2011. A fiasco of volcanic proportions?
   Eyjafjallajökull and the closure of European airspace. *Mobilities* 6: 31–40.
Chambers, J. 1992. Dialect acquisition. *Language* 68: 673–705.
Cheshire, J., and S. Fox. 2009. Was/were variation: A perspective from London.
   Language Variation and Change 21: 1–38.
Cheshire, J., P. Kerswill, S. Fox, and E. Torgersen. 2011. Contact, the feature pool and
   the speech community: The emergence of multicultural London English. *Journal
   of Sociolinguistics* 15: 151–196.
Coupland, N. 2010. The authentic speaker and the speech community. In C. Llamas and
   D. Watt (eds.), *Language and Identities*. Edinburgh University Press, 99–112.
Cresswell, T. 1997. Imagining the nomad: Mobility and the postmodern primitive. In
   G. Benko and U. Strohmayer (eds.), *Space and Social Theory: Interpreting
   Modernity and Postmodernity*. Oxford: Blackwell, 360–379.
   2006. *On the Move: Mobility in the Modern Western World*. London: Routledge.
   2011. Mobilities I: Catching up. *Progress in Human Geography* 35: 550–558.
   2012. Mobilities II : Still. *Progress in Human Geography* 36: 645–653.
   2014. Mobilities III: Moving on. *Progress in Human Geography* 38: 712–721.
Cresswell, T., and C. Martin. 2012. On turbulence: Entanglements of disorder and
   order on a Devon beach. *Tijdschrift voor Economische en Sociale Geografie* 103:
   516–529.
Czaika, M., and H. De Haas. 2014. The globalisation of migration: Has the world
   become more migratory? *International Migration Review* 48: 283–323.
Eckert, P. 2003. Sociolinguistics and authenticity: An elephant in the room. *Journal of
   Sociolinguistics* 7: 392–431.
Ellis, A. 1889. *On Early English Pronunciation: Part V*. London: Truebner and Co.
Fox, S. 2007. *The Demise of Cockneys? Language Change in London's 'Traditional'
   East End*. PhD dissertation, University of Essex.
   2015. *The New Cockney: New Ethnicities and Adolescents' Speech in the Traditional
   East End of London*. Basingstoke: Palgrave Macmillan.
Freudendal-Pedersen, M. 2009. *Mobility in Daily Life: Between Freedom and
   Unfreedom*. Farnham: Ashgate.
Gregory, D. 1985. Suspended animation: The stasis of diffusion theory. In D. Gregory
   and J. Urry (eds.), *Social Relations and Spatial Structures*. London: Macmillan,
   296–336.
Hall, T. 2009. Footwork: Moving and knowing in local space(s). *Qualitative Research*
   9: 571–585.
Hannam, K., M. Sheller, and J. Urry. 2006. Editorial: Mobilities, immobilities and
   moorings. *Mobilities* 1: 1–22.
Heidegger, M. 1962 [1927]. *Being and Time*. Oxford: Blackwell.
Hernández Campoy, J. M. 2003. Exposure to contact and the geographical adoption
   of standard features: Two complementary approaches. *Language in Society*
   32: 227–255.
Horvath, B. 1985. *Variation in Australian English: The Sociolects of Sydney*.
   Cambridge: Cambridge University Press.
Inoue, F. 2010. Gravity model of diffusion for Tokyo new dialect forms. *Leeds Working
   Papers in Linguistics and Phonetics* 15: 92–100.
Jeffries, S. 2010. Clear sky thinking. *The Guardian* G2, April 20, 8–11.

Jensen, O. 2011. Emotional eruptions, volcanic activity and global mobilities: A field account from a European in the US during the eruption of Eyjafjallajökull. *Mobilities* 6: 67–75.

Kabachnik, P. 2010. Place invaders: Constructing the nomadic threat in England. *The Geographical Review* 100: 90–108.

Kerswill, P. 1993. Rural dialect speakers in an urban speech community: The role of dialect contact in defining a sociolinguistic concept. *International Journal of Applied Linguistics* 3: 33–56.

Kerswill, Paul, and A. Williams. 2000. Creating a new town koine. *Language in Society* 29: 65–115.

Labov, W. 1966/2006. *The Social Stratification of English in New York City*, 2nd ed. Cambridge: Cambridge University Press.

  1982. Building on empirical foundations. In W. Lehmann and Y. Malkiel (eds.), *Perspectives in Historical Linguistics*. Amsterdam: John Benjamins, 79–92.

  2001. *Principles of Linguistic Change*, vol. 2: *Social Factors*. Oxford: Blackwell.

  2007. Transmission and diffusion. *Language* 83: 344–387.

  2010. *Principles of Linguistic Change*, vol. 3: *Cognitive and Cultural Factors*. Oxford: Wiley.

Larmouth, D. 1981. Gravity models, wave theory and low-structure regions. In H. Warkentyne (ed.), *Methods IV: Papers from the 4th International Conference on Methods in Dialectology*, University of Victoria, Canada, 199–219.

Makoni, S. 2012. A critique of language, languaging and supervernacular. Uma crítica à noção de língua, linguagem e supervernáculo. *Muitas Vozes, Ponta Grossa* 1:189–199.

Malkki, L. 1992. National geographic: The rooting of peoples and the territorialization of national identity among scholars and refugees. *Cultural Anthropology* 7: 24–44.

Massey, D. 1993. Power-geometry and a progressive sense of place. In J. Bird, B. Curtis, T. Putnam, G. Robertson, and L. Tucker (eds.), *Mapping the Futures: Local Cultures, Global Change*. London: Routledge, 59–69.

Matsumoto, K., and D. Britain. 2003. Contact and obsolescence in a diaspora variety of Japanese: The case of Palau in Micronesia. *Essex Research Reports in Linguistics* 44: 38–75.

Mendoza-Denton, N. 2008. *Homegirls: Language and Cultural Practice among Latina Youth Gangs*. Oxford: Blackwell.

Merriman, P. 2012. *Mobility, Space and Culture*. London: Routledge.

Milroy, J. 1992. *Linguistic Variation and Change*. Oxford: Blackwell.

Milroy, J., and L. Milroy. 1985. Linguistic change, social network and speaker innovation. *Journal of Linguistics* 21: 339–84.

Milroy, L. 1980. *Language and Social Networks*. Oxford: Blackwell.

  2002. Mobility, contact and language change – working with contemporary speech communities. *Journal of Sociolinguistics* 6: 3–15.

Mougeon, R., and E. Beniak (eds.). 1994. *Les origines du français québécois*. Sainte-Foy: Les Presses de l'Université Laval.

Office for National Statistics (ONS). 2005. *Reversal of the Southward Population Flow since Start of the New Century: Focus on People and Migration*. London: ONS.

  2012. *Internal Migration by Local Authorities in England and Wales, Year Ending June 2011*. London: ONS.

Orton, H., and E. Dieth. 1962. *Survey of English Dialects: Introduction.* Leeds: E. J. Arnold and Son.

Papazachariou, D. 1998. Linguistic variation in intonation: Language and the construction of identity among Northern Greek adolescents. PhD dissertation, University of Essex.

Penny, R. 2000. *Variation and Change in Spanish.* Cambridge: Cambridge University Press.

Peters, P., A. Kloppenburg, and S. Wyatt. 2010. Co-ordinating passages: Understanding the resources needed for everyday mobility. *Mobilities* 5: 349–368.

Piller, I. 2014. Superdiversity: Another Eurocentric idea? Available at www.languageonthemove.com/language-globalization/superdiversity-another-eurocentric-idea.

Pooley, C., J. Turnbull, and M. Adams. 2005. *A Mobile Century? Changes in Everyday Mobility in Britain in the Twentieth Century.* Aldershot: Ashgate.

Rampton, B. 2013. Drilling down to the grain in superdiversity. *Tilburg Papers in Culture Studies* 48: 2–15.

Sayers, D. 2014. The mediated innovation model: A framework for researching media influence in language change. *Journal of Sociolinguistics* 18: 185–212.

Schilling, N. 2013. *Sociolinguistic Fieldwork.* Cambridge: Cambridge University Press.

Schivelbusch, W. 1986. *The Railway Journey: Trains and Travel in the Nineteenth Century.* Oxford: Blackwell.

Sharma, D. 2011. Style repertoire and social change in British Asian English. *Journal of Sociolinguistics* 15: 464–492.

Sheller, M., and J. Urry. 2006. The new mobilities paradigm. *Environment and Planning A* 38: 207–226.

Trudgill, P. 1974. Linguistic change and diffusion: Description and explanation in sociolinguistic dialect geography. *Language in Society* 3: 215–246.

1983. *On Dialect.* Oxford: Blackwell.

1986. *Dialects in Contact.* Oxford: Blackwell.

2004. *New Dialect Formation: The Inevitability of Colonial Englishes.* Edinburgh: Edinburgh University Press.

Urry, J. 2000. *Sociology Beyond Societies: Mobilities for the Twenty-first Century.* London: Routledge.

2007. *Mobilities.* Cambridge: Polity.

Vannini, P. 2010. Mobile cultures: From the sociology of transportation to the study of mobilities. *Sociology Compass* 4: 111–121.

Vertovec, S. 2007. Super-diversity and its implications. *Ethnic and Racial Studies* 30: 1024–1054.

Weinreich, U., W. Labov, and M. Herzog. 1968. Empirical foundations for a theory of language change. In W. Lehmann and Y. Malkiel (eds.), *Directions for Historical Linguistics.* Austin: University of Texas Press, 97–195.

Woods, N. 1997. The formation and development of New Zealand English: Interaction of gender-related variation and linguistic change. *Journal of Sociolinguistics* 1: 95–126.

Woods, M. 2011. *Rural.* London: Routledge.

Yeoh, B. 2006. Mobility and the city. *Theory, Culture and Society* 23: 150–152.

Zlotnik, H. 1999. Trends of international migration since 1965: What existing data reveal. *International Migration* 37: 21–61.

11 From mobility to complexity in sociolinguistic theory and method

Jan Blommaert

Introduction

In a celebrated article, Aaron Cicourel emphasized that "it is important to locate the analysis of language and social interaction in a wide variety of social activities that are implicitly and explicitly known to the participants and the investigator" (1992: 296). The case built in that article revolved around the challenge, notably in conversation analysis and other branches of discourse analysis, to do justice to the tremendous complexity characterizing real social environments – a medical environment in Cicourel's concrete study – and the need, consequently, to employ "several types of ethnographic and textual materials in order to underscore ... unavoidable aspects of organizational and local constraints and processes that are integral to rethinking 'context'" (p. 309). If we accept, like Cicourel, that any form of human communication is set in a real social environment and draws on real and actual bodies of knowledge and experience of participants operating as "context" in social encounters, then tracing the sources of knowledge and experience of participants becomes a key issue, because "[a]s long as we continue to reify terms like 'social structure', 'culture' and 'language', we shall miss the contextual and cognitive significance of everyday social organization" (Cicourel 1973: 9) and we shall continue to impute our own, researchers', assumptions and biases to the people we study.

Such reifications, of course, are a legacy of structuralism and found their way into the standard methodologies of a good deal of contemporary social and human sciences. In sociolinguistics, Glyn Williams's (1992) critique of work as widely diverse as Labovian variationism, Fishmanian sociology of language, and Schegloffian conversation analysis demonstrated the lasting and pervasive influence of structural-functionalist consensus models handed down from Talcott Parsons (drawing in turn heavily on Durkheim). Such models, Williams explained, would imagine any social environment as an integrated 'complete' system displaying an elementary form of equilibrium, in which every individual member would know what was expected from him or her, and in which such knowledge would be accessible to all members. Thus, in mainstream sociolinguistics, "[t]he general discourse is ... the normative consensus view of society"; as for the speaker, he or she is imagined as a "free, rational individual capable of employing language not only to express meaning, but to convey a social identity"; groups tend "to be seen as the aggregate of individual rational behavior" (1992: 230–232);[1] and as for society,

[t]he society within which the free, rational subject exists is a very specific form of society. It is an open society full of opportunity of which the rational and enterprising individual actor, operating on the basis of an inherent desire for social status, will be able to take full advantage. (p. 232)

Williams observes "that this model of society is very close to the North American world view, and to the individual liberalism which it encapsulates" (p. 234). It also stresses, and presupposes, clear, distinct, and stable social units that can become sociolinguistic units: the speech community, the dialect or language area, and language (or dialect, sociolect, etc.) itself (cf. Rampton 1998). Those are, evidently, the reifications that Cicourel saw as fundamental flaws in social and humanities research.

Recent decades have witnessed growing numbers of sociolinguists interrogating and unthinking these reifications. In the words of Blommaert and Rampton (2011: 3),

there has been ongoing revision of fundamental ideas (a) about languages, (b) about language groups and speakers, and (c) about communication. Rather than working with homogeneity, stability and boundedness as the starting assumptions, mobility, mixing, political dynamics and historical embedding are now central concerns in the study of languages, language groups and communication.

Unsurprisingly, these efforts often have their roots in the field, broadly taken, of multilingualism – one of sociolinguistics' core areas – and introductory textbooks on multilingualism now definitely look different from those published a couple of decades ago, to the extent that one might speak of a "post-Fishmanian" paradigm shift (e.g., Blackledge and Creese 2010; Weber and Horner 2012; see also Pennycook, this volume, (Chapter 9).

In this paradigm shift, new fundamental theoretical developments have been absorbed and incorporated into the analytical framework. An important one is the development of language ideologies as a field of macro- and micro-sociolinguistic research (e.g., Kroskrity 2000), now enabling a far more sophisticated view of "the contextual and cognitive significance of everyday social organization" emphasized above by Cicourel. We can now see how

---

[1] One of the most perfect examples of these views applied to sociolinguistics is Carol Myers-Scotton's well-known "Markedness Model" for code-switching. See Myers-Scotton (1992); an early but extensive critique of this model can be found in Blommaert and Meeuwis (1994).

institutionalized interlanguage relationships and forms of sociolinguistic stratification are driven by particular ideological imaginings of language, culture,
identity, and political structure (e.g., Blommaert 1999; Gal and Woolard 2001;
Makoni and Pennycook 2006; see also Part I of this volume, Chapters 2–5),
how languages and language varieties themselves can be analyzed as ideological constructs having a strong bearing on everyday language behavior,
providing behavioral and discursive templates *in* language usage (e.g., Silverstein and Urban 1996; Agha 2007; Seargeant 2009). These developments have
refocused sociolinguistic analysis, from reified notions of language (and dialect, sociolect, etc.) to a new kind of unit: an ideologically configured and
indexically ordered set of specific linguistic-semiotic resources, sometimes
coincident with what is commonly accepted as a language (e.g., English),
but most often coincident with more specific notions such as "register",
dynamically developing as "repertoires" in the course of people's social lives,
and deployed in highly context-sensitive metalinguistically regimented social
practices (e.g., Silverstein 2003 and this volume, Chapter 2; Rampton 2006;
Agha 2007; Coupland 2007; Rymes 2014).

I have deliberately given some space to the importance of language
ideologies as a keystone for what I qualified as the "post-Fishmanian"
paradigmatic shift, because their impact is quite often overlooked or downplayed. But it is due to this development that we can now investigate
sociolinguistic phenomena and processes that are defined in terms of fundamentally different units – flexible, unstable, dynamic, layered, and mobile
ones. If studies of multilingualism now look quite different from those of a
generation ago, it is to a large extent because researchers now can draw on a
far more analytically precise vocabulary derived from language ideologies
research. It is by means of this vocabulary that we can tackle the challenges
earlier defined by Cicourel and Williams: to get rid of the reifying legacy of
structuralism and to do justice to the complexity of sociolinguistic phenomena and processes.

In what follows, I shall outline these challenges and their paradigmatic
potential for sociolinguistic theory and method at some length. I will sketch
two steps: first, a move from stability to mobility – a move that is now largely
accomplished; and second: from mobility to complexity – a move still very
much in its initial stages.[2] My discussion of the first move will be retrospective, as a consequence, while the second move can be discussed only program-
matically. It will be followed by some remarks on the development of new
methods for sociolinguistic research, after which I shall conclude with more
general reflections.

---

[2] An earlier version of the following two sections can be found in Blommaert (2013: 6–14).

From stability to mobility

As mentioned earlier, the paradigmatic shift has been most noticeable in the field of multilingualism, and the reason for that is straightforward: Multilingualism is a feature of sociocultural diversity, often associated with migration and sensitive to influences at both macro- and micro-levels, leading to highly complex, "messy," and hybrid sociolinguistic phenomena that defy established categories. To start with the macro-levels: Migration as a force behind multilingualism compels analysts to consider *mobile* people – people who do not stay in the place where their languages are traditionally used, to put it simply – whose linguistic resources and communicative opportunities are affected by such forms of mobility. New forms of migration due to post–Cold War globalization processes combined with the emergence of online technologies as current features of social life – what Steven Vertovec called "superdiversity" (2007) – have generated complex social-communicative environments and webs of mobile people, semiotic modes and forms, and meanings.

The study of these environments called for a sociolinguistics of globalization, and the central notion in early attempts in that direction was *mobility* (Coupland 2003; 2010; Pennycook 2007; Blommaert 2010). In itself, this move represents a major theoretical effort, for it disrupts the long tradition, reviewed by Glyn Williams, in which language, along with other social and cultural features of people, was primarily imagined as relatively fixed in time and space, as sedentary, so to speak. A language or language variety was something that "belonged" to a definable (and thus bounded) "speech community"; that speech community lived in one place at one time and, consequently, shared an immense amount of contextual knowledge. That is why people understood each other: They knew all the social and cultural diacritics valid in a stable sociolinguistic community and could, thus, infer such contextual knowledge in interactions with fellow members of that community. Roles and expectations were clear and well understood in such contexts – children had respect for elder people and so forth. And people reproduced patterns that were seen as anchored in a timeless tradition – the rules of language usage are what they are, because the rules of society are what they are (for a critique, see Rampton 1998). Social and linguistic features were members of separate categories between which stable and linear correlations could be established.

From the very early days of sociolinguistics, however, alternative views were available. John Gumperz and Dell Hymes (1972), for instance, quickly destabilized these assumptions in their programmatic work on ethnographies of communication, and they did so with one apparently simple theoretical intervention: They defined social and linguistic features not as separate-but-connected but as *dialectic*, that is, co-constructive and, hence, *dynamic*. Concretely: The reiteration of specific patterns of language usage – say, the use of "yes sir" as an answer in a hierarchical speech situation – creates a social structure (hierarchy) which in turn begins to exert a compelling effect on subsequent similar speech situations. It has become a 'rule' or a 'norm' and so becomes an ideologically saturated behavioral expectation and an aim for effect in communication. But such 'rules' or 'norms' have no abstract existence; they have an existence only in iterative communicative enactment. People need to perform such ideologically saturated forms of behavior – their behavior must be iterative in that sense – but small deviations from that rule have the capacity to overrule the whole of norm-governed behavior. Saying "yes sir" with a slow and dragging intonation, for instance ("yeeees siiiiiiiir"), can express irony and so entirely cancel the norm, and even become the onset of an alternative norm.

The importance of this simple but fundamental change in perspective is massive, even if it took a while before it was fully taken on board, for it introduced a dimension of contingency and complexity into sociolinguistics that defied the static correlational orthodoxies. Deviations from norms, for instance, can now be the effect of a whole range of factors, and it is impossible to make an a priori choice for any of them. The dragging intonation in our example above can be the result of intentional subversiveness, but it can also be the effect of degrees of 'membership' in speech communities – whether or not one 'fully' knows the rules of the sociolinguistic game. So, simple correlations do not work anymore; they need to be established by means of ethnographic examination (Hymes 1996: 31–32). Such examination, while always more complicated than anticipated, was easier in communities that displayed a relative sociocultural homogeneity, and a significant part of research in the ethnography of communication focused on group-internal ways and rules of speaking (e.g., Schieffelin 1990). Investigating more "mixed" contexts, such as interethnic communication in British professional contexts (e.g., Gumperz 1982) or ethnically heterogeneous inner-city schools in urban Britain (Rampton 1995), made clear that when people move around the globe, their communicative resources are affected by such moves: Accents, styles, modes of conversational arrangement all proved to be sensitive to mobility, and what worked well in one part of the world proved to lose functional efficacy in another. Reasons for such differences are rarely "linguistic" in the strict sense of the term: They are *indexical* (cf. Part I of this volume, Chapters 2–5). It is the language-ideological framing-in-uptake of accents, styles, and so on that changes whenever people move from one place to another, and the complex processes of (re-)contextualization central to John Gumperz's work are in fact indexical in nature (a point acknowledged in his later work; see Gumperz 2003: 110–113). Mobility, sociolinguistically, is therefore a matter of determining the different orders of indexicality through which communication travels, and their effect on communicative conditions and outcomes (Blommaert 2010: 41–43; also Jacquemet 2005).

Taking mobility as the central concept in a sociolinguistics of globalization has, in my view, three major methodological effects: (1) it creates a degree of unpredictability in what we observe, and we can solve this unpredictability only (2) by close ethnographic inspection of the minutiae of what happens in communication and (3) by keeping in mind the intrinsic limitations of our current methodological and theoretical vocabulary – thus, by accepting the need for new images, metaphors, and notions to cover adequately what we observe. The challenge of mobility is paradigmatic, not superficial (cf. also Rampton 2006; Jaworski and Thurlow 2010; Pennycook 2010; 2012).

The paradigmatic nature of the challenge is hard to escape when one addresses the many forms of multilingual communicative behavior that appear to characterize the present world and for which scholars have developed terms such as 'languaging', 'polylanguaging', 'crossing', 'metrolingualism', 'transidomatic practices', and so forth (Blommaert and Rampton 2011 provide a survey; see also Pennycook, this volume, Chapter 9). In superdiverse environments (both on- and offline), people appear to take any linguistic and communicative resource available to them – a broad range, typically, in superdiverse contexts – and blend them into hugely complex linguistic and semiotic forms. Old and established terms, such as 'code-switching' and indeed even 'multilingualism', appear to rapidly exhaust the limits of their descriptive and explanatory adequacy in the face of such highly complex 'blends' (cf. Creese and Blackledge 2010; Sharma and Rampton 2011; Backus 2012).

And not only that: Two additional issues emerge. First, the question of the origin and trajectory of the actual resources that constitute the blend, how they have been acquired, and what kind of 'competence' they would represent is equally difficult to answer. Contemporary repertoires are tremendously complex, dynamic, and unstable and *not* predicated on the forms of knowledge-of-language one customarily assumes, since Chomsky, with ordinary language users. Important issues of what it means to "know" and "use" a language emerge here (e.g., Rampton 1995; Moore 2012; Blommaert and Backus 2013; Rymes 2014; Zentz 2015). Profoundly sociolinguistic issues such as the specific communicative resources deployable and deployed in discourse and differential fluency in and command over such resources between participants in communication were central to the research programs of Gumperz (e.g., 1982) and Hymes (e.g., 1996); in the context of globalization, they are back with a vengeance, as work on, for example,e.g., asylum seekers in the West – mobile people par excellence – has shockingly demonstrated (e.g., Maryns 2006; see Eades 2010 for an overview).

Second, the sociolinguistic environments in which such forms circulate and are being deployed also demand further attention. While many of the "messy" forms of language use currently analyzed as aspects of sociolinguistic superdiversity may have precedents in earlier eras, they now operate in a sociolinguistic environment which, certainly due to the massive presence of online and long-distance communicative contexts, contains features not previously attested. In other words, while superdiversity may not have brought many really "new" *linguistic* phenomena, the new *sociolinguistic* aspects cannot be avoided. There are new and extraordinarily large online (i.e. "transidiomatic", in the sense of Jacquemet 2005) communities developing specialized modes of communication on their platforms involving new identity performance opportunities as well as new norms for appropriate communicative behavior and requiring new kinds of visual literacy-based semiotic work in new genres and registers (e.g., Androutsopoulos 2006; Varis and Wang 2011). These new online and long-distance contexts challenge established understandings of core features of "natural" communication (such as physical co-presence, sharedness of medium and communicative resources, and oral performance as the elementary form of language) and invite new forms of research – if for nothing else, because of the ways in which online contexts affect more conventional "offline" communicative environments. There is now a genuinely global contextual scale level, which combines space–time scope with speed and volume in ways previously unthinkable, creating a poorly understood new level of globalized mobility.[3] Consequently, the sociolinguistic economies of contemporary societies – the entire range of resources circulating in societies, their distribution, and their mutual relationships – need to be investigated anew, and pending that it is safe to assume that these economies display important differences with those of preceding generations.

Let me summarize the argument so far. Globalization as a sociolinguistic phenomenon has made scholars increasingly aware of the deficiencies of earlier theoretical models and analytical frameworks, based on imageries of stable, resident and sedentary speech communities in an integrated society; it has compelled them to see sociolinguistic phenomena and processes as objects fundamentally characterized by mobility. Taking mobility as a paradigmatic principle of sociolinguistic research dislodges several major assumptions of mainstream sociolinguistics and invites a more complex, dynamic, and multifaceted view of sociolinguistic realities. As announced above, I consider this move to be largely accomplished, even if much important work remains to be done. Such work, however, can benefit from an additional move: from mobility to complexity.

From mobility to complexity

The point of departure for this second move is the need to *reimagine* the sociolinguistic phenomena and processes we intend to study, now detached

---

[3] To judge these developments from within a broader historical perspective, Burke (2011) is commendable.

from the older imagery discussed and dismissed above. To reimagine can be taken literally here: What is needed is a set of images and metaphors that appear to offer more and better analytical opportunities because they correspond better to the phenomena and processes we observe. I would suggest that chaos (or complexity) theory offers us such images and metaphors, and I will allow myself to be inspired in this direction by two early works: Conrad Waddington's (1977) *Tools for Thought* about complex systems and Ilya Prigogine and Isabelle Stengers's (1984) classic *Order out of Chaos*. Note, and I emphasize this, that what follows is not an attempt to bring Chaos Theory (with capitals) into sociolinguistics; it is merely an attempt at drawing inspiring images and metaphors from those sources into sociolinguistics. As said, this second move can only be programmatic, and adequate images and metaphors help us construct a deep level of theorizing. We can use complexity as a *perspective*, not as a compulsory vocabulary or theoretical template. It offers a *freedom to imagine*, not an obligation to submit.

The two books, when they appeared, introduced a universe of complex systems: systems that are open and unfinished, in and on which several apparently unrelated forces operate simultaneously but without being centrally controlled or planned, so to speak. In such systems, change is endemic and perpetual, because of two different dynamics: interaction with other systems (an external factor), and intrasystem dynamics and change affected by such exchanges with others but also operating autonomously (an internal factor). Consequently, no two interactions between systems are identical, because the different systems would have changed by the time they entered into the next ('identical') interaction. Repeating a process never makes it identical to the first one, since repetition itself is a factor of change. The authors also stressed the importance of contingency and accident – the 'stochastic' side of nature. General patterns can be disrupted by infinitely small deviations – things that would belong to statistical 'error margins' can be more crucial in understanding change than large 'average' patterns. And they emphasized the non-unified character of almost any system, the fact that any system can and does contain forces and counterforces, dominant forces and 'rebellious' ones.

Particularly inspiring, of course, is the insight that chaos is not an absence of order but a *specific form of order*, characterized, intriguingly, by the increased interaction, interdependence, and hence coherence between different parts of a system. And the assumption that such general chaotic patterns can be found at every scale level – authors usually distinguish the microscopic world from the macroscopic one – is both challenging and productive as well. Finally, but more speculatively, the notion of entropy can be useful to keep in mind: Systems inevitably develop entropy, a loss of the energy that characterizes their nonequilibrium state, and tend to develop towards uniformity. Their internal pattern of change, in other words, tends towards homogeneity and the reduction of the intense energy of diversity.

Those ideas are decades old by now, and many of them have become common sense. But not, I observe with regret, in sociolinguistics and many other branches of the human and social sciences, nor in public policy. They have more influence and are much better understood in New Age movements than in the EU Commission or in any university department of sociolinguistics, and this is a pity.[4] When we apply them to sociolinguistics, we arrive at an entirely new range of baseline images for "complex sociolinguistics", which I can summarize in a set of theoretical propositions.

1. A sociolinguistic system is a *complex system* characterized by internal and external forces of perpetual change, operating simultaneously and in unpredictable mutual relationships. It is therefore always dynamic, never finished, never bounded, and never completely and definitively describable, either. By the time we have finished our description, the system will have changed. As for the notion of 'sociolinguistic system', it simply stands for any set of systemic – regular, recurrent, nonrandom – interactions between sociolinguistic objects at any level of social structure.

2. Sociolinguistic systems are *not unified*, either. In earlier work, I used the notion of '*polycentricity*' to identify the fragmentation and the interactions between fragments of a sociolinguistic system (Blommaert 2010: 32–41). A sociolinguistic system is always a 'system of systems', characterized by different *scale levels* – the individual is a system, his or her peer group is one, his or her age category another, and so on; we move from the smallest 'microscopic' or 'nanosociolinguistic' level (Parkin 2012: 74) to the highest 'macroscopic' scale level. Centers in a polycentric system typically occupy specific scale levels and operate as foci of *normativity*, that is, of ordered indexicalities (Silverstein 2003; Blommaert 2005; Agha 2007). The norms valid in a small peer group are different from those operating on the same individuals in a school context, for instance.

3. Going back to what was established earlier: Sociolinguistic systems are characterized by *mobility*; in the constant interaction within and between systems, elements move across centers and scale levels. In such forms of mobility, the characteristics of the elements change: Language varieties that have a high value here can lose that value easily by moving into another 'field of force', so to speak – another sociolinguistic system. Concretely, an accent in English that bears middle-class prestige in Nairobi can be turned into a stigmatized immigrant accent in London.

---

[4] I am being unfair here towards the very interesting attempts made by some people in our field to adapt complexity/chaos theory to linguistic and sociolinguistic phenomena; see, e.g., Diane Larsen-Freeman's work on language learning (Larsen-Freeman 1997).

4. The reason for such changes is *historical*: The value and function of particular aspects of a sociolinguistic system are the outcome of historical and local processes of becoming. At the lowest level of language, word meanings are 'conventional', that is, 'historically entrenched as meaning x or y'; historicity creates recognizability, grounded in indexical attributions: I hear x, and I recognize it as conventionally and indexically meaning y. This also counts for higher-order levels such as genres, styles, discourse traditions, and other forms of intertextuality and interdiscursivity.

5. In a complex system, we will encounter *different historicities* and different *speeds of change* in interaction with each other, collapsing in synchronic moments of occurrence. Long histories – the kind of history that shaped 'English', for instance – are blended with shorter histories – such as the one that produced hip-hop jargon, for instance. I called this 'layered simultaneity' in earlier work (2005: 126): In communication, resources are used that have fundamentally different historicities and therefore fundamentally different indexical loads. The process of lumping them together, and so eliding the different historicities inscribed in them, I called "synchronization". Every synchronic act of communication is a moment in which we "synchronize" materials, each of which carries very different historical indexicalities, an effect of the intrinsic polycentricity that characterizes sociolinguistic systems.

6. The previous statement, when initially formulated, was a general typification of discourse, from individual utterance to text and discourse complex. We can make the same statement with respect to larger units as well, as a typification of entire zones of communication and of communicative systems in general, because of *'fractal recursivity'*: the fact that phenomena occurring on one scale level also resonate at different scale levels (Irvine and Gal 2000). The intrinsic hybridity of utterances (something, of course, introduced by Bakhtin a long time ago) is an effect of interactions within a much larger polycentric system.

7. The "synchronization" mentioned earlier is an act of interpretation in which the different historical layers of meaning are folded into one 'synchronic' set of meanings. This is a reduction of complexity, and every form of interpretation can thus be seen as grounded in a reduction of the complex layers of meaning contained in utterances and events – a form of *entropy*, in a sense. People appear to have a very strong tendency to avoid or reduce complexity, and popular 'monoglot' language ideologies (Silverstein 1996), as well as 'homogeneistic' language and culture policies, can exemplify this tendency. While the default tendencies of the system are towards entropy – uniformity, standardization, homogenization – the perpetual 'chaotic' dynamics of the system prevent this finite state. In sociolinguistic systems, we are likely to always encounter tensions between tendencies

towards uniformity and tendencies towards heterogeneity. In fact, this tension may characterize much of contemporary social and cultural life (see Blommaert and Varis 2012).

8. In line with the previous remarks, change at one level also has effects at other levels. Every instance of change is at least potentially *systemic*, since changes in one segment of the system have repercussions on other segments of that system. Every "micro" occurrence, therefore, can also be read as a "macro" feature. A simple example is the way in which parents can be influenced by their teenage children's Internet gaming jargon and effectively adopt it in their own speech, even when these parents themselves have never performed any online gaming in their lives. A change in one segment (the teenagers) affects other segments (their parents) and is provoked by higher-scale features (the often global jargon of online gaming communities). Similarly, as noted earlier, the introduction and spread of the Internet and other mobile long-distance communication instruments has changed the entire sociolinguistic economy of societies; the change, thus, affects not just those who intensively use such technologies, but also those who lack access to them.

9. The latter remark has a methodological consequence. The loci of macroscopic change can be microscopic and unpredictable; large-scale change can be triggered by individual contingencies or recurrences of seemingly insignificant deviations – the stochastic side of sociolinguistic systems. A jurisprudence-driven legal system is a good illustration (cf. Eades, this volume, Chapter 17): A single highly contingent ruling by a judge can change the whole system of legislation on related issues. This means that microscopic and detailed investigation of cases – ethnography, in other words – is perhaps the most immediately useful methodology for investigating systemic sociolinguistic aspects (cf. Rampton 2006; Blommaert and Rampton 2011). The precise *direction* of change is unpredictable as well because of the unpredictability of the other factors. We know that systems change irreversibly – we know, thus, that there is a *vector* of change – but what exactly the outcome of change will be is hard to determine. We can *believe* in a certain direction of change, but we will not necessarily see it happen. The history of language planning across the globe is replete with unexpected (and often unwelcome and unhappy) outcomes.

10. In view of all this, the task of analysis is not to reduce complexity – to reiterate, in other words, the synchronization of everyday understanding – but to demonstrate complexity, to unfold the complex and multifiliar features and their various different origins that are contained in synchronized moments of understanding. The recognition that the synchrony of linguistics and sociolinguistics (the so-called Saussurean synchrony) is in actual fact an ideologically plied habit of synchronization evidently destroys that synchrony (cf. Blommaert 2013: 117–119).

I realize that all of these points sound rather abstract and perhaps daunting; I can reassure my readers, however, that these points merely summarize and reformulate insights repeatedly established in sociolinguistic and linguistic-anthropological literature by now; they represent the second move of the paradigm shift, which merely extends and broadens the acquired insights of the first move. The terms in which I have couched my points are there because they enable us to imagine the sociolinguistics of superdiversity as organized on an entirely different footing from that which characterized the Fishmanian, Labovian, and Schegloffian sociolinguistic world. In fact, several of the points flatly contradict some of the most common assumptions in the study of language in society – the boundedness of speech communities; the stability, linearity, and even predictable nature of sociolinguistic variation; the linear nature of linguistic and sociolinguistic evolution; the autonomy and bounded-ness of language itself; the assumption of sharedness of resources among speakers; and so forth – the structuralist reifications identified by the likes of Cicourel and Williams. They have now been replaced by a baseline imagery of openness, dynamics, multifiliar and nonlinear development, unpredictability. What used to be considered deviant and abnormal – complexity, hybridity, and other forms of 'impurity' in language use – has become, in this perspective, normal.

Towards method

Recall Cicourel's insistence, quoted at the outset, on the need to employ "several types of ethnographic and textual materials in order to underscore . . . unavoid-able aspects of organizational and local constraints and processes that are integral to rethinking 'context'" (Cicourel 1992: 309). We need an aggregate of methods that reflects the complexity of the cases we investigate, and methods that do not simplify these cases to a one-dimensional skeleton structure. I have repeatedly gestured towards ethnography as a privileged set of instruments for studying complexity, but that in itself is not sufficient and the issue is not all that simple. Let me briefly review some important aspects of the task of designing methods for a complex sociolinguistics.

1. The biggest challenge in research is how to avoid statifying and stabiliz-ing what is, in effect, a dynamic and unstable given. In other words, we need methods that enable us to focus on *change* itself, on how and why sociolin-guistic environments do *not* stay the same over time and in different condi-tions. The points that follow sketch aspects of this issue.

2. As outlined earlier, events always emerge under the influence of different (and often unclearly related) forces. Given this non-unified nature of sociolin-guistic events and of speech deployed in them, simple notions of "context" will not do. It is good to return to Cicourel's (1992) remarks here, directed, as we

know, against the deeply flawed notion of context, interpreted as directly inferenceable (and explicitly enacted) sociocognitive information; this was the interpretation that Cicourel had detected in Schegloffian conversation analysis. Cicourel's argument was that, in order to just describe what participants in the medical encounters he had studied actually do in the way of meaning-making, it was vital to identify several very different bodies of "contextual" material influencing their actions – most of it *in*visible in the interaction itself but definitely present as assumptions, identity categories, action templates, and frames for understanding in the encounters. It was possible, drawing on this richer set of "contextual" levels, to see such medical encounters not as just one (sequentially developing) activity but as an agglomerate of different sequential and interlocking activities, "nested" in other activities and involving small and delicate, but interpretively substantial, genre and footing shifts, some oriented to the interaction here-and-now, others pointing to different (present or absent) participants or anticipating subsequent steps in the activity. As for the latter, medical encounters typically also lead to post hoc case discussions by the medical team, to iterative uptake in later encounters with other patients, to archived case files, reports, and publications, and so forth – and all of these play a role in the single and uniquely situated ("micro") encounter itself, which thereby acquires a *systemic* ("macro") dimension.[5] Such encounters, thus, constituted not just one context (that of the encounter itself) but several related yet very different "contexts" (cf. also Briggs 1997). The encounter was *polycentric*, we would now say.

It is an elementary step in the development of method, I believe, to assume that every case of actual social interaction we study is couched in layers upon layers of relevant contexts and that awareness of the salience of different context levels is not sidelined whenever we focus on specific ones. Every momentary context is shaped by conditions created earlier and has the potential to shape ulterior conditions as well, and any adequate "contextual" sociolinguistic analysis must identify these "transcontextual" influences.

3. This point has a bearing on the ways in which we currently use standard "data" artifacts, such as transcribed recordings. Transcripts have a tendency to suggest one *single* sequentially organized activity in which every turn can be read as responding to a previous one hearable in the audio-recording – while in fact, it was an activity in its own right or responded to an entirely different prompt signaling a different participation framework. The uniformity of activity (and thus of context, as we saw) can never be taken for granted. Neither can the *nature* of activity be taken for granted: We very often take transcripts to

---

[5] Cicourel's *The Social Organization of Juvenile Justice* (1968) developed this issue in spectacular detail and remains, therefore, a methodological classic. See also the discussion of "forgotten contexts" in Blommaert (2005: 56–66).

represent a "conversation", whereas closer inspection reveals frequent genre and register shifts *within* a conversation, with micro-narratives, shouts, or shifts from one-to-one to group-oriented speech – all being extraordinarily important to understand what goes on. The complexity of communicative events needs to be reflected in the data artifacts we employ to study them. To rephrase Cicourel, "textual materials" such as transcripts need to be complemented by "ethnographic materials" providing clues about how to use the transcript.

4. As for quantitative methods (now including "big data" mining techniques), the stochastic nature of sociolinguistic systems ought to sensitize us to the fact that statistical frequencies or averages might not be the key to understanding a sociolinguistic environment; the really relevant elements – triggers of large-scale change, for instance – can be exceptional, deviant, and statistically insignificant. Really influential forces, as we know, may be characterized precisely by their *in*frequency of occurrence. Survey work needs to be driven by ethnographically established and ecologically valid questions and insights, and quantitative outcomes need to be ethnographically verified (Cicourel 1964; also Blommaert and van de Vijver 2013; for examples, see Sharma and Rampton 2011; Rampton 2012).

5. A set of methods needs to be designed for addressing the new sociolinguistic environments, mentioned earlier, that characterize superdiversity. Some work has been done already on online ethnography (e.g., Beaulieu 2004; Androutsopoulos 2008); but work on the interaction between online and offline sociolinguistic life very much awaits development (Varis 2014 provides a survey). As mentioned earlier, the presence of new communication and information technologies has reshuffled the sociolinguistic economies of contemporary societies, leading to new repertoires and forms of semiotic work characterized by visual literacy-driven resources and practices. This is disturbing for a science more at ease with (and privileging) spoken language usage as the baseline material for sociolinguistic inquiry and traditionally rather poorly equipped for addressing literate materials (Lillis 2013). New multimodal methods of analysis need to come into circulation in order to adequately tackle the various challenges posed by these new and very rapidly evolving sociolinguistic environments.

Accepting and foregrounding the complexity of sociolinguistic phenomena and processes evidently does not make life easier for sociolinguists; indeed, it renders the job of adequate analysis vastly more complex. We must realize that a paradigmatic shift such as the one outlined here will involve the disqualification, not so much of actual analytical techniques (we will forever be recording and transcribing talk), but of the assumptions we hold about them and about their results. Far more multifaceted forms of research will have to be constructed, combining (in demanding ways) advanced skills in a variety of methods and approaches, but held together and made coherent by a clearly established and defined research object. It is to be anticipated that the next decade will see a flurry of innovation in the field of sociolinguistic method; it will also undoubtedly see developments in research ethos and strategy, with more attention (and respect) for interdisciplinarity, "mixed methods" and teamwork. This, I believe, is to be welcomed.

Conclusion

Dell Hymes opened his essay "Models of the Interaction of Language and Social Life" with this simple sentence: "Diversity of speech has been singled out as the main focus of sociolinguistics" (Hymes 1972: 38). In defining the object of sociolinguistics in this way, he reacted against the hegemony of a science of language that focused on the static, the stable, the eternal, and the universal in language, and proposed a science that would explain the actual ways in which language operated in social life and played a role in structuring society. These ways were diverse, and that meant that they were not deducible from general rules of grammar or cognition, not stable over time nor unaffected by history and human agency.

I find this definition of the scope of sociolinguistics still the clearest and most convincing argument in favor of sociolinguistics, its unique raison d'être. But accepting it involves accepting diversity as *change*, both in the nature and structure of our object and in the approaches we develop for analyzing it. The fact that paradigmatic shifts, such as the ones outlined here, occur and even intensify is testimony of the usefulness of existing approaches: They took us to the point where we experienced their limits and the need to revise and improve them. We have in the past decades come to recognize language in society as a domain that has undergone deep and fundamental changes at all levels, as part of deep and fundamental changes of the world at large. The "creative destruction" (to use Schumpeter's well-worn term) involved in this recognition leads us to a more accurate and precise science, of greater relevance to other disciplines and more useful to the people and communities we observe and study.

REFERENCES

Agha, Asif. 2007. *Language and Social Relations*. Cambridge: Cambridge University Press.
Androutsopoulos, Jannis. 2006. Multilingualism, diaspora, and the Internet: Codes and identities on German-based diaspora websites. *Journal of Sociolinguistics* 10, 4: 520–547.
    2008. Potentials and limitations of discourse-centred online ethnography. *Language@Internet* 5, article 9. www.languageatinternet.org/articles/2008/1610/androutsopoulos.pdf.

Backus, Ad. 2012. A usage-based approach to borrowability. *Tilburg Papers in Culture Studies*, paper 27.

Beaulieu, Anne. 2004. Mediating ethnography: Objectivity and the making of ethnographies of the internet. *Social Epistemology* 18: 139–163.

Blackledge, Adrian, and Angela Creese. 2010. *Multilingualism: A Critical Perspective.* London: Bloomsbury.

Blommaert, Jan. 2005. *Discourse: A Critical Introduction.* Cambridge: Cambridge University Press.

2010. *The Sociolinguistics of Globalization.* Cambridge: Cambridge University Press.

2013. *Ethnography, Superdiversity and Linguistic Landscapes: Chronicles of Complexity.* Bristol: Multilingual Matters.

(ed.). 1999. *Language Ideological Debates.* Berlin: Mouton de Gruyter.

Blommaert, Jan, and Ad Backus. 2013. Superdiverse repertoires and the individual. In Ingrid de Saint-Georges and Jean-Jacques Weber (eds.), *Multilingualism and Multimodality: Current Challenges for Educational Studies.* Rotterdam: Sense Publishers, 11–32.

Blommaert, Jan, and Michael Meeuwis. 1994. The Markedness Model and the absence of society: Remarks on codeswitching. *Multilingua* 13, 4: 397–423.

Blommaert, Jan, and Ben Rampton. 2011. Language and superdiversity. *Diversities* 13, 2: 1–22.

Blommaert, Jan, and Fons van de Vijver. 2013. Combining surveys and ethnographies in the study of rapid social change. *Working Papers on Urban Language and Literacies* 108.

Blommaert, Jan, and Piia Varis. 2012. Culture as accent. *Tilburg Papers in Culture Studies* 18.

Briggs, Charles. 1997. Notes on a "confession": On the construction of gender, sexuality, and violence in an infanticide case. *Pragmatics* 7, 4: 519–546.

Burke, Peter. 2011. *The Social History of Knowledge,* vol. 2: *From the Encyclopaedia to Wikipedia.* Cambridge: Polity.

Cicourel, Aaron. 1964. *Method and Measurement in Sociology.* New York: Free Press.

1968 [2013]. *The Social Organization of Juvenile Justice.* New Brunswick, NJ: Transaction Publishers.

1973. *Cognitive Sociology: Language and Meaning in Social Interaction.* Harmondsworth: Penguin Education.

1992. The interpenetration of communicative contexts: Examples from medical encounters. In Alessandro Duranti and Charles Goodwin (eds.), *Rethinking Context: Language as an Interactive Phenomenon.* Cambridge: Cambridge University Press, 291–310.

Coupland, Nikolas. 2007. *Style: Language Variation and Identity.* Cambridge: Cambridge University Press.

(ed.). 2003. *Journal of Sociolinguistics* 7/4 (Thematic issue on *Sociolinguistics and Globalisation*).

(ed.). 2010. *The Handbook of Language and Globalization.* New York and London: Wiley Blackwell.

Creese, Angela, and Adrian Blackledge. 2010. Towards a sociolinguistics of superdiversity. *Zeitschrift für Erziehungswissenschaften* 13: 549–572.

Eades, Diana. 2010. *Sociolinguistics and the Legal Process*. Bristol: Multilingual Matters.

Gal, Susan, and Kathryn Woolard (eds.). 2001. *Languages and Publics: The Making of Authority*. Manchester: St. Jerome.

Gumperz, John. 1982. *Discourse Strategies*. Cambridge: Cambridge University Press.

2003. Response essay. In Susan Eerdmans, Carlo Prevignano, and Paul Thibault (eds.), *Language and Interaction: Discussions with John J. Gumperz*. Amsterdam: John Benjamins, 105–126.

Gumperz, John, and Dell Hymes (eds.). 1972. *Directions in Sociolinguistics: The Ethnography of Communication*. New York: Holt, Rinehart and Winston.

Hymes, Dell. 1972 [1986]. Models of the interaction of language and social life. In John Gumperz and Dell Hymes (eds.), *Directions in Sociolinguistics: The Ethnography of Communication*. London: Basil Blackwell, 35–71.

1996. *Ethnography, Linguistics, Narrative Inequality: Toward an Understanding of Voice*. London: Taylor & Francis.

Irvine, Judith, and Susan Gal. 2000. Language ideology and linguistic differentiation. In Paul Kroskrity (ed.), *Regimes of Language*. Santa Fe, NM: SAR Press, 35–83.

Jacquemet, Marco. 2005. Transidiomatic practices: Language and power in the age of globalization. *Language and Communication* 25, 3: 257–277.

Jaworski, Adam, and Crispin Thurlow. 2010. Language and the globalizing habitus of tourism: Towards a sociolinguistics of fleeting relationships. In Nikolas Coupland (ed.), *The Handbook of Language and Globalization*. Oxford: Wiley-Blackwell, 255–286.

Kroskrity, Paul (ed.). 2000. *Regimes of Language*. Santa Fe, NM: SAR Press.

Larsen-Freeman, Diane. 1997. Chaos/complexity science and second language acquisition. *Applied Linguistics* 18, 2: 141–165.

Lillis, Theresa. 2013. *The Sociolinguistics of Writing*. Edinburgh: Edinburgh University Press.

Makoni, Sinfree, and Alastair Pennycook (eds.). 2006. *Disinventing and Reconstituting Languages*. Bristol: Multilingual Matters.

Maryns, Katrijn. 2006. *The Asylum Speaker: Language in the Belgian Asylum Procedure*. Manchester: St. Jerome.

Moore, Robert M. 2012. "Taking up speech" in an endangered language: Bilingual discourse in a heritage language classroom. *Working Papers in Educational Linguistics* 27, 2: 57–78.

Myers-Scotton, Carol. 1992. *Social Motivations for Codeswitching: Evidence from Africa*. Oxford: Clarendon Press.

Parkin, David. 2012. From multilingual classification to translingual ontology: Concluding commentary. *Diversities* 14, 2: 71–85.

Pennycook, Alastair. 2007. *Global Englishes and Transcultural Flows*. London: Routledge.

2010. *Language as a Local Practice*. London: Routledge.

2012. *Language and Mobility: Unexpected Places*. Bristol: Multilingual Matters.

Prigogine, Ilya, and Isabelle Stengers. 1984. *Order out of Chaos: Man's New Dialogue with Nature*. New York: Bantam Books.

Rampton, Ben. 1995. *Crossing: Language and Ethnicity among Adolescents*. London: Longman.

1998. Speech community. In Jef Verschueren, Jan-Ola Östman, Jan Blommaert, and Chris Bulcaen (eds.), *Handbook of Pragmatics, 1998 Installment*. Amsterdam and New York: John Benjamins, 1–30.

2006. *Language in Late Modernity*. Cambridge: Cambridge University Press.

2012. Drilling down to the grain in superdiversity. *Working Papers in Urban Language and Literacies* 98.

Rymes, Betsy. 2014. *Communicating beyond Language: Everyday Encounters with Diversity*. New York: Routledge.

Schieffelin, Bambi. 1990. *The Give and Take of Everyday Life: Language Socialization of Kaluli Children*. Cambridge: Cambridge University Press.

Seargeant, Philip. 2009. *The Idea of English in Japan: Ideology and the Evolution of a Global Language*. Bristol: Multilingual Matters.

Sharma, Devyani, and Ben Rampton. 2011. Lectal focusing in interaction: A new methodology for the study of superdiverse speech. *Working Papers in Urban Language and Literacies* 79.

Silverstein, Michael. 1996. Monoglot "Standard" in America: Standardization and metaphors of linguistic hegemony. In Donald Brenneis and Ronald Macaulay (eds.), *The Matrix of Language*. Boulder, CO: Westview Press, 284–306.

2003. Indexical order and the dialectics of sociolinguistic life. *Language and Communication* 23: 193–229.

Silverstein, Michael, and Greg Urban (eds.). 1996. *Natural Histories of Discourse*. Chicago, IL : University of Chicago Press.

Varis, Piia. 2014. Digital ethnography. *Tilburg Papers in Culture Studies* 103.

Varis, Piia, and Xuan Wang. 2011. Superdiversity on the internet: A case from China. *Diversities* 13, 2: 71–83.

Vertovec, Steven. 2007. Super-diversity and its implications. *Ethnic and Racial Studies* 30, 6: 1024–1054.

Waddington, Conrad H. 1977. *Tools for Thought*. St. Albans: Paladin.

Weber, Jean-Jacques, and Kristine Horner. 2012. *Introducing Multilingualism: A Social Approach*. London: Routledge.

Williams, Glyn. 1992. *Sociolinguistics: A Sociological Critique*. London: Routledge.

Zentz, Lauren. 2015. "Is English also the place where I belong?" Linguistic biographies and expanding communicative repertoires in Central Java. *International Journal of Multilingualism* 12, 1: 68–92.

Part IV

Power, mediation and critical sociolinguistics

12 Critical debates: Discourse, boundaries and social change

Sari Pietikäinen

1. Introduction: shifting boundaries, transforming critique

Language boundaries and categories are a classical sociolinguistic issue in accounts of linguistic diversity and change. However, the status of boundaries and categories is called into question in the complex and shifting terrain of theoretical and political debates (cf. Blommaert, this volume, Chapter 11). How should such boundaries and categories be best understood and defined? One important perspective, adopted in this chapter, is that the construction of sociolinguistic boundaries always involves questions of power. That is, we need to ask when, how, on what grounds, and by whom they are defined and operationalized. These questions have consequences for many key issues of interest in sociolinguistics, including identity and social inequalities. This perspective is often taken as a form of critical language research, although we also need to question what is actually meant by the concept of 'criticality'.

As a heterogeneous and debated project in itself, the concept of the critical is frequently used in different strands of research into language, power, and social change (see, e.g., Fairclough 1992; Pennycook 2001; 2012; Mesthrie 2009; Heller 2011; Duchêne et al. 2013). Often, theorization of the complex relationships between language, power, and social change, as developed by Foucault, Bourdieu, Bakhtin, and Voloshinov, forms the baseline of critical perspectives, but there are obviously different historical developments and emphases within language research interested in these issues (see, e.g., Woolard 1985; Blommaert 2005; Heller 2011; Wodak 2011). For instance, we can trace back uses of the term 'critical' to Critical Linguistics, a perspective developed by linguists and literary theorists at the University of East Anglia in the United Kingdom (Fowler et al. 1979; Kress and Hodge 1979) during the 1970s, aiming to explore relationships between language use and ideologies, basing their work on Halliday´s systemic functional linguistics. This work continued in the 1980s under the label of Critical Discourse Analysis (CDA), a heterogeneous approach to the study of language use as part of social practice, with a focus on reproduction of social and political hegemony and power relations (see, e.g., Fairclough 1992; van Dijk 1993; Wodak 1996).

In other fields of language research too, for example in critical applied linguistics (Pennycook 2001), the term 'critical' marks a focus on the ways in which power and inequality figure in the arenas of language teaching, language policy, and language testing. In sociolinguistics, we can trace the roots of critical research in the work of Hymes (1974) and Gumperz (1982) in emphasizing an understanding of language as embedded in larger social systems and in the structuration of social difference, as well as reflecting the impact of Bourdieu's work in exploring the role language plays in the political field and in processes of social (re)production (see, e.g., Hanks 2005; Heller 2011). Contemporary critical stances in sociolinguistics often evolve around questions of social difference and inequality in relation to linguistic diversity, particularly under the new, shifting conditions of mobility, globalization, and new economy, often accompanied by the argument that we need research that is aligned to a more ethnographic approach (cf. Blommaert 2010; Heller 2011; Duchêne et al. 2013). What these various ways of using the term 'critical' seem to have in common is that they mark a step away – or perhaps a step forward – from "merely" descriptive approaches to language research and that they challenge the idea of objectivist sociolinguistic research. Rather, a starting point is found in the idea that power always matters in sociolinguistic affairs and that research needs to investigate how language figures and is figured in changing relationships of power.

The prevalence of the term 'critical' nowadays is hardly surprising, as the term evokes important questions that relate to power, inequality, resistance, and change. Also the growing demands of various research funding and assessment enterprises, insisting that research must have demonstrable social relevance, give renewed currency to critical work (cf. Curry and Lillis 2013). At the same time, research done under the critical label has itself been critiqued for its arguably deterministic and biased views of social change and of the directions it should take, for its a priori assumptions about relationships between language and power, and for losing its groundings and relevance under new conditions (e.g. Hammersley 1997; Toolan 1997; Breeze 2011). Yet many researchers continue to use the term 'critical', albeit with an attempt to renew its meaning and scope, at times indexed by newly coined terminology, such as "postcritical", by emphasizing transdisciplinary work (such as multi-sited ethnography, nexus analysis, and discourse ethnography), or through foregrounding the work's time–space aspects (in using concepts such as circulation and trajectories).

'Critical' has become a problematic term under current circumstances, if we agree that societies are suffering crises of authority and legitimation of any knowledge or of any political action (Phillips 2000: 14). The critical tag is not alone in these crises, as many other concepts that were conceived in the modernist frame – such as language, nation, and citizen – have also become problematic concepts (Pennycook 2010). What 'critical' meant thirty or sixty years ago may not map onto the concerns and interests of current research, being undertaken in a context where the understanding of centres and margins is shifting and where power bases are tending to become polycentric. Also, various disciplinary developments around critical research have created different ontologies and epistemologies, not all of which are compatible. Criticality comes in different shapes and forms, and what the term means in sociolinguistics may or may not be synonymous with the sense(s) invoked in critical approaches in discourse studies, applied linguistics, sociology, and so forth. These problems associated with the term 'critical' do not mean that questions related to language, power, or social change are currently less important or pressing, but rather that what critical means now is partly ambiguous and is certainly changing.

Starting from a core interest in language, power, and social change, critical language research has become a complex enterprise with rhizomatic connections to a wide range of theories, methods, and questions. While much of critical language research seems to continue to question and reflect on what is taken for granted – especially in terms of ideological critique (cf. Thomas 1993; Määttä and Pietikäinen 2014) – we seem to be at a point of ontological and epistemological transition as regards understanding what 'critical' means. Criticality is not alone in this transition, as similar kinds of ontological and epistemological questioning can be found in other fields researching language in society. For example, Reyes (2014: 367) discusses what she calls the "Super-New-Big" trend in examining large-scale changes in the contemporary moment. Otsuji and Pennycook (2010, and see Pennycook, this volume, Chapter 9) reflect on the various prefixes (metro/trans/poly) now being attached to 'language' or 'lingualism' as ways of exploring multilingual language use without necessarily endorsing established disciplinary assumptions. These transitions are part of the development of theories and concepts. As Foucault ([1969] 1972: 3) reminds us, discussing disciplinary changes, beneath apparent continuity and development there are always interruptions, displacements, and transformations of traditions and concepts. The concept of 'critical' is no different. Similarly to the three waves of feminist studies (Eckert, this volume, Chapter 3) or to the several 'turns' in sociology and cultural studies, critical language research has also gone through various phases (see, e.g., Pennycook 2001).

In the remainder of this chapter,[1] I explore some more specific ways in which the term 'critical' has been employed in language research regarding

---

[1] This chapter has benefited from discussions on critical language research in the Jyväskylä Discourse Think Tank (2013), and I wish warmly to thank all the participants. Nikolas Coupland, Alexandre Duchêne, Monica Heller, and Helen Kelly-Holmes have provided very helpful

language, power, and social change. To exemplify these developments, I locate the discussions around debates regarding sociolinguistic boundaries in a context of the multilingual indigenous Sámi community in Finland. Similarly to many other indigenous and minority language communities, the Sámi community continues to undergo intersecting linguistic, political, and economic changes related to, for example, indigenous language rights and revitalization, political and cultural sovereignty, contested legal definitions of the category of Sámi, and an economic change from primarily production to service industries, mainly tourism (Lehtola 2012; Pietikäinen 2013). All these changes disturb boundaries and create debates about the "right" course of action on Sámi identity and language politics, economic development, and other issues (Pietikäinen 2013; 2014; Pietikäinen and Kelly-Holmes 2013). Various appropriations and applications of the concept of criticality appear to be in circulation, and further reflections upon how the term may help or hinder research into language and social change is needed.

In the following, I treat the various approaches to criticality as themselves forming a discourse contingent upon particular historical conditions, claims for "the truth", actors, and possibilities (cf. Luke 2002: 97) in the changing Sámi context. Foucault (as quoted in Weedon 1987: 108) argues that discourses are ways of constituting knowledge, together with the social practices, forms of subjectivity, and power relations that inhere in such knowledges and relations between them. This conceptualization includes the very idea that discourses have a material power and systematically form, shape, and change the definitions of objects circulating within them (Pennycook 2010; Määttä and Pietikäinen 2014). I focus on three concurring and intersecting discourses about the critical, stemming from previous critical language research and operating in the indigenous Sámi context. In an attempt to highlight the logics of each discourse, I call these (1) emancipatory critique, (2) ethnographic critique, and (3) carnivalesque critique. I end with a discussion of criticality as an unfinished project and on the concept of rhizome (Deleuze and Guattari 1987) as a way forward.

2.   Emancipatory critique

One broad, influential approach to examining language, power, and social change has been through the work known as critical theory, a tradition of work associated with the Frankfurt school, a group of German philosophers and social theorists from the latter part of the twentieth century who worked

comments on the various versions of this chapter and I am grateful for them. The chapter is produced in the context of the Peripheral Multilingualism research project, funded by the Academy of Finland.

within a Western European Marxist tradition (cf. Agar 1991; Bronner 1994; Pennycook 2001). Agar (1991: 107) describes how a "critical" theory may be distinguished from a "traditional" theory, according to a specific practical purpose: A theory is critical to the extent that it seeks human emancipation, "to liberate human beings from the circumstances that enslave them" (Horkheimer 1982: 244).

This version of critical work, with its normative dimension, has been popular in various social and political movements, including those supporting minority and indigenous language rights. This is no wonder, as this version of the critical seems to provide a clear criterion and direction for both social change and political action. Within the field of language research, a discourse of emancipatory critique of this kind became popular towards the end of the twentieth century, especially (as noted above) in research carried out under the umbrella term CDA (cf. Blommaert 2005; Pennycook 2010; Forchtner 2011). While in itself a heterogeneous enterprise that incorporates various strands and foci, the CDA approach is characterized by a concern for language, power, and emancipation that is largely inherited from the critical theory tradition (Forchtner 2011; Zhang et al. 2011). For example, one of the grounding scholars of CDA, Norman Fairclough (1995: 132), suggests that CDA is about investigating how "practices, events and texts arise out of and are ideologically shaped by relations of power and struggles over power; and to explore how the opacity of these relationships between discourse and society is itself a factor securing power and hegemony" (see also Kelly-Holmes, this volume, Chapter 7). Luke (2002: 106) argues that the prevailing project of CDA is that of the critique of ideology, which it shares with most forms of textual analysis and the presupposition of normative orders. As the pioneering CDA scholar Ruth Wodak concludes (2011: 52), CDA aims at "producing enlightenment and emancipation".

CDA has been acknowledged to have been successful in putting questions of language, power, and domination in the foreground; in presenting an explicit agenda for change; and in bringing linguistic and textual analysis into a dialogue with (critical) sociological theories. At the same time, it has also inherited many of the same objections as critical theory in general. These relate to CDA's lack of reflexivity on its own philosophical foundations, its readiness to take some key categories unproblematically for granted, and its tendency to orient itself towards unproblematized and static assumptions about power relations (oppressors/oppressed, majority/minority), as well as its belief in the awareness of inequality as a step towards emancipation (see, e.g., Hammersley 1997; Schegloff 1997; Slembrouck 2001; Verschueren 2001; Luke 2002; Blommaert 2005; Heller and Pujolar 2009; Pennycook 2010; also Heller and Duchêne, this volume, Chapter 6). Pennycook (2012: 129–130) points out how the unproblematized and nonlocalized use of some key concepts creates

new kinds of problems: "reaffirm[ing] concepts such as emancipation, awareness, rationality, objectivity, quality, democracy and transformation which,
from another perspective, may be viewed as products by the same system that
gives rise to those very problems that this framework aims to critique. Thus, it
both critiques and reproduces at the same time". This kind of reproduction of
problematic boundaries, particularly between centres and margins, as well as
internal hierarchies, can be found in many minority and indigenous language
contexts (Heller 2011; Pietikäinen 2014), as a kind of a recursive echo of
nation–state logics.

    These typical strengths and problems of emancipatory critique materialize in
the Sámi context, where this kind of critique operates with a particular long-
standing view of the power imbalance between what is considered to be the
centre (the nation–state, the ethnic and linguistic majority) and the periphery or
minority (the Sámi community, Sámiland), and, moreover, with a default set of
strategies for overcoming this power imbalance. These include promoting
equal status, access, and rights for Sámi people and for their cultural, political,
linguistic, and economic practices. In some cases these strategies translate into
the active promotion of particular rights for the Sámi, applicable in their
domicile area or when interacting with authorities. Importantly, for emancipatory critique to work, sociolinguistic boundaries need to be fixed: There need
to be clear criteria, or at least a consensus, as to what counts as Sámi, indigenous, endangered, and minority, and how these can be identified, accounted,
maintained, or developed. This rather fixed view of power relations, of who is
Sámi and who is Finnish, and of the objects and tools for critiquing and
ultimately changing these relationships, continues to be the dominant frame
informing much political mobilization in the Sámi context. It has been successfully employed in promoting indigenous legal, political, and linguistics
rights; in implementing the cultural sovereignty of the Sámi people; and in
informing many Sámi language and cultural revitalization projects. It plays a
crucial role in various enumerative practices (of the number of Sámi language
speakers, of the number of Sámi living in the Sámi domicile area, etc.), feeding
into the logics of emancipatory discourse: The relatively small or large
numbers of Sámi language speakers, for example, have been used as indicators
of how necessary (in the case of small or decreasing numbers) or effective (in
the case of large or increasing numbers) language revitalization projects are.

    At the same time, emancipatory critique is problematic in the Sámi context.
It reproduces its own centres and margins, in fact in ways that are quite similar
to how the modernist nation–state system that it sets out to critique does, by
endorsing fixed boundaries around the category of Sáminess. In the process, it
includes some bodies, histories, and practices and excludes others. At the same
time, there is an increasing need to account for the multiplicity, complexity,
and ambiguity around being and becoming Sámi. There are more and more

bodies, repertoires, experiences, and trajectories that do not fit comfortably into these official categories. This situation generates increasing critique "from the ground up", directed at this fixedness of categories and at the policing of linguistic and ethnic boundaries. For example, new speakers of the endangered Sámi languages (cf. O'Rourke et al. 2015) – those who have learnt the Sámi languages outside the family context, typically later in life, and especially those learners who do not have Sámi heritage – disturb the category of "Sámi speaker", which has so far mainly referred to people with Sámi heritage. This is also a political and legal question, as competence in Sámi languages and the ways it has been acquired are part of a legal dispute around who counts as Sámi, what criteria are used, and who gets to decide (Valkonen 2009; Joona 2013). In this moment of transition, the current official legal definition of the category of "Sámi", provided by the Finnish Sámi Parliament, the highest legal authority in Finnish Sámi issues, has been criticized as being too narrow and exclusive, and the counter-critique to this critique has been described as interference in the internal issues of Sámi community and as an attempt to colonialize the Sámi community from the inside (Sarivaara 2012).

The Sámi example illustrates how emancipatory critique may not be as straightforward on the ground as it first seems. It may have both intended as well as unintended impacts. It can be a powerful strategy for engaging with various legal and educational institutions operating with similar kinds of normative frameworks. At the same time, it tends to create local tensions between what is now perceived as the "elite Sámi", with acknowledged statuses and legally granted rights, on one hand, and those with far more hybrid and complex genealogies, on the other. In this sense, the emancipatory critique is simultaneously both part of the solution and part of the problem. The example also illustrates how sociolinguistic boundaries result from the discursive processes and objectives of social contests: What becomes fixed – at least for a while – as denoting "being Sámi" is the result of discourse work and a precarious yet strategic use of essentialism (Spivak 1988; cf. Wee, this volume, Chapter 15).

The changing conditions of globalization, as well as novel spaces, modes, and understandings of activism and social change, have all created theoretical and empirical challenges for emancipatory critical research (cf. Luke 2002; Zhang et al. 2011). Investment in one view of power relations and in one way to change them may limit the possibilities for emancipatory critical work to engage locally and to think of alternative strategies for social change and related political projects. At times, this makes emancipatory work mistrustful of approaches which start with the premises of locally embedded, decentred, and networked views on language, power, and social change. Next, I turn to look at this kind of critical work, which I refer to as ethnographic critique.

3.   Ethnographic critique

If emancipatory critique starts with a set view of what seems to be the problem and with a set of strategies to solve it, ethnographic critique begins from the other end. It rejects the totalizing tendency of the emancipatory critical view to create a single universal knowledge or truth and simple dualisms (powerful/ powerless, just/unjust, etc.) that go with it. Instead, it locates knowledge production in multiple positions, in changing local conditions, and in individual stories. Ethnographic critique is in an alliance with postmodern thinking insofar as it explicitly rejects totalizing perspectives on history and society – grand narratives – and attempts to explain the world in terms of patterned interrelationships (Agar 1991: 116). What becomes the focus of interest, then, is the ways in which different social experiences, conditions, and consequences of (say) being a Sámi are framed by various discourses at a given historical moment, how people make sense of them, and, importantly for the critical dimension, how they map upwards or are linked to wider social, historical, and economic structurations. The attempt here is to explore particular event- and process-based configurations of power and knowledge that emerge at a particular time and place within encounters that are historically conditioned (Patton 2006: 268). When discussing critical sociolinguistics and ethnography, Heller (2011: 34) describes 'critical' to mean "describing, understanding and explaining the relations of social difference and social inequality that shape our world". The critical stance manifests itself in ethnographic work with research foci related to social issues and power relations as they emerge in local or individual practices and experiences, as part of wider patterning of social organization. To research "small" things is simultaneously to examine "big" things (cf., e.g., Heller 2011; Madison 2012).

Ethnographic critique emphasizes material and historical dimensions – that is, how social relations came to be the way they are (Pennycook 2001: 6; Cook 2013: 966) – and what becomes fixed under what kind of conditions, and with what consequences (Heller 2011). Here we can see a link between ethnography and the Foucauldian idea that power and knowledge are the same thing (cf. Ball 1994). Foucault ([1969] 1972) insists that knowledge must be traced to different discourses that frame the knowledge formulated within them, and which are constituted historically. In much critical language research, this position of Foucault's has been interpreted as a call for an ethnographic approach – an examination of what counts as knowledge in a particular time and place, according to what criteria, and decided by whom. This includes reflections of the position of the researcher as a knowledge producer and the ways in which knowledge is obtained and constructed (Madison 2012).

A story told by a Sámi man that I call here Antero, in the context of ethnographic research on language biographies, is a story of boundary work related to language-ideological debates over who owns the Sámi languages, and on what grounds. Antero is a senior Sámi with a multilingual repertoire, including Inari Sámi, one of the least common Sámi languages, which has about 400 speakers (Kulonen et al. 2005). The story illustrates how power and knowledge are intertwined with real, material consequences on the construction of sociolinguistic boundaries, and impacting on individuals' legitimacy as Sámi language speakers. In terms of language biography, Antero is a typical example of his generation of Sámi. In his childhood, before the Second World War in preindustrialized Finnish Lapland, Antero learnt and used Inari Sámi at home and in his village, hearing other Sámi languages and Finnish occasionally being used by travellers and by relatives. Entering the Finnish school system at the age of seven changed his linguistic practices drastically. At boarding school, a strict Finnish-only language policy was applied, and Antero learnt to read and write in Finnish only. Because of the long distances, Antero was able to visit home only during a few holidays in the school year, and gradually his language practices shifted from Inari Sámi to mainly Finnish. Over the next decades, Finnish became his main language for everyday activities, relating to work opportunities and a family life with non-Inari Sámi speakers. Only later in life, when Antero decided to establish a tourism business as a part of the ongoing economic development of the area, the Inari Sámi language acquired new value as an index of authenticity. At this time in his life, at least partly prompted by the example set by his grandchildren who were taking part in Inari Sámi-medium education, Antero decided to take part in an Inari Sámi language course designed for speakers lacking literacy skills. But in the end he stayed there for only a few days, as he got into a language-ideological argument with the teachers over the correct pronunciation of one particular word.

The story of Antero illustrates local conditions and complexities related to sociolinguistic boundaries: how the criterion for being a Sámi speaker can change over time and space, how it is possible to be a legitimate Sámi speaker "here" but not "there". The story also shows how the aims of language revitalization, typically framed by emancipatory goals, are actually a highly complex issue "on the ground", in the everyday life of the people and community. Using Inari Sámi as a language of education turns out to work well for some people in certain situations, and not so well for others in other situations (cf. Heller 2011). Being classified as a Sámi speaker (or as a new speaker, or as not being a Sámi speaker) may have both desirable and undesirable consequences for the same people (Sarivaara 2012), as this kind of boundary work has to do with the construction of social stratification and differentiation (Heller 2001: 197; 2011: 34–35; Blackledge and Creese 2010: 5). As Antero's story illustrates, sociolinguistic boundaries are not natural objects but discursive constructions, or what Heller (2011: 36) describes as "ideas that people struggle over, sometimes working hard to make them real ... and sometimes trying to redefine or even destroy them". A similar kind of discursive work can be found in the language-ideological tensions that exist between the categories of dialect and language (cf. Duchêne 2008: 10).

The typical limitation associated with ethnographic critique relates to its lack of universality, and consequently its difficulties in connecting small, local practices with the big picture (cf. Heller 2001: 198). Further, in critical (minority) language research, ethnographic critique is at times seen to be too relativistic and postmodernist, which can be interpreted as unhelpful, and even harmful, to social and political action. For example, recent sociolinguistic discussions about what a "mother tongue" or a "first language" is and where boundaries around particular languages are positioned can be interpreted as relativistic and giving in too much to a postmodernist deconstruction, undermining and disregarding attempts by many minority and indigenous language communities to strengthen their languages (see, e.g., Olthuis et al. 2013: 177–184). At the same time, Heller (2011: 10) emphasizes that ethnography is a powerful way to examine how what happens locally is not distinct from wider patterns of social organization or from the ways in which categorization is used to reproduce or challenge social inequality. Ethnographic critique may thus help in understanding processes underlying the ways in which categories and boundaries, such as "Inari Sámi speaker" or "mother tongue", became what they are at a particular moment and place, and the local conditions under which they operate (cf. Blackledge and Creese 2010; Heller 2011). It also sheds light on various particular debates about boundaries, the consequences of particular categories, and the ways in which people cope and strategize with them. While ethnographic critique helps in problematizing boundaries, the next version of the critique sheds light on ways in which they can be transgressed.

4.   Carnivalesque critique

Perhaps more than the two previous versions of critique, carnivalesque critique has a flavour of counter-culture, grass-roots, perhaps even lightness and marginality to it. Rather than being part of more "established" versions of critique, that is, part of a political movement or a social project, carnivalesque critique is typically found in fleeting moments of popular culture, such as graffiti, political parodies, and various media "mash-ups". In these contexts, playful and ironic carnivalesque critique is used to poke fun at and disturb fixed categories and boundaries with humor. It is used to shed light on the absurdity of fixed relations between language, culture, ethnicity, nationality, and geography and to explore how such relations are resisted, defied, or rearranged with appropriations of hybridity, exaggeration, and unfinishedness (Bakhtin 1986; Pennycook 2010).

In this version of criticality, ambivalence, fleeting temporality, and humor become the method of critique (Clifford 2013; Pietikäinen 2013). In the Sámi context, carnivalesque critique seems to be linked to emerging imaginations and practices of being and becoming Sámi – to be found, for example, in hybrid comedy shows, tourism performances, and progressive arts. In the field of critical language research, interest in carnivalesque critique, as both a research topic and a mode of critique of language boundaries and categories, is relatively recent, as it has perhaps so far been seen as too ephemeral and light to be taken seriously (see, however, Pennycook 2007; Lamarre 2014; Pietikäinen 2014).

Despite its apparent lightness, carnivalesque critique is serious about language, power, and social change. In the current era of multiple transitions, cross-sections and mobilities, it has become a promising concept for examining the dynamics of power in multidirectional and intersecting social and political changes. It engages with critical discussions and activism by troubling essentializing notions of identity and by recognizing that identities shift and change over time and space, just as the institutions and structures that delineate them shift and change (Wilson 2013: 3). Carnivalesque strategies are used to challenge hegemonic social orders through grotesque realism and inversion of hierarchies and exaggeration, inviting audiences to critically reflect upon the constructed nature of the social world (Martin and Renegar 2007). This multiplicity with a critical edge has made carnivalesque critique popular among many current political identity projects related to gender, sexuality, race, ethnicity, and others, which aim to start with multiplicity and intersectionality rather than dichotomic categorization. For critical language researchers, it provides a nexus point, a conjuncture to explore overlapping practices of politics, popular culture, and social change in a moment of transition and multiplicity (cf. Pietikäinen 2014; Pietikäinen et al. forthcoming).

Here again, the works of Michel Foucault have been used to unravel the transgressive potential of carnival and what it might offer in terms of critique. Foucault (1997 [1963]) argues that "transgression is an action which involves the limits ... limit and transgression depend on each other" (p. 33). He continues, "[T]ransgression forces the limit to face the fact of its imminent disappearance, to find itself in what it excludes or to be more exact to recognize itself for the first time" (p. 34). Transgression therefore does not deny limits or boundaries but rather exceeds them, thus completing them while disclosing a reflexive act of denial and affirmation. This understanding of transgression opens up alternative ways of thinking critically about what is perceived as normative, standard, or taboo (sacred) and what is perceived as counter-normative, opposite, or deviant (profane), and, importantly, how these boundaries can be problematized and changed. Going back to our earlier discussion about languages and boundaries, the idealized models of bounded and autonomous languages that are used in many projects framed by emancipatory critique tend to conflict with the hybrid, mixed, and changing multilingual practices and identities that characterize the lived reality of many minority language speakers, highlighted by ethnographic critique. Transgressive, carnivalesque critique, then, starts from the status quo and aims to go beyond prevailing boundaries by problematizing existing fixed ontologies of sociolinguistic boundaries, while also providing alternative ways to move forward that capture both fluidity and fixedness – the dynamics of power (cf. Pennycook 2007). It also challenges us to rethink the very notion of critique itself, as well as the social change it promises to bring.

These alternative imaginations of being and becoming Sámi seem to foreground heteroglossia (Bakhtin 1986; see also Blackledge and Creese 2014) as a starting point and push for novel ways to account for and to validate change, multiplicity, and ambiguity. Bakhtin argues (1968: 10) that "carnival can be seen as a temporal liberation from the prevailing truth and from the established order". Carnival is transgressive in its very nature – a "genuine transgression", Bakhtin (1968) suggests. Carnival is transgressive because it stirs up and shakes thought that is based on the logics of identity categories and boundaries (Lechte 1990: 109). The attempt – or at least the spirit – of carnival is to dislocate, counterbalance, and disturb normalizing and totalizing categories and boundaries and to show that they too are products of a system of discourses and practices, and as such are subject to change. Thus, one possible way to bring critical reflection into this system is through "carnivalization".

In the Sámi context, with ongoing debates around categories and boundaries, carnivalesque critique can be found in some particular shifts and moments related to ways of understanding, using, and talking about Sámi resources. An example of this is a highly popular, albeit somewhat controversial Sámi TV comedy show called *Märät Säpikkäät/Njuoska Bittut*. A key element of the program is performing and trying out alternative Sámi identities and intersecting various linguistic, ethnic, and gender boundaries. The show portrays and makes jokes about iconic and easily recognized characters visiting Sámiland, including ignorant tourists, "wanna-be-Sámis", "fake-Sámis", and Helsinki people (people from the capital of Finland, in the country's southern centre), as well as iconic Sámi figures such as "Super-Sámis" (Sámi activists) and "city-Sámis". The show seems to escape from – or at least to laugh at – some of the traditional, fixed boundaries, including the Sámi/Finnish, minority/majority, North/South, centre/periphery, and female/male distinctions, and their absurdity in everyday life, which is characterized by an intersection of various simultaneous identities and complex ways of belonging (Pietikäinen 2014). The show is about critiquing and transgressing these boundaries: Laughter is a way to make stereotypes and fixed categories visible, perhaps to shake them, and potentially to open a space for reflection. It allows people in the show to perform "taboo" or "profane" things behind the protective shield of humor (again see Pietikäinen et al. forthcoming). The viewer may see the show as just humor, political critique, or simply as being offensive and in bad taste, and the reception of the *Märät Säpikäät/Njuoska Bittut* show seems to include all these options (cf. Aikio et al. 2013).

The comedy show marks a point in history where carnivalization and laughter in the context of Sámi identity have become possible. In the Bakhtinian sense of the carnival world, laughter shakes up the authoritative notion of boundaries, making room for a multiplicity of voices and meanings. The pregiven, regular categories and conventions are broken, reversed, and subverted through mockery, parody, and humor. The show is a playful, though carefully planned, strategic (and economically viable) performance. It purposefully moulds together the requirement of ownership and appropriation of Sámi languages, as well as the need for entertainment, into a TV show that licenses laughing and play as well as temporal crossings between categories and positions, with potential for more serious, political implications. Carnivalesque critique simultaneously plays with and against these norms. It can be simultaneously reflective, banal, critical, and humorous, allowing ambivalent voices to address diverse audiences and trying to articulate the ongoing, ever-shifting, multidimensional, heterogeneous, and ambiguous aspects that constitute the current local Sámi predicament and its diverse realities. Given its humorous character, carnivalesque critique may be disregarded because it fails the test of amounting to "proper" critique. It has indeed been criticized as not presenting any way forward, only "turning everything into a big joke". Also its ephemerality has been thought to make it irrelevant to the deeper and more extensive temporality of projects oriented towards social change.

At the same time, it can, I suggest, be seen as an alternative model of critique, celebrating as it does processes of becoming, change, and renewal, while being hostile to all that is static or complete. In the Sámi context carnivalesque critique seems to provide a way to address multiple, shifting norms and diverse realities by creating practices and performances that are important for emerging ways of being and doing Sáminess. Such performances and practices critique the prevailing categories and norms. They employ both fixity and fluidity to create a polyphony that plays with previous orders and norms. The dissolution of the division between the sacred (norm) and the profane (its opposite) invites us to reflect on what boundaries are sanctioned, what novel boundaries and crossings are allowed, which identities are uplifted, and which boundaries are saved. These performances and practices make sense locally and are meaningful in relation to the constantly changing social, spatial, and symbolic environments in which they are enacted and interpreted. For example, the character portrayals of the "wanna-be Sámi" and the "Super-Sámi" are recognizable types within the community, and the question of who would best fit these characterizations is subject to discussion. Finally, the Sámi version of carnivalesque critique has managed to involve new participants in the discussion about sociolinguistic boundaries, people who are typically absent from more emancipatory critique: young people, the non-Sámi-language speakers, and others from the margins of dominant ways of doing critique in the Sámi context.

5.   Unfinished critique: roots and rhizomes

When discussing critique and sociolinguistics, Heller (2001: 197) talks about "the project of critique" when dealing with various ongoing developments and shortcomings in different disciplines' engagement with the construction of relations of social difference and inequality. To me this underlines the fact that any kind of critique is an ongoing and unfinished process, embedded in a particular time and space, and that rather than trying to find "the truth" or "the best version" of a critical stance, where the alternative is to abandon the whole project, it makes more sense to try to understand the conditions and conse-quences of meanings and usages of criticality in a given time and space – how critique is understood, developed, and applied; by whom; and in whose name.

In this chapter, I have tried to show what kinds of lenses are offered by three versions of critique – emancipatory, ethnographic, and carnivalesque – to provide insight into shifting and complex sorts of boundary work in shifting multilingual, indigenous Sámi contexts. Each of these modes of critique obviously has its pros and cons. Emancipatory critique seems to work when there is a consensus on the goals and on the means to achieve them, but falls short when it encounters disagreement, complexities, or multiplicities. The strength of the ethnographic critique is in problematizing categories found "on the ground" and in bringing local practices into view in relation to wider social and cultural processes, but it faces challenges in terms of its grounding for political projects, and it potentially struggles to escape the dangers of excessive relativism (Pennycook 2012). Carnivalesque critique seems to provide alterna-tive spaces, audiences, and practices for political identity projects, but raises doubts through its fleeting and apparently noncommittal attitude towards social, political, and economic structures and their long-term development. However, all three take language as a key focus of critique, and discourse as a resource for constructing that critique.

This in turn points towards the centrality of discourse in any critical project. If we take as our starting point the Foucauldian view of discourse as socially constructed and constitutive to our ways of knowing and talking about that knowledge, then the conditions, trajectories, and consequences of circulating discourses about the issue under scrutiny become directly relevant for critical sociolinguistic research. Such a view is neither just a description of abstract processes and structures nor merely a bland theory of language in society or discourse as social action; it in fact amounts to a politics of social organization (cf. Pennycook 1990; Heller 2001). In this view, "reality" and "construction" are not opposite; rather, this dichotomy dissolves. Critical questions concern the workings of discourses: their logics, their genealogy and anatomy, and their ecology.

One possible way forward in developing the project of critique can be found in the rhizomatic ontology developed by French philosophers Deleuze and Guattari (1987); this is a provocative critique of modernity's discourses and institutions and provides a promising starting point for thinking about critique in terms of its complexity, connectivity, and intersectionality of discourses. The rhizome can be seen as a theoretical metaphor of an interconnected and irreducible multiplicity of ongoing processes. It is a metaphorical representation of knowledge that could account for interconnectivity and multiplicity among the nodes in a network. It resists tree-like knowledge charting causality along chronological lines, and instead favours a nomadic system of movement (Heckman 2002; Wallin 2010).

I would like to argue this kind of rhizomatic thinking can be useful in describing the complex dynamics and manifold interrelationships between discourse and economics, between shifting sociopolitical forces and language practices, between environment, culture, and identity. It can help in finding new ways forward beyond fixed, a priori categorizations of people, languages, and places, in situations where static categories are no longer sufficient to account for current complexities and multiplicities. In this sense a rhizomatic approach provides a critique of the dichotomous representations of fixed boundaries, unchanging categories, and totalizing politics which were typical of modernist thinking, and which now prove to be inadequate to the task of explaining what is happening on the ground. It enables us to envision a system of dynamic changes that are never complete. The risks with a rhizomatic approach relate to a danger of depoliticizing practices that are crucial for many identity struggles or to the risk of a certain kind of romanticization of processual rhizomatic approach, which may lack deep engagement with the powers of orders and taxonomies (Wallin 2010). Also Deleuze and Guattari themselves caution against celebratory approaches to rhizomatics in writing that "there exist tree or root structures in rhizomes; conversely, a tree branch or root division may begin to burgeon into a rhizome" (p. 15). Taking up these potentials and limitations with a rhizomatic approach, one way of moving forward could be to start with the assumption that neither the rhizome (the potential for things to deterritorialize and enter into new assemblages) nor the root tree (the stratification of things into orders, taxonomies, or structures) is primary. Sometimes more stability is what is required; at other times more fluidity is needed to overcome overtly rigid systems or open up new innovations.

Consequently, a rhizomatic discourse approach to boundary work at a particular time and space is not a closed or unchanging perspective, but rather an open system that emerges and transforms in the course of interaction. The relationships between language practices and their networked characteristics are implied and are seen in connection with historical, social, economic, and political practices and processes. They are neither linear nor separate, but instead any text, sign, or speech act potentially includes several interlinked discourses, which are connected to and across each other. Thus discourse can be seen as a historically embedded practice of knowledge construction, with material consequences and with rhizomatic connections to other spaces, times, and practices. What becomes crucial, then, is to understand which processes, actors, and resources are brought together under the logics of a particular discourse, and what the conditions and consequences of the discourse are. Using a rhizomatic discourse approach, it is possible to trace, map, and connect the historicities and the emergence of discourses across spaces and practices, while shifting away from fixed, ahistorical, static meanings. As discourses are productive as well as reflective of social relations, the focus is on "becoming" rather than on "being".

These intersecting discourses on criticality offer lenses into the questions of language, power, and social change. The tensions and developments around them imply differences in the organization of social and political actions and become an important terrain of debates and dialogues. The issue to me is not whether or not to be critical, but to oppose dogmatic unities, singular truths, and unidirectional courses of action. Perhaps the project of criticality is a case of recognizing the ways in which all critique rests within a rhizome of relationships with other processes.

REFERENCES

Agar, Michael. 1991. The right brain strikes back. In Nigel G. Fielding and Raymond M. Lee (eds.), *Using Computers in Qualitative Research*. London: Sage, 181–194.
Aikio, Kirste, Esa Salminen, and Suvi West. 2013. *Sápmi Underground: Saamelaisten käyttöopas* [Sámi Underground: A Sámi Manual]. Helsinki: Johnny Kniga.
Bakhtin, Mikhail. 1968. *Rabelais and His World*. Trans. Helene Iswosky. Bloomington: Indiana University Press.
    1986. *Speech Genres and Other Late Essays*. Austin: University of Texas Press.
Ball, Stephen. 1994. *Education Reform: A Critical and Post-structural Approach*. Buckingham: Open University Press.
Blackledge, Adrian, and Angela Creese. 2010. *Multilingualism: A Critical Perspective*. London: Continuum.
    (eds.). 2014. *Heteroglossia as Practice and Pedagogy*. Dordrecht: Springer.
Blommaert, Jan. 2005. *Discourse: A Critical Introduction*. Cambridge: Cambridge University Press.

2010. *Sociolinguistics of Globalization*. Cambridge and New York: Cambridge University Press.

Breeze, Ruth. 2011. Critical discourse analysis and its critics. *Pragmatics* 21, 4: 493–525.

Bronner, Stephen Eric. 1994. *Of Critical Theory and Its Theorists*. Oxford: Blackwell.

Clifford, James. 2013. *Returns: Becoming Indigenous in the Twenty-first Century*. Cambridge, MA: Harvard University Press.

Cook, Deborah. 2013. Adorno, Foucault and critique. *Philosophy & Social Criticism* 39, 10: 965–981.

Curry, Mary Jane, and Theresa Lillis. 2013. Introduction to the thematic issue: Participating in academic publishing – Consequences of linguistic policies and practices. *Language Policy* 12, 3: 209–213.

Deleuze, Gilles, and Félix Guattari. 1987. *A Thousand Plateaus*. Minneapolis: University of Minnesota Press.

Duchêne, Alexandre. 2008. *Ideologies across Nations: The Construction of Linguistic Minorities at the United Nations*. Berlin: Mouton de Gruyter.

Duchêne, Alexandre, Melissa Moyer, and Celia Roberts (eds.). 2013. *Language, Migration and Social (In)equalities*. New York: Multilingual Matters.

Fairclough, Norman. 1992. *Discourse and Social Change*. Cambridge: Polity Press.

1995. *Critical Discourse Analysis*. Boston: Addison Wesley.

Finnish Sámi Parliament. 2013. Sámi in Finland. Available at www.samediggi.fi/ index.php?option=com_content&task=blogcategory&id=105&Itemid=104.

Forchtner, Bernhard. 2011. Critique, the discourse-historical approach, and the Frankfurt School. *Critical Discourse Studies* 8, 1: 1–14.

Foucault, Michel. [1969] 1972. *The Archaeology of Knowledge and the Discourse on Language*. New York: Pantheon.

[1966] 1994. *The Order of Things: An Archaeology of the Human Sciences*. New York: Vintage Books.

1977. *Language, Counter-memory, Practice: Selected Essays and Interviews by Michel Foucault*. Ed. Donald F. Bouchard. Ithaca, NY: Cornell University Press.

Fowler, R., B. Hodge, G. Kress, and T. Trew. 1979. *Language and Control*. London: Routledge and Kegan Paul.

Gumperz, John J. 1982. *Language and Social Identity*. Cambridge: Cambridge University Press.

Hammersley, Martyn. 1997. On the foundations of critical discourse analysis. *Language & Communication* 17, 3: 237–248.

Hanks, William. 2005. Pierre Bourdieu and the practices of language. *Annual Review of Anthropology* 34, 1: 67–83.

Heckman, Davin. 2002. "Gotta Catch 'em All": Capitalism, the war machine and the Pokemon trainer. *Rhizomes* 5.

Heller, Monica. 2001. Critique and sociolinguistics: Analysis of discourse. *Critique of Anthropology* 21, 2: 192–198.

2011. *Paths to Post-nationalism: A Critical Ethnography of Language and Identity*. New York: Oxford University Press.

2014. Gumperz and social justice. *Journal of Linguistic Anthropology* 23, 3: 192–198.

Heller, Monica, and Joan Pujolar. 2009. The political economy of texts: A case study in the structuration of tourism. *Sociolinguistic Studies* 3, 2: 177–201.

Horkheimer, Max. 1982. Egoism and the freedom movement: On the anthropology of the bourgeois era. *Telos* 54: 10–16.

Hymes, Dell. 1974. *Foundations in Sociolinguistics: An Ethnographic Approach.* Philadelphia: University of Pennsylvania Press.

Joona, Tanja. 2013. Vielä sananen ILOsta – alkuperäiskansasopimus ja Suomen haasteet [ILO Convention and the challenges in Finland]. In Erika Sarivaara, Kaarina Määttä, and Satu Uusiautti (eds.), *Kuka on saamelainen ja mitä on saamelaisuus – identiteetin juurilla* [Who is Sámi and what is Sámi identity]. Rovaniemi: Lapin yliopistokustannus, 145–163.

Kress, Gunther, and Robert Hodge. 1979. *Language as Ideology.* London: Routledge & Kegan Paul.

Kulonen, Ulla-Maija, Irja Seurujärvi-Kari, and Risto Pulkkinen (eds.). 2005. *The Sámi: A Cultural Encyclopaedia.* Helsinki: Suomalaisen Kirjallisuuden Seura.

Lamarre, Patricia. 2014. Bilingual winks and bilingual wordplay in Montreal's linguistic landscape. *International Journal of the Sociology of Language* 228: 131–151.

Lechte, John. 1990. *Julia Kristeva.* London: Routledge.

Lehtola, Veli-Pekka. 2012. *Saamelaiset suomalaiset: kohtaamisia 1896–1953* [Sámi Finns: Encounters 1869–1953]. Helsinki: Suomalaisen Kirjallisuuden Seura.

Luke, Allan. 2002. Beyond science and ideological critique: Developments in critical discourse analysis. *Annual Review of Applied Linguistics* 22: 96–110.

Madison, Soyini. 2012. *Critical Ethnography: Method, Ethics and Performance.* Los Angeles, CA: Sage.

Martin, Paul, and Varie Renegar. 2007. The man for his time: *The Big Lebowski* as carnivalesque social critique. *Communication Studies* 58, 3: 299–313.

Mesthrie, Rajend. 2009. Critical sociolinguistics: Approaches to language and power. In Rajend Mesthrie, Joan Swann, and Ana Deumert, *Introducing Sociolinguistics.* Edinburgh: Edinburgh University Press, 309–343.

Määttä, Simo, and Sari Pietikäinen. 2014. Ideology. In J.-O. Östman and J. Verschueren (eds.). *Handbook of Pragmatics.* Amsterdam and Philadelphia: John Benjamins.

Olthuis, Kivelä, and Skutnabb-Kangas. 2013. *Revitalising Indigenous Languages: How to Recreate a Lost Generation.* Bristol: Multilingual Matters.

Otsuji, Emi, and Alastair Pennycook. 2010. Metrolingualism: Fixity, fluidity and language in flux. *International Journal of Multilingualism* 7, 3: 240–254.

O'Rourke, Bernadette, Joan Pujolar, and Fernando Ramallo. 2015. *New Speakers of Minority Languages: The Challenging Opportunity* (Special Issue). *International Journal of the Sociology of Language.*

Patton, Paul. 2006. Foucault, critique and rights. *Critique Today* 1: 264–288.

Pennycook, Alastair. 1990. Towards a critical applied linguistics for the 1990s. *Issues in Applied Linguistics* 1, 1: 8–28.

　　2001. *Critical Applied Linguistics: A Critical Introduction.* Mahwah, NJ: Lawrence Erlbaum.

　　2007. *Global Englishes and Transcultural Flows.* London: Routledge.

　　2010. Critical and alternative directions in applied linguistics. *Australian Review of Applied Linguistics* 33, 2: 16–31.

　　2012. *Language and Mobility: Unexpected Places.* Bristol: Multilingual Matters.

Phillips, John. 2000. *Contested Knowledge: A Guide to Critical Theory.* London and New York: Zed Books.

Pietikäinen, Sari. 2013. Multilingual dynamics in Sámiland: Rhizomatic discourses on changing language. *International Journal of Bilingualism.* 19 (2), 206–225.

2014. Circulation of indigenous Sámi resources across media spaces: A rhizomatic discourse approach. In Jannis Androutsopoulos (ed.), *Mediatization and Sociolinguistic Change.* Berlin: De Gruyter, 515–538.

Pietikäinen, Sari, Helen Kelly-Holmes, Alexandra Jaffe, and Nikolas Coupland. Forthcoming. *Sociolinguistics from the Periphery: Small Languages in New Circumstances.* Cambridge: Cambridge University Press.

Pietikäinen, Sari, and Helen Kelly-Holmes (eds.). 2013. *Multilingualism and the Periphery.* Oxford: Oxford University Press.

Reyes, Angela. 2014. Linguistic anthropology in 2013: Super-new-big. *American Anthropologist* 116, 2: 366–378.

Sarivaara, Erika. 2012. Statuksettomat saamelaiset: paikantumisia saamelaisuuden rajoilla [Non-Status Sámi. Locations within Sámi Borderlands]. Doctoral thesis. Guovdageaidnu: Sámiallaskuvla.

Schegloff, Emanuel. 1997. Whose text? Whose context? *Discourse and Society* 8: 165–187.

Slembrouck, Stef. 2001. Explanation, interpretation and critique in the analysis of discourse. *Critique of Anthropology* 21, 1: 33–57.

Spivak, Gayatri 1988. Subaltern studies: Deconstructing historiography. In Ranajit Guha and Gayatri Chakravorty Spivak (eds.), *Selected Subaltern Studies.* New York and Oxford: Oxford University Press, 3–32.

Thomas, Jim. 1993. *Doing Critical Ethnography.* Newbury Park, CA: Sage.

Toolan, Michael. 1997. What is critical discourse analysis and why are people saying such terrible things about it? *Language and Literature* 6, 2: 83–102.

Valkonen, Sanna. 2009. *Poliittinen saamelaisuus* [Political Sáminess]. Tampere: Vastapaino.

van Dijk, Teun. 1993. *Elite Discourse and Racism.* Newbury Park, CA: Sage.

Verschueren, Jef. 2001. Predicament of criticism. *Critique of Anthropology* 21, 1: 59–81.

Wallin, Jason. 2010. Rhizomania: Five provocations on a concept. *Complicity: An International Journal of Complexity and Education* 7, 2: 83–89.

Weedon, C. 1987. *Feminist Practice and Poststructuralist Theory.* Oxford: Blackwell.

Wilson, Angelia. 2013. *Situating Intersectionality: Politics, Policy, and Power.* New York: Palgrave Macmillan.

Wodak, Ruth. 1996. *Disorders of Discourse.* London and New York: Longman

2011. Critical linguistics and Critical Discourse Analysis. In Jan Zienkowski, Jan-Ola Östman, and Jef Verschueren (eds.), *Discursive Pragmatics.* Amsterdam and Philadelphia: John Benjamins, 50–70.

Woolard, Kathryn. 1985. Language variation and cultural hegemony: Toward an integration of sociolinguistic and social theory. *American Ethnologist* 12, 4: 738–748.

Zhang, Hongyan, Paul Chilton, Yadan He, and Wen Jing. 2011. Critique across cultures: Some questions for CDA. *Critical Discourse Studies* 8, 2: 95–107.

13　Theorizing media, mediation and mediatization

Jannis Androutsopoulos

1.　Introduction

Sociolinguistics is currently facing the challenge of how to conceptualize the rapid expansion of its main object of study, socially meaningful linguistic differentiation, beyond the domain of spoken language in face-to-face interaction. This expansion moves into two distinct but interrelated directions: the rise of digitally mediated language as a new type of everyday language-in-use, and the circuit of mediatized representation, uptake, and recontextualization of linguistic fragments. This chapter discusses the three concepts flagged in the title in terms of their status in sociolinguistic theory and their usefulness in responding to these processes.

Discussing media, I first suggest that the concept is currently either erased from the discipline's canonical knowledge or reified as a catch-all notion that obscures the differentiation of the domain it denotes. I also suggest that a lot of thinking about language and media in sociolinguistics is shaped by metaphors which obscure, rather than illuminate, this relationship. Ultimately, I argue, 'the media', widespread as it might be as a descriptive cover term, is a theoretical cul-de-sac. Instead, understanding the implications of media for linguistic differentiation and its social meaning will fare better with conceptual alternatives, including mediation and mediatization.

Discussing mediation, I develop an understanding of the term that centres on technologically facilitated production and reception of linguistic signs. Digitally mediated written language represents a historically new type of mediation, which boosts the importance of writing as an everyday modality of language. I suggest that the sociolinguistic impact of digital mediation is more than its being a written representation of preexisting spoken-language variability and that we need to understand how digital mediation expands the boundaries of visually constituted linguistic heterogeneity.

Discussing mediatization, I introduce the concept's currently predominant readings in linguistic anthropology and communication studies and explore their implications for the study of sociolinguistic differentiation and change. These include the mediatized representation of sociolinguistic differentiation and its language-ideological implications, techniques of staging involved in these representations, and practices of uptake and circulation. Overall, I argue that mediatization and mediation take us further in opening up the black-box notion of 'the media', in transgressing unproductive distinctions such as the one between 'mass' and 'new media', and in understanding media in terms of performance, staging, uptake, and recontextualization.

2.   'The media' in sociolinguistics: erasure, reification, differentiation

An informal survey of the term 'media' in sociolinguistic literature yields two main findings. The first we can refer to as 'erasure': Discussions of language and media are largely absent from canonical systematizations of sociolinguistic knowledge. This becomes obvious by looking a few years back. For example, there is no article on language and media in the second edition of a multivolume handbook (Ammon et al. 2004); there is one article referencing media ("Interaction and the Media") in a more recent handbook (Wodak et al. 2010). Discussions of language and media are missing from earlier publications on sociolinguistic theory (e.g. Coupland et al. 2001), as they are from most international introductions to sociolinguistics. The term 'media' rather comes up in absentia, as 'influence' to be denied or a factor of linguistic change deemed implausible (cf. Chambers 1998). This is not to deny early and still influential research on variation and style in media language, notably by Allan Bell (2011) or the recent interest in media, which is rapidly rising in the context of various theoretical advances.[1] Language and media issues are an emerging theme but do not represent canonical knowledge.

The second term, reification, aims to capture what happens when media are eventually thematized in sociolinguistic literature, especially in variationist sociolinguistics. The dominant understanding of 'media' is mass media and basically boils down to television. It evokes the social functions of mass media as institutions of mass communication that are fundamental to the production and reproduction of a nation-wide public sphere and imagined national community (Anderson 2006). This is complemented by a dominant understanding of 'media language' as a type of language that is professionally scripted and acts as a "working definition of the standard language" (Bell 2011: 178). A mainstream understanding of 'the media' in sociolinguistics is that of a centripetal force whose effect on language in

---

[1] See, among others, Blommaert 2010 (globalization), Bell and Gibson 2011 (performance), Androutsopoulos 2014a (sociolinguistic change; see also Chapter 20 of this volume), and a debate on media and language change in the *Journal of Sociolinguistics* 18, 2 (2014).

the community can be imagined only as a pull towards homogenization. This is how sociolinguists such as Trudgill (2014) and Chambers (1998) justify their rejection of media influence on language use, with the argument that no evidence for such homogenization exists. Were language systematically affected by the media, Trudgill (2014) argues, speakers of British English would have adopted American English accents.[2]

For researchers who dismiss a priori any impact of 'media' on language use, the media are coextensive with mass media and conceived as a force of linguistic convergence. Digitally mediated communication, including the now-popular social media, are deemed a different issue altogether. Exposure to media language and social interaction (as a prerequisite of linguistic diffusion) are apparently considered distinct processes that somehow never interrelate. In this view, the argument for a potential (but refuted) impact of media on language apparently boils down to the claim that "language change must come from the television" (Trudgill 2014: 220).

A sociolinguistic problem with this understanding of media is that it is reductive and in many ways outdated. Not only does it erase digitally mediated communication, where extensive variability in public written language undermines the assumption that 'media language' equates to standard language, it also erases the diversity in mass media language itself. This diversity has evolved – in Europe at least since the liberalization of the television market in the 1980s – into a rich repertoire of speech styles, themselves encased in a repertoire of genres. There are worlds of difference between, for example, standardized news language and speech styles by candidates in reality television shows. As Busch (2006) argues, rather than thinking of media as a centripetal, standardising force, they are more aptly viewed as heteroglossic, yet hierarchically ordered spaces, whose orders of indexicality draw on the audience's life worlds and speak back to them. However, traditional sociolinguistic views of language and media hardly examine media language itself but rather operationalize media consumption or 'exposure' as an independent variable (see discussion in Androutsopoulos 2014b; Sayers 2014; Stuart-Smith 2014).

For scholars beyond linguistics, such as media theorists and anthropologists, an undifferentiated entity termed 'the media' is theoretically and analytically a cul-de-sac. Asif Agha (2011a: 171) argues that the 'mass media' construct "obscures the characteristics of cultural forms that emerge

---

[2] Trudgill's response to the debate on media and language change (2014) offers a compact presentation of the 'received view' (Kristiansen 2014) on media and language change, which can be summarized as follows: The diffusion of linguistic changes below the level of awareness, i.e. in grammar and phonology, requires density of interpersonal interaction. Diffusion of features above the level of awareness, i.e. lexis, idioms, etc., can also take place via mass media.

and spread through" practices of mediatization, to which I turn below. As media scholar Nick Couldry puts it,

the term 'media', and notoriously the phrase 'the media', result from a reification. Indeed, media processes involve a huge complexity of inputs (what are media?) and outputs (what difference do media make, socially, culturally?), which require us to find another term to differentiate the levels within and patterns across this complexity. (Couldry 2008: 379)

The reification of 'media' offers fertile ground for a number of old and influential metaphors, which can promote deterministic and homogenising views on language/media relationships. One is derived from the container metaphor of communication, which conceptualises messages as 'containers' for 'thoughts' or 'meanings' (Krippendorff 1994). Applied to media, this metaphor separates 'containers' (media technologies) from 'content' (the messages transmitted and their characteristics). Its traces are evident in constructions such as 'language *in* the media' (Johnson and Ensslin 2007). Taking this trope one step further, the type of medium (or 'container') is viewed as the most important determinant for classifying and explaining linguistic patterns, so that the language of, for example, newspapers is viewed as distinct from that of radio or television. Similar 'containers' are expected to bring 'content' with similar linguistic patterns. No doubt there is some empirical validity in this, as a comparison between, say, live sports reporting on radio and on television quickly demonstrates. Varying the transmission channel while keeping everything else constant demonstrates the impact of channel at the level of genre, register, and linguistic structure. So, language use is constrained to some extent by the technology of mediation, but this is not the same as a technologically determinist view, which creates an entirely compartmentalized conception of media and language and thereby obscures the relevance of factors such as audience design and speaker design, which cut across transmission channels.

The container metaphor pairs up with a second, theoretically even more consequential metaphor, that of media 'influence' on language. I find it striking how common this and associated metaphorical expressions (such as 'flooding') are, not just in popular lay concerns about media-driven language decay (see Chambers 1998), but also among researchers who clearly move beyond a wholesale dismissal of media importance and even take speakers' engagement with media seriously into consideration.[3] The influence metaphor assigns 'the media', an impersonal entity whose status between technologies and institutions remains obscure, the capacity to influence 'language', cast here

---

[3] See Sayers 2014; Stuart Smith 2014; Tagliamonte 2014; and discussion in Androutsopoulos 2014a.

as another underspecified entity. However, once we develop a differentiated view of processes of representation, stylization, uptake, circulation, and engagement, a putative causal link between a media construct and a linguistic system just makes no sense.

Against this backdrop, it should come as no surprise that alternative views on the language/media relationship come without these metaphors or with different metaphors altogether. Perhaps the strongest alternative is the interest in media representations of sociolinguistic differentiation. The prototypical objects of study here are media texts whose speakers, often fictional characters, are differentiated from one another by some pattern of sociolinguistic heterogeneity. Interested sociolinguists examine things such as the allocation of language style to characters, the deployment of features from one or more dialects or registers in constructing a speaker persona, the voicing of social identities and intergroup relations in media performance, and the commodification of vernacular features in heavily styled multimodal texts such as commercial advertisements.[4] Sociolinguistics and linguistic anthropology develop a language-ideological critique of such representations: What values underpin them, and what kind of metalinguistic knowledge must audiences bring to bear on their viewing in order to interpret the socio-stylistic contrasts in representation? How do these representations reproduce or challenge inequality, discrimination, and racism (Hill 1995; Lippi-Green 1997)? And how do the features indexing social groups relate to empirically documented variation in nonmediated contexts? This line of research is boosted by, and in turn contributes to, theoretical input from the notion of enregisterment (Agha 2003), notably the suggestion that the mediatized performance of speech styles contributes to the construction of their typical or 'exemplary' speakers. I return to this issue in Section 4.

Unlike the exposure-and-influence paradigm, this line of scholarship is compatible with research on audience practices with the media. Unlike the rhetoric of 'influence', the perspective on media engagement emphasizes the agency and creativity of audiences in how they deal with media language (e.g. Spitulnik 1997). Understanding how representations of sociolinguistic differentiation are read by audiences can offer a much-needed complement to linguistic media analysis (Johnstone 2011; Androutsopoulos 2014b). So, understanding whether patterns of media language might have an impact on audiences' own linguistic practices requires analysis of genres and styles of media language, on the one hand, and of media engagement practices, on the other. Issues of impact are raised here too, but in a more contextualized, qualitatively bolstered way. Not least, this line of research goes to show how fuzzy the boundary between media language and language in the community

---

[4] See Androutsopoulos 2010 for a research survey; Coupland 2007; Jaffe 2009; Bell and Gibson 2011; Johnstone 2011; Queen 2015.

has become, with the former staging the latter, the latter recontextualizing fragments of the former.

Metaphors such as circuit and circulation, unelaborated as they still may be at present, are useful in opening up the 'media' construct and developing the shift of perspective to 'new media', a term which is equally inadequate at a theoretical level. The analytical distinction between 'mass' and 'new media', handy as it may be for quick reference, will not take us far in an era where media technologies, institutions, and publics give rise to hybrid combinations of institutional and participatory discourse and new opportunities for digital circulation and rescaling of utterances. New theoretical metaphors are required here, too. Space is one such metaphor, in the sense that digital technologies provide the infrastructure by which virtual spaces for interaction and discourse are semiotically constructed by institutions and publics. This understanding of space becomes topical and timely as engagement with media ceases to be exclusively in the receiving and consuming mode. Space does not just refer to the physical site of co-present viewing. In online communication, the metaphor of space connotes movement, presence, interaction, and agency. People go to and act in virtual spaces (being on Facebook, in a forum, or on a chat channel); people move in virtual space through their avatars (e.g. in *Second Life* or a multiplayer online game); and they discursively construct these spaces by means of mediational tools, including those that enable the production of digital written language.

3.   Mediation: digital written language as a sociolinguistic object

The meaning of mediation advanced here is semiotic materialization, its premise being that all realizations of language depend on technologies of mediation. Agha (2011b: 163; 2011a: 174) uses the term "mediation" to refer to all semiotic means by which people relate to each other within frameworks of communicative activity (see also Bucholtz and Hall, this volume, Chapter 8). Kristiansen (2014) points out:

Language as such is "mediated" in the sense that a formed substance is necessary to express linguistic meaning. In order to form the substance, we make use of technologies. We use "physiological technologies" to form sound waves that make sense in spoken language, and gestures that make sense in signed language. We apply writing and printing technologies to a multitude of substances in forming "strokes" to be made sense of in written language. (Kristiansen 2014: 99)

Mediation thus refers to "the technological aspect of speaking, signing and writing", Kristiansen continues (p. 99), which is "inherent to language in this fundamental sense". Following up on Kristiansen, 'primary' and 'secondary' technologies of mediation can be distinguished. Primary mediation is embodied, in the sense that spoken language is mediated through verbal cords and facial movement; sign language is mediated through gestural and facial movement (again, see in this volume Bucholtz and Hall, Chapter 8, and Lucas and Bayley, Chapter 16). Secondary mediation depends on mediational tools – a term familiar from mediated discourse analysis (Norris and Jones 2005), by which the recording and transmission of signs are amplified. Mediated language of the secondary type is defined by Kristiansen (2014: 99) as "language use based on some technology that 'liberates' the transmission/construction of meaning from the contextual constraints of face-to-face interaction". All written language relies as a sine qua non condition on mediational tools, with the tools themselves changing in the course of time. An elaborate classification of mediational tools, as found in semiotics, would further distinguish these processes according to their material conditions, technical complexity, historical depth, and so on. On this basis we can think of speech events as drawing on and combining various technologies of mediation in generically conditioned ways, so that, for example, a stage performance involves both primary and secondary mediational tools, and digitally mediated interaction involves the mediation of written language via keyboards and screens (Jucker and Dürscheid 2012).

It could be argued at this point that processes of mediation as such are of primary interest to phoneticians and graphologists, whereas sociolinguists are interested in their outcome, that is, spoken and written language. One reason to evoke mediation in sociolinguistics is in my view the ongoing change in the social status of digital written language, which is aptly captured with the term "mass literacy" (Brandt 2015). In my own phrasing, we are witnessing a new scale of unregimented writing in society at large: "more people write, people write more, and unregimented writing goes public" (Androutsopoulos 2011). One consequence of this turn to mass literacy is, I believe, that everyday informal language, the subject matter of sociolinguistics, is now expanding into a new domain. Rather than being restricted to specific purposes and occasions (and segments of the population), language mediated by keyboards and screens is now being used by almost everyone and to all sorts of purposes, including spontaneous and informal networked writing (Androutsopoulos 2011).[5] The widespread assumptions that authentic language in the community is limited to spoken language and that written language is the most homogenous, or invariant, area of language, seem no longer tenable.

Once the notion of authentic language in the community is extended across mediational borders, the question is how linguistic differentiation in digital

---

[5] By this, I do not mean to deny the persisting digital divide and inequalities of Internet access across countries and continents but to emphasize that at least in Europe, North America, and parts of Asia, computer literacy and online access are available to the vast majority of people.

written language relates to that in spoken language (other things being equal); or, differently phrased, how sociolinguistic heterogeneity can be theorized across modalities of language. My impression is that the hitherto predominant response has followed the phonocentric assumption, or spoken-language bias, that by and large predominates in sociolinguistics. By this I mean the notion, which goes back to early structuralism, that written language is a secondary mode, a mere 'rerendering' of spoken. In research on computer-mediated communication, this phonocentric view is reflected in the assumption that socially meaningful variation emerges only in the relation of digital language to (or its simulation of) spoken-language variability, for example when regional features are represented in writing. To be sure, there is ample evidence for the written representation of spoken-language variation in digital sociolinguistics research, and important questions to be asked: Which socially diagnostic variables from a given vernacular are represented in networked writing, and how do they relate to orthographic norms? Why are some features represented and others not? (see Siebenhaar 2006; Dorleijn and Nortier 2009; Vandekerckhove and Nobels 2010). Questions of this kind have important theoretical implications for a transmodal view of language in society. However, they are still based on the assumption that the patterns of linguistic variation that matter are those that reproduce spoken-language variability.

By contrast, my intent here is to suggest that digital mediation gives rise to graphic variability that is not just a mirror-image of phonic variability but emerges against the backdrop of the orthographic representation of a given linguistic item in a given language. To the extent that a writing system enables two or more spelling variants, these can be mobilized, conventionally or in ad hoc ways, provided they are still within the realm of recognisability. Sebba (2007) establishes that spelling variants can be socially meaningful even without encoding phonic differences, that is, as heterographic homophones. One of Sebba's examples is the word *dog*, which can also be represented as <dogg>, with potential indexical associations to hip-hop, or <dög>, with added "heavy metal umlaut" (Spitzmüller 2012). However, the spelling <Dd@gG> probably isn't a socially recognisable representation of the word *dog*.

The status of orthography as a mode-specific point of reference for graphic variability extends to punctuation and diacritics. The apostrophe in English (Squires 2012) is a good example. Squires analyses the use of the possessive apostrophe in texting by female and male students and revisits sociolinguistic theory of language and gender in interpreting the results. The apostrophe is systematic enough to be treated as a sociolinguistic variable, and its variability clearly goes beyond being a mere reflex of phonic variation. Another similar example is the graphic signalling of gender-inclusiveness in German nouns, a process termed *Movierung*. In past usage, the morphologically masculine form was the noun's generic form. One way of signalling inclusiveness is by repetition of the noun in masculine and feminine (suffixed) form. For instance, the noun *Mitarbeiter* (literally 'co-worker', i.e. 'associate') has the feminine form *Mitarbeiterin*, and together they build the gender-inclusive plural construction *Mitarbeiterinnen und Mitarbeiter* ('staff'). Such plural constructions are often abbreviated by means of a separator between the base form and the gender-marked plural suffix. The most common separators in institutional and public texts are the slash </> and word-internal capital <I>, hence *Mitarbeiter/innen* or *Mitarbeiter-Innen*. We currently see in the discourse of German universities, notably in circular emails, a number of new separators, such as <*> and <_>, hence *Mitarbeiter*innen* and *Mitarbeiter_innen*, respectively (readers are invited to look these up on the Internet). There is a metapragmatic awareness of these variants being preferred by younger members of staff who seem to be deliberately avoiding the institutionally unmarked separators. In the metapragmatic discourse that evolves around this instance of variation, the visual shape of some innovative separators gains symbolic meaning, e.g. in the suggestion that the underscore, <_>, iconizes the prevailing gender gap.

The same logic of analysis can be extended from single graphemic variables (like the above) to digital writing styles such as the notorious (and underinvestigated) "Leet speak", where letters are replaced by similar-looking digits (hence, *L33t*) or the typographic practices by young female bloggers studied by Vaisman (2011), where elements from different scripts, substitution of graphs by visually similar digits, decorative usage of punctuation and other resources are tied together in creative visual expressions of social identities.

A second aspect of genuinely graphic variability emerges within multilingual and multiliteral repertoires. As discussed in Androutsopoulos (2015), digital language practices are constrained by participants' languages of alphabetization and socially asymmetric conventions for written usage. In postcolonial societies such as Jamaica or Senegal, language choices for spoken conversation and written discourse have traditionally parted ways, with vernacular repertoires of spoken interaction not being used for writing. Informal digital communication can offer new opportunities for reducing this gap (cf. Deumert and Lexander 2013). In such settings, the relation of informal digital language to spoken usage is in flux, with digital written language becoming a resource for overcoming the hegemony of postcolonial language regimes.

My intent against this backdrop is to emphasise the opportunities provided by the availability of two or more orthographies or scripts for local heterographic practices in networked writing. The practice of writing utterances in one language in the orthography or script of another can crystallize in patterns of computer-mediated digraphia for languages regularly written in the Latin script online, such as Greek and Serbian (Androutsopoulos 2009; Ivkovic 2013). It can also materialize in more fleeting, smaller-reach, often ad hoc moments of what I term 'trans-scripting' (Androutsopoulos 2015). This can be observed with for example, young speakers of Greek writing English or German items in the Greek script, or speakers of Turkish spelling German words and phrases in Turkish orthography, so that *Deutsch* is cast as *Doyc* (Hinnenkamp 2008). These variants are homophones, so *Doyc* indexes not a Turkish accent but rather a Turkish view of things.

Trans-scripting, then, is a practice by which conventionalized values attached to scripts can be evoked as impromptu contextualization cues in digital written language (see also Su 2003). The contextualization perspective has broader relevance in this respect (see also Rampton, this volume, Chapter 14). Following Gumperz (1982), contextualization cues cover all semiotic means by which interlocutors provide hints to the sociocultural placement of their contribution in interactional context and its preferred interpretation. Georgakopoulou (1997) was one of the first researchers to observe that in the absence of familiar prosodic, segmental, and visual cues, contextualization work in computer-mediated discourse largely relies on what can be encoded with a keyboard and mouse. She also observes that the lack of ordinary resources for contextualization "results in an increased reliance on code-centred contextualization cueing, which would be otherwise delegated to different signals" (Georgakopoulou 1997: 158). Spelling or punctuation variants of different kinds can accomplish pragmatic work that would probably draw on prosody in face-to-face conversation.

The issue here is how to conceive of the relationship of graphically realized cues to their presumable phonic counterparts. While a phonocentric approach would assume that graphic contexualization cues in digital writing replicate spoken ones, the graphocentric approach advocated here suggests an analysis in terms of iconic contrasts. A case in point are iterations of graphemes or punctuation signs, which are extremely common in the social media data with which I am familiar. The following examples are status updates or comments among young female users in semi-public exchanges on Facebook (for a detailed discussion of these data, see Androutsopoulos 2015). Their base language is Greek in (1)–(4), English in (5), and German in (6) and (7), and they all include one or more items with iterated graphemes as well as multiple punctuation signs, especially exclamation marks. The items with iterated graphemes are in italics in the English glosses below.

1. simera to bradu partyyyy xD naiii eimai sta high mou :D agaaapes m thnxx :*
   'tonight there's *party* xD *yes* I'm in great mood :D my *loves thnxx* :*'
2. hahaha....aurio mwro m 3ekourasou...gt anamainetai megalh vra-
   diaaaaaaaaaaaaa! !
   'hahaha....tomorrow get some rest baby...because we're expecting a great
   evening! !'
3. mwrhhhhhhhhhhhhhhhhhhhhhhh!!!ti kaneis?. h noula?... xa8hkateeeee!
   '*hey you*!!! how are you?. what about [friend's name]?... we *lost* you!'
4. to na mou les psemmata...enw ta kserw ollllllla....
   'that you are lying to me...while I know *everything*.....'
5. hahahah ooo yesssss xD
   'hahahah *o yes* xD'
6. ICH BIN TOOOOOOOOOOD !!!! DAS WAR SOOO WITZIG GES-
   TERN HAHAHAHAH
   'I'm *dead* !!!! That was *so* funny yesterday hahahahah'
7. LLLEEEEECCCCKKKKERRR !!!
   '*tasty* !!!'

In social media conversations, utterances of this kind are generally understood as expressing an emotional stance towards the interlocutor and/or the propositional content of the contribution. A phonocentric analysis seems to work well for some iterations. For example, *partyyyy* in (1) or the term of address *mwrhhhhhhhhhhhhhhhhhhhhhhh* in (2) will be understood as conveying a vowel lengthening the speaker/writer would have produced in speech. It works less well when the iterated graphs are less likely to represent phonation, as with noncontinuant consonants in the examples (4), (5), and (7). Considering the last example, the expressive surplus of *LLLEEEEECCCCKKKKERRR* is obvious, thanks to an iconic analogy of more graphs equating more expressive emphasis. However, its phonic correspondent is less straightforward. The hyperarticulation of the onset lateral is phonically plausible, but less so that of the mid-word /k/. In German, /r/ is usually vocalized in postvocalic final position, [ɐ], which is often lengthened for emphasis. However, the writer here does not attempt to represent in spelling the vocalized pronunciation, [ɐ], which could look like <leckaaa>, but keys expressiveness by modifying the word's orthographic shape. Tannen (2013: 106–108) comes to the same conclusion in a discussion of repetition as a marker of enthusiasm in digital media conversations. Some repetitions index a likely pronunciation; others work as a purely visual means of emphasis.

A phonocentric approach also comes to its limits with regard to the repetition of punctuation signs. For example, whether a contribution comes with two, four, or more <!> is iconically understood as conveying degrees of expressivity or emotional involvement, but probably less as conveying discrete differences in pitch or facial expression. Examples of this sort suggest that the direction of mediational mapping can be reversed: Instead of typing what they allegedly would have said, networked writers key their expressiveness and may perhaps retrospectively attempt to voice what they just spelt.

Clearly, much more research is needed in order to substantiate these suggestions. The point I wish to make here is that sociolinguistic approaches to networked writing require a framework that conceptualises visible language as a distinct level of stylistic practice in a third-wave sense (Eckert 2012; also this volume, Chapter 3). A broader premise here could be the hypothesis that mass digital literacy brings along a heightened awareness of visual aspects of linguistic signifiers (cf. Kelly-Holmes, this volume, Chapter 7). Put differently, the cultural sensitivity to the auditory channel for the perception of linguistic variation is being complemented by a visual sensitivity for the subtleties of graphic variability and the ways it sometimes indexes a primary phonic, itself socially enregistered, materialization of language, and sometimes emerges through the contrast of a particular graphic materialization to normative orthography or local conventions of digital written language. And even though this discussion focuses on interactive written language online, it should be obvious that such heightened awareness of visible language is also at play in other contemporary practices of typographic and scriptural design (see, e.g., Spitzmüller 2012).

4.   Mediatization

The concept of mediatization has a range of understandings in communications studies and linguistic anthropology, and its reception in sociolinguistics is still diffuse (cf. discussion in Androutsopoulos 2014b). My aim is to discuss two predominant conceptions and consider their usefulness in opening up the black box of 'the media', not least in view of the need for new concepts and theoretical metaphors identified above.

The first conception is by Agha (2011a,b) who offers an explicit conceptual relation of mediation to mediatization. While mediation refers to semiotic realizations of language in communicative context, mediatization is understood as a "narrow special case of mediation" and refers to "institutional practices that reflexively link processes of communication to processes of commoditization" (Agha 2011b: 163). Agha writes:

Today, familiar institutions in any large scale society (e.g., schooling, the law, electoral politics, the mass media) all presuppose a variety of mediatized practices as conditions on their possibility. In linking communication to commoditization, mediatized institutions link communicative roles to positions within a socioeconomic division of labor, thereby expanding the effective scale of production and dissemination of messages across a population, and thus the scale at which persons can orient to common presuppositions in acts of communication with each other. And since mediatization is a narrow special case of mediation, such links also expand the scale at which differentiated forms of uptake and response to common messages can occur, and thus, through the proliferation of uptake formulations, increase the felt complexity of so-called "complex society" for those who belong to it. (Agha 2011b: 163)

Agha's mediatization is not limited to mass media in the narrow sense. At its core is the link of communication and commoditization, with the latter a much broader notion than consumerism (Agha 2011a). I focus here on those aspects in particular that tie in well with sociolinguistic interests. One is the dual focus on practices by institutions as well as members of a population. Institutionally, mediatized messages are designed for and oriented to large audiences, thereby expanding the dissemination of a message across a population and providing "massively parallel inputs to recontextualization" (Agha 2011a: 167). This does not preclude a variety of potential responses. Different people may respond to mediatized messages in many different ways, but they engage with the same messages and treat these "as indexical presuppositions of whatever it is they do or make" (p. 167).

The second take on mediatization originates in European communications studies where mediatization is defined as a large-scale, metaprocess of social and cultural change through the development of communications media (see Krotz 2009; Livingstone 2009; Hepp 2014; Lundby 2014). The central question of mediatization research is how changes in media bring about changes in human communication, cultural practices, and social formations. The notion of media deployed here is a broad one, which includes not only mass media but all kinds of mediational tools in a Scollonian sense (Scollon 2001). Mediatization as a long-term process, Krotz (2009) argues, begins with the development of secondary mediation technologies and extends to ever more complex configurations of mediated and mediatized communication, which, at the present historical stage, permeate all aspects of private and institutional life. In this sense the notion of 'mediatized childhood' refers to the ways in which media at large, that is, use of mediational tools as well as consumption of media content, transforms the social configuration of childhood, including the practices of communication to and among children. As this example suggests, mediatization research rejects a media-effects approach in favour of a view centred on communicative practices with media.

Both readings of mediatization incorporate mediation, though in a slightly different sense in each case. From a sociolinguistic angle, both can be useful in abandoning the 'media influence' view towards an understanding of how, to use Agha's terminology here, mediatized messages and subsequent acts of mediated communication are intertwined or, in a communication studies wording, how an increasing range of language practices becomes entangled in complex configurations of mediational tools and mediatization technologies.

Elsewhere (Androutsopoulos 2016) I suggest that the communication-studies concept of mediatization together with a nexus-of-practice approach (Scollon 2001) are useful for the analysis of mediatized practices. By this I mean the recontextualization of communicative practices through the use of digital media: We write emails to do things we used to do in person, send text messages instead of calling, or complement audience talk by tweeting about the show we are watching. Some mediatized practices are modelled on pre-digital ones. For example, audience talk on Twitter resembles familiar practices of audience engagement in face-to-face interaction. Other mediatized practices constitute a new nexus of practice for new institutional activities, for example, new practices of online journalism, such as the management of user comments in social media sites (cf. Androutsopoulos 2016). In this sense, mediatized practices act as mediators, as it were, between macrolevel social processes of mediatization and microlevel patterns of digitally mediated language use.

Returning to Agha's theory of mediatization, I focus on two aspects: the implications of mediatized representations for the formation of registers and their 'exemplary speakers', and the implications of uptake for the circulation and diffusion of linguistic features. Agha's study of the enregisterment of Received Pronunciation in Britain (Agha 2003) established the impact of mediatized messages on the association of linguistic forms with social groups or activities. This association is constituted through metapragmatic stereotypes, which link speech forms with recognizable speaker stereotypes and social contexts of use (Johnstone 2011). They include the discursive construction of typical or exemplary speakers, which can change in the course of time (Agha 2003: 265). Typifications of a register can occur in a range of media genres, each having a specific scale of circulation; examples in Agha's data include newspaper glosses, weekly 'pennies', and schoolbooks. The relevance of this framework for contemporary audiovisual media (such as commercials, film, soap operas, or reality shows) is boosted by the observation that not only do mediatized forms of vernacular speech proliferate in these genres, but metapragmatic typifications are extremely common too. For instance, audiovisual fiction regularly draws on register contrasts as a resource for the mediatized presentation of social types and their interpersonal relations in a fictional narrative, and commercials regularly commodify features of regional dialects by linking them to advertized products (cf. Coupland 2009). What makes audiovisual media texts particularly relevant to the study of enregisterment is the visual presentation and embodied conduct of typical speakers, which may enable a richer construction of their characterological features.

Taking the study of enregisterment into the domain of audiovisual narratives requires taking into consideration how representations of linguistic differentiation are contextualized in terms of media genre, interactional key, and techniques of staging. Depending on genre, a dialect speaker can be keyed as, for example, funny, rustic, gross, or down-to-earth, with different implications for potential practices of uptake in which fragments of mediatized dialect can be evoked to perform a range of speech activities, for example, to categorise a speaker. By staging, I mean "all the representational choices involved in the production and editing of text, image, and talk in the creation of media products" (Jaffe 2009: 572; Jaffe herself uses here the term "mediatization"; see also Jaffe, this volume, Chapter 4). In audiovisual media, staging includes a variety of techniques of postproduction. In reality television formats, for example, utterances and interactions by lay participants (e.g. candidates in a casting show) are staged by means of montage, overlaid music tracks, written-language inserts or added subtitles. Such techniques of staging can act as contextualization cues that guide viewers' perceptions of media characters. For example, superimposed inserts typify speakers in terms of social categories or discourse positions; overlaid music can key an utterance as dramatic, witty, or dumb; intralingual subtitling indexes programme-makers' assumptions about the intelligibility of nonstandard varieties for the sake of a nationwide audience (Vandekerckhove et al. 2009). To give another example, Cole and Pellicer (2012) show that the staging of a mediatized fragment creates constraints around interpretation. The case is Hillary Clinton's use of 'black' rhetorical forms in a campaign event, and the analysis shows that the televized mediatization of a decontextualized fragment of Clinton's speech leads to devaluing interpretations, which do not match those of the audience at the campaign event.

A sociolinguistic analysis of mediatized messages, then, can benefit from considering techniques of staging, in the context of media institutions and genres and in relation to enregisterment. Describing and understanding these processes requires, here too, a new analytical vocabulary, whose inception in current research draws, among other things, on the framework of performance and intertextuality proposed by Bauman and Briggs (1990). For example, the study by Cole and Pellicer (2012) introduces a set of terms such as "premediatized event" (e.g. a live speech), "premediatization audience" (the audience to this speech), "mediatized fragment" (e.g. an excerpt from that speech that is broadcast), and "postperformance mediatization" (the metapragmatic and metadiscursive processes that follow up on this broadcast).

Extending Agha's perspective, Cole and Pellicer (2012: 451) define uptake as "a kind of perception or awareness of a fragment of semiotic behaviour that can lead to the recycling or reinterpretation of the fragment". One way of examining practices of uptake is by focusing on here-and-now audience responses during reception, thereby following the ethnographic tradition of audience studies (see discussion in Androutsopoulos 2014b: 18–25). There is ample evidence in this research that fragments from mediatized texts are recontextualized in audience practices of voicing, quoting, evaluating, and so on. However, the subsequent trajectory of uptake fragments is often left to speculation. It is therefore theoretically and methodologically useful to examine uptake both as a practice of media engagement and as a series of subsequent mediatized messages, the two of them not being sharply separate. Understanding the trajectory from ad hoc moments of uptake to the broader circulation, and eventually diffusion, of mediatized fragments can only benefit by the availability of both types of data. This seems extremely pertinent in dealing with social media, where the boundaries between a mediated contribution (e.g. a status update, comment, or tweet) and its rescaling and mediatization on the part of institutional actors (e.g. journalists who quote this comment in their own online story) are particularly fuzzy.

A rare attempt to reconstruct this trajectory in detail is a case study by Squires (2014), which distinguishes between adoption (defined as direct uptake of a mediatized fragment by audience members), circulation (the "use-in-practice of the feature from adopters to new users, who are media consumers"), and diffusion ("spread of the feature from adopters to new users, who may or may not be media consumers"; Squires 2014: 43). The second and third steps differ from the first in that they detach the fragment from the context of its immediate reception, and the third step differs from the second in terms of a process Squires terms "indexical bleaching". In her definition, this happens when "a feature retains its semantic meaning and pragmatic force" but loses its social meaning" (p. 43). Through bleaching, Squires suggests, a features ceases to be part of "media language", that is, loses its metapragmatic connection to a specific mediatized representation and its characters, and enters the lexical or idiomatic repertoire of a speech community. Androutsopoulos (2014b: 23) terms this process "intertextual bleaching", defined as "decreasing interactional relevance of the fragment's intertextual link, so that its media origin is made ever less relevant in the actual instance of recontextualization"(p. 23).

In either wording, indexical/intertextual bleaching is a useful notion, as it lends itself to corpus-based operationalization. Squires (2014) does this with Twitter data, which recycle a phrase that originates in a television show, and distinguishes these tweets by discursive domain, topical reference, and formal variation. Other potential data come to mind, such as newspaper corpora or ethnographically documented everyday talk. Understanding how different types of postmediatized data can shed light to different facets of circulation and diffusion is a task for future research. Regardless of data, semantic and pragmatic criteria can be used to identify whether a mediatized fragment has reached the stage of bleaching. This is the case when the use of this fragment bears no cue to its mediatized origin, e.g. it is not part of media stylization and does not raise subsequent metapragmatic justification or hedging.

5.   Conclusion

As it happens, the end of this discussion meets Trudgill's suggestions on media influence on the spread of lexical innovations: "People hear new words and phrases on the TV, and sometimes start using them themselves. That's about it"(Trudgill 2014: 220). The preceding discussion suggests there is much more complexity in this process and new ideas on how to uncover it. There is good reason at this point, therefore, to recall Blommaert's plea for a new vocabulary in sociolinguistics. "What is needed is a new vocabulary to describe events, phenomena and processes, new metaphors for representing them, new arguments to explain them" (Blommaert 2010: 1–2; cf. Blommaert, this volume, Chapter 11). I argued that sociolinguistics needs new vocabulary, metaphors, and arguments in order to cope with rapidly changing language practices involving media. That said, I take 'new' here to include a critique of received definitions and arguments, notably relating to media and its influence on language (Section 2) and a rediscovery of established concepts, such as mediation (Section 3).

As pointed out in the beginning, language and media research in sociolinguistics is in flux. There is a rising amount of research on both areas covered in this chapter, that is, interpersonal computer-mediated communication and mass-mediated discourse. My intention was not to suggest that these areas are still uncharted territory but to emphasise that results from this research have not yet become canonical knowledge in the discipline. The view of media as something distinct from everyday language, and peripheral to its development, is still around. Sociolinguistics is therefore still in the process of normalising media, mediation, and mediatization as aspects of language in society. Part of this process is to acknowledge that the use of mediational tools and the uptake of mediatized messages are common language practices in a mediatized society and fundamental to the circulation and diffusion of semiotic innovations in the digital age.

REFERENCES

Agha, Asif. 2003. The social life of cultural value. *Language and Communication* 23: 231–73.

   2011a. Large and small scale forms of personhood. *Language & Communication* 31, 3: 171–180.

   2011b. Meet mediatization. *Language & Communication* 31, 3: 163–170.

Ammon, Ulrich, Norbert Dittmar, Klaus J. Mattheier, and Peter Trudgill (eds.). 2004. *Sociolinguistics: An International Handbook of the Science of Language and Society*, 2nd ed. 3 vols. Berlin: De Gruyter.

Anderson, Benedict. 2006. *Imagined Communities: Reflections on the Origin and Spread of Nationalism*, revized ed. London and New York: Verso.

Androutsopoulos, Jannis. 2009. 'Greeklish': Transliteration practice and discourse in a setting of computer-mediated digraphia. In A. Georgakopoulou and M. Silk (eds.), *Standard Language and Language Standards*. Farnam: Ashgate, 221–249.

2010. The study of language and space in media discourse. In Peter Auer and Jürgen E. Schmidt (eds.), *Language and Space: An International Handbook of Linguistic Variation*. Berlin and New York: De Gruyter, vol. 1, 740–758.

2011. Language change and digital media: A review of conceptions and evidence. In Tore Kristiansen and Nikolas Coupland (eds.), *Standard Languages and Language Standards in a Changing Europe*. Oslo: Novus, 145–161.

2014a. Beyond 'media influence'. *Journal of Sociolinguistics* 18, 2: 242–249.

2014b. Mediatization and sociolinguistic change. Key concepts, research traditions, open issues. In Jannis Androutsopoulos (ed.), *Mediatization and Sociolinguistic Change*. Berlin: De Gruyter, 3–48.

2015. Networked multilingualism: Some language practices on Facebook and their implications. *International Journal of Bilingualism* 19, 2: 185–205.

2016. Mediatisierte Praktiken: Zur Rekontextualisierung von Anschlusskommunikation in den Sozialen Medien. In Arnulf Deppermann, Helmuth Feilke, and Angelika Linke (eds.), *Sprachliche und kommunikative Praktiken*. Berlin: De Gruyter, 337–368.

Bauman, Richard, and Charles L. Briggs. 1990. Poetics and performance as critical perspectives on language and social life. *Annual Review of Anthropology* 19: 59–88.

Bell, Allan. 2011. Leaving home: De-europeanisation in a post-colonial variety of broadcast news language. In Tore Kristiansen and Nikolas Coupland (eds.), *Standard Languages and Language Standards in a Changing Europe*. Oslo: Novus, 177–198.

Bell, Allan, and Andy Gibson. 2011. Staging language: An introduction to the sociolinguistics of performance. *Journal of Sociolinguistics* 15, 5: 555–572.

Blommaert, Jan. 2010. *The Sociolinguistics of Globalization*. Cambridge: Cambridge University Press.

Brandt, Deborah. 2015. *The Rise of Writing: Redefining Mass Literacy in America*. Cambridge: Cambridge University Press.

Busch, Brigitta. 2006. Changing media spaces: The transformative power of heteroglossic practices. In Clare Mar-Molinero and Patrick Stevenson (eds.), *Language Ideologies, Policies and Practices*. Basingstoke: Palgrave Macmillan, 206–219.

Chambers, J. K. 1998. TV makes people sound the same. In Laurie Bauer and Peter Trudgill (eds.), *Language Myths*. London: Penguin, 123–131.

Cole Debbie and Régine Pellicera. 2012. Uptake (un)limited: The mediatization of register shifting in US public discourse. *Language in Society* 41, 4: 449–470.

Couldry, Nick. 2008. Mediatization or mediation? Alternative understandings of the emergent space of digital storytelling. *New Media Society* 10: 373–391.

Coupland, Nikolas. 2007. *Style, Language Variation and Identity*. Cambridge: Cambridge University Press.
2009. The mediated performance of vernaculars. *Journal of English Linguistics* 37, 3: 284–300.
Coupland, Nikolas, Srikant Sarangi, and Christopher N. Candlin (eds.). 2001. *Sociolinguistics and Social Theory*. London: Longman.
Deumert, Ana, and Kristin Vold Lexander. 2013. Texting Africa: Writing as performance. *Journal of Sociolinguistics* 17, 4: 522–546.
Dorleijn, Margreet, and Jacomine Nortier. 2009. Code-switching and the internet. In B. E. Bullock and A. J. Toribio (eds.), *The Cambridge Handbook of Linguistic Code-Switching*. Cambridge: Cambridge University Press, 127–141.
Eckert, Penelope. 2012. Three waves of variation study: The emergence of meaning in the study of sociolinguistic variation. *Annual Review of Anthropology* 41: 87–100.
Georgakopoulou, Alexandra. 1997. Self-presentation and interactional alliances in e-mail discourse: The style- and code-switches of Greek messages. *International Journal of Applied Linguistics* 7, 2: 141–164.
Gumperz, John J. 1982. *Discourse Strategies*. Cambridge: Cambridge University Press.
Hepp, Andreas. 2014. Mediatization: A panorama of media and communication research. In Jannis Androutsopoulos (ed.), *Mediatization and Sociolinguistic Change*. Berlin: De Gruyter, 49–66.
Hill, Jane. 1995. Junk Spanish, covert racism and the (leaky) boundary between public and private spheres. *Pragmatics* 5, 2: 197–212.
Hinnenkamp Volker. 2008. Deutsch, Doyc or Doitsch? Chatters as languagers – The case of a German-Turkish chat room. *International Journal of Multilingualism* 5, 3: 253–275.
Ivković, Dejan 2013. Pragmatics meets ideology: Digraphia and non-standard orthographic practices in Serbian online news forums. *Journal of Language and Politics* 12, 3: 335–356.
Jaffe, Alexandra. 2009. Entextualization, mediatization and authentication: Orthographic choice in media transcripts. *Text & Talk* 29, 5: 571–594.
Johnson, Sally, and Astrid Ensslin (eds.). 2007. *Language in the Media: Representations, Identities, Ideologies*. London: Continuum.
Johnstone, Barbara. 2011. Dialect enregisterment in performance. *Journal of Sociolinguistics* 15, 5: 657–679.
Jucker, Andreas H., and Christa Dürscheid. 2012. The linguistics of keyboard-to-screen communication: A new terminological framework. *Linguistik Online* 56, 6. www.linguistikonline.org/56_12/juckerDuerscheid.html.
Krippendorff, Klaus. 1994. Der verschwundene Bote. Metaphern und Modelle der Kommunikation. In Klaus Merten, Siegfried J. Schmidt, and Siegfried Weischenberg (eds.), *Die Wirklichkeit der Medien. Eine Einführung in die Kommunikationswissenschaft*. Opladen: Westdeutscher Verlag, 79–113.
Kristiansen, Tore. 2014. Does mediated language influence immediate language? In Jannis Androutsopoulos (ed.), *Mediatization and Sociolinguistic Change*. Berlin: Mouton de Gruyter, 99–126.
Krotz, Friedrich. 2009. Mediatization: A concept with which to grasp media and societal change. In Knut Lundby (ed.), *Mediatization: Concept, Changes, Consequences*. New York: Peter Lang, 19–38.

Lippi-Green, Rosina. 1997 *English with an Accent: Language, Ideology, and Discrimination in the United States*. London and New York: Routledge.

Livingstone, Sonia M. 2009. On the mediation of everything. *Journal of Communication* 59: 1–18.

Lundby, Knut (ed.). 2014. *Mediatization of Communication*. Berlin: Mouton de Gruyter.

Norris, Sigrid, and Rodney H. Jones (eds.). 2005. *Discourse in Action: Introducing Mediated Discourse Analysis*. London and New York: Routledge.

Queen, Robin. 2015. *Vox Popular: The Surprising Life of Language in the Media*. Malden, MA: Wiley-Blackwell.

Sayers David. 2014. The mediated innovation model: A framework for researching media influence in language change. *Journal of Sociolinguistics* 18, 2: 185–212.

Scollon, Ron. 2001. *Mediated Discourse: The Nexus of Practice*. London: Sage.

Sebba, Mark. 2007. *Spelling and Society: The Culture and Politics of Orthography around the World*. Cambridge: Cambridge University Press.

Siebenhaar, Beat. 2006. Code choice and code-switching in Swiss-German Internet relay chat rooms. *Journal of Sociolinguistics* 10, 4: 481–509.

Spitulnik, Debra. 1997. The social circulation of media discourse and the mediation of communities. In Alessandro Duranti (ed.), *Linguistic Anthropology: A Reader*. Oxford: Oxford University Press, 95–118.

Spitzmüller, Jürgen. 2012. Floating ideologies: Metamorphoses of graphic 'Germanness'. In Alexandra Jaffe, Jannis Androutsopoulos, Mark Sebba, and Sally Johnson (eds.), *Orthography as Social Action: Scripts, Spelling, Identity and Power*. Berlin: Mouton de Gruyter, 255–288.

Squires, Lauren. 2012. Whos punctuating what? Sociolinguistic variation in instant messaging. In Alexandra Jaffe, Jannis Androutsopoulos, Mark Sebba, and Sally Johnson (eds.), *Orthography as Social Action: Scripts, Spelling, Identity and Power*. Berlin: Mouton de Gruyter, 289–324.

2014. From TV personality to fans and beyond: Indexical bleaching and the diffusion of a media innovation. *Journal of Linguistic Anthropology* 24, 1: 42–62.

Stuart-Smith, Jane. 2014. No longer an elephant in the room. *Journal of Sociolinguistics* 18, 2: 250–261.

Su, His-Yao. 2003. The multilingual and multi-orthographic Taiwan-based Internet: Creative uses of writing systems on college-affiliated BBSs. *Journal of Computer Mediated Communication* 9, 1. Available at: http://dx.doi.org/10.1111/j.1083-6101.2003.tb00357.x.

Tagliamonte, Sali A. 2014. Situating media influence in sociolinguistic context. *Journal of Sociolinguistics* 18, 2: 223–232.

Tannen, Deborah. 2013. The medium is the metamessage. In D. Tannen and A. M. Trester (eds.), *Discourse 2.0*. Washington, DC: Georgtown University Press, 99–117.

Trudgill, Peter. 2014. Diffusion, drift, and the irrelevance of media influence. *Journal of Sociolinguistics* 18, 2: 213–222.

Vaisman, Carmel. 2011. Performing girlhood through typographic play in Hebrew blogs. In C. Thurlow and K. Mroczek (eds.), *Digital Discourse: Language in the New Media*. Oxford: Oxford University Press, 177–196.

Vandekerckhove, Reinhild, and Judith Nobels. 2010. Code eclecticism: Linguistic variation and code alternation in the chat language of Flemish teenagers. *Journal of Sociolinguistics* 14, 5: 657–677.

Vandekerckhove, Reinhild, Annick De Houwer, and Aline Remael. 2009. Between language policy and linguistic reality: Intralingual subtitling on Flemish television. *Pragmatics* 19, 4: 609–628.

Wodak, Ruth, Barbara Johnstone, and Paul E. Kerswill (eds.). 2010. *The Sage Handbook of Sociolinguistics*. London: Sage.

14 Foucault, Gumperz and governmentality: Interaction, power and subjectivity in the twenty-first century

Ben Rampton

This chapter explores what the work of John Gumperz can contribute to our understanding of power relations in the twenty-first century. It does so by emphasising the critical dimension of his work (Rampton 2001; Blommaert 2005) and by considering its relevance to Foucault's notion of 'governmentality'.[1] As a concept developed in his later work, governmentality has not featured very prominently in explicit appropriations of Foucault in linguistics, but it cries out for interactional sociolinguistic analysis and has been at the centre of discussion among social theorists about the changing character of contemporary power.

To pursue this agenda – consistent with the larger programme sketched by Arnaut (2012) – I shall begin by reviewing the rather different ways in which U.S. linguistic anthropology and (mainly) European critical discourse studies relate to Foucault's thought (Section 1). I shall then move into a more detailed consideration of how John Gumperz's work resembles some of the later Foucault's, not just in its discourse constructionism and its attention to discursive technologies of power, but also in its attention to an 'antagonism of strategies' and its understated practice-focused politics (Section 2). After that, I summarise the shifts in governmentality identified by Fraser, Deleuze, Rose, and others, dwelling in particular on the new forms and functions of digital surveillance (Section 4); in Section 5, I return to Gumperz and interactional sociolinguistics, arguing that their tracking of real-time attention and inferencing, their recognition of discrepant but hidden communicative preferences, and their critique of the legibility of populations all remain highly relevant, although to cope properly with the new digital environments, interactional sociolinguistics will need to be updated with some quite challenging new types of analysis. But even without these, the Gumperzian framework can make an important contribution to understanding subjective experiences of digital

---

[1] This chapter is very much indebted to interactions with Karel Arnaut, Jan Blommaert, Nik Coupland, Kamran Khan, Celia Roberts, and Piia Varis, though any misunderstandings are very much my own.

surveillance, and the chapter concludes with a sketch of what the empirical sociolinguistic study of contemporary governmentalities might look like.

1.   Foucault in studies of language in society

Foucault's work spans (a) the human sciences, (b) institutions and their 'dividing practices', and (c) the formation of subjectivity, with the 'subject' understood in two ways: as "subject to someone else by control and dependence" and as "tied to his [or her] own identity by a conscience or self-knowledge" (Foucault 1982: 208, 212; 2003: 55). In North American linguistic anthropology, there is a great deal of research on themes like these. In research in linguistic anthropology on language ideologies, for example, issues of power and domination are pursued in (i) historical critiques of models and theories in linguistic science, (ii) institutional analyses of language policy and practice, and (iii) accounts of ordinary people, their metapragmatic ideas, and their everyday linguistic activities (see, e.g.. Kroskrity 2004). Elsewhere in linguistic anthropology, there are eloquent descriptive case studies of what amount to Foucauldian power/knowledge regimes in action (e.g. Goodwin 1994; Mehan 1996), and there are also substantial programmes of investigation where Foucault is a central inspiration (cf. Briggs on interviews [2002] and communicability [2005]).

Foucault, however, also invites us to combine careful empirical analysis with the investigation of gradual but widespread change in Western societies, and on this, U.S. linguistic anthropology has often had less to say, perhaps partly due to its ethnographic relativism outside matters of language, or maybe because of anthropology's traditional focus on countries of the global South (Collins 2003: 36–37; however, see Heller 1999; Duranti 2003: 332–333; Briggs and Hallin 2007). In contrast, in critical discourse traditions outside the United States, Foucault serves as a foundational and repeated reference point for linguistic studies that foreground large-scale historical shifts of the kind indexed by terms like 'the new economy', 'marketisation', 'globalisation', and 'modernity'. These transformations are studied in sociolinguistic processes such as the conversationalisation of public discourse and the technologisation of discourse and in new accounts of the circulation of texts (e.g. Fairclough 1989; Pennycook 1994; Blommaert 2005). Text types and genres are viewed as Foucauldian technologies of power, positioning discourse recipients as particular types of subject, and the comparison of texts produced at different times or places serves as a way of illustrating very general social changes. All this positions critical discourse studies as a substantial interdisciplinary contribution, with an empirical reach into the detailed discursive workings of power unmatched elsewhere in the social sciences. In this way, this non-American tradition is not only more explicit than linguistic anthropology in its engagement with Foucault, but also more ambitious.

There is, however, at least one way in which U.S. linguistic anthropology is generally stronger in its capacity to engage empirically with Foucault's thinking. This is Foucault's idea of 'governmentality', which refers to

all endeavours to shape, guide, direct the conduct of others, whether these be the crew of a ship, the members of a household, the employees of a boss, the children of a family or the inhabitants of a territory. And it also embraces the ways in which one might be urged and educated to ... control one's own instincts, to govern oneself ... Practices of government are deliberate attempts to shape conduct in certain ways in relation to certain objectives ... [Studying governmentality, it is vital to] track force relations at the molecular level, as they flow through a multitude of human technologies, in all the practices, arenas and spaces where programmes for the administration of others intersect with techniques for the administration of ourselves. (Rose 1999: 3–5; Foucault 1978/2003: 229–245)[2]

According to Foucault (1982), "[t]o govern ... is to structure the possible field of action of others" (p. 221), and "a relationship of power ... is a mode of action which ... acts upon the actions [of others]: an action upon an action, on existing actions or on those which may arise in the present or future" (p. 220). There is an obvious parallel here with the conversation analytic notion of the adjacency pair – two utterances in sequence produced by different people, with the first turn setting up a limited range of possible second turns (offers require acceptances or rejections, questions expect answers, etc.). Adjacency pairs are a fundamental unit of conversational organisation (Levinson 1983: 304), and in linguistic anthropology, the routine incorporation of conversation analysis within linguistic anthropology's more comprehensive programme for the study of language in institutions and society produces a framework that is very well suited to investigation of Foucault's 'capillary micro-physics of power' (Foucault 1977: 29; Goodwin and Duranti 1992: 30–31; Ahearn 2012: 263–265). Foucault also sees *struggle* as crucial to power relations, with the subordinated subject "acting or being capable of action" so that "[e]very power relationship implies, at least *in potentia*, a strategy of struggle" (1982: 220, 225),[3] and this is

---

[2] Fraser defines governmentality as "small-scale techniques of coordination [widely diffused throughout society] [which] organised relations on the 'capillary' level: in factories and hospitals, in prisons and schools, in state welfare agencies and private households, in the formal associations of civil society and informal daily interaction ... Organising individuals, arraying bodies in space and time, coordinating their forces, transmitting power among them, this mode of governmentality ordered ground-level social relations according to expertly designed logics of control" (2003: 162).

[3] Foucault (1984b) helpfully spells out the relationships between power relations, government, and domination: "I am not ... sure if I made myself clear, or used the right words, when I first became interested in the problem of power. Now I have a clearer sense of the problem. It seems to me that we must distinguish between power relations understood as strategic games of liberties – in which some try to control the conduct of others, who in turn try to avoid allowing their conduct to be controlled or try to control the conduct of others – and the states of

also something that can be studied empirically if the moment-to-moment, real-time processing of interactional discourse forms part of the analytic agenda (as in U.S. linguistic anthropology). In contrast, for the European critical discourse tradition, this movement between action and response in the struggle over power is more difficult to track, because the focus is more on written texts than on spoken interaction. As a result, it is also harder to bring empirical precision to Foucault's argument that these struggles over power are 'immediate':

> In such struggles people criticise instances of power which are the closest to them, those which exercise their action on individuals. They do not look for the 'chief enemy', but for the immediate enemy. Nor do they expect to find a solution to their problem at a future date (that is, liberation, revolutions, end of class struggle). (Foucault 1982: 211–212; Rose 1999: 279–280)

But this is no problem if research is able to draw on conversation analysis and microethnography. With microanalysis in the analytic repertoire, it is possible to pick out the exact point in a prior turn that sparks a resistant utterance, and interactive silences, hesitations, nuances, slightings, and speakings-in-disguise are all staple concerns.[4]

This brief sketch of links to Foucault in studies of language and society brings out three elements central in what follows: an interest in widespread

---

domination that people ordinarily call 'power'. And between the two, between the games of power and states of domination, you have technologies of government [a.k.a. governmentality] – understood, of course, in a very broad sense that includes not only the way institutions are governed but also the way one governs one's wife and children. The analysis of these techniques is necessary because it is often through such techniques that states of domination are established and maintained. There are three levels to my analysis of power: strategic relations, techniques of government, and states of domination" (pp. 40–41). This also entails the view that "power relations are not something that is bad in itself ... The problem ... is to acquire the rules of law, the management techniques, and also the morality, the *ethos*, the practice of the self, that will allow us to play these games of power with as little domination as possible ... I see nothing wrong in the practice of a person who, knowing more than others in a specific game of truth, tells those others what to do, teaches them, and transmits knowledge and techniques to them. The problem in such practices where power – which is not in itself a bad thing – must inevitably come into play is knowing how to avoid the kind of domination effects where a kid is subjected to the arbitrary and unnecessary authority of a teacher, or a student put under the thumb of a professor who abuses his authority" (pp. 39–40). See also Lemke 2000 and Section 2d of this chapter.

[4] Although they never mention him, Varenne and McDermott's (1998) description of doing interaction analysis looks especially close to Foucault's approach to struggles with relations of power: "When we perform practical research tasks ..., apparently paradoxical things happen as we notice how actors are both continually sensitive to matter they cannot be said to have constructed, and also slightly 'off' the most conventional version of what they could have been expected to do ... [W]hat subjects construct in the real time of their activity can never be said to be what it would be easiest to say it is. What subjects construct may never be any particular thing that any audience may label it to be. We, as analysts, must always take the position that it is something more, something other, something that cannot be named without replacing it within the very frame the act attempted to escape" (p. 177).

social change in the West (as in critical discourse studies), an interdisciplinary aspiration (ditto), and an empirical commitment to the importance of micro-interactional processes (as in U.S. linguistic anthropology). To draw these subdisciplinary tendencies closer together (Blommaert 2005: chapters 2 and 3), I shall focus on the work of John Gumperz.

2.   Foucault and Gumperz

Although they overlapped at the University of California at Berkeley, where Gumperz worked from 1956 to 1991 and Foucault visited regularly from 1975 until his death in 1984,[5] it is hard to find any reference to Foucault in Gumperz's publications (or vice versa). Nor does Gumperz give the centre of the stage to the 'big D' Discourses (Gee 1999) that feature most prominently in sociolinguistic appropriations of Foucault. But beyond my own personal alignment (e.g. Rampton 2001), there are two sets of reasons for focusing on Gumperz in an exploration of sociolinguistics and governmentality.

First, Gumperz has played a central role in the formation of contemporary linguistic anthropology from the 1970s onwards, embracing a "dynamic view of social environments where history, economic forces and interactive processes ... combine to create or to eliminate social distinctions" (Gumperz 1982: 29). Situated moment-to-moment interaction occupies an especially prominent place, and the methodology he developed – interactional sociolin-guistics – involved a deep and flexible integration of ethnography, ethno-methodology, linguistics, cognitive science, discourse, and conversation analysis (1982: 9–37). Where Gumperz has led, others have followed.

Second, there are at least four areas of loose but important compatibility between Gumperz and Foucault, especially if we are "less concerned with being faithful to a source of authority than with working within a certain ethos of enquiry, with fabricating some conceptual tools that can be set to work in relation to the particular questions that trouble contemporary thought and politics" (Rose 1999: 5; Foucault 1974/1994;[6] also Haggerty and Ericson 2000: 608; Fraser 2003: 161). These cover (a) their assumptions about the social world and discourse, (b) their attention to the discursive technologies of power, (c) their tactical approaches to empirical analysis, and (d) the element of low-key activism in their commitment to 'practical systems' as the focus of enquiry.

---

[5] I am grateful to Johanna Woydack for pointing this out.

[6] Foucault said of his books: "I would like my books to be a kind of tool-box which others can rummage through to find a tool which they can use however they wish in their own area ... I would like the little volume that I want to write on disciplinary systems to be useful to an educator, a warden, a magistrate, a conscientious objector. I don't write for an audience, I write for users, not readers" (1974/1994).

(a) Foucault rejected the view that events and activities are determined by hidden forces or universal structures (e.g. 2003: 53–54) and instead set out to discover "the connections, encounters, supports, blockages, plays of forces, strategies and so on which at a given moment establish what counts as being self-evident, universal and necessary" (1980/2003: 249). He also famously rejected the idea of a social world prior to discourse, holding that "practices [themselves] ... systematically form the objects of which they speak": "Discourses are not about objects; they do not identify objects, they constitute them and in the practice of doing so conceal their own invention" (Foucault 1974: 49). Gumperz was focused more narrowly on communication than on social reality per se, but he refused to "treat communication as merely reflecting other presumably more basic forces" (1982: 40), insisted that "the relationship of ... social factors to speech form is quite different from what the sociologist means by correlation among variables" (Gumperz and Hernández-Chavez 1972: 98), and proposed "an important break with previous approaches to social structure and to language and society. Behavioural regularities are no longer regarded as reflections of independently measurable social norms; on the contrary, these norms are themselves seen as communicative behaviour" (Blom and Gumperz 1972: 432).[7]

(b) In terms of substantive focus, there are overlaps in the technologies of power that Foucault and Gumperz attend to. In Foucault's account of the technologies of knowledge/power, two basic methodologies in the human sciences stand out (1982: 213; 1978: 139ff.). In institutional 'dividing practices', there is a central role for quantifying techniques concerned with the management of populations, objectifying people as measured bodies fitting into the administration of factories, schools, hospitals, barracks, and so on (Foucault 1977; Dreyfus and Rabinow 1982: chapter 7). Conversely, with the formation of subjectivity/subjectification, 'confession' and the hermeneutic interpretations of experts play a key part turning the speech of individuals into truths about them(selves) (Dreyfus and Rabinow 1982: chapter 8). Turning to sociolinguistics, Gumperz's analysis of the interview resonates with Foucault's

---

[7] According to Gumperz 1990, "there's no denying that politics and economic conditions are extremely important in race relations, and that ultimately redressing the balance of discrimination is a matter of power. But communication *is* power. Our social position depends on our ability to communicate, we get things in life by communicating. If we want to get a flat, we need to go to the housing authorities. To get a position in employment, we have to go through job interviews. We are tested in school at every turn, at every transition, and how we do in these tests determines how we do in later life. In all these cases, communication can make the difference. We need to communicate even to keep what we have. So communication is power – that I think is the point" (p. 52; also in Harris and Rampton 2003: 272). Compare Foucault (1982: 213): "It is certain that the mechanisms of [discursive] subjection cannot be studied outside their relation to the mechanisms of exploitation and domination. But they do not merely constitute the 'terminal' of more fundamental mechanisms."

critique of 'confession'. The interview is a very widespread contemporary genre which, suggests Foucault, derives from the confession and operates as a subjectifying 'technology of the self', feeding into dividing practices as well (Briggs 2002: 913). In Gumperz's work on 'gatekeeping', there is a profound challenge to the 'truths' – to the asymmetrical but authoritative personal and institutional judgements – that interviews produce. This is achieved, first, by foregrounding the active role played by interviewer interpretation, a role that is generally erased in the self-understandings and institutional documents that interviews subsequently generate. Second, this is achieved by showing how interpretation of the propositional messages produced in interview speech are continuously influenced in unnoticed and highly contingent ways by an incessant stream of heterogeneous semiotic signs – 'contextualisation cues' – that can easily lead to misunderstanding, especially when the participants inhabit different social and communicative networks (1982: chapter 6; Roberts et al. 1992). The 'truths' from the interview, in other words, are ineradicably partial and situated.

(c) Gumperz always treats wider discourses and ideologies as one vital dimension in the investigation of conduct,[8] but his analyses never begin with particular theories, policies, or 'Discourses', setting out to examine their implementation or effects. Instead, the initial stages of empirical research of interactional sociolinguistics involve ethnography, looking for "insight into the local communicative ecology" (Gumperz 1999: 465). But this approach itself chimes with Foucault, who advises against beginning an empirical enquiry with a particular model or theory, and instead suggests "another way to go further towards a new economy of power relations, a way which is more empirical":

[this] consists of taking the forms of resistance against different forms of power as a starting point. To use another metaphor, it consists of using this resistance as a chemical catalyst so as to bring to light power relations, locate their position, find out their point of application and the methods used . . . it consists of analysing power relations through the antagonism of strategies. (1982: 211)

There is a good case for saying that 'trouble' (if not actual resistance) and the 'antagonism of strategies' serve both as the entry point and as the central preoccupation for Gumperz's analyses. The initial stages of fieldwork include checking out "how local actors handle the problems they encounter" (1999: 465), and in his research on interviewing, it is the communicative trouble generated in the dissonance of institutional logics and minority worker

---

[8] This is apparent when he says, for example, that "our task as interactional sociolinguists in modern educational settings is to chart the process by which models of educability [ideas about what types of children can be educated how] are put into daily practice and to uncover the implicit theory of learning that informs our choice of model" (1986: 67–68).

expectations that opens into a detailed theory of discursive interaction (1982). Similarly in Gumperz's work on code-switching in the early 1970s, the incongruence and conflict between local community speech and the standard language prioritised in official transactions serve as the matrix for a far-reaching description and theorisation of the social organisation of linguistic difference (Blom and Gumperz 1972; Gumperz and Hernandez-Chavez 1972; Section 4 below).

(d) In a paper on the possibilities of enquiry – 'What Is Enlightenment?' (2003) – Foucault sees the "acquisition of capabilities and the struggle for freedom" as two driving aspirations. But because the development of human capabilities is technologised and regimented, the growth of capacity normally undermines freedom, forming "the paradox of the relations of capacity and power" (p. 55). This raises the question: "how can the growth of capabilities be disconnected from the intensification of power relations?" (p. 55; see also note 2 above). To explore the possibilities, Foucault says that diverse enquiries should focus on concrete practices and that these should be conceptualised simultaneously as "technological type[s] of rationality and as strategic games of liberties" (p. 56):

This leads to the study of what could be called "practical systems". Here [the domain of reference is] not the representations that men give of themselves, nor the conditions that determine them without their knowledge, but rather what they do and the way they do it. That is, the forms of rationality that organise their ways of doing things (this might be called the technological aspect) and the freedom with which they act within these practical systems, reacting to what others do, modifying the rules of the game, up to a certain point (this might be called the strategic side of these practices). (2003: 55)

These practical systems, we could say, are Gumperz's central concern. The "ground-level social relations [ordered] according to expertly designed logics of control" (Fraser 2003: 162) form one part of the dynamic in focus, with either the interview genre or the standard language operating as governing technologies of power. But by entering these systems through the 'antagonism of strategies' – by also attending, in other words, to miscommunication and to the mixing and alternation of codes – Gumperz brings in the 'strategic game of liberties'. Indeed, when these descriptive accounts are themselves turned into materials for consciousness-raising discussion with both managers and subordinates, as in the *Crosstalk* project (Gumperz et al. 1979; Jupp et al. 1982; Roberts et al. 1992), Gumperz adopts a path towards low-key, partial, and specific transformations similar to the one outlined by Foucault: "analyzing and reflecting on limits" in order to open "the possibility of no longer being, doing, or thinking what we are, do, or think", "practical critique that takes the form of a possible crossing-over", "grasp[ing] the points where change is possible and desirable" (Foucault 2003: 53–54; 1984a/2003: 23; also e.g. Rose 1999: 282–284; Ball 2013: 125).

My comparison of Gumperz and Foucault started out from the widely held view that sociolinguistics can provide the Foucauldian agenda with a microscope, sharpening its empirical grasp of how "power reaches into the very grain of individuals, touches their bodies and inserts itself into their actions and attitudes, their discourses, learning processes and everyday lives" (Foucault 1980: 39). But even though Foucault obviously works across a far larger canvas than Gumperz, there are several other points of quite profound connection, and these increase the relevance of interactional sociolinguistics for Foucauldian analysis. So if Foucault is invoked in far-reaching interrogations of contemporary social change, there may be a good case for bringing in Gumperz as well. To take this further, we must first review some recent discussions of governmentality in social theory.

3.   Repositioning Foucault

In a 2003 paper entitled 'From discipline to flexibilisation? Rereading Foucault in the shadow of globalisation', Nancy Fraser asks: "How does power [now] operate after the decentering of the national frame?" (p. 170). "[I]t would be hard to formulate a better guiding question as we seek to understand new modes of governmentality in the era of neoliberal globalization" (p. 170), although the relevance of Foucault's work is not straightforward, because Foucault

was the great theorist of the fordist mode of social regulation ... Viewed through his eyes, social services became disciplinary apparatuses, humanist reforms became panoptical surveillance regimes, public health measures became deployments of biopower, and therapeutic practices became vehicles of subjection. (2003: 160)

Now, however, "we ... see ourselves as standing on the brink of a new, postfordist epoch of globalisation", and

[i] the ordering of social relations is undergoing a major shift in scale, equivalent to *denationalisation* and *transnationalisation* ... [N]ational ordering is not disappearing, [but] it is in the process of being decentered as its regulatory mechanisms become articulated ... with those at other levels ... At the same time, [ii] regulation is also undergoing a process of *desocialisation*. In today's hegemonic – neoliberal – variant of globalisation, massive, unfettered, transnational flows of capital are derailing the Keynesian project of national economic steering. The tendency is to transform the fordist welfare state into a postfordist 'competition state', as countries scramble to cut taxes and eliminate 'red tape' in hopes of keeping and attracting investment. The resulting 'race to the bottom' fuels myriad projects of deregulation, as well as efforts to privatize social services, whether by shifting them onto the market or by devolving them onto the family (which means, in effect, onto women) ... Finally, [iii] as fordist discipline wanes in the face of globalisation, its orientation to self-regulation tends to dissipate too. As more of the work of socialisation is marketised, fordism's labour-intensive individualising focus tends to drop out. In

psychotherapy, for example, the time-intensive talk-oriented approaches favoured under fordism are increasingly excluded from insurance coverage and replaced by instant-fix pharma-psychology ... In the US, accordingly, some observers posit the transformation of the social state into a 'prison-industrial complex', where incarceration of male minority youth becomes the favored policy on unemployment. The prisons in question, moreover, have little in common with the humanist panopticons described by Foucault. Their management often subcontracted to for-profit corporations, they are less laboratories of self-reflection than hotbeds of racialized and sexualized violence – of rape, exploitation, corruption, untreated HIV, murderous gangs, and murderous guards. If such prisons epitomize one aspect of postfordism, it is one that no longer works through individual self-governance. (2003: 165–166, emphases in original)

With changes like these, says Fraser, Foucault's portrait of the disciplinary societies looks outdated,[9] but she insists that the study of governmentality – of the rational ordering of ground-level social relations – remains a vital project.

Fraser identifies several ways of taking this forward,[10] and these include investigation of "[the] objects of intervention, [the] modes of subjectification,

---

[9] Bauman (1987) also offers an influential metaphor to encapsulate these changes when he proposes that the state is changing from 'gardener' to 'gamekeeper'. "The gardening state presumes exceptional concern with pattern, regularity and ordering, with what is growing and what should be weeded out. Legislators have been central to the gardening state, as using their reason to determine what is and what is not productive of order. The social sciences have been part of that application of reason to society through facilitating the husbandry of societal resources ... [By contrast, t]he new global order involves ... the gamekeeper state ... [Such a gamekeeper state is] not bothered to give society an overall shape ... The gamekeeper [is] concerned with regulating mobilities, with ensuring that there [is] sufficient stock for hunting in a particular site but not with the detailed cultivation of each animal in each particular place" (Urry 2000: 188, 189). Picking up on Foucault in particular, Deleuze (1992) speaks of a shift from disciplinary societies to 'societies of control': "We are in a generalised crisis in relation to all the environments of enclosure – prison, hospital, school, family ... [U]ltrarapid forms of free-floating control [replace] the old disciplines operating in the time frame of a closed system ... In the disciplinary societies one was always starting again (from school to the barracks, from the barracks to the factory), while in societies of control one is never finished anything ... The disciplinary societies have two poles: the signature that designates the *individual*, and the number or administrative numeration that indicates his or her position within a *mass* ... In the societies of control ... what is important is no longer either a signature or a number, but a code: the code is a *password*, while on the other hand the disciplinary societies are regulated by *watchwords* ... The numerical language of control is made of codes that mark access to information, or reject it. We no longer find ourselves dealing with the mass/individual pair. Individuals have become '*dividuals*', and masses [have become] samples, data, markets, or '*banks*' ... The disciplinary man was a discontinuous producer of energy, but the man of control is undulatory, in orbit, in a continuous network. Everywhere *surfing* has already replaced the old *sports* ... Types of machine are easily matched with each type of society ... [D]isciplinary societies equipped themselves with machines involving energy, with the passive danger of entropy and the active danger of sabotage; the societies of control operate with machines of a [different] type, computers, whose passive danger is jamming and whose active one is piracy and the introduction of viruses ... Man is no longer enclosed, but man is in debt" (pp. 4–6).

[10] She also specifies the need for analysis of (1) the specifically transnational character of postfordist regulation, involving a profound reorganisation of security, policing and legal functions (2003: 167; also Bigo 2002; 2006) as well as an increasing tendency to "'govern-at-a-distance', through

and [the] mix of repression and regulation" that characterise post-fordist governmentality (p. 167). Rather than being self-regulated citizens who understand "themselves to be a member of a single integrated national society" (Rose 1996: 334), Fraser argues that the preferred subject participates in "(market) choice [as] a consumer of services ... obligated to enhance her quality of life through her own decisions. In this new 'care of self', everyone is an expert on herself, responsible for managing her own human capital to maximal effect" (Fraser 2003: 168; Rose 1996: 343). In the production of this consumer of services, surveillance plays a crucial part, but it no longer operates as a process of disciplinary 'soul training', as it did in Foucault's panopticism (Haggerty and Ericson 2000: 615). Instead, it feeds profiling and establishes

new forms of (transnational) segmentation. Working largely through population profiling, [post-fordist regulation] separates and tracks individuals for the sake of efficiency and risk prevention[, s]orting the capable-and-competitive wheat from the incapable-and-noncompetitive chaff ... In this "dual society", a hypercompetitive, fully networked zone coexists with a marginal sector of excluded low-achievers. (Fraser 2003: 169)

The importance of new forms of postpanoptic surveillance facilitated by digital technology is addressed by other scholars. Haggerty and Ericson speak of a 'surveillant assemblage' which they describe as "a host of different phenomena and processes working together, ... operat[ing] across both state and extra-state institutions, ... [seeking to] introduce breaks and divisions into otherwise free-flowing phenomena" (2000: 608, 610). Boundaries and enclosures of all kinds – hospitals, factories, schools, families – may be giving way to the flows of people, objects, and information associated with neoliberal marketisation, but "ultrarapid forms of free-floating control [are replacing] the old disciplines operating in the time frame of a closed system" (Deleuze 1992: 4), and digital surveillance is central in this. It plays a major role in the processes by which "the population is increasingly constituted as consumers and seduced into the market economy", "constructing and monitoring consumption" (2000: 615; Bauman and Lyon 2013: 16, 121ff.; van Dijck 2013), although for the most part, it does not operate as a centralised Orwellian 'Big Brother'. Countering a totalising view of surveillance, Rose proposes that

it is better seen as conditional access to circuits of consumption and civility, constant scrutiny of the right of individuals to access certain kinds of flows of consumption goods: recurrent switch points to be passed in order to access the benefit of liberty. (Rose 1999: 243)

flexible, fluctuating networks that transcend structured institutional sites" (p. 167; also Bauman 2000: 11; Bauman and Lyon 2013: 13), and (2) increasing reliance on dispersed and marketised modes of governmentality (p. 168), in which competition is introduced to social services; clients are turned into consumers; and auditors and accountants replace service professionals as the frontline disciplinarians (p. 168; Rose 1996).

There are some, however, for whom older forms of regulation are still useful:

> As ... mechanisms of regulation through desire, consumption and the market ... come to extend their sway over larger and larger sectors of the population, earlier bureaucratic and governmental mechanisms of self-formation and self-regulation become less salient and can begin to be dismantled and refocused upon marginalised individuals who through ill will, incompetence or misfortune are outside these webs of 'consuming civility' ... They are, no doubt, the 'usual suspects' – the lone parent, the delinquent juvenile, the school truant, the homeless person, the alcoholic. (Rose 1999: 87, 88, 89)

Indeed there are some – poorer foreigners, asylum seekers, immigrants, and ethnic minorities – who become subject to what Bigo calls the '*Ban*opticon' (2002; 2006). This is a surveillant assemblage that treats these groups as potential enemies and exceptional risks who require forms of attention which go beyond normal democratic accountabilities. This is managed by a proliferating transnational 'archipelago' of security experts (police, intelligence, military, immigration control, private companies, specialist lawyers, and academics) that is ever seeking, for example, to extend the integration of police files with data from social security, taxes, insurance, credit bureaus, supermarkets, and so on. The Banopticon turns schools, hospitals, and services into security auxiliaries, and it encourages fear and unease in the general public (see also Bauman and Lyon 2013; Huysmans 2014).

These shifts in regulation are obviously complex and varied, and it is important not to exaggerate the changes. In Fraser's paper, the title is framed as a *question*; the later Foucault himself considered *post*disciplinary power (Lemke 2003; Caluya 2010); and Rose (1999) warns against overstatements about epochal transformation, proposing instead that "we should seek to identify the emergence of new control strategies and the reconfiguration of old ones" (p. 240). But if these are issues that "trouble contemporary thought and politics" (p. 5), if Foucault's governmentality is seen as an important resource for engaging with them, and if Gumperz's interactional sociolinguistics is very closely tuned to Foucault's governmentality, then it is worth trying to specify in more detail the relevance of Gumperz's work to the new forms of regulation now emerging in the twenty-first century.

4.   Gumperz and contemporary digital governmentalities

Gumperz's major work antedates one of the most significant ways in which linguistic anthropology is able to engage with 'free-floating control' in post-disciplinary conditions where enclosures have given way to flows – through the detailed transcontextual analysis of how meanings and texts move through and across events over time, developed in the 1990s (Bauman and Briggs 1990; Silverstein and Urban 1996; Blommaert 2005; Briggs 2005). Nevertheless,

Gumperz situated all of his work in a realisation that the boundaries between social groups are disappearing, that distinctive group norms are weakening, and that "individuals are freer to alter their social personae with circumstances" (1982: 26; Gumperz and Hernández-Chavez 1972: 291). In place of 'community', Gumperz stressed the sociocommunicative significance of interpersonal networks (Blom and Gumperz 1972; Gumperz 1982), opening the door to empirical investigation of Fraser's suggestion that networks are "emerging as important new vehicles for postfordist governmentality" (2003: 169).

But to capitalise on the distinctive capacity of interactional sociolinguistics to engage with the situated 'nanodynamics' of postfordist power, the everyday use of digital technologies presents itself as a prime object of analysis. These technologies impact on the interaction order (Goffman 1981), and they play a central role in surveillance, 'soft' and 'hard', seducing and excluding. Larsen, Urry, and Axhausen suggest, for example, that with mobile phones,

distinctions between presence and absence, attention and inattention ... partially dissolve. Goffman argued that "co-presence renders persons uniquely accessible, available, and subject to one another" (1963: 22), but it seems that many young adults' social meetings are now typified by brief moments of 'inattention' and 'mobilities', as phone calls are answered, text messages are sent, new faces arrive while others leave. (2008: 650)

"The scarce resource", says Wellman, "is attention, not information" (2001: 236), and this is targeted in the 'attention economy', where "the interest of consumers needs to be caught as eyeballs migrate from television to tablet to mobile phone to laptop" (van Dijck 2013: 122). In the words of the manual *Hooked: How to Build Habit-Forming Products*:

Habit-forming technology is already here, and it is being used to mold our lives. The fact that we have greater access to the web through our various connected devices – smartphones and tablets, televisions, game consoles, and wearable technology – gives companies far greater ability to affect our behaviour. As companies combine their increased connectivity to consumers, with the ability to collect, mine, and process customer data at faster speeds, we are faced with a future where everything becomes potentially more habit-forming ... [This book] *Hooked* seeks to unleash the tremendous new powers innovators and entrepreneurs have to influence the everyday lives of billions of people. (Eyal 2014: 8, 9)[11]

This is governmentality – "the deliberate attempt ... to shape conduct in certain ways in relation to certain objectives" (Rose 1999: 4) – in postfordist form, and there are at least three elements in Gumperz's analytic agenda that help us orient to this, though adaptations are necessary with each one. These interests are (a) the dynamics of real-time attention and inferencing, initially

---

[11] I am indebted to Alex Nunes for this reference.

developed in Gumperz's work on code-switching; (b) the role played by unrecognised communicative preferences, which Gumperz called 'communicative styles' and originally articulated in his studies of cross-cultural interaction; and (c) the mistaken faith placed by institutional assessments in the stable transparency of lexicogrammatical meaning (cf. Eades, this volume, Chapter 17), an issue in both the code-switching and the cross-cultural work.

(a) In code-switching, people switch between different languages or registers in the course of their talk, and in the account that Gumperz developed in the 1970s and early 1980s, when actors notice elements from a different code entering the stream of speech they are listening to, their sense-making engages more or less simultaneously with two levels of meaning: the more general cultural connotations of the registers brought into juxtaposition (e.g. their indexical associations with home, work, or recreation or with particular social groups) and the rhetorical and interactional implications of the code-switch for what's going on right now ('Does it add or subtract from the authority or authenticity of what's being said?'; 'Is it humorous, serious or accidental?'; 'Is it addressed to a different participant?'; etc.) (Rampton 2009: 151–153, 173 n. 4). As well as showing that code-switches "can act as powerful instruments of persuasion in everyday communicative situations" (Gumperz and Cook-Gumperz 1982: 6), this account puts real-time attentional tracking, cognitive inferencing, and shifts of cultural positioning together in a single analysis, and as such, it provides a vivid point of entry into the subtle reconfiguring of social relations continuously unfolding in interaction, a point picked up by Goffman (1981: 126–127). In fact the integration of these elements also looks promising as a way of engaging with the commercial app designer's efforts to catch and hold our attention in new habits of consumption, although to take this further, Gumperz's framework would need to expand beyond just registers and languages to different media. But this is not conceptually difficult. Elaborating both Goffman and interactional sociolinguistics, Scollon 1998 offers tools for analysing multitasking, where "keep[ing] open several competing sites of [media] engagement" simultaneously is "the normal attention pattern" (p. 256), and Schegloff (2002), for example, provides a glimpse of the complex social calculations that go into the decision about whether or not to pick up a phone call ('Is this important enough to warrant a switch of attention? Will the interruption be justified? How much time will it take? Is this the right moment?').

So Gumperz's work on code-switching initially established that attention, inferencing, and social positioning can be studied together as a dynamic interactional process, and in fact in any empirical investigation of ideas about fluctuating control versus disciplined enclosure (Deleuze 1992), some version of this is going to be important.

(b) In his work on intercultural miscommunication during the 1980s, Gumperz developed another concept that can be extended and applied to the analysis of digital governmentality. Although there are always contingencies in play, Gumperz argued that there are patterned tendencies in how different groups produce and construe semiotic signs and their indexical connotations, even when they are using the same language, and he called these 'communicative styles'. These are expressive and interpretive dispositions that are "learned in the course of previous interactive experience, [that] form part of our habitual and instinctive linguistic knowledge" (1982: 162) and that encompass many different kinds of linguistic and discursive preference, ranging from ways of using particular intonation contours to expectations about the organisation of genres. But these preferences often go unrecognised, and this can generate "special problems ... in a modern society where people have widely varying communicative and cultural backgrounds" (1982: 167): when there is a communicative mismatch, this is often misattributed to ability or attitude rather than to differences in style. This diagnosis has major investigative implications: although analysis of real-time processing in the here-and-now is vital, it is never sufficient. Beyond the understandings articulated by co-present individuals, there are historically shaped and potentially discrepant communicative sensibilities operating unnoticed in the background, and to grasp their influence on what unfolds in any given interaction, researchers need know about communicative practice in different participants' social networks beyond the event itself (Prevignano and di Luzio 2002: 10, 11, 23).

Gumperz's own analyses tended to focus on the unrecognised influence of nondominant communicative styles and to describe, for example, the ways in which British-born gatekeepers failed to apprehend the distinctive discursive expectations shaping the spoken English of Indian immigrants with Hindi-speaking backgrounds. But online Web 2.0 environments introduce an additional set of influential but often unrecognised 'communicative styles', and rather than disadvantaging their carriers, these are "expertly designed logics of control" (Fraser 2003: 162), often seeking commercial profit. According to van Dijck,

Sociality is not simply "rendered technological" by moving to an online space; rather, coded structures are profoundly altering the nature of our connections, creations and interactions ... Algorithms, protocols, and defaults profoundly shape the cultural experience of people active on social media platforms ... Online sociality has increasingly become a coproduction of humans and machines ... [A] platform [like Facebook, YouTube or Wikipedia] ... shapes the performance of social acts instead of merely facilitating them. Technologically speaking, platforms are the providers of software, (sometimes) hardware, and services that help code social activities into a computational architecture; they process (meta)data through algorithms and formatted

protocols before presenting their interpreted logic in the form of user-friendly inter-
faces with default settings that reflect the platform owner's strategic choices . . . The
challenge is to make the hidden layer visible . . . (2013: 20, 32, 33, 29)

Users don't necessarily accept the patterning of online social behaviour
inscribed in these designs and algorithms, and van Dijck sets out to chart the
"ongoing clash between user tactics and platform strategies", invoking de
Certeau's account of how people negotiate the practices arranged for them
by institutions (2013: 20, 6). But, she says, the "information apparatus that has
come to produce everyday life" is "powerful, oblique and only partially
visible", a "technological unconscious" (2013: 32). Admittedly, *all* communication is shaped in normally unremarked ways by the linguistic and discursive
resources that it draws on, but rather than simply being a stock of sedimented
preferences tacitly activated in the here-and-now, as in Gumperz's account,
these technocultural 'communicative styles' are themselves interactive and
fast-moving, continuously updating, customising, filtering in response to the
users' online conduct, operating, one might say, more as busy personal
assistants 24/7 than sets of (slowly updated) reference resources (see Eisenlauer 2014).

In sum: Gumperz's notion of communicative style emphasised hidden
discrepancies in the prestructuring of here-and-now communication, insisting
on the potentially destabilising influence of the particular histories that different participants bring to an encounter, introducing unconscious partiality and
bias. This challenge to ideas about consensual interactional organisation
carries over into studies of digital communication, as does the need to go
beyond the encounter in order to better understand it. But with the interactivity
of the Web, it may be more apt to speak of 'implicit participants' (van Dijck
2013: 33) than 'hidden discrepancies'.

(c) If Gumperz's 'communicative style' points to how discrepant communicative *hinterlands* can prestructure the social dynamics of real-time attention
and inferencing in asymmetrical face-to-face encounters (his central object of
analysis), the *outcomes* of such encounters are at stake in his efforts to unseat
lexicogrammar as a central point of reference in educational and workplace
assessments. Gumperz distinguishes between two broad sources of meaning:
(1) the propositional meaning formulated with syntax, lexis, and semantics,
codified in linguistics, preserved in writing, and taught and assessed at school,
and (2) the huge and diffuse constellation of less regimented features that he
calls 'contextualisation cues', "by which speakers signal and listeners interpret
what the activity is, how semantic content is to be understood and how each
sentence relates to what precedes or follows" (1982: 131). Gumperz dwells
on intonation as one of the most important of these less codified features, but

"a contextualisation cue is any feature of linguistic [or indeed semiotic] form that contributes to signalling contextual presuppositions", and these depend both on the situated contingencies of the moment and on "the historically given repertoire of the participants" (1982: 131; cf. 'communicative style' above). With this broad distinction in place, Gumperz criticises institutions operating in ethnically diverse environments for relying too heavily on the aspects of meaning that seem to be stabilised in lexicogrammar and for overlooking the crucial contribution of less standardised contextualisation cues. As a result, minority speakers are given poor ratings in institutional encounters, not necessarily just because institutional representatives are prejudiced but because their comprehension is flawed, whether this is focused on code-switching at school or cross-cultural English in job interviews.

James Scott's (1998) *Seeing like a State* helps us to situate this social problem within fordist modernity. In terms that resonate with Foucault, Scott focuses on

a state's attempt to make society legible, to arrange the population in ways that simplified the classic state functions of taxation, conscription, and prevention of rebellion ... The pre-modern state was, in many crucial respects, partially blind; it knew precious little about its subjects, their wealth, their landholdings and yields, their location, their very identity ... As a result, its interventions were often crude and self-defeating ... How did the state gradually get a handle on its subjects and their environment? ... [P]rocesses as disparate as the creation of permanent last names, the standardization of weights and measures, the establishment of cadastral surveys and population registers, the invention of freehold tenure, *the standardization of language and legal discourse*, the design of cities, and the organization of transportation [can be seen] as attempts at legibility and simplification. In each case, officials took exceptionally complex, illegible, and local social practices, such as land tenure customs or naming customs, and created a standard grid whereby it could be centrally recorded and monitored ... (1998: 2; emphasis added)

Gumperz's work can be read as a critique of institutional ideas about the linguistic legibility of populations, as a reassertion of the importance of the "complex, illegible and local", and as the development of an analytic apparatus for understanding this. But with the emergence of postfordism, to what extent is this still relevant?

Within the surveillant assemblage described by Haggerty and Ericson (2000), the legibility of populations is less dependent on language, standard or otherwise:

[a] great deal of surveillance is directed toward the human body ... [and breaks the body] down into a series of discrete signifying flows ... For example, drug testing striates flows of chemicals, photography captures flows of reflected lightwaves, and lie detectors align and compare assorted flows of respiration, pulse and electricity. The

body is itself, then, an assemblage comprised of myriad component parts and processes which are broken-down for purposes of observation ... It is then reassembled in different settings through a series of data flows. The result is a decorporealised body, a "data double" of pure virtuality. The monitored body is increasingly a cyborg: a flesh-technology-information amalgam ... These hybrids can involve something as direct as tagging the human body so that its movements through space can be recorded, to the more refined reconstruction of a person's habits, preferences, and lifestyle from the trails of information which have become the detritus of contemporary life. The surveillant assemblage is a visualizing device that brings into the visual register a host of heretofore opaque flows of auditory, scent, chemical, visual, ultraviolet and informational stimuli. Much of the visualization pertains to the human body, and exists beyond our normal range of perception. (2000: 611, 612)

Indeed, within the kinds of site that Gumperz analysed,

[c]urrent organisational surveillance practices feature the collection of information from the body and provide detailed data about individuals, their habits and lifestyles that they might not ordinarily reveal in face-to-face interactions such as the recruitment interview. (Ball 2005: 90, 91)

There is still a great deal of substance in Gumperz's critique of the superficiality with which individuals are construed and assessed:

Rather than being accurate or inaccurate portrayals of real individuals, ['data doubles'] are a form of pragmatics: differentiated according to how useful they are in allowing institutions to make discriminations among populations ... [S]urveillance is often a mile wide but only an inch deep ... These new forms of reputation lack ... deep subjective nuances ... Instead, knowledge of the population is now manifest in discrete bits of information which break the individual down into flows for purposes of management, profit and entertainment. (Haggerty and Ericson 2000: 614, 618, 619)

But compared with the interviewing manager or classroom teacher targeted in Gumperz's interventions, the judges here are now much more remote, 'governing at a distance', while critical deconstruction of the authority of the semiotic codes on which institutional assessments are based now needs to focus on much more than relatively standard lexicogrammars.

So in proposing that Gumperz's framework holds relevance to new forms of governmentality in 'societies of control', I have suggested that the account of code-switching needs to be extended beyond languages to different media, that analysis of the hidden influence of discrepant communicative styles should engage with the codes inscribed in Web 2.0 platforms, and that critiques of the semiotic basis of institutional assessment should now extend to the "flows of auditory, scent, chemical, visual, ultraviolet and informational stimuli" that inform the surveillant assemblage. But is this ridiculously overambitious? There can be no doubting the obstacles. There is the technical challenge of finding and understanding the codes, algorithms, and protocols – "embedded, hidden, off-shored and merely forgotten about" (van Dijck 2013: 29) – that shape online sociality and translate bodies into digital information. And there are the practical problems of identifying and gaining access to the "scattered centres of calculation", the "forensic laboratories, statistical institutions, police stations, financial institutions, and corporate and military headquarters" where "the information derived from flows of the surveillant assemblage are reassembled and scrutinized in the hope of developing strategies of governance, commerce and control" (Haggerty and Ericson 2000: 613). But there is still, it seems, at least one gap in the study of postfordist governmentality where Gumperzian interactional sociolinguistics can help start to make some inroads.

Writing from a base in business studies, Kirstie Ball argues that "the *experience of surveillance* has not yet been addressed in any detail ... The fact that individuals sometimes appear to do little to counter surveillance does not mean that surveillance means nothing to them" (2009: 640; emphasis added). She locates this experience in "[t]he moments between the surveillance system's hailing of the subject, and the subject's response" (2009: 645), and elsewhere, she addresses "resistance strategies ... breaking or disrupting [the relations] between watcher and watched" (2005: 93), proposing that arguments about "resistance ... challenge the totalising impulse of surveillance practice [and] are welcome in the face of government and private sector rhetoric about its desirability" (2005: 89). The moment between interpellation and response is of course a space where interactional sociolinguistics offers an especially sensitive lens. And regardless of whether or not they are (macro-)politically valuable, "forms of resistance" and the "antagonism of strategies" are, as we have seen in Section 2c, a productive Foucauldian starting point for the study of power relations, potentially leading from there into analysis of "the system of differentiations", the "forms of institutionalisation", the "degrees of rationalisation" (Foucault 1982: 223) where closer engagement with the software shaping the user interface in digital technologies may or may not become more important as the analysis proceeds.

So in concluding, it is worth looking at the shape that (neo-)Gumperzian investigation of twenty-first-century governmentalities might take.

5.   Empirical projects

To be consistent with the discussion in this chapter, interactional sociolinguistic research on twenty-first-century governmentalities should

(1) situate itself in issues that "trouble contemporary thought and politics" (Gumperz 1982: 29; Rose 1999: 5; Eerdmans et al. 2002: 9)
(2) attend to the microdynamics of interaction in which new technologies play some part, looking ethnographically for moments of friction

(3) watch out for "the emergence of new control strategies and the reconfiguration of old ones" (Rose 1999: 240; Ball 2005: 99–100)

(4) try to involve comparison across time, juxtaposing datasets both before and after the ascendance of mobile digital technologies, to help to avoid overstatements about epochal change, and

(5) develop collaborative interventions that build on Foucault's low-key but practice-focused commitment to helping us "to step back from [a] way of acting or reacting, to present it to oneself as an object of thought and to question it as to its meaning, its conditions, and its goals, . . . reflect[ing] on it as a problem" (1984a/2003: 23). The interventions should also recognise that this kind of critical "[t]hought is not, cannot be, an external evaluation" (Rabinow and Rose 2003: xix; Section 2d, above).

Studies of this kind could be conducted in a range of institutions, but guided by the background of my own work, I will briefly make the case for schools as a good site.

To begin with, schools are places where the traditional discipline intersects with marketised consumption, and it is very widely claimed, for example, that digital technologies have transformed learning in ways that are really difficult for schools to cope with, an issue with which research has yet to come to grips[12] (Sefton-Green and Erstad 2013: 88; Rampton and Harris 2010: 254–257). Power relations at school can also be productively probed with microanalysis. In data from the mid-1990s, I was able to show, for example, that the disciplinary regimes of standard language pedagogy *failed* to generate the 'linguistic insecurity' predicted by sociolinguists who overlook interaction (Rampton 2006: 271–277, 319–320). Rather than producing "discipline, obedience, order-following routine, uniformity and a reduction of options", a number of pupils responded to the standard language curriculum with "initiative, adventurousness, experimentation, self-assertion, emotionality, pleasure and entertainment seeking" (Bauman and Lyon 2013: 57–58; Rampton 2006: chapter 8) – a heteroglossic mix which partly attests to the influence of consumer subjectivities but could also be read as Foucauldian 'games of liberty' (Rampton 2006: 120–123). Updating to 2005–2006 when mobile digital devices had become quite common, Georgakopoulou (2014) has examined the ways in which the subjectivity of teenage girls is affected by their everyday interactional involvement with technopopular media, concluding that these media engagements "serve as major structuring forces in peer-group

---

[12] The editor of the journal *Learning Media and Technology* recently complained that "educational technology and media research [focus] firmly on the *state-of-the-art* rather than the *state-of-the-actual*", and called instead for "in-depth, forensic accounts of . . . the ordinary rather than extra-ordinary aspects of how digital media and technology are being used (and not being used)" (Selwyn 2011: 211–212).

interactions, shaping the individuals' distinct sense of self . . ., their sense of heterosociability, their ethical scenarios about how to display oneself, and their social relations inside and outside school" (p. 241). Practical negotiations of the relationship between media culture and formal education are obviously complex and very varied, and there is a great deal of scope for close comparative analysis of, for example, the experience of different forms of surveillance (the teacher's gaze, CCTV in the corridor, playground gossip, smartphone snapshots) or, alternatively, for comparative accounts of the here-and-now constraints and affordances of different platforms and technologies (MSN, WhatsApp, pens and paper [Varis, forthcoming]). With two datasets of this kind, one pre- and the other postdating the spread of mobile technologies, there would be a potentially workable base for historical comparison, and in fact in an earlier study, we started this task with a broad quantitative survey of pupils' practical engagements with technopopular culture (Rampton et al. 2008: 7–9; Rampton and Harris 2010: 256–257, 261 n. 15). After that, following in the tradition of *Crosstalk* (Section 2c above), recordings and transcripts of interaction in familiar settings can also feed into awareness-raising discussion material for teachers, as in Harris and Lefstein 2011 (viz. pp. 46–64 on new media in class).

At the point where it becomes necessary to investigate directly the hidden codes that shape online conduct and the nonlinguistic semiotics that make populations legible in digital surveillance (Sections 4b and 4c), interactional sociolinguists need to collaborate with computer scientists, but Gumperzian methodology can still make a useful and distinctive contribution to the discussion of issues such as privacy or 'algorithmic regulation',[13] even in its current form. People may be shocked when, for example, they are shown what really happens to their personal details (Mulgan 2014: 18), but the formulation of workable strategies has to engage with the ways in which people actually experience – use, enjoy, and depend on – digital technologies in their everyday practice. In their innovative *Crosstalk* programme (as well as in a good deal of subsequent training material), Gumperz, Jupp, and Roberts sought to facilitate a rethinking that engaged fully with the complex lived relationship between situated actions and their longer term influences and effects, focusing in their case on institutional encounters and race discrimination. But this kind of awareness-raising could also address Ball's 'experience of surveillance', fully mindful that "[t]he notion of resistance, at least as it has conventionally functioned within the analyses of self-proclaimed radicals, is too simple and flattening . . . [Instead,] one [s]hould examine the [much smaller] ways in which creativity arises out of the

---

[13] This is Morozov's term, and it refers to the way in which certain parts of the political process can now be automated due to the advent of Big Data, enabled by the proliferation of cheap sensors and data-storing devices.

situation of human beings engaged in particular relations of force and meaning, and what is made out of the possibilities of that location" (Rose 1999: 279).

Drawing on historical analyses, Foucault saw everyday practices as being central to relations of power, and Gumperz pioneered empirical tools and procedures for understanding these practices in the ethnographically situated here-and-now of their enactment, motivated by a similar commitment to the possibility of their operating differently. Fraser and others argue that although Foucault predates the twenty-first century, rereading and reworking what he wrote will help us better understand the modes of regulation now emerging. The same applies to Gumperz.

REFERENCES

Ahearn, L. 2012. *Living Language: An Introduction to Linguistic Anthropology.* Malden, MA: Wiley-Blackwell.

Arnaut, K. 2012. Super-diversity: Elements of an emerging perspective. *Diversities* 14, 2: 1–16.

Ball, K. 2005. Organisation, surveillance and the body: Towards a politics of resistance. *Organization* 12, 1: 89–108.

2009. Exposure: Exploring the subject of surveillance. *Information, Communication and Society* 12, 5: 639–57.

Ball, S. 2013. *Foucault, Education and Power.* London: Routledge.

Bauman, R., and C. Briggs. 1990. Poetics and performance as critical perspectives on language and social life. *Annual Review of Anthropology* 19: 59–88.

Bauman, Z. 1987. *Legislators and Interpreters.* Cambridge: Polity.

2000. *Liquid Modernity.* Cambridge: Polity.

Bauman, Z., and D. Lyon. 2013. *Liquid Surveillance.* Cambridge: Polity Press.

Bigo, D. 2002. Security and immigration: Toward a critique of the governmentality of unease. *Alternatives* 27: 63–92.

2006. Globalised (in)security: The field and the Ban-opticon. In N. Sakai and J. Solomon (eds.), *Translation, Biopolitics, Colonial Difference.* Hong Kong: Hong Kong University Press.

Blom, J. P., and J. Gumperz. 1972. Social meaning in linguistic structure: Codeswitching in Norway. In J. Gumperz and D. Hymes (eds.), *Directions in Sociolinguistics.* Oxford: Blackwell, 407–434.

Blommaert, J. 2005. *Discourse: A Critical Introduction.* Cambridge: Cambridge University Press.

Blommaert, J., J. Collins, M. Heller, B. Rampton, S. Slembrouck, and J. Verschueren (eds.). 2001. Discourse and Critique. Special issue of *Critique of Anthropology* 21, 1, and 21, 2.

Briggs, C. 2002. Interviewing, power/knowledge, and social inequality. In J. Gubrium and J. Holstein (eds.), *Handbook of Interview Research: Context and Method.* London: Sage, 911–922.

2005. Communicability, racial discourse and disease. *Annual Review of Anthropology* 34: 269–291.

2007. Anthropology, interviewing and communicability in contemporary society. *Current Anthropology* 48, 4: 551–580.

Briggs, C., and D. Hallin. 2007. Biocommunicability: The neoliberal subject and its contradictions in news coverage of health issues. *Social Text* 25, 4: 43–66.

Caluya, G. 2010. The post-panoptic society? Reassessing Foucault in surveillance studies. *Social Identities* 16, 5: 621–633.

Cheney-Lippold, J. 2011. A new algorithmic identity: Soft biopolitics and the modulation of control. *Theory, Culture and Society* 28, 6: 164–181.

Collins, J. 2003. Language, identity, and learning in the era of 'expert-guided' systems. In S. Wortham and B. Rymes (eds.), *Linguistic Anthropology of Education*. Westport, CT: Praeger, 31–60.

de Certeau, M. 1984. *The Practice of Everyday Life*. Berkeley: University of California Press.

Deleuze, G. 1992. Postscript on the societies of control. *October* 59: 3–7.

Dreyfus, H., and P. Rabinow. 1982. *Michel Foucault: Beyond Structuralism and Hermaneutics*. New York: Harvester Wheatsheaf.

Duranti, A. 2003. Language as culture in US anthropology. *Current Anthropology* 44: 323–347.

Eerdmans, S., C. Prevignano, and P. Thibault. 2002. *Language and Interaction: Discussions with John J. Gumperz*. Amsterdam: John Benjamins.

Eisenlauer, V. 2014. Facebook as a third author: (Semi-)automated participation framework in social network sites. *Journal of Pragmatics*. Available at http://dx.doi.org/10.1016/j.pragma.2014.02.006.

Eyal, N. 2014. *Hooked: How to Build Habit-Forming Products*. Available at www.hookmodel.com.

Fairclough, N. 1989. *Language and Power*. London: Longman.

1992. *Discourse and Social Change*. Cambridge: Polity.

Foucault, M. 1974. *The Archaeology of Knowledge*. London: Tavistock.

1974/1994. Prisons et asiles dans le mécanisme du pouvoir. In *Dits et Ecrits,* vol. 11. Paris: Gallimard. Quotation at www.michel-foucault.com/quote/2004q.html.

1977. *Discipline and Punish*. Harmondsworth: Penguin.

1978. *The Will to Knowledge: The History of Sexuality I*. London: Penguin Books.

1978/2003. Governmentality. In P. Rabinow and N. Rose (eds.), *The Essential Foucault: Selections from Essential Works of Foucault 1954–1984*. New York: The New Press, 229–245.

1980. *Power/Knowledge*. New York: Harvester Wheatsheaf.

1980/2003. Questions of method. In P. Rabinow and N. Rose (eds.), *The Essential Foucault: Selections from Essential Works of Foucault 1954–1984*. New York: The New Press, 246–258.

1982. The subject and power. In H. Dreyfus and P. Rabinow, *Michel Foucault: Beyond Structuralism and Hermaneutics*. New York: Harvester Wheatsheaf, 208–226.

1984a/2003. Polemics, politics and problematisations: An interview with Michel Foucault. In P. Rabinow and N. Rose (eds.), *The Essential Foucault: Selections from Essential Works of Foucault 1954–1984*. New York: The New Press, 18–24.

1984b/2003. The ethics of concern of the self as a practice of freedom. In P. Rabinow and N. Rose (eds.), *The Essential Foucault: Selections from Essential Works of Foucault 1954–1984*. New York: The New Press, 25–42.

2003. What is enlightenment? In P. Rabinow and N. Rose (eds.), *The Essential Foucault: Selections from Essential Works of Foucault 1954–1984*. New York: The New Press, 43–57.

Fraser, N. 2003. From discipline to flexibilisation? Rereading Foucault in the shadow of globalisation. *Constellations* 10, 2: 160–171.

Gee, J. 1999. *An Introduction to Discourse Analysis: Theory and Method*. London: Routledge.

Georgakopoulou, A. 2014. Girlpower or girl (in) trouble? Identities and discourses in the (new) media engagements of adolescents' school-based in interaction. In J. Androutsopoulos (ed.), *Mediatization and Sociolinguistic Change*. Berlin: De Gruyter, 217–244.

Goffman, E. 1963. *Behaviour in Public Places*. New York: Free Press.

1981. *Forms of Talk*. Philadelphia: Pennsylvania University Press.

Goodwin, C. 1994. Professional vision. *American Anthropologist* 96, 3: 606–633.

Goodwin, C., and A. Duranti. 1992. Rethinking context: An introduction. In A. Duranti and C. Goodwin (eds.), *Rethinking Context*. Cambridge: Cambridge University Press, 1–42.

Gumperz, J. 1982. *Discourse Strategies*. Cambridge: Cambridge University Press.

1986. Interactional sociolinguistics and the study of schooling. In J. Cook-Gumperz (ed.), *The Social Construction of Literacy*. Cambridge: Cambridge University Press.

1990. Interview with John Gumperz. In J. Twitchin, *Crosstalk: An Introduction to Cross-Cultural Communication*. London: BBC, 46–55.

1999. On interactional sociolinguistic method. In S. Sarangi and C. Roberts (eds.), *Talk, Work and Institutional Order*. Berlin: Mouton, 453–471.

Gumperz, J. 2002.

Gumperz, J., and J. Cook-Gumperz. 1982. Introduction: Language and the communication of social identity. In J. Gumperz (ed.), *Language and Social Identity*. Cambridge: Cambridge University Press, 1–21.

Gumperz, J., and Hernández-Chavez. 1972. Bilingualism, bidialectalism, and classroom interaction. In C. Cazden, V. John, and D. Hymes (eds.), *Functions of Language in the Classroom*. New York: Teachers College Press, 84–110.

Gumperz, J, T. Jupp, and C. Roberts. 1979. *Crosstalk*. Southall, UK: BBC/National Centre for Industrial Language Training.

Haggerty, K., and R. Ericson. 2000. The surveillant assemblage. *British Journal of Sociology* 51, 4: 605–622.

Hanks, W. 1996. *Language and Communicative Practices*. Boulder, CO: Westview Press.

Harris, R., and A. Lefstein. 2011. *Urban Classroom Culture: Realities, Dilemmas, Responses*. London: Centre for Language Discourse and Communication, King's College London. Available at www.kcl.ac.uk/sspp/departments/education/research/ucc/ucculture.aspx.

Harris, R., and B. Rampton (eds.). 2003. *The Language, Ethnicity and Race Reader*. London: Routledge.

Heller, M. 1999. *Linguistic Minorities and Modernity: A Sociolinguistic Ethnography*. London: Longman.

Huysmans, J. 2014. *Security Unbound*. London: Routledge.

Jupp, T, C. Roberts, and J. Cook Gumperz. 1982. Language and disadvantage: The hidden process. In J. Gumperz (ed.), *Language and Social Identity*. Cambridge: Cambridge University Press, 232–256.

Khan, K. 2014. Citizenship, securitization and suspicion in UK ESOL policy. *Working Papers in Urban Language and Literacies* 130. Available at www.kcl.ac.uk/ldc.

Kroskrity, P. 2004. Language ideologies. In A. Duranti (ed.), *A Companion to Linguistic Anthropology*. Oxford: Blackwell, 496–517.

Larsen, J., J. Urry, and K. Axhausen. 2008. Coordinating face-to-face meetings in mobile network societies. *Information, Communication and Society* 11, 5: 640–658.

Lemke, T. 2000. Foucault, governmentality and critique. Available at www.andosciasociology.net/resources/Foucault$2C%2BGovernmentality$2C%2Band%2BCritique%2BIV-2.pdf.

2003. Comment on Nancy Fraser: Rereading Foucault in the shadow of globalisation. *Constellations* 10, 2: 172–179.

Levinson, S. 1983. *Pragmatics*. Cambridge: Cambridge University Press.

Mehan, H. 1996. The construction of an LD student: A case study in the politics of representation. In Michael Silverstein and Greg Urban (eds.), *Natural Histories of Discourse*: Chicago, IL: University of Chicago Press, 253–276.

Morozov, E. 2014. The rise of data and the death of politics. *Observer*, July 20. Available at www.theguardian.com/technology/2014/jul/20/rise-of-data-death-of-politics-evgeny-morozov-algorithmic-regulation.

Mulgan, G. 2014. Is people-powered data possible? The future of citizen control. *Understanding Society* July: 17–18. London: Ipsos-MORI Social Research Institute.

Parkin, D. 2012. From multilingual classification to translingual ontology: Concluding commentary. *Diversities* 14, 2. Available at www.unesco.org/shs/diversities/vol14/issue2/art5.

Pennycook, A. 1994. *The Cultural Politics of English as an International Language*. London: Longman.

Prevignano, C., and A. di Luzio. 2002. A discussion with John Gumperz. In S. Eerdmans, C. Prevignano, and P. Thibault (eds.), *Language and Interaction: Discussions with John J. Gumperz*. Amsterdam: John Benjamins, 7–30.

Rabinow, P., and N. Rose. 2003. Introduction: Foucault today. In In P. Rabinow and N. Rose (eds.), *The Essential Foucault: Selections from Essential Works of Foucault 1954–1984*. New York: The New Press, vii–xxxv.

Rampton, B. 2001. Critique in interaction. *Critique of Anthropology* 21, 1: 83–107.

2009. Interaction ritual and not just artful performance in crossing and stylisation. *Language in Society* 38, 2: 149–176.

2006. *Language in Late Modernity: Interaction in an Urban School*. Cambridge: Cambridge University Press.

Rampton, B., and R. Harris. 2010. Change in urban classroom culture and interaction. In K. Littlejohn and C. Howe (eds.), *Educational Dialogues*. London: Routledge, 240–264.

Rampton, B., R. Harris, A. Georgakopoulou, C. Leung, L. Small, and C. Dover. 2008. Urban classroom culture and interaction: End-of-project report. *Working Papers in Urban Language and Literacies* 53.

Roberts, C., E. Davies, and T. Jupp. 1992. *Language and Discrimination*. London: Longman.

Rose, N. 1996. The death of the social? Re-figuring the territory of government. *Economy and Society* 25, 3: 327–356.

   1999. *The Power of Freedom*. Cambridge: Cambridge University Press.

Schegloff, E. 2002. Beginnings in the telephone. In J. Katz and M. Aakhus (eds.), *Perpetual Contact*. Cambridge and New York: Cambridge University Press, 284–300.

Scollon, R. 1998. *Mediated Discourse as Social Interaction: A Study of News Discourse*. London: Longman.

Scott, J. 1998. *Seeing like a State*. New Haven, CT: Yale University Press.

Sefton-Green, J., and O. Erstad. 2013. Digital disconnect? The 'digital learner' and the school. In O. Erstad and J. Sefton-Green (eds.), *Identity, Community and Learning Lives in the Digital Age*. Cambridge: Cambridge University Press.

Selwyn, N. 2011. Technology, media and education: Telling the whole story. *Editorial in Learning, Media and Technology* 36, 3: 211–213.

Silverstein, M. 1985. Language and the culture of gender. In E. Mertz and R. Parmentier (eds.), *Semiotic Mediation*. New York: Academic Press, 219–259.

Silverstein, M., and G. Urban (eds.). 1996. *Natural Histories of Discourse*. Chicago, IL: University of Chicago Press.

Urry, J. 2000. *Sociology beyond Societies: Mobilities for the 21st Century* London: Routledge.

Urry, J. 2003. *Global Complexity*. Cambridge: Polity.

van Dijck, J. 2013. *The Culture of Connectivity*. Oxford: Oxford University Press.

Varenne, H., and R. McDermott. 1998. *Successful Failure*. Boulder, CO: Westview Press.

Varis, P. Forthcoming. Digital ethnography. In A. Georgakopoulou and T. Spilioti (eds.), *Routledge Handbook of Language and Digital Communication*. London: Routledge.

Wellman, B. 2001. Physical place and cyberspace: The rise of personalised networking. *International Journal of Urban and Regional Research* 25, 2: 227–252.

Part V

Sociolinguistics, contexts and impact

15   Are there zombies in language policy?
Theoretical interventions and the continued
vitality of (apparently) defunct concepts

Lionel Wee

Introduction

The conditions of late modernity have led to calls for the reevaluation of the
theoretical value of concepts generally developed in connection with modernist perspectives on language and society. Beck (Slater and Ritzer 2001: 262)
describes as 'zombie categories' those concepts that are of questionable
relevance:

I think we are living in a society, in a world, where our basic sociological concepts are
becoming what I call 'zombie categories'. Zombie categories are 'living dead' categories which govern our thinking but are not really able to capture the contemporary
milieu. In this situation I don't think it's very helpful only to criticize normal sociology,
and to deconstruct it. What we really need is to redefine, reconstruct, restructure our
concepts and our view of society.

The most influential zombie categories for Beck are those connected with nationalism, such as the nation-state and the national language (Škabraha 2005; Beck
2011), and he sees a need to move away from categories that are 'nation-state
centred' to those that are more 'non-nation-state centred' (Slater and Ritzer 2001:
262–263). In a somewhat similar vein, Heller (2008: 513) points out that even
though 'nation-states have scarcely disappeared as relevant actors and constraints
on action ... [i]t is increasingly difficult for them to impose fictive (linguistic,
cultural) homogeneity within their boundaries', and she calls for a 'critical
ethnographic sociolinguistics' (2011) that understands the various processes by
which language, community and identity, among other concepts, come to constructed as 'regimes of truth' (Heller 2011: 6, citing Foucault 1984).

It is important to note, however, that zombies may also be found beyond the
nation-state (Beck 2002: 24). This is worth bearing in mind because the nation-
state is by no means the only domain where language policy operates. As
Spolsky (2009) points out, a number of other domains also come within the
purview of language policy, such as the family, religion, the workplace, the
military, the media, schools, and various international organizations, including
NGOs. The expansion of the scope of language policy involves more than just

the inclusion of other domains, however. The very idea of what we might mean by language policy has to also be understood in much more inclusive terms than it used to be. This is because there is greater awareness amongst language policy scholars of the fact that language policies are inevitably formulated under the influence of particular ideological assumptions about identity, culture, community, and, of course, language – however implicit these may be. Even in cases where no explicit language policy is being formulated, ideology still 'operates as "default" policy' (Lo Bianco 2004: 750).

The pervasive influence of ideologies was not always appreciated, though. Particularly in the 1960s and 1970s, scholars tended to adopt a highly technocratic approach to language policy, where the goal was to deal with language 'problems', especially those faced by newly independent nation-states, by identifying rational 'solutions'. As Blommaert (1996: 202) observes, there was 'an abnormalization of the Other' so that recently decolonized Third World states or emergent states such as Israel were seen to be in particular need of language problem-solving, whereas patterns of language distribution in Western countries were considered 'normal' and 'stable'. Even when language policy turned its attention to Europe in the later 1970s, and attention focused on the national minorities in European countries, such as the Basques, the Bretons, and the Welsh, 'the abnormalization was continued, even exacerbated ... multilingualism is a problem, not because it would be an unworkable situation for administrative and educational practice, but because it is politically denied' (Blommaert 1996: 203). Thus, 'successful language planning, or degrees of it, was understood in terms of the efficacy of planned policy measures as well as the target populations' propensity to comply with the public policies pertaining to language planning' (Das Gupta and Ferguson 1977: 6). The field of language policy then consisted mainly of investigations into the processes of language selection, codification, and elaboration and how these might be best implemented (Haugen 1966).

However, as reflections over the limitations of a technocratic approach to language policy gained momentum (Luke et al. 1990; Tollefson 1991), scholarly concerns started to widen, going beyond the nation-state and a narrow understanding of language to how communicative practices in general might be ideologically constrained. Concomitantly, the identification of a language problem is no longer taken at face value, since definitions of what counts as a problem often reflect vested interests. Instead, a critical orientation is nowadays much more in evidence. As Lo Bianco (2004: 739) observes, the early aspiration to be a 'science of the field':

... has had to be discarded as all the human sciences acknowledge, if not enjoy, the philosophical logic of postmodernity with its insistence on the impossibility of interest-free knowledge. Research conducted to sustain policy development is organically invested with dilemmas about how knowledge designed for action, for application, in contexts of contending interests and ideologies, is implicated in these processes and cannot in any absolute sense rise above interests and ideology.

Language policy scholars are now more prepared to engage with the ideological underpinnings affecting the interconnections between linguistic and nonlinguistic elements, such as ethnicity, gender, age, and religious beliefs (Spolsky 2004: 39ff.). Perhaps most significantly, the appreciation of ideological influences means that language policy no longer treats debates over what is meant by 'language' as irrelevant, given that such ontological issues are themselves ideologically informed, and whatever understandings of language that are arrived at will inevitably go on to shape the communicative practices and thus the language policies of the associated domains.

The more inclusive nature of contemporary language policy studies means that the range of potential zombies in language policy has to be understood as being commensurately broad rather than being restricted to the nation-state. This range can include any kind of social context where ideologies have led to the naturalization and entrenchment of certain communicative practices at the expense of critically engaging with other possibilities (see examples below).

Debating modes of intervention

The impetus for talking about zombies comes from the fact that societies, as a result of rapid social and technological developments, are becoming detraditionalized. Where language policy is concerned, this means raising questions about whether traditional assumptions concerning the relationship between linguistic and nonlinguistic elements are still sustainable.

Here are two examples to show that such traditional assumptions are not easily dislodged. The first is from the domain of religion, and concerns the relationship between gender and language. Ong (2006: 42–43) describes the struggles faced by the Sisters of Islam, a Malaysian feminist group, as they attempt to gain legitimacy for 'women's intellectual and moral capacity to interpret Islam for themselves' rather than having to rely on the interpretations provided by traditionally male Islamic scholars, known as *ulamas*.

The second, from the domain of the workplace, concerns the relationship between ethnicity and language. Park (2013) discusses 'diversity management' in a multinational corporation, where he shows how even the embrace of cultural and ethnic diversity can become a social mechanism of control. Koreans, for example, were characterized as having English that was good enough for routine tasks but 'inadequate for more serious and fast-paced discussions and debates in strategic meetings' (Park 2013: 8–9). Thus,

... diversity management attributes any inequality that is experienced by such groups to their cultural essence – such as Koreans' "reluctance" to speak out their views – rather than to social conditions. It thus becomes the responsibility of the group members to overcome such essential characteristics – even though they are simultaneously trapped within those characteristics by the very discourses that define them as essential to the group. *This also explains why older discourses of identity that reify national difference do not disappear in the age of commodification of language and identity*; they serve as important resources for explaining, rationalizing, and reframing issues of inequality as something innocent, something that can be transformed into a justification for the dominant social order of the workplace. (Park 2013: 17, emphasis added)

The older/traditional discourses identified by Ong (2006) and Park (2013) show how deeply established and widespread ideological assumptions involving language can be, which raises the issue of social intervention.

At this point, it is also worth keeping in mind that Beck's own invocation of zombies does not actually focus on the issue of intervention. For Beck, concepts are outmoded because 'normal sociology' is unable to 'capture the contemporary milieu' (see above). Beck, then, is primarily concerned with how scholarly discourses are best able to adequately describe current social conditions. But once the issue of intervention is raised, we then have to focus on questions such as 'Why are the traditional assumptions involving language so persistent?', 'How can the shift away from these assumptions be instituted?', and 'What kinds of resistance might any such attempted shifts face?'

The field of language policy does have a history of being interventionist, though awareness of the critical influence of ideologies has caused language policy scholars to be particularly appreciative of the difficulties involved once the question of intervention is raised (Wee 2011a: 21). These difficulties arise for a number of reasons. One, given the ideological nature of language policy, scholars have to be up-front about the fact that any intervention on their part, however objectively intended, inevitably involves them taking a position on highly political issues (Blommaert 1999: 437):

Taking sides is unavoidable: it comes along with doing a particular type of questioning of linguistic reality. An attempt at providing a history of language, which takes into account social and political factors, forces us to voice interpretations of these factors. And in social and political reality, interpretations are partisan, and they almost automatically align the one who formulated the interpretation with one or another political bloc. So be it.

What this means, as I point out elsewhere (Wee 2011a: 15), is that linguists involved in language policy cannot be blind to class interests or political factionalism. Rather, it means being aware that, by acting as expert consultants to groups, communities, institutions, or states, linguists have to be clear about and comfortable with the goals of the clients, or even engage the clients in critical discussions about the viability and appropriateness of the goals.

Two, there is the issue of the realistic and feasible translation of theoretical concepts into practical implementation,[1] given that relevant stakeholders in language policy (families, communities, organizations, and nation-states, among many others) operate under highly differentiated constraints of time, economic resources, and investments in the status quo. Three, theories can change – as Beck's invocation of 'zombie categories' itself exemplifies – and while theorists can afford to shift their theoretical inclinations at relatively small cost to themselves, changing infrastructural and other investments according to the dictates of what is theoretically 'in' versus what is 'out' is a much more difficult affair, not least because the lives of individuals and communities may be drastically affected to varying degrees.

Four, these already tricky issues arguably become even trickier in the specific case of language policy. This is because there may well be language managers (Spolsky 2009) who not only are authorized but might even be obligated to act by introducing specific language policies – despite imperfect or contentious theoretical knowledge, or in the face of less than ideal practical conditions. Given all these considerations, we need to exercise caution when dealing with the interface between theory and social intervention. The factors that become significant when we move from theoretical debates per se to debates about how or whether to intervene are qualitatively different, since we now also need to take into account debates about what would be appropriate modes of intervention.

Therefore, while I am all for innovations in sociolinguistic theorizing, I want in this chapter to argue for a somewhat more cautious position once we move into talking about social intervention. Returning to Beck's metaphor, I want to suggest that what may appear to be zombies from a primarily theoretical perspective are in fact still very much alive and kicking when we bring in social intervention. This is not to deny that certain traditional ideas about language ought to be challenged and, if possible, rendered defunct. But it is important to be sensitive to the possibility of opposition and resistance, especially if traditional ideas are still vital because individuals and communities have stakes in them. Dismissing these ideas as zombies when the discourse is amongst scholars is one thing, since this is in the nature of

---

[1] I do not think that there is such a thing as 'impracticable theory', that is, theory that is inherently impractical either because it is simply unworkable or because it meets with predictable and sustained opposition. Given the appropriate social conditions, just about any theory, however initially farfetched, might find acceptance and translation into practice. This is a position that is consistent with the notion of the double hermeneutic (below), which highlights that humans are in principle capable of modifying their behavior in the light of theoretical findings. The issue has to do with developing the social conditions that would be conducive to putting into practice whatever theory one happens to be promulgating, and this requires appreciating the kinds of resistance that might currently be in place and that therefore might need to be dislodged. I thank Nik Coupland for raising this point.

academic theorizing and debate. Dismissing these as zombies when the focus is on social intervention is very much another, since this would bring us dangerously close to scholarly vanguardism, a point I return to at the end of this chapter.

I organize the remainder of this chapter into two parts. I first consider a number of examples (strategic and nonstrategic essentialism, linguistic rights and linguistic citizenship, fixed and fluid multilingualism) to demonstrate how social intervention complicates theoretical debates in different ways. I then identify some general considerations (academics as gatekeepers, the double hermeneutic) that transcend specific theoretical controversies and that might help us move forward as we consider the nexus between theory and intervention.[2]

Essentialism: strategic and nonstrategic

If we have to list one concept that is widely accepted in academic circles as lacking theoretical plausibility, it would probably be essentialism. But though essentialism may be widely criticized in sociolinguistics (and, more broadly, in the humanities and social sciences), it continues to prove extremely difficult to displace among the various stakeholders involved in language policy.

An enduring example concerns the status of the native speaker, which remains influential especially in language education, despite important critiques (Rampton 1990; Davies 2003). For parents who want assurances that their children are learning the language properly, for education policymakers who want to be able to assure parents that the teachers are indeed knowledgeable about the language they teach, the assumption that there is an essential link between racial identity and language competence provides a convenient fiction where physically identifiable characteristics become icons (Gal and Irvine 1995; see also Gal, this volume, Chapter 5) of the less tangible language competence.

It is also important to note the directionality of the iconization process: The physically and thus more readily identifiable feature is the proxy for the less easily ascertainable, rather than the other way round. This observation holds even when language itself becomes an icon, as when a Southern (U.S.) drawl (where the otherwise short vowels in words like *pet and pit* are followed by a glide and, in some cases, a schwa as well) is seen to

---

[2] I use the phrase 'nexus between theory and intervention' as a rhetorical reminder of the fact that bringing in the issue of intervention complicates otherwise primarily theoretical discussions. I am by no means suggesting that modes of intervention are themselves devoid of theoretical considerations.

signify laziness (Kuipers 1998: 18). Relative to an attribute such as laziness, manifestations of language practices in speech or writing are more readily identifiable. This directionality is significant. Essentialism is difficult to displace precisely because there is a need for assurance or stability in how we navigate the social world, and the more complex the world becomes, the greater this need. Essentialism – in spite of or perhaps because of its discriminatory nature – provides for the user an uncomplicated if simple-minded guide as to the nature of the social world: How it is (or appears to be) and how it ought to be (or not to be).

One relevant sociolinguistic debate raised by essentialism is whether there are circumstances where it might be acceptable or defensible. Some scholars (McElhinny 1996; Bucholtz 2003) appear to consider essentialism acceptable if it is strategic. In strategic essentialism, the user does not actually subscribe to the essentialist assumptions but only acts as though he or she does in order to achieve particular social objectives. Unfortunately, the distinction between strategic and nonstrategic essentialism, while theoretically valid, becomes neutralized once we move into the realm of actual social intervention. For example, consider that Solomon Bandaranaike, who headed the 1956 Sri Lankan government, had a strategic essentialist orientation towards his own championing of Sinhala (Wee 2011b: 35). But his later attempts to moderate his own earlier extremist position resulted in protests from 'other Sinhalese demagogues with political ambitions of their own . . .' (Sowell 2004: 86) and even, ultimately, his assassination. Thus, even if a political leader adopts a stance of strategic essentialism, he or she is often able to convince other stakeholders to follow only because, for them, the essentialism is all too real or nonstrategic.

Since effective language policy requires the collaboration or 'buy in' from groups of people, many of whom may have different reasons for being willing to collaborate, the theoretical distinction between strategic and nonstrategic essentialism becomes difficult to sustain in actual practice.

Linguistic human rights and linguistic citizenship

The problem of essentialism is exacerbated in the context of a rights discourse (Wee 2011b), and this brings up the particularly controversial question of whether it is appropriate or even coherent to talk about linguistic human rights (Phillipson and Skutnabb-Kangas 1995: 483), because these assume 'an almost ineluctable connection between language and (ethnic) identity' (May 2005: 327).

Linguistic human rights are intended to protect ethnic minority languages, so that ethnic minorities can 'reproduce themselves as distinct groups, with their own languages and cultures' (Skutnabb-Kangas 2000:

498). The notion of linguistic human rights therefore relies on particularly strong essentialist assumptions. It aims to preserve the historically contingent boundaries that define groups rather than treating these boundaries as social inventions whose naturalness may need to be critiqued. Thus, it tries to lock in constellations of socio-cultural-political features that are becoming increasingly delinked in a rapidly globalizing world of migration, mobility, and advances in communication and transportation technologies.

The point to note is that a critique of linguistic human rights does not entail a dismissal of boundaries as unimportant or irrelevant. Instead, it calls for a more reflexive approach to the social construction of boundaries, how these have come about, and what interests their preservation might serve. Even Beck (Slater and Ritzer 2001: 266) acknowledges this when he remarks that boundaries will still be need to drawn even if they are 'fictive'. In this regard, a more sophisticated alternative to linguistic human rights is linguistic citizenship (Stroud 2001; 2009), which refers to 'the situation where speakers themselves exercise control over their language, deciding *what* languages are, and what they may *mean*, and where language issues ... are discursively tied to a range of social issues – policy issues and questions of equity' (Stroud 2001: 353, emphasis in original).

The sophistication of linguistic citizenship arises from its clear recognition that the meanings attributed by speakers to their languages change over time. As Stroud (2009) explains:

A notion of linguistic citizenship is thus attuned to the implications of a multitude of identities, subject positions, and positions of interest that suggest reframing semiotic practices of citizenship away from a totalizing sense of language and toward such notions as *fracturedness*, *hybridity*, *partiality*, and *perspective*. Rather than the idea of language, central to linguistic citizenship are the notions of genre and multilingual repertoires. (p. 209, emphasis in original)

While more coherent as a scholarly concept and certainly more in tune with late modernist approaches, the nonessentialist stance of linguistic citizenship does not, however, easily lend itself to rallying cries or to conceptual sound bites that policymakers can quickly grasp and then convey to other stakeholders. This makes linguistic citizenship a more complex and less straightforward conceptual tool for influencing language policy. As already noted, uptake from policymakers and their constituents is critical if any language policy to succeed. This is perhaps one reason why linguistic citizenship has not captured the hearts of activists or policymakers as prominently as linguistic human rights. The latter has the advantage of combining the moralistic overtones associated with a rights discourse with essentialist assumptions.

Fixed and flexible multilingualism

The distinction between fixed and flexible multilingualism (Blackledge and Creese 2010; Weber and Horner 2012: 108) has been gathering momentum in sociolinguistic debates. Fixed multilingualism assumes that different languages ought to be kept separate and 'pure' (Heller 1999). Flexible multilingualism, in contrast, treats the boundaries between languages as relatively porous.

As I have discussed elsewhere (Wee 2015), insofar as organizations are at all concerned with multilingualism, they tend to construe it in fixed rather than flexible terms. This is because organizations are in the main social actors whose continued legitimacy often depends on them conforming to various regulatory requirements and institutional myths. In the case of language, one powerfully pervasive myth is that languages are stable and discrete and need to be kept separate. Any attempt by organizations to challenge or renounce this way of understanding language has to confront the question of why they are embracing a view of language that (as yet) lacks institutional hegemonic force, such as that associated with flexible multilingualism. Nevertheless, this organizational tendency towards fixed multilingualism is often presented as being in conflict with the 'fluid multilingual realities of today's world' (Weber and Horner 2012: 117), a fluidity that scholars have variously characterized as translingualism (Canagarajah 2013), translanguaging (García 2009), poly-languaging (Jørgensen 2008), and metrolingualism (Otsuji and Pennycook 2010; see also Pennycook, this volume, Chapter 9).

There is a perceived tension, then, between the flexible multilingualism that speakers are characterized as being engaged in, on the one hand, and the fixed multilingualism that organizations are associated with, on the other (Otsuji and Pennycook 2010: 24)). The flexible multilingualism of speakers tends to be construed as being negatively constrained by the fixed multilingualism of organizations (García 2009; see also Weber and Horner 2012: 115).

In the case of language education policy, however, we need to ask how students can be best prepared for a multilingual reality that also includes organizations, since it is an inescapable fact that many graduates will end up working for organizations – which are entities that tend to prefer fixed rather than flexible multilingualism. Students need to be prepared for institutional realities where the mixing of resources associated with distinct language systems is frowned upon and even penalized. One possibility might be to highlight to students the relationship between these two types of multilingualism as a topic for critical discussion, as an issue that does not allow for any easy resolution but one of which the students nevertheless need to be aware as they prepare to enter the workplace. This would require getting students to examine their own ideological assumptions about language.

There are already acknowledgements that fixed multilingualism may have a place in education (Weber and Horner 2012: 132) and cautions against the blind celebration of flexible multilingualism (Otsuji and Pennycook 2010: 243). But we need to go beyond a grudging tolerance of fixed multilingualism. Rather than seeing the relationship between fixed and flexible multilingualism as antagonistic, it is more important to explore pedagogically meaningful ways of connecting them.

General considerations

We have seen that different theoretical controversies face different problems when the issue of social intervention is raised. The distinction between strategic and nonstrategic essentialism becomes harder to sustain when we look at actual policy implementation. In the case of linguistic human rights and linguistic citizenship, there appears to be a trade-off between scholarly sophistication and the ability to find broad public appeal. With the different kinds of multilingualism, there is a need, particularly in the context of education, to find ways of getting students to critically explore how the flexible language practices of individuals can coexist with the fixity preferred by organizations.

It would be premature in all these cases to write off or dismiss as zombies the more conservative positions. Such examples could quite easily be multiplied, so that, as we move to look at other theoretical debates, these may yet throw up further intervention-related problems that would be specific to the notions under consideration.

What I want to do next, therefore, and what I think is more fruitful, is to consider from a more general perspective some of the factors that cut across the specificities of particular theoretical debates and their relationships to social intervention. A consideration of these factors would provide us with a sense of what sociolinguists and applied linguists need to keep in mind when we move from primarily theoretical considerations to matters of intervention.

Academics as gatekeepers

One immediate consideration is that those sociolinguists and applied linguists who are in a position to do so should contribute to changing language policy in ways that are informed by their own theoretical commitments. This can take a variety of forms. Consider what is often described as the parallel language ideology, where in 2006, the Nordic ministers for education and culture collectively issued a declaration on the importance of reinforcing the status of local European languages vis-à-vis the growing use of English (Bolton and Kuteeva 2012: 430).

However, there remain a number of questions about how the parallel language ideology ought to be implemented in practice, since the conception of the ideology may have been motivated by administrative considerations rather than a proper appreciation of the constraints and limitations that inevitably come into play when the considerations have to do with actual learning, teaching, and disciplinary expectations instead (Airey 2009).

Thus, in Sweden, the Swedish Language Council (1998: 16, quoted in Kuteeva 2011: 6) has mandated that 'encouragement should be given to educational development work aimed at enhancing students' ability to use Swedish and English in parallel in their subjects'. But given the uncertainty surrounding how this ideology ought to be operationalized, there is a great deal of on-the-ground improvisation and variation. Some departments in Stockholm University apparently allow their students to decide whether they want to write their projects in English or Swedish. The default appears to be that the teachers decide on the language to be used, and also if the course is taught in Swedish, the exam will mostly likely be in Swedish (and vice versa). There are instances, however, when students are allowed to choose for themselves. A student from the United Kingdom, for example, was allowed to submit her final assignment in English although the Master's course was mainly in Swedish and all the other students wrote their assignments in Swedish.[3]

There are also important disciplinary differences that need to be borne in mind. In their study of Stockholm University, Bolton and Kuteeva (2012: 10–11) emphasize that:

[c]ontent-based lectures are very common in the Science faculty, and the difference in terms of content transmitted through a lecture in English or Swedish is small . . . Thus, it appears that transmitting knowledge in English may not present as many challenges as constructing knowledge through discussion in English, a core pedagogical method for the Humanities and Social Sciences.

Bolton and Kuteeva (2012: 438–439) quote one academic from the Department of Biochemistry and Biophysics as saying, 'It would be stupid trying to reduce the dominance of English, since very few of our collaborators would understand a word of Swedish'. In contrast, another academic, this time from the Department of Social Anthropology, finds that '[t]eaching, especially lecturing, in English when it is not your native language usually makes for less lively and engaging lessons, which is pedagogically detrimental'. The full implications of parallel language use therefore remain unclear.

In this case, linguists are in a position not only to contribute descriptions as to how the concept is being implemented, but also, on the basis of these

---

[3] My thanks to Tove Larsson (personal communication) for these observations.

descriptions, to make recommendations about issues arising from educational difficulties (for educators as well as students), fairness in evaluations, and whether the ideology is actually contributing in any meaningful way towards the broader goal of sustaining Swedish in response to perceived competition from English. Given that some linguists might be involved in the language policies of their own universities, attempts to help clarify and, where necessary, challenge the ideological bases on which policies such as the concept of parallel language use are formulated and how they might be implemented would be useful.

Another example comes from Canagarajah (2010), who observes that 'it appears as if World Englishes scholars feel increasingly under pressure to practice what they preach', that is, to provide spaces in academic contexts for the use of otherwise stigmatized varieties of English. Canagarajah describes an edited collection, *English as a Lingua Franca* (Mauranen and Ranta 2009), and quotes one of the editors, Mauranen, who explained the editorial decision as follows:

Some of the papers in this book have been written by native speakers of English, others not, but all have been written by expert users of English. No policy of having the L2 [second language] authors' texts checked by native speakers for linguistic correctness has been applied, because this was regarded as an irrelevant practice in a book presenting international scholarship.

Canagarajah himself suggests that 'whether to use nativized English or not is a rhetorical decision' and that the author has to 'take into consideration the dominant discourse and readership of the journal to choose the extent to which he/she can introduce variant language and discourse'. This is admittedly not an easy enterprise given various institutional constraints (e.g. publishers may insist on standard varieties to ensure that contents are accessible to the widest possible readership; authors may prefer not to use stigmatized varieties in their own works in order to maintain a sense of prestige).

These are examples of language policy at work where linguists can have some immediate impact, albeit in admittedly relatively restricted academic domains. Any possibility of strong resistance might be mitigated by the fact that academics are dealing with fellow academics.

For a wider kind of impact, however, we have to take a longer and less certain view of things. This is where the double hermeneutic comes in.

The double hermeneutic

The double hermeneutic (Giddens 1987) refers to the fact that there is a two-way relationship between lay/everyday concepts and social scientific ones. Unlike the natural sciences where the objects and phenomena studied by scientists (e.g. chemical processes) lack awareness, those studied by social scientists (i.e. people, society) not only are capable of appreciating social scientific concepts such as 'citizen' and 'sovereignty' (Giddens 1987: 20), but also are able to use these themselves in ways that inform their own behaviors and values. As Giddens (1987: 18–19) puts it:

... the subjects of study in the social sciences and the humanities are concept-using beings, whose concepts of their actions enter in a constitutive manner into what those actions are ... [U]nlike in the natural sciences, in the social sciences, there is no way of keeping the conceptual apparatus of the observer – whether in sociology, political science or economic – free from appropriation by lay actors.

An example of the double hermeneutic at work in language policy can be found in the case of Singapore, when Lee Kuan Yew, the country's first prime minister, was concerned about gross differences in economic development across the various ethnic groups:

One of the problems which has worried me is the uneven rate of development within the community, because the Chinese, Indians, Ceylonese and Eurasians progress at a faster rate than our Malays. If we do not correct this imbalance, then, in another 10 to 20 years, we will have a Harlem, something not to be proud of. So from politics I have had to go to anthropology and sociology to seek the reason for this. (Speech to Southeast Asia Business Committee, May 12, 1968; cited in Han et al. 1998: 181)

Lee consulted the works of sociologist Judith Djamour and cultural anthropologist Bryan Parkinson, both of whom emphasized differences in cultural values between the Malays and the Chinese, and came to the conclusion that the most feasible policy was one where ethnic enclaves were eliminated and the different ethnicities encouraged to interact. This led to the recognition of English as an official language that would serve as the interethnic lingua franca, in the hopes that interethnic interaction would allow the otherwise separate communities to learn from each other:

We have diminished the problem by making them [different ethnic groups] live together ... You know, a Chinese neighbor can be just as friendly ... But you will never dispel that sense of distinctiveness ... I was making a visit last week to some families who have upgraded ... One of the families was a Malay family. And he's bought an executive flat, beautiful marble floor. All he had was 'O' levels in Malay language in Maju School, and his wife too. But he has learnt English ... And he is acting just like a Chinese. You know, he's bouncing, running around, to-ing and fro-ing. In the old culture, he would not be doing that. I'm not saying all of them have become like that. But here is one who has moved, shifted gears and has made his life a success. (Lee, quoted in Han et al. 1998: 184).

As academics, many of whom are involved in public discussions and in university education, we can therefore hope that some of the sociolinguistic concepts that are being debated will at some point become appropriated by lay actors, even if this is a longer term result of current cohorts of students ultimately graduating, finding themselves in positions of influence, and recalling (perhaps vaguely) what they learnt in their sociolinguistics classes. However, we also have to accept that one very real consequence of such appropriations is that concepts might be reinterpreted in ways academics might not necessarily agree with. What this could mean, to return to some of the examples previously discussed, is that the differences between strategic and nonstrategic essentialism, between linguistic human rights and linguistic citizenship, and between fixed and flexible multilingualism, among others, might then be borne in mind by influential lay actors who shape language policy – even if their understandings of these differences should differ from what they were initially taught (or what we as academics might be comfortable with).[4]

Conclusion

By way of closing, I want to return to the question that forms the title of this chapter and explain why I think there aren't (at least not yet, anyway) any zombies in language policy. I am certainly not suggesting that there is no need to rethink essentialist stances, language rights, or fixed multilingualism. But a more cautious view towards so-called modernist notions is necessary because, in the context of social intervention, many of the notions that might otherwise be dismissed as outdated or zombie categories are still highly influential.

As I have tried to emphasize in this chapter, it is a difficult balancing act trying to document revolutionary changes that are indeed occurring (and that therefore merit conceptual innovations) while also taking care not to be too hasty in assuming the completeness of any such transitions. We therefore need to be careful not to slip into a kind of scholarly vanguardism, where, as academic elites, we assume a level of intellectual class-consciousness that may be only apparently in advance of the very societies that we are both studying as well as members of.

By this, I do not mean at all to suggest that the theoretical ideas critiquing modernist perspectives are automatically guilty of vanguardism or lack merit. Nor am I suggesting that the more conservative ideas ought to be left alone. The fact that more conservative positions are not zombies does not mean that they should be allowed to live. But there is a big difference between, on the one hand, trying to help shift social attitudes towards ideas that are more in line with a social reality that is only ever going to become more complex and, on the other, simply dismissing (as Beck seems to do) still powerful and

---

[4] It is true that some policymakers may be academics, and vice versa. But the categories 'lay' and 'academic' are distinct. They constitute different identities and involve different responsibilities, even if the same individuals might sometimes happen to be occupying them.

influential conservative positions as irrelevant. The key issue concerning theoretical innovations, when we consider the matter of social intervention, is to be sensitive to the conditions that are keeping ostensible zombies very much alive and to be more appreciative of the practical difficulties involved in putting the more conservative views to rest. In the case of language policy, we have seen that language issues are inevitably connected to historical issues and involve matters that go beyond language alone to include, among many other possibilities, assumptions about gender, age, ethnicity, nationalism, class, and religion (Lo Bianco 2004: 738). The danger in trying to implement some specific sociolinguistic theoretical innovation is that we might well then be engaging in 'linguistics applied' rather than 'applied linguistics'. The former, as Widdowson (2000: 5) reminds us, no matter how carefully theorized, can only ever provide 'a partial view' of 'experienced language':

This does not invalidate it. On the contrary, its very partiality yields insights which would be impossible otherwise. But it does set limits on its claims to represent reality in the round and to provide an authoritative basis for intervention. Difficulties arise when these limits are not recognized and when its partiality is imposed: in other words, when linguistics is directly applied.
. . .
In the case of applied linguistics, intervention is crucially a matter of mediation . . . Applied linguistics is in this respect a multilateral process which, of its nature, has to relate and reconcile different representations of reality, including that of linguistics without excluding others.

What this means is that a major factor keeping the process of zombification at bay is the multidimensional nature of language issues, and any attempt to put into place some theoretical innovation has to take into account this multidimensionality. Consequently, social intervention should not be predicated on the assumption that zombification has already occurred. Rather, it has to take place alongside the very concepts that it aims to dislodge in the hope that gradual changes will (perhaps via the double hermeneutic discussed above) ultimately lead to those concepts indeed becoming zombified.

REFERENCES

Airey, John. 2009. *Science, Language, and Literacy: Case Studies of Learning in Swedish University Physics*. Uppsala: Acta Universitatis Upsaliensis.

Beck, Ulrich. 2002. The cosmopolitan society and its enemies. *Theory, Culture and Society* 19, 1–2: 17–44.

2011. More justice through more Europe: An interview with Ulrich Beck. Interviewed by Nikola Tietze and Ulrich Bielefeld. Mittleweg 36. Available at www.eurozine.com/articles/2011-12-29-beck-en.htm.

Blackledge, Adrian, and Angela Creese. 2010. *Multilingualism: A Critical Perspective.* London: Continuum.

Blommaert, Jan. 1996. Language planning as a discourse on language and society: The linguistic ideology of a scholarly tradition. *Language Problems and Language Planning* 20, 3: 199–222.

    1999. The debate is closed. In Jan Blommaert (ed.), *Language Ideological Debates.* Berlin: Mouton, 425–438.

Bolton, Kingsley, and Maria Kuteeva. 2012. English as an academic language at a Swedish university: Parallel language use and the 'threat' of English. *Journal of Multilingual & Multicultural Development* 33, 5: 429–447.

Bucholtz, Mary. 2003. Sociolinguistic nostalgia and the authentication of identity. *Journal of Sociolinguistics* 7: 398–416.

Canagarajah, Suresh. 2010. World Englishes in academic journals. Blog entry dated October 19, 2010. Available at www.personal.psu.edu/asc16/blogs/TQeditor/.

    2013. Literacy and mobility: Toward pedagogies of traveling texts. Talk delivered at the Department of English Language and Literature, National University of Singapore. August 21, 2013.

Davies, Alan. 2003. *The Native Speaker: Myth and Reality.* Clevedon: Multilingual Matters.

Das Gupta, Jyotirinda, and Charles A. Ferguson. 1977. Problems of language planning. In Joan Rubin, Bjorn H. Jernudd, Jyotirinda Das Gupta, Joshua A. Fishman, and Charles A. Ferguson (eds.), *Language Planning Processes.* The Hague: Mouton, 3–8.

Foucault, Michel. 1984. Truth and power. In Paul Rabinow (ed.), *The Foucault Reader.* New York: Pantheon, 51–75.

Gal, Susan, and Judith T. Irvine. 1995. The boundaries of languages and disciplines: How ideologies construct difference. *Social Research* 62: 967–1001.

García, Ofelia. 2009. *Bilingual Education in the 21st Century: A Global Perspective.* Malden, MA, and Oxford: Wiley-Blackwell.

Giddens, Anthony. 1987. *Social Theory and Modern Sociology.* Cambridge: Polity Press.

Han, Fook Kwang, Warren Fernandez, and Sumiko Tan. 1998. *Lee Kuan Yew: The Man and His Ideas.* Singapore: Singapore Press Holdings.

Haugen, Einar. 1966. *Language Conflict and Language Planning: The Case of Modern Norwegian.* Cambridge, MA.: Harvard University Press.

Heller, Monica. 1999. *Linguistic Minorities and Modernity: A Sociolinguistic Ethnography.* London: Longman.

    2008. Language and the nation-state: Challenges to sociolinguistic theory and practice. *Journal of Sociolinguistics* 12, 4: 504–24.

    2011. *Paths to Post-Nationalism.* Oxford: Oxford University Press.

Jørgensen, J. Normann. 2008. Polylingual languaging around and among children and adolescents. *International Journal of Multilingualism* 5, 3: 161–176.

Kuipers, Joel C. 1998. *Language, Identity, and Marginality in Indonesia.* Cambridge: Cambridge University Press.

Kuteeva, Maria. 2011. Editorial: Teaching and learning in English in parallel-language and ELF settings: Debates, concerns and realities in higher education. *Iberica* 22: 5–12.

Lo Bianco, Joseph. 2004. Language planning as applied linguistics. In Alan Davies and Catherine Elder (eds.), *Handbook of Applied Linguistics*. Oxford: Blackwell.

Luke, Allan, A. McHoul, and Jacob Mey. 1990. On the limits of language planning: Class, state and power. In Richard B. Baldauf and Allan Luke (eds.), *Language Planning and Education in Australasia and the South Pacific*. Clevedon: Multilingual Matters.

Mauranen, Anna, and Elina Ranta (eds.). 2009. *English as a Lingua Franca: Studies and Findings*. Newcastle: Cambridge Scholars Publishing.

May, Stephen. 2005. Language rights: Moving the debate forward. *Journal of Sociolinguistics* 9: 319–347.

McElhinny, Bonnie. 1996. Strategic essentialism in sociolinguistics of gender. In Natasha Warner, Jocelyn Ahlers, Leela Bilmes, M. Oliver, Susan Wertheim, and Melissa Chen (eds.), *Gender and Belief Systems*. Berkeley, CA: Berkeley Women and Language Group, 469–480.

Ong, Aihwa. 2006. *Neoliberalism as Exception: Mutations in Citizenship and Sovereignty*. Durham, NC: Duke University Press.

Otsuji, Emi, and Alastair Pennycook. 2010. Metrolingualism: Fixity, fluidity and language in flux. *International Journal of Multilingualism* 7: 240–254.

Park, Joseph. 2013. Metadiscursive regimes of diversity in a multinational corporation. *Language in Society* 42: 1–21.

Phillipson, Robert, and Tove Skutnabb-Kangas. 1995. Linguistic rights and wrongs. *Applied Linguistics* 16: 483–504.

Rampton, Ben. 1990. Displacing the 'native speaker': Expertise, affiliation, and inheritance. *ELT Journal* 44, 2: 97–101.

Škabraha, Martin. 2005. Ulrich Beck's reconstruction of modernity. Available at http:// vulgo.org/index.php?option=com_content&view=article&catid=118:politics&id= 344:ulrich-becks-reconstruction-of-modernity.

Skutnabb-Kangas, Tove. 2000. *Linguistic Genocide in Education, or Worldwide Diversity and Human Rights?* Mahwah, NJ: Lawrence Erlbaum.

Slater, Don, and Ritzer, George. 2001. Interview with Ulrich Beck. *Journal of Consumer Culture* 1, 2: 261–277.

Sowell, Thomas. 2004. *Affirmative Action around the World*. New Haven, CT: Yale University Press.

Spolsky, Bernard. 2004. *Language Policy*. Cambridge: Cambridge University Press.
2009. *Language Management*. Cambridge: Cambridge University Press.

Stroud, Christopher. 2001. African mother tongue programs and the politics of language: Linguistic citizenship versus linguistic human rights. *Journal of Multilingual and Multicultural Development* 22, 4: 339–355.
2009. Towards a postliberal theory of citizenship. In John E. Petrovic (ed.), *International Perspectives on Bilingual Education: Policy, Practice and Controversy*. New York: Information Age Publishing, 191–218.

Swedish Language Council. 1998. Draft action programme for the promotion of the Swedish language. Available at www.sprakradet.se/servlet/GetDoc?meta_id_ 2285.

Tollefson, James. 1991. *Planning Language, Planning Inequality*. New York: Longman.

Weber, Jean-Jacques, and Kristin Horner. 2012. *Introducing Multilingualism: A Social Approach*. London: Routledge.

Wee, L. 2011a. Language policy and planning. In James Simpson (ed.), *Handbook of Applied Linguistics*. London: Routledge, 11–23.

Wee, Lionel. 2011b. *Language without Rights*. Oxford: Oxford University Press.

2015. *The Language of Organizational Styling*. Cambridge: Cambridge University Press.

Widdowson, Henry. 2000. On the limitations of linguistics applied. *Applied Linguistics* 21, 1: 3–25.

16   Quantitative sociolinguistics and sign languages: Implications for sociolinguistic theory

Ceil Lucas and Robert Bayley

Introduction

Quantitative sociolinguistics has been part of the language research landscape since the early 1960s, beginning with the work of William Labov in New York and Martha's Vineyard (Labov 1969; 1972a,b). In an early and often-cited study on the raising and centralization of vowels on Martha's Vineyard, Labov (1972b) found that centralization corresponded with certain age groups and with the speaker's orientation towards traditional life on the island. These findings represented one of the earliest uses of quantitative methods for arriving at conclusions about the structure and use of language. The results showed that linguistic variation is not random, that it is quantifiable, and that understanding variation is essential to understanding how language works. Numerous studies in the variationist tradition established by Labov have taught us a great deal about language structure and language change. This chapter focuses on what quantitative sociolinguistics has taught us about variation in sign languages and the implications of that knowledge for sociolinguistic theory and for linguistic theory more generally.

In contrast to the study of variation in spoken languages, the study of variation in sign languages is still in the relatively early stages. The first large-scale study of variation in American Sign Language (ASL) appeared only in 2001 (Lucas et al. 2001b). That study, based on data collected in the mid-1990s in seven areas of the United States, was following by similar studies in Australia and New Zealand (Schembri et al. 2009; McKee et al. 2011), the United Kingdom (Schembri et al. 2013), and Italy (Cardinaletti et al. 2011; Geraci et al. 2011; 2015), as well as by a study of Black ASL, the variety of ASL that developed in the segregated schools of the U.S. South before the civil rights era of the 1960s (McCaskill et al. 2011). Although we have ethnographically oriented studies of smaller signing communities, such as Green's (2014) work on Nepali Sign Language, as well as earlier work involving individuals or small groups of signers (see Patrick and Metzger 1996 for a review), large-scale surveys in several countries have provided the primary insights into the relationship between variation in sign languages and sociolinguistic (and linguistic) theory.

We are fully aware of the advantages of recent trends in sociolinguistics that have combined close ethnographic observation with quantitative methods and sometimes focused on marginal members (e.g. Bucholtz 1999; Eckert 2000). We suggest, however, that such studies depend crucially on earlier work that provided the backdrop against which those studies were undertaken. Eckert (2000), for example, reports that the Michigan high school "jocks" and "burn-outs" she studied differed in the extent of their participation in the Northern Cities Vowel Shift. That finding would not have been possible had not earlier large-scale research previously established the direction and parameters of the Northern Cities Vowel Shift. Our focus, then, is on the insights gained from the large-scale variationist studies of sign languages.

Principles of quantitative analyses

A basic tenet of quantitative sociolinguistics is that, if our ultimate goal is to produce a model of language structure, that model must account for variation in a principled way. Bayley (2013: 85) states:

The central ideas of . . . [a variationist approach] are that an understanding of language requires an understanding of variable as well as categorical processes and that the variation that we witness at all levels of language is not random. Rather, linguistic variation is characterized by orderly or "structured heterogeneity" (Weinreich et al. 1968). That is, speakers' choices between variable linguistic forms are systematically constrained by multiple linguistic and social factors that reflect underlying grammatical systems and that both reflect and partially constitute the social organization of the communities to which users of the language belong.

As Hazen (2007) explains, Weinreich et al. challenged Chomsky's idealization of the "homogeneous speech community" (1965) and "the corresponding theoretical irrelevance of diversity. They instead offer a different view of change, where variation and irregularity are both an integral part of language change" (p. 74). Quantitative sociolinguistics provides us a way to study this structured heterogeneity. Bayley (2013: 86–87) explains three basic principles of quantitative sociolinguistics:

1. The principle of quantitative modeling: The forms that a variable takes can be closely examined, and the features of the context that co-occur with a variable form can be noted. Context includes the surrounding linguistic environment and the social factors that co-occur with the variable.
2. The principle of multiple causes: It is unlikely that any single contextual factor can explain the variability observed in natural language data.
3. The principle of accountability: As formulated by Labov (1969) and Sankoff (1990), "any variable form (a member of a set of alternative ways of 'saying the same thing') should be reported with the cases in which the

form did occur in the relevant environment, compared to the total number of cases in which it might have occurred" (Bayley 2013: 89). In other words, researchers must account for all of the data and cannot pick and choose examples to fit particular theories.

What quantitative sociolinguistics looks like in sign languages

These principles may be applied to variation in sign languages. We continually observe variation at all levels of sign language structure. In phonology, for example, we see variation in handshape, location, palm orientation, movement, and number of articulators (Lucas et al. 2001b; Schembri et al. 2009; McCaskill et al. 2011).[1] Studies of morphosyntactic variation in sign languages include investigations of variation in null and overt subject personal pronouns in ASL, Australian Sign Language (Auslan), and New Zealand Sign Language (NZSL) (McKee et al. 2011; Wulf et al. 2002), variation in the position of *wh*-signs in Italian Sign Language (LIS) (Geraci et al. 2015), and repetition of lexical items and phrases in Black ASL (McCaskill et al. 2011). Research has also examined variation in discourse, including conversational openings and closings and back-channeling (Metzger and Bahan 2001). Finally, as in traditional dialect studies, a number of studies examined lexical variation in several different languages (e.g. Cronberg 1965; Lucas et al. 2001a; Geraci et al. 2011; McCaskill et al. 2011; Stamp et al. 2014). These studies have shown that lexical variation is governed by a wide range of regional and social differences.

As seen in Table 1, James Woodward completed the first studies of phonological variation in ASL in the 1970s, focusing on sign lowering and centralization, handedness (two hands or one), thumb extension, and lexical variation. Beginning with Sutton-Spence, Woll, and Allsop (1990), variationist studies have extended beyond ASL to include studies of other languages and dialects. Table 2 illustrates the number of sites and the number of signers involved in these studies. Table 3 illustrates some of the variables that have been examined by these studies and the number of examples analyzed.

We can see that large amounts of data have been used for all of these analyses. These studies provide evidence about (1) the nature of the system, (2) how the system changes, and (3) how varieties come about.

---

[1] In sign language linguistics, the term phonology refers to the features of a sign such as movement, hold, handshape, palm orientation, etc. These are seen as analogous to the features of phonemes in spoken languages and can be described in similar ways. For further information see, e.g., Brentari (2011) and Liddell and Johnson (1989).

Table 1. *Variationist Studies of Sign Languages*

1970s	James Woodward led the first studies of phonological variation in ASL. Variables included lowering/centralization, handedness, thumb extension, and lexical variation.
1990	Sutton-Spence, Woll, and Allsop (1990). Variation in fingerspelling in British Sign Language.
1994–2001	Lucas, Bayley, and Valli (2001b), *Sociolinguistic Variation in American Sign Language*
2007–2011	McCaskill, Lucas, Bayley, and Hill (2011), *The Hidden Treasure of Black ASL: Its History and Structure*
2003–	Schembri and Johnston, Variation in Auslan: Schembri et al. (2009), McKee et al. (2011)
2005–	McKee and McKee, Variation in New Zealand Sign Language: Schembri et al. (2009), McKee et al. (2011).
2008–2010	Schembri et al., Variation in British Sign Language: Schembri et al. (2013)
2008–	Geraci, Cardinaletti, Cecchetto, and Donati, Variation in Italian Sign Language (LIS): Cardinalette et al. (2011), Geraci et al. (2011)

Table 2. *What Do We Mean by Quantitative?*

Study	Sites	Signers
Sutton-Spence et al. 1990	Various British, from a TV program *See Hear*	485
Lucas et al. 2001	7 U.S. sites	207
Schembri et al. 2013	8 British sites	249
Schembri et al. 2009 and McKee et al. 2011	5 Australian sites, 3 New Zealand regions	205 in Australia, 138 in New Zealand
McCaskill et al. 2011	6 U.S. sites	96
Geraci et al. 2011	10 Italian sites	165

The nature of the system

Among the more important findings of studies of variation in sign languages has been the documentation of the role of grammatical function in phonological variation. In earlier studies based on small groups of signers, claims were made that the only factors involved in phonological variation were phonological ones. It was claimed, for example, that the location of the preceding sign and of the following sign explained the lowering of signs like KNOW[2] from the forehead to the cheek or lower, the movement of the sign DEAF from ear to chin or chin

---

[2] ASL signs are conventionally written in capitals. KNOW, for example, refers to the ASL sign, not to the English word with which it is glossed.

Table 3. *Sociolinguistic Variables Studied in Sign Languages*

Language	Variable	Number of Tokens
ASL	1 handshape	5195
	Location	2862
	DEAF	1618
	Pro-drop	429
Black ASL	2 hand → 1 hand	818 (+ 2258 earlier study)
	Location	877 (+ 2862 earlier study)
	Size of signing space	2247
	Clausal or phrasal repetition	172
	Mouthing	221
	Constructed dialogue/constructed action	1021
BSL	Finger spelling	19,450
Auslan/NZSL	Location	2267 Auslan, 2096 NZSL
	Pro-drop	997 Auslan, 2195 NZSL
LIS	Wh- signs	884 annotated, 413 coded

Table 4. *Linguistic Constraints on Phonological Variation in ASL: DEAF and the Location of Signs like KNOW*

Variable	Analysis	Constraint ranking
DEAF	+cf vs. –cf	Grammatical function > discourse genre
	Chin to ear vs. contact cheek	Grammatical function > location of following segment
Location of KNOW, etc.	+cf vs. –cf	Grammatical function > contact of following sign with body > location of preceding sign

to ear, or the change of a one-handshape sign from 1 to L or 5 (see Woodward and DeSantis 1977; Liddell and Johnson 1989).[3] However, Table 4 and Table 5 show the results of a large quantitative study of sociolinguistic variation in ASL conducted between 1994 and 2001 (Lucas et al. 2001b). Based on large numbers of examples of the variables collected from 207 signers, the quantitative analysis

---

[3] In early studies of variation in ASL, Lucas (1995) and Bayley et al. (2000) focused on the sign DEAF because it occurred very frequently in interview data and because it had also been examined by Liddell and Johnson (1989). As Bayley et al. explain, DEAF can be used in a range of different grammatical functions. Moreover, the two main variants that diverge from the citation form illustrate the processes of metathesis and metathesis followed by deletion. Finally, there is considerable variation in the forms signers in different U.S. regions prefer. This combination of factors made DEAF a good candidate for initial explorations of the nature of variation in ASL. From a theoretical perspective, the results of the 1995 and 2000 studies provided the first indication of the importance of grammatical function in conditioning variation in sign languages.

Table 5. *Linguistic Constraints on Phonological Variation in ASL: 1 Handshape Signs*

Analysis	Constraint ranking
+cf vs. –cf	Grammatical function > features of preceding and following handshapes
L handshape vs. all others	Features of preceding and following handshapes > grammatical function
1 handshape vs. all others	Grammatical function > features of preceding and following handshapes

showed that the grammatical function of the variable played a central role in explaining the variation.

That is, whether the variable itself is a noun, verb, or adjective is central to understanding the variation. For example, in the case of DEAF, the ear to chin variant (the citation form that is found in dictionaries and taught in sign language classes) occurs mostly with verbs, while the chin to ear variant occurs with nouns and adjectives. Prepositions and interrogative signs like WHY tend to be lowered from the forehead, while verbs and nouns resist lowering. The first person pronoun that corresponds to "I" tends to maintain the citation 1 handshape (index open, all other fingers and thumb closed), while other pronouns permit variation, as do nouns and verbs. Studies of location variation in Auslan and NZSL found interaction between grammatical function and frequency, leading to a new category, "sign type", and showed that nouns, adjectives, and high frequency verbs were more likely to be produced at the forehead level (Schembri et al. 2009). This is not to say that phonological factors are entirely thrown out. Table 4, Table 5, and the Auslan and NZSL results all show that phonological factors play some role but that grammatical function is now usually the main explanation for the variation.

The main question emerging from these studies is Why do grammatical and prosodic constraints seem to have a more important role than the features of the preceding and following signs in conditioning phonological variation in ASL? The first answer is simply that, as in spoken languages, phonological variation in ASL is not constrained exclusively by phonological factors. The focus heretofore may have been on features of the preceding and following signs, but large data-based quantitative studies show that grammatical factors must also be considered.

A second answer concerns differences between spoken and sign languages. Having established that sign languages are indeed "real" languages, research on all aspects of sign language structure has begun to show some fundamental differences between languages in a spoken or signed modality. Of most relevance to the present discussion are the basic differences in how morphology functions and how the differences manifest themselves in variation. In many of the spoken languages in which phonological variation has been extensively explored, morphology is a "boundary phenomenon". That is, meaningful segments are added to the beginning or end of other units in the language in the form of plural markers, person and tense markers, derivational affixes, and so forth. These units are essentially added to an existing phonological environment. It stands to reason that when variation occurs, a good place to look for the cause of this variation is the immediate environment to which units have been added (i.e. the preceding and following segments). In fact, many studies of spoken language variation have demonstrated the key role of the immediate phonological environment in governing variation.

However, morphology in sign languages is by and large not a boundary phenomenon, at least not to a great extent. There exist very few sequential affixes. Morphological distinctions are accomplished by altering one or more features in the articulatory bundle that makes up a segment or by altering the movement path of the sign. For example, segments are not usually added to other segments to provide information about person or aspect. Rather, the location feature of a segment (e.g. near or away from the signer) indicates person, and movement between locations indicates the subject and object of the verb in question. Similarly, a particular movement path indicates continuative or inceptive aspect. As Emmorey (1999) states with specific regard to aspect marking in ASL:

In many spoken languages, morphologically complex words are formed by adding prefixes or suffixes to a word stem. In ASL and other signed languages, complex forms are most often created by nesting a sign stem within dynamic movement contours and planes in space ... ASL has many verbal inflections that convey temporal information about the action denoted by the verb, for example, whether the action was habitual, iterative, continual. Generally, these distinctions are marked by different movement patterns over-laid onto a sign stem. This type of morphological encoding contrasts with the primarily linear affixation found in spoken languages. For spoken languages, simultaneous affixation processes such as template morphology (e.g. in Semitic languages), infixation, or reduplication are relatively rare. Signed languages, by contrast, prefer nonconcatenative processes such as reduplication; and prefixation and suffixation are rare. Sign languages' preference for simultaneously producing affixes and stems may have its origins in the visual-manual modality. (p. 173)

The results of the quantitative studies in ASL, Auslan, and NZSL indicate that these fundamental differences manifest themselves in the variable components of the language. That is, the immediate phonological environment turns out not to play the major role in governing phonological variables, in part because the variables themselves are not affixes. The grammatical category to which the variable in question belongs is consistently the first-order linguistic constraint.

This finding has important implications for our understanding of variation in spoken and signed languages. As the modality differences between spoken and signed languages manifest themselves in the basic phonological, morphological, and syntactic components of the language, so they also seem to appear in the patterns of linguistic variation. As the phonological and morphological processes go, so apparently goes variation.

How the system changes

We know from many studies that variation is often the very first indication of a change in progress in a language. We will look at three examples from sign languages here. The first concerns the lowering of signs like KNOW, as mentioned in Table 4. In both ASL and Auslan, age differences are seen: In both languages, younger signers markedly prefer the lowered forms and older signers prefer the nonlowered citation forms. This lowering or centralization of signs has been documented starting with Frishberg (1975), and the differences noted in these studies may well indicate increased centralization from one generation to the next.

The second example concerns the use of repetition, as analyzed in the project on Black ASL. One hundred and seventy-two examples were drawn from twenty-six ten-minute conversations, from both Black and White signers. The researchers coded each clip for the total number of events containing instances of repetition. Thus, "an utterance in which the same sign phrase was repeated at least twice was counted as one event, not as two or three" (McCaskill et al. 2011: 110). The researchers also coded the form and function of the repeated phrase as follows:

> Noun: #DAY STUDENT, #DAY STUDENT?[4][question directed at another signer]
> Adjective/Adverb: 2-DAY-AGO ... 2-DAY-AGO, 2-DAY-AGO [response]
> Verb/predicate: SAME, LEAVE, LEAVE, LEAVE, LEAVE.
> WH sign: KILL, WHY, WHY?
> Function word (including pronouns): PRO.1, PRO.1, THAT ...
> Verb Phrase/full sentence: PRO.2 BRAVE, PRO.2 BRAVE.
> Token response: RIGHT, RIGHT, RIGHT, RIGHT [response]

According to McCaskill et al.,

---

[4] As noted in note 2, uppercase is used for the English glosses of ASL signs, and # is used to mark fingerspelling that has become lexicalized. A translation of the first example would be "Were you a day student?", past tense determined by the context of the discourse and the lexicalized form of the fingerspelled 'day'.

The category verb/predicate is justified since many signs that might ordinarily be considered adjectives (SICK) or nouns (HOME) can function as predicates in ASL. As for verb phrase/full sentence, we were most likely to find verb phrases repeated. For events in this category, we only coded if the phrase or sentence was immediately and fully repeated. We counted responses and instances of back-channeling such as RIGHT and TRUE as token responses. We did not code for events in which the repetition was clearly morphological in nature, e.g. LEARN, LEARN, LEARN, where the signer's meaning was clearly "repeatedly learn" as opposed to a simple repetition of the lexical sign. And we kept in mind signs in which repetition is a part of the structure. For example, CHURCH is usually signed with two contacts of the dominant hand on the base hand. This was not counted as an instance of repetition, of course. But one signer signed this sign with six total contacts, clearly three instances of the sign, so we counted this as an example of repetition of the sign. (p. 111)

The results are summarized in Table 6, which illustrates a striking difference between Black signers and White signers in the use of repetition, with Black signers, both old and young, showing three times the number of repetitions as the White signers. And this is seen also within the specific age categories. It is particularly striking when we consider that eighteen of the nineteen examples from older White signers were produced by one signer. Without those eighteen instances, the ratio becomes fifty-seven instances from the Black signers compared with one from the White signers.

It would seem, then, that repetition is a feature that distinguishes Black signers from White signers. We also see an interesting change in the Black population, with more repetition among the older signers than among the younger signers. What seems to be occurring here, then, is much like what is occurring with other variables. Integration has resulted in a partial convergence of Black and White ASL varieties, whether in number of citation forms in the case of lowering or two-handed signs or in characteristics that have nothing to do with the citation/noncitation distinction such as repetition, which seems to have a pragmatic function. The idea that repetition serves a pragmatic function is supported by the fact repetitions in all grammatical categories are predominantly declarative statements rather than questions.

A final example comes from Italian Sign Language (LIS). Geraci et al. (2015), based on the data from the Italian project described above, examined variation in the position of *wh-* signs, which can occur before the predicate, after the predicate, or both before and after. Such variation can be seen across signers and even within the signing of a single signer. For example, Geraci et al. (2015) report that a signer from Trani produced all three variants in a

Table 6. *Repetition by Grammatical Function by Race, Gender, and Age*

Group	Noun	Adj/ adv	Verb/ predicate	WH	Function sign (incl. pronoun)	Verb phrase/ full sentence	Token response	Total
Black male, old	10	4	20	0	2	14	1	51
Black female, old	3	1	9	2	2	13	7	37
Black male, young	7	1	0	0	0	7	1	16
Black female, young	4	1	1	0	0	12	8	26
White male, old	2	1	6	0	0	7	3	19*
White female, old	2	1	1	0	0	1	0	5
White male, young	2	1	1	0	0	4	0	8
White female, young	1	1	2	0	1	5	0	10
Total	31	11	40	2	5	63	20	172

*18 from one signer.
Source: McCaskill et al. 2011: table 6.2.

brief elicitation task in which signers answered questions about a hypothetical automobile accident:

(1) HAPPEN WHERE
    Where did that happen?
(2) IX-2[5] WHERE BUMP-cl
    Which part of the car did you bump into?
(3) IX-2 WHERE CRASH WHERE?
    Where did the accident happen?

Geraci et al. report that the positions of *wh-* signs were constrained by the clause type, with direct questions and objects favoring the position before the predicate, the option that is congruent with spoken Italian, and nondirect questions and subjects favoring republication or the position following the predicate. Interestingly, younger, better-educated signers strongly disfavored the position before the predicate, in contrast to the older signers with less formal education, who favored this position. That is, at least with this aspect of the grammar, the younger, better-educated signers were diverging from the option that is congruent with spoken Italian. Geraci et al. suggest that this

---

[5] IX stands for 'index', with IX-2 meaning 'second person, you'.

result may represent "an increased awareness of the status of their own language" (2015: 146) on the part of the younger more highly educated signers.

The results from Geraci et al. (2015), while they provide an indication of a growing awareness of the autonomy of LIS on the part of younger, well-educated members of the Italian Deaf[6] community, also have implications for linguistic theory and serve to illustrate a possible typological difference between spoken and sign languages. In the overwhelming majority of spoken languages, *wh-* phrases either occur at the left edge of the sentence or remain in situ. In fact, the World Atlas of Language Structures online database covers several hundred spoken languages that place *wh-* phrases at the left edge and several hundred that place *wh-* phrases in situ, but only one language (Tennet, spoken in South Sudan) that places *wh-* phrases at the end of sentences (Dryer 2011). The situation is quite different with sign languages. Cecchetto (2012) summarizes the literature and argues that in some languages the right periphery of the clause is the only natural position for *wh-* items. He notes that clear cases include LIS, Indo-Pakistani Sign Language, and Hong Kong Sign Language, while Israeli Sign Language, Catalan Sign Language, Spanish Sign Language, Sign Language of the Netherlands, and Japanese Sign Language are possible candidates.

An empirical study of a possible change in LIS, then, has served to illustrate a possible difference in typology between languages in the visual-gestural modality and languages in the aural-oral modality. Results such as those we have summarized here, we suggest, provide evidence of how studies of variation can contribute to both sociolinguistic theory and linguistic theory more generally.

How varieties come about

This discussion of the use of repetition by Black and White signers brings us to the discussion of how quantitative sociolinguistics can help us see how varieties come about in the first place, with the example of Black ASL. As Rickford (1999) notes in his discussion of African American English (AAE), "all languages, if they have enough speakers, have dialects – regional or social varieties that develop when people are separated by geographic or social barriers" (p. 320). The geographical and social boundaries include settlement patterns, migration, geographic features, language contact, economic ecology,

---

[6] The use of uppercase "Deaf" here indicates cultural deafness, as opposed to the strictly audiological condition indicated by lowercase "deaf." Both uses are conventional in the literature on deafness.

social stratification, social interaction (e.g. social practices, speech communities), and group and individual identity (Wolfram and Schilling-Estes 2006).

The same geographic and social factors that promote the formation of spoken language varieties are also implicated in the formation of Black ASL. Not surprisingly, Black deaf people were affected both by the same racial discrimination of the era that affected Black hearing people and by the same social isolation and marginalization due to race that contributed to the development and maintenance of AAE. Racial discrimination was present in local, state, and regional organizations in the Deaf community. For example, the National Association of the Deaf (NAD) was founded in 1880. At first the association welcomed Black Deaf Americans. However, in 1925, the Cleveland Conference of the NAD revoked the membership of the Black members, changing the bylaws to prohibit Black Deaf membership (Burch 2002; Tabak 2006). The effect of desegregation on the public education of Black Americans has received much attention in the literature; however, very little attention has been focused on the effects of desegregation on Black Deaf and hard-of-hearing Americans. Aramburo (1989) and Hairston and Smith (1983) demonstrated that for more than a century and a half, White Deaf children in America had been educated in special schools, while Black Deaf children, especially those in the Southern states, had been relegated to segregated schools. In seventeen states, public school systems required that White Deaf and Black Deaf students be taught separately, and, in some cases, the laws even required that only Black teachers could teach Black students (Doctor 1948). Moreover, in some states, there were no special provisions for Black Deaf children until many years after the end of the Civil War and the abolition of slavery. Louisiana, for example, did not establish a school for Black Deaf children until 1938 and the state resisted integration until 1978, twenty-four years after the U.S. Supreme Court's ruling in *Brown v. Board of Education* that segregated schools violated the Constitution.

The sociohistorical reality characterized by geographically and socially isolated residential schools led to the development of a distinct variety of ASL, especially in the South. Hairston and Smith (1983) state that there is "a Black way of signing used by Black deaf people in their own cultural milieu – among families and friends, in social gatherings, and in deaf clubs" (p. 55). Tabak (2006) also remarks that the differences about Black signing include lexical variation, the size of signing space, and voiceless mouthing, based on his research on Black Deaf Texans.

Burch and Joyner (2007) also report about the difference in the signing at the former Raleigh school. The reports acknowledge the existence of Black ASL, but they are based on anecdotes and observations. However, in the last forty-plus years, researchers who noticed the differences between Black and

White signing in the South did produce some data to support the claims of the differences. In his appendices to the 1965 *A Dictionary of American Sign Language*, co-authored with William Stokoe and Dorothy Casterline, Croneberg discusses these differences as a consequence of the segregation of deaf schools in the South. Based on responses to a 134-item sign vocabulary list, he reports "a radical dialect difference between the signs" of a young North Carolina Black woman and those of White signers living in the same city (Croneberg 1965: 315). Many other studies of Black ASL dealing with specific linguistic features are small scale. They include work on phonology (Woodward et al. 1976; Woodward and DeSantis 1977; Lucas et al. 2001b), lexical variation (Aramburo 1989; Guggenheim 1993; Lucas et al. 2001b), language attitudes (Lewis et al. 1995), and parallels between Black ASL and African American speech styles (Lewis 1998).

However, the research on Black ASL is not nearly as rich as the research on AAE. The early phonological studies in the 1970s relied on self-reported data and small numbers of participants, and most of the other studies were on lexical variation. In contrast, McCaskill et al. (2011) filmed ninety-six Black signers in six of the seventeen states, in free conversation and interviews, and also elicited lexical items. Signers were divided into two groups, those over fifty-five who attended segregated schools and signers under thirty-five who attended integrated schools. During the course of the study, the researchers investigated an inventory of eight linguistic features that distinguish Black signing from the ASL used by white signers. These were:

1. Use of two-handed rather than one-handed signs
2. Use of signs produced at the forehead rather than lowered variants
3. Greater use of repetition
4. Use of a larger signing space
5. Less use of mouthing
6. Use of role shifting (Constructed action/constructed dialogue)
7. Vocabulary differences
8. Incorporation of features of AAE into ASL.

These features include phonological ones such as two-handed versus one-handed signs; signs located at the forehead as opposed to lowered versions of those signs; the size of the signing space; syntactic features such as the use of repetition (discussed earlier) and the use of constructed action and constructed dialogue; features resulting from contact with English, such as mouthing and AAE words and phrases; and lexical differences. The study found that Black signers, both young and old, prefer two-handed and non-lowered signs, a larger signing space, and repetition. No big differences were found in the use of constructed action or constructed dialogue.

Older Black signers show markedly less mouthing, while younger Black signers incorporate words and phrases from AAE into their signing. Finally, there are numerous lexical differences between Black signing and White signing, some of which overlap with regional differences. Overall, the study found Black ASL to be a distinct variety of ASL, which is changing as a result of the integration of schools and mainstreaming for deaf students. For example, while all Black signers use more two-handed signs and forehead-level signs than White signers, the younger Black signers use more one-handed and lowered signs than do the older Black signers.

The description of the emergence and existence of a distinct variety of ASL was made possible by the methods of quantitative sociolinguistics, as were the insights about the differences in the nature of variation in spoken languages and sign languages (the nature of the system) and about generational differences in the lowering of signs and mouthing (how the system changes). If quantitative analysis did not reveal facts about how the system works and about how it comes about and changes, then it might simply be an interesting parlor game. But it clearly does reveal such facts, so we need to pay attention to what it tells us about the claims that we make about the structure and use of language and about what we include in our models of language. In addition, quantitative sociolinguistics has produced important changes in linguistic practice in general. As Hazen (2007) observes, "It is more common today for claims to be supported by empirical evidence; in addition, claims of more or less now require statistical support" (p. 88). Moreover, without collecting the kind of real language data required for quantitative analyses, whether the data are from spoken or signed languages, we run the risk of missing the communities that use these languages, communities that are the heart of the languages that we study. Finally, we suggest that the kind of large-scale variationist studies of sign languages that we have described here are necessary precursors to more intensive ethnographic studies of smaller groups of signers. In an argument in favor of the community of practice approach, Bucholtz (1999) criticized Labov's speech community model on the grounds that, among other things, it prefers studying "central members of the community as opposed to those on the margins" (p. 207). We do not dispute the point that marginal members of a community are worthy of study. However, until we understand the central tendencies in a community, how can we know who is on the margins? Thanks to recent variationist studies of a number of different sign languages, we now have a basis to begin more in-depth studies of particular signing communities and to explore in greater detail the signing of Deaf communities around the world.

Conclusion

For many years, studies of sign languages and studies of linguistic variation existed in separate disciplinary realms. As we have discussed, recent decades have seen the development of a number of large-scale studies of variation in signed languages. Thanks to the rich and expanding number of studies of variation in ASL, Auslan, BSL, LIS, and NZSL, among other languages, we are now in a position to begin the comparative sociolinguistic study of sign language variation, as demonstrated by the work of Schembri et al. (2009) on variation in location in ASL, Auslan, and NZSL and of McKee et al. (2011) on variable subject presence or absence in the same three languages. Such work has the potential to inform us about what types of variation are particular to specific signed languages, which patterns are shared across signed languages, and which are common to all human languages, regardless of modality.

REFERENCES

Aramburo, A. 1989. Sociolinguistic aspects of the Black Deaf community. In C. Lucas (ed.), *The Sociolinguistics of the Deaf Community*. New York: Academic Press, 103–122.

Bayley, R. 2013. The quantitative paradigm. In J. K. Chambers and N. Schilling (eds.), *The Handbook of Language Variation and Change*, 2nd ed. Malden, MA: Wiley-Blackwell, 85–107.

Bayley, R., C. Lucas, and M. Rose. 2000. Variation in American Sign Language: The case of DEAF. *Journal of Sociolinguistics* 4: 81–107.

Bayley, R., A. Schembri, and C. Lucas. 2015. Variation and change in sign languages. In A. Schembri and C. Lucas (eds.), *Sociolinguistics and Deaf Communities*. Cambridge: Cambridge University Press, 61–94.

Brentari, D. 2011. Sign language phonology. In J. Goldsmith, J. Riggle, and A. C. L. Yu (eds.), *The Handbook of Phonological Theory*, 2nd ed. Malden, MA: Wiley-Blackwell, 691–721.

Bucholtz, M. 1999. "Why be normal?" Language and identity practices in a community of nerd girls. *Language in Society* 28: 203–223.

Burch, S. 2002. *Signs of Resistance: American Deaf Cultural History 1900–1942*. New York: New York University Press.

Burch, S., and H. Joyner. 2007. *Unspeakable: The Story of Junius Wilson*. Chapel Hill: University of North Carolina Press.

Cardinaletti, A., C. Cecchetto, and C. Donati (eds.). 2011. *Grammatica, Lessico e Dimensioni di Variazione nella LIS*. Milan: Franco Angeli.

Cecchetto, C. 2012. Sentence types. In R. Pfau, M. Steinbach, and B. Woll (eds.), *Sign Language: An International Handbook*. Berlin: Mouton de Gruyter, 292–315.

Cecchetto, C., S. Giudice, and E. Mereghetti. 2011. La raccolta del Corpus LIS. In A. Cardinaletti, C. Cecchetto, and C. Donati (eds.), *Grammatica, Lessico e Dimensioni di Variazione nella LIS*. Milan: Franco Angeli, 55–70.

Chomsky, N. 1965. *Aspects of the Theory of Syntax*. Cambridge, MA: MIT Press.

Croneberg, C. 1965. Appendix D: Sign language dialects. In W. C. Stokoe, D. C. Casterline, and C. G. Croneberg, *A Dictionary of American Sign Language*. Silver Spring, MD: Linstok, 313–319.

Doctor, P. V. 1948. Deaf Negroes get a break in education. *The Silent Worker*, November.

Dryer, M. S. 2011. Position of interrogative phrases in content questions. In M. S. Dryer and M. Haspelmath (eds.), *The World Atlas of Language Structures Online*. Munich: Max Planck Digital Library. Available at http://wals.info/chapter/93.

Eckert, P. 2000. *Linguistic Variation as Social Practice: The Linguistic Construction of Identity in Belten High*. Oxford: Blackwell.

Emmory, K. 1999. The confluence of space and language in signed languages. In P. Bloom, M. A. Peterson, L. Nodel, and M. F. Garrett (eds.), *Language and Space*. Cambridge: MIT Press, 171–209.

Frishberg, N. 1975. Arbitrariness and iconicity: Historical change in American Sign Language. *Language* 51: 696–719.

Geraci, C., K. Battaglia, A. Cardinaletti, C. Cecchetto, C. Donati, S. Guiduce, and E. Mereghetti,. 2011. The LIS corpus project: A discussion of sociolinguistic variation in the lexicon. *Sign Language Studies* 11: 328–374.

Geraci, C, R. Bayley, A. Cardinaletti, C. Cecchetto, and C. Donati. 2015. Variation in Italian Sign Language (LIS): The case of *wh-* signs. *Linguistics* 53: 125–151.

Green, E. M. 2014. The nature of signs: Nepal's Deaf society, local sign, and the production of communicative sociality. Ph.D. dissertation, University of California, Berkeley.

Guggenheim, L. 1993. Ethnic variation in ASL: The signing of African Americans and how it is influenced by topic. In E. Winston (ed.), *Communication Forum*. Washington, DC: School of Communication, Gallaudet University, 51–76.

Hairston, E., and L. Smith. 1983. *Black and Deaf in America: Are We That Different?* Silver Spring, MD: TJ Publishers.

Hazen, K. 2007. The study of variation in historical perspective. In R. Bayley and C. Lucas (eds.), *Sociolinguistic Variation: Theories, Methods, and Applications*. Cambridge: Cambridge University Press, 70–89.

Labov, W. 1969. Contraction, deletion, and inherent variability of the English copula. *Language* 45: 715–762.

    1972a. *Language in the Inner City: Studies in the Black English Vernacular*. Philadelphia: University of Pennsylvania Press.

    1972b. *Sociolinguistic Patterns*. Philadelphia: University of Pennsylvania Press.

Lewis, J. 1998. Ebonics in American Sign Language: Stylistic variation in African American signers. In *Deaf Studies V: Toward Unity and Diversity. Conference Proceedings*. Washington, DC: College for Continuing Education, Gallaudet University, 229–240.

Lewis, J., C. Palmer, and L. Williams. 1995. Existence of and attitudes toward Black variations of sign language. In L. Byers, J. Chaiken, and M. Mueller (eds.), *Communication Forum 1995*. Washington, DC: School of Communication, Gallaudet University, 17–48.

Liddell, S., and R. E. Johnson. 1989. American Sign Language: The phonological base. *Sign Language Studies* 64: 195–278.

Lucas, C. 1995. Sociolinguistic variation in ASL: The case of DEAF. In C. Lucas (ed.), *Sociolinguistics in Deaf Communities*. Washington, DC: Gallaudet University Press, 3–25.

Lucas, C., R. Bayley, R. Reed, and A. Wulf. 2001a. Lexical variation in African American and white signing. *American Speech* 76: 339–360.

Lucas, C., R. Bayley, and C. Valli 2001b. *Sociolinguistic Variation in American Sign Language*. Washington, DC: Gallaudet University Press.

McCaskill, C., C. Lucas, R. Bayley, and J. Hill. 2011. *The Hidden Treasure of Black ASL: Its History and Structure*. Washington, DC: Gallaudet University Press.

McKee, D., R. McKee, and G. Major. 2008. Sociolinguistic variation in NZSL numerals. In R. M. de Quadros (ed.), *Sign Languages: Spinning and Unraveling the Past, Present and Future: Papers from the 9th Theoretical Issues in Sign Language Research Conference*. Petrópolis, RJ, Brazil: Editora Arara Azul, 296–313.

McKee, R., A. Schembri, David D. McKee, and T. Johnston. 2011. Variable subject expression in Australian Sign Language and New Zealand Sign Language. *Language Variation and Change* 23: 375–398.

Metzger, M., and B. Bahan. 2001. Discourse analysis. In C. Lucas (ed.), *The Sociolinguistics of Sign Languages*. Cambridge: Cambridge University Press, 112–144.

Patrick, P., and M. Metzger. 1996. Sociolinguistic factors in sign language research. In J. Arnold, R. Blake, B. Davidson, S. Schwenter, and J. Solomon (eds.), *Sociolinguistic Variation: Data, Theory, and Analysis, Selected Papers from NWAV23 at Stanford*. Stanford, CA: Center for the Study of Language and Information, 229–242.

Rickford, J. R. 1999. *African American Vernacular English: Features, Evolution, Educational Implications*. Oxford: Blackwell.

Sankoff, G. 1990. The grammaticalization of tense and aspect in Tok Pisin and Sranan. *Language Variation and Change* 2: 295–312.

Schembri, A., J. Fenlon, R. Rentelis, S. Reynolds, and K. Cormier. 2013. Building the British Sign Language corpus. *Language Documentation and Conservation* 7: 136–154.

Schembri, A., D. McKee, R. McKee, S. Pivac, T. Johnston, and D. Goswell. 2009. Phonological variation and change in Australian and New Zealand sign languages: The location variable. *Language Variation and Change* 21: 193–231.

Stamp, R., A. Schembri, J. Fenlon, R. Rentellis, B. Woll, and K. Cormier. 2014. Lexical variation and change in British Sign Language. *PLOS One* 9, 4: 1–14.

Stokoe, W. C. 1960. Sign language structure: An outline of the visual communication system of the American Deaf. Occasional Paper 8. Buffalo: State University of New York Linguistics Department.

Sutton-Spence, R., B. Woll, and L. Allsop. 1990. Variation and change in fingerspelling in British Sign Language. *Language Variation and Change* 2: 324–330.

Tabak, J. 2006. *Significant Gestures: A History of American Sign Language*. Westport, CT: Praeger.

Weinreich, U., W. Labov, and M. Herzog. 1968. Empirical foundations for a theory of language change. In W. P. Lehmann and Y. Malkiel (eds.), *Directions for Historical Linguistics: A Symposium*. Austin: University of Texas Press, 95–188.

Wolfram, W., and N. Schilling–Estes. 2006. *American English: Dialects and Variation*, 2nd ed. Oxford: Blackwell.

Woodward, J. 1976. Black southern signing. *Language in Society* 5: 211–218.

Woodward, J., and S. DeSantis. 1977. Two to one it happens: Dynamic phonology in two sign languages. *Sign Language Studies* 17: 329–46.

Woodward, J., C. Erting, and S. Oliver. 1976. Facing and hand(l)ing variation in American Sign Language. *Sign Language Studies* 10: 43–52.

Wulf A., P. Dudis, R. Bayley, and C. Lucas 2002. Variable subject presence in ASL narratives. *Sign Language Studies* 3: 54–76.

17 Theorising language in sociolinguistics and the law: (How) can sociolinguistics have an impact on inequality in the criminal justice process?

Diana Eades

1. Introduction

A common complaint about the legal system is that lawyers can manipulate people with complex language, such as "big words" and "tricky questions". But sociolinguistic research, beginning in the early 1980s and examining a number of legal contexts, demonstrates many more ways in which language is implicated in the widespread popular dissatisfaction with the law. For example, research in criminal courts shows how defendants and witnesses are controlled, coerced, and manipulated through the rigid and asymmetrical discourse structure of courtroom hearings, which restricts the interactional rights of witnesses to providing answers to specific questions (see Eades 2010 for references). More recently, considerable sociolinguistic attention has turned to how competing stories can, or must, be told, retold, and evaluated throughout the criminal justice process. This chapter examines a theoretical dissonance between how sociolinguistics and the law see language, which is highlighted in this research.[1]

Section 2 sets out this difference, between the sociolinguistic view of language as a dynamic, "non-neutral medium" (Duranti 2011) used for a wide range of social purposes and the law's view of language as a fixed and transparent means of reference. In Section 3, I consider the sociolinguistic focus on context as integral to the understanding of any spoken or written text. Current research examines the ways that interactions are entextualised and texts are recontextualised as they travel through the legal process and reveals some important consequences of transformations occurring along the way. In contrast, Section 4 introduces the impact throughout the law of the central role of authoritative written texts and the concomitant legal view that the texts have a fixed meaning, in the consideration of which context is irrelevant.

---

[1] The scope of this chapter is limited to the common law, that is, the legal system found in England and the countries it colonised.

Section 5 turns to the law's treatment of individuals in terms of their legal categories and roles, divorced from their social, cultural, historical, and political context. This focus on decontextualised individuals can erase difference, consistent with the view of language as a neutral and transparent means of reference. But in confusing equal treatment with same treatment, the erasure of sociolinguistic difference in language use can compromise the principle of equality before the law. The example in Section 6 highlights this consequence of the view of language as "stable, denotational and context-free" (Ehrlich 2012: 58), in combination with other language ideologies central to the legal process. The chapter concludes in Section 7 by arguing that it is both possible and necessary for sociolinguists to pursue opportunities for dialogue with practitioners and scholars of the law, dialogue that can problem-atise law's referential theory of language and other related language ideolo-gies, while opening for challenge and correction problematic sociolinguistic approaches to law.

2.   A fundamental theoretical dissonance

Sociolinguists and linguistic anthropologists know language as a "non-neutral medium, that is, a tool that plays a role in the ways in which speakers think and act as well as in the ways in which social activity is organized" (Duranti 2011: 46). As this tool is socially created, manipulated, and changed, any questions about the meaning of a spoken or written text have to take account of its situatedness (although debates within sociolinguistics contest the ways in which this situatedness can be taken into account; see Section 3).

But a rather different view which is widespread in Western society sees language as a neutral tool for communication, which is typically taken to have the purpose of transmitting referential meaning. In Woolard and Schieffelin's (1994: 71) terms this is a language ideology in which there is "the tendency to see propositionality as the essence of language"; see also Silverstein (1996: 287). An indication of the central position of this tendency is found in dictionary definitions of "language". For example, the *Macquarie Dictionary* (of Australian English) defines language in terms of "communication", which in turn is defined as "the imparting or interchange of thoughts, opinions, or information by speech, writing, or signs". This dominant theory of language contrasts with the axiomatic sociolinguistic understanding that passing on information is just one of the vast array of actions for which language is used.

In the last two decades anthropological linguists have written about this dominant referential theory of language (or Woolard and Schieffelin's "propositionality"), explaining that this approach also holds that language meaning is neutral, inherent, transparent, and fixed, or immutable. I will use the term "referentialism" to refer to this language ideology or theory, which is at the heart of the law's approach to language and which others have also called "textualism" (Collins 1996: 204),[2] "literalism" (Solan and Tiersma 2005; Eades 2008: 245), "referential transparency" (Haviland 2003), "textualist or referentialist ideology" (Mertz 2007: 48; Ehrlich 2012), and the "correspondence theory of language" (Ainsworth 2008).

It is not surprising that the referential theory of language is important in both the principles and practice of the law, given its ideological, taken-for-granted status in Western society generally. An examination of sociolinguistic findings on language in the legal process supports Ainsworth's (2008: 14) claim that what she refers to as the "correspondence theory of language" is the "linchpin of legal ideology of language". This referentialist ideology can be seen, for example, in the widespread expectation that court interpreters should act as "a kind of transparent filter through which referential meanings pass from an opaque source language into the official target language" (Haviland 2003: 768; see also Hale 2004: 8; Angermeyer 2014: 434).

Research by U.S. law professor-linguists Ainsworth (e.g. 2008) and Solan and Tiersma (2005) on interactions between police officers and citizens highlights the impact of this referential theory of language on fundamental human rights. Ainsworth (2008) finds that this language ideology (or linguistic ideology) underlies the legal insistence in the United States that, for suspects to exercise their constitutional right to a lawyer in a police interview, they must use a bald and completely unmodified imperative, such as "Give me a lawyer", or another relatively direct speech act such as "I want a lawyer". The law's failure to recognise indirect speech acts (e.g. in "I think I would like to talk to a lawyer") is premised on the conception of language as "essentially a transparent and objective medium of communication" (p. 16). And this referentialist view results in a situation in which the legal rules governing suspects' rights in police interviews are "applied acontextually, without regard for either conversational implicature or for the ways in which power asymmetry may affect register selection" (p. 16). Thus, according to Ainsworth, these rights are "perilously easy to waive and nearly impossible to invoke" (p. 19).

3.   From context to (re)contextualisation

Ainsworth's exposure of the acontextual assessment by police and the courts of suspects' attempts to invoke their rights underlines the central role played by the concept of context and contextualisation in sociolinguistic approaches to language.

---

[2] As Section 4 explains, the term "textualism" has a specific meaning in legal scholarship and commentary, related to but more narrowly focused than the way in which Collins uses the term.

The approach to context which has most typically characterised much of variation sociolinguistics is referred to by Coupland (2007: 18) as deterministic: The researcher determines which contextual features or variables (such as social class, region, age, sex, and ethnicity) need to be examined for their correlation with language variables, in fine-grained quantitative studies of language variation and its role in language change. In contrast, the constructionist approach, which is at the heart of discursive and interactional sociolinguistics, views context not primarily in terms of social structures, such as class or sex, but in social actions and meanings, from which, however, social structures cannot be divorced (cf. Part 1 of this volume, Chapters 2–5). From the late 1970s, the work of Gumperz (e.g. 1982) precipitated a shift in focus from inherent meaning to conversational inference, that is, "the situated or context-bound process of interpretation, by means of which participants in a conversation assess each other's intentions, and on which they base their responses" (p. 153). This perspective resonated with the shift already taking place among linguistic philosophers such as Austin, from semantics to pragmatics, and from language to communication (Blommaert 2011: 123). Consistent with his focus on the process of conversational inference, Gumperz also shifted the analytic emphasis from that of a collection of static variables defining context to the dynamic process of contextualisation, the term for the "interpretive practices by means of which discourse is connected to and made meaningful in terms of context" (Blommaert 2005: 251).

Within constructionist sociolinguistic approaches there is a difference – between linguistic ethnographers and others including critical discourse analysts, on the one hand, and conversational analysts, on the other – in the role of the analyst in the decision about which aspects of context warrant attention (see Billig and Schegloff 1999; Blommaert 2005: 50–56; D'hondt 2009: 4–8). For Conversation Analysis, it is the demonstrated relevance of particular aspects of context to participants in an interaction that warrants treating them as analytically relevant. My alignment is with the other stance, which holds that "identifiable traces" (following Blommaert 2005: 57) of social structure are not necessarily present in every text and that "contexts are not features of single texts but of larger economies of communication and textualisation".

Constructionist theorisation of context and contextualisation has more recently drawn on work on intertextuality by poststructuralists such as Kristeva and Derrida, who were influenced by the work of semioticians such as Bakhtin, to understand that no text, whether spoken or written (or signed; see Chapter 16) is completely independent. This work on connections between texts was first introduced to sociolinguistics through the work of linguistic anthropologists such as Silverstein and Urban (e.g. 1996) and Bauman and Briggs (e.g. 1990) on the processes of creating text (entextualisation) and transforming text (through decontextualisation and recontextualisation).

As the terms indicate, this work places context as an integral part of textual meaning, even breaking down a clear-cut distinction between texts, with context shaping text as much as text shapes context (following Duranti and Goodwin 1992: 31; see also Mertz 2007: 45).

The processes of entextualisation, decontextualisation, and recontextualisation have become a particularly fitting focus of sociolinguistic research in the legal system (e.g. Trinch 2003; Maryns 2006; Ehrlich 2007; Eades 2008), given that it revolves around the telling, retelling, and adjudication of competing stories. Heffer et al.'s (2013) collection of current language and law work in this area uses Blommaert's (2005: 78–83) term "textual travel" to refer to "the way that texts move through and around institutional processes and are shaped, altered, and appropriated during their journeys" (Rock et al. 2013: 5). These transformations of legal texts can include "form, propositional content, function, intended meaning or interpretation" (p. 11). As Rock et al. (2013: 4) put it, "the management of textual travel, including such phenomena as entextualisation and [de-/re-] contextualisation, comprise the very core of argumentation in and around the law". Ehrlich (2013; see also 2012) presents an example of such textual travels in the legal system in tracing the way a complainant's account in a rape trial is transformed in the judge's summary in an appeal decision. While most of the research in Heffer et al.'s (2013) collection examines processes in common law (which is an adversarial system), the papers drawn together by D'hondt and Van der Houwen (2014) in a special issue of the journal *Language and Communication* examine similar processes of transformations of legal texts in continental law (which predominantly uses an inquisitorial system).

While sociolinguistics pays increasing attention to the management of text through various recontextualisations[3] as it travels through the legal process, the law itself sees 'the story' as being (or expected to be) 'the same', as it travels and is transplanted into different contexts. For example, being well aware of their duty to present one version of a story, and to discredit any competing version, in courtroom hearings lawyers search for inconsistencies between different recontextualisations of a witness's account. The central cross-examination strategy known as "raising prior inconsistent statements" contrasts a witness's earlier version of an event or situation with what he or she says about it in answer to questions in cross-examination. Any evidence of inconsistency thus exposed between two accounts by the same person is used to argue that the person is unable to present his or her story (or a part of it) consistently and is therefore lacking in credibility and/or reliability. This process ignores the way that different interviewers' questions can

---

[3] Given that recontextualisation implies decontextualisation, I follow the convention of referring to this process simply as recontextualisation in several places in this chapter.

recontextualise and fragment a witness's account, often deciding what can be told and how, and in this way resulting in interactionally achieved inconsistency (Matoesian 2001: 38; Eades 2012). (This is not to ignore the fact that individual failings of memory and/or honesty can also be implicated in inconsistency.)

Thus, there is a considerable and consequential dissonance between the constructionist sociolinguistic understanding of the central role of contextualisation in how any text is produced and received, on the one hand, and, on the other hand, a legal system that works by the frequent removal of context from its consideration, as it focuses on (often microscopic) analysis of the surface forms of utterances and their propositional content. (The law's predominant acontextualism is also at odds with the determinist sociolinguistic theory of language, which will not be further dealt with in this chapter.) In the examination below of the contextualisation of courtroom utterances and their subsequent de- and recontextualisation, I follow scholars such as Verschueren (2012) in considering context as comprising the linguistic context of the text being examined, as well as the immediate context of situation and the wider context (here, social, cultural, political, and historical).

4.   Textualism in the law

While sociolinguists find interviews with police and lawyers and in courtroom hearings to be rich sites for exploring intertextuality, in the everyday work of lawyers and judicial officers intertextuality involves more than the texts (written and oral) specific to a particular case. They must also interpret and apply to the case relevant parts of authoritative legal texts (statutes and, in common law, case judgments also). In this work, the authoritative written text is central (Tiersma 2001) and the referential theory of language is often highly visible.

This is particularly so in the United States, in relation to the way that the law deals with arguments over meaning in a legal document, such as a statute or a contract. Thus, the "plain meaning rule" holds that "when the language [in a legal document] is clear, courts have no authority to go beyond the words of the statute or contract, but must apply the clear language of the document to the facts before them" (Solan 1993: 93). Tiersma (1999: 126) explains that the effect of this rule is to focus the attention of courts "on the meaning of words and sentences, rather than on the speaker's [or writer's] intent, even though that intent is legally what should decide the issue". There has been much debate in U.S. courts about the extent to which "legislative intent" (or speakers'/writers' meaning) should be taken into account, and where and when the plain meaning rule should be invoked. And in recent years, there has been a strong "revival" of this plain meaning rule (p. 127), in the approach to statutory interpretation referred to in legal scholarship and commentary as "textualism". Supreme Court Justice Antonin Scalia is at the forefront of this legal textualism, arguing "forcefully" that "texts, in particular the Constitution, have a fixed, determinate meaning" (Ainsworth 2008: 15).

While this approach guides courts in their interpretation of legal documents, including judicial decisions and written laws, it seems to impact also on how courts deal with issues of the spoken language of individuals who come before them. Thus, the seemingly absurd situation revealed by Ainsworth's study of judicial decisions about the speech act required in order for suspects to invoke their right to a lawyer makes some kind of "sense" when we understand the role of textualism in legal interpretation.

However, not all jurisdictions take the strong version of textualism which currently prevails in the United States. Gray (2012: 137), who was a judge of the Federal Court of Australia for twenty-eight years, points out that the "passionate disagreement" in the United States about statutory interpretation has no counterpart in Australia. Section 15 of the Australian 1901 Acts Interpretation Act requires courts "to consider the desirability of people being able to rely on the ordinary meaning conveyed by the text, *taking into account its context and the purpose or object underlying the Act* [being examined], as well as the need to avoid prolonging legal or other proceedings without compensating advantage" (p. 137, emphasis added).

5.   Social context and "equality before the law"

However, regardless of the extent to which the original legislative context and purpose of a law is taken into account, at the heart of the world view and the operation of the legal system is what Mertz (2007: 132) calls the "bracketing of social context". The essence of how and why social context can become irrelevant in the law is captured in Mertz's 2007 monograph, which uses anthropological linguistics in the examination of how law schools in the United States train students to "think like a lawyer". She explains that the law "derives its legitimacy in part from an act of translation of social events and actors into their corresponding legal categories and roles" (p. 131). So, lawyers are trained to transform people into parties to a legal action, and to strip away as much personal and contextual detail as possible, in order to see how the events and situations fit the relevant statute law and legal authorities, that is, earlier binding cases (see also Conley and O'Barr 1990: 196).

However, this transformation from people to parties, stripped of many contextual particulars, presents a challenge for the central principle of all legal systems, namely "equality before the law", which is enshrined in Article 7 of the Universal Declaration of Human Rights (1948). This principle requires equal treatment *in the law* (i.e. laws should not discriminate against anyone), and *by the law* (i.e. no one should be discriminated against in the way they are treated in the legal process). It underlies the oath taken by judicial officers (judges and magistrates) to administer the law "without fear or *favour*, affection or ill-will" (emphasis added). As Philips (1998) has shown, this principle can be interpreted in practice as treating all people in the same way in the legal process. Thus, in the Arizona guilty plea events she studied, Philips found that some judges asked identical questions of each defendant in establishing that they were pleading guilty knowingly and voluntarily. On the other hand, other judges tailored the hearing to the individual, taking particular account of contextual factors such as their level of education and other social background details in guiding their interaction with the defendants to establish the same issues about pleading knowingly and voluntarily. Philips's detailed ethnographic interviews with the judges led her to the conclusion that those who tailored the guilty plea to individuals, taking account of their social background, were those with a liberal ideological stance. These judges held the view that people are not all equally capable of protecting their own liberty and that the state should take on the role of protector of human liberties, particularly for powerless people. On the other hand, the judges who treated all defendants in the same way in taking their guilty plea were those with a conservative ideological stance, believing that all individuals are equally capable of taking care of themselves and that they do not need the state to help.

Although Philips's findings about the diversity in Arizona judges' approach to equality before the law are probably indicative of practice in many other jurisdictions around the world, a much-cited 1991 Australian High Court case makes it clear that equal treatment does not necessarily mean same treatment. As Judge McHugh explained in *Waters v Public Transport Corporation* (1991),

discrimination can arise just as readily from an act which treats as equals those who are different as it can from an act which treats differently persons whose circumstances are not materially different.

It appears to be in civil law areas, such as litigation about discrimination (e.g. in access to public transport), and sentencing decisions in criminal law that courts are most likely to consider the relevance of social context. In sentencing, judges usually have discretion in exercising their responsibility to balance the main aims of retribution, deterrence, and rehabilitation. However, they must also take into account a wide range of relevant "material facts" concerning the nature of the offence, the nature of the offender, and the effect of the offence and the penalty (Findlay et al. 2005: chapter 9). Thus, for example, an influential Australian High Court case established that an offender's Aboriginality may often be a relevant consideration, with Justice Gerard

Brennan holding that "the same sentencing principles are to be applied irrespective of the offender's ethnic or other group but a court can take into account facts which exist only by reason of the offender's membership of such a group" (*Neal v R* 1982: 326).

Paying attention in sentencing practices to such dimensions of context as the offender's ethnic background is consistent with the common law focus on the need to protect the rights of the accused and convicted (while not ignoring the protection of society). But it seems that, when it comes to questions concerning language use, such as in relation to grammatical, lexical, or pragmatic features of a witness's account, the law can often have problems with recognising difference and, as a result, problems with how it hears and assesses witnesses' stories. It is the argument of this chapter that this is due in no small part to the law's referential view of language and a number of other associated language ideologies. The next section explains this argument with an example from an Australian case which is the subject of extensive sociolinguistic analysis (e.g. Eades 2008, 2012; 2016).

6.   Example

This example comes from a lower court hearing[4] in which three young teenage Aboriginal boys were prosecution witnesses in the case against the six police officers charged with their abduction. There was never any dispute that the boys had been approached by armed police officers late one night, who then took them "for a ride" in three separate vehicles 14 kilometres out of town and abandoned them in a swampy industrial wasteland. The boys were not under arrest or charged with any offence, and their removal was contrary to legislated guidelines for police engagement with children. The defence case was that there was no abduction because the children had willingly gone with the police. The first stage in the case against the police officers was a hearing in front of a magistrate (a lower court judge) in which the cross-examination of the teenage complainants was more extreme than many experienced lawyers had ever seen. This was arguably because of the important role this case played in the two-century struggle between Aboriginal people and the state over the freedom of Aboriginal people in public places (as detailed in Eades 2008).

An example from the evidence of one of the three complainant children – thirteen-year old Albert[5] – exemplifies the central cross-examination strategy known as "raising prior inconsistent statements", referred to in Section 3 above, about whether or not the boys had been "grabbed" by police. Shortly before Extract 1, the first of the two defence counsel (DC1) had read from the

---

[4] *Crawford v Venardos & Ors* 1995 Unreported, Brisbane Magistrates' Court, February 24.
[5] Personal names in this chapter are pseudonyms. See Appendix for transcription conventions.

376 Sociolinguistics, contexts and impact

transcript of the audio-recorded interview by the initial investigators some ten months earlier, in which Albert had said that the police had *grabbed* him and his two friends. DC1's recontextualisation of this part of Albert's account then proceeded with DC1 challenging Albert (a few minutes before Extract 1) that it *didn't happen at all (.) did it? (2.0) that you were grabbed (.) it DIDN'T HAPPEN (.) did it?* Albert's softly spoken answer of *°No°* had then led to a tirade from the lawyer about why he had lied about this (see Eades 2008: 103–104 for the full extract, which is also discussed in Eades 2012).

These accusations of lying rely on an acontextual approach to utterance meaning, which ignores a number of social and linguistic contextual factors. For example, it is not clear whether Albert had used the word *grab* in his earlier report to mean physically take hold of or in the more colloquial sense of taking him aside, such as in "I tried to leave early but the boss grabbed me", where no physical contact is intended or understood. Or could the earlier use of the word have been childish exaggeration, avoided in court following legal advice?

Extract 1 highlights the main parts of the cross-examination exchange about this *lie* about being *grabbed* by the police:

Extract 1

5. DC1:   I'll suggest this answer to you (.) that you were TRYING TO MAKE
            THINGS LOOK WORSE FOR THE POLICE (.) is that the correct answer?
            (27.8) is that the correct answer?
6. ALBERT: (1.4) °No°.

Nine turns later the question was asked in a slightly different way:

15. DC1:   YOU LIED TO MAKE THINGS LOOK BAD FOR THE POLICE (,) DIDN'T YOU? (1.2)
            DIDN'T YOU?
16. ALBERT: (3.5) °Yes°.

On the face of it, the contrast between Albert's answers in Turns 6 and 16, recorded in the official transcript as "No" and "Yes", respectively, appears to show a witness changing his mind, a situation always counted as a success for any cross-examining lawyer. More importantly, the answer of *°Yes°* to the shouted question *YOU LIED TO MAKE THINGS LOOK BAD FOR THE POLICE– DIDN'T YOU? (1.2) DIDN'T YOU?* achieved a major victory for defence counsel: It seemed to indicate the witness's acceptance of the presupposition that his report of being "grabbed by police" had been a lie, and that he told this lie to investigators in order to create problems for police. What could be clearer, we might think, than Albert's "Yes" answer in Turn 16? From the legal evidential perspective the lawyer has succeeded in a major cross-examination goal, namely, eliciting from the witness a favourable admission (Mauet and McCrimmon 2011: 194). But the following discussion of the problems with this literal interpretation highlights how, as expressed by Ehrlich (2007: 468) "the [usual] process of interpretation or meaning making is radically underdetermined by linguistic evidence".

This is because, to interpret Albert's°*Yes*° here as unequivocal acceptance of the defence counsel's proposition and its presupposition requires an interpretation that ignores a multitude of contextual considerations. This was a starkly asymmetrical interaction between a middle-aged, highly paid barrister and a thirteen-year-old Aboriginal part-time street kid with a history of sporadic school attendance. It took place in an adult court with none of the protections afforded to child witnesses when they are accused or when they are complainants in sexual abuse cases. The courtroom setting indexed the asymmetrical relationship between the defendant police officers and the three child witnesses, with the front rows of the public gallery filled with the six accused police officers and their families, including several children in school uniforms. Albert had already been subjected to aggressive cross-examination, which included much shouting, for more than an hour (with none of the judicial restraint that is often used in such situations). The linguistic context of the two apparently contradictory monosyllabic answers might suggest that Albert was also an evasive witness, given the very low volume of his two answers, and the pauses of 27.8, 1.4, 1.2, and 3.5 seconds before these answers. On the other hand, further linguistic contextualisation comprising the defence counsel's shouting and the repetition of the two tag questions (*is that the correct answer?* and DIDN'T YOU?) might suggest that the prosodic features of Albert's answers were consistent with a child witness responding under bullying and intimidation.

Thus, the immediate, linguistic, and social contextualisation of the seemingly least subtle answers possible – "no" and "yes" – problematises the meaning of this interaction, particularly casting doubt on a literal interpretation of the "yes" answer. And cultural contextualisation further problematises a literal interpretation of the answer and sheds light on the interpretation of the long silences in this extract. Research summarised in Eades (2008: 92–96) reveals widespread Aboriginal Australian use of gratuitous concurrence, that is, answering "yes" to a question (or "no" to a negative question), regardless of actual agreement with, or even understanding of, the question. On many occasions a "yes" (or "yeh" or "mm") answer may signal something like "It's easiest if I agree with your questioning, and I hope that this answer will help bring the questioning to an end." On the other hand, it may signal agreement to a proposition. And it is often impossible, for either an interlocutor or an analyst, to be sure of the speaker's intention. Thus, it can often be dangerous to rely for important questions on literal interpretations of "yes" answers from Aboriginal witnesses to cross-examination questions which can easily elicit gratuitous concurrence. This is particularly the case with Aboriginal witnesses (like Albert) who have not had opportunities to develop bicultural abilities in using English.

Further, the widespread Anglo convention of interpreting silences as indicating that something is not working in an interaction (e.g. Jefferson 1989) is not shared with Aboriginal people, who often use lengthy silences in either formal or informal interaction and who find them neither uncomfortable nor remarkable (e.g. Eades 2008: 107–109; Mushin and Gardner 2009). Thus, in making sense of this extract, we cannot rely on negative Anglo assumptions about the use and meaning of silence in interactions. The noticeable silences, up to 27 seconds in this extract, were likely an indication that Albert was thinking carefully about serious questions in a bullying environment.

But it is not surprising that there appeared to be no room for contextual factors to be considered in the interpretation of Albert's answers. How could a legal system based on the conception of language meaning as neutral, inherent, transparent, and fixed find that the°Yes° answer in Turn 16 could mean anything other than agreement to the incriminating proposition in Turn 15?

However, the uptake of this answer went further than simply being taken as his acceptance of a shouted insistent proposition. In its textual travel from cross-examination interaction to closing address monologue, this°Yes° answer was recontextualised and presented as a damning twenty-five-word utterance by the second of the two defence counsel, who told the court:

Extract 2
Albert told [the other defence counsel] in cross-examination that the reason that he'd said the police had grabbed him and forced him into the car was to make (.) things (.) look (.) worse (.) for (.) the (.) police.

But the propositional content attributed here to Albert cannot be found in any of his evidence. Of his 544 answers, 66% were *Yes, No,* or *I dunno* (or variant forms such as *Yeh*), with his longest utterance being the ten-word *You don't have to know my things what I do.* The only evidence for the assertion in Extract 2 is the exchange presented above as Extract 1. So, how can Albert's one-word, monosyllabic response be recontextualised and counted as his having uttered a damning twenty-five-word statement? To understand this requires recognition of the consequences of the referential theory of language and some of the other ideologies of language which support it.

Conventional courtroom practice in reporting admissions by witnesses often frames these admissions with reporting verb phrases such as "The witness accepted that . . .". But DC2's strategy here was to present the utterance which had been authored and animated by DC1 in Turn 15 (Extract 1), so that it now appeared to have been originally authored and animated by Albert (in

Goffman's 1981 terms). There is no indication here of the extent of the inaccuracy in this apparent reporting of what Albert "told" the first defence counsel. And while this change of footing was achieved by reading Albert's "yes" answer as indication that he was (co-)principal of DC1's utterance, the analysis above shows the flawed nature of this reading and its reliance on a context-free denotational approach to meaning.

Further, this change of footing needs to be understood in the context of the frequent cross-examination practice of questioning witnesses about decontextualised extracts from earlier interviews, relying on strategic prosodic and paralinguistic choices in reading aloud from official transcripts, which do not record these features. This is a central strategy in the way in which direct quotes from transcripts of earlier interviews are used in raising prior inconsistent statements (see Section 3 above). The transcripts' obscuring of such linguistic recontextualisation of the earlier interview is consistent with the law's focus on the propositional meaning of words and is enabled by the "ideology of decontextualised fragments", that is, the assumption that individual words or fragments taken from a story can be understood without their context (Eades 2012: 477; see also Eades 2008: 320–322 and Matoesian's 2000: 909 "theory of decontextualised meaning"). Arguably this ideology was at work as DC2 prepared the statement in Extract 2: Albert's softly spoken monosyllabic°*Yes*° answer was taken from the transcript, stripped of its immediate, linguistic, social, and cultural context, to count as unequivocal agreement to the shouted bullying assertion by DC1. But in contrast to the use of direct reported speech often used in raising prior inconsistent statements, DC2's recontextualisation used indirect reported speech, relying on the reporting speech verb "told", in his transformation of this monosyllabic transcript extract into the twenty-five-word incriminating statement.

This significantly misleading recontextualisation is further supported by an approach to legal interviews which was first pointed out by Jönsson and Linell (1991) in relation to police interviews. That is, while written witness or suspect statements result from an interactional process, namely, an interview, they are presented as the product of a single person, the interviewee. The results are "monologized versions of dialogic interaction" (D'hondt and Van der Houwen 2014: 4) which are presented as if they are faithful renditions of what the interviewee had said (e.g. Komter 2013). An important consequence of this transformation of interviews into apparently being the product of the interviewee alone is what Jönsson and Linell (1991: 434) term "the blurring of source distinctions". In the police written witness statements they studied it was impossible to know which information originated in the proposition of a police officer question and which was initiated by the interviewee (see also Rock 2001; Komter 2013). This "blurring of source distinctions" is made possible by the language ideology, found more widely in the institutional production of written statements following interviews, which ignores the contribution made by an interviewer to an interview and which Trinch (2003) terms "the ideology of narrator authorship". In the recontextualisation of the cross-examination exchange in DC2's closing address, the ideology of narrator authorship goes further than enabling the "blurring of source distinctions", to result in actual switching of author attribution.

This switch of author attribution appears to have been persuasive. The magistrate's 447-word decision to drop the charges against the police officers included specific reference to the inconsistency over the use of the word *grabbed* between Albert's interview with the investigators and his evidence in court, while completely ignoring the contextualisation of this inconsistency (see Eades 2008: 276–277, 320–321). Further, the two defence counsel succeeded in recontextualising the boys' unwavering assertions in court that they were *told* and *forced* to go with police (Eades 2016). The court decided that there had been no "unlawful deprivation of liberty", because, in effect, the boys had consented to go with police. This decision legitimised the well-known and discriminatory police practice of removing Aboriginal people from public places (Eades 2008).

The issue of consent is one of the foundational principles of Western liberal legalism, and its discursive construction in a number of legal settings is the focus of analyses in Ehrlich, Eades, and Ainsworth (2016). The erasure of context in rape cases has resulted in decisions that consent has been freely given in situations where women have reacted to violent threats with submission rather than physical resistance (Ehrlich 2016; also 2007; 2012). As with the boys in this chapter in relation to armed police officers, complainants are seen to be on a "level playing field" with a sexually predatory man or a group of them. And in court, all complainants are taken to be on the same "level playing field" with cross-examining lawyers. As Mertz (2007: 132) has pointed out, the "bracketing of social context, along with the translation of people and events into legal categories and roles, is deemed to be a crucial way in which the law achieves objectivity and lawyers achieve dispassionate professional competence". But this resulting objectivity and dispassionate professional "competence" comes at a heavy cost: The erasure of social context is responsible for problematic interpretations of consent, as the work of Ehrlich and this author shows (see also Ehrlich and Eades 2016). And it can result in the legitimisation, and thus perpetuation, of neocolonial (Eades) and patriarchal (Ehrlich) control.

7.   Conclusion: impact of sociolinguistics on law?

However, the law is not monolithic, and despite being slow to change, it is not immutable. New laws can be codified, and existing laws can be amended, but this is only part of how change can be effected. In common law, judgments in specific cases also act to renew, revise, and refine the law. And part of what is involved here is the wide-ranging reading and participation in conferences and judicial training that enable judicial officers to learn more about a multitude of complexities that can impact individual cases they must decide. These powerful mechanisms for change in the law can provide opportunities for sociolinguistics to reach beyond the discipline and the wider academy to address the fundamental problems with the law's theory of language. But in order to engage in dialogue with legal scholars and practitioners, we need to learn how to talk about sociolinguistic research to nonlinguists. Consistent with Conley and O'Barr's (2005: 155) point that language ideology "both deserves and is capable of straightforward exposition", it is important to recognise complex negative connotations associated with the word "ideology". We don't have to use this term outside the academy; instead, we can talk about assumptions about how language works, and how these depend on social, historical, and cultural factors (see Eades 2015b).

Australian sociolinguists have been welcomed into dialogue with judicial officers and legal professionals in a number of oral and written forums about several different topics. Judicial leadership in relation to Aboriginal ways of using English comes from Justice Mildren from the Northern Territory, whose publications and judicial practice recognise such issues as the role of gratuitous concurrence in rendering some Aboriginal people too suggestible for the fair use of leading questions in cross-examination. In pointing out to fellow judicial officers and lawyers the relevance to some Aboriginal witnesses of the judge's power "to disallow questions, or forms of questioning which are unfair" (Mildren 1997: 14), Mildren is clearly bringing cultural and linguistic context into the law. Further, recommendations about and/or versions of jury directions about Aboriginal ways of using English, originating from Mildren and often used in the Northern Territory, are now found in three states in publications such as judicial benchbooks (which provide guidelines for judicial officers about day-to-day practice in court). Often referred to as "Mildren directions" or "Mildren-type directions" and drawing considerably on sociolinguistic research, these directions have been considered in several appeal cases.

Reading these cases, it is apparent that a major judicial concern is the extent to which such jury directions could be used to stereotype Aboriginal witnesses, an issue which goes to the heart of the law's focus on individuals and which resonates with contemporary sociolinguistic concerns about essentialism (see Eades 2013: chapter 1). Mildren anticipates this issue, with an important feature of the directions being the frequent use of modifying expressions such as "many Aboriginal people", "often", and "may", indicating that the directions should be impossible to apply in a categorical manner. And jurors are explicitly reminded that:

You are the judges of fact in this case. It is therefore your function to decide which evidence you accept, and which evidence you reject. You, and you alone, are the judges of the facts ... you may be assisted by what I am about to tell you. (Mildren 1997: 21)

So, a question to be asked by juries, judges, and sociolinguists is, Why (and how) might this witness's Aboriginality be relevant to his or her communication in legal interviews? This question has to be answered in two ways. First, and in general terms, Aboriginality is always relevant – and it always has been – to interactions between Aboriginal people and the criminal justice process, as I have argued in Eades (2008; 2012), drawing on a wealth of historical and criminological research. Second, and more specifically, when we focus on conversational inference in interviews, the issue is whether the Aboriginality of the witnesses is likely to impact on their choice of pragmatic, lexical, or grammatical features of their evidence. So, the question about the relevance of Aboriginality has to be considered in the light of linguistic repertoires available to speakers. In what community (or communities) has the witness been socialised? Is it possible that he or she might use and interpret silence, gratuitous concurrence, and other pragmatic features in Aboriginal ways? And what opportunities have they had to develop bicultural proficiency in using English? That is, judges' and sociolinguists' concerns about essentialist stereotyping of an Aboriginal witness's use of English need to be addressed by sociolinguistically informed understandings about the central role of socialisation within sociocultural groups. (There is arguably also scope for some "strategic essentialism", given the well-documented two centuries of disadvantage and discrimination suffered by Aboriginal people in the law; see Eades 2012).

In Eades (2015a) I discuss judicial consideration of the use of Mildren-type directions by an appeal court in Western Australia and a trial judge in New South Wales.[6] In both cases this consideration was informed, partly at least, by the erroneous assumption that the Aboriginal ways of using English discussed in the directions, such as gratuitous concurrence, are not relevant to witnesses who speak English and do not speak any traditional Aboriginal language. These cases underline the need for sociolinguistic awareness-raising about the continuity of Aboriginal cultural and linguistic practices in contemporary communities of speakers of varieties of English.

But in the 2011 Western Australian *Bowles* case, there was no evidence of any such assumption about the Aboriginal use of gratuitous concurrence

---

[6] It is not my intention to comment on legal reasoning or to analyse the complexity of these cases or the decision made, and nor do I have the expertise required.

(and this is not the place to consider the number of reasons which may have contributed to the different outcome on this issue). The appeal court in this case refused to rule that the trial judge's use of Mildren directions (e.g. about gratuitous concurrence) were unbalanced and/or unfair, saying:

There may be a danger that a jury drawn from the dominant culture will unthinkingly assess a witness based upon their own unconscious assumptions ...
[I]t may be necessary for a judge to suggest to a jury that they may need to use care in respect of a particular witness in applying these assumptions. (*Bowles v WA* [2011] WASCA 191; 52)

This appeal court statement, referring to the Aboriginal witness's answers of *yes*, encapsulates an essential challenge to the referential theory of language and goes to the heart of cultural presuppositions which impact meaning.

Cases such as *Bowles* therefore highlight the way in which the law is beginning to take a different approach to language and gives encouragement for sociolinguists to take our research to the law. In doing this, we must negotiate the law's frequent preference for precision and definiteness, which can result in an overly deterministic approach to context, in those situations when context is admitted as relevant. (This was evident in the two cases mentioned above, in the mistaken reliance on proficiency in a traditional Aboriginal language as an indicator of the relevance of information about Aboriginal ways of using English.) How can we explain to legal practitioners the dynamic, complex, and subtle nature of Aboriginal identities, and that equality before the law will be better served by an approach to language and meaning which acknowledges the reciprocal relationship between text and context in the complex processes of contextualisation and recontextualisation? The answer, I believe, lies partly in ongoing dialogue, in which we can build on the law's firm commitment to the consideration of complexity, in endeavours such as the determination of guilt and the evaluation of individual "material facts" which are relevant to sentencing. Can sociolinguistics show how such a commitment is also needed in relation to difference in the language practices of witnesses, as demonstrated by the judge's ruling in the *Bowles* case about the "need to use care" in "applying ... assumptions"?

Another important reason for the increasing interdisciplinary dialogue between sociolinguistics and legal practitioners (and scholars) is to address ignorance and misconceptions held by many sociolinguists about how the law works,[7] referred to by Conley and O'Barr (2005: 155) as "linguists' ideologies of law". It is somewhat ironic, for a discipline so focused on context, that (socio)linguistic work on language in the law often ignores important aspects

---

[7] But note the leadership taken by language and law scholars who combine sociolinguistic expertise with legal training and expertise, e.g. Ainsworth (2008) and Haworth (2006).

of the specific legal context being analysed. Thus, if we want to make a contribution to understanding the impact of language use in court, it is important to know about legal reasons for interactional constraints. For example, (socio)linguistic outrage about manipulative cross-examination questions must be contextualised in the understanding that defence lawyers are professionally required to "cross-examine competently, effectively and with the 'maximum zeal permitted by law'" (Boyd and Hopkins 2010: 155–156, citing Luban 1999: 140). Further, when a defence lawyer is representing a client who has pleaded not guilty, the lawyer is legally obliged to challenge the truthfulness of the complainant(s). Thus defence strategies to challenge and deny witness's truthfulness go beyond individual or professional linguistic trickery and have to be seen in their structural context. These strategies are allowed, even required, as part of the central work of testing a witness's truthfulness and are facilitated by a language ideology problematised in Eades (2012), namely, that repeated questioning enables the truth to emerge. Yet again, the understanding about how the law works comes back to assumptions about how language works which are at odds with the findings of sociolinguistic research. But in order to have an impact on law's flawed ideologies of language, we need to address (socio)linguistics' flawed ideologies of law (following Conley and O'Barr 2005).

"The failure of the law to live up to its ideal of equal treatment" (Conley and O'Barr 2005: 139) is a repeated finding of the systematic and scholarly study of how language is used in the legal process. Sociolinguists have a responsibility to use evidence-based research findings to take our research beyond the academy. This chapter has argued that the law's referential theory of language is at the heart of its failure to afford the basic human right of "equality before the law" to witnesses giving evidence in common law courts. But given that the view of language as a neutral tool for communication is much more widespread than the legal system, we need to also work in diverse ways throughout society, formally and informally, to explain and exemplify the most fundamental sociolinguistic knowledge: that language is always situated – socially, culturally, linguistically, historically, politically – and that this situatedness is at the heart of meaning.

APPENDIX   Transcription conventions

°	An utterance spoken at very low volume
(.)	An untimed pause within a turn of less than 0.5 of a second
(3.2)	A number in parentheses indicates the length of a pause in seconds.
YES	Small capitals indicate raised volume.
yes	Underlining indicates emphasis.

CASES CITED

Bowles v Western Australia 2011 WASCA 191.

Crawford v Venardos & Ors 1995 Unreported, Brisbane Magistrates' Court, February 24.

Neal v R 1982 *Commonwealth Law Reports* 149, 305–326 (High Court).

Waters v Public Transport Corporation 1991 *Commonwealth Law Reports* 173, 349–416 (High Court).

REFERENCES

Ainsworth, Janet. 2008. "You have the right to remain silent . . . But only if you ask for it just so": The role of linguistic ideology in American police interrogation law. *International Journal of Speech, Language and the Law* 15, 1: 1–22.

Angermeyer, Philipp Sebastian. 2014. Monolingual ideologies and multilingual practices in small claims court: The case of Spanish-speaking arbitrators. *International Journal of Multilingualism* 11, 4: 430–448.

Bauman, Richard, and Charles L. Briggs. 1990. Poetics and performance as critical perspectives on language and social life. *Annual Review of Anthropology* 19: 59–88.

Billig, Michael, and Emanuel Schegloff. 1999. Critical discourse analysis and conversational analysis: An exchange between Michael Billig and Emanuel A. Schegloff. *Discourse and Society* 10, 4: 543–582.

Blommaert, Jan. 2005. *Discourse*. Cambridge: Cambridge University Press.
    2011. Pragmatics and discourse. In Rajend Mesthrie (ed.), *The Cambridge Handbook of Sociolinguistics*. Cambridge: Cambridge University Press, 122–137.

Boyd, Russell, and Anthony Hopkins. 2010. Cross-examination of child sexual assault complainants: Concerns about the application of s41 of the Evidence Act. *Criminal Law Journal* 34: 149–166.

Collins, James. 1996. Socialization to text: Structure and contradiction in schooled literacy. In Michael Silverstein and Greg Urban (eds.), *Natural Histories of Discourse*. Chicago, IL: Chicago University Press, 203–228.

Conley, John M., and William M. O'Barr. 1990. *Rules versus Relationships*. Chicago, IL: University of Chicago Press.

2005. *Just Words: Law, Language and Power*. Chicago, IL: University of Chicago Press.

Coupland, Nikolas. 2007. *Style: Language Variation and Identity*. Cambridge: Cambridge University Press.

D'hondt, Sigurd. 2009. The pragmatics of interaction: A survey. In Sigurd D'hondt, Jan-Ola Östman, and Jef Verschueren (eds.), *The Pragmatics of Interaction*. Amsterdam: John Benjamins, 1–19.

D'hondt Sigurd, and Fleur Van der Houwen. 2014. Quoting from the case file: How intertextual practices shape discourse at various stages in the legal trajectory. *Language and Communication* 36: 1–6.

Duranti, Alessandro. 2011. Linguistic anthropology: The study of language as a non-neutral medium. In Rajend Mesthrie (ed.), *The Cambridge Handbook of Sociolinguistics*. Cambridge: Cambridge University Press, 28–46.

Duranti, Alessandro, and Charles Goodwin. 1992. *Rethinking Context: Language as an Interactive Phenomenon*. Cambridge: Cambridge University Press.

Eades, Diana. 2006. Lexical struggle in court: Aboriginal Australians vs the state. *Journal of Sociolinguistics* 10, 2: 153–181.

2008. *Courtroom Talk and Neocolonial Control*. Berlin: Mouton de Gruyter.

2010. *Sociolinguistics and the Legal Process*. Bristol: Multilingual Matters.

2012. The social consequences of language ideologies in courtroom cross examination. *Language in Society* 41, 4: 471–497.

2013. *Aboriginal Ways of Using English*. Canberra: Aboriginal Studies Press.

2015a. Judicial understandings of Aboriginality and language use in criminal cases. In Peter Toner (ed.), *Strings of Connectedness: Essays in Honour of Ian Keen*. Canberra: ANU Press, 27–51.

2015b. Communicating with Aboriginal witnesses in court. *Precedent (Journal of the Australian Lawyers Alliance)* 126: 44–48.

2016. Erasing context in the courtroom construal of consent. In Susan Ehrlich, Diana Eades, and Janet Ainsworth (eds.), *Discursive Constructions of Consent in the Legal Process*. Oxford: Oxford University Press, 71–91.

Ehrlich, Susan. 2007. Legal discourse and the cultural intelligibility of gendered meanings. *Journal of Sociolinguistics* 11: 452–477.

2012. Text trajectories, legal discourse and gendered inequalities. *Applied Linguistics Review* 3, 1: 47–73.

2013. Post-penetration rape and the decontextualization of witness testimony. In Chris Heffer, Frances Rock, and John Conley (eds.), *Legal-Lay Communication: Textual Travels in the Law*. Oxford: Oxford University Press, 189–205.

2016. Post-penetration rape: Coercion or freely-given consent? In Susan Ehrlich, Diana Eades and Janet Ainsworth (eds.), *Discursive Constructions of Consent in the Legal Process*. Oxford: Oxford University Press.

Ehrlich, Susan, and Diana Eades. 2016. Introduction: Linguistic and discursive dimensions of consent. In Susan Ehrlich, Diana Eades and Janet Ainsworth (eds.),

Discursive Constructions of Consent in the Legal Process. Oxford: Oxford
   University Press 1–20.
Ehrlich, Susan, Diana Eades, and Janet Ainsworth (eds.). 2016. *Discursive
   Constructions of Consent in the Legal Process*. Oxford: Oxford University Press.
Findlay, Mark, Stephen Odgers, and Stanley Yeo. 2005. *Australian Criminal Justice*,
   3rd ed. (1st ed. 1994). Oxford: Oxford University Press.
Goffman, Erving. 1981. *Forms of Talk*. Philadelphia: University of Pennsylvania Press.
Gray, Peter. 2012. Review of *The Language of Statutes: Laws and Their Interpretation*
   by Lawrence M. Solan (2010). *International Journal of Speech, Language and the
   Law* 19, 1: 135–140.
Gumperz, John. 1982. *Discourse Strategies*. Cambridge: Cambridge University Press.
Hale, Sandra. 2004. *The Discourse of Court Interpreting: Discourse Practices of the
   Law, the Witness and the Interpreter*. Amsterdam: John Benjamins.
Haworth, Kate. 2006. The dynamics of power and resistance in police interview
   discourse. *Discourse and Society* 17, 6: 739–759.
Haviland, John. 2003. Ideologies of language: Some reflections of language and U.S.
   law. *American Anthropologist* 105, 4: 764–774.
Heffer, Chris, Frances Rock, and John Conley (eds.). 2013. *Legal-Lay Communication:
   Textual Travels in the Law*. Oxford: Oxford University Press.
Hymes, Dell. 1974. *Foundations of Sociolinguistics: An Ethnographic Approach*.
   Philadelphia: University of Pennsylvania Press.
Jefferson, Gail. 1989. Preliminary notes on a possible metric which provides for a
   "Standard Maximum" silence of approximately one second in a conversation.
   In Derek Roger and Peter Bull (eds.), *Conversation: An Interdisciplinary
   Perspective*. Clevedon: Multilingual Matters, 166–196.
Jönsson, Linda, and Per Linell. 1991. Story generations: From dialogical interviews
   to written reports in police interrogations. *Text* 11, 3: 419–440.
Judicial Commission of New South Wales. 2009. *Equality before the Law Benchbook*.
   Sydney: Judicial Commission of New South Wales.
Komter, Martha. 2013. Travels of a suspect's statement. In Chris Heffer, Frances Rock,
   and John Conley (eds.), *Legal-Lay Communication: Textual Travels in the Law*.
   Oxford: Oxford University Press, 126–146.
Luban, David. 1999. Twenty theses on adversarial ethics. In Michael Lavarch and
   Helen Stacy (eds.), *Beyond the Adversarial System*. Sydney: Federation Press,
   134–154.
Maryns, Katrijn. 2006. *The Asylum Speaker: Language in the Belgian Asylum
   Procedure*. Manchester: St. Jerome Press.
Matoesian, Gregory. 2000. Intertextual authority in reported speech: Production
   media in the Kennedy Smith rape trial. *Journal of Pragmatics* 32: 879–914.
   2001. *Law and the Language of Identity: Discourse in the William Kennedy Smith
   Rape Trial*. Oxford: Oxford University Press.
Mauet, Thomas, and Les McCrimmon. 2011. *Fundamentals of Trial Technique*,
   3rd Australian ed. (1st ed. 1993). Sydney: Thomson Reuters.
Mertz, Elizabeth. 2007. *The Language of Law School: Learning to Think like a Lawyer*.
   Oxford: Oxford University Press.
Mildren, Dean. 1997. Redressing the imbalance against Aboriginals in the Criminal
   Justice System. *Criminal Law Journal* 21, 1: 7–22.

Mushin, Ilana, and Rod Gardner. 2009. Silence is talk: Conversational silence in Australian Aboriginal talk-in-interaction. *Journal of Pragmatics* 41: 2033–2052.

Philips, Susan. 1998. *Ideology in the Language of Judges: How Judges Practice Law, Politics and Courtroom Control*. New York: Oxford University Press.

Rock, Frances. 2001. The genesis of a witness statement. *Forensic Linguistics* 8, 2: 44–72.

Rock, Frances, Chris Heffer, and John Conley. 2013. Textual travel in legal-lay communication. In Chris Heffer, Frances Rock, and John Conley (eds.), *Legal-Lay Communication: Textual Travels in the Law*. Oxford: Oxford University Press, 3–32.

Silverstein, Michael, and Greg Urban. 1996. The natural history of discourse. In Michael Silverstein and Greg Urban (eds.), *Natural Histories of Discourse*. Chicago, IL: Chicago University Press, 1–17.

(eds.). 1996. *Natural Histories of Discourse*. Chicago, IL: Chicago University Press.

Solan, Lawrence M. 1993. *The Language of Judges*. Chicago, IL: Chicago University Press.

Solan, Lawrence M., and Peter M. Tiersma. 2005. *Speaking of Crime: The Language of Criminal Justice*. Chicago, IL: University of Chicago Press.

Tannen, Deborah. 1989. *Talking Voices: Repetition, Dialogue, and Imagery in Conversational Discourse*. Cambridge: Cambridge University Press.

Tiersma, Peter M. 1999. *Legal Language*. Chicago, IL: University of Chicago Press.

2001. Textualizing the law. *Forensic Linguistics* 8, 2: 73–92.

Trinch, Shonna. 2003. *Latinas' Narratives of Domestic Abuse: Discrepant Versions of Violence*. Amsterdam: John Benjamins.

Verschueren, Jef. 2012. *Ideology in Language Use: Pragmatic Guidelines for Emprirical Research*. Cambridge: Cambridge University Press.

Woolard, Kathryn A., and Bambi B. Schieffelin. 1994. Language ideology. *Annual Review of Anthropology* 23: 55–82.

Part VI

The evolution of sociolinguistic theory

18   Succeeding waves: Seeking sociolinguistic theory for the twenty-first century

Allan Bell

This chapter examines developments in sociolinguistic theory since the 1990s, mainly as they can be traced in the pages of the *Journal of Sociolinguistics*.[1] First published in 1997, the Journal set itself a theorizing remit from the start, and it has remained committed to that intention. From my perspective as founding co-editor with Nikolas Coupland – and sole editor since 2008, with a team of associate editors – I here review trends in the contents of the Journal, put forward some editorial-insider perspectives derived from reading (to date) more than 2500 submissions across nearly twenty years, and look forward to the future of sociolinguistics.

1.   Three sociolinguistics

Dell Hymes was sociolinguistics' founding theorist, and any consideration of trends in the field tends to find its way back to his early writings as a means of clarifying where we have come from. In a programmatic essay published more than forty years ago, Hymes distinguished three ways in which (socio) linguistics may view the relationship between the social and the linguistic (1974: 195):

(1) ***the social as well as the linguistic***: addressing social issues which have a language component
(2) *socially realistic linguistics*: basing linguistic investigation on real-society data
(3) *socially constituted linguistics*: affirming that language is inherently social and society is inherently linguistic.

[1] My thanks to Nik Coupland for this commission and for his insightful editorial inputs to the final version. In reflecting on the *Journal of Sociolinguistics* over nearly twenty years, I want to acknowledge him as founding co-editor, and the others who have worked on the Journal in the past – Adam Jaworski, Virpi Ylänne, Monica Heller, Lionel Wee, Susan Shaw, Rakesh Bhatt. And in particular the current team, some of whom are long serving: David Britain, Bonnie McElhinny, Devyani Sharma, Joseph Park, Andy Gibson, Trish Brothers. I am indebted to Andy Gibson, the Journal's Reviews and Editorial Associate, for some of the content analyses presented in the chapter.

The development of sociolinguistics across its more than half a century of history could be seen broadly as a movement from (1) and (2) towards (3), a socially constituted discipline. The way in which language constitutes the social, and the social constitutes language, is now taken as a given in much sociolinguistic work.

The first approach above remains a strong driver in our field – addressing social issues which have a language component. This has always been a goal for sociolinguists of all kinds: to apply their knowledge for the benefit of those they are researching. Often such social intervention has itself been an impetus for conducting the research. Engaged, interventionist research in language maintenance, policy and planning, education, literacy, and other areas (cf. Part 5 of this volume, Chapters 15–17) are staples of sociolinguistic work now, as they were in the 1990s and 1960s. Such commitments were often the prime motivations for our field's founders undertaking a particular project, and they have continued to spur successive generations of sociolinguists. These are an outworking of the engagement to research *with* communities as well as *for* them, and to eschew just researching *on* a community (Cameron et al. 1992). This commitment is reflected throughout the pages of the *Journal of Sociolinguistics* from early in its publishing history. In volume 3 (1999) Heller brought together a suite of opinion pieces on 'Sociolinguistics and public debate'. 'What do we have to say about the language debates of our time?', Heller asked, and the responses included Rickford's reflections on 'the Ebonics controversy in my backyard'.

Hymes's second approach – basing our investigations on real-world data – remains a cornerstone of the field. It is no accident that sociolinguistics dates from the period in which audio-recording technology became readily available and portable. What counts as 'real-society data' may change or be contested, but it is hard to imagine a sociolinguistics in which recorded data of some kind will not be central, even if the nature of the data and the technology used to capture it may change. Most of the articles that get published in the *Journal of Sociolinguistics* are based on empirical data that has been recorded – be it videoed, downloaded, transcribed, or otherwise – in some area of social life.

However, in his third approach, Hymes envisaged something more fundamental and comprehensive – not only improvement in people's linguistic conditions but a challenge to the foundations of linguistic discrimination and inequity. There is a critical function in sociolinguistics just as there is in discourse analysis (see Pietikäinen, this volume, Chapter 12). In opting for a socially constituted linguistics Hymes emphasised a concern for social equity and how it is evidenced and substantiated in the voices of society – who speaks, who is listened to, who is valued, who is disregarded. 'One way to think of the society in which one would like to live is to think of the kinds of voices it would have', he wrote (1996: 64). In this he aligned (unknowingly) with the Russian theorist Bakhtin (1981), to whose contribution I will return in concluding.

What might a socially constituted sociolinguistics look like? Here I will focus the conversation not on linguistics as a whole, which is what Hymes envisaged, but specifically on *socio*linguistics. A socially constituted sociolinguistics would:

(1) be engaged, critical, interventionist, advocating for linguistic equity – that is, encompassing Hymes's first approach above and more

(2) deal with data from across the real world – a broad version of Hymes's second approach. There would be an intentional diversification of data sources to include the margins, new digital genres, vernacular, and disadvantaged contexts. As J. Milroy observed in a 2001 article in the *Journal of Sociolinguistics*, the data of sociolinguistics have remained largely (if now decreasingly) monolingual and from standard-language cultures

(3) address and seek to resolve issues of social theory and significance as well as linguistic issues; would ask the question 'What is society?' as well as 'What is language?'

(4) build on the principle that language itself is socially constituted, and interaction is its basic material

(5) build on the principle that society is to a considerable degree linguistically constituted, and seek to unpack that at all levels of language structure, for example, in the operation of linguistic ideologies, and

(6) be essentially dialogical in character (Bakhtin 1981), that is, taking full account of listeners and audiences as well as of speakers.

Such a sociolinguistics invites engagement, and it has been one ambition for the *Journal of Sociolinguistics* that its contents should make a contribution to language equity, however we may define that. As a first take on the character of the Journal and its place in the field, let us examine that part of its content that the Journal itself has commissioned or instigated or encouraged, as compared with the three-quarters of published content which originated as volunteered submissions. In the *Journal of Sociolinguistics*, commissioned content has been of two main kinds: themed issues, usually proposed and guest-edited by one or more scholars from outside the editorial team, and orchestrated exchanges around an issue in the field, usually in this journal titled 'Dialogue' or 'Debate', sometimes instigated by one of the editors.

In the eighteen volumes from 1997 to 2014, the Journal has published thirteen theme issues and six Dialogues/Debates (details are given in the Appendix). There are many ways in which one could thematize the trends in these suites. The following classifications are permeable, but the overall thrust is clearly the desire to stimulate something new in the field:

- **fresh or incoming themes or issues**: from realist social theory (2000), through globalisation (2003), authenticity (2003), communities of practice (2005), and computer-mediated communication (2006), to the sociolinguistics of performance (2011) and of tourism (2014)
- **new takes on existing issues**: style (1999), orthography (2000), dialect contact (2002), acquisition of sociolinguistic competence (2004), the sociolinguistics of writing (2013), and the role of media in language change (2014)
- **redefining and reshaping the field and its neighbours**: linguistic ethnography (2007) and linguistic anthropology (2008), and an exchange between Hymes and Samarin on the historical emergence of sociolinguistics (2000), and
- **sociolinguistics and society**: public debate of sociolinguistic issues (1999), language rights (2005), and multilingualism in South Korea and its diaspora (2012).

Such initiatives seem to me one service that a journal and its editors can offer their field, particularly in the use of formats or the focus on topics that would not be published, for example, in book form. As the *Journal of Sociolinguistics* approaches twenty years of publication, our editorial policy is turning to encouraging and commissioning an increasing amount of evaluative and opinionated material. We intend that these should continue to reflect, inform, and enrich the field.

2.   The place of the social in sociolinguistics

The movement towards a socially constituted sociolinguistics is in part a knock-on effect of intellectual developments outside of our field. The late-twentieth-century 'turn to language' in the social sciences in general, and the accompanying rise of constructivism as the dominant paradigm, had its repercussions in sociolinguistics. Quite suddenly, it seemed, the object of enquiry in our field – language in use – had become everybody's object of enquiry.

The social-scientific turn to language was well set by the time the *Journal of Sociolinguistics* was founded in the mid-1990s. Part of the response within sociolinguistics was a complementary 'turn to society'. The editorial statement (largely initiated by Coupland) from the original manifesto on the inside back cover of the Journal's first issue (1997) reflects this trend:

The Journal promotes sociolinguistics as a thoroughly linguistic and thoroughly social-scientific endeavour . . . Language is regarded as not only a reflection of society but as itself constituting much of the character of social life. The Journal promotes the building and critique of sociolinguistic theory and encourages the application of social theory to linguistic issues.

Successive editorial teams have reviewed this declaration over the years but have always chosen to endorse and continue with it as capturing a central goal of the Journal. The statement appears still on the inside covers of each issue. The Journal has always insisted that articles do justice to both social and linguistic dimensions. A recurrent reason for submissions to the Journal being declined is that their engagement with the social is inadequate (less often, their engagement with the linguistic). In particular, in the twenty-first century, papers are increasingly expected to go beyond dealing in simple demographic categories without, for example, unpacking or interrogating those categories. The kind of quantitative, correlational analysis with which variationist socio-linguistics was established, and which served it so well in its early decades, is now expected to be enriched with nuanced attention to the social. While in the 1990s a straightforwardly correlational paper may have got through to publi-cation in the Journal, this has become increasingly unlikely. If such a submis-sion is accepted, it is likely to end up as a short, circumscribed Research Note because of its limited social dimensions.

Data sets are also expected to consist not just of counts that are abstracted from the social realities of the speech from which they are drawn. Quantitative data need to be complemented with qualitative stretches of actual used lan-guage. This reflects change in the nature of variationist sociolinguistics itself, which in this century is using much more diverse databases and blending with ethnographic methodologies to produce work that is richer in its social content.

The first issue of the Journal (volume 1/1, 1997) reflected the fact that these trends were already in the making. This was fortuitous, because we founding editors did not prearrange articles for the early issues but were subject to what was submitted. The first article in the first issue, by Wolfram, Hazen, and Tamburro, brought impeccable variationist credentials and method but applied that to examination of just one speaker, against the background of what was already known from Wolfram and colleagues' extensive studies of the island dialect of Ocracoke, North Carolina. That was followed by a multimodal study from Ron Scollon of handbills and their distribution in public places in Hong Kong. The third article of the issue focused on Cajun identity and its linguistic reflexes (Dubois and Melançon), and the fourth was a variationist study of the development of New Zealand English (Woods). This founding issue can be seen, then, as both affirming existing traditions of sociolinguistics and its diverse strands and foreshadowing further developments – more focus on individuals, a concern with identity, and emphasis on the role of language and discourse in public life.

Sociolinguists do not raise the question 'What is language?' often enough (Bell 2014: 2), compared with the frequently debated 'what is a language?'. We have asked even less the parallel question that our field's name invites: 'What is society?' (2014: 323). Most sociolinguists are linguists by background rather than sociologists, thus we have not been strong on meshing our work with social theory. We have preferred to cobble up our own bric-a-brac answers to questions that have long been addressed in sociology or to adopt second-hand socioscientific solutions as givens, without due consideration for where they came from or where they are going to: 'The social analysis in quantitative sociolinguistics is relatively shallow. Frequently, there is no explicit recognition that social class analysis depends on a theory of social class' (Milroy 2001: 546). This is no new challenge. Woolard (1985: 738) formulated the issue well a decade before the Journal was founded:

> In developing descriptions of and explanations for variation in speech, sociolinguists have often borrowed sociological concepts in an ad hoc and unreflecting fashion, not usually considering critically the implicit theoretical frameworks that are imported wholesale along with such convenient constructs as three-, four-, or nine-sector scalings of socioeconomic status. In other cases those of us interested in sociolinguistic variation have invented or at least elaborated our own favorite explanatory concepts, developing through these what amount to partial social theories to account for our immediate empirical data. In either case, the enterprise often amounts to a reliance on implicit rather than explicit social theory, with little consideration given to how sociolinguistic findings might be modified by the adoption of a different theoretical frame of investigation, or in turn might validate or modify grander theories of how society works.

In the twenty-first century our field calls for explicit engagement with the social and its theorization. But across its near-twenty-year lifetime the *Journal of Sociolinguistics* has been witness to two contrary trends in the relations of language and society. The first and prevailing impetus has indeed been to engage much more directly with social theories and incorporate them critically into the discipline. In the early volumes of the Journal this was explicit in directly social-theoretic articles such as Carter and Sealey (2000: 3) on language, structure, and agency; and Fairclough (2000: 163) on discourse, social theory, and social research. The tendency of later articles has been to simply incorporate social theory (e.g. Heller et al. 2014) rather than thematise it. This could be interpreted as some indication of its naturalization within sociolinguistics.

In his introduction to the 2001 Coupland, Sarangi, and Candlin volume on sociolinguistics and social theory, Nikolas Coupland outlines three positions he sees sociolinguistics taking on theory:

(1) Sociolinguistic theory is proper linguistic theory. That is, sociolinguistics does linguistics the way linguistics should be done.
(2) Sociolinguistics is an accumulation of socially relevant mini-theories. It has theories but no theory.
(3) Sociolinguistic theory is (or should be) social theory. That is, sociolinguistics necessarily involves social-theoretical content.

The last position is a starting place. In sociolinguistics, whether we like it or not, we are working with social theory merely by plying our trade. We will be adopting a theory even if we are not aware what it is. Arguably it is better to do so consciously and selectively than by default. Early variationist sociolinguistics took over the prevailing structural-functionalism of the mid-twentieth century. It was a theory that naturalizes social difference and discrimination, minimizes social conflict, and thus implicitly supports the status quo – even though these early researchers were anything but social conservatives. Models such as social networks (Milroy 2002) and communities of practice (Eckert and Wenger 2005) are attempts to import paradigms from other social-scientific fields and theorize the social dimension of sociolinguistics using alternatives that are oriented to social process rather than structure. They represent an effort to access more of the cultural lifeblood of 'class' differences in lived-out experience, particularly of those on the social margins.

A second and countervailing trend to the engagement with social theory is a retreat from the social, positioning some sociolinguistic behaviours as mechanistic rather than socially driven. It is a curious twist that two of the founding and leading figures of variationist sociolinguistics, Labov and Trudgill, have in the twenty-first century markedly reduced the role of the social in their accounts of language variation and change, heading away from rather than towards an encounter between sociolinguistics and social theory. Social psychological drivers have been sidelined in favour of more mechanistic factors which see sociolinguistic outcomes as resulting straightforwardly from calculable linguistic inputs or social interactions.

In his early work Labov (1972) made language evaluation and style central issues on the sociolinguistic agenda, although his working definition of 'style' was reductionist, positing that it was a direct reflex of varying amounts of attention paid to speech. Simultaneously he resisted the label 'sociolinguistics' in his introduction to what was one of the first books with the term in its title – 'since it implies that there can be a successful linguistic theory or practice that is not social ... a socially realistic linguistics seemed a remote prospect in the 1960's' (p. xiii). His earlier preface to *The Social Stratification of English in New York City* (2006 [1966]), the foundation study of variationist sociolinguistics, is instructive:

[S]ociolinguistics is more frequently used to suggest a new interdisciplinary field – the comprehensive description of the relations of language and society. This seems to me an unfortunate notion, foreshadowing a long series of purely descriptive studies with little bearing on the central theoretical problems of linguistics or of sociology. My own intention was to solve linguistic problems, bearing in mind that these are ultimately problems in the analysis of social behaviour. (Labov 2006: viii)

It is worth noting that although Labov states that his own focus was linguistic issues, there is an implicature embedded above which indicates a converse – an appropriate sociolinguistics will also legitimately address issues in social theory. It will avoid just describing and will not be atheoretical on its social dimension any more than on the linguistic. It is also a pertinent question, to which I will return later, whether sociolinguistics has now become an 'interdisciplinary field' and, if it has, whether it has fallen into a trap of simple descriptivism.

Labov's more recent work largely sets aside the role of evaluation and attitudes as forces in linguistic change. Instead it adopts a mechanistic 'principle of density', which says that people influence each other's language merely through encountering and talking to each other. What matters is not their social psychological motivations and responses but the simple fact that they have interacted (Labov 2001: 19). Gauging sociolinguistic influence then becomes a matter of mathematically calculating interaction densities in the manner of traffic flows:

> The principle of density implicitly asserts that we do not have to search for a motivating force behind the diffusion of linguistic change. The effect is a mechanical and inevitable one; the implicit assumption is that social evaluation and attitudes play a minor role. (Labov 2001: 20)

In an important article assessing the role of social values and attitudes in Labov's work, Kristiansen (2011) concludes in favour of Labov's earlier rather than later approach. In his Philadelphia work, Labov supplanted attitudes as a driving force with an account based on measuring interaction patterns among people. However, the role of ideologies and covert values proved to be central drivers of linguistic change in Kristiansen's own research in Denmark.

Trudgill had published the first article which introduced the social psychological theory of speech accommodation into sociolinguistics in 1981. His later work on New Zealand English speculated that the front vowel shift in that dialect derived from identity motivations. In an early *Journal of Sociolinguistics* paper, he argued that New Zealanders did not want to sound like Australians; therefore, they differentiated their own vowels from Australian representations (Trudgill et al. 1998). But Trudgill (2004) soon began to adopt the view that the process of colonial dialect formation in such situations is linguistically mechanistic and inevitable and that identity characteristics play no part in it (although they may follow as a consequence). The accommodation that takes place is an automatic process of behavioural coordination between speakers and not at all motivationally driven. This contrasts interestingly with Schneider's 'dynamic model' of the development of colonial Englishes (2007). Schneider's key claim is that 'identity constructions and realignments, and their symbolic linguistic expressions, are ... at the heart of the process of the emergence of Post-Colonial Englishes' (2007: 28). While Trudgill holds that the process of colonial English formation is purely linguistic, for Schneider it is an 'identity-driven process of linguistic convergence' (p. 30).

Labov and Trudgill surely have it right that linguistic and mechanistic factors must be considered in the causal mix as well as social psychological drivers. But for my part I would not want to see that lead to the sidelining of the social in sociolinguistics. It seems to me to be the unique contribution of our field that we treat seriously and skilfully the analysis and theorization of society and language *together* and that we not endorse that they are separate or separable entities. Our drive should be to theorize both society and language in an ever more well-founded and integrated way, which seems to be a legitimate reading of the position Labov was taking in 1966. Hymes also, in an essay on 'why linguistics needs the sociologist' (1974: 69ff.) advocated for incorporating the social sciences into the sociolinguistic enterprise. His call was for integration:

It should be clear that a mechanical amalgamation of standard linguistics and standard sociology is not likely to suffice ... Adding a speechless sociology to a sociology-free linguistics can yield little better than post-hoc attempts at correlation between accounts from which the heart of the relevant data will be missing. (p. 76)

This brings us to consider a central issue in social theory and its place in recent sociolinguistic thought.

3.   The place of structure and agency

The interplay in social life between agency and structure has proved to be a central matter for sociolinguistic practice as well as a contested question in social theory. On the one hand, social structure constrains how we live. We start not with a blank slate but with what we inherit from our parents and our environment (linguistically as well as socially). On the other hand, agency is our freedom to live as we choose. Even in the most regimented milieu, there is room for human agency to create something new. Our relationship with space, for example, is constrained by how other humans and their social structures have already shaped the space we inherit – but we in turn reshape that and create new spaces from old. Humans and society, then, are simultaneously both free and fettered.

I said above that when sociolinguistics arose in the mid-twentieth century, structure ruled in the functionalist paradigms of the time. In the twenty-first century, agency dominates and constructivist approaches prevail. Different strands of sociolinguistics have been heirs to opposite sides in this dualism. Variationist sociolinguistics and the sociology of language clearly derive from an empiricist social science tradition and sit squarely on the structure side of the equation. By contrast, the more anthropological strands of sociolinguistics have been leaning towards the agentive for several decades since the waning of structural anthropology.

Constructivism has become the default approach in sociolinguistics as in all the social sciences. We can endorse its premise that a person is more than a static bundle of sociological categories. But to say that someone is male, or Anglo, or middle class does tell us something, even though these categorizations are not sufficient representations of a whole person. On the other hand, he or she is also more than an ever-shifting kaleidoscope of personas created in and by different situations, with no stable core – even though to say that we appear as child to our parents, employee to our boss, partner to our partner does tell us something about the person. A part of our behaviour is a reflection of the social characteristics of groups we are associated with, but we do not recreate ourselves moment by moment out of nothing. The counterpoint to radical constructivism is that, to the present, we bring the shapings of our past, of our relationships, of our environment, although we are indeed more than the sum of those things.

In her programmatic paper on social meaning in sociolinguistics, Eckert (2012) characterizes the nature of the shift in the field since the 1960s like this:

> The entire view of the relation between language and society has been reversed. The emphasis on stylistic practice ... places speakers not as passive and stable carriers of dialect, but as stylistic agents ... It has become clear that patterns of variation do not simply unfold from the speaker's structural position in a system of production, but are part of the active – stylistic – production of social differentiation. (Eckert 2012: 97)

This is neatly summarized – but also partially. Speakers are not the untrammelled agents that the quotation may imply, any more than they were the social automatons of mid-twentieth-century social theory. Sociolinguistics has gained greatly in richness, nuancing, and insight through the constructivist paradigm. But this pendulum has arguably swung too far towards agency, and our field is in danger of forgetting the inescapable impact of structure on speakers. This is strange, for who should be more aware than we sociolinguists of the role that the language environment of our first twenty years plays in moulding the shape of our linguistic future?

Many social thinkers have devoted themselves to seeking a way through the structure/agency duality. One attempt is Giddens's theory of structuration (1984), which treats structures as the ongoing creation of human agency. The everyday routines of hundreds or thousands or millions of individuals groove paths that define the shape of the areas and regions we live in. We may commute daily to work, make weekly trips to the supermarket, monthly visits to the hairdresser, and take annual holidays in a sunny place. These are the routines that also produce our repeated everyday interactions with workmates, shop assistants, or sports club members. Talk is central to these regular encounters, which provide much of the stuff of what sociolinguists study.

Another approach – expounded with remarkable clarity and brevity in an article published in the *Journal of Sociolinguistics* by Carter and Sealey in 2000 – is 'realist' sociology (see also their full-length book, Sealey and Carter 2004). They treat both structure and agency as present and necessary. Social structure is at once prior to action and modified as a result of action. But structure is also more than just the sum of individual actions: Its shape becomes independent of the individuals who have contributed to it.

4.   The centering of style and ideology in sociolinguistic theorizing

The *Journal of Sociolinguistics* has always been strong on style, which is not surprising given the research histories of its two founding editors. Individual articles have appeared frequently across the Journal's publishing history, from Kiesling's now-classic study of ING use in an American college fraternity (1998) to Rickford and Price's soon-to-be-classic article on 'Girlz II women' (2013). Alongside many individual papers there have been some strategic theme issues. The first special issue that the Journal ever published was 'styling the other', edited by Ben Rampton (1999), and a more recent issue focused on 'the sociolinguistics of performance' (Bell and Gibson 2011).

In the early twenty-first century the issue of style – and the issues that style raises – has moved from the periphery to the centre of sociolinguistic theorization. The Journal has probably played a part in that sea-change. Certainly, the development can be documented through a word search of two relevant terms in the first five volumes of the Journal (eighteen issues, 1997–2001) compared with a more recent four-volume run (twenty issues, 2010–2013). Two terms that have increasingly clustered with 'style' are 'social meaning' and 'index/ indexicality', and their usage may offer us some indication of trends in coverage over the past twenty years. A search for 'social meaning' in the early period (1997–2001) finds it appearing in 8 percent of articles. That rises to 27 percent in the recent sample (2010–2013). More strikingly, the terms 'index/indexicality' occurred in just 18 percent of articles early on, but that rose to over half of all articles in the later period (60 percent).

It is here that the interplay of structure and agency is at its sharpest and clearest, here that the debate over these polarities is most obviously required and joined. The most influential proposal in this area has been Eckert's 'three waves' model of the development of variationist sociolinguistics. Her examination of the role of social meaning reflects the shift from structure to agency, as the quote above indicated. This has major repercussions for the shape and conduct of the discipline, beginning with how we view language and languages and the use of language. Eckert has reinterpreted the history of variationist sociolinguistics from an agentive standpoint, proposing that we are now in a 'third wave' of its development.

Putting forward a thesis that circulated from 2005 (at least in North America), although it was not formally published till 2012, Eckert interpreted variationist sociolinguistics as developing in three waves:

(1) The first was based on survey methodology and establishing correlations between linguistic variation and sociodemographic categories, from Labov's New York study onwards.
(2) Then came the use of ethnographic methods to identify local categories that affect variation. This began with the Milroys' Belfast studies and included Eckert's own Belten High project (2000).
(3) In the third wave, variation itself constructs social meaning, and styles are the focus. It includes Eckert's more recent research.

This frame rapidly became the new orthodoxy on the history and shape of variationism. Many younger American scholars began positioning themselves as part of the 'third wave', and claims to that effect became routine components of the introductions to many submissions to the *Journal of Sociolinguistics*. Not all those papers lived up to their claims, and at times the would-be 'third wave' study was transparently traditional-variationist in its approach. But quite apart from the impact and follow-through, how defensible are Eckert's three waves and their characteristics?

There are at least three critiques to be made of the interpretations in Eckert (2012), although I can touch on them only briefly in this chapter. The first has already been addressed above – the overweighting of agency relative to structure. As Carter and Sealey write:

Too great an emphasis on structures denies actors any power and fails to account for human beings making a difference. Too great an emphasis on agency overlooks the ... very real constraints acting on us in time and space. (Carter and Sealey 2000: 11)

Secondly, the identification of these three historical phases represents a reductionist interpretation of the way in which even variationist sociolinguistics has developed, let alone the wider field. Although dominant in North America, variationism cannot be treated as an undertaking isolated from the rest of sociolinguistics. If the canvas was broadened to incorporate the anthropological and ethnographic strands of sociolinguistics, the meaning of that history would look very different. The importation of Silverstein's account of indexicality (e.g. 1979), for example, has had a considerable impact, including in Eckert's own work. What we have seen over the life of the *Journal of Sociolinguistics* is a quiet revolution in the character of variationist sociolinguistics. It has been broadened and enriched by inputs from ethnography, by qualitative approaches, and by wider social theorization, to the extent that the enterprise looks very different now from how it appeared forty years ago. It is arguably a postvariationism. And that is how it should be.

Thirdly, the history of style and social meaning that Eckert puts forward is partial – in both senses. It does justice to only one part of the work that has been accomplished on style over the past decades. On the American scene, for example, Ervin-Tripp (1972) undertook seminal pioneering work. Giles (with Powesland, 1975), Bell (1982), and Coupland (1984) were all publishing direct accounts of style by the early 1980s from the United Kingdom and New Zealand, including research which used variationist techniques to address new questions in the field. The overlooking of such precursors also makes Eckert's interpretation partial in the sense of privileging a particular interpretation of the history of style in sociolinguistics. An alternative account would provide a fuller and more firmly based history which does not identify and divide into these claimed three waves.

The *Journal of Sociolinguistics* has borne witness to the shift from the publication of traditional variationist work in its early years (Budzhak-Jones and Poplack 1997) to inventive niche research such as studies of mandative adjectives in physicians' speech (Hesson 2014) and Sarah Palin's use of demonstratives (Acton and Potts 2014). This has also entailed a movement beyond correlation, with an acceptance of the need to locate and evidence the social meanings of linguistic forms rather than assuming that a statistical distribution itself constitutes adequate evidence of social meaning.

Interest in social meaning in language has been accompanied by a growing emphasis on the role of ideologies (cf. Gal, this volume, Chapter 5, and also many other chapters). A focus on language ideologies goes back to Hymes, but research and reflection began to flourish in linguistic anthropology in the 1990s – that is, more or less coincident with the first few years of the *Journal of Sociolinguistics*. The foundation publications of language ideology research were a series of edited collections published over the next few years, including *Regimes of Language* (Kroskrity 2000), particularly the opening chapters by Kroskrity and Irvine and Gal; and *Language Ideologies* (1998), edited by Schieffelin, Woolard, and Kroskrity, particularly Woolard's introduction and Gal's epilogue. The collections edited by Blommaert (1999) and Gal and Woolard (2001) followed and provided a list of strong and diverse contributions.

Linguistic ideologies sometimes surface in open debates about language, but more often they remain unspoken and unconscious. While they may have major social and political effects – from individual discrimination through to armed conflict – most of the time people are scarcely aware of their existence. These ideologies are 'naturalized' – they represent commonsense views of language and society that people take for granted. They need no justification; they just describe the way the world is.

But while self-presenting as neutral descriptions, ideologies have repercussions which are far from unaligned.

Approaches to the ideological loading of language were spelled out in the
programmatic articles by Woolard (1998) and Irvine and Gal (2000). Woolard
identified several features of ideologies which affect language:

(1) Ideologies serve the interests of social groups and are differentiated
    according to those interests. As Irvine and Gal observe, 'there is no "view
    from nowhere," no gaze that is not positioned' (2000: 36). Most
    approaches can agree on this characterization of ideology.
(2) Prevalent ideologies serve the interests of the social elite; they legitimate and
    sustain subordination. Not all approaches are prepared to cross the divide
    from (1) to accept (2), a 'critical' take that ideologies are about power.
(3) Such ideologies disguise the operation of domination from the nonelite
    groups.

It seems that language ideological research was relatively slow to enter the
pages of the *Journal of Sociolinguistics*. In the first nine volumes (1997–2005),
only three articles had the word 'ideology' (or a derivative) in their titles.
But the next volume (10, 2006) carried three articles, followed by nine more
across the succeeding eight volumes (2007–2014) – that is, about one per year.
Counting the appearance of 'ideology' in titles is a rough and ready measure,
but it is clear at a glance that many – perhaps even most – Journal articles deal
with the ideological dimensions of language. Of those which foreground
ideology in their titles, the coverage of situations and languages on the ground
is diverse – Singapore, Rumania, the Arab world, American English, Korean,
French, Danish, Swedish, British English, German, and so on. Issues have
included monolingualism, standardisation, and orthography, as well as the
operation of ideologies in situations as diverse as family exchanges, media
debates, and sociolinguistic interviews.

5.   The diversification of sociolinguistics

Our field has grown exponentially in the past fifteen years. I was contracted to
write an introductory textbook in 1999, then long delayed actually finishing it.
I found I had made my own task much more difficult by the delay. Between
conception and completion of the text – eventually published as *The Guidebook to Sociolinguistics* in 2014 – the field grew exponentially in both size and
diversity. Encompassing that range in a single book became much more of a
challenge than it had been in the 1990s. Originally I had gauged that the topics
of most chapters in my book had already had their own book-length introduction and/or dedicated journal. By the time the book was finished, the field was
of such a size that virtually every section of every chapter had bred its own

publication – linguistic landscape, dialect birth, style, folk linguistics, communities of practice, and so on, for dozens of subfields. My dilemma reflected the broadening and diversification of the discipline as a whole, and that trend continues.

Alongside the rise of style as a core interest of sociolinguistics there has been a broadening of the allowable databases. While the anthropological strand of the field has always been eclectic in its data sources, variationist sociolinguistics began with a commitment to locating and recording the vernacular, defined as a speaker's least monitored speech style. There were early breaks with this principle (e.g. Bell 1977; Hindle 1979), but generally until the 1990s 'the vernacular' was seen as the holy grail of sociolinguistic data. However, styles and styling by definition disrupt this restriction, so that there was an increase in recording and studying performed and mediated genres of language both in their own right as linguistic products and for the light they could cast on styling.

The *Journal of Sociolinguistics* has always been hospitable to papers on performed or mediated materials, and they were strongly represented in our first, 1997 volume: printed handbills (Scollon), film (Marriott), graffiti (Adams and Winter), diachronic radio language (Van de Velde, van Hout, and Gerritsen), and advertising (Jones). Such data sources have made regular appearances since, but there has been a further, technology-driven shift over the past decade: the use of Internet data. The theme issue edited by Androutsopoulos in 2006 on computer-mediated communication in sociolinguistics was an early assemblage of innovative work. In some cases the sociolinguistics of the Internet has been the focus of a study (e.g. Divita 2012; Seargeant et al. 2012), particularly in the Internet's interactive forms such as social media and often as enabled by mobile technology. In other instances, the Internet has served as a means of access to data generated elsewhere, such as stage performances and televised programmes (e.g. the papers in Bell and Gibson 2011).

The turn to media and the Internet for data has required expanded analytical methods. It has become increasingly clear that digital materials must be analysed not just in their linguistic dimension – phonetics, syntax, discourse. Their 'multimodal' affordances are also crucial, including their interaction with strictly linguistic aspects of texts: visuals, appearance, soundtrack, movement (e.g. the theme issue on sociolinguistics and tourism, edited by Jaworski et al. 2014). While the Journal maintains an insistence that language and its analysis must be present in published papers, there are some data sets that cannot be adequately addressed without also focusing on their multimodal affordances.

From Hymes and Labov onwards, sociolinguists have always analysed discourse of various kinds, so discourse analysis and sociolinguistics have never been easy to tell apart. They have increasingly melded over the past two decades, and the attempt to make a distinction is now more or less fruitless. Discourse work, especially of the critical kind, has brought to sociolinguistics over these twenty years an expectation of intellectual engagement with social theory and critical engagement with social problems. It is through discourse studies that a good deal of broader social thought has made its way into sociolinguistics, and sociolinguistics itself is now a broader field because of it.

One consequence of the wider social-scientific turn to language, together with the broadening of data sources and analytical methods, has been a putative increasing contribution from nonlinguists since the 1990s. This is perhaps most obviously displayed at the two-yearly European Sociolinguistics Symposium, which has been the *Journal of Sociolinguistics'* natural 'home conference' since we launched the Journal there in 1996. The Symposium showcases hundreds of presentations arising from a range of disciplinary approaches that is at once stimulatingly eclectic and bewilderingly broad. It invites the question: Can a field this wide maintain its focus and build a core of theory and method?

Together with diversifications in disciplines and data has come the development of a new and particular strand in sociolinguistic research, absent in the 1990s but prevalent by 2015. Globalisation was the subject of an early theme issue of the Journal (Coupland 2003), and many papers since have framed their content in terms of this diverse phenomenon. Often studying Internet or media materials, an increasing number of submissions to the Journal deal with the globally connected nature of contemporary linguistic life – witness the theme issue on English in transnational South Korea (Lo and Park 2012). Globalisation is also tightly interwoven with the ever-developing digital technologies. Simultaneously with their face-to-face talk, speakers may be streaming a video from a remote site and texting a friend half a world away. The embedding of digital affordances into our co-present interactions is extraordinarily important and a challenge to some of the foundation assumptions of conducting research in our field (D'Arcy and Young 2012; Sharma 2012). Often this kind of work does not follow former identifiable strands of sociolinguistic research but cuts across variation, discourse, and ethnographic methods and interests.

Finally, 'identity' as an issue is no newcomer to sociolinguistic research; it has been there from the start. Over the years it has been one of the most used and least specified terms in sociolinguistic studies. Some have tried to avoid it – but hundreds of submissions to the Journal show that we seem to not be able to do without some concept of identity, even if we prefer to pluralize it to 'identities'. Identity includes both agentive and structural dimensions, which different scholars will weight differently. It is partly product – you cannot choose where you were born. It is partly process – you can make choices that re-present your self. Papers published in the Journal have especially focused on gender and ethnic identity, often looking at how these are performed linguistically. But as both Labov and Trudgill have pointed out, sociolinguists have too often proposed identity as an explanation of variation or change without any data other than the variation itself to support it. Like other aspects of social meaning, identities need independent warranting. They continue to contribute a strong thread to sociolinguistic research as our field seeks fresh ways to theorize what 'identity' may mean in the twenty-first century.

6. Conclusion

Returning, then, to Hymes's socially constituted (socio)linguistics, how far have we come? Are we there yet? Here is how Hymes himself foresaw it, looking forward to the turn of the millennium in his closing plenary at the 1972 Georgetown University Round Table, one of the foundation conferences of sociolinguistics:

The final goal of sociolinguistics, I think, must be to preside over its own liquidation. The flourishing of a hybrid term such as sociolinguistics reflects a gap in the disposition of established disciplines with respect to reality. Sometimes new disciplines do grow from such a state of affairs, but the recent history of the study of language has seen the disciplines adjacent to a gap themselves grow to encompass it ...

What are the chances for such a history to be written, say, from the vantage point of the year AD2000? To see, in retrospect the flourishing of 'sociolinguistics' as a transitional stage in the transformation of linguistics and adjacent social science disciplines to encompass what I have called 'socially constituted linguistics'? The chances, I think, are quite uncertain. (Hymes 1974: 206)

I do not see that we have yet experienced the transformation of linguistics into something socially constituted nor, gazing into my own crystal ball in 2016, can I envisage a future in which that will happen. General/theoretical linguistics shows little sign of encompassing sociolinguistics, still less adopting it as the best way to do linguistics. Hence my deduction that here we are talking about a socially constituted *socio*linguistics rather than linguistics. However, there has been one major change since Hymes's 1972 manifesto: The 'adjacent social science disciplines' have been refashioned by the turn to language. They now regard society as in at least some degree linguistically constituted. And over the past decade or so there has been growing interchange between those social sciences and sociolinguistics, which can only be productive. From this it will be clear that, pace Hymes, I do not see a dissolution into adjacent disciplines as a future for sociolinguistics.

In pursuit of a socially constituted sociolinguistics, I see us proceeding to incorporate social theory and theories as a natural part of how we approach language in society. We can do this consciously, not just de facto pulling scraps out of a bag of sociotheoretical rags. I think this is probably best achieved by one of the most obvious and most productive cross-fertilization procedures in scholarship: collaboration. For sociologists and linguists to work together is not unheard of, but it is certainly uncommon. We should actively seek out opportunities to bring social theorists into our research undertakings and be prepared to be challenged by them – to have our assumptions confronted, our methods questioned, and our analytical techniques scrutinized. We are not necessarily looking for the very latest social theory here but for productive lines of enquiry, some of which may be new but others just unknown to us. Social network theory, for example, was well established in social anthropology before being brought into sociolinguistics. There are other paradigms that could be equally productive for our discipline if only we knew about them. One avenue for this cross-fertilization may well be through the discourse side of our field. Discourse analysts have long been more closely connected with and energized by social theories from different places and traditions. We can encourage them to bring transparent versions of such approaches into the mainstream of our field.

In this enterprise I envisage sociolinguistics contributing to social theory as well as taking from it. Our field may have grown out of linguistics, and most of us may be trained linguists, but the centrality of language and its place in all human interactions, structures, and undertakings positions us to contribute something to social theorization. Ideally working with collaborators, sociolinguists can offer answers to the questions 'What is society?' and 'What is language?'. As J. Milroy has noted (1992), an adequate sociolinguistic theory is a contribution to social science in general.

In social theory, for example, structure will make – is already making – a comeback against the tide of the agentive and the constructive. I welcome that. The pendulum has been needing to swing back – but not too far. We need to hold the two in tension, and not just revert to the former structure-dominant, agent-poor stances and theories of the mid-twentieth century. We must retain the gains made through two decades of focus on agency, while we return to adequate accounting for and theorization of the structured in verbal interaction. That will enable us to achieve a level of generalization in our analyses and interpretations and to escape from the anarchy of insisting that a focus on the local and the temporal means there is nothing that can be generalized across contexts.

Sociolinguistics is set to keep on diversifying. Our data sources will continue to broaden, at very least because of the continuing creation of new digital affordances and genres. We cannot tell how these will play out or what the shape of new things will be like in twenty years' time. Who could have envisaged in the 1990s the details of our current digital present? Certainly, with diversifying data will come the need for new and broader methods to analyze them. What we now call multimodality may, a decade from now, look reductionist as a set of techniques for understanding the digital (and other) genres that are to come.

Are there dangers in diversification? Could it lead to the dilution of rigorous linguistic analysis and theorization and a descent into unproductive descriptivism, as Labov feared in 1966 (quoted above)? It could, but it need not. Opening up sociolinguistics to include those who deal with language in society but lack linguistic-analytical training is a challenge, but it has a solution, whose name again is collaboration. In 1974 Hymes gave an address on 'why linguistics needs the sociologist'. We need the knowledge and capabilities of the social scientists, but they equally need our language-analytic skills if they are to make the most of their encounters with language data. Hymes provides what is in effect a manifesto for cross-disciplinary collaboration:

Such work requires skills that are partly linguistic and partly social ... A certain amount of linguistics is needed simply to perceive the relevant features of the data – that a pronunci-ation has altered, that a word order is reversed, that a grammatical category is surprisingly frequent or absent ... What one needs at the base of the enterprise is something neither social science nor linguistics separately much provide – a social inquiry that does not abstract from verbal particulars, and a linguistic inquiry that connects verbal particu-lars, not with a model of grammar or discourse in general, but with social activities and relationships ... The social scientist lacks the observational skills and the linguist lacks the framework for making the connections. (Hymes 1996: 87)

Interdisciplinarity is not a 'good' in its own right but, rightly plied, can produce findings and insights which the separated disciplines would not yield. We can note in passing that there has not yet been significant change in the situation since Hymes made this diagnosis in the 1970s. If we seek to progress through mutual rapprochement with the wider social sciences, the key issue for sociolinguists will be not to lose our linguistic heart in the process but to maintain the centrality to our humanness of language itself.

Advocacy for linguistic equity will remain a hallmark of sociolinguistics in the future, as in the past. Here I return to Bakhtin, because we can learn from his subversive position on language diversity (1981). The stabilizing, central-izing impetus of linguistic standard and convention seeks to define and name languages and is always in tension with the decentralizing, momentary, creative use of language. Bakhtin has often been regarded as a herald of constructivist, agentive approaches, but he is equally adamant about lan-guage's simultaneous and inseparable normativity (1981: 272). The efforts of the centripetal powers of academies, educators, politicians, and pedants will always seek to constrain the centrifugal forces which are whirling language apart into diversity, spinning new words, new dialects, new languages, new voices. For this we need a politics of voice, a sociolinguistics which celebrates the profusion of voices that is its subject matter and which is committed to an equitable hearing for all those voices (see essays in Hymes 1996 for his take on linguistic inequality).

I believe that Bakhtin can also help us address central questions of sociolinguistic theory (Bell 2007; 2014). His dialogical approach to language is tailored to the needs of a forward-looking sociolinguistics. It is built around irony, parody, quotation, hybridity, and the like – the sort of phenomena that make strong linguists blanche and turn elsewhere for their research goals. But just because Bakhtin places these intractable characteristics at the heart of his theory, it is an enormously promising way of approaching the complexities of everyday language. This forms part of a dialogical theory of language, which emphasises addressivity, responsiveness, and the heteroglossia that is society's answer to the establishment's attempts to prescribe a standard. J. Milroy (1992) has suggested that sociolinguistic theory should be speaker-based rather than system-based; I would argue that it should be speaker–hearer based. Central to our theorization is sociolinguistics' interest in hearers as well as speakers. We should no more conceive of language without listeners than of a language that has no speakers.

This is one way, perhaps *the* way, towards the realization of a socially constituted linguistics, a discipline that is thoroughly linguistic and thoroughly social, refusing to play light on either front, as well as resisting the temptation to see the social and the linguistic as separable. We may maintain, with Labov, that the nature of linguistic data can make sociolinguistics the most exact of the social sciences (Milroy 1992). The capturability of language also makes the material that we study arguably the most usable data available through which to examine many sociotheoretic postulates. Such an enterprise will continue to position language style as a central issue and testing ground. The balance between agency and structure, for example, is perhaps more evident and more penetrable in the study of style than it is in many other social and linguistic areas.

What should the field expect of its journals in this situation? I believe it can ask editors and their teams to risk taking a lead, to look out for fresh trends, to bring new possibilities in from other fields; to commission a range of opinion and assessive material – state-of-the-art overviews, evaluative theme issues, position pieces, debates on key questions, historical reviews, and commentaries; to offer a sense of the past of sociolinguistics as a basis for a bold approach to its future.

What we still lack is a satisfactory broader social-theoretical frame for our work. Paradigms such as structural functionalism and constructivism are encompassing but found wanting. Proposals such as social networks and the community of practice are too limited to undergird our whole enterprise.

We are, I think, in need of something new and overarching. I have suggested that a dialogical approach may offer that. In any case, such a progression will probably come through intelligent cross-fertilization from outside our field, and we will continue to look for and encourage that in the scholarship that appears in the *Journal of Sociolinguistics*.

REFERENCES

Acton, Eric K., and Christopher Potts. 2014. That straight talk: Sarah Palin and the sociolinguistics of demonstratives. *Journal of Sociolinguistics* 18: 3–31.

Adams, Karen L., and Anne Winter. 1997. Gang graffiti as a discourse genre. *Journal of Sociolinguistics* 1: 337–360.

Androutsopoulos, Jannis (ed.). 2006. Sociolinguistics and computer-mediated communication. Theme issue of *Journal of Sociolinguistics* 10, 4.

Bakhtin, M. M. 1981 [1935]. Discourse in the novel. In M. M. Bakhtin, *The Dialogic Imagination* (ed. Michael Holquist, trans. Caryl Emerson and Michael Holquist). Austin: University of Texas Press, 259–422.

Bell, Allan. 1977. The language of radio news in Auckland: A sociolinguistic study of style, audience and subediting variation. PhD thesis, University of Auckland.

1982. Radio: The style of news language. *Journal of Communication* 32: 150–164.

2007. Style in dialogue: Bakhtin and sociolinguistic theory. In Robert Bayley and Ceil Lucas (eds.), *Sociolinguistic Variation: Theories, Methods and Applications*. New York and Cambridge, UK: Cambridge University Press, 90–109.

2014. *The Guidebook to Sociolinguistics*. Malden, MA, and Oxford: Wiley Blackwell.

Bell, Allan, and Andy Gibson (eds.). 2011. The sociolinguistics of performance. Theme issue of *Journal of Sociolinguistics* 15, 5.

Blommaert, Jan (ed.). 1999. *Language Ideological Debates*. Berlin: Mouton de Gruyter.

Budzhak-Jones, Svitlana, and Shana Poplack. 1997. Two generations, two strategies: The fate of bare English-origin nouns in Ukrainian. *Journal of Sociolinguistics* 1: 225–258.

Cameron, Deborah, Elizabeth Frazer, Penelope Harvey, M. B. H. Rampton, and Kay Richardson. 1992. *Researching Language: Issues of Power and Method*. London: Longman.

Carter, Bob, and Alison Sealey. 2000. Language, structure and agency: What can realist social theory offer to sociolinguistics? *Journal of Sociolinguistics* 4: 3–20.

Coupland, Nikolas. 1984. Accommodation at work: Some phonological data and their implications. *International Journal of the Sociology of Language* 46: 49–70.

(ed.). 2003. Sociolinguistics and globalisation. *Theme issue of* Journal of Sociolinguistics 7, 4.

2007. *Style: Language Variation and Identity*. Cambridge: Cambridge University Press.

Coupland, Nikolas, Srikant Sarangi, and Christopher N. Candlin (eds.). 2001. *Sociolinguistics and Social Theory*. Harlow: Pearson Education.

D'Arcy, Alexandra, and Taylor Marie Young. 2012. Ethics and social media: Implications for sociolinguistics in the networked public. *Journal of Sociolinguistics* 16: 532–546.

Divita, David. 2012. Online in later life: Age as a chronological fact and a dynamic social category in an Internet class for retirees. *Journal of Sociolinguistics* 16: 585–612.

Dubois, Sylvie, and Megan Melançon. 1997. Cajun is dead – Long live Cajun: Shifting from a linguistic to a cultural community. *Journal of Sociolinguistics* 1: 63–93.

Eckert, Penelope. 2000. *Linguistic Variation as Social Practice: The Linguistic Construction of Identity in Belten High.* Malden, MA: Blackwell.

2012. Three waves of variation study: The emergence of meaning in the study of sociolinguistic variation. *Annual Review of Anthropology* 41: 87–100.

Eckert, Penelope, and Etienne Wenger. 2005. What is the role of power in sociolinguistic variation? *Journal of Sociolinguistics* 9: 582–589.

Ervin-Tripp, Susan M. 1972. On sociolinguistic rules: Alternation and co-occurrence. In John J. Gumperz and Dell Hymes (eds.), *Directions in Sociolinguistics.* New York: Holt, Rinehart & Winston, 213–250.

Fairclough, Norman. 2000. Discourse, social theory, and social research: The discourse of welfare reform. *Journal of Sociolinguistics* 4: 163–195.

Gal, Susan, and Kathryn A. Woolard (eds.). 2001. *Languages and Publics: The Making of Authority.* Manchester: St. Jerome Publishing.

Giddens, Anthony. 1984. *The Constitution of Society: Outline of the Theory of Structuration.* Cambridge: Polity Press.

Giles, Howard, and Peter F. Powesland. 1975. *Speech Style and Social Evaluation.* London: Academic Press.

Heller, Monica. 1999. Ebonics, language revival, *la qualité de la langue* and more: What do we have to say about the language debates of our time? *Journal of Sociolinguistics* 3: 260–266.

Heller, Monica, Joan Pujolar, and Alexandre Duchêne. 2014. Linguistic commodification in tourism. *Journal of Sociolinguistics* 18: 539–566.

Hesson, Ashley. 2014. Medically speaking: Mandative adjective extraposition in physician speech. *Journal of Sociolinguistics* 18: 289–318.

Hindle, Donald M, 1979. The social and situational conditioning of phonetic variation. PhD dissertation, University of Pennsylvania.

Hymes, Dell. 1974. *Foundations in Sociolinguistics: An Ethnographic Approach.* Philadelphia: University of Pennsylvania Press.

1996. *Ethnography, Linguistics, Narrative Inequality: Toward an Understanding of Voice.* London: Taylor & Francis.

Irvine, Judith T., and Susan Gal. 2000. Language ideology and linguistic differentiation. In Paul V. Kroskrity (ed.), *Regimes of Language: Ideologies, Polities, and Identities.* Sante Fe, NM: School of American Research Press, 35–83.

Jaworski, Adam, Crispin Thurlow, and Monica Heller (eds.). 2014. Sociolinguistics and tourism. Theme issue of *Journal of Sociolinguistics* 18, 4.

Jones, Rodney H. 1997. Marketing the damaged self: The construction of identity in advertisements directed towards people with HIV/AIDS. *Journal of Sociolinguistics* 1: 393–418.

Kiesling, Scott Fabius. 1998. Men's identities and sociolinguistic variation: The case of fraternity men. *Journal of Sociolinguistics* 2: 69–99.

Kristiansen, Tore. 2011. Attitudes, ideology and awareness. In Ruth Wodak, Barbara Johnstone, and Paul Kerswill (eds.), *The Sage Handbook of Sociolinguistics*. London: Sage, 265–278.

Kroskrity, Paul V. (ed.). 2000. *Regimes of Language: Ideologies, Polities, and Identities*. Sante Fe, NM: School of American Research Press.

Labov, William. 1972. *Sociolinguistic Patterns*. Philadelphia: University of Pennsylvania Press.

2001. *Principles of Linguistic Change*, vol. 2: *Social Factors*. Malden, MA: Blackwell.

2006 [1966]. *The Social Stratification of English in New York City*, 2nd ed. Cambridge: Cambridge University Press.

Lo, Adrienne, and Joseph Sung-Yul Park. 2012. Globalization, multilingualism and identity in transnational perspective: The case of South Korea. Theme issue of *Journal of Sociolinguistics* 16, 2.

Marriott, Stephanie. 1997. Dialect and dialectic in a British war film. *Journal of Sociolinguistics* 1: 173–193.

Milroy, James. 1992. The theoretical status of sociolinguistics. In Kingsley Bolton and Helen Kwok (eds.), *Sociolinguistics Today: International Perspectives*. London and New York: Routledge, 356–360.

2001. Language ideologies and the consequences of standardization. *Journal of Sociolinguistics* 5: 530–555.

Milroy, Lesley. 2002. Introduction: Mobility, contact and language change – Working with contemporary speech communities. *Journal of Sociolinguistics* 6: 3–15.

Rampton, Ben. 1999. Styling the other. Theme issue of *Journal of Sociolinguistics* 3–4.

Rickford, John R. 1999. The Ebonics controversy in my backyard: A sociolinguist's experiences and reflections. *Journal of Sociolinguistics* 3: 267–282.

Rickford, John, and Mackenzie Price. 2013. Girlz II women: Age-grading, language change and stylistic variation. *Journal of Sociolinguistics* 17: 143–179.

Scollon, Ron. 1997. Handbills, tissues, and condoms: A site of engagement for the construction of identity in public discourse. *Journal of Sociolinguistics* 1: 39–61.

Sealey, Alison, and Bob Carter. 2004. *Applied Linguistics as Social Science*. London: Continuum.

Seargeant, Philip, Caroline Tagg, and Wipapan Ngampramuan. 2012. Language choice and addressivity strategies in Thai-English social network interactions. *Journal of Sociolinguistics* 16: 510–531.

Schieffelin, Bambi B., Kathryn A. Woolard, and Paul V. Kroskrity (eds.). 1998. *Language Ideologies: Practice and Theory*. New York: Oxford University Press.

Schneider, Edgar W. 2007. *Postcolonial English: Varieties around the World*. Cambridge: Cambridge University Press.

Sharma, Bal Krishna. 2012. Beyond social networking: Performing global Englishes in Facebook by college youth in Nepal. *Journal of Sociolinguistics* 16: 483–509.

Silverstein, Michael. 1979. Language structure and linguistic ideology. In Paul R. Clyne, William F. Hanks, and Carol L. Hofbauer, *The Elements: A Parasession on Linguistic Units and Levels*. Chicago, IL: Chicago Linguistic Society, 193–247.

Trudgill, Peter. 1981. Linguistic accommodation: Sociolinguistic observations on a sociopsychological theory. In C. S. Masek, R. A. Hendrick, and M. F. Miller (eds.), *Papers from the Parasession on Language and Behavior*. Chicago, IL: Chicago Linguistic Society, 218–237.

2004. *New-Dialect Formation: The Inevitability of Colonial Englishes*. Edinburgh: Edinburgh University Press.

Trudgill, Peter, Elizabeth Gordon, and Gillian Lewis. 1998. New-dialect formation and Southern Hemisphere English: The New Zealand short front vowels. *Journal of Sociolinguistics* 2: 35–51.

Van de Velde, Hans, Roeland van Hout, and Marinel Gerritsen. 1997. Watching Dutch change: A real time study of variation and change in standard Dutch pronunciation. *Journal of Sociolinguistics* 1: 361–391.

Wolfram, Walt, Kirk Hazen, and Jennifer Ruff Tamburro. 1997. Isolation within isolation: A solitary century of African-American Vernacular English. *Journal of Sociolinguistics* 1: 7–38.

Woods, Nicola J. 1997. The formation and development of New Zealand English: Interaction of gender-related variation and linguistic change. *Journal of Sociolinguistics* 1: 95–125.

Woolard, Kathryn A. 1985. Language variation and cultural hegemony: Toward an integration of sociolinguistic and social theory. *American Ethnologist* 12: 738–748.

1998. Introduction: Language ideology as a field of inquiry. In Bambi B. Schieffelin, Kathryn A. Woolard, and Paul V. Kroskrity (eds.), *Language Ideologies: Practice and Theory*. New York: Oxford University Press, 3–47.

Appendix   *Journal of Sociolinguistics* 'commissioned' content, 1997–2014

Volume	Genre	Title and Contributors
Vol. 3, 1999	Dialogue	*Sociolinguistics and Public Debate* (ed. Heller) Heller; Rickford; Laforest; Cyr
Vol. 3, 1999	Theme issue	*Styling the Other* (ed. Rampton) Rampton; Cutler; Bucholtz; Lo; Rampton; Johnstone; Bell; Hill
Vol. 4, 2000	Dialogue	*What Can Realist Social Theory Offer Sociolinguistics?* Carter and Sealey; Potter; Fairclough
Vol. 4, 2000	Dialogue	*'Sociolinguistics as I See It'* Samarin; Hymes
Vol. 4, 2000	Theme issue	*Non-standard Orthography and Non-standard Speech* (ed. Jaffe) Jaffe; Androutsopoulos; Miethaner; Jaffe and Walton; Berthele; Preston
Vol. 6, 2002	Theme issue	*Investigating Change and Variation through Dialect Contact* (ed. L. Milroy) L. Milroy; Britain; Watt; Schilling-Estes; Anderson; Dyer; Chambers
Vol. 7, 2003	Dialogue	*Sociolinguistics and Authenticity: an Elephant in the Room* Eckert; Bucholtz; Coupland
Vol. 7, 2003	Theme issue	*Sociolinguistics and Globalisation* (ed. Coupland) Coupland; Heller; Machin and van Leeuwen; Pennycook; Meyerhoff and Niedzielski; House; Thurlow and Jaworski; Blommaert
Vol. 8, 2004	Theme issue	*The Acquisition of Sociolinguistic Competence* (ed. Bayley and Regan) Bayley and Regan; Wolfram, Carter, and Moriello; Preston and Yamagata; Young and Lee; Mougeon, Rehner, and Nadasdi; Dewaele
Vol. 9, 2005	Theme issue	*Debating Language Rights* (ed. May) May; Ricento; Patrick; Blommaert; Canagarajah; Grin
Vol. 9, 2005	Dialogue	*Communities of Practice in Sociolinguistics* Davies; Eckert and Wenger; Gee; Meyerhoff

cont.

Volume	Genre	Title and Contributors
Vol. 10, 2006	Theme issue	*Sociolinguistics and Computer-Mediated Communication* (ed. Androutsopoulos) Androutsopoulos; Herring and Paolillo; del-Teso-Craviottto; Siebenhaar; Kelly-Holmes; Androutsopoulos; Georgakopoulou
Vol. 11, 2007	Theme issue	*Linguistic Ethnography: Links, Problems and Possibilities* (ed. Rampton, Maybin, and Tusting) Tusting and Maybin; Rampton; Scollon and Wong Scollon; Tsitsipis; Sealey; Wetherell; Blommaert; Hammersley
Vol. 12, 2008	Theme issue	*Sociolinguistics and Linguistic Anthropology: Strengthening the Connections* (ed. Bucholtz and Hall) Bucholtz and Hall; Woolard; Eckert; Sidnell; Heller; Rampton; Gumperz and Cook-Gumperz
Vol. 15, 2011	Theme issue	*The Sociolinguistics of Performance* (ed. Bell and Gibson) Bell and Gibson; Coupland; Gibson; Bell; Johnstone; Bucholtz and Lopez; Bauman
Vol. 16, 2012	Theme issue	*Globalization, Multilingualism and Identity in Transnational Perspective: The Case of South Korea* (ed. Lo and Park) Park and Lo; Kang; Shin; Song; Cho; Jeon; Lo and Kim; Block
Vol. 17, 2013	Theme issue	*Sociolinguistics of Writing* (ed. Lillis and McKinney) Lillis and McKinney; Blommaert; Trimbur; Gillen; Deumert and Lexander; Maybin
Vol. 18, 2014	Debate	*Media and Language Change* Sayers; Trudgill; Tagliamonte; Kristiansen; Androutsopoulos; Stuart-Smith; Gunter; Sayers; Coupland
Vol. 18, 2014	Theme issue	*Sociolinguistics and Tourism* (ed. Jaworski, Thurlow, and Heller) Heller, Jaworski, and Thurlow; Thurlow and Jaworski; Coupland and Coupland; Kelly-Holmes and Peitikainen; Heller, Pujolar, and Duchêne

19 Language theory in contemporary sociolinguistics: Beyond Dell Hymes?

Barbara Johnstone

Introduction

As a long-time reader and editorial board member of *Language in Society* (*LiS*) and its editor from 2005 to 2014, I have had the opportunity to observe changes in the field of sociolinguistics through the lens of its oldest journal.[1] *LiS* was founded, in 1972, specifically to publish research related to "all the interrelations of language and social life" (Hymes 1972: 2). The journal's founding editor, Dell Hymes, hoped that the journal would help lead to "a reconstruction of social theory in the light of linguistic methods and findings, and of linguistic theory on a social basis" (p. 2). When it came to the latter of these goals, Hymes hoped for a "broad conception of language and its relevance" (p. 3), broader than that of the "central thread" of twentieth-century linguistic theory, with its focus on reference at the expense of other kinds of meaning, its insistence on the autonomy of levels of language (phonology, morphology, syntax, and semantics) and on the autonomy of language as an object of study, and its lack of attention to what people do with language (p. 3). Hymes hoped for an "integrative" theory of language that would question the very notions of "language" and "dialect" and that would start from the assumption that structure follows function rather than the other way around, as "the significance of features of language cannot be assessed without knowledge of their social matrix" (p. 5). This was not a modest set of aims. For Hymes, the goal of sociolinguistics, "if such research is to be more than a novel name for a hodge-podge of pre-existing activities, pursued helter-skelter," was "to change the terms of reference for scientific, and informed public discussion, of 'language' ... to put an end to theory and research in terms of 'language' and 'languages,' and to replace it by theory and research in terms of the true forms in which

[1] I started work on this chapter while I was a visiting fellow at the Netherlands Institute for Advanced Study (NIAS) in June 2014. I am grateful to Leonie Cornips and Vincent de Rooij for making that visit possible. Kathryn Woolard, who was also a fellow at NIAS, had many useful suggestions. Nik Coupland provided very helpful feedback on an earlier draft.

417

linguistic resources are organized, change and are changed, in human lives" (p. 10).

LiS has always been multidisciplinary. Its original associate editors were William Labov, a linguist, and Allan Grimshaw, a sociologist; Hymes had academic degrees in linguistics and anthropology and taught mainly in the latter field. From the beginning, the journal has published research by people with disciplinary homes in linguistics, anthropology, sociology, education, and elsewhere, who employ ethnography, conversation analysis, quantitative variation analysis, discourse analysis of various stripes, and experimentation. As broad as its remit is, however, work published in *LiS* is still, more than forty years after its founding, intended to be about "speech and language as aspects of social life" (*LiS* Editorial Policy, front flyleaf). Thus it is fair to expect that research published in *LiS* is based on some way of understanding what "speech and language" are, explicit or not, and it is fair to ask whether its founder's aims for the journal have been fulfilled. In this chapter I focus on the second of Hymes's hopes, the hope that *LiS* would lead to a reconstruction of "linguistic theory on a social basis." What is the linguistic theory that underlies the work published in *LiS* in the twenty-first century, and is it the sort of theory that Hymes hoped for in 1972? Has the journal devolved into a forum for "a hodge-podge of pre-existing activities," or has it resulted in a new way of understanding language? To answer these questions, I explore how shifting theories of speech and language have informed research published in *LiS* during the first decade and a half of the twenty-first century.

Whether or not this is made explicit in the work itself, *LiS* articles have come increasingly to reflect the Hymesian view of language as first and foremost social practice and of linguistic practice as embedded in practices of meaning-making more generally. I focus in what follows on three closely related theoretical trends that have characterized linguistics, linguistic anthropology, and research in the "language and social interaction" areas of communication studies and sociology over the past two decades. The first is the move away from thinking of languages, dialects, and other named varieties as autonomous bundles of grammar and lexicon that linguists and dialectologists need to describe and towards thinking of languaging (cf. Pennycook, this volume, Chapter 9) as the process by which interactants create meaning intersubjectively, linking forms with meanings as they draw on repertoires that may be associated with multiple ways of speaking. The second body of work I touch on asks what gives rise to the idea that there are autonomous, clearly bounded languages with identifiable sets of speakers, some "native" and some whose authority to use the languages is more tenuous. The third trend is the move from describing linguistic interaction in isolation to describing it as it is embedded in and dependent on embodied interactional practices of gesturing, moving, and gazing, and technologies ranging from orthography to electronic communication systems.

Language and languaging: interaction and the details of talk

As Hymes hoped, one broad trend in language study in general over the last fifty years has been a gradual move away from structuralist theories of language to approaches that theorize language as social practice. Many linguists have come to think of "language" and "languages" as cultural constructs that arise for particular political and social reasons, and to think of our object of study, by contrast, as "languaging" (Becker 1991; 1995) or discourse (Harris 1981; Hopper 1988; Hanks 1996). We have come to see the patterns that we traditionally thought of as perduring as being, rather, emergent (Hopper 1988), always arising out of the things people do, for the particular reasons they do them, as they speak. This shift is by no means equally advanced across the discipline, and different theories of language use and language change make different assumptions about the process. Systemic-functional linguistics is perhaps the most influential of the usage-based theories of language, but it has been slow to take hold in North America and continental Europe. On the other hand, the study of grammaticalization is well advanced in historical linguistics.

This theoretical thread is evident in sociolinguistics, too. It is particularly visible in several kinds of work that have appeared in *LiS* in the last decade or two: research about style and enregisterment, about stylization and voicing, and about "text-metricality" and its role in creating meaning. With its roots in linguistics, this body of work tends towards particularity, focusing on small details of language and linking them with the interactional exigencies and outcomes of the moment.

Variation, style, and "social meaning"

In recent work, many variationists have supplemented or replaced the demographic categories traditionally used to account for their findings (sex, socio-economic class, level of education, etc.) with categories that are demonstrably relevant in the situations and to the people they study. Sparked by Eckert's ground-breaking work on linguistic variation as social practice (Eckert 2000; cf. Eckert, this volume, Chapter 3), many variationists are now interested in how linguistic variants enter into "styles" associated with groups of people who engage in repeated activities with one another. The study of style has a long and complicated history in sociolinguistics (Eckert and Rickford 2001; Coupland 2007), but variationists influenced by Eckert's work tend to see styles as ways of doing things – sets of orientations, symbols, ways of dressing, patterns of activity, ways of speaking, and so on – that are associated with and used to evoke and create communities of practice (Eckert 2000: 41–45). Using one or another of a set of possible linguistic choices is one of the things speakers do when they adopt styles associated with communities of practice they participate in. To study styles, variationists have required new methods, including ethnography and interviewing, and new theory about what speakers accomplish by using the resources provided by linguistic variation and about what "social meaning" is and how it becomes attached to linguistic variants.

Several articles by students of Eckert's that were published in *LiS* in the early 2000s reflect this shift in focus. Zhang (2005) compares the frequency of variants of several phonological variables in the speech of two groups of young, well-educated Chinese: people who work in international businesses, and people who work in state-owned businesses. Members of the international business group use a combination of features associated with Beijing speech and features associated with several other varieties of Chinese to construct and project a cosmopolitan style that is in some ways unlike the local standard, while people who work for state-owned businesses tend to use more Standard Mainland Mandarin variants. Zhang explains these findings in terms of linguistic marketplaces in which people use styles of speech to adopt new Yuppie identities. Moore and Podesva (2009) explore how English adolescents construct and use tag questions, showing that members of different self-defined groups ("populars," "townies," and "geeks") typically use different types of tags to different effects, both to construct different stances in the moment and to align with different styles in the longer term. In a study of how American university students interpret others' use of the alveolar variant of *-ing*, Campbell-Kibler (2008) shows that listeners, as well as speakers, use multiple social and linguistic resources to construct images of the people they hear, so that listeners who are told different things about speakers hear the same speech samples as representing styles associated with different personality types.

Work like this on variation and style has led sociolinguists to think about how ways of speaking get linked with "images of personhood" (Agha 2007: 177), like yuppies, "townies," and such. The semiotic process known as "enregisterment" (Agha 2003; 2007; Johnstone et al. 2006) has proven a useful conceptual tool in studies of the ways in which linguistic features or sets of features come to be associated with styles or varieties of speech, and what using these styles or varieties comes to mean. In *LiS*, Henry (2010) describes competing ways in which "Chinglish" has come to be imagined and evaluated in China. Outsiders, such as Western ESL teachers, sometimes see Chinese-influenced English as evidence that English is a poor fit for Chinese expressive needs. According to their linguistic-relativist ideology of language, Chinglish is valuable in that it provides windows onto the Chinese mind. For Chinese language professionals, on the other hand, oriented to the idea that nonstandard uses of any language are evidence of low personal standards and carry negative social value, Chinglish is simply evidence that Chinese students are not learning standard English well enough. Cole and Pellicier (2012) explore the role of mediatization in establishing a dominant, perduring social meaning for a way of speaking. Cole and Pellicier analyze the uptake of a speech that a white U.S. presidential candidate gave to a group of African American leaders. The candidate's use of features of African American preaching style was seen as effective in the moment, when the audience interpreted it as a sign that the candidate was aligning with them by moving toward a style of speech they valued. Later, however, the candidate's style-shifting was represented in the media as inappropriate mockery of a way of speaking that, from the point of view of mainstream language ideology, is stigmatized.

Stylization and (multi)voicing

Sociolinguistics' shift toward a more practice-oriented theory of language is also reflected in research on stylization and voicing, often in the context of verbal performance. Ground-laying work published in *LiS* at or before the turn of the twenty-first century includes Rampton's (1991; 2002) work on "crossing" and Coupland's (2001) on "styling." The focus in this work is on how people use resources associated with multiple personas or situations and with multiple ways of speaking and on what doing this can accomplish. In *LiS*, for example, Buescher et al. (2013) describe how a nonlocal way of speaking, Lingala, is used to claim several kinds of identity in Goma, a town on the Rwandan border in the Kiswahili-speaking part of the Democratic Republic of the Congo. Because of the unstable political situation on the Rwandan-Congolese border, it has become important for Congolese there to claim "Congolité," or true Congoleseness, and using bits of Lingala (a language which most inhabitants of Goma do not actually speak well) can serve this function. Because of its use by the military, Lingala also indexes power and authority, and because it is the language of the capital city it can also stake a claim to urban sophistication. Levon (2012) shows how gay Israeli men use *oxtšit*, a slang lexicon that is associated with gayness, not to claim gay identities but to perform humorous critiques of the idea that there is a single "gay identity." More mainstream gay men, men who value assimilation with heterosexual speech norms, actually use this highly feminine, stereotypically gay-sounding variety more than gay men engaged in subverting heterosexual norms. Levon claims that mainstream gays' uses of *oxtšit* are instances of "vari-directional voicing," a term Levon borrows from Bakhtin. Mainstream gay men use *oxtšit* among themselves to parody nonmainstream gay men and thus index their own normative gay identities. Also interested in voicing, or whose identity is being indexed in acts of language crossing, Tetreault (2009) shows how urban French teens of Algerian descent use a register associated with TV talk-show hosts to shift their footing vis-à-vis co-present teens, putting others on the footing of talk-show guests so as to mock them. In the course of her interviews, the teens would sometimes appropriate Tetreault's microphone and audio-recorder, using them as props in the performance of the TV-host persona. This persona is identified with a standard register of French, a variety that the teens did not actually claim as theirs. Using this register positioned the teens to caricature their peers, ritually defaming them, but in such a way as to mitigate the speaker's responsibility for his words (because he is speaking in a way that is perceived as inauthentic for him) and increase the force of his words (because they are spoken in a way associated with official, institutionally sanctioned speech). Britt (2011) also describes how variety-crossing can accomplish shifts in footing in speeches by prominent African Americans who move into black preaching style to "cloak themselves with the status and respect associated with black preachers" (p. 211). Thompson (2010) shows how a Tanzanian musician styles himself as "the Maasai rapper" by using pronunciation features associated with Maa and transposing syllables in Swahili, apparently undermining the ideology that privileges Standard Swahili but at same time mocking stereotypical Maasai-ness.

Text-metricality and semiotic calibration

Linguistic anthropology's traditional concern with the role of language in the transmission of culture has led to a recurring interest in how language and social interaction can serve to organize and calibrate interactants' experience of the world. With the focus firmly on language as system, Sapir (1921) and his student Whorf (1941) first suggested ways in which linguistic categories reflect and shape cultural ones. In the latter decades of the twentieth century, Sherzer (1987) and others (Hill and Mannheim 1992; Urban 1994; Lucy 1997) suggested that the calibration of culture happened not in language-as-system but in discourse, language-in-interaction. As Roman Jakobson had shown for folk poetry decades earlier, linguistic parallelism is crucial to this process (Jakobson 1960; 1966; 1968). Sounds or structures juxtaposed in similar contexts invite audiences to work out the connections between them. In work that has received renewed attention in the 2000s, Michael Silverstein revives Jakobson's insight into the role of juxtaposition in the transmission of language and culture and brings Jakobson's insight from the level of the text to the level of the interaction. Silverstein uses the term "text-metricality" to describe the ways in which both monological texts and conversational, multi-vocal "interactional texts" can calibrate interpretations through parallelism. In Silverstein's adaptation of the semiotic theory of American philosopher C. S. Peirce, parallelism is treated as one of the "metapragmatic" practices by which interlocutors signal how to interpret what they say and do (Silverstein 1985, 1993).

This strand of Silverstein's thought is visible in a number of recent *LiS* articles. For example, in an analysis of Tibetan Buddhist debate, Lempert (2008) shows how interactants use similarities and differences in the stances they take with regard to propositions to point to their interactional stances with regard to one another. In these highly formalized speech events, a less experienced, lower-ranking "defender" argues with a more experienced, more senior "challenger" about the meaning of a segment of a Buddhist text. The conduct of the debate has to do with both epistemic matters (who knows better what the text means and how each argues for his interpretation) and social alignments associated with rank and seniority. Arguers' stances toward textual interpretations serve as models for stances vis-à-vis each other. For example, the challenger in a debate might repeatedly respond to the defender's claims about what "I know" with claims about what "everybody knows," brushing off the defendant's expertise as common knowledge and thereby enacting the challenger's higher status. Wilce (2008) shows how, despite efforts to "scientize" how psychiatry is talked about in Bangla in order to dispel traditional Bangladeshi psychiatry's aura of magic and religion, the correspondence between psychiatrists writing for a popular magazine and the people who write to ask them questions is characterized by the kind of parallelism that is associated with ritual language. Howard (2009) explores how expectations set up by patterns of repetition can serve as jumping-off points in Thai children's language games, places where humor can be created via the use of unexpected words and meanings. The games thus tweak adult cultural models, "decalibrating" expectations while at the same time drawing attention to them.

Constructing languages and speakers

Even before Hymes gave voice to it, the idea that languages are clearly bounded entities that can be neatly divided up into varieties was felt to be problematic. Linguists have known since the earliest attempts to trace the history of languages or map variant forms that the world does not present itself to us with neat linguistic boundaries waiting to be discovered. Contemporary dialectology suggests that rather than starting with relatively small sets of prechosen variable features (different ways of saying the same word, different words for the same thing, different grammatical or discourse patterns for the same purpose) and looking for dialect boundaries by aggregating the dividing lines between variants of them, we need to look at how much larger numbers of variant tokens cluster together, trying to remain agnostic about what the clusters represent and to pay attention not just to the centers of clusters but to their peripheries (Goebl 1982; Viereck 1985; Kretzschmar 1996). Once our aim is no longer to find and describe "varieties" or "languages," but rather to find and describe the spatial patterns that emerge in large corpora of speech, we are led to reimagine varieties and languages not as empirical objects but as ideological ones, concepts that come into being in particular historical and material contexts, via particular sets of discursive practices. *LiS* authors exploring these processes have typically taken a broad historical approach, linking the cultural production of languages and speakers with historical processes like colonialism and imperialism, industrialization and deindustrialization, and global flows of people and money, as well as ideologies associated with nationalism and, more generally, how language, place, and identity are thought to map onto each other, and ideologies associated with language standardization.

Language ideology, standardization, and linguistic expertise

In *LiS*, Makoni et al. (2007) trace how colonial powers in southern Africa created the idea of timeless, primordial, culturally authentic "indigenous" languages, and how this idea has made it difficult to see how language shift is really happening in urban Zimbabwe. Makoni et al. critique the idea, associated with research on language endangerment and language death, that indigenous languages are autonomous and timeless, intimately linked to traditional culture. They show that it was, rather, the colonial powers and the missionaries who came with them who divided up southern African ways of speaking into "dialects," created standard varieties of them in order to translate the Christian Bible, and assigned national "languages" to the new, arbitrarily bounded countries they had created.

Working in the framework of language ideology research associated with Gal, Woolard, and other American linguistic anthropologists (Schieffelin et al. 1988; Woolard and Schieffelin 1994; Gal and Irvine 1995), Frekko (2009) explores the standardization of Catalan. The ideology associated with European nationalism required a nation to be associated with a single national language that was both available for public use and helped create a national public (Anderson 1991). However, there were "missing registers" in Catalan, because there were things that had never needed to be done in Catalan. Further, Catalan was strongly indexical of a particular persona, so it could not index Catalonianness in general the way Castilian could index Spanishness. This worried Catalan language professionals, who were concerned that Catalan could not function as a national standard because it did not map onto a national public. Exploring how language professionals can erase boundaries between languages as well as create them, Woolard and Genovese (2007) describe an early modern written genre in Spain in which words that could be read as either Spanish or Latin were used strategically to illustrate the superiority of Spanish over other vernaculars. This "strategic bivalency" both drew on and unsettled the idea that Latin and Spanish were different languages by blurring the boundaries between them.

As languages and varieties have come to be seen as cultural products rather than taken-for-granted units of analysis, sociolinguists like these are asking new questions about who gets thought of as a language expert and what expertise consists of and accomplishes. In *LiS*, French (2009) describes the work of revolutionary linguist Eoin MacNeill in linking Irish, in all its variety, with quintessential Irish national identity, and Samuels (2006) shows how Bible translation practices led the San Carlos Apache to think of language as a purely referential system. What it means to be a "speaker" of a language has also received attention in studies by McEwan-Fujita (2010) and O'Rourke and Ramallo (2013) of new speakers of Scottish Gaelic and Galician, respectively.

Language ideology and social inequality

Ideas about language are also the focus in a number of *LiS* articles about how ideas about languages, varieties, and speakers can create and justify social inequality. For example, Barrett (2006) studied a Mexican restaurant in the United States where the English-speaking managers believed that their ways of accommodating linguistically to monolingual Spanish-speaking employees were sufficient to make their directions understandable to the employees. The managers' impoverished idea of what is required to speak Spanish allowed them to ignore Spanish grammar and to rely on "Mock Spanish" (Hill 1998) practices such as adding [o] to English words to make them sound Spanish. The Spanish-speakers were often blamed for the resulting miscommunications. Andrus (2012) shows how the idea behind the "excited utterance" exception to the exclusion of hearsay evidence in Anglo-American law – the idea that under certain conditions people are not the agents or owners of their own words – can disempower victims of domestic violence, when words they uttered to police officers at the scene of the complaint can be put into evidence in court without their consent. Carter (2014) explores how national and institutional ideology about language, identity, and ethnicity intersect with local experience in a North Carolina school to encourage the idea that all Latino students are monolingual Spanish speakers and that Latinos use Spanish as a dangerous secret code. In a study of an addiction treatment program in the United States, Carr (2006) describes the "ideology of internal reference" that underlies how therapists encourage clients to talk only about psychological aspects of their illness, and how this ideology contributes to the political isolation of the clients. Maryns (2013) shows how the institutional privileging of written text over other modes of discourse erases important aspects of the identities of asylum-seekers in Belgium.

Multimodal semiosis

A third body of work that reflects Hymes's concern with "language in its social matrix" is research that moves away from studying linguistic behavior in isolation toward studying language as it is embedded in other modes of meaning-making. Like the move from language as object to languaging as practice, this shift is predicated on a theory of language as nonautonomous, arising from and shaped by the work of human interaction. This shift in focus has led some sociolinguists to describe meaning-making with language in the same terms as they describe meaning-making in other modes. In multimodal research on discourse-in-interaction, language is seen as one of a number of communicative resources that interactants draw on as they jointly create meaning.

Embodied interaction

Research questions that might once have been addressed through studies of code choice or code-switching or with reference to "paralinguistic" features are increasingly being addressed through studies of sociolinguistic repertoires in multiple modes. Sociolinguists are increasingly interested in describing the procedures by which people attempt to create intersubjectivity in particular situations (sometimes those made visible in the complex, diverse societies created by global mobility), drawing on linguistic and nonlinguistic resources that may have multiple origins. For example, Paugh (2005) describes how children in rural Dominica, forbidden to speak Patwa in favor of English, nonetheless use "verbal resources and physically embodied social action" (p. 63) to create situations in their play in which Patwa is appropriate. Higgins (2007) describes "tactics of intersubjectivity" (Bucholtz and Hall 2004) in a conversation among Tanzanian journalists that includes a joke in Swahili and English that they understand in different ways.

Describing a set of communicative resources that includes both language and the body (cf. Bucholtz and Hall, this volume, Chapter 8), Edwards (2012) explores how some Deaf-Blind people and their interpreters work toward mutual senses of what is going on around them by using conventional hand-signing embedded in the emergent practice of moving the Deaf-Blind people's hands through space. Edwards draws explicitly on William Hanks's "practice approach to language" (Hanks 1996) inspired in some ways by the work of Pierre Bourdieu (1977). In this approach, linguistic systems (like hand-signing) are seen as relatively "prefabricated" and reusable, but always underspecified, dialectically related to and dependent on emergent strategies that arise as they are needed. Matoesian (2012) is also interested in how the conventional and the creative interact in a focus group in which participants invoke and construct symbolic collectivities. Matoesian shows how gesture and gaze interact with linguistic choices such as pronoun use and tense in an "iconic interpenetration among talk, bodily conduct, and sociocultural context" (p. 365).

Ethnomethodology and interaction analysis

Other explorations of multimodality in interaction start from the premises of conversation analysis, with interest in how interaction is ordered and sustained in the moment. In this view, resources associated with language (such as words) have equal footing with gesture, gaze, and timing, and the focus is less often on the small details of language. Researchers' questions are about how people manage to come to a shared understanding of what they are doing and how to do it. Moore (2008) describes how customers in an American print shop use names, descriptions, and gestures to identify the services they want. Pasquandrea (2011) explores how Italian doctors interact with Chinese patients through interpreters, using bodily orientation and gaze along with the management of transition-relevant points to make it clear who is talking to whom at what point. Mondada (2012) shows how participants in a meeting use the resources of language and the body to manage code choice and participation, such that a participant sitting silently in the last row, who does not speak the initial language of the meeting, becomes a recognized expert, and the language of the meeting changes to accommodate her. Keating and Sunakawa (2010) describe how a team of online gamers, sitting together in a room, manage their interactions in the virtual world of the game and in the real space they share and how they transition between these worlds. The resources of language (ranging from prosody to grammatical deixis) and the body (orientation and coordination of movement) work together; the focus of the analysis is not talk but interaction.

Discussion

As this very partial overview has suggested, if Dell Hymes were to read *LiS* today he would find great deal of evidence that his call for a "broad conception of language and its relevance" has been taken up. It is harder than it once was to imagine that linguistic variation simply reflects differences in linguistic input in childhood (though see Bell, this volume, Chapter 18). It is harder than it once was to talk about "languages" and "dialects" without specifying whose categories these are and what gave rise to them. And it is harder than it once was to analyze discourse as if it consisted entirely of words. One wonders, however, why it has taken so long, particularly in view of the fact that Hymes's claims about language were not new when he made them. A full answer to this question would require an extended excursion into the sociology of science and the history of linguistics. For example, Hymes and his cofounders of *LiS* were motivated in large part by their opposition to Chomskyan generative linguistics, which treated language as a cognitive disposition described in very abstract terms and was explicitly not interested in what people do with language or how communicative practice shapes communicative resources. Although many sociolinguists would still view their understanding of language as incompatible with Chomskyan theory, it is less important now to make that incompatibility explicit or to frame one's work as a response to it.

Another part of the answer, however, has to do with what sociolinguists have been in a position to notice, and when. Some of the shifts in focus visible in *LiS* over the past fifteen years reflect shifts in sociolinguists' attention resulting from economic and political changes that were hardly on the horizon in 1972. For example, the variety of multiethnic, multinational, multilingual ways of being that have become particularly visible as a result of globalization have encouraged sociolinguists to move beyond the idea that each person has a single "native" language and that multilingual discourse is necessarily the result of switches between discrete, self-contained linguistic systems called "languages." Geographic and social mobility have brought once localized, isolated ways of speaking to the attention of people whose parents and grandparents spoke as they did largely because everyone with whom they interacted spoke that way. This has led to new, or newly visible, performances of second-order representations of regionally or socially marked speech and new scholarly attention to performance and the multivoiced quality of performance.

Shifts in sociolinguists' attention also reflect shifts in ways of working that are made possible by new technologies for data collection, transcription, and analysis. For example, while the study of the nonverbal elements of communication has a long history (Birdwhistell 1959; Kendon 1972), interest in multimodality in face-to-face interaction has spread, as video recording has become easier and cheaper (as Bell also notes, this volume, Chapter 18). (Likewise, scholarship on multimodality in written communication, though less often represented in *LiS*, tracks change in the increasing ease with which writers can combine words and images.) Access to computers has made it easier to store large amounts of data, and increasingly sophisticated concordance software and software for automatic linguistic tagging and voice recognition has made it easier to transcribe and analyze the data. Concomitantly, some sociolinguists now work with large corpora of data that make it possible to find patterns in usage that were once hard to spot.

Still, even if economic and technological change have drawn some early twenty-first-century sociolinguists' attention back to aspects of language in social life that Hymes wanted us to think about, it is clear that neither the journal nor the field of sociolinguistics as a whole have "chang[ed] the terms of reference for scientific ... discussion of 'language.'" "Autonomous" linguistics, focused on the study of structures largely divorced from contexts, still dominates the field of language study in many parts of the world, and public understanding of language is still dominated by the idea that there are discrete, clearly bounded languages with better and worse varieties and that the function of language is to denote things in the world (Joseph and Taylor 1990; Lippi-Green 1997). Perhaps a real paradigm shift will have happened only once it is no longer possible to imagine a journal called *Language in Society*, because we will have reached the point at which we can no longer imagine extracting "language" from the process of meaning-making.

REFERENCES

Agha, A. 2003. The social life of a cultural value. *Language and Communication* 23: 231–273.
   2007. *Language and Social Relations*. New York: Cambridge University Press.
Anderson, B. 1991. *Imagined Communities: Reflections on the Origin and Spread of Nationalism*. London and New York: Verso.
Andrus, J. 2012. Language ideology, fractal recursivity, and discursive agency in the legal construction of linguistic evidence. *Language in Society* 41, 5: 589–614.
Barrett, R. 2006. Language ideology and racial inequality: Competing functions of Spanish in an Anglo-owned Mexican restaurant. *Language in Society* 35, 2: 163–204.
Becker, A. L. 1991. A short essay on languaging. In F. Steier (ed.), *Research and Reflexivity*. Thousand Oaks, CA: Sage, 226–234.
   1995. *Beyond Translation: Essays toward a Modern Philology*. Ann Arbor: University of Michigan Press.
Birdwhistell, R. L. 1959. *Introduction to Kinesics: An Annotation System for Analysis of Body Motion and Gesture*. Washington, DC: U.S. Department of State Foreign Service Institute.
Bourdieu, P. 1977. *Outline of a Theory of Practice*. Cambridge: Cambridge University Press.
Britt, E. 2011. "Can the church say amen": Strategic uses of black preaching style at the State of the Black Union. *Language in Society* 40, 2: 211–233.
Bucholtz, M., and K. Hall. 2004. Theorizing identity in language and sexuality research. *Language in Society* 33, 4: 469–515.
Buescher, K., S. D'hondt, and M. Meeuwis. 2013. Recruiting a nonlocal language for performing local identity: Indexical appropriations of Lingala in the Congolese border town Goma. *Language in Society* 42, 5: 527–556.
Campbell-Kibler, K. 2008. I'll be the judge of that: Diversity in social perceptions of (ING). *Language in Society* 37, 5: 637–659.
Carr, E. S. 2006. "Secrets make you sick": Metalinguistic labor in a drug treatment program for homeless women. *Language in Society* 35, 5: 631–653.
Carter, P. 2014. National narratives, institutional ideologies, and local talk: The discursive production of Spanish in a "new" US Latino community. *Language in Society* 43, 2: 209–240.

Cole, D., and R. Pelicier. 2012. Uptake (un)limited: The mediatization of register shifting in US public discourse. *Language in Society* 41, 4: 447–470.

Coupland, N. 2001. Dialect stylization in radio talk. *Language in Society* 30, 3: 345–375.

2007. *Style: Language Variation and Identity*. Cambridge: Cambridge University Press.

Eckert, P. 2000. *Linguistic Variation as Social Practice*. Oxford: Blackwell.

Eckert, P., and J. R. Rickford (eds.). 2001. *Style and Sociolinguistic Variation*. Cambridge and New York: Cambridge University Press.

Edwards, T. 2012. Sensing the rhythms of everyday life: Temporal integration and tactile translation in the Seattle Deaf-Blind community. *Language in Society* 41, 1: 29–71.

Frekko, S. E. 2009. "Normal" in Catalonia: Standard language, enregisterment and the imagination of a national public. *Language in Society* 38, 1: 71–93.

French, B. 2009. Linguistic science and nationalist revolution: Expert knowledge and the making of sameness in pre-independence Ireland. *Language in Society* 38, 5: 607–625.

Gal, S., and J. T. Irvine. 1995. The boundaries of languages and disciplines: How ideologies construct difference. *Social Research* 62: 967–1001.

Goebl, H. 1982. *Dialektometrie*. Vienna: Oesterreichischen Akademie der Wissenschaften.

Hanks, W. 1996. *Language and Communicative Practice*. Boulder, CO: Westview.

Harris, R. 1981. *The Language Myth*. New York: St. Martin's Press.

Henry, E. S. 2010. Interpretations of "Chinglish": Native speakers, language learners and the enregisterment of a stigmatized code. *Language in Society* 39, 5: 669–688.

Higgins, C. 2007. Shifting tactics of intersubjectivity to align indexicalities: A case of joking around in Swahinglish. *Language in Society* 36, 1: 1–24.

Hill, J. H. 1998. Language, race, and white public space. *American Anthropologist* 100: 680–689.

Hill, J. H., and B. Mannheim. 1992. Language and world view. *Annual Review of Anthropology* 21: 381–406.

Hopper, P. J. 1988. Emergent grammar and the a priori grammar postulate. In D. Tannen (ed.), *Linguistics in Context: Connecting Observation and Understanding*. Norwood, NJ: Ablex, 117–134.

Howard, K. M. 2009. Breaking in and spinning out: Repetition and decalibration in Thai children's play genres. *Language in Society* 38, 3: 339–363.

Hymes, D. 1972. Editorial introduction to *Language in Society*. *Language in Society* 1, 1: 1–14.

Jakobson, R. 1960. Concluding statement: Linguistics and poetics. In T. Sebeok (ed.), *Style in Language*. Cambridge, MA: MIT Press, 350–377.

1966. Grammatical parallelism and its Russian facet. *Language* 42: 399–429.

1968. Poetry of grammar and grammar of poetry. *Lingua* 21: 597–609.

Johnstone, B., J. Andrus, and A. E. Danielson. 2006. Mobility, indexicality, and the enregisterment of "Pittsburghese." *Journal of English Linguistics* 34, 2: 77–104.

Joseph, J. E., and T. J. Taylor (eds.). 1990. *Ideologies of Language*. New York: Routledge.

Keating, E., and C. Sunakawa. 2010. Participation cues: Coordinating activity and collaboration in complex online gaming worlds. *Language in Society* 39, 3: 331–356.

Kendon, A. 1972. Some relationships between body motion and speech. In B. Pope (ed.), *Studies in Dyadic Communication*. New York: Pergamon, 177–213.

Kretzschmar, W. B. 1996. Quantitative areal analysis of dialect features. *Language Variation and Change* 8: 13–39.

Lempert, M. 2008. The poetics of stance: Text-metricality, epistemicity, interaction. *Language in Society* 37, 4: 569–592.

Levon, E. 2012. The voice of others: Identity, alterity and gender normativity among gay men in Israel. *Language in Society* 41, 2: 213–235.

Lippi-Green, R. 1997. *English with an Accent: Language, Ideology, and Discrimination in the United States*. London and New York: Routledge.

Lucy, J. A. 1997. Linguistic relativity. *Annual Review of Anthropology*, 26.

Makoni, S., J. Brutt-Griffler, and P. Mashiri. 2007. The use of "indigenous" and urban vernaculars in Zimbabwe. *Language in Society* 36, 1: 25–49.

Maryns, K. 2013. Procedures without borders: The language-ideological anchorage of legal-administrative procedures in translocal institutional settings. *Language in Society* 42: 71–92.

Matoesian, G. M. 2012. Gesture's community: Social organization in multimodal conduct. *Language in Society* 41, 3: 365–391.

McEwan-Fujita, E. 2010. Ideology, affect, and socialization in language shift and revitalization: The experiences of adults learning Gaelic in the Western Isles of Scotland. *Language in Society* 39, 1: 27–64.

Mondada, L. 2012. The dynamics of embodied participation and language choice in multilingual meetings. *Language in Society* 41: 213–235.

Moore, E., and R. J. Podesva. 2009. Style, indexicality, and the social meaning of tag questions. *Language in Society* 38, 4: 447–485.

Moore, R. J. 2008. When names fail: Referential practice in face-to-face service encounters. *Language in Society* 37, 3: 385–413.

O'Rourke, B., and F. Ramallo. 2013. Competing ideologies of linguistic authority amongst new speakers in contemporary Galicia. *Language in Society* 42, 3: 287–305.

Pasquandrea, S. 2011. Managing multiple actions through multimodality: Doctors' involvement in interpreter-mediated interactions. *Language in Society* 40, 4: 455–481.

Paugh, A. L. 2005. Multilingual play: Children's code-switching, role play, and agency in Dominica, West Indies. *Language in Society* 34, 1: 63–86.

Rampton, B. 1991. Interracial Panjabi in a British adolescent peer group. *Language in Society* 20: 391–422.

2002. Ritual and foreign language practices at school. *Language in Society* 31: 491–525.

Samuels, D. W. 2006. Bible translation and medicine man talk: Missionaries, indexicality, and the "language expert" on the San Carlos Apache Reservation. *Language in Society* 35, 4: 529–557.

Sapir, E. 1921. *Language*. New York: Harcourt, Brace and World.

Schieffelin, B. B., K. A. Woolard, and P. V. Kroskrity (eds.). 1988. *Language Ideologies: Practice and Theory*. New York: Oxford University Press.

Sherzer, J. 1987. A discourse-centered approach to language and culture. *American Anthropologist* 89: 295–305.

Silverstein, M. 1985. On the pragmatic "poetry" of prose: Parallelism, repetition, and cohesive structure in the time course of dyadic conversation. In D. Schiffrin (ed.), *Meaning, Form, and Use in Context: Linguistic Application*. Washington, DC: Georgetown University Press, 181–198.

    1993. Metapragmatic discourse and metapragmatic function. In J. A. Lucy (ed.), *Reflexive Language*. Cambridge: Cambridge University Press, 33–58.

Tetreault, C. 2009. Cité teens entextualizing French TV host register: Crossing, voicing, and participation frameworks. *Language in Society* 38, 2: 201–231.

Thompson, K. D. 2010. "I am Masai": Interpreting ethnic parody in Bongo Flava. *Language in Society* 39, 4: 457–492.

Urban, G. 1994. Repetition and cultural replication: Three examples from Shokleng. In B. Johnstone (ed.), *Repetition in Discourse: Interdisciplinary Perspectives*, vol. 2. Norwood, NJ: Ablex, 145–161.

Viereck, W. 1985. Linguistic atlases and dialectometry: The Survey of English Dialects. In J. M. Kirk, S. Sanderson, and J. D. A. Widdowson (eds.), *Studies in Linguistic Geography*. London: Croon Helm, 94–112.

Whorf, B. L. 1941. The relation of habitual thought and behavior to language. In L. Spier (ed.), *Language, Culture, and Personality: Essays in Memory of Edward Sapir*. Menasha, WI: Sapir Memorial Publication Fund, 75–93.

Wilce, J. M. 2008. Scientizing Bangladeshi psychiatry: Parallelism, enregisterment, and the cure for a magic complex. *Language in Society* 37, 1: 91–114.

Woolard, K. A., and E. N. Genovese. 2007. Strategic bivalency in Latin and Spanish in early modern Spain. *Language in Society*, 36, 4: 487–509.

Woolard, K. A., and B. Schieffelin. 1994. Language ideology. *Annual Review of Anthropology* 23: 55–82.

Zhang, Q. 2005. A Chinese yuppie in Beijing: Phonological variation and the construction of a new professional identity. *Language in Society* 34, 3: 431–466.

20 Five Ms for sociolinguistic change

Nikolas Coupland

Sociolinguistic change

In a few earlier publications I have lobbied for sociolinguists to begin working with a conception of *sociolinguistic change* (Coupland 2009; 2014a,c). Androutsopoulos (2014a) uses this concept in titling his comprehensive volume, *Mediatization and Sociolinguistic Change*, and in his introduction to that book (2014b) he points out that the phrase has been in fitful circulation for some years with a range of different meanings. To my mind the idea of sociolinguistic change is both liberating and focusing for sociolinguistics. It liberates the field to look beyond 'language change', which has set its sights on highly constrained sorts of change. The idea of sociolinguistic change focuses sociolinguistics by requiring it to be specific about what other sorts of change are then in question (principally in relation to what is generally called social change). In other words, theorising sociolinguistic change will entail reconsidering what priorities sociolinguistics should have in connection with change, why, and with what implications.

The present chapter firstly (in the rest of this section) extends this view of sociolinguistic change, vis-à-vis language change and social change; sociolinguistic change is broadly defined as *consequential change over time in language–society relations*. Then, in later sections, several of the main themes that have emerged in the earlier chapters of this book are reconsidered – all of them explicitly relevant to sociolinguistic change in this sense and able to contribute to the further theorising of this concept.[1] The five themes, or thematic clusters, can be referred to (without undue artificiality) by five 'm'-led keywords: *markets*, *mobility*, *modalities*, *media*, and *metacommunication*. Overlaps between this list and earlier sections and chapters of this book are, therefore, easily visible. It is unlikely that the whole of what we should call sociolinguistic change can ultimately be contained within changes in these five thematic dimensions. On the other hand, separately and together, they account

---

[1] The five themes discussed in this chapter extend my earlier attempts to establish the remit of sociolinguistic change, but with particular reference to the contents of the present volume.

for a substantial part of the changes in language–society relations that have already been debated in earlier chapters.

My brief comments on *social theory* in Chapter 1 pointed to ambiguity in the use of this term, but also to repeated efforts in the social sciences to establish, in broad theoretical terms, how a given society stands in its historical trajectory, from different critical standpoints. That is, *social change* is a dominant concern in social theory. The prominent journal *Theory, Culture and Society* gives us a snapshot of social-theoretic interests by listing its fifty most-read articles.[2] As I write, the current list includes individual papers by Ahmed, Appadurai, Beck, Featherstone, Hannerz, Rose, and Thompson, and these are names that we see being occasionally cited in contemporary sociolinguistic research. Topics included in the list of fifty articles include global interconnectedness, cosmopolitanism and localism, neoliberalism, feminism, materiality, embodiment, multiethnicity, diversity, media, performance, rhetoric, popular culture, and, above all, power and inequality. Foucault is a very common point of reference, but so are Bourdieu and Marx, and of course many of the other great names from the histories of the humanities and the social sciences. In the journal as a whole there is a good deal of reflexive discussion about the evolution and current standing of these disciplines and their subfields and about transdisciplinarity. 'Discourse', 'meaning', and 'language' are liberally used concepts.

The above summary is intended to show that sociolinguistic theory, as it has been represented in the present book, is not a distant cousin to social theory. But how should we view this relationship in more particular terms? How should we negotiate it and develop it to mutual advantage? Firstly, it would evidently be foolish for sociolinguists to pursue their theoretical agenda without reference to social theory. But the two endeavours are different. Sociolinguistic theory need not simply be incorporated into social theory; sociolinguists do not need to see themselves as servicing preexisting social-theoretic debates. As has just been observed, social theorists are already aware of the importance of language and discourse, but society and culture are their targeted domains, and language is, understandably, for the most part an ancillary issue, typically not seen as bearing its own theoretical load. When it comes to modelling change, social theory and sociolinguistic theory will have some shared but also some different agenda. As with social theory, not all sociolinguistic theory will be about change. We also need what we might call 'universalist' theorising of language in society, to be able to generalise about how language always embeds a metapragmatics of social meaning (cf. Part I in this volume, Chapters 2–5), how speaking is always in some

---

[2] Available at http://tcs.sagepub.com/reports/most-read.

key ways an embodied practice (cf. Bucholtz and Hall, Chapter 8), and so on. But an orientation to sociolinguistic change is also necessary in order to establish what *is* universal and what is 'of the current epoch'.

In the name of sociolinguistic change specifically, sociolinguists should parallel social theorists' persistent questioning of 'how things are now', from a range of critical standpoints and in diverse sociolinguistic environments, *but with specific reference to the language–society interface.* How does the social world of language and language use stand now, here as opposed to there, and how is it changing? Is language taking on new, more, or less significance in particular respects? Is social life changing by virtue of new orientations to, and new uses of, language? Returning to Hymes (as Bell and Johnstone both did in Chapters 18 and 19), we may well agree that language and society should be viewed as, to a large extent, mutually constitutive, and the idea of a language–society 'interface' may therefore be misleading. Yet social change is not universally and wholly constituted as change in language practices, just as changes in language practices are not always socially meaningful (see below). Sociolinguistic change research should therefore seek out the ways in which aspects of social change *are* carried through changing language practices, or through changes in language ideology, or in some other specifiable language-related sense. It should also find principled ways to establish which changes in language practices over time are socially meaningful and consequential, and which are not.

Some well-theorised social changes, or at least particular aspects of those changes, have language and discourse at their centre. To take just one example for the moment, Fairclough (1992; 2006) shows how the material economic and cultural changes that we refer to as globalisation are ideologically natural-ised and made legitimate through a 'globalist' (and sometimes a 'hyperglob-alist') discourse. Neoliberalism is associated with distinctive ways of speaking and ways of representing. It is an analysable discourse about employment and life chances, although Fairclough points out that there is a countercurrent of 'scepticism', too, associated with a sceptical discourse. Globalist discourse, or discursive globalism, is (or in the recent past was) a new discursive practice. It is (or was) the result of a sociolinguistic change that moved into specific environments and took hold as a 'normal' way to talk about some aspects of being in the world. This example helps us to recognise that globalism and globalisation are not the same thing, just as sociolinguistic change and social change are not the same thing. Fairclough may well have become sensitised to the fact of there being a new discourse by engaging with interdisciplinary accounts of globalisation, and it is true that sociolinguistics was 'late getting to the party' (as I suggested, in a poorly chosen phrase, in Coupland 2003; see also 2010). But Fairclough was making an observation on sociolinguistic change that was to some extent independent of accounts of new social trends regarding demographic mobility, increasing economic interdependency, and so on. Similar arguments can be made about there being potentially independent sociolinguistic treatments of change under each of my five 'm'-headed themes, below.

The sociolinguistic account of *language change* does not orient to social change in any significant theoretical sense. I am not suggesting that this is necessarily the case, or necessarily a limitation when it is the case. In fact, the theoretical coherence and empirical apparatus of classical approaches to language change, a.k.a. variationism, depend on suppressing considerations of social change. Generalising about the social basis of language change and the 'driving forces' involved, Labov writes that '[i]n one form or another, they [the driving forces] involve the association of social attributes with the more advanced forms of a change in progress: local identity, membership of communities of practice, social class, age or gender' (Labov 2010: 368). Labov treats some of the 'social factors' as being 'cultural', defined as being 'broad cultural patterns, which transcend small group behavior' (p. 368), such as gender differentiation. In order to explain language change in this way, variationists have to assume that the social and cultural 'factors' that they recognise to be the driving forces of change *do not themselves change*. Language change is interpreted to be the difference between the state of a linguistic system for a given social group at two different points in time, studied (where possible) in real time, otherwise in apparent time (assuming that older speakers' speech at 'time 2' is representative of their earlier speech at 'time 1'). Language change is strictly interpreted, therefore, to be the changing linguistic patterns of an identified social group over time, on the presumption that the group has a social profile that does not change over time; 'language' in this specific sense may change, but social structure and the social constitution of social categories endure. This view contrasts sharply with, for example, Silverstein's view (in Chapter 2) of (socio)linguistic change as 'movement of a sociological structure of repertoires of enregisterment'.

But social theory points us to multiple dimensions of social change, including changes in the meanings of the categories of class, gender, and age with which variationism has mainly worked. For example, Savage (2007) draws on real-time comparative data from the British Mass-Observation Survey (sampled in 1949 and in 1990) to draw conclusions about the changing nature of class in Britain post World War II. He concludes that the earlier data indicated 'the power of class as a form of ascriptive inscription' (i.e. social class *in*scribed on people's identities, having been *a*scribed to them from birth), whereas the later sample showed that people entertained 'a reflexive and individualised account of their mobility between class positions'. (Coupland 2009 reviews some other sociological evidence suggesting, similarly, that class and class-based configurations of consumption and taste are changing the meanings of class in Britain, and hence that there are likely to be changing indexicalities of 'standard' and 'nonstandard' language.) Changing meanings of gender over time and across disciplines (e.g. Sandford 2015) have been a prominent theme in social theory, as have changing meanings of ageing under neoliberal conditions (e.g. Macnicol 2015).

There is no suggestion here that social-theoretic accounts can simply be drafted into variationism; they clearly cannot be, without undermining its reliance on static categories of social structure. But if, as many chapters in this book suggest, we need to reinterpret language (including dialect) variation in terms of social semiotic processes, then there must be a theoretical space where sociolinguistic interpretations of social meaning engage with social change, opening up a view of sociolinguistic change. As dialects change over time, do they carry the same potential for social stigmatisation or as markers of elite practice, or are new language-ideological circumstances arising in relation to particular ways of contextualising dialectal speech in particular contexts? (The case for 'vernacularisation' as a sociolinguistic change arising in British broadcast media is considered in Coupland 2014c.)

For variationism itself, the important question arises of how to theorise the social significance of particular instances of language change. Labov incorporates analysis of 'natural misunderstandings' into his approach; he presents a taxonomy of misunderstandings that includes moments when listeners misanalyse homonyms, when they 'hear' linguistic items according to 'the wrong' dialect norms (Labov 2010: chapter 2). This is one way of demonstrating that language change can be consequential. But dialect misunderstandings are relatively rare, and we need to establish criteria for when language-implicated change is and is not consequential in more profound senses. In line with sociolinguistics' long-standing concern for social equity (as discussed in Chapter 1), we might start with criteria relating to status and opportunity, as they feature in Hymesan conceptions of voice and 'narrative inequality' (Hymes 1996; see also chapters by Gal [Chapter 5], Bucholtz and Hall [Chapter 8], Bell [Chapter 18], and others in this book). In a theory of sociolinguistic change we need to recognise that many aspects of language change are *not* socially consequential, although they may well be significant for theory in historical linguistics (cf. the debate over how to distinguish trivial from significant aspects of language change in the various papers in *Journal of Sociolinguistics* 18, 2 [2015]). Turning the issue of consequentiality on its head, a sociolinguistic change perspective is also necessarily interested in *why* language change happens, that is, asking what social and ideological processes are consequential for language change (Kristiansen and Jørgensen 2005).

We can now turn to the 'm'-headed keywords which can elaborate different perspectives on sociolinguistic change. The fact that it is possible, in several cases, to use examples and arguments from the earlier chapters of this book implies that the infrastructure of sociolinguistic change already exists in many different contributions to sociolinguistic theory, even though it has not been so named.

Markets and the capitalisation of sociolinguistic practice

Since Bourdieu (1991) it has been difficult to avoid seeing traces (and often much more than traces) of exchange-value and 'capital' attaching to ways of speaking, and seeing these values being transacted in many contexts of language use (Blommaert 2015). Mautner (2015) refers to 'the marketisation of public discourse', by which she means an increasing tendency for social domains previously considered public to have come under the control of private individuals, organisations, and institutions, so that language use and users come under new regimes of scrutiny and normativity. Styles of language associated with business have, Mautner argues, influenced discourse in many other domains. These claims mesh very well with arguments developed by Heller and Duchêne (Chapter 6) and by Kelly-Holmes (Chapter 7); see also Kelly-Holmes and Mautner (2010), Block et al. (2012), and Holborow (2015).

'Marketisation' and 'capitalisation' are process nominals that imply change over time, and they can readily be assumed into Fairclough's account (above) of 'discursive neoliberalisation', understood as a sociolinguistic change. Elsewhere Fairclough discusses another facet of the same broad change – the 'technologisation of discourse', which includes 'the application of technical-instrumental rationality in processes of designing and redesigning semiotic "objects", for instance interview genres in various institutional contexts, or telephone sales talk' (Fairclough 2007: 134). He has in mind the sorts of controlled, systematised, and often scripted communicative routines that Cameron has described. Cameron (2000) mentions 'new' and 'post-Fordist' ways of working and 'new forms of linguistic and other agency that workers must in principle develop to meet the demands of the new capitalism' (p. 323), so there is no doubt that Cameron views these developments as being based in social change. But we should note that an expression like 'new ways of working' could refer to changing social and organisational patterns alone, or it could refer to a sociolinguistic change in the sense we are considering here. In fact it refers to both. Following Cameron's interpretation, we are confronting a change that has shifted relationships between language and society in specific social circumstances and in specific regards. So, 'language' refers to new or newly required styles and newly restricted forms of discursive agency at work, and 'society' refers to changing designs for workplaces, new employer–employee relations, and so on. The shifts are certainly consequential, both for employees (in the immediate sense of what they can and cannot do) and (more abstractly) for how the public faces of some organisations are corporatised by regimenting the talk of employed individuals.

In Chapter 7, Kelly-Holmes similarly refers to 'the marketised economy', echoing Heller and Duchêne's use of 'The New Economy', so 'newness' and change are again in the air. But Kelly-Holmes also raises the metatheoretical problem of establishing what is new and what is not, at which level(s) of generality. It might be possible to locate three scales at which generalisations about sociolinguistic change can be established. At the most local scale, sociolinguistic change (in the broad field of capitalisation/marketisation/ commodification, and so on) can be empirically established (not so differently from how it is established in variationist accounts of language change) as observable change over time in documented language practices. The sources cited in this section give us ample direction in how this can be done, in investigating historical trends in specific contexts of public signage, university administration (one of Fairclough's empirical domains), call centres, and so on. At a second, more inclusive scale, we can combine these sets of empirical findings to reach generalisations about sociolinguistic change for which one or more chosen '-isation' concept would be then be more fully validated. (Relevant here are the risks of premature theoretical generalisation and [to use Wee's term] vanguardism that were briefly discussed in Chapter 1.) This is to suggest that inductive generalisation from multiple empirical initiatives remains the most secure way of building sociolinguistic theory.

At a third scale of generalisation (which in fact might be foundational for the other two) there needs to be universalist sociolinguistic theory – theory that explains and generalises about the basic affordances of linguistic/ semiotic meaning that make sociolinguistic change possible. In the case of capitalisation/marketisation, that theory is already in place in Gal and others' conceptualisation (e.g. in Chapter 5; see also Gal 1989) of language ideology, symbolic economies, metalevel semiosis, and the uptake of signs. Because, as Gal has shown, language-in-use *always* functions in particular symbolic economies and markets, and because language ideologies *always* have a 'materialist' dimension, language-in-use has the theoretical potential that we have seen being exploited and actualised in the consequential modes of sociolinguistic change discussed in this section. This three-level model of sociolinguistic theory-building – local empirical analysis, inductive generalisation across instances, and exposition of universalist principles of social meaning – may well be relevant in other cases, where it might clarify the relationship between sociolinguistic theory in general and the theorising of sociolinguistic change.

Mobility and (super)diversification

The idea of mobility and ideas about the consequences of mobility are densely represented through contemporary social theory and critical theory and, not surprisingly, then, through sociolinguistic theory. Demographic and spatial mobility – the geographical movement of people – provides a starting point for these ideas, although, as Britain points out in Chapter 10, it should not be taken for granted that there actually has been an increase in mobility. Mobility of course refers to far more than the movement of people. Globalisation is also theorised as the global mobility of economic principles and practices (see above), cultural norms, images, styles, and values (Coupland 2010). Then there is another general sort of mobility, what we could call 'the internal mobility of categories' – constant appeals to hybridity (that theoretical 'master trope'; Kraidi 2002), contingency, emergence, and the impact of seeing the social world through the lens of social constructionism.

We may have reached a metatheoretical peak in the fetishising of mobility and the antagonistic critiquing of structure, stability, and stasis. Britain's discussion of the ideologies of sedentarism and nomadism is particularly helpful when we try to assess 'where we (sedentarily) are and where we (nomadically) are going'. As Pennycook asks in Chapter 9, are our 'mobile terms' a response to our 'mobile times'? The tropes of '-ation' and '-isation', laying emphasis on process, not product, and on 'endless becoming', can be added to the tropes of 'trans-', 'super-', 'poly-', and 'metro-' that Pennycook discusses (see also Pennycook 2012). Giddens's sociological theory of structuration (displacing structure itself; see Giddens 1984) was influential in 'processifying' labels and perspectives across many academic disciplines – hence we have seen 'detraditionalisation' (Wee [Chapter 15], again following Giddens), 'carnivalisation' (Pietikäinen [Chapter 12], following Bakhtin), but also 'identification' preferred to 'identity', 'authentication' preferred to 'authenticity' in sociolinguistics, and so on (cf. Bucholtz and Hall 2004; Coupland 2014b).

Sociolinguistics was founded on the ideas of diversity and diversification (reviewed and reinterpreted in Gal, Chapter 5), and diversity can itself be seen as a kind of internal mobility. Variationists have always argued that linguistic diversity is a prerequisite for linguistic change, and mobility in more direct senses has always featured strongly in the variationist project. For example, Labov (2010) theorises 'forks in the road', patterns of dialect divergence, sometimes associated with population shifts. 'Dialects in contact' was a perspective pioneered by Trudgill (1986; see also 1999) – a dialectological response to demographic mobility and complexity. There was also Labov's (1972) approach to contextual style, or 'speaker-internal variation', linked to social aspiration and therefore to social mobility, and the sociolinguistic idea of style was quickly picked up by social psychologists and reinterpreted as 'accent mobility' (Giles 1973). So sociolinguistics is no stranger to mobility in general, and it is understandable that the will to upgrade our sensitivities and theoretical responses to (actual or perceived) increasing mobility has resulted in hyperbolic affixing. Diversity itself may no longer be sufficient, hence 'superdiversity' (Vertovec 2007; Blommaert and Rampton 2011; Blommaert 2013; Rampton et al. 2015).[3]

The migration crisis of 2015, with very large numbers of people from the Middle East and North Africa moving or attempting to move at great human cost into Europe, can reasonably be referred to as hypermobility, relative to postwar trends. Its demographic scale and the scale of associated suffering, disruption, and political turmoil are intense. The crisis is also associated with politicised category disputes: Governments are asking whether individuals 'are' (in that essentialising use of 'to be') 'refugees', 'asylum-seekers', or 'economic migrants', and 'where are they from?' The sociolinguistic implications of the crisis are as yet far from clear, although existing scholarship in the area of superdiversity will provide a strong foundation (e.g. Madsen et al. 2013; 2015; Blackledge and Creese 2014; Jørgensen and Møller 2014). It is predictable that more traditional sociolinguistic research will also be needed alongside critical ethnographies, including surveys of the distribution of languages and ethnicities, which in today's theoretical climate might be seen as strategically essentialist research based on fixed categories of language and ethnicity, of the sort that might, nevertheless, be able to speak to public institutions and agencies on their own terms (in the manner that Eades recommends in Chapter 17).

However, even if mobility is 'everywhere', it is still necessary to ask what precisely we can identify as sociolinguistic changes linked to mobility. One useful line of inquiry relates to what Gilroy and others (Gilroy 2004; Goebel 2015) have called conviviality, which is relevant here if we take it as a positively valenced overview of how people and groups in ethnically complex and fluid situations 'get along'. Rampton (2014) introduces methodological issues into this sort of debate, although he (provisionally) concludes that 'the temptation to look for conviviality in contemporary superdiversity – to

---

[3] Rampton et al. (2015) cite Vertovec's well-known phrase defining superdiversity as 'a diversification of diversities', although they also observe that Vertovec's conceptualisation of superdiversity is 'limited in "grand narrative" ambitions or explicit theoretical claims'. This raises questions about how well this terminological innovation maps onto the realities of a putative sociolinguistic change: How much 'more diverse' is the condition of superdiversity, and more than what? (The terminological innovation that introduced 'superconductivity', for example, was intended to represent a wholly new condition for cooled metals, not even able to be equated with 'perfect conductivity'.) We might therefore need to locate the value of the term 'superdiversity' as being its potential to invite questions about new conditions of mobility and diversity, rather than its ability to generalise about them.

dwell on creative translingual sociability or polylingual business-oriented improvisation – needs to be tempered by attention to fear, unease and their systematic cultivation as modes of control'. There are signs of conviviality in some European politicians' responses to the migration crisis and in incipient, apparently spontaneous, mass movements to welcome refugees into some European cities (and not others). Convivial actions and discourses do not themselves constitute a sociolinguistic change, although they could be this, if there were sufficient evidence of conviviality settling into relevant domains of public discourse to displace what is currently (in Britain) a seemingly predominant concern about threats to bordered sovereignty and integrity.

Related to this, sociolinguistics has begun to contribute to the topic of cosmopolitanism (see, e.g., Canagarajah 2013; Theodoropoulou 2014), a concept that has been widely canvassed in social theory for some time. For example, Beck (2002) asks how cosmopolitanism 'from below' is realised in the mundane practices of communities, such as in their engagement with popular culture and in many aspects of their symbolic exchanges. Following this line (which is a line that suits sociolinguists' typical inclinations) would allow us to assess cosmopolitanism as a routine and perhaps globalising practice, outside the realms of statist accounts of 'the integration of migrant minorities' or 'intercultural relations'. Beck and Levy (2013) consider how cosmopolitanism should be theorised in terms of the group or the collectivity. Bringing language into this debate may facilitate an extension of already-productive but inconclusive sociolinguistic debates about concepts such as 'speech community', 'community of practice', 'communities of contact' and 'communities of value' (cf. Cohen 2010; Coupland 2010).

Contemporary demographic mobility falls into different types (as discussed by Britain in Chapter 10). Some of those types are primarily recreational, and rural as well as urban, so they stand outside the current remit of superdiversity research. Sociolinguists have pioneered new perspectives on 'language in tourism' which are sensitive to the nuances of social interaction in different sorts of tourist encounters (cf. Thurlow and Jaworski 2010; 2011; Pietikäinen et al. 2016). (Jaworski et al. 2014 is an edited collection of articles on sociolinguistics and tourism.) Tourism is another productive domain of social theory research, not least following Urry's classic analysis of 'the tourist gaze' (Urry and Larsen 2012). Tourism itself, certainly as a mass, highly globalised activity, spanning both vernacular and elite experience, has a rather short history, and it is clearly evolving into new modes, some of which are associated with new ways of experiencing language, culture, and otherness. Jaworski and Thurlow have been interested, for example, in the 'fleeting relationships' of tourist encounters, and they have pointed to the theoretical importance of new genres of talk, display and performance based on partial competence, formulaicity, code-crossing, verbal play, and so on.

Modalities and the theorising of 'language'

The more sociolinguistics aligns its understanding of social meaning with semiotics, the less possible and desirable it becomes to ignore the multimodal constitution of language in use. This does not call into question the 'linguistics' that is morphologically the head component of 'sociolinguistics'; it simply enriches the sense of 'linguistics' that is relevant here. As Bucholtz and Hall argue in Chapter 8, language-in-use is fundamentally a material as well as a social and cognitive process, and to ignore the multiple modes of semiosis that attach to this materiality, and to the contextualisation of speaking in so many other respects, is to impoverish sociolinguistics. There has never been such a thing as 'unimodal' communicaion, so that 'unimodality' has simply been an analytic constraint and preference. On the other hand, Kress and van Leeuwen (2001) propose that 'multimodal discourse' is the basis of a 'contemporary' theory of communication, suited to the age of interactive multimedia and multiskilling. So once again we encounter a possible split between universalist theorising of language as a multimodal resource and extrapolations of that theory that might illuminate forms and contexts of sociolinguistic change.

Many chapters in this book have shown how sociolinguistic theory needs to relate to semiotic dimensions beyond the strictly 'linguistic' (textual/written and oral/aural). In Chapter 3 Eckert interprets cultural and subcultural styles as multimodal complexes – linguistic/phonological styles that interconnect with visual/dress- and appearance-related modes of self-presentation, all aspects of which can be actively displayed and manipulated in the service of group-level social identification. Style as a holistic accumulation of things said, done, and 'liked' is also in evidence in Jaffe's analysis in Chapter 4 of *Stuff White People Like*. Androutsopoulos explains in Chapter 13 how any adequate sociolinguistic perspective on mediation and 'new media' needs *not* to inherit the phonocentrism that sociolinguistics has been drawn to in the past, and so on. These and other instances show that sociolinguistics is already aware of needing to orient to multimodality, even if that need is more recognised than fulfilled. In another sense, sociolinguistics is already attuned to classical social-theoretic studies of taste and distinction (Bourdieu 1984; Elias 2000), but we should recall that Elias's study of 'the civilising process' was fundamentally multimodal. He traced how 'manners', including conventions of eating, speaking, dressing, and so on, attracted judgements of good taste and modernity in different ways over different epochs. Bax and Kádár (2011) have added a historical perspective to politeness theory, bringing it within the scope of sociolinguistic change, but politeness also needs to be theorised multimodally.

In the earlier discussion of capitalisation and commodification, and in Chapter 7, by Kelly-Holmes, we saw how the visual attributes of particular languages can be put to work in promotional marketing. Use of so-called Celtic font in the marketing of Welsh and Irish products in global marketplaces is one instance, but as Kelly-Holmes (2005) and Jaffe et al. (2012) also show, orthography has much wider semiotic utility in a wide range of contemporary contexts (also discussed by Androutsoloupos in Chapter 13). Visual culture is on the rise as screen-based technologies steadily become more ingrained in our social lives, and many sociolinguistic changes arise through new ways of managing the interface between textual/oral and visual signalling. Visual signalling is the near-exclusive modality for Deaf language use. But here, too, as Lucas and Bayley show in Chapter 16, social changes have impacted directly on the gestural character of particular sign languages. Whether and how sign language interpreting is embedded in TV broadcasting has sometimes been a focus of disagreement and disparaging commentary, reminiscent of the 'complaint tradition' centred on the broadcasting of vernacular accents and dialects.[4] Far more opportunities will arise to embed signed versions of spoken language and interactions through new media technologies, and new ways of contextualising language are in general an important nexus for theorising sociolinguistic change.

As suggested above, sociolinguistics has always had an opportunity to offer its neighbouring disciplines and subdisciplines better-described, better-informed, and better-theorised accounts of language and discourse. This has been the great achievement of linguistic anthropology vis-à-vis anthropology itself. Linguistic anthropology has been able to demonstrate that, descriptively, analytically, and theoretically, anthropology certainly 'needs language'. Anthropology, a discipline founded on the issues of culture and meaning, and indeed change, cannot dispense with expertise in the areas of language and social interaction. The situation is not quite the same with regard to sociology and the social sciences, where language and discourse, though acknowledged to matter, are not so ingrained. So it seems to be particularly important for sociolinguistics (defined inclusively) to 'offer back' its semiotically elaborated theorising of language to those parts of social science where it is most relevant.

Media and mediatisation

As Androutsopoulos explains in introducing Chapter 13, it formerly seemed possible to very largely ignore 'the media' in sociolinguistics, but this was also

---

[4] In September 2015 the online version of the U.K. newspaper *The Telegraph* carried a feature under the heading 'Get these manic sign-language gnomes off our television screens', where the writer put the case that on-screen sign language interpreters amounted to 'infuriating intrusions'. See http://blogs.telegraph.co.uk/news/geraldwarner/5026396/.

the case in much of the social sciences. Broadcast media could be construed as projecting illegitimate versions of both language and society, versions that were even more suspect because they sometimes purported to be (as well as to represent) reality, in disciplinary climates where the priority for linguistic and social research was to engage with the 'really real'. In sharp contrast to this view, and acknowledging Androutsopoulos's argument that the concept is grossly underspecified, 'the media' are nowadays inescapably relevant to sociolinguistics. In Chapter 18, for example, Bell identifies a 'turn to media' in sociolinguistic research over the life to date of the *Journal of Sociolinguistics*.

Terminology in this area can be troublesome. In its most abstract sense, mediation is a fundamental aspect of language. As Androutsopoulos (2014b) writes (following Norris and Jones 2005 and Agha 2011; see also Coupland 2007), '[a]ll symbolic communication is mediated by semiotic means' (p. 10), which establishes mediation (alongside contextualisation, for example) at the theoretical heart of what sociolinguistics is about. But the more specific process of mediatisation can be argued to have a place there too. Androutsopoulos reviews different definitions of 'mediatisation', where one of its key senses refers to historical change across most societies into a condition where many aspects of day-to-day life routinely involve electronically mediated exchange and consumption. Because mediatisation has impacted on language–society relations, and because aspects of these changes are consequential, mediatisation is obviously a locus for sociolinguistic change. Important aspects of marketisation and mobility (discussed above) involve mediatised circulation, which is increasingly multimodal in form.

The question of whether and how 'the media' influence language change is a difficult and contentious one, and, under scrutiny, it proves to be a question that is not particularly well formed (cf. Coupland 2014a). But beyond language change itself, Androutsopoulos (in Chapter 13, but see also 2014b) identifies several different perspectives from which mediatisation can be shown to be associated with sociolinguistic change. Broadcast media can, for example, bring linguistic fragments (and more) into wider circulation in social interaction within and across communities. Spitulnik observes that in large-scale mass-mediated societies, 'people have frequent interactions or *frequent acts of consumption* with certain media forms' and that there is '*large-scale exposure* to a common communication form' (Spitulnik 2009: 94, emphasis in original). She is interested in how mass media can facilitate circulation of particular linguistic forms, styles, and interactional routines, and in how that circulation in turn facilitates collective identification and 'the formation of community in a kind of subterranean way' (p. 95). A different perspective is on the changing sociolinguistic norms of mass media themselves, which may play a role in promoting particular ideological priorities for how public discourse should more generally be enacted (cf. Bell 2011). A further perspective again is on how media draw attention to, comment on, and play a part in culturally enregistering ways of speaking (cf. again Agha 2007).

In other words, media of different sorts – 'old' and 'new', and the mediatised world of language in general – cannot be hived off from the 'everyday language' that early sociolinguistics took to be its object of study. Mediatised language *is* everyday language, and (borrowing again from Androutsopoulos, Chapter 13) there are permeable boundaries between what we might take to be 'mediated' and 'unmediated' sociolinguistic practices, whether or not media can be shown to be causally implicated in language change. On the other hand, mediatisation *is sociolinguistic* change, and, taken as a composite shift across countless specific loci of change, it changes the terms of our engagement with language, in some general and sometimes highly particular ways. For example, in Chapter 12, Pietikäinen shows how a Finnish television show parodies Sámi language and culture in a way that destabilises traditionally respectful attitudes to Sámi affairs. The potential intensity of media representations and performances, allied to their extensive reach (as Spitulnik notes), is salient in this example.

Taking a long view of media and social change, social theorists have linked mediatisation to the development of new quantities and qualities of 'visibility' (Thompson 1995; 2005), which sociolinguistics could easily analyse and retheorise in more precise ways. People we call 'public figures' have become more readily visible to us, as 'ordinary' members of society, through their appearances on television and radio. This once-new visibility at a distance has supplanted the norm of 'co-present publicness' of earlier times. But Thompson also notes that mediated vision (e.g. how we 'see' our politicians on television) is selective and determined by various sorts of editorial framing and projection – that is, by 'mediatisation' in Jaffe's (2011) alternative sense of the term. So visibility is accompanied by new forms of *in*visibility too. Critical interpretation of mass-mediated representations and performances has steadily become more complex and more necessary as a dimension of citizenship (Ramanathan 2013), and indeed central to the politics of 'citizen sociolinguistics' (Rymes and Leone 2014). There is also a tension between seeing and being seen. We consider public figures to be visible to audiences, but we may fail to see how we ourselves are under scrutiny and surveillance (cf. Rampton's account of governmentality in Chapter 14; also Couldry 2012; Rampton 2015).

Surely the most pervasive long-term sociolinguistic changes associated with mediatisation are in connection with performance and performativity. 'Old media' soon positioned almost all members of society as 'viewers', 'listeners', and 'audiences', with all of the potentiated attributes and demands that Bauman and others have recognised in these roles (e.g. Bauman 1977; 1992; see also Bell and Gibson 2011). Obviously to highly varying degrees (because audiences are so diverse), audiences need to recognise and interpret genres, and identify continuities and discontinuities in relation to genres. They need to evaluate, and may sometimes comment explicitly and metacommunicatively on, particular performances, although relative passivity is also a characteristic of the typical 'old media' audience identity. They need to appreciate the aesthetics of performance, and the framings of performances, and to become aware of the mise-en-scène devices through which media institutions and their production teams create their own versions of social reality and approximations to reality (i.e. verisimilitude; Jaffe 2011). Some audience members will engage in all of these responsive actions, and if they do, they have acculturated themselves into one important form of incumbency in 'mediatised society'. Then, with the expansion into 'new media', particularly in interactive formats, they have acquired rights and obligations to perform.

'Performance talk' is of course not a new sociolinguistic mode in itself, although there are ever-more social contexts of work and leisure, off-line as well as online, where a premium is placed on 'style' (personal style, corporate style, relational style, etc.; see the discussion of Cameron's research, above). Self-styling is implied to be a matter of personal responsibility in individualised societies (cf. Bauman 2000; Castells 2001), although there are also considerable opportunities (e.g. for young people online) to manufacture multiple versions of their own identities and to build (what Castells calls) 'portfolios of sociability' (cf. also Hodkinson 2007). Performativity and (multimodal) style in general become more salient, as more and more people have to function in particular style economies and markets. All of this implies that language use is increasingly negotiated with greater reflexivity, metacommunicatively, and we turn to this final 'm' theme immediately below.

Metacommunication and the reflexive imperative

Reflexivity can be theorised as being, on the one hand, a universal characteristic of sociolinguistic meaning and, on the other hand, a variable quality of the social environment in which language use takes place. Both approaches are necessary, and this gives us another case of how sociolinguistic theory needs to be both universalist and specifically oriented to change.

In earlier chapters several contributors have explained how the sociolinguistic theory that they espouse needs to incorporate 'meta' processes of different kinds. In his theorising, Silverstein in Chapter 2 has built a detailed infrastructure of metapragmatics around language use, which is where all the sociolinguistic 'stuff' of ideology and social evaluation takes place. In Chapter 3 Eckert endorses Agha's account of the metadiscursive practices that consolidate the social meanings of styles or registers, and her concept of the indexical field points us to complex repertoires of meaning that are selectively accessed and put to work in particular instances. For Jaffe (Chapter 4), stance is a recursively reflexive position taken up by a participant in discourse (recursive because stances can be taken towards other stances), and this theoretical framework helps her to model the layers of indexical meaning that build up around a blog about race and taste (see also Jaffe 2009). Gal (Chapter 5) reviews the concept of metasign in semiotics and places it at the centre of her theorising of language ideology.

All these accounts build on Jakobson's (1960) early insight about the metalinguistic function of language (see also Lucy 1993; Gumperz 1996). Agha (2007) provides a comprehensive discussion of the roles played by reflexive processes not only in language use but in the establishment of cultural normativity and change. What is most important in all these perspectives is that much of what is distinctively *social* about language resides in its metacommunicative aspects. This is where the social is embedded into linguistic practice, and how language use comes to be a socially constituted practice. The meanings structured around ways of speaking can usefully be seen as being sustained through reflexive (metapragmatic) representations. Sociolinguistics has for some time recognised the importance of incorporating reflexivity into its theory in multiple ways (cf. Jaworski et al. 2004). But there is another way of looking at reflexivity, one that looks back at and into language and discourse from social and cultural perspectives on change. It asks how we get to know what our social conditions are and how our culture stands in its history of inevitable change. (In other words, it asks the classical questions of social theory.) The answer inevitably has to do with language, discourse, and representation, and specifically with their metasocial and metacultural functions (Urban 2001). But these functions and processes are constrained or facilitated/necessitated by *changing social conditions*.

Giddens (e.g. 1990; 1996) theorised social change in relation to reflexivity. This is not reflexivity in its universal function as an element of pragmatics and social meaning, but reflexivity as a changing and consequential quality of modern life:

The reflexivity of [late-][5] modern social life consists in the fact that social practices are constantly examined and reformed in the light of incoming information about those very practices, thus constitutively altering their character ... [O]nly in the era of modernity is the revision of convention radicalised to apply (in principle) to all aspects of human life. (Giddens 1990: 38–39)

ı

---

[5] The phrase 'late modernity' has overtaken Giddens's use of 'modernity' to refer to the epoch in which he was writing. Giddens mainly contrasts 'modernity' with 'tradition', hence he sees 'detraditionalisation' as a feature of the contemporary globalised epoch.

Many of the social and sociolinguistic changes discussed in this chapter find their basis in the fact that contemporary social and linguistic life, in globalised societies, is distinctive for its *heightened levels of reflexivity*. Mediatisation has brought us into repeated contact with multiple, densely reflexive representations and versions of social and linguistic ways of being. We construe (and cannot avoid construing) alternatives to what we take to be the sociolinguistic norms that allow us to make sense of our experiences; 'the media' are replete with densely packed fictional or would-be real representations. Normativity and indeed reality are qualities that fall within media institutions' fields of action and representation – technological media have their own resources for distinguishing the real from the unreal, and for determining what matters in such distinctions. At the same time, the diminishing authority of traditional social and sociolinguistic structures results in more individualised social conditions, and more complex life politics, which Giddens saw as including 'ecological problems and dilemmas ... linked to wider questions of identity and lifestyle choice' (1996: 231). Commodification itself disrupts the meanings of traditional forms and resources (cf. Heller and Duchêne, Chapter 6, and the pride-to-profit reframing of minority languages; also Kelly-Holmes, Chapter 7, on new marketised conditions for language use). Mass-mediated cultural representations become more dynamic, vivid, and (most commonly) multimodal, just at the point where the relative certainty and predictability of lives lived 'in the community' (if this implies in smaller, face-to-face networks) becomes less constraining.

'Reflexive modernisation' was the phrase that expressed Giddens and his colleagues' overview of the social changes that have brought us to 'where we are now' (Beck et al. 1994). More recent treatments of the growth of social reflexivity have emphasised its disruptive power. Archer (2003; 2007; 2012) gives us a complex account of the different modes of reflexivity that she finds in her empirical research, based on interviews with university students. She argues that reflexive and individualistic choice-making increasingly becomes an onerous demand, or an 'imperative', which some young people find impossible to live up to. They are unable to align themselves with any particular normative lifestyle or identity, and they get trapped, Archer argues, in types of contingent, weakly motivated practices that amount to 'presentism' and 'shapelessness'. Archer offers this as one way of explaining the often quite shallow bases of social encounters enacted through social media, for example (Archer 2012: 308; see Pietikäinen et al. 2016: chapter 2 for a discussion of metacommunication, metaculture, and reflexivity in relation to 'small languages').

The high reflexivity of the contemporary, globalised sociolinguistic world has begun to be recognised in sociolinguistic treatments of a wide range of concepts – some new and some not so new – that have 'meta'-processing as their point in common: performance and performativity, style and stylisation, stance and positionality, parody and irony, transgression, metadiscursive practices, and so on. Reflexivity also underlies a wave of new research on mediation in all of its manifestations, particularly on changes in media practices and media as sites and resources for the enactment or thematising of change (e.g. Mortensen et al. forthcoming; Thøgersen et al. forthcoming). In this research there are always 'old' theoretical resources to draw on, as well as new theoretical frameworks of the sort we have seen being canvassed throughout this book. Reflexivity can in fact be interpreted as another type of mobility – movement across layers of representation in response to the multiple layers of social meaning that a changing social world confronts us all with, and that an evolving sociolinguistics needs to be ready to theorise.

REFERENCES

Agha, Asif. 2007. *Language and Social Relations*. Cambridge: Cambridge University Press.
    2011. Meet mediatisation. *Language and Communication* 31, 3: 163–170.
Androutsopoulos, Jannis (ed.). 2014a. *Mediatization and Sociolinguistic Change*. Berlin: Mouton de Gruyter.
    (ed.). 2014b. Mediatization and sociolinguistic change: Key concepts, research traditions, open issues. In J. Androutsopoulos, *Mediatization and Sociolinguistic Change*. Berlin: Mouton de Gruyter, 3–48.
Archer, Margaret. 2003. *Structure, Agency and the Internal Conversation*. Cambridge: Cambridge University Press.
    2007. *Making Our Way through the World: Human Reflexivity and Social Mobility*. Cambridge: Cambridge University Press.
    2012. *The Reflexive Imperative in Late Modernity*. Cambridge: Cambridge University Press.
Bauman, Richard. 1977. Verbal art as performance. *American Anthropologist* 77, 2: 290–311.
    1992. *Folklore, Cultural Performances and Popular Entertainments: A Communications-Centered Handbook*. Oxford: Oxford University Press.
Bauman, Zygmund. 2000. *The Individualized Society*. New York: John Wiley.
Bax, Marcel, and Dániel Z. Kádár (eds.). 2011. *Understanding Historical (Im) politeness: Relational Linguistic Practice over Time and across Cultures*. Amsterdam: John Benjamins.
Beck, Ulrich. 2002. The cosmopolitan society and its enemies. *Theory, Culture & Society* 19: 17–44.
Beck, Ulrich, and Daniel Levy. 2013. Cosmopolitanized nations: Re-imagining collectivity in world risk society. *Theory, Culture & Society* 30: 3–31.
Beck, Ulrich, Anthony Giddens, and Scott Lash. 1994. *Reflexive Modernization: Politics, Tradition and Aesthetics in the Modern Social Order*. Stanford, CA: Stanford University Press.
Bell, Allan. 2011. Leaving home: De-europeanisation in a post-colonial variety of broadcast news language. In T. Kristiansen and N. Coupland (eds.), *Standard*

Languages and Language Standards in a Changing Europe. Oslo: Novus, 177–198.

Bell, Allan, and Andy Gibson (eds.). 2011. Staging language: An introduction to the sociolinguistics of performance. Thematic issue of *Journal of Sociolinguistics* 15, 5: 555–572.

Blackledge, Adrian, and Angela Creese (eds.). 2014. *Heteroglossia as Practice and Pedagogy.* Dordrecht: Springer.

Block, David, John Gray, and Marnie Holborow. 2012. *Neoliberalism and Applied Linguistics.* London: Routledge.

Blommaert, Jan. 2013. Language and the study of diversity. *Tilburg Papers in Culture Studies* 74. Available at www.tilburguniversity.edu/upload/2648cf26-31f2-4138-83d3-3176cabc28b0_TPCS_74_Blommaert.pdf.

Blommaert, J. 2015. Pierre Bourdieu and language in society. *Working Papers in Urban Language and Literacies* 153, King's College London. (This and other papers from the King's College collection are available at www.kcl.ac.uk/innovation/groups/ldc/publications/workingpapers/.)

Blommaert, Jan, and Ben Rampton. 2011. Language and superdiversity. *Diversities* 13, 2. Available at www.mmg.mpg.de/fileadmin/user_upload/Subsites/Diversities/Journals_2011/2011_13-02_art1.pdf.

Bourdieu, Pierre. 1984. *Distinction: A Social Critique of the Judgement of Taste* (trans. R. Nice). Cambridge, MA: Harvard University Press.

1991. *Language and Symbolic Power.* Oxford: Polity Press.

Bucholtz, Many, and Kira Hall. 2004. Theorizing identity in language and sexuality research. *Language in Society* 33, 4: 469–515.

Cameron, Deborah. 2000. Styling the worker: Gender and the commodification of language in the globalized service economy. *Journal of Sociolinguistics* 4, 3: 323–347.

Canagarajah, Suresh. 2013. *Translingual Practice: Global Englishes and Cosmopolitan Relations.* Abingdon and New York: Routledge.

Castells, Manuel. 2001. *The Internet Galaxy.* Oxford: Oxford University Press.

Cohen, Anthony P. 2010. *The Symbolic Construction of Community.* London and New York: Routledge.

Couldry, Nick. 2012. *Media, Society, World: Social Theory and Digital Media Practice.* Cambridge: Polity.

Coupland, Nikolas. 2003. Sociolinguistics and globalisation. *Journal of Sociolinguistics* 7, 4: 465–472.

2007. *Style: Language Variation and Identity.* Cambridge: Cambridge University Press.

2009. Dialects, standards and social change. In Marie Maegaard, Frans Gregersen, Pia Quist, and J. Normann Jørgensen (eds.), *Language Attitudes, Standardization and Language Change* (Festschrift for Tore Kristiansen). Oslo: Novus, 27–50.

2010. The authentic speaker and the speech community. In Carmen Llamas and Dominic Watts (eds.), *Language and Identities.* Edinburgh: Edinburgh University Press, 99–112.

2014a. Language change, social change, sociolinguistic change: A meta-commentary. *Journal of Sociolinguistics* 18, 2: 277–286.

2014b. Language, society and authenticity: Themes and perspectives. In Véronique Lacoste, Jakob Leimgruber, and Thiemo Breyer (eds.), *Indexing Authenticity: Sociolinguistic Perspectives*. Berlin: Mouton de Gruyter, 14–39.

2014c. Sociolinguistic change, vernacularization and broadcast British media. In Jannis Androutsopoulos (ed.), *Mediatization and Sociolinguistic Change*. Berlin: Mouton de Gruyter, 67–96.

Elias, Norbert. 2000. *The Civilizing Process: Sociogenetic and Psychogenetic Investigations*, revised ed. Oxford: Wiley-Blackwell.

Fairclough, Norman. 1992. *Discourse and Social Change*. Cambridge: Polity Press.

2006. *Language and Globalization*. London and New York: Routledge.

2007. Global capitalism and change in higher education: Dialectics of language and practice, technology, ideology. Proceedings of the British Association for Applied Linguistics conference 2007. Available at www.baal.org.uk/proc07/36_norman_fairclough.pdf.

Gal, Susan. 1989. Language and political economy. *Annual Review of Anthropology* 18: 345–367.

Giddens, Anthony. 1984. *The Constitution of Society: Outline of the Theory of Structuration*. Cambridge: Polity Press.

1990. *The Consequences of Modernity*. Stanford, CA: Stanford University Press.

1996. *In Defence of Sociology: Essays, Interpretations and Rejoinders*. Cambridge: Polity.

Giles, Howard. 1973. Accent mobility: A model and some data. *Anthropological Linguistics* 15, 2: 87–105.

Gilroy, Paul. 2004. *After Empire: Melancholia or Convivial Culture?* Abingdon: Routledge.

Goebel, Zane. 2015. *Language and Superdiversity: Indonesians Knowledging at Home and Abroad*. New York: Oxford University Press.

Gumperz, John J. 1996. The linguistic and cultural relativity of conversational inference. In J. J. Gumperz and S. Levinson (eds.), *Rethinking Linguistic Relativity*. Cambridge: Cambridge University Press, 359–406.

Hodkinson, Paul. 2007. Interactive online journals and individualisation. *New Media and Society* 9, 4: 625–650.

Holborow, Marnie. 2015. *Language and Neoliberalism*. Abingdon: Routledge.

Hymes, Dell. 1996. *Ethnography, Linguistics, Narrative Inequality: Toward an Understanding of Voice*. London: Taylor & Francis.

Jaffe, Alexandra (ed.). 2009. *Stance: Sociolinguistic Perspectives*. New York: Oxford University Press.

2011. Sociolinguistic diversity in mainstream media: Authenticity, authority and processes of mediation and mediatization. *Journal of Language and Politics* 10, 4: 562–586.

Jaffe, Alexandra, Jannis Androutsopoulos, Mark Sebba, and Sally Johnson (eds.). 2012. *Orthography as Social Action: Scripts, Spelling, Identity and Power*. Berlin: De Gruyter.

Jakobson, Roman. 1960. Linguistics and poetics. In T. Sebeok (ed.), *Style in Language*. Cambridge, MA: MIT Press, 350–377.

Jaworski, Adam, Nikolas Coupland, and Darius Galasiński (eds.). 2004. *Metalanguage: Social and Ideological Perspectives*. Berlin and New York: Mouton de Gruyter.

Jaworski, Adam, Crispin Thurlow, and Monica Heller (eds.). 2014. Sociolinguistics and tourism. Thematic issue of *Journal of Sociolinguistics* 18, 4.

Jørgensen, J. Normann, and Janus Møller. 2014. Polylingualism and languaging. In Constant Leung and Brian V. Street (eds.), *The Routledge Companion to English Studies*. Abingdon: Routledge, 67–83.

Kelly-Holmes, Helen. 2005. *Advertising as Multilingual Communication*. Basingstoke and New York: Palgrave-Macmillan.

Kelly-Holmes, Helen, and Gerlinde Mautner (eds.). 2010. *Language and the Market*. Basingstoke: Palgrave Macmillan.

Kraidy, M. M. 2002. Hybridity in cultural globalization. *Communication Theory* 12, 3: 316–339. http://dx.doi.org/10.1111/ j.1468–2885.2002.tb00272.x.

Kress, Gunther, and Theo van Leeuwen. 2001. *Multimodal Discourse: The Modes and Media of Contemporary Communication*. London: Edward Arnold.

Kristiansen, Tore, and J. Normann Jørgensen. 2005. Subjective factors in dialect convergence and divergence. In P. Auer, F. Hinskens, and P. Kerswill (eds.), *Dialect Change: Convergence and Divergence in European Languages*. Cambridge: Cambridge University Press, 287–302.

Labov, William. 1972. *Sociolinguistic Patterns*. Philadelphia: Pennsylvania University Press.

2010. *Principles of Linguistic Change: Cognitive and Cultural Factors*. Malden, MA, and Oxford: Wiley-Blackwell.

Lucy, John A. 1993. Reflexive language and the human disciplines. In J. A. Lucy (ed.), *Reflexive Language: Reported Speech and Metapragmatics*. Cambridge: Cambridge University Press, 9–32.

Macnicol, John. 2015. *Neoliberalising Old Age*. Cambridge: Cambridge University Press.

Madsen, Lian Malai, Martha Sif Karrebæk, and Janus Spindler Møller. 2013. The Amager project: A study of language and social life among minority children and youth. *Kings College Working Papers in Urban Language and Literacies* 102.

(eds.). 2015. *Everyday Languaging: Collaborative Research on the Language Use of Children and Youth*. De Gruyter.

Mautner, Gerlinde. 2015. Marketization of public discourse. In C. Ilie (ed.), *The International Encyclopedia of Language Social Interaction*. Oxford: Wiley-Blackwell. DOI: 10.1002/9781118611463.wbielsi132.

Mortensen, Janus, Nikolas Coupland, and Jacob Thøgersen (eds.). Forthcoming. *Style, Mediation and Sociolinguistic Change: Perspectives on Talking Media*. New York: Oxford University Press.

Norris, Sigrid, and Rodney Jones (eds.). 2005. *Discourse in Action: Introducing Mediated Discourse Analysis*. London and New York: Routledge.

Pennycook, Alastair. 2012. *Language and Mobility: Unexpected Places*. Bristol: Multilingual Matters.

Pietikäinen, Sari, Helen Kelly-Holmes, Alexandra Jaffe, and Nikolas Coupland. 2016. *Sociolinguistics from the Periphery: Small Languages in New Circumstances*. Cambridge: Cambridge University Press.

Ramanathan, Vaidehi (ed.). 2013. *Language Policies and (Dis)citizenship: Rights, Access, Pedagogies*. Clevedon: Multilingual Matters.

Rampton, Ben. 2014. Conviviality and phatic communication? *Working Papers in Urban Language & Literacies* 140. King's College London.

2015. Post-panoptic standard language. *Working Papers in Urban Language and Literacies* 162, King's College London.

Rampton, Ben, Jan Blommaert, Karel Arnaut, and Massimiliano Spotti. 2015. Superdiversity and sociolinguistics. *Tilburg Papers in Culture Studies* 130.

Rymes, Betsy, and Andrea R. Leone. 2014. Citizen sociolinguistics: A new media methodology for understanding language and social life. *Working Papers in Educational Linguistics* 29, 2: 25–43.

Sandford, Stella. 2015. Contradiction of terms: Feminist theory, philosophy and transdisciplinarity. *Theory, Culture and Society*. doi:10.1177/0263276415594238.

Savage, Mike. 2007. Changing social class identities in post-war Britain: Perspectives from mass-observation. *Sociological Research Online* 12, 2. Available at www.socresonline.org.uk/12/3/6.html.

Spitulnik, Debra. 2009. The social circulation of media discourse and the mediation of communities. In A. Duranti (ed.), *Linguistic Anthropology: A Reader*, 2nd ed. Malden, MA: Wiley-Blackwell, 93–113.

Theodoropoulou, Irene. 2014. *Sociolinguistics of Style and Class in Contemporary Athens*. Amsterdam: John Benjamins.

Thompson, John B. 1995. *The Media and Modernity: A Social Theory of the Media*. Cambridge: Polity.

2005. The new visibility. *Theory, Culture & Society* 22: 31–51.

Thøgersen, Jacob, Nikolas Coupland, and Janus Mortensen (eds.). Forthcoming. *Media, Language Ideology and Change*. Oslo: Novus Press.

Thurlow, Crispin, and Adam Jaworski. 2010. *Tourism Discourse: Language and Global Mobility*. London: Palgrave Macmillan.

2011. Tourism discourse: Languages and banal globalization. *Review of Applied Linguistics* 2: 285–312.

Trudgill, Peter. 1986. *Dialects in Contact*. New York: Basil Blackwell.

1999. Dialect contact, dialectology and sociolinguistics. *Cuadernos de Filología Inglesa* 8: 1–8.

Urban, Greg. 2001. *Metaculture: How Culture Moves through the World*. Minneapolis: University of Minnesota Press.

Urry, John, and Jonas Larsen. 2012. *The Tourist Gaze 3.0*, 3rd ed. London: Sage.

Vertovec, Steven. 2007. Super-diversity and its implications. *Ethnic and Racial Studies* 30, 6: 1024–1054.

Index